Bandido

Tiburcio Vasquez, May 18, 1874. (Author's collection)

Bandido

The Life and Times of Tiburcio Vasquez

John Boessenecker

University of Oklahoma Press : Norman

Also by John Boessenecker

Badge and Buckshot: Lawlessness in Old California (Norman, 1988)

The Grey Fox: The True Story of Bill Miner, Last of the Old Time Bandits (with Mark Dugan) (Norman, 1992)

Lawman: The Life and Times of Harry Morse, 1835–1912 (Norman, 1998)

Against the Vigilantes: The Recollections of Dutch Charley Duane (Norman, 1999)

Gold Dust and Gunsmoke: Tales of Gold Rush Outlaws, Gunfighters, Lawmen, and Vigilantes (New York, 1999)

Library of Congress Cataloging-in-Publication Data

Boessenecker, John, 1953-
    Bandido : the life and times of Tiburcio Vasquez / John Boessenecker.
        p. cm.
    Includes bibliographical references and index.
    ISBN 978-0-8061-4127-5 (hardcover : alk. paper)
    1. Vasquez, Tiburcio, 1835–1875. 2. Outlaws—California—Biography. 3. California—Biography. I. Title.
    HV6452.C3V3 2010
    364.1092—dc22
    [B]

                                                                    2009050434

The paper in this book meets the guidelines for permanence and durability of the Committee on Production Guidelines for Book Longevity of the Council on Library Resources, Inc. ∞

Copyright © 2010 by John Boessenecker. Published by the University of Oklahoma Press, Norman, Publishing Division of the University. Manufactured in the U.S.A.

2 3 4 5 6 7 8 9 10

For Bill Secrest and the late J. E. "Jack" Reynolds

Bandidos such as Tiburcio Vasquez . . . functioned like Mexican Robin Hoods.

National Park Service, *Civil Rights in America,* 2004

Everybody thinks Vasquez was a kind of a hero, when really he was just a thief.

John Steinbeck, *The Pastures of Heaven,* 1932

Contents

Illustrations

Preface and Acknowledgments

Once, California was for Californios. A distant and pastoral province of Mexico, it was an isolated, sparsely settled frontier. Then came the gold rush of 1849. Americans and Europeans flooded in, and almost overnight the Californios, California's Spanish-speaking people, became a tiny minority, strangers in their own land. Today Latin Americans have reclaimed their place in the state. Fully one-third of California's population is Hispanic. Los Angeles is the second largest Mexican city on earth. Hispanic immigration, both legal and illegal, is a compelling national issue. The economic, political, and cultural power and influence of Hispanics increase every day. Tiburcio Vasquez could not have foreseen this change, but he would have liked it.[1]

Tiburcio Vasquez (Tee-BOOR-see-oh BAS-kes) is, next to Joaquín Murrieta, America's most famous Hispanic bandit. At the end of his life, the *Chicago Tribune* called him "the most noted desperado of modern times." The judgment of the *New York Times* was harsher: "With the single exception of Joaquin Murrieta . . . Vasquez is the most thoroughly hardened ruffian that ever terrified a community in the state."[2]

Why write a biography of such an outlaw? Although famous to western history buffs and to generations of Hispanics, who revere him as a Robin Hood–like folk hero, he is unknown to the majority of Americans. In fact, he is often confused with Murrieta, the gold rush bandit who was slain by the California Rangers in 1853.[3] Tiburcio Vasquez led an extraordinary life, filled with high drama. His is a rip-roaring story of romance, adventure, violence, and retribution in the Old West, fraught with shootouts, robberies, lynchings, prison breaks, love affairs, manhunts, and betrayals. Of more substance, his life also illustrates important issues of racism and social injustice on the frontier, the lost history of Mexican Americans, their culture, their role in the West, and their legacy. His story raises many questions. Why did he become a *bandido?* Was he driven to it? Or was he an opportunist who seized on racial strife to justify his crimes? Why did so many Hispanics protect and harbor him and his band? Why have so many in subsequent generations, especially among Hispanics, revered him as a romantic hero, an enduring symbol of resistance to oppression? Why did so many Anglos revile him as a heartless robber and killer? And does his story reveal larger truths about racism and social injustice? By examining his life and times, perhaps we can find answers.

The story of Tiburcio Vasquez is shrouded in mystery and myth. After he was captured near Los Angeles in 1874, newspaper editor Ben C. Truman published a little pamphlet, *The Life, Adventures, and Capture of Tiburcio Vasquez,* a compilation of news articles that had been published in the Los Angeles press. A year later, two more brief paperbacks appeared, also written by newspapermen: Eugene Sawyer's *The Life and Career of Tiburcio Vasquez, the California Bandit and Murderer,* and George Beers's more ambitious *Vasquez; or, the Hunted Bandits of the San Joaquin.*[4] Almost everything that has subsequently appeared in print about Vasquez was based on one or all of these sources. None is remotely complete, as all deal mainly with the final years of his life, and contain myriad errors and omissions. During the past century, hundreds of magazine articles, newspaper stories, and book passages have been devoted to Vasquez, repeating the mistakes multifold. No full-length biography telling Tiburcio Vasquez's true and complete story has ever been written. That is a significant oversight I seek to address.

For forty-one years I have collected material on Vasquez, first researching and writing about him when I was a young student, and later delving into court records, newspaper archives, and private recollections. A great deal of information in this biography has never been published before. Outlaws are by nature shadowy and secretive; they don't leave diaries, correspondence, or detailed records of their lives. Researching them is exceedingly difficult. I could never have completed this work without the generous assistance of many people. First to come to my aid were J. E. "Jack" Reynolds and William B. Secrest. Jack Reynolds, a well-respected

California bookseller, began researching Vasquez in 1946, intending to write a biography. He conducted research until the 1960s, amassing a voluminous collection of data. His Vasquez book never came to fruition, however, and in 1989 he and I agreed to collaborate on the bandit's biography after I completed several other writing projects. When Jack passed away in 1993, before we could begin work, his widow, Rosalie, kindly gave me his files and research notes. My old compadre Bill Secrest, Fresno historian and author, began his own research on Tiburcio Vasquez in the 1950s, and authored a number of magazine articles and book chapters about the bandit and members of his gang. Bill unselfishly shared with me his extensive research, lent me rare photographs, prepared the maps found herein, helped me track down countless historical items, and faithfully answered my never-ending calls and e-mails for help. It is fitting that I dedicate this book to Bill Secrest and Jack Reynolds.

Information about Tiburcio Vasquez's early years is especially sparse, and I could not have reconstructed that period of his life without the invaluable assistance of my friend Dennis Copeland, historian and director of the California History Room and Archives at the Monterey Public Library. Dennis's detective work uncovered many hitherto unknown facts about Tiburcio's boyhood, his family, and his friends. Dennis's fine research skills have greatly enriched this book, and I am deeply indebted to him for his generous help and fellowship. Another good friend, Deborah Melendy Norman, descendant of a pioneer mountain family of San Benito County, provided invaluable help. An astute researcher and genealogist, Debbie located all manner of data about Tiburcio's family, friends, and associates, as well as providing much background information about the mountain region and its people, on whom Vasquez relied for support during the 1860s and 1870s.

My friend Phil Reader, historian and expert on crime in early Santa Cruz, generously lent me his files and provided much information about Vasquez and the members of his band. Ray Iddings of the New Idria Preservation Project, a nonprofit organization dedicated to saving the ghost town of New Idria, took me on a tour of the isolated San Benito County mountains and showed me Tiburcio's hangouts and hideouts. I also owe special thanks to Genevieve Troka of the California State Archives; Gary Kurutz of the California State Library; Susan Snyder of the Bancroft Library at the University of California, Berkeley; John M. Cahoon of the Natural History Museum of Los Angeles County; William P. Frank

of the Huntington Library; James Reed of History San Jose; and Robert
Chandler of the Wells Fargo Bank History Department, all of whom made
materials in their respective collections available to me.

Many more people helped me, and my thanks go out to Christopher
Brennen; Daniel Buck; Sven Crongeyer of the Los Angeles County
Sheriff's Department; Harold L. "Lee" Edwards; Gary Engle; Carlo M.
De Ferrari; Mona Gudgel of the Monterey County Historical Society;
Georgianna Gularte; Phil Hudner; Charles Johnson of the Ventura County
Museum; Ron Lerch; Patsy Ludwig; Pat Mazzini of the Sonoma County
Historical Society; Robert G. McCubbin; Bobby McDearmon; John
McWilliams; Rubén G. Mendoza, Ph.D.; Charles C. Miller; Jocelyn Moss
of the Marin History Museum; Kevin J. Mullen; Jay O'Connell; Steve
Patsis; Daniel J. Patterson; Chris Penn; Sheila Lee Prader; Elayne Silva
Reyna; Jo Ellen Rismanchi; Dan Schmidt; Brother Lawrence Scrivari;
the late Albert Shumate; Ray Silvia; Peter Sonne; Phil Spangenberger;
Corinne Stasinos; Glen Swanson, Paul Trejo; Troy Tuggle; Elisabeth Waldo;
Bill Williams; Beatriz C. Wing; Daniel Woodhead; Marian Wydo; and
Conrad Yamamoto.

I owe a special debt of gratitude to those friends and colleagues who
read the manuscript and offered their helpful advice and criticism: Dennis
Copeland, Deborah Melendy Norman, Jay O'Connell, Bill Secrest, and
his son, historian Bill Secrest, Jr. Thanks also to my editors, Alice Stanton
and Kirsteen Anderson.

Lastly, heartfelt thanks to my wife Marta S. Diaz, for her love, support,
advice, proofreading, Spanish translations, and especially, for her efforts
to cultivate in her gringo husband an understanding of the customs and
culture of old Mexico.

Finally, a brief comment on my linguistic choices. I use "Californios"
in referring to native-born, Spanish-speaking Californians; "Mexicans"
in referring to natives of Mexico; and "Indians" in referring to Native
Americans. Often, however, the historical record does not designate the
nativity of a Spanish-speaking person, who generally belonged to one of
frontier California's three main Spanish-speaking groups—Californio,
Mexican, or Chileno—and in such cases I refer to the individual as
Hispanic. I also employ the widely used term "Hispanic" in a generic
sense for Spanish-speaking residents of California. For the same reason I
use the term "Anglo" to refer to California's white, English-speaking population, although it included Irish and many other European heritages.

The inclusion of Spanish words and phrases conveys a flavor of the times and sometimes is necessary for specificity. I am very aware, however, that most of my readers will be English speakers with little or no knowledge of Spanish. Therefore, I treat terms borrowed from Spanish using English conventions: capitalizing Californio, for example, and not inflecting the term for gender to create a potentially confusing alternation between "Californio" and "California." I generally accent Hispanic names as they would be in Spanish, but make an exception for the Vasquez family, because in historical sources, the name was almost invariably spelled Vasquez, not Vásquez. Spanish-language place-names within the United States are spelled according to current conventions, without accents (for example, San Jose, California).

Bandido

Tiburcio Vasquez's

CALIFORNIA

■ Yreka

■ Redding

Oroville
■
Grass Valley
■
Marysville
■
SIERRA

Hopland
■
Santa Rosa
■ Petaluma
Sacramento
■
Jackson
■
Mokelumne Hill
San Quentin
Stockton
■
Oakland
■ Sonora
San Leandro
San Francisco
Livermore
●
SAN
JOAQUIN
NEVADA

COAST
San Jose
■ Pacheco Pass
Gilroy
●
San Juan Bautista
Firebaugh's
Tres Pinos
Ferry
Santa Cruz
New Idria
Rancho de
los Californios
Millerton
■
■ Fresno
Lone Pine
■

Monterey
Cantua Canyon
●
Kingston
■
● Visalia
Cerro Gordo
■

RANGE
● Poso Chane
● Tulare Lake
VALLEY

Coyote Holes
●

San Emigdio
●
■ Bakersfield
San Luis Obispo
■
● Tejon Pass
MOJAVE DESERT

TEHACHAPI MTS.

Elizabeth Lake
●
Soledad Canyon
●
Santa Barbara
■
Rock Creek Canyon
●
Greek George's
House
●
Ventura
■ Los Angeles

N

0   50   100

Campo
■
Fort Yuma
San Diego
■

Map by William B. Secrest.

CHAPTER ONE

Sons of the Conquistadores

The heat came up out of Sonora and struck them like a drawn blade. Juan Atanasio Vasquez, his wife, and three sons bent over their horses as they trudged north through the Mexican desert. With them were almost two hundred fellow travelers—neighbors, friends, and strangers; women and children; the poorest of the poor, *soldados, peones,* and campesinos— recruited in Sinaloa and Sonora to make the long trek to California. The hooves of five hundred horses and mules shook the ground and stirred up clouds of dust, turning the men's white *pantalones* brown. Women swayed in their saddles, clutching their *rebozos* tightly over their heads as protection from the merciless sun. Amidst the neighing of horses and the groaning of pack mules was an overwhelming sense of fear and anticipation. But they were sturdy and strong, spurred on by the promise of a little money, clothing, and livestock; the protection of the Virgin of Guadalupe; and hope for a new life in a distant land.

Their leader was Lieutenant Colonel Juan Bautista de Anza, a nails-tough Indian fighter and trailblazer, commander of Tubac presidio, the last of the conquistadores. A year earlier he had led a party of leather-jacketed soldiers from Tubac to the Mission San Gabriel, near what is now Los Angeles, and then north to Monterey. For the first time an overland route, 1,200 miles long, had been blazed from northern Mexico to Alta (Upper) California.

California had first been explored more than two hundred years earlier by Juan Rodríguez Cabrillo, who sailed up the Pacific Coast in 1542, and

Sebastian Vizcaino, who mapped the coast in 1602, reaching Monterey Bay at year's end. They found a landscape of mild climate, populated only by Indians, lush with flowing streams, high grass, dense forests, wild game, flocks of fowl, and endless rolling hills and pastureland perfect for grazing cattle. By 1767, a string of Catholic missions had been established on the Baja California peninsula. In 1769, Gaspar de Portolá, at the head of an exploring party that included Father Junípero Serra, landed by ship in San Diego. They established a mission and presidio, then marched north through Alta California to San Francisco Bay. Portolá and Serra returned to Monterey the following year, founding another mission and presidio there. A year later Father Serra established Mission Carmel four miles south of Monterey at the mouth of the Carmel River. Eventually twenty-one missions would be built in Alta California, from San Diego in the south to Sonoma in the north. Each was a day's ride apart, about thirty miles, and connected by a dusty trail: El Camino Real, The King's Highway. At the missions, Franciscan priests strove to convert the Indian population to Catholicism and train them in trades and farming skills. Their religious mandate was to save souls, but their political purpose was to make the Indians loyal subjects of Spain.

The province was a raw frontier, and the Spanish government, fearing it would be claimed by Great Britain or Russia, wanted colonists to settle it. In early 1775, Juan Bautista de Anza was ordered to bring a contingent of settlers to Alta California on the trail he had pioneered. He set out personally to recruit colonists in the dusty, impoverished, mixed-race pueblos of Sonora and Sinaloa. On March 28, 1775, he began seeking volunteer soldiers and *pobladores* (settlers) in the plaza at Culiacán, the principal town of Sinaloa. Each family was offered two years' pay, five years of rations, new clothes, weapons, horses, and cattle. Anza's popularity and stature attracted many potential recruits, but only the most desperately poor seriously considered the dangerous journey. The first man to sign Anza's roster, enlisting as an army private, was forty-year-old campesino (farm laborer) Juan Atanasio Vasquez. He was listed as a *mulato*—of mixed Spanish and African blood, a descendant of one of the many slaves brought to Mexico by the Spanish. Like most volunteers, Vasquez agreed to bring along his family: wife María Gertrudis Castelo, and sons José Tiburcio, age twenty; José Antonio, age eight; and Pedro José, age seven. In September, most of the company assembled at San Miguel de Horcasitas, the adobe capital of Sonora, then departed for the presidio of Tubac, two hundred miles distant on the northern frontier in what is now southern Arizona. Along the way, the eldest Vasquez son, José Tiburcio, became enamored with María Ana Bojorques, the fifteen-year-old daughter of another colonist. She was a *mestiza,* of mixed Spanish and Indian blood.

On October 23, Anza left Tubac at the head of a column of 240 men, women, and children, including thirty-eight soldiers. They numbered among them many of the founding families of California: Moraga, Pico, Bernal, Castro, Soto, Alviso, Pacheco, Bojorques, García, Peralta, Berreyesa, Valencia, Sánchez, Sotelo, Galindo, Linares, Higuera, Tapia, and Feliz. Due to the size of the company, which included 340 horses, 320 head of cattle, and 165 mules laden with provisions, they traveled slowly, covering only ten to twenty miles a day. Two days out they arrived at Mission San Xavier del Bac, just south of what is now Tucson, Arizona. In the morning the young lovers, José Tiburcio Vasquez and María Ana Bojorques, along with two other couples, were married in the mission by Father Pedro Font, the company chaplain. Within hours they resumed the northward march. Passing through the little presidio of Tucson, they pressed on to the Gila River, following it west to its junction with the Colorado. Fortunately, they had no trouble with Indians, but the trip took months and was arduous in the extreme. Long stretches without water forced well-digging, which yielded but a few quarts of alkali liquid. The blistering heat of Sonora was soon replaced by bitter cold and lashing rain, hail, and snowstorms. There was little wood for fires, and many fell sick. Others continually had to chase cattle that strayed to find water, and a hundred head died of thirst. But Anza pushed the colonists on relentlessly across the Mojave Desert.

On January 4, 1776, amidst great rejoicing, the settlers finally arrived at Mission San Gabriel. Here they rested for six weeks, before setting off north behind Anza. Although slowed down by heavy rain, deep mud, and flooded streams, they reached Monterey on March 10. Along the way, there had been but one death—of a woman in childbirth—and eight new colonists had been born along the trail from Sonora. Two weeks later Anza led an exploring party of soldiers farther north to explore San Francisco Bay and locate the site for a presidio. On his return to Monterey, Anza ordered his lieutenant, José Joaquín Moraga, to lead twenty soldiers plus a small group of settlers, including the Vasquez family, to San Francisco Bay. Arriving on June 27, 1776, they built brush huts the following day, and a day later celebrated mass under a brush arbor at a spot that would become Mission Dolores. These events marked the founding of the city of San

Francisco, six days before the signing of the Declaration of Independence, a continent away.[1]

Small communities quickly grew up around the missions, especially at San Diego, Monterey, San Luis Obispo, and Santa Barbara. In 1797 Mission San Juan Bautista and its satellite San Juan pueblo were established in the Pajaro River valley, east of the Gabilan Mountains and thirty miles from Monterey.[2] In addition to founding missions, the Spanish government established civilian pueblos at San Jose, Los Angeles, and Branciforte, now part of Santa Cruz. Despite these developments, California became even more isolated in 1781, when mistreated Yuma Indians retaliated against the Spanish. They attacked the missions and settlements near the Colorado River crossing, killing all the male adults and herding the women and children into slavery. The Yuma Massacre effectively closed the Anza trail to California, halting overland immigration. With few incoming settlers, the original families of the Anza expedition intermarried, and within several generations many Californios were related through blood or marriage. At the same time, the horses and cattle brought by Anza multiplied into vast herds which ranged and fattened freely on the grassy hills. California's non-Indian population of 600 in 1781 grew to about 3,700 forty years later.

Juan Atanasio Vasquez remained at the San Francisco presidio, but within a year his son José Tiburcio—along with the latter's wife, infant daughter, and sixty-three other soldados and pobladores—were persuaded to try their luck at starting a new pueblo at the south end of San Francisco Bay. Lieutenant Moraga led them to a spot eight miles below the southern tip of the bay, where on November 29, 1777, ground was broken. This new settlement, a few miles southeast of Mission Santa Clara, which had been founded earlier that year, was christened San Jose. As was customary, the Spanish government provided the settlers with enough basic necessities to start a new life. José Tiburcio Vasquez and his wife, like almost everyone in the little pueblo, received an allotment of one horse, one mule, two mares, two oxen, two cows, one calf, two sheep, and two goats. Thus, in little more than a year the Vasquez family had helped establish what would become two of the largest cities in the western United States.[3]

In the new pueblo José Tiburcio Vasquez was, like his father before him, listed in government records as a *mulato*. Yet this did not prevent him from becoming a prominent citizen of San Jose. Of the nine heads of families in the pueblo, only he could read and write. He lived out his life in San Jose, serving in 1794, 1802, and 1807 as *alcalde* (chief town administrator, a combination of mayor and judge). José Tiburcio and his wife had thirteen children, of whom four died in early childhood. Their fifth was a son, José Hermenegildo Vasquez, born in 1784. In time, Hermenegildo would sire Tiburcio Vasquez, the *bandido*.[4]

Like his grandfather, Hermenegildo Vasquez served as a Spanish soldier. In 1808 he was stationed at the garrison in Monterey, where he served for many years. There he met María Guadalupe Cantúa, first-born daughter of Juan Bautista Cantúa. Her grandfather, Ignacio Cantúa, was likewise a soldier who had been garrisoned at Monterey in 1782, and remained there long past his retirement in 1813. Hermenegildo Vasquez and Guadalupe Cantúa were married in the Royal Presidio Chapel in Monterey on February 26, 1821. Hermenegildo was thirty-six and Guadalupe just sixteen. Their twenty-year age difference was not unusual in that era; because of the lack of women, older men commonly married teenage girls. The relationship was undoubtedly passionate, for when they wed, Guadalupe was already six months pregnant.[5]

Among the upper classes, courtships were rigidly conducted, and señoritas were not allowed in the company of suitors unless a *dueña,* or chaperone, was present. This was frequently not true of the lower economic classes, however, who often could not afford elaborate customs to preserve their daughters' chastity. Often young unmarried women of the Vasquez family's social class were allowed to mingle freely with men and boys, and as a result, premarital sex was more common than among the wealthy *ranchero* families. Despite the active efforts of Catholic priests and government officials to suppress illicit sex, Mexican California saw a fairly high degree of illegitimate births.[6]

The couple's first child, Fernando Vasquez, was born on May 30, 1821, and baptized at Mission Carmel the next day. Infant death was common, and in less than three weeks the baby was dead. The grief-stricken couple promptly conceived another child, a daughter, Manuela, born the following year. Like most Californios of that era, they raised a large family. In 1824 a son, José Miguel Pedro, who was always known by the nickname Claudio, was born. More children quickly followed: Antonio María in 1826, María Concepción in 1828, Francisco (nicknamed "Chico") in 1830, José Joaquín in 1832, María Antonia in 1833, Tiburcio in 1835, and finally María Josefa, 1837.[7]

For the first five years of their marriage, Don Hermenegildo and Doña Guadalupe Vasquez lived in the Monterey area. He quit soldiering, and in 1826 they moved north with their growing brood to San Jose, where they lived near his father, José Tiburcio. The elder Vasquez, then in ill health, died a year later and was buried at Mission Santa Clara. Like his father, Hermenegildo was a prominent citizen of San Jose. He too could read and write, and served for a year as *regidor* (councilman). An unpaid position, it was nonetheless an office of prestige. After living in San Jose for six years, he and his family moved to the area of Rancho San Ysidro, near what is now Gilroy, forty miles north of Monterey. Doña Guadalupe's uncle, Julián Cantúa, was the son-in-law of the rancho's owner, Ignacio Ortega, and Cantúa and his wife had been granted a 4,000-acre section of the rancho. Hermenegildo went to work for the Ortegas. Possibly he was a vaquero, but as an educated man, he probably also performed clerical duties. Hermenegildo, however, longed for his own rancho.[8]

The Spanish government at first required that settlers live in the pueblos. Much of the range land was set aside for support of the missions and controlled by the mission padres, who opposed private landownership. They believed that the settlers, if allowed to commingle with their Indian wards, would corrupt them morally. The Spanish government soon allowed private land grants, provided that they were outside the pueblos and did not conflict with mission lands or Indian villages. After Mexico won independence from Spain in 1821, grants of land became even more liberal. In 1790 there were but nineteen private ranchos in California; by 1830 there were fifty, with fourteen in the Monterey district alone. The smallest grants were four leagues, almost 18,000 acres. By the 1830s some of the most desirable grants, such as those in the Salinas and Pajaro river valleys, had been subdivided into much smaller tracts. In 1834 the Mexican government secularized the missions, and hundreds of square miles of verdant grazing land were opened to private ownership. Now, any Mexican citizen could apply for a land grant, and by 1840 there were more than one thousand private grants in California, large and small. Retired soldiers were also granted small plots of land. In the Monterey district, the number of private grants increased to ninety-five during the 1830s.

Some of the ranchos were vast indeed. Francisco Pacheco, who owned several ranchos in what would become Monterey and Merced counties, held a total of more than 125,000 acres, with 500 horses, 14,000 head of cattle, and 15,000 sheep. David Spence, a transplanted Scot who married into a prominent Californio family, owned 25,000 acres and 4,000 cattle on the Salinas River. Most ranchos in the Monterey district were far more modest, however, ranging from 2,000 to 8,000 acres. In such a vast, under-populated territory, land was plentiful and the borders of ranchos were vaguely defined. Fences were unknown. Rancheros allowed their half-wild cattle to graze widely. As most local rancheros were related by blood or marriage, there were few complaints when cattle strayed onto a neighbor's land.[9]

Ranch life in California produced some of the world's finest horsemen. Californios learned to ride in early childhood, becoming so attached to their mounts that laws were passed prohibiting the riding of horses into places of business. Men were commonly bowlegged and pigeon-toed from spending much of their lives in the saddle. California mustangs (from the Spanish word *mesteño*) were sturdy, fast, well adapted to working with cattle, and unlike American horses, could be fed on grass rather than grain. Stock herders, or *vaqueros* (a term later corrupted by Anglos into "buckaroo") were the prototypes of the American cowboy. The cowboy's hat, chaps (*chaparreras*), lariat (*la reata*), saddle, spurs, and branding irons were all adapted from those of the vaqueros of California and Texas. Because the California range was open and unfenced, cattle were rounded up in rodeos and marked with the owner's brand. Californios herded sheep and cattle on the same range, a tradition that carried over into the American era. The result was that California saw little of the conflict between cattlemen and sheep men that was so common in the West during the second half of the nineteenth century.

Cattle raising became the cornerstone of California's economy. Although most Californios lived near the ocean, few ate fish. Beef was the principal food. Cattle hides provided leather for boots, saddles, reatas, and even door hinges. Fat from butchered cattle was boiled and melted into tallow to make candles and soap. In the mid-1820s Yankee merchant ships from New England began making regular visits to California ports, principally San Diego, Los Angeles, and Monterey. Soon a bustling trade developed, with Californios obtaining both necessities and luxuries from Yankee traders in exchange for hides and tallow. So important was this trade that Yankee merchants called a dried steer hide, which had a value of one dollar, a "California bank note." The larger merchant ships could carry as many as 30,000 hides back to the New England shoe industry. Many Yankee traders settled permanently in California, learned to speak Spanish, were baptized in the Catholic faith, married Californio women, and became socially and politically prominent. During the 1830s, American trappers began to arrive in California. These rough, uneducated mountain men were less likely than the merchants and seafarers to embrace Catholicism and the Californio culture.[10]

Class lines were strictly defined in Mexican California. The *ricos*—rancheros and *hacendados*—and families claiming pure Spanish extraction were at the top; mestizos, those of mixed Spanish-Indian blood, were below them; and Christianized Indians were relegated to the bottom. Many mestizos and even mulatos became landed ricos through distinguished military or government service.

California's remoteness from Mexico prompted its people to become self-reliant and independent. They resented politicians and military figures sent from Mexico to govern them. By the time of Tiburcio's birth, Californios increasingly saw their homeland as separate and distinct from Mexico. They dubbed themselves *hijos del país* (native sons) and Californios instead of Mexicans. Prior to the American occupation, the term "Californio" described the elite class of propertied rancheros. During the gold rush, Anglos came to apply the label to all native-born, Spanish-speaking Californians, regardless of class or degree of Indian blood, so as to distinguish them from Mexican and South American immigrants. After 1850, Californios were increasingly referred to as Californians by Anglo newspaper editors.

Social life revolved around the family, and Californio families were indeed large. Because women married young, frequently in their mid-teens, they sometimes gave birth to ten or even twenty children. Catholicism was central to the life of Californios; everyone attended Sunday mass. Religious festivals were celebrated with elaborate feasts in the pueblos that could last for days. Rancheros wore their finest outfits and rode their best horses; women and children arrived in creaky, two-wheeled carts called *carretas*. Beeves were butchered and barbecued over large outdoor fires. The central plaza was blocked off with brush fences so that bloody battles between bulls and grizzly bears could be staged. Cockfighting and horse racing were also highly popular, as was *carrera del gallo*, a contest of skill in which vaqueros, riding at top speed, would attempt to swing down from the saddle and snatch up a live rooster, half-buried in the ground. Californios, both men and women, loved to gamble, and betting was heavy at such events, with the stakes often being horses, cattle, or land.[11]

At such feasts, carne asada, frijoles, enchiladas, and tamales would be washed down with the Californios' favorite liquor, *aguardiente,* a coarse brandy often made from a mixture of rum and mescal. Guitar playing and singing were highly valued skills, but dancing was the most popular of all social pastimes. Californios were almost fanatical in their love for *bailes,* or dances. As Walter Colton, later alcalde of Monterey, pointed out, "A Californian would hardly pause in a dance for an earthquake, and would renew it before the vibrations ceased." In an isolated frontier offering little in the way of entertainment, dances were the height of Californio social life. Dancers wore elaborate and colorful costumes, and to the strains of the guitar and the clicking of castanets, they danced the popular styles of the era: *la jota, la bamba, el jarabe tapatío, el son,* and *el fandango.* So popular was the last that the term "fandango" became synonymous with dancing, and during the gold rush, all Spanish-Mexican dance halls were called fandango houses. Bailes provided prime opportunities for young men and women to meet, and were scenes of much wooing and courting. In one favorite tradition, *los cascarones,* eggs would be emptied and colored, then filled with perfume and sealed with wax. At fiestas, young Californios of both sexes would playfully break the eggshells on the heads of those they favored, hoping thereby to begin a courtship.[12]

Under Mexican law, women were allowed to own separate property in their own right. Doña Guadalupe may have received a small inheritance from her father or grandfather, for in 1834 she purchased an adobe house on a 150-foot-by-150-foot lot, situated on a gentle hill overlooking Monterey. It was a typical Monterey adobe, having a narrow single story forty feet long and fifteen feet wide, with a peaked tile roof and just two rooms; a large *sala,* or living room, on the north end and a combined bedroom and kitchen on the south. In front was a long covered portico with two doors that opened directly into the rooms; each room also had a back door, opening directly into the yard behind. The mud-brick walls, two and a half feet thick, provided insulation that helped keep the house warm in winter and cool in summer. The adobe (although remodeled in 1924 with a second story and a ground-floor addition) still stands at 546 Dutra Street and is now owned by the city of Monterey. From the house

The Vasquez family home in Monterey. The adobe and the huge Monterey cypress tree in front are still standing. (California History Room, Monterey Public Library)

was a gentle, sloping grade to the little pueblo below, with sweeping views of Monterey Bay beyond. It was a picturesque and idyllic place to raise a family.[13]

Guadalupe was already expecting her ninth child when she and Hermenegildo moved their brood from Rancho San Ysidro into this hillside Monterey home. In this crowded but comfortable little adobe a son was born five months later, on April 10, 1835. The same day the family and relatives walked the short distance to the Capilla de Monterey, the Royal Presidio Chapel (which is still standing), where the infant was anointed with holy oils and baptized Tiburcio Vasquez by Monterey's padre. He was named after both his grandfather and uncle. His namesake, St. Tiburtius, was a Roman, martyred in A.D. 286. The feast day of San Tiburcio is August 11, so in the Spanish tradition, Tiburcio's birthday was celebrated on this saint's day. Thus Tiburcio Vasquez always said that his birth date was August 11, 1835. Tiburcio's godmother, Mariana Escamilla, was the young wife of James Watson, an Englishman who had settled in Monterey. Their one-year-old son, Tomás, would become sheriff of Monterey County and play a prominent role in Tiburcio's life.[14]

Tiburcio once recalled, "The first years of my life were spent . . . in the usual manner of the young of my life and class." There were many children in Monterey. Two doors away from the Vasquez house, less than two hundred feet north, stood the large adobe of Raymunda Castillo, the beautiful young mistress of California Governor Juan Bautista Alvarado. Alvarado had the house built for her in 1831, and she lived there for nine years. In this adobe, still standing at 510 Dutra Street, Raymunda bore five daughters by her lover. Alvarado openly acknowledged and supported the girls, and gave them his last name. Due to their father's prominence, they were socially accepted in Monterey, even though they were illegitimate. The girls were undoubtedly playmates of the younger Vasquez children. One of them, Estefana, was a year older than Tiburcio, and another, Francisca, was a year younger. They undoubtedly shared many childhood experiences with the future bandit children. Like other Monterey children, they rode wooden hobby horses in the hills and played *gallina ciega* (blind man's bluff), *vaquela* (throwing stones at a mark on the ground), *cana* (skipping stones), *tagamo* (peg toss), and on rainy days, *naipes* (cards).[15]

Monterey served as the capital of California from 1776 to 1849, under the flags of Spain, Mexico, and the United States. During Tiburcio's

The street that Tiburcio Vasquez grew up on. The Vasquez adobe is at the left; in the center, at the end of the street, is the large adobe of Raymunda Castillo. (California History Room, Monterey Public Library)

childhood it was the most important town on the Pacific Coast. Montereños were proud of their little adobe pueblo, which at the time of Tiburcio's birth had a population of about one thousand, a number that would remain more or less constant until 1880. But when Sir George Simpson, head of the Hudson Bay Company, visited in 1841, he was not impressed. He described Monterey as "a mere collection of buildings, scattered as loosely on the surface as if they were so many bullocks at pasture; so that the most expert surveyor could not possibly classify them into crooked streets." Simpson, an Englishman who was not above denigrating the Californios, saw nothing picturesque:

> The dwellings, some of which attain the dignity of a second story, are all built of adobes, being sheltered on every side from the sun by overhanging eaves, while toward the rainy quarter of the southeast they enjoy the additional protection of boughs of trees, resting like so many ladders on the roof. . . . Externally the habitations have a cheerless aspect in consequence of the paucity of windows. . . . As to public buildings this capital of a province may, with a stretch of charity, be allowed to possess four. First is the church, part of which is going to decay, while another part is not yet finished; its only peculiarity is that it is built, or rather half built, of stone. Next comes the castle, consisting of a small house, surrounded by a low wall, all of adobes. It commands the town and anchorage, if a garrison of five soldiers and a battery of eight or ten rusty and honey-combed guns can be said to command anything. Third is the guard-house, a paltry mud hut without windows. Fourth and last stands the custom-house, which is, or rather promises to be, a small range of decent offices; for though it has been building for five years it is not yet finished.[16]

As a former soldier, Hermenegildo was entitled to seek a grant of land from the Mexican government, and did so six months after Tiburcio's birth. He sent a petition to Governor José Castro, asserting that he had "a numerous family and having no other means to maintain them than his personal exertions . . . asks for five hundred *varas* of land" on the Pajaro River near San Juan Bautista. Eight months later Hermenegildo was granted a small section of land measuring four hundred varas by five hundred varas, about forty acres, situated on a bend of the Pajaro River about three miles northwest of San Juan Bautista and just west of its confluence with San Benito Creek. This land had once been owned by Mission San Juan Bautista, but was taken over by the Mexican government when the missions were secularized. Here Hermenegildo built an adobe house, cultivated the rich fields, grew vegetables, and raised a small herd of cattle. It was known as the Felix, or Feliz, rancho. Hermenegildo's brothers had been much more fortunate than he, due no doubt to their better political connections. The same year Felipe Vasquez was granted the 2,700-acre Rancho El Chamisal bordering Pilarcitos Canyon, east of Monterey. In 1839 José Tiburcio Vasquez was granted the nearly 4,500-acre Rancho Corral de Tierra, in San Mateo County, and became the first settler at Half Moon Bay.[17]

Don Hermenegildo owned several ox-drawn carretas, which he used to bring produce to market in Monterey. Sometimes, he would rent them out, particularly to his neighbor, Manuel Larios, a wealthy ranchero of San Juan Bautista. But in 1840 his wealthy neighbor failed to return them and pay for their use, so Hermenegildo sought assistance from the local magistrate to force Larios to give back the carts. Soon his teenage sons, Claudio and Antonio María, were working for their father as teamsters, hauling produce, tallow, soap, hides, and lumber between San Juan Bautista, Monterey, the Gilroy rancho, and Santa Cruz. Claudio and Antonio were hardworking and evidently had a corner on the market, as one prominent merchant repeatedly hired them to bring lumber and other heavy goods to his Monterey store, and complained when they were too busy to work for him.[18]

In 1838 Tiburcio's eldest sister, fifteen-year-old Manuela, was courted by a carpenter, Tomás Salgado, age twenty-three, whose family had recently emigrated from Mexico and settled in San Juan Bautista. On April 22, at Mission San Juan Bautista, they were married amidst great celebration. Because guests often traveled long distances from outlying ranchos, wedding fiestas might last from three days to a week. A contemporary described the typical scene: "The married couple then enter the house, where the near relatives are all waiting in tears to receive them. They kneel down before the parents of the lady, and crave a blessing, which is bestowed with patriarchal solemnity. On rising, the bridegroom makes a signal for the guests to come in, and another for the guitar and harp to strike up. Then commences the dancing, with only brief intervals for refreshment, but none for slumber: the wedded pair must be on their feet." Manuela and Tomás Salgado quickly began raising a large family. They later moved permanently to the little pueblo at San Juan Bautista. Tiburcio would be a regular visitor to their home, and San Juan became, next to Monterey, his favorite haunt.[19]

Tragedy struck when Tiburcio's youngest sister, María Josefa, died in early childhood. In 1841 there was more grief when his brother, José Joaquín, three years his senior, died a few weeks before his tenth birthday. A year later, Tiburcio's brother Claudio, then eighteen, romanced a teenage girl named Dolores Espinosa. She was half California Indian and had been raised in San Juan. In July 1843 she gave birth out of wedlock to a daughter, Concepción Espinosa. Apparently neither Claudio nor Dolores was able to provide for the child, for Doña Guadalupe took her new granddaughter into her home and raised the child as one of her own. Concepción Espinosa, who was always treated as a sister, would play an important role in Tiburcio's adult life. The relationship between Claudio and Dolores soon ended, although Dolores remained close to the Vasquez family. She was later courted by Francisco Chávez, a young *borreguero,* or sheepherder, from New Mexico. At the same time, Jesús Soto, a thirty-year-old Monterey musician, began wooing Tiburcio's teenage sister, Concepción. On August 6, 1845, in a triple wedding at Mission Carmel, the two couples married, as did Jesús Soto's brother, Lorenzo. Francisco and Dolores Chávez raised a large family in San Juan, and their son, Clodoveo Chávez, would become very important in Tiburcio Vasquez's life.[20]

Concepción Vasquez and Jesús Soto moved into a small adobe located just north of the Vasquez house on her mother's large lot. Here they raised three children. The Vasquez family was close-knit, and Doña Guadalupe always lived with or near her daughters. The family was middle class, as Tiburcio later recalled: "My parents were people in ordinarily good circumstances, owning a small tract of land, and always had enough for their wants."

Tiburcio was especially close to his sister María Antonia, two years his senior, whom he once said was like a mother to him. In 1847, when she was just thirteen, María found herself in the same predicament as Dolores: unmarried and expecting a baby. In May she gave birth to a healthy boy. Perhaps she endeavored to keep the birth from her parents, for he was not baptized until six weeks later, something most unusual in that era. The child was christened Jesús, but María declined to tell the priest who the father was. Doña Guadalupe could not have been angry with her daughter for long. After all, as a young girl she had done the same thing, but did not have the misfortune of being abandoned by her lover. Like Concepción Espinosa, Jesús would be raised by Doña Guadalupe and her daughters.[21]

Amidst a close and loving family, Tiburcio Vasquez would grow to manhood in the fog-swept adobe pueblo. Like everything else in California, he was an amalgamation of the old world and the new. In the boy's veins ran the blood of the Spaniard, the African, and the Indian. But, born and bred, he was all Californio.

CHAPTER TWO

In Old Monterey

To understand Tiburcio Vasquez, one must know old Monterey. Today it is a picturesque seaside town, a tourist's paradise, and together with neighboring Carmel, a great artists' colony. Its simple beauty and serenity, its breathtaking landscapes and ocean views, and its quaint *paisano* culture attracted many of the great artists and literary figures of the late nineteenth and twentieth centuries. The Monterey Bay Aquarium, Cannery Row, Fisherman's Wharf, and the historic adobes of the "Old Spanish Capital" are among America's most popular tourist destinations. But long before Robert Louis Stevenson lived in the village, long before there was a John Steinbeck or a *Tortilla Flat* or a *Cannery Row* or an aquarium, there was another Monterey altogether. The public memory of that Monterey has completely vanished.

Dozens of ancient adobes line the old streets of the town, each a visible link to the distant past, each a silent witness to extraordinary events of Tiburcio's youth, ironically now forgotten: wide-eyed, barefoot boys following a mounted bandido as he canters down Calle Principal, a heavy pair of Colt's Dragoons in pommel holsters and a string of severed ears draped around his saddle horn; a murdering outlaw publicly hanged, and then freed when the rope miraculously breaks; the historic two-story Cooper-Molera adobe and the ancient Monterey cypress behind, its branches decorated with the dangling corpse of a lynched gambler; a vicious feud over a beautiful widow's fortune that left ten men dead; lonely travelers robbed and murdered on the roads leading out of the pueblo; public officers shot down in broad daylight; and desperate gun battles between heavily armed ruffians in saloons and fandango houses.

This was the Monterey region that saw forty murders in three years and spawned some of the worst outlaws of the Old West: the sinister robber-killers Salomon Pico, Domingo Hernández, Mariano Hernández, and Capistrano López; Anastacio García, who reportedly confessed to fourteen murders; the notorious brigand William Otis Hall; "English Jim" Stuart and his gang of Australian freebooters; the gunfighting Bushton boys; the desperado Obispo Arceo; and last but certainly not least, its native son who would become the last great bandido chieftain, Tiburcio Vasquez. This is a Monterey that does not fit well with the modern image of a romantic artists' colony or picturesque vacation resort. It is a Monterey that the city's boosters, arts and historical associations, museums, and chamber of commerce do not readily publicize. It is a Monterey that won't be found in the city's highly promoted Path of History, the walking tour of historic adobes. But it cannot be completely buried, for it is there, if only in dusty court records, forgotten memoirs, moldering newspaper archives, and the mute memory of ancient adobe walls.

Nineteenth-century writers such as Hubert Howe Bancroft painted Mexican California as a pastoral arcadia where crime and violence were all but unknown. That was hardly true. Mexican California saw significant rates of murder, theft, assault, and domestic violence. Long before the Americans arrived, Monterey had been a town of political intrigue, turmoil, rebellion, and occasional violent crime. An early historian said that Monterey County "had hundreds of disreputable characters, vagabonds and convicts forced upon her. . . . The Mexican government for several years made Monterey a dumping ground for her worthless class."[1] There were other dangers as well. In 1818 the notorious French privateer Hippolyte de Bouchard, at the head of 350 cutthroats from Argentina, sailed into Monterey Bay and sacked and burned the town. The Spanish garrison was too weak to oppose them. All Hermenegildo Vasquez and his fellow soldiers could do was to flee into the hills with everyone else. In 1823 the infamous Indian outlaw Pomponio terrorized the settlements between Monterey and Sonoma. He raided the missions, kidnapped women, and murdered numerous fellow Indians, even killing several of his own men after they were wounded by pursuers. He was finally captured near Novato, brought to Monterey for trial, and executed by firing squad there on September 6, 1824.[2]

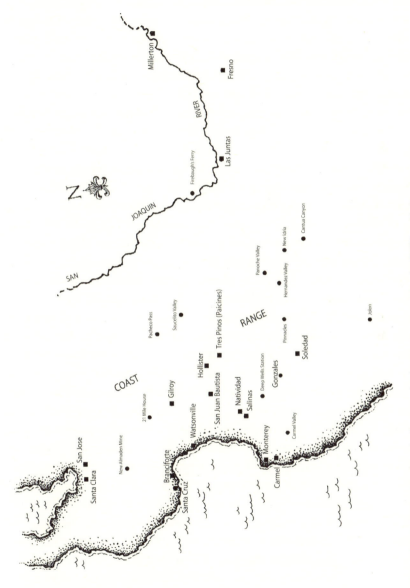

Central California, showing the haunts of Tiburcio Vasquez. Map by William B. Secrest.

By the time of Tiburcio's birth, Californios' increasing independence from Mexico was leading them to seek home rule. In 1836, when Tiburcio was little more than a year old, the patriot Juan Bautista Alvarado put together a ragtag army of revolutionaries. It consisted of some 175 Californios armed with antiquated and inaccurate *escopetas* (muskets) and the traditional Californio weapon, the lance, made from a butcher knife affixed to the tip of a long willow pole. Alvarado was joined by the notorious Tennessee mountain man Isaac Graham, owner of a whiskey distillery in nearby Natividad, who led a motley band of fifty American fur trappers and sailors, plus Indians and Mexicans, many armed with modern rifles. They seized the Monterey presidio without bloodshed, captured the Mexican-appointed governor, and sent him back to Mexico by ship. Two years later Alvarado, despite his rebellion, was confirmed as governor by the Mexican government. But he mistrusted Isaac Graham and his men, whom he saw as violent, drunken troublemakers. In 1840, suspecting that Graham was plotting to overthrow him, Alvarado sent the mountain man and forty-five of his followers to Mexico in chains. After a year in exile in Mexico, they were acquitted of all charges and given free passage back to California. In July 1841, when Tiburcio was six, Montereños were surprised to see Graham and two dozen fellow ruffians, armed with rifles and swords, disembark from a schooner in the bay. The presence of these restless and quarrelsome Americans in the pueblo would foreshadow bitter changes for the Californios.[3]

In 1842 a new Mexican governor, Manuel Micheltorena, arrived in Monterey, accompanied by a battalion of three hundred *cholos,* convicts who had been conscripted into military service. Though Micheltorena was an able governor, he proved highly unpopular as his cholo army engaged in much petty thievery and molested women, much to the outrage of Californios. Former Governor Juan Bautista Alvarado and General José Castro of Monterey led a revolt against him. In February 1845, after a battle with the rebels at Cahuenga Pass near Los Angeles, Micheltorena agreed to leave California with his cholos, and the prominent Californio Pío Pico became governor. These events demonstrated to the U.S. government how weak was Mexico's hold on its northernmost frontier.[4]

In addition to civil unrest, sporadic violent crime made life in Monterey dangerous. But the greatest danger to rancheros came from raids by Indians from the San Joaquin Valley and the foothills of the Sierra Nevada.

Californios in the Salinas and Pajaro valleys were especially vulnerable to Indian marauders who crossed the Coast Range to plunder their herds. Such raids were of great concern to Hermenegildo Vasquez and his neighbors on the Pajaro River. When Tiburcio was five, in January 1841, Indians attacked the nearby pueblo of San Juan Bautista. Two months later they drove off two hundred horses from ranchos near Monterey. Such raids were so frequent that two years later several Monterey rancheros petitioned the governor for military protection. Thomas O. Larkin, writing in 1845, complained that Indians stole several thousand head of horses annually, making it almost impossible for Monterey-area rancheros to herd their cattle. In October 1846 Indian raiders ran off two dozen horses from ranchos near Mission Carmel. The biggest raid came in December, when a large band of Indians descended from the mountains and stole every horse they could find within thirty miles of Monterey. Rarely did the rancheros follow the thieves across the Coast Range, for the Indians would lie in wait in the mountain passes and ambush pursuers.[5]

It was an exciting time for a young Californio boy in Monterey. Tiburcio, like all Montereños, loved to watch ships come into harbor, and people would flock to the customshouse to see the newest goods and hear the latest news from the outside world. He spent time with his father on his tiny Rancho Felix on the Pajaro, and on his uncle Felipe Vasquez's rancho near Pilarcitos Canyon. There he learned, like all Californio youths, to ride and rope, to herd livestock, to shear sheep and tie wool, and to butcher cattle and sheep. From his father Tiburcio acquired the rough masculine skills so highly respected by Californios. Wrote George Beers, one of his biographers, "He was an excellent marksman when a mere boy, and was noted for his superb horsemanship; in fact, he excelled in the chase and in all manly sports engaged in by the Mexican population." But Tiburcio developed little interest in the life of a vaquero. It was the social life of Monterey he liked best.[6]

Tiburcio was Doña Guadalupe's youngest and favorite son. Early Montereños remembered Tiburcio's mother as a "short, stout woman, always at prayers." She was as devoted to the church as she was to her children. Even when visiting a relative's ranch outside town, she would walk for miles back into Monterey, rebozo over her head, so as not to miss mass. It troubled her greatly that her youngest son showed little interest in the church. Tiburcio was especially close to his mother and his elder sisters

Manuela and María. From them he learned to play guitar and developed a love for music, song, and dance. But above all he loved women. Early on he learned to banter and flirt with neighborhood women and girls.[7]

There was little in the gentle, fun-loving youth that would make anyone suspect he would turn into a fearsome outlaw. But he could be mischievous. Near what is now the corner of Aguajito Road and Fremont Street were a number of springs, known as Los Aguajitos (Little Waterholes) to the Californios and as Washerwoman's Bay to the Anglos. There, at stone washing tubs, Californio and Indian servants congregated to do laundry and swap gossip. One old Montereño recalled that Tiburcio "would squat on the banks and give and take gossip with the women as they scrubbed the clothes of their employers. And when he left, not infrequently the clothes were found to have hard knots tied in [the] arms or legs."[8]

In those years it was customary for Montereños to take boys to see public executions and punishments as a warning to obey authority. If Tiburcio attended such, the lessons did not sink in. Nor did the local *calabozo* (jail) instill dread in him. Monterey's adobe jail was notably harsh and its conditions notorious. A Mexican government commission examined it in 1842, reporting, "It was without any floor but the bare earth, and so wet that a stick would sink some distance into it. The walls were black, and so dark that an object could not be seen more than a yard off. There was neither light nor ventilation, except through two small skylights; it was very unhealthy, and the more so when many people had to sleep therein. They had to use a barrel as a privy, and the whole place was a sink-hole of filth."[9]

Jacob R. Leese, who was born in Monterey in 1839 to an American father and a Californio mother and later served as the county's undersheriff, recalled, "I knew Tiburcio Vasquez; everybody knew him, especially the women and children. . . . He was born . . . of Mexican parents, both of whom were descendants of good families. His father and mother were plain, honest people, with a family of four sons and one [*sic*] daughter, all of whom turned out well with the exception of Tiburcio."[10]

Tiburcio's charming good nature and love of fun made him popular among young people in the pueblo. Always well dressed and well groomed, he was a ladies' man even in his youth. Said George Beers, "He was a great favorite with all the senoritas on account of his good looks and graceful deportment, and was the recipient of constant flattery, both from them

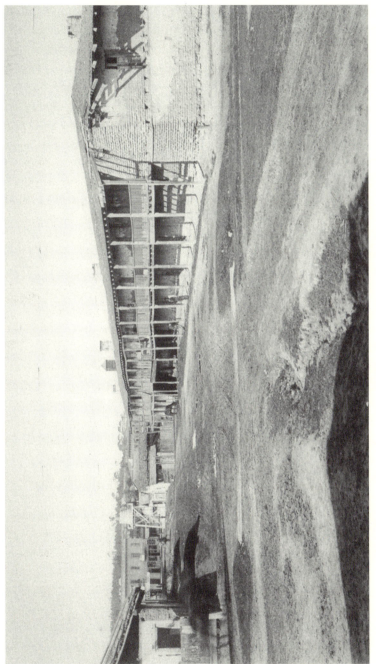

Monterey, showing at right the Government House (El Cuartel), where young Vasquez attended dances. Although this photo was taken in the 1880s, Monterey had changed little since the days of Tiburcio's youth. (Author's collection)

and his male companions and friends." Young Vasquez loved to attend the balls and dances that were so popular in Monterey. One of Tiburcio's childhood friends was Juan Pombert who was born in Monterey in 1831, the son of a French-Canadian trapper who married an elder sister of Salomon Pico's. Years later, in 1871, Pombert would be an unsuccessful candidate for Monterey County sheriff. In his old age, Pombert recalled that balls were held in the Government House (El Cuartel), which had a large hall. In this ballroom Pombert watched young Vasquez master the popular dances of the day.[11]

Tiburcio and his brothers divided their time between the Rancho Felix and their house in Monterey. Apparently, marital discord developed between Hermenegildo and Doña Guadalupe, for by the time Tiburcio was in his early teens, Hermenegildo lived primarily on the Rancho Felix on the Pajaro River, and Doña Guadalupe in Monterey. At some point the couple evidently separated, and Hermenegildo stopped living in the Monterey adobe. Neither the 1850 federal census nor the 1852 California state census show him residing there. For a time in 1852 Hermenegildo lived with his brother, José Tiburcio Vasquez, on the latter's rancho at what is now Half Moon Bay in San Mateo County. Hermenegildo's sons helped their father with his crops and cattle, and in their free time attended dances, sometimes as far away as the Rancho Bolsa del Pajaro in what is now Watsonville. In the late 1840s Tiburcio, probably with one or more of his elder brothers, would ride ten miles to fandangos hosted by the rancho's owner, Sebastián Rodríguez. The ranchero's niece, Catarina Rodríguez, who was a year older than Tiburcio, recalled attending dances there with the future bandit chieftain.[12]

In Monterey Governor Alvarado established a free public school in 1842. Some three hundred boys were taught in three spacious rooms in a large Monterey adobe. The principal, Henri Cambuston, was a quarrelsome, hard-drinking Frenchman. Juan Pombert recalled that in 1845 and for some years thereafter, young Vasquez attended this school. "He was a bright, intelligent lad," said George Beers, "and received the rudiments of an English education." Tiburcio was taught by Cambuston, from whom he learned to speak imperfect English which improved greatly over the years, and by Vicente Gómez, from whom he learned beautiful, ornate penmanship. There were few textbooks, so students were assigned to copy existing books into manuscript form. They learned reading, writing, arithmetic, history, geography, and drawing. Vasquez was not an exceptional student, but he learned to read and write proficiently. He enjoyed reading romantic Spanish novels. He especially loved poetry, and as Pombert recalled, "often humorously addressed his friends in rhyme." As Tiburcio grew older, he continued to read books in Spanish, and he enjoyed writing poems to his female admirers. He wrote with a flourish, and was immensely proud of both his poetry and his penmanship. Tiburcio was full grown by his mid-teens and of slight build. He stood but five feet six inches tall and never weighed much more than 130 or 140 pounds. But his handsome features, graceful manners, and stylish dress made him a favorite with the pueblo's señoritas.[13]

During Tiburcio's youth Montereños began to witness extraordinary events that would forever change their lives. In 1842 the pueblo's residents were shocked when two American men-of-war appeared in the bay. The American commander, Commodore Thomas Ap Catesby Jones, was under the mistaken belief that war had broken out between the United States and Mexico. His forces captured the town without firing a shot and raised the U.S. flag over the presidio. When his error was made clear, an embarrassed Jones withdrew his forces and made formal apologies, but this incident again showed Montereños how poorly defended the pueblo was and how vulnerable they were to American expansionism.[14]

Over the ensuing four years, relations between the United States and Mexico rapidly deteriorated. War broke out on the Texas border in May 1846. But the conflict had already spread to California. In December 1845, Captain John C. Frémont, the American explorer, had arrived in California at the head of a sixty-man expedition. They rode to Monterey, where Frémont met with the garrison commander, General José Castro. Frémont and his men were ostensibly on a scientific expedition, but Californios were highly suspicious because most of Frémont's men were soldiers and scouts, not scientists. Castro granted Frémont permission to winter in California but ordered him to stay out of the coastal pueblos. In March 1846, Frémont led his command to Gabilan Peak, twenty-five miles east of Monterey, built a log fort, and raised the American flag in defiance of the Mexican officials. Only when he became convinced that a Californio force would attack him did Frémont and his men retreat north toward Oregon.

Frémont's rash action outraged Californios, and events would soon turn violent. In June the so-called Bear Flag Revolt broke out. American trappers, frontiersmen, and ruffians who had drifted into the Sacramento

Valley became agitated by rumors of pending war and seized the head-quarters of General Mariano Vallejo in Sonoma. This was a foolish act, for Vallejo was a friend and supporter of the Americans. The Bear Flaggers also captured a large band of Californios' horses that they believed were to be used by General Castro for a campaign against them. Castro sent a force north to confront the Bear Flaggers, led by Joaquín de la Torre of Monterey, a thirty-four-year-old professional soldier and ranchero. Energetic, a natural leader, and possessing great courage, de la Torre was strongly opposed to American intervention in California. His fifty horsemen, armed with willow lances and inaccurate escopetas, encountered twenty well-armed Bear Flaggers at Olompali Rancho, near what is now Novato. There, on June 24, a short skirmish took place that left one Californio dead and several wounded by modern American rifles. Realizing that he was outgunned, de la Torre withdrew to the south and managed to evade the pursuing Americans.[15]

The slain Californio was Manuel Cantúa, a younger brother of Doña Guadalupe's and one of Tiburcio's uncles. The anguish of the Vasquez and Cantúa families can only be imagined. But they had little time for grieving. Just two weeks later, on July 7, 1846, Montereños were thrown into panic when a U.S. naval force led by Commodore John Drake Sloat landed and raised the American flag at the customshouse. He proclaimed a state of war and that California was now part of the United States. President James Polk and most Americans believed it was their "manifest destiny" to annex California and the Southwest to the United States. Hostilities in California, fortunately, would prove tame compared to the bloodletting that took place along the Rio Grande and in Mexico.

In addition to the three gunships in the harbor, Montereños soon saw another potent example of American military force. At sundown on July 20, the earth shook as Captain Frémont, Kit Carson, and two hundred gringo horsemen, leading a herd of three hundred captured mustangs, rode down Calle Principal toward the customshouse. A witness, Walter Colton, recorded the scene: "The citizens glanced at them through their grated windows. Their rifles, revolving pistols, and long knives glittered over the dusky buckskin which enveloped their sinewy limbs, while their untrimmed locks, flowing out from under their foraging caps, and their black beards, with white teeth glittering through, gave them a wild, savage aspect." Frémont's men camped on a hill under the Monterey pines and their songs filled the clear night air. The paisanos gathered on a nearby hilltop and watched the Americans' night fires and the long shadows of their sentries. At dawn the Montereños, no doubt the Vasquez family among them, again flocked to the hilltop, and heatedly debated what to do about the armed strangers in their midst. Finally one *viejo* raised his fist and shouted, "Viva la república y muerte a los gringos!"[16]

Such sentiments soon prompted many of the young Californio fighting men in Monterey to take part in the only significant engagement in Northern California, the Battle of Natividad. Some of the combatants would play important roles in the early life of Tiburcio Vasquez. It began when John C. Frémont, after a campaign in Southern California, returned to Monterey in late October to recruit more men and horses. American forces were now in firm control of the little pueblo. At Frémont's request, Captain Charles Burroughs brought twenty-two men and five hundred horses and mules from Sutter's Fort, located in what is now the city of Sacramento. En route to Monterey, Burroughs camped at San Juan Bautista on the night of November 15. There they were joined by a motley and multiethnic group of thirty-five frontiersmen led by Captain Bluford "Hell Roaring" Thompson. But their movements had been detected by the Californios. A 150-man force, led by Manuel Castro, cousin of the general, and his lieutenant, Joaquín de la Torre, set out to intercept the Americans. Riding with the Californios were Bernardino "Three Finger Jack" García, who was already notorious for torturing and killing two Bear Flaggers in Sonoma County; the soon-to-be-infamous outlaws Domingo Hernández and Capistrano López; Doña Guadalupe's first cousin Juan Ignacio Cantúa; and José Antonio García, who was related to the Vasquez family by marriage. The two forces met the next day, November 16, at Rancho Natividad, just north of what is now Salinas. In a sharp, close-quarters fight, a half dozen American volunteers, including their commander, Captain Burroughs, were slain, and the same number wounded. The Californios suffered an equal number of casualties. Juan Ignacio Cantúa was badly wounded.[17]

The bloodshed, taking place so near to their home and involving members of their family, would profoundly affect the Vasquez and Cantúa families, imbuing in them a long-lasting distrust of gringos. Two of Doña Guadalupe's closest male relatives, one of them her own brother Manuel Cantúa, killed five months earlier, had been struck down by American rifle fire during the Mexican War. Tiburcio, who was only eleven at the time but certainly aware of these tragedies, does not appear to have been deeply moved by them, however. And if he was, an eventful youth would made him forget. Years later, when asked by a reporter whether any of his family had been killed by Anglos, he did not think of his uncle Manuel Cantúa. He replied, "I . . . never had any relative killed by an American that I know of."[18]

While the Vasquez family tried to make sense of the tumult around them, hostilities continued in Southern California. Several more engagements took place, but Californio commander Andrés Pico, without a regular army, was outmanned and outgunned. In January 1847 he formally surrendered to John C. Frémont, thus ending the war in California. A year later Mexico signed the Treaty of Guadalupe Hidalgo, ceding its northern territories, including Alta California, to the United States. For Tiburcio's family, and for all Californios, life would never be the same.[19]

In April 1847 there arrived in Monterey four companies of Colonel Jonathan D. Stevenson's New York Regiment of Volunteers. Many of the rank and file were young ruffians recruited from the street gangs of New York, and they would be responsible for a great deal of crime and violence in California in the decade to come. To Montereños, they were an unwelcome sight, and their rowdy behavior was certainly resented by the Vasquez family and their fellow paisanos. The New York Volunteers were garrisoned in the pueblo for a year until they were ordered discharged into the civilian population. Their members would play prominent roles in Monterey, some good, many bad.[20]

For Californios, still reeling from the conquest, the greatest shock was yet to come. In January 1848 gold was discovered at Sutter's Mill in the isolated Sierra Nevada foothills. Within weeks after news of the gold strike reached Monterey in May, most of the able-bodied men had departed for the mining region, soon to be dubbed the "Mother Lode." On July 2, a Monterey correspondent wrote, "A very large company left Monterey today for the gold scene—some on horses, some in wagons, some in carts, some on foot, and some on crutches." Said Monterey merchant Thomas O. Larkin, "Every bowl, tray, and warming pan has gone to the mines. Everything in short that has a scoop in it and will hold sand and water." His fellow Montereyan Walter Colton added, "The gold mines have upset all social and domestic arrangements in Monterey; the master has become his own servant, and the servant his own lord. The millionaire is obliged to groom his own horse, and roll his wheelbarrow."[21]

Barely thirteen when news of the bonanza reached Monterey, Tiburcio was too young to make the long and dangerous trip to the mines. However, his older brothers, Claudio, Antonio María, and Francisco undoubtedly joined the rush to riches. It is doubtful that their father, Hermenegildo, went with them, for at sixty-four he was an old man in that era. Many Californios, the first to reach the diggings, struck gold that initial season in the mines, then returned home for the winter. By December, news of the gold discovery had reached the East Coast, setting off one of history's great mass migrations. When Californios went back to the mining region in the spring of 1849, they found the country flooded with new American arrivals who resented all Spanish-speaking miners and often greeted them with violence. In April 1849, one ranchero wrote to a friend, "Don't go to the mines on any account. They are . . . loaded to the muzzle with vagabonds from every quarter of the globe, scoundrels from nowhere . . . and assassins manufactured in Hell for the express purpose of converting highways and byways into theaters of blood."[22]

In 1848 California's population consisted of about 14,000 whites, the majority of them Californios, and perhaps 100,000 Indians. By early 1849 news of the gold discovery had spread throughout the world, and gold-seekers flooded into California from around the globe. Within ten years the new state's population would explode to 380,000. Californios were completely outnumbered, their vast ranch holdings invaded by squatters and land sharks. They did not understand American laws and business practices. Many unwittingly borrowed money at usurious rates from unscrupulous Anglos. The loans were secured by their land, and when they were unable to repay they lost their ranchos by foreclosure. The gold rush, more than anything else, completely changed the lives of the Californios and began their rapid economic and political decline. By the 1860s much of their property and power had evaporated. Californios, especially the peones, vaqueros, and campesinos, became a displaced people.[23]

None of Tiburcio's brothers had any significant landholdings, and if any of them attempted to strike it rich in the gold rush, they did not succeed. Soon they were back at home, engaged in their usual agrarian pursuits. When Tiburcio was twelve, the Americans began construction of a new city hall directly across the street from the Vasquez adobe. Its builder, Walter

Colton, wrote that it was made by "the labor of the convicts, taxes on liquor shops, and fines on gamblers." Young Tiburcio watched stonecutters removing rock from a quarry on a nearby hill, teamsters hauling it to the sloping meadow across from his house, and masons erecting a large, two-story building. When Colton Hall was completed after a year of labor, it was the most impressive public building in California, with schoolrooms on the ground floor and a large assembly room on the second story. In September and October 1849, Colton Hall was the scene of California's first constitutional convention. Like other neighborhood boys, young Vasquez no doubt peered through the windows to watch the proceedings, from which his paisanos were largely, though not totally, excluded.

Colton Hall now partly blocked the family's panoramic views of the pueblo and the ocean, but provided an opportunity to Guadalupe. She opened a small restaurant in her home, where she and her daughters Manuela and María made and sold tamales, no doubt catering to the delegates across the street. Tiburcio may have been humiliated to see his mother and sisters waiting on foreigners. He developed a strong dislike of gringos, and soon had many negative experiences with them. One of Tiburcio's early encounters took place in 1849 or 1850. Cora Older, a journalist who in 1916 interviewed old Montereños who had known Vasquez, recorded the incident:

> Tiburcio had several pretty sisters. Among them were María Antonia and Manuela. They helped their mother in serving tamales. Often foreign visitors came to the Vasquez adobe, which commands a charming view of the bay, and there bought the native dishes. One day . . . there arrived a group of American soldiers in uniform. They were gay, thoughtless young men, bent on amusement among these funny "greasers." They admired the senoritas, and they showed it. Seated around the little table on the Vasquez porch they made eyes at the Vasquez girls. The girls blushed. After all it was business to be polite to the Americans. They were good customers.
>
> Tiburcio was not quite 15, but he seemed older. He furtively watched the advances of the soldiers to his sisters as they fetched coffee, frijoles, and tamales. Next to his mother he adored his sisters. It hurt him that they would be exposed to the advances of strange men. The soldiers did not notice the lad glaring back,

walking past them. As the visitors started to leave after paying their bill two of the soldiers started to kiss the Vasquez girls.

With a leap Tiburcio was at the throats of the Americans. "Gringos!" He thought he was speaking English, but he was shouting at them in Spanish. "You've stolen our country. You've killed our men. Now you attack our women!"

The soldiers did not know what the lad was saying. They brushed aside the pale, trembling youth, who so violently interrupted their attempted flirtation, and went down the hill laughing.[24]

It was not long before the youth had more confrontations with Americans. According to Vasquez, his earliest fight took place in 1850: "My first difficulty occurred in Monterey in a ball room, when I was fifteen years of age. I was engaged in a fight, but no blood was shed." Vasquez later gave additional details of his early troubles with the newcomers: "About the year 1852, myself and friends were in the habit of giving little balls among ourselves. These balls were frequently interrupted, and the participants rudely insulted and outraged by parties calling themselves native Americans. Whatever their nationality, they were a low order of men. From these insults arose my inclination to play the part which I have since acted. The events I allude to transpired in the county of Monterey, and resulted in one or two personal collisions, which, however, passed off without bloodshed."[25]

Conflict between Anglos and Hispanics became commonplace in gold rush California. This was particularly true in the mining region, where by early 1849 some ten thousand Mexicans, many of them experienced miners, had flooded into the Mother Lode. Many Anglo gold-seekers were Mexican War veterans, and they detested Californios and Mexicans who owned land, mining claims, or businesses in the new territory that they believed had been won with the blood of their fallen comrades. On the other hand, Californios and Mexicans resented the Anglos as unwanted invaders. Competition from experienced and successful Mexican and Chileno miners resulted in the racist Foreign Miners' Tax of 1850, which forced noncitizens to pay a monthly license fee, causing much resentment and violence. Ruffians of both races, contemptuously referring to each other as greasers and gringos, fought and killed over gold, mining claims, land, and Hispanic women. A great deal of violence was committed by members of both groups, though on balance, Hispanics got the worst of it. Although Monterey experienced similar levels of violence, less of it was racially motivated. As violent and volatile as it was, Monterey was still more stable than the unsettled, largely ungoverned mining camps of the early gold rush. Nonetheless, racial conflict made a profound impact on young Vasquez.[26]

Despite the ethnic disharmony, Tiburcio's family knew many happy moments. On May 3, 1850, Tiburcio's brother, Antonio, now twenty-three, wed twenty-year-old widow María Asunción Boronda, at Mission San Carlos de Monterey. In September, the first census was taken by the new American government. In the adobe on Dutra Street, Tiburcio was enumerated as living with his mother and her granddaughter, Concepción Espinosa. Hermenegildo was not in the household. Next door lived Tiburcio's elder sister, Concepción, her husband, Jesús Soto, and their children. Antonio and his wife lived first on her family's rancho in the Carmel Valley, then acquired a house in Monterey, today known as the Frémont Headquarters adobe, located at 539 Hartnell Street. Tiburcio's brother Chico moved south to Los Angeles. Like Antonio, he was honest, law-abiding, and hardworking. Chico Vasquez was tall, handsome, and powerfully built, with large dark eyes and a shock of black curly hair. In Los Angeles he worked as a laborer and met and wooed a young Californio woman, María Villa. The two were wed in the Catholic church on the plaza on October 10, 1853. They lived in the little pueblo for a few years, then moved to Ventura and began raising a large family. Later, after 1860, they settled near what is now Acton in Soledad Canyon, north of Los Angeles. Chico worked as a farmer and stock raiser, and later as a miner in the Soledad Mines.[27]

For many Californio youths like Vasquez these were traumatic times. They had been completely unprepared for the rapid and complete conquest. The traditions that rooted Californios to their heritage were under constant attack from the new Anglo culture. The pastoral Californio customs, their old way of life, were fast disappearing. Californios were losing control over their own lives, their future was dark and uncertain. Perhaps because Tiburcio's siblings were older, they adapted well to these changes. They led busy lives, filled with child rearing and hard work. His sisters and especially his mother were devoted to their Catholic faith, which gave them hope and taught them to forgive and forget the ill treatment they received from Anglos. But Tiburcio was cut from different cloth.

Early on he rejected the church and its teachings. Beneath his gentle, good-humored nature, he harbored deep hatred against gringos. At the same time he loved the social life of Monterey and its fiestas, bailes, and fandangos. His poetry, singing, and guitar playing brought him success in serenading and wooing the pueblo's señoritas. Although he had learned the traditional skills of hunting, herding cattle, and butchering livestock, he had no interest in the simple life of a vaquero. He began to reject the traditional Californio values of hard work, Catholicism, frugality, and self-restraint, and became increasingly fascinated by the pursuit of leisure, young women, personal independence, and sexual freedom. Reaching maturity in a time of great social upheaval, Tiburcio stood on the threshold of an entirely different kind of life in old Monterey.

CHAPTER THREE

A Boyhood among Bandits

During the gold rush period of the 1850s, Monterey was a wide-open town, roiling with ethnic and political turmoil and governed by corrupt officials. The county had two things the mining region did not have: cattle and women. Monterey's livestock brought high prices in the Mother Lode country, and its Californio women attracted unmarried prospectors, cattle buyers, and fortune hunters at a time when the state was 90 percent male. Monterey's new arrivals included numerous Anglo, Australian, and Mexican desperadoes. The commingling of these ruffians with home-grown Californio badmen was a deadly brew. Monterey quickly became one of the most violent communities in America, with some of the highest murder rates in our nation's history. During one three-year period in the mid-1850s Monterey County saw forty homicides. For a county of only four thousand people, that calculates to a per-capita homicide rate thirty times greater than the modern national rate. During the 1850s Monterey was a gunfighters' town that made Dodge City, Deadwood, and Tombstone look peaceful by comparison.[1]

Monterey's violence and corruption were exemplified by its first county sheriff, William F. Roach, who served from 1850 to 1853. He had come to Monterey in 1847 as a twenty-seven-year-old sergeant in Company D of the New York Volunteers. Roach's undersheriff was Aaron "Ned" Lyons, his good friend and fellow ex-sergeant of Company D. Thoroughly corrupt, Bill Roach would become one of early Monterey's most controversial figures. He first achieved notoriety as a result of a robbery of the Monterey customshouse. This crime was committed by Australian career criminals from San Francisco. (Many Australians in California were ex-convicts from the Australian penal colony and were known as "Sydney Ducks.") On December 8, 1850, burglars entered the customshouse and stole $14,000, most of which belonged to the collector of customs, Andrew Randall. The thieves were all Sydney Ducks, members of a gang headed by the notorious "English Jim" Stuart. In the pueblo the Australian ruffians were conspicuous by their loud, colorful clothes and boisterous conduct. They were quickly suspected of the theft and arrested the same day by the justice of the peace, who lodged them in the decrepit adobe jail. The five were searched and about $14,000 was found in their possession and confiscated. There was little other evidence against them, however.

Subsequently each was released on $5,000 bail. English Jim Stuart and another gang member, Sam Whittaker, traveled from San Francisco to attend the trial in April 1851. Both took the stand under assumed names and testified that the accused were all of good character. The trial resulted in a hung jury. Stuart later confessed that the accused men were in fact guilty but, "There was a great deal of false swearing and bribery." He also revealed that Sheriff Roach "received seven hundred dollars and a gold watch for packing the jury and other services." Stuart admitted that a juror was given a one-hundred-dollar bribe, and that "Dennis McCarthy, the constable, received one hundred dollars from the prisoners for false swearing. He first swore for the prosecution, and then swore back in favor of the prisoners."[2]

Andrew Randall had filed a civil lawsuit against the burglars. Desperate to recover at least a portion of his loss, Randall agreed to a settlement whereby he would keep half the stolen money and the five thieves would keep the other half. Thoroughly disgusted and disillusioned, Randall gave a succinct description of early Monterey law enforcement: "I don't believe there is so corrupt a clique extant in any civilised country as exist in Monterey." Randall, however, was soon to get a measure of revenge. A few months later, English Jim Stuart and Sam Whittaker were arrested in San Francisco for other crimes and were publicly hanged by its newly formed Committee of Vigilance.[3]

But the excitement created by the customshouse robbery was nothing compared to that caused by the depredations of bandit chieftains Salomon

Pico and Domingo Hernández. Salomon Pico was born near San Juan Bautista in 1821 to a highly prominent family. His first cousins were Pío Pico, last governor of California under Mexican rule, and Andrés Pico, the dashing warrior who had commanded Californio troops during the Mexican War. Tiburcio, as a youth, knew Salomon Pico, who was married to his first cousin Juana Vasquez. During the hostilities, Salomon Pico took an active hand battling against the Americans, and after the conquest he harbored deep hatred for them. He claimed that he had been "cheated out of his property by Americans" and vowed that he "would kill every American falling into his hands." He was suspected of robbing and killing many travelers along El Camino Real between Monterey and Los Angeles during the early 1850s, and later boasted of having slain thirty-nine Americans. There were numerous accounts of Salomon Pico carrying the severed ears of his victims on a leather thong draped around his saddle horn. During the Spanish and Mexican eras, soldiers who took part in punitive expeditions against Indian horse thieves traditionally removed their ears to prove that they had killed their quarry. So Pico, a former soldier, may well have obtained his string of ears from slain Indians, or perhaps they really were from his Anglo victims. Tiburcio Vasquez, like many in the poorer classes of Californios in Monterey, Santa Barbara, and Los Angeles, viewed Salomon Pico as a hero and patriot. Other Californios, however, particularly the ricos and rancheros, as well as most Anglos, were terrified of him, so much so that one early chronicler said that in Monterey "the very adobes of the ancient capital trembled at the mention of his name."[4]

Associated with Salomon Pico was another exceptionally dangerous bandido, Domingo Hernández. Tiburcio would become good friends with the latter's younger brother, Agustín Hernández. Domingo, born near San Juan Bautista in 1815, was "of medium stature, bronze complexion, with large head and broad shoulders. . . . His mouth was enormous, and the teeth set wide apart, so that however horrible might be his frown, his laugh was worse." During the Mexican War he and his compadre Capistrano López had served under Joaquín de la Torre, but after the Battle of Natividad they deserted and became cattle thieves. Hernández was suspected of numerous murders on the roads between San Jose and Monterey. According to one early account, "He boasted of the way he used to kill travelers who had the appearance of foreigners. He would ask the victim for a cigar, or a light, and pretending to be occupied with the cigar, he would let the traveler advance a few steps, and then shoot him from behind." Like Salomon Pico, Domingo Hernández was widely reported to carry a string of severed ears on his saddle horn. How many men were robbed and killed by Pico, Hernández, and their fellow bandidos will never be known. As late as 1872, a traveler on the lonely trail between Monterey and Mission Carmel found a number of wooden crosses on the roadside, placed there in the 1850s, marking the graves of murdered men.[5]

Tiburcio Vasquez was thirteen in early 1849 when Domingo Hernández's most famous exploit took place in Monterey. The bandido had been tried for horse and cattle theft and the alcalde, Florencio Serrano, sentenced him to death by hanging. A large crowd attended the execution, including many of his desperado compadres. The ruffians, according to Serrano, were "the riffraff of the free [discharged] Volunteers" who were drunk and "supplied with arms of all types, yelling threats and insults" in protest of what they believed was an unfair hanging. A detachment of U.S. soldiers was assigned to prevent a rescue. When the trap was sprung, the rope broke and Hernández plunged to the ground, uninjured. A loud cheer went up from his Californio and Anglo friends. Many of the Californio onlookers, as well as the Catholic priest, exclaimed that it was a miracle and that he had been spared by the Virgin Mary. Hernández, now a heroic figure to the crowd, was taken back to the old adobe jail, surrounded by admirers and well-wishers. Serrano, believing that Hernández would soon be lynched anyway, ordered him released. That night a celebration and fandango was held in the desperado's honor. Domingo Hernández got roaring drunk, stabbed a man, and fled Monterey.[6]

Capistrano López was every bit as bad. During the revolution against Governor Micheltorena in 1845, the governor's wife sent eight hundred dollars in gold by a dispatch rider from Monterey to her husband in Los Angeles. Capistrano López waylaid the rider on a rancho south of what is now Salinas, and robbed and killed him, leaving the body to rot on the trail. According to Californios, López betrayed his own people for money during the Mexican War. While John C. Frémont was entrenched in the Gabilan Mountains in 1846, Capistrano López and Domingo Hernández were sent to spy on him. Instead, López visited the Americans' camp and, after accepting a bribe, informed Frémont of the Californios' plans to attack. That night Frémont and his men slipped away. Later the same year, when Thomas Larkin, the American consul, was held prisoner by Mexican forces at San Luis Obispo, Capistrano López unsuccessfully plotted to help him escape.[7]

In the winter of 1850–51, bandit gangs, some of them organized by Salomon Pico and Domingo Hernández, embarked on a spree of robbery and stock theft unseen since the era of the Indian raids. In November, the prominent Francisco Pacheco, owner of two large ranchos east of San Juan Bautista, was robbed of $15,000 in gold. In February 1851, Juan Anzar, a wealthy ranchero of San Juan Bautista, lost his entire herd of saddle horses. Early in March, 150 horses were stolen in a raid near Mission Soledad. On the night of March 13, thieves raided the rancho of Teodoro Gonzáles in the Salinas Valley and made off with most of his saddle animals. Francisco Pacheco was victimized again when his Rancho San Luis Gonzaga lost a large number of horses and nine hundred head of cattle. According to a Monterey report, on a night in late March "every stable in the town was broken open, and all the horses stolen." Four ranchers were killed by outlaws near Soledad and San Luis Obispo in attempts to recover their stolen stock. In San Luis Obispo so many horses were stolen that not a mount was left with which to pursue the thieves.

On April 15, 1851, one of Salomon Pico's men had a falling out with him. He defected from the gang and rode into Monterey with a chilling story to tell. Pico planned to raid Marcelino Escobar's rancho on the Carmel River and murder its American majordomo, Josiah Swain. The next day a posse of twenty-five Anglos and Californios was raised in Monterey by state senator and former U.S. naval officer Selim E. Woodworth, and Philip A. Roach, the town's former mayor. Later that day, after a brief hunt, they captured Salomon Pico and four of his gang, together with a band of stolen horses. One of the captured bandidos was reportedly Domingo Hernández; the others were Cecilio Mesa, Reyes Torres, and William Otis Hall, the last a notorious American horse thief. The posse brought their prisoners into Monterey and a vigilante court was promptly convened. In Hall's pocket was found a memorandum book containing the names of potential victims and listing livestock brands for ranchers in Monterey and Los Angeles counties. Domingo Hernández and Cecilio Mesa were released, but Salomon Pico, Reyes Torres, and William Otis Hall were sentenced to death by hanging. At the last moment Sheriff William Roach appeared and seized the prisoners, whom he lodged in the town's leaky adobe jail. Two days later Salomon Pico was released on bond, but he promptly jumped bail and vanished. On April 27 William Otis Hall broke out of the jail with the help of members of Jim Stuart's gang.[8]

That May the governor commissioned Senator Woodworth to raise a company of twenty rangers to break up the gangs of robbers and horse thieves in the coastal counties. Woodworth reported that one band of outlaws "consisted of whites and Indians, under the command of a negro." This "negro" may have been the dark-complected Domingo Hernández or perhaps another noted bandit chieftain, Francisco "Negro" García. Woodworth led his rangers on a manhunt into the San Joaquin Valley, scouring all the country between Monterey and Tulare Lake. They caught but one thief, an unnamed American, "who was made to confess and disclose the names of his white confederates." The prisoner was sent back to Monterey under guard, but he was shot dead trying to escape. Woodworth and his rangers returned from their manhunt empty-handed, having recovered none of the stolen horses and costing the state the then-exorbitant sum of $9,000 for one month's service.[9]

Meanwhile, one of the witnesses against William Otis Hall was found murdered. Hall and Salomon Pico fled south, probably to avoid Woodworth's rangers. In June, Captain John Caldwell, the mail rider between Monterey and Santa Barbara, was slain south of San Luis Obispo. Hall and Pico were suspected of killing him. The dangerous pair ended up in Los Angeles, where Hall was recognized by a former constable from Monterey and arrested. He was returned to Monterey, convicted of horse theft, and sentenced to four years in San Quentin. He never got there. On the night of August 9, 1851, Monterey City Marshal Charles Clapp was awakened by a loud pounding on the door of the adobe jail. Thinking it was another officer he had been expecting, Clapp swung open the door and was confronted by half a dozen armed, masked men, wearing serapes and cloaks. Clapp later reported that one of them spoke English; the others were evidently Californios. They seized Clapp, bound and gagged him, and demanded the keys to Hall's cell. When Clapp refused, the masked men broke down the cell door with an axe. They found a terrified William Otis Hall handcuffed and chained by the waist and legs to a stout post driven into the earthen floor. Since it was clear that he could not be removed from his cell, the masked men wrapped a rawhide reata around his neck and strangled him to death. This lynching, Monterey's first, caused great excitement. Some townsfolk believed that members of Salomon Pico's gang had lynched Hall to prevent him from talking, but it seems more probable that the lynchers were members of Monterey's fledgling vigilance committee. Since Californios at that time owned most of the ranchos and livestock in the Monterey area, they had the most to lose from cattle rustlers and consequently were active in the early days of Monterey's vigilante movement. Many other men would be lynched by Monterey's vigilantes during the 1850s.[10]

Salomon Pico continued to operate with impunity in Southern California, where he rode with the infamous gold rush bandit Joaquín Murrieta. He was accused of more robberies and murders and had narrow escapes from the sheriffs of both Santa Barbara and Los Angeles counties. Finally, in 1857, Pico fled to Baja California, where his violent exploits continued unabated until he was arrested and executed by firing squad in 1860. Despite his enduring reputation as a folk hero to many Hispanics, Pico's close association with American and Australian robbers, coupled with Californios' efforts to capture him and his execution by Mexican forces, demonstrate that he was a career criminal rather than a political outlaw or rebel.[11]

Such distinctions were unimportant to young Tiburcio Vasquez, who became increasingly fascinated with Monterey's bandidos. He especially admired Anastacio García, who was eleven years his senior and married to Tiburcio's second cousin, the beautiful María Guadalupe Vasquez. Anastacio García was respected by the rough Anglo element of Monterey. Like Capistrano López, he had been paid to spy for the Americans during the Mexican War, but his treachery did not dim Tiburcio's adulation of him. Six feet tall with a muscular build, García was an expert vaquero and hunter, and a dead shot with rifle and revolver. One Montereyan described him as "a man of uncommon personal attractions—large and finely proportioned, with regular features, dark eyes and a profusion of curly hair—the very *beau ideal* of a brigand." García owned sixty acres on Rancho El Tucho, where he built an adobe home. His little ranch was situated on the Salinas River, twelve miles northeast of Monterey, near the present-day intersection of Blanco and Cooper roads. Next to Anastacio's claim was a sixty-acre tract owned by his brother, Encarnación García, who was married to one of Tiburcio's first cousins. Anastacio had four young children, and his mother and another brother, José Antonio, lived nearby in small adobe huts, known as *jacales*. Anastacio García was a good friend of Henry Cocks, an Englishman married to a Californio woman who owned a rancho on the Salinas. Cocks served as justice of the peace and, despite Anastacio García's reputation for treachery and violence, appointed him his constable. García had powerful Anglo friends in Monterey, among them Sheriff Ned Lyons and political boss Lewis Belcher.[12]

Hermenegildo Vasquez seems to have been involved little in Tiburcio's life after 1850, and Anastacio García increasingly took his place as a father figure. From García Tiburcio developed a taste for easy money, fine horses, fast women, and hard liquor. Andrew Wasson, later Monterey sheriff, said that young Vasquez "was a sort of good-for-nothing, listless fellow, who seldom or never worked, preferring to hang around the saloons of the town." Vasquez and García enjoyed socializing and drinking together in the cantinas and gambling halls. But although Tiburcio liked aguardiente and American whiskey—he often carried a bottle in his pocket—he was never a heavy imbiber, claiming that he "drank liquor only to be sociable." Unlike many Californios and Mexicans, Tiburcio never smoked cigarettes, but he did enjoy a good cigar.[13]

Due to his small size, wiry strength, and wonderful skill in the saddle, young Vasquez became a popular rider in horse races at Monterey, San Juan, and Santa Cruz. In the last town was a straight, mile-long racecourse that is now North Branciforte Avenue, which Tiburcio knew well. Said Charles H. Lincoln, later Santa Cruz County sheriff, "I remember Vasquez used to come to Santa Cruz when he was a boy and ride in scrub races." Tiburcio preferred large American horses over native California mustangs, as they could easily carry his light weight. Such horses would prove to be of great advantage to him in later years.[14]

Gambling was heavy at such events, and Tiburcio's interest in betting on horses developed into a passion for gambling and card playing. When not riding as a jockey, he spent much of his time in Monterey's gaming halls and fandango houses, which were frequented by both Anglos and Californios. By age sixteen, young Vasquez was associating with an exceedingly rough crowd. On September 20, 1851, Tiburcio was with a group of ruffians including Alejandro Ramos, a thirty-year-old Californio, and José García, probably the older brother of Anastacio. Although existing court records present a hazy picture, there was a fight near the Abrego store in which Ramos killed an unidentified man. The murder was witnessed by several prominent citizens, including merchant José Abrego and John M. O'Neil, later a Union cavalry major in the Civil War. Ramos was promptly arrested and lodged in Monterey's crumbling jail. His preliminary examination was held two days later in the mayor's court, and Ramos was held to answer on a charge of manslaughter. The trial took place a month later, on October 27. Tiburcio attended it and testified on behalf of Ramos, as did José García and another compadre, Juan Alvarez. Abrego, O'Neil, and Undersheriff Thomas Munk were among the witnesses for the prosecution. The trial lasted one day and the jury found Ramos guilty of manslaughter. Ramos got one month in jail and a fifty-dollar fine. Life was cheap in old Monterey.[15]

Yet another notorious outlaw well known to Tiburcio Vasquez was Mariano Hernández. Often confused with Domingo Hernández, to whom he was not related, Mariano was born in San Francisco in 1810. Mariano's eldest sister, María, was married to Tiburcio's uncle and namesake, José Tiburcio Vasquez. Mariano Hernández was granted the thirteen-thousand-acre Rancho del Puerto in what is now San Joaquin County. In 1843, well before the American period, he was charged with stealing cattle by fellow Californios. During the gold rush, American settlers overran his rancho, igniting his deep hatred for gringos. He quickly became a notorious horse thief and highway robber. One of his most brutal crimes occurred in May 1850 when he and a companion robbed and stabbed to death two Anglo gold miners in Mariposa County. In August, Hernández was arrested in San Jose and lodged in jail, but a month later he escaped.[16]

By 1852 Mariano Hernández was stealing horses in Santa Cruz County with Domingo Hernández and Capistrano López. Mariano was captured and locked up in the Santa Cruz jail. Soon thereafter, on the night of July 20, Domingo Hernández was captured by vigilantes at a house in Santa Cruz and lynched. The next morning the vigilantes broke into the jail and removed Mariano Hernández. Before he died he made a confession, naming the members of his gang and identifying Capistrano López as one of the leaders. That afternoon the same vigilantes captured Capistrano López and brought him into Santa Cruz. He was tried before a jury of twelve, chosen from the assembled crowd. The horse he was riding was stolen, and witnesses testified that he "frequently boasted of killing and robbing Americans." The lynch court found him guilty, and he was hanged on the vigilantes' gallows. Although most vigilantes in California were Anglo, these ones were primarily Californios who had suffered heavily from horse and cattle thieves. In one fell swoop, they had eliminated three of the worst desperadoes on the Pacific Coast.[17]

Two months later bandidos caused even more excitement. Claudio Feliz, brother-in-law of Joaquín Murrieta, the infamous "Marauder of the Mines," led a small band of freebooters into the Salinas Valley. At that time it was Claudio, not Joaquín, who was the leader of a rampaging gang of young Mexicans and Californios that for almost two years had been robbing and killing in both the San Francisco Bay Area and the Mother Lode country. On September 13 they held up a Mexican on the Salinas River, taking his horse and serape. He immediately reported the theft to Henry Cocks, justice of the peace of Alisal Township, in what is now Salinas. Cocks quickly raised a seven-man posse that included his constable (and Tiburcio's compadre) Anastacio García. They tracked the outlaws to an adobe on the west bank of the Salinas River, across from El Tucho. It was dark when Cocks's men surrounded the house. In a pitched gun battle, Claudio Feliz and one of his gang were slain. The posse later captured another of the band and killed a fourth. Anastacio García's heroism in this affair would soon be eclipsed by the murderous career he was about to begin. Any opportunity for him to influence Tiburcio in a positive direction quickly evaporated.[18]

Young Vasquez, between stints of gambling and horse racing, worked for various ranchos as a vaquero in the early 1850s. He disliked the work, but gambling did not keep him fed. One of his employers was Catherine Cole, who owned a portion of the Rancho Potrero de San Carlos, located along Potrero Canyon in what is now Carmel Valley. Living in Carmel Valley was James Meadows, an English sailor who had married a local Indian woman. Their daughter, Isabel Meadows, who was born in 1846, recalled years later that Tiburcio fathered a son, Luis, out of wedlock. The child's mother was María Cano, a fifteen-year-old Mexican girl, who gave birth to the boy in August 1852. María later married Dolores Tarango, who adopted the youth, known thereafter as Luis Tarango. While no definite proof has surfaced that Luis Tarango was Tiburcio's son, Isabel Meadows was a reliable source. Luis Tarango became a well-known figure in Carmel Valley, and when he died in Monterey in 1926 the local newspaper called him "an intimate friend of the notorious bandit, Vasquez." Luis Tarango would not be the last illegitimate child linked to Tiburcio.[19]

Young Vasquez soon began an occupation that brought him into increasingly frequent contact with American ruffians. Jacob Leese, a boyhood friend, recalled, "A bright boy naturally, when he was sixteen years old he thought he had learned enough at the common schools of the times and set out in life for himself. He did not like to work—not a bit—so he set up a dance house, which was his ruin." Tiburcio was actually seventeen when he opened a combination saloon, dance hall, and gambling parlor in Monterey. One of Anastacio García's Anglo friends was William Pyburn, a merchant, liquor dealer, gambler, and real estate speculator. Pyburn owned a small, square-shaped adobe (no longer standing) on what is now Abrego Street. It was located directly across from the Casa Abrego, owned by José Abrego, which still exists on the corner of Webster and Abrego streets. In late 1852 or 1853, Pyburn either leased this adobe to Tiburcio Vasquez or hired him to run it as a fandango house. Pyburn apparently also paid for a gambling license. In those days, dances were generally given in private residences, and everyone in town was welcome to attend. This led to the custom, practiced by some Montereños, of operating cafes, saloons, and gambling parlors in their homes. Although Pyburn's adobe was just a small house, it soon became a popular hangout for Monterey's rough crowd, both Californios and Anglos. Tiburcio, though not yet eighteen, lived there with a girl and served aguardiente, ran monte and other card games, and held bailes at night.[20]

Jacob Leese recalled that Anastacio García "was a regular visitor at Tiburcio's dance house." Young Vasquez had wooed Anastacio's youngest sister, María Antonia García, who was seven months older than Tiburcio. By all accounts Anastacio was an exceptionally handsome man, and his sister María was probably equally good-looking. The couple was engaged to marry, and she was undoubtedly the girl with whom Tiburcio lived in the little adobe on Abrego Street in 1853 and 1854. With flashing dark eyes and a thick mane of silky black hair cascading over her bare shoulders, she danced, sang, and played guitar to entertain mesmerized customers, both Hispanic and Anglo. One of the main attractions of Tiburcio's dance house, she would be the cause of several violent encounters between young Vasquez and newcomers to the pueblo. He recalled, "When I lived in Monterey County I kept a dance house and sold liquor. The Americans used to come in and beat and abuse me and mistreat my woman." He would later repeatedly blame his career of banditry on the abuse he suffered from Anglo ruffians.[21]

Tiburcio now had regular contact with the roughest men in Monterey, both Anglo and Hispanic. Racial disturbances, fueled by whiskey and aguardiente, often took place in saloons, gambling halls, and fandango

The earliest known photograph of Monterey, an ambrotype taken in 1859 or 1860. The small white adobe, center left, housed Tiburcio's dance hall and saloon. The large white adobe on the right is the Casa Abrego, and rear left is San Carlos Church, where Tiburcio was baptized. The latter two buildings are still standing. (Dennis Copeland collection)

houses. In Monterey such quarrels were often caused by competition for young Californio women, as women of any ethnicity were much sought after and fought over. Prior to the American conquest, many of the most desirable Californio girls of the ranchero class had married Yankee merchants and seafarers, often causing resentment among young Californio men. Now such resentment spread to the poorer classes, as gold-seekers competed for the attentions of the daughters of peones and campesinos. One such disturbance in Tiburcio's little adobe dance hall was recalled in later years by an elderly Montereño:

> Across from the Abrego house in Monterey, on Abrego Street, Tiburcio Vasquez had a saloon and dance hall. Sailors from American boats in Monterey harbor would swagger into the saloon, demand liquor, and pushing the native habitués of the

place roughly aside, would flirt and make free with the dance-hall girls. This happened a number of times, with Tiburcio's anger and indignation mounting at each affront. One day he was knocked cold by a sailor who was considerably more than "half seas over" from too free imbibing of his unwilling host's whiskey, and who resented interference in his clumsy mauling of one of the girls who played the guitar and sang in the place. Recovering, [Tiburcio] let out a yell and started to clean up the establishment, with the able assistance of a dozen Montereyans who, as regular hangers-on of the place, had also had quite enough of the sea-going Gringos muscling in. No one was killed in the enthusiastic free-for-all, but the cock-sure Americanos were pretty well bashed up, with some broken bones, a loosely flapping ear or two, and a liberal sprinkling of black eyes, bloody noses, and missing teeth.[22]

Although Anastacio García had many Anglo friends, his young protégé by now had a bitter hatred for gringos. To Tiburcio these events justified his entering into a life of banditry. By his account, he was motivated not by the political and economic discrimination against Californios, but by social and racial prejudice. He later recalled: "My career grew out of the circumstances by which I was surrounded. As I grew up to manhood I was in the habit of attending balls and parties given by the native Californians, into which the Americans, then beginning to become numerous, would force themselves and shove the native born men aside, monopolizing the dance and the women. This was about 1852. A spirit of hatred and revenge took possession of me. I had numerous fights in defense of what I believed to be my rights and those of my countrymen.... I believed we were unjustly and wrongly deprived of the social rights that belonged to us.... I went to my mother and told her I intended to commence a different life. I asked for and obtained her blessing, and at once commenced the career of a robber."[23]

Guadalupe Vasquez was a devout Catholic whose life centered around her children and her church. Despite Tiburcio's claim, it is untrue that she gave her blessing to her son's career of robbery. As descendants of his brother Antonio later recalled, "She was devout and deplored her youngest son's waywardness and tried futilely to change him." Tiburcio himself later characterized his parents and his upbringing in a way that was undoubtedly more accurate: "I affirm they did all they could to bring me up in the right way; circumstances which they could not control threw me among the vicious, and I disobeyed their teachings." For Californios, much of public and private life revolved around the church, but Tiburcio in adulthood was not a practicing Catholic, a fact that no doubt grieved his mother greatly.[24]

Vasquez always said it was at this time that his career of banditry began. He recalled, "My first exploit consisted of robbing some peddlers of money and clothes in Monterey County. My next was the capture and robbery of a stage coach in the same county. I had confederates with me from the first, and was always recognized as the leader. Robbery after robbery followed each other as rapidly as circumstances allowed." Tiburcio's claims cannot be confirmed, and no report of such a stagecoach robbery has been located. What is certain is that Anastacio García, not Vasquez, was then the *caudillo* (chief) of the bandits, for he came to be widely recognized as one of the most dangerous desperadoes in the coastal region. García had a paramour in Monterey, and she later told Truman Beeman, then a Monterey County deputy sheriff, that he had confessed fourteen murders to her. One of the most cold-blooded took place in Monterey in 1854, when García convinced the young Indian servant of an army officer to break into his trunk and steal a sack of gold coin. The next day the murdered corpse of the servant was found on the beach, and the coin was gone. Although his early biographer George Beers claimed that Tiburcio Vasquez had committed this murder, Anastacio García was later indicted for it by the Monterey County grand jury.[25]

Before long, Tiburcio's friendship with Anastacio García would result in more bloodshed. Vasquez gave several accounts of this incident. In one interview he recalled, "At this time I was . . . charged with having assisted Anastacio García in a difficulty which took place in a ball-room, in which García killed an employee of the sheriff. This imputation arose from the fact that on the day succeeding the affair, García called on me at my mother's house, and we went off together throughout the country." In another account he said: "The boys had a fandango one night. I was there with Anastacio García. During the evening García got into a quarrel with José Guerra [Higuera] and while they were fighting, the constable came in. There was a great uproar, and the constable was shot through the heart. The next morning José Guerra was hanged by the vigilantes for the crime. . . . I was then running with García, and was engaged to marry García's sister. Many persons thought for these reasons I was concerned. That night I slept in the house of Chona García. I did not run away."[26]

Neither of Tiburcio's statements is complete or correct. According to contemporary news accounts, the facts are that on Saturday night, September 2, 1854, Vasquez, García, José Higuera, and a compadre named Feliz attended a fandango in a Monterey adobe. A contemporary account called it a "low dance house." According to journalist Cora Older, this adobe was located near the intersection of what is now Munras and Webster streets. Jacob Leese, however, implied that the location was actually Tiburcio's fandango house. As was customary, the crowd was a mixture of Californios, Mexicans, and Anglos, all vying for the attentions of the dancing señoritas. Vasquez and his companions were half-drunk on aguardiente when a quarrel broke out. Anastacio García struck one of the guests a strong blow over the head with a water pitcher. In an instant a brawl was on, and someone ran to fetch Constable William Hardmount. The well-liked Hardmount was a twenty-five-year-old New Yorker who had come to California in 1847 with the New York Volunteers. As a popularly elected constable, he took his duties seriously. Hardmount rushed to the dance house and pushed his way through the crowd toward Anastacio García. The outlaw drew his pistol and ordered Hardmount to stand back. Vasquez, Higuera, and Feliz sprang to García's side, revolvers drawn. As Hardmount attempted to persuade García to put up his weapon, one of the four men fired, hitting the constable in the head and killing him instantly. A bystander was wounded in the shoulder by a stray bullet. The four desperadoes fled, but Higuera didn't get far. He was shot in the stomach and captured. At noon the next day he was dragged from his bed by vigilantes and hanged from a beam projecting from the roof of the dance house.[27]

A more detailed account comes from Deputy Sheriff Truman Beeman. According to Beeman, Hardmount, in attempting to arrest García, was shot dead by Vasquez. Tiburcio immediately fled the adobe, but Anastacio García and José Higuera remained at the fandango. Anastacio's friend, Sheriff Ned Lyons, was called to the scene. He entered the adobe to arrest García, who held off the sheriff at gunpoint. Lyons's friend Jack Robinson, armed with a double-barreled shotgun, stepped inside to assist the sheriff. At that, García and Higuera bolted for the back door. As Higuera swung the door open, Robinson put a load of buckshot into him. García fled through the doorway with Robinson close behind. Robinson fired the second barrel and one buckshot struck García in the wrist, causing him to drop his revolver. García broke into a dead run and vanished into the night. José Higuera was alive though badly wounded. At daylight a lynch mob surrounded the adobe, dragged him outside, and hanged him on the front porch.[28]

In yet another version, it was reported that as Constable Hardmount approached Anastacio García, Vasquez seized Higuera's pistol, thrust it under García's outstretched gun hand, and fired the fatal shot. Vasquez, apparently due to the conflicting testimony, was never charged with Hardmount's murder. Although Tiburcio always proclaimed his innocence, one of his gang, Abdon Leiva, later said that Vasquez admitted his guilt: "He told me that he killed the constable and that his friends got him out of the scrape."[29]

Tiburcio fled Monterey and never again appeared openly in the pueblo. His lover, María García, soon married another man. Although Vasquez never admitted it, her change of heart apparently caused him deep bitterness. Never again would he consider marriage, and in later years would say that he never trusted women. Until the end of his life, women would be ever-changing sexual partners and nothing more.

Tiburcio's involvement with Anastacio García also marked him permanently. García was largely responsible for Tiburcio's decision to enter into a life of banditry. After 1854, there is scant evidence that Vasquez ever attempted to reform or to live a different life. He enthusiastically assumed the role of a highway robber. He became addicted to the excitement and easy money, which in turn gave him ready access to gambling tables and women of uncertain virtue. He was now a fugitive, as his boyhood friend Jacob Leese pointed out: "Dead broke, a hunted dog by the law, and with the hatred of the Mexican for the gringo planted in his heart, what could one expect that this hot-headed boy should go from bad to worse?"[30]

Vasquez was hardly alone in his choice of a larcenous career. Between 1851 and 1880, 1,207 Hispanics were sentenced to the state prison at San Quentin. During the period 1851 to 1860, Spanish-surnamed inmates made up 19.2 percent of the prison population. In 1850, California was 12.7 percent Hispanic; by 1860, their proportion in the overall state population had declined to only 4.3 percent. Hispanics were thus significantly overrepresented in the prison population. The reasons for Hispanic banditry are complex and seem to be closely tied to the causes of violent crime on the frontier. Violence and theft were commonplace in California during the 1850s. Homicide rates were vastly higher then than today. Hordes of ambitious young men of many races and nationalities flocked to California, motivated by greed, adventure, or desperation. The development of Colt's revolving pistol, a huge improvement over the old single-shot weapons, made it possible for every man to carry sixfold firepower in his holster. Although the term *machismo,* an exaggerated sense of masculinity or male superiority, was unknown in Tiburcio's day and did not come into common use until the 1930s, a similar concept of personal honor was paramount. For Anglos and Hispanics alike it was a rough ethic that required a man to answer insults with deadly force and never to back down from a fight. This, coupled with the ready availability of bowie knives, six-shooters, and liquor, was a recipe for carnage in the unsettled gold rush society.[31]

With human life so cheap, it is no wonder that some men held little regard for property rights. Claim jumping, land squatting, sluice robbing, highway robbery, and livestock theft were common during the gold rush. Many young men who came to the mining frontier were by nature adventuresome and perhaps somewhat reckless. Although most were consumed by gold fever, the majority did not strike it rich. At or near the bottom of the socioeconomic heap were the poorest of the Hispanics. Bad blood between Americans and Mexicans had been stirred up in the Mexican War, and many on both sides looked upon the other as the enemy. Racism, fueled by ignorance, intolerance, and religious bigotry, was the order of the day. Many Hispanics were driven from the mines, savaged by callous Anglos, and occasionally flogged or hanged without just cause by vigilantes. The gold rush uprooted young Californio males and Mexican immigrant miners from their pastoral occupations and traditional rural families, imposing on them a rough frontier society from which they were systematically excluded while riches were everywhere. It is not surprising that numerous Hispanics, denied an honest means to earn a decent living, turned to robbery and stock theft. While some were career criminals, many others, especially Californios, simply saw little wrong in stealing from the very Anglos who had appropriated their land and their heritage.

For every bandido or cattle thief caught, many others escaped detection. Californio bandidos knew the country better than Anglo newcomers, were the best horsemen, and rode the best saddle animals. With wide networks of family and friends willing to aid them, many easily eluded capture.

And though Tiburcio had seen that violent criminals sometimes paid for misdeeds with their lives, the lesson that the nineteen-year-old learned in Monterey was an important one: in gold rush California a man could commit murder and get away with it.

CHAPTER FOUR

The Roach-Belcher Feud

Anastacio García laid low in El Tucho until the excitement from the Hardmount killing died down, thirsting for revenge against the vigilantes who had lynched José Higuera. Three weeks later, on the night of September 24, 1854, he boldly rode into Monterey at the head of a band of well-armed desperadoes. Tiburcio, his loyal follower, was undoubtedly with him. They searched in vain for the lynchers, then stole several fresh horses before galloping out of town. Although Montereños were too cowed to oppose him, García and Vasquez did not press their luck. They soon turned their horses toward Mendocino County, far to the north.[1]

Tiburcio's first cousin, María Águila, twenty-nine years his senior, was married to Fernando Feliz, grantee of the Rancho de Sanel in Mendocino County. At that time Mendocino County was extremely isolated and very sparsely populated, with only a few hundred rugged settlers amongst a substantial and hostile Indian population. It had no county government and no sheriff; its municipal affairs were administered by its neighbor to the south, Sonoma County. There were no roads, no newspapers, no telegraph, and very little communication with the outside world. In short it was an ideal place for fugitives to hide, and to the Rancho de Sanel the two outlaws made a hard, 250-mile ride. They found Tiburcio's cousin and her family living in a large adobe hacienda near the Russian River, at what later became the town of Hopland. Here the outlaws worked as herders in exchange for the Felizes' hospitality. It is doubtful the isolated ranchero knew that Vasquez and García had been involved in a murder in

Monterey. He was probably happy just to have experienced vaqueros to help him work his cattle.[2]

Anastacio García appears to have soon returned to his home on Rancho El Tucho, where he kept a low profile and, with the help of influential friends like Henry Cocks, Ned Lyons, and Lew Belcher, avoided both lynch law and legal prosecution. But Tiburcio stayed in Mendocino County, and it was not long before he was again in trouble. As he later recalled, "I gathered together a small band of cattle and went into Mendocino County, back of Ukiah and Falis [Feliz] Valley. Even here I was not permitted to remain in peace. The officers of the law sought me out in that remote region, and strove to drag me before the courts." Vasquez explained further, "I took a few cattle and went into the hills near Ukiah. . . . The officers soon learned where I was and again attempted to arrest me, but after another fight, in which no one was killed, I escaped."[3]

Feliz Creek, named after the ranchero, drained the hills to the west of the Rancho de Sanel and flowed into the Russian River not far from the Feliz hacienda. Ukiah, which later became the county seat, did not exist at that time; it is situated about twelve miles to the north. Tiburcio did not reveal whose cattle he "took" into the Feliz Valley, but he was obviously suspected of stealing them. He fled south from Mendocino County. The details of this incident have been lost to history, and his subsequent movements are difficult to trace. Tiburcio may have stayed for a time at the large Sonoma County rancho of his first cousin Guadalupe Vasquez. Her husband, Mark West, a Scot who had been granted the 6,600-acre Rancho San Miguel, had died five years before. Their big hacienda, which also served as a general store and post office, was located on Mark West Creek seven miles north of Santa Rosa. Guadalupe had seven children, owned 1,500 cattle and more than 500 horses, and may have needed the help of a skilled vaquero like Tiburcio.[4]

According to one early chronicler, Vasquez next turned up with his younger sister in Sonora, an important mining town of the Southern Mines in the Sierra Nevada foothills. It had a large Hispanic population and was named after the many miners from Sonora, Mexico, who had settled there in the early years of the gold rush. O. P. Fitzgerald, a Methodist bishop who later served as California's superintendent of schools, wrote that during the winter of 1854–55, Tiburcio "stabbed big John Davis for rudeness to his sister when he [Davis] was drunk at the Tigre." El Tigre (The Tiger) was Sonora's red-light district. Fitzgerald recalled:

I had met the young sister of Vasquez, Anita by name, in the little school that had been opened by my wife in the camp. The pupils were of many nationalities and shades of complexion, but they were molded into delightful unity by the kind, patient, and unselfish little schoolmistress. The Mexican girl was the beauty and pet of the school, having gentle ways, a pretty face, and a voice of remarkable sweetness. At that time social lines were not very rigidly drawn in Sonora, and little Anita was not held responsible for the wild doings at the Tigre. As she grew in stature and beauty, many were the conjectures as to what would be her fate. . . .

The highwaymen, or "road agents," as they were facetiously called, became so daring that they actually robbed the banker D. O. Mills within sight of his banking house in Columbia, a neighboring camp which was a rival of Sonora both in the laxity of its morals and in the richness of its gold diggings.

It was suspected and whispered among the miners that Vasquez, the young Mexican, had a hand in these robberies, and the Tigre was known to be a favorite resort of a number of desperate characters who lived nobody knew how, coming and going mysteriously between sunset and sunrise. A robbery and murder of peculiar boldness and atrocity at Algerine Camp, a rich mining district a few miles west of Sonora, roused the whole country round about, and the perpetrators were pursued with such spirit that most of the band, including both Americans and Mexicans, were captured. It was discovered that Vasquez was one of the gang, but he managed to escape.[5]

Fitzgerald's story is open to question, and it is possible he confused Vasquez with another bandit. Although he had no sister named Anita, it was later reported that he had once lived briefly in Sonora. The raid Fitzgerald describes may be the so-called Rancheria Tragedy of August 6, 1855, involving a gang of eight Mexican robbers and one American. In a raid on the little mining camp of Rancheria in Amador County, this murderous band killed five men and one woman. Four suspects were captured and lynched; three were slain resisting arrest, including one at Algerine Camp.[6]

Vasquez's trail picks up again by the fall of 1855, when he was back in Monterey County, riding with Anastacio García. Before long both were embroiled in the bloodiest feud of the California gold rush. At that time the wealthiest man in Monterey County, which then included present-day San Benito County, was José María Sánchez. He had emigrated to Monterey from Mexico in 1825, as an ambitious young man of twenty-one. By 1850 Sánchez had acquired three large ranchos, totaling 44,000 acres. A capable and shrewd businessman, he owned large herds of cattle and horses as well as holding mortgages on neighboring ranchos. During the gold rush, Sánchez's wealth soared. His cattle, which before 1849 had sold for four dollars per head, now brought seventy to ninety dollars each from buyers at the meat markets of San Francisco, Stockton, and Sacramento. His horses, which had brought no more than ten dollars a head, now sold at prices from one hundred to two hundred dollars each. Sánchez was often paid in gold dust and nuggets.

On the stormy Christmas Day of 1852, Sánchez and his vaqueros were returning from a cattle-selling trip carrying saddlebags loaded with gold dust. Anxious to get home for Christmas, Sánchez attempted to cross the rain-swollen Pajaro River, but the current swept him away and he drowned. He left behind his twenty-eight-year-old wife, Encarnación, nicknamed Chona, and their five young children. Chona Sánchez, like many Californio women of that period, could neither read nor write, and she knew little of cattle raising or business affairs. But she was slender, green-eyed, and stunningly beautiful. As heir to her dead husband's $300,000 estate (the equivalent of about $8 million today), she was the target of every American adventurer in Monterey County. Chona, at the same time, was fully aware that many Californios had lost their land to squatters, land speculators, and their opportunistic lawyers. To protect herself she quickly married Thomas Godden, a lawyer newly arrived in San Juan Bautista. Godden showed his true colors by arranging for a crooked gambler friend, Samuel Head, to be appointed as administrator of the estate. But not long after, Godden died in a steamboat explosion on San Francisco Bay.

Chona had now lost two husbands in less than four months. She did not grieve long, however, for two months later she married a young doctor, Henry L. Sanford. Unknown to Chona, Samuel Head had quickly looted the Sánchez estate, taking $45,000 from the sale of cattle and another $23,000 by paying fraudulent creditors' claims filed by his cronies. In June 1853, just three months after Head had been appointed, the district court judge removed him as administrator and ordered him either to pay back the money or have his bondsmen cover the loss. But Head had hidden the stolen gold and his bondsmen turned out to be destitute gamblers.[7]

Monterey County's crooked sheriff, William F. Roach, now arranged for his crony, the corrupt probate judge Josiah Merritt, to appoint him guardian of the Sánchez children. Then he resigned as sheriff and set out to loot the Sánchez estate himself. Chona's new husband, Henry Sanford, quickly accused Roach of embezzlement and asked Judge Merritt to remove the ex-sheriff as guardian. Merritt refused. Sanford sought help from his good friend Lewis F. Belcher, a twenty-eight-year-old rancher and cattle broker, popularly known as the "Big Eagle of Monterey." Belcher hired a tough and highly capable lawyer, David S. Terry of Stockton. Terry brought a lawsuit against Roach for stealing $73,000 in gold from the estate and obtained a change of venue to Stockton on the grounds that Roach had bribed Merritt.[8]

The Stockton judge appointed Lew Belcher as a receiver to recover the stolen gold from the ex-sheriff in Monterey. However, Belcher discovered that Roach had skipped town and was fleeing on horseback to Mexico. Belcher employed a retinue of gunmen to protect his interests, among them Anastacio García and Bill Byrnes. The latter was a famous manhunter and Indian fighter who as lieutenant of the California Rangers had helped break up Joaquín Murrieta's band two years earlier. Belcher ordered Byrnes to track down the fleeing Roach. Byrnes, using relays of fresh horses, pursued the former sheriff, capturing him at San Buenaventura (now called Ventura) and bringing him to jail in Stockton. The Stockton court found William Roach guilty of embezzlement and ordered him jailed until he returned the stolen gold. At first Roach refused, but after six months behind bars he finally relented. In exchange for his release, Roach told David Terry that the treasure was hidden in the Monterey adobe of his brother-in-law, Jeremiah McMahon. Terry, accompanied by Lew Belcher, raced to the adobe and tore part of it down in a futile search for the gold. Belcher was enraged at being duped. He gathered together a band of hired gunfighters, which included Bill Byrnes and Anastacio García, and ordered them to find and kill Roach. Anastacio García would soon draw his young protégé, Tiburcio Vasquez, into the simmering conflict. William Roach went into hiding, protected by his own band of hired bodyguards, including Monterey badman George Bushton.[9]

On March 15, 1855, Dr. Sanford, Chona's new husband, and Jerry McMahon, Roach's brother-in-law, were in Monterey to attend court hearings on the case. Sanford tried to avoid McMahon, but later that day the two encountered each other in the barroom of the Washington Hotel. McMahon, an Irish ruffian and strong Roach partisan, denounced Sanford in what one newspaper called "language of the most insulting nature." During the violent years of the gold rush, such an affront to personal honor justified a deadly response. Dr. Sanford jerked his pistol, but a saloon patron seized his arm and the revolver exploded harmlessly into the ceiling. McMahon fled, but fifteen minutes later he burst back into the barroom, six-shooter in hand. "Sanford, God damn you, where are you now?" McMahon shouted. Each man went for his gun and opened fire at close range. Both aimed true, and both fell with a bullet in the heart. In moments the two combatants were dead and the Roach–Belcher feud had begun.[10]

Lew Belcher now got himself appointed guardian to replace the deceased Dr. Sanford. He filed lawsuits to recover the missing gold and also sued Roach's bondsmen, but they were unable to make the loss good. Roach remained in hiding, but his partisans retaliated by repeatedly attempting to ambush Belcher on the road between Monterey and his Carmel Valley ranch. Now more than ever, Belcher needed the protection of hired gunmen like Anastacio García, the most feared desperado in Monterey. For a year García and Tiburcio Vasquez had stayed out of Monterey. Local tradition maintained that García had a hideout in a mountain gorge ten miles south of Carmel Valley, known to this day as Anastasia Canyon, and that he and Tiburcio were harbored there by a friend, Agustín Escobar. The two outlaws often made secret visits to friends and family in Monterey and El Tucho.[11]

Anastacio García could not appear openly with Lew Belcher because the year-old Hardmount murder charge was still hanging over his head. According to a contemporary, García remained in hiding "until the witnesses all disappeared." On October 2, 1855, perhaps at Belcher's urging, he rode into Monterey alone to face the charges against him. Said Cora Older, "Early Montereyans . . . told the writer what an imposing figure . . . was Anastacio as, a pistol in each hand, he came on his swift horse down from his hiding place." García turned himself in to Sheriff Lyons and demanded a court hearing on the murder charges. As the *Monterey Sentinel* reported, "The prosecution not being able to find any testimony against García, the proceeding was dismissed, and he is now at liberty." García's friendship with Sheriff Lyons no doubt aided him in evading the murder charge. Anastacio García was now free to appear openly in Monterey and to take an active part in the feud by protecting Lew Belcher and retaliating against Roach and his men. Vasquez seems to have followed him willingly into the Belcher faction. Unlike García, however, Vasquez did not appear openly in Monterey. Fearing punishment for the constable's murder, even though he was never formally charged with it, he made surreptitious visits at night and kept out of sight during the daytime.[12]

William Roach's attorney was Isaac Wall, a former speaker of the state assembly. On Friday afternoon, November 9, 1855, Wall and a young ex-constable, Thomas Williamson, rode south out of Monterey on horseback, leading one pack horse. They told friends that they were headed to Southern California. Belcher's men, however, believed that their pack animal carried a portion of the stolen gold, which Wall and Williamson were taking to Roach. Half an hour later, Anastacio and another Belcher partisan mounted up and followed the pair out of town. According to then Monterey Deputy Sheriff Truman Beeman, the second man was Tiburcio Vasquez.[13]

Wall and Williamson rode twenty-five miles south to the Rancho Guadalupe on the Salinas River, owned by Mariano Malarin. Soon afterward, Anastacio and a compadre—perhaps Tiburcio—rode up. There was to be a large rodeo the next day, so it was not unusual for vaqueros to drift into the rancho for work. Wall and Williamson spent the night as guests of Malarin. At seven the next morning they saddled up, loaded their pack horse, and set off south on El Camino Real. Shortly after that, García and his compadre mounted and rode out of the rancho. Malarin's vaqueros thought it strange that the two left before the rodeo.

Wall and Williamson didn't get far. Several miles to the south was the rancho of Teodoro Gonzáles, located in what is now the town of Gonzales. The rancheros heard gunfire across the Salinas River, and before long, Wall's riderless mount galloped up to the hacienda. It had been shot in the flank, the bullet passing through the saddle. Soon Williamson's frightened horse raced up, the ex-constable's rifle still lashed to the saddle. The rancheros galloped across the river to investigate and found the body of Isaac Wall in a small arroyo known as Lime Kiln Gulch just off the

Isaac B. Wall, murdered in 1855 during the Roach–Belcher feud. Anastacio García and Tiburcio Vasquez were the prime suspects in his death. (William B. Secrest collection)

main road. He had been shot in the back of the head and in the left wrist. His body had been dragged from the road and thrown into the ravine. His ring, derringer pistol, and ivory-handled Colt's revolver were gone. The robbers had overlooked his money belt, which was found to contain $1,000. Nearby the pack horse's saddlebags were found opened and the contents scattered about. One of the rancheros raced into Monterey to spread the alarm.

At this time the undersheriff of Monterey County was Joaquín de la Torre, the former soldier who was highly regarded by both Anglos and Hispanics. He and his brother, Gabriel, Monterey's justice of the peace, rode out to the murder scene with a posse of citizens. They made a further search and thirty yards from Wall's body, hidden in the brush, they discovered Thomas Williamson's corpse. He too had been shot in the back of the head. The wound had been delivered at very close range, as most of one ear had been torn away by the force of the gunshot. His Colt's Navy revolver was gone, but two hundred dollars was found hidden in his saddlebags. The tracks of at least seven horses were found, leading them to believe that a band of at least seven men had committed the murders (although the tracks may simply have been those of the vaqueros from the Gonzáles rancho). In the absence of the county coroner, Justice Gabriel de la Torre conducted an inquest, then his brother set out to investigate the murder.

Joaquín de la Torre was well aware that El Camino Real was infested with bandits who often murdered their victims so as to leave no witnesses. He knew both Wall and Williamson well. They had been heavily armed for the trip, each carrying a rifle and revolver, and would never have allowed strangers to approach them on the road, especially not from behind. That, coupled with the fact that the victims had been shot at close range, made it clear that they had been killed by someone they knew. Over the next few days de la Torre searched the area, rode to nearby ranchos, and interviewed witnesses. At the Malarin rancho he learned that Anastacio García had left Monterey shortly after the murdered men, had apparently followed them to the rancho, and then had left soon after the two had departed on Saturday morning. García had then returned to the rancho the same day and had taken part in the rodeo. That night he returned to his adobe at El Tucho. De la Torre determined that Wall and Williamson both knew Anastacio García, and that there had been an "old enmity" between Williamson and García. Isaac Wall, however, had been on friendly terms with García. What, if anything, de la Torre was able to learn about Vasquez's possible part in the crime is unknown, but according to Truman Beeman, García was accompanied by Tiburcio Vasquez. It was later reported that García had made statements to vaqueros at the Malarin rodeo which made them suspect he had been involved in the killings.[14]

The murders of two prominent citizens caused a public uproar. California's governor offered a $1,000 reward for the killers. James B. Wall, brother of Isaac, rode down from San Jose to help hunt down the murderers, offering an additional $1,000 in bounty. Anastacio García was almost immediately and publicly suspected of the crime. It was widely rumored in Monterey that Lew Belcher had paid García to rob and kill the two to keep them from meeting up with William Roach. By the time Joaquín de la Torre returned to Monterey, he believed that he had enough evidence to arrest García. De la Torre and García were bitter enemies, as each had accused the other of treachery during the war, but de la Torre had assembled some particularly incriminating evidence against the latter. Five days after the murders, on the night of November 15, de la Torre testified before District Court Judge William Rumsey that Wall and Williamson had been killed by Anastacio García at the head of a band of seven or eight outlaws. The judge issued a warrant for García's arrest.[15]

At three o'clock the next morning Monterey County Sheriff John Keating and a well-armed posse rode out of Monterey toward Anastacio García's adobe at El Tucho. With Sheriff Keating were Joaquín de la Torre; Charles Layton, a former soldier and keeper of the lighthouse at Point Pinos; A. C. Beckwith, a hotel keeper; James Wall, brother of the murdered man; and a Sonoran named Sierra. The adobe was situated in a dense thicket of willows and brush on the north side of the Salinas River. Asleep inside were García, Guadalupe, and their children. According to Deputy Sheriff Beeman, Tiburcio Vasquez was also with them. The possemen surrounded the house in the foggy darkness. De la Torre called out in Spanish, "Come out and surrender to the sheriff."

The posse got no reply. In a bold but foolhardy move, Joaquín de la Torre stepped quickly up to the front door and kicked it in. García was ready for him. Two balls from his six-gun struck de la Torre full in the face, killing him instantly. The posse responded by pouring lead into the adobe. As muzzle flashes lit the foggy blackness, Sheriff Keating and his men saw that one other man was in the adobe with García. The posse came under a furious barrage of rifle and pistol fire from the adobe, making it clear that García was not alone. One of the possemen recalled, "The bullets flew around like cold peas on a hot shovel."

García fought like a madman. He stepped into the doorway holding Guadalupe in front of him as a shield, believing that the sheriff's men would not shoot a woman. Firing his pistol over her shoulder, he shot Beckwith in the left hand and thigh. The possemen thought that Guadalupe had fired the shot. Layton fired back, putting a ball in her breast, and she collapsed, badly wounded. Anastacio García fired again and Layton reeled, a bullet in his stomach.

"The damned fellow has shot me in the guts," the light keeper gasped. Seconds later gunfire from the adobe ripped off one of Layton's fingers and he cried. "Here's a finger drawn, too."

One of the posse called loudly for matches to set fire to the thatched tule roof of the adobe, shouting, "We will burn him out!"

Tiburcio Vasquez's pistol, a massive .44 caliber Colt's Second Model Dragoon revolver, serial no. 9381, manufactured in 1850 or 1851. (Author's collection)

But before this could be done, García and his compadre, brandishing rifles and revolvers, burst out of the adobe. García, six-shooter flaming, ran directly at James Wall, whose pistol was empty. Wall was able to escape his brother's fate, however, as he dodged the bullets and leaped for cover. The two outlaws plunged into the riverbank thicket and disappeared. Sheriff Keating sent word to Monterey for reinforcements, and by mid-day a huge posse of 150 Anglos and Californios was searching the brush along the Salinas River. Montereyans, already reeling from the cold-blooded murder of two prominent citizens, were stunned. Reported one Monterey correspondent that afternoon, "Express after express has been running between the town and the river all day and the citizens are greatly excited at times, and at times completely dumbfounded at the reports thus heard." Said the *Monterey Sentinel,* "During the whole day, the most fearful excitement has existed in our community and a general feeling of insecurity and danger is experienced."

At one o'clock the sheriff's brother, George Keating, with Constable Kellogg of Alisal, a vaquero named Coleman, and several other volunteers, were scouring the riverbank thicket not far from the adobe. Suddenly, they encountered one or both of the outlaws. A barrage of gunfire wounded Coleman in the shoulder and Keating in the breast. Constable Kellogg returned fire with his shotgun and several buckshot ripped into Anastacio García's chest. But the bandit chieftain was not seriously injured and once again the killers disappeared into the brush. According to Cora Older, García briefly appeared at the door of his mother's adobe and called out in Spanish, "Mother, pray for Joaquín de la Torre. I just sent his soul to heaven." He and Vasquez then fled down the river toward Pilarcitos Canyon, then a notorious hideout for outlaws, thieves, and fugitives from justice.

Three wounded possemen were brought into Monterey, along with the body of Joaquín de la Torre. Charles Layton had become separated from his comrades in the predawn darkness. Although gut-shot, he staggered six miles toward town until he was found by a Californio who brought him into Monterey. Doctors did not think his wounds were serious, but his condition quickly worsened and three days later he died. The other men wounded in the shootout at El Tucho recovered, as did Guadalupe García.[16]

Joaquín de la Torre's body was taken to his brother Gabriel's home, which is still standing in Monterey at the corner of Polk and Hartnell streets. Later that day a Montereyan recorded the scene: "We went down to see the body, and it was a sad and awful sight. The dead man lay on the bed with a dreadful wound in the face. He was a tremendous strong man; full robust and well proportioned. He lay stretched out on the bed like a giant. The wailings of the old mother, howling with grief; the suffocating sobs of the wife and sisters of the dead man, while fondly embracing the corpse of one who only yesterday was in the vigor of manhood, were distressing to witness. . . . Poor Joaquin, a brave, honest, and generous man, was killed by two balls right through the mouth and eyes. We had shaken hands with him only the night before."[17]

Sheriff Keating came under heavy criticism for his handling of the affair at El Tucho. One pioneer recalled, "It was said by García's friends, among the whites, that if Sheriff Keating had approached the door alone, or with one man, that García would have delivered himself up" but that he would never have surrendered to Joaquín de la Torre, "his bitter enemy." According to García's friend Henry Cocks, "If a little more coolness and judgment had been shown, it is more than likely he would have delivered himself up or been taken unawares. Too much bravery amounts to rashness." Cocks gave a long interview to the *Monterey Sentinel* in which he recounted a series of circumstances that led him to believe a mounted band of Sonoran outlaws had slain Wall and Williamson before fleeing south. Due to his friendship with García his account was given little credence in Monterey, and soon the grand jury indicted García for murdering the two men.[18]

But García did not immediately flee Monterey County. A week later, on the evening of November 23, a settler named Jackson saw him on the Salinas River near Pilarcitos Canyon. García told Jackson he "would not be taken." García remained in hiding in Monterey County for several more weeks, probably recovering from his wounds. Then he rode south to Los Angeles County, where he hid out with relatives near San Juan Capistrano. Tiburcio Vasquez later recalled that he also rode to Southern California, where he "became employed to a man named Manuel Paul [Poli]." A physician from Spain, Manuel Antonio Rodríguez de Poli was one of the largest rancheros in the portion of Santa Barbara County which later became Ventura County. He was owner of the former lands of Mission San Buenaventura, almost forty-nine thousand acres. Tiburcio was a vaquero for Poli for no more than eight months.

In August 1856 Poli and some of his vaqueros, Vasquez likely among them, drove a herd of cattle north to Monterey County, intending to cross through Pacheco Pass and sell them at the cattle market in Stockton. On August 29 they reached Tres Pinos, now Paicines, nineteen miles south of San Juan Bautista. Poli's horse spooked and fell backward. The pommel of the saddle struck his breast, killing him. Several vaqueros took the body back to Ventura. Tiburcio was likely there, given that his favorite sister, María, twenty-three, was to be married in San Juan the following week. On September 8 she wed Mariano Serena, a twenty-seven-year-old immigrant from Mexico, at Mission San Juan Bautista. Despite their estrangement, Don Hermenegildo and Doña Guadalupe were present, as was undoubtedly the rest of their family. It is doubtful that María would have married without Tiburcio present, and her wedding may well have prompted him to join the cattle drive north. Vasquez knew better than to hang around Monterey County, and he soon returned to Ventura. He now hired on as a borreguero (sheepherder) for another prominent ranchero, Ysidro Obiols. Like Poli, Obiols was a Spaniard. He spoke English fluently and was popular with both Hispanics and Anglos, who a year later elected him to a seat on the county board of supervisors. Tiburcio lived in his hacienda on Ventura Street in San Buenaventura and herded his sheep on the hillside above the mission.[19]

Meanwhile in Monterey, the Roach-Belcher feud continued unabated. Early in December, William Roach's clerk and former undersheriff, Thomas Munk, while playing poker in a Monterey gambling hall, accused a professional gambler of cheating. Munk publicly declared, "Shooting is too good for you. You should be taken out and hanged." These words proved prophetic, for in the morning the gambler was found lynched from a Monterey cypress behind the big house of J. B. R. Cooper, now called the Cooper-Molera adobe. Munk was to testify in favor of Roach in the Sánchez estate lawsuits, but Lew Belcher warned him he was about to be indicted for murder and tried to persuade him to flee. Munk refused and was promptly arrested for the killing, but he was soon released for lack of evidence. Munk maintained that Belcher's men, in order to prevent him from testifying for Roach, had lynched the gambler and then tried to frame him.[20]

By this time Lew Belcher had the upper hand in the feud. While William Roach remained in hiding, Belcher appeared openly in public, protected by his bodyguards. On the night of June 18, 1856, he was having a drink with Deputy Sheriff Truman Beeman at the bar of the Washington Hotel in Monterey. Suddenly Belcher was shot by an unknown assassin concealed behind a pillar in the hotel corridor. The "Big Eagle of Monterey" dropped to the floor, grievously wounded, and died the next day. Before he died, Belcher accused William Roach, ex-sheriff Ned Lyons, Anastacio García, and three other enemies of being his murderers. All except Roach and García, who were in hiding, quickly proved alibis. While it is remotely possible that García secretly returned to Monterey to exact revenge on Belcher for embroiling him in the feud, it is highly improbable that either he or Roach did the deed. Belcher's assassin, although never identified, was almost certainly one of Roach's partisans, however.[21]

In October Los Angeles City Marshal William C. Getman and Undersheriff William H. Peterson got a tip that Anastacio García was hiding out near San Juan Capistrano. With a small posse they headed toward the mission town. Thirteen miles from the pueblo they encountered Anastacio García and two compadres riding toward them. Getman and Peterson drew their guns, and García, though armed with two six-shooters and a sixteen-inch bowie knife, gave up peaceably. The murderer was returned to Monterey by steamship and lodged in the new granite jail that had been built next to Colton Hall, directly across the street from the Vasquez house. García was charged with six murders: those of Hardmount, Wall, Williamson, de la Torre, Layton, and the Indian boy. For three months he languished in jail, awaiting trial. Then, in the morning blackness of February 16, 1857, a masked mob entered the jail and seized and bound the sheriff and jailer. Dragging García from his cell, they looped a lariat around his neck. The rope was thrown over a beam and the out-law's feet were tied to a heavy log. The weight of the log nearly severed the brigand's head when he was hoisted up.

Who lynched Anastacio García? There are two credible theories. Con-temporary newspapers reported that several of the Juan Flores–Pancho Daniel gang had been spotted near Monterey, having fled vigilantes in Los Angeles County. It was believed that the band, which included Faustino García, brother of Anastacio, planned to free him, prompting local vigi-lantes to take quick and lethal action. But in later years another story became widely accepted in Monterey: From his jail cell García had warned the surviving leaders of the Belcher faction that if they did not help him he would confess that they had paid him to kill Wall and Williamson. Belcher's men promised to break him out of jail, but hanged him instead. This account has the ring of truth, for it was García's political connection with Belcher that had helped him escape punishment before.[22]

Although the death of Anastacio García effectively ended the Roach-Belcher feud, the vendetta would claim one more victim. William Roach came out of hiding and bought a farm in Santa Cruz County, about twenty-five miles north of Monterey. A heavy drinker, he would boast of his lawless exploits during the vendetta when under the influence. On September 3, 1866, unknown killers crushed his skull with a rock and threw his body into a well. It was generally believed that Roach had been killed either by Belcher's friends or by his own partisans who feared his drunken boasting would lead to their arrests for murder.[23]

An understanding of the Roach-Belcher feud is central to an under-standing of Tiburcio Vasquez. As it illustrates, 1850s Monterey was an unstable community. A new Anglo society had been superimposed on the preexisting Californio one; its courts had become incompetent and corrupt; law enforcement was ineffective and partisan; its gold rush economy was of the boom–and–bust type; citizens were more interested in making money than civic affairs; and politics were controlled by a few powerful individuals. These conditions, which gave rise to the Roach-Belcher feud, were not unique, for they appeared at various other times during the frontier period, most notably in San Francisco's vigilance movements of 1851 and 1856; Montana Territory's vigilante uprising of 1863–65 involving outlaw-sheriff Henry Plummer and organized thievery; New Mexico's Lincoln County War of 1878–79; and the cowboy troubles of southern Arizona, 1880–82, in which Wyatt Earp and his brothers became prominent. Such conditions combined to create a vacuum of legal and moral order. In some cases, vigilantes stepped in to fill this void; in others, bloody feuds resulted. Monterey got both.[24]

The conditions that caused and fueled the feud, coupled with Tiburcio's conflict with Anglo society, had a profound impact on him. He was young and impressionable, and in the absence of his father, he fell under the influence and tutelage of one of the worst desperados in California. He wholeheartedly embraced the wild life of Monterey's fandango houses, monte parlors, grog shops, and bordellos. He resented Anglos, especially the gringo ruffians who had abused and humiliated him. He was surrounded by greed, violence, ethnic and religious intolerance, and political corruption. City and county officials abused the public trust, judges were bought, crooked lawyers defrauded Californios, and prominent men used the legal system for their own financial benefit. In such an atmosphere, it was easy enough to justify robbing and stealing. Thus was the character of Tiburcio Vasquez forged in a crucible of crime, corruption, and racism in old Monterey.

CHAPTER FIVE

He Never Showed
the White Feather

By the fall of 1856 Tiburcio Vasquez was back in Ventura. Although ostensibly a borreguero for Ysidro Obiols, he was now, by his own admission, a thief. He later said that by this time he intended "to live off the world, and perhaps suffer at its hands." According to an early account, he engaged in stock theft in the San Joaquin Valley. For almost a year he was not caught, or for that matter, suspected. He undoubtedly also spent time with his brother Chico, who had moved to Ventura. His wife, María, had just given birth to their first child, Felicita, who years later would feature prominently in Tiburcio's life.[1]

Whether Tiburcio had any contact with his father is unknown. Hermenegildo was now seventy-two, suffering from the infirmities of age, and impoverished. In 1853 he had filed a claim to prove ownership of his little rancho on the Pajaro River. To prove his case he needed to bring witnesses to San Francisco to testify in court, but he could not afford to pay for their travel. In 1855 he sought additional time to prove his claim. His attorney wrote that he was "old and infirm and has been unable on account of his poverty to procure the attendance of his witnesses," and that he was "entirely dependent on his friends for assistance." Two months later, on March 27, 1855, when his case came before the court, Hermenegildo and his witnesses failed to appear, and the court rejected his claim. It was a bitter and final blow to a proud man who had lost his family, his land, and his birthright. Hermenegildo's niece had married Secundino Robles, prominent owner of the Rancho Santa Rita in what is now the city of

Palo Alto. In 1857 they took in the ailing old soldado and cared for him. His health continued to decline, and by the end of the year he was seriously ill. He died on January 16, 1858, and was buried in a simple ceremony at Mission Santa Clara two days later.[2]

By this time his youngest son had suffered serious misfortunes in Los Angeles County. Tiburcio recalled, "A friend of mine stole some horses and pawned them. The officers got after him, and as I was with him when they came upon us, they arrested me also. When in jail I told him to make certain statements which would clear him. He did so and got free, and I was sent to the State Prison for five years. I didn't intend to convict myself, but made a fool of myself and got nipped. I was wholly innocent." Vasquez later provided more details, saying that he "had $200 in money and while here [Los Angeles] met a man with ten horses and a mule" and they "went in together and sold the animals" but Tiburcio "was arrested and lodged in jail for grand larceny." Tiburcio claimed that when he was told the charge against him was stealing horses, he said, "If selling the horses was the offense, then I myself am the guilty party." The other man was then released, and Vasquez was convicted. Tiburcio once gave a different account to a journalist, who wrote, "Vasquez, though then but twenty-two years of age, was well versed in the hooks and crooks of his own profession, and also tolerably familiar with the complicated machinery of the courts. . . . He suggested to his comrade that the latter should make certain statements in court on the day of trial which he (Vasquez) would get clear, and then, in return, he would perform a like service. The other promised, but a talk with the officers induced him to change his tactics somewhat. When the case was called for trial, the partner of Vasquez turned State's evidence." Tiburcio was then convicted.[3]

Vasquez's stories, as would become a habit with him, skirted the truth. The simple facts are that on July 15, 1857, Tiburcio, with two young Indians known only as Juan and José, raided the rancho of Luis Francisco on the Santa Clara River in northern Los Angeles County. His compadres, like many California Indians of that period, had no surnames. The theft was reported to Undersheriff William H. Peterson, the captor of Anastacio García. Two days later Peterson arrested the horse thieves and recovered three of the stolen animals. Vasquez and his compadres were lodged in the county jail in Los Angeles. José apparently turned state's evidence, as the charges against him were dropped. Tiburcio and Juan hired Kimball H. Dimmick—a prominent lawyer, former judge, and veteran of the New York Volunteers who was known as "a defender of horse thieves, gamblers, and desperadoes"—to defend them. Dimmick wasn't able to do much for the pair. They were indicted for grand larceny on August 11. Two days later Tiburcio and his partner, faced with conclusive evidence, pleaded guilty. Juan got one year in state prison; Tiburcio, apparently seen as the ringleader, received five years.[4]

Vasquez was stunned at the severity of his sentence; he had expected only one year. But it was a bad time for horse thieves in Los Angeles. The county was still in a state of feverish excitement due to the so-called Juan Flores "revolution." Just five months before Tiburcio's arrest Juan Flores, an escaped convict from San Quentin, with Pancho Daniel, a former member of Joaquín Murrieta's band; Faustino García, younger brother of Anastacio; and a dozen other bandidos had terrorized Los Angeles County, killing Sheriff James Barton and three of his posse in a wild gun battle. In a massive manhunt and vigilante uprising by both Anglos and Californios, two of the gang were shot to death and ten more suspects were lynched, including Flores.

Tiburcio's stern sentence, five times longer than his codefendant's, was partly a result of strong anti-bandido sentiment caused by the murders of Sheriff Barton and his possemen. Among Spanish-speaking people in Los Angeles there was a widespread belief that the criminal justice system did not treat them fairly. But that dynamic seems to have been only part of the reason for Tiburcio's sentence. Although there is no doubt of his guilt, and seven of the seventeen grand jurors who indicted him were Hispanic, his punishment was harsh for a first conviction. In Los Angeles, at least, that was not the norm for Hispanic defendants. A recent study of more than 1,200 court cases for theft, assault, and homicide in Los Angeles County from 1850 to 1875 found that Hispanics and Anglos were treated substantially the same way. A statistical analysis of ethnic composition and conviction rates demonstrated that "criminal justice administration was not skewed dramatically against Spanish-language surnamed defendants nor significantly tilted in favor of Europeans and Americans." In frontier California, Hispanics were, for the most part, treated fairly in the courts. Far more often it was vigilantes who mistreated them.[5]

Some writers have incorrectly claimed that Tiburcio Vasquez was by this time a famous bandit and a renowned hero to Californios. In fact in 1857 he was an exceedingly obscure criminal. His involvement in the Roach-Belcher feud was unknown outside of Monterey and only came to light when he achieved national notoriety many years later. His arrest for horse theft in Los Angeles received a small, nine-line notice in the *Los Angeles Star.* More significantly, no mention at all of his arrest appeared in the Los Angeles Spanish-language newspaper *El Clamor Público.* Had Vasquez been a prominent or heroic figure, *El Clamor Público,* which was widely read by Californios, would certainly have reported his capture.

Tiburcio and his Indian compadre, along with three other convicted felons, were placed in irons by Sheriff Elijah Bettis and taken north on the steamer *Senator* to San Francisco, and from there to the state prison at San Quentin. Tiburcio entered the penitentiary on August 26, 1857, just six weeks after his cattle raid in Los Angeles County. His name was recorded in the prison register as Tiburcio Basquez, height 5 feet, 5 and ⅜ inches, dark complexion, dark eyes, and black hair. In an effort to obscure his identity, Tiburcio told the officers he was nineteen. In this era before mug photographs, the Bertillon system of measurements, and fingerprinting, he was stripped and his body minutely examined for scars and other identifying features, all duly recorded in the register: "scar on left breast, scars on left forefinger, 2 small scars on left thumb." Tiburcio was assigned convict number 1217. For almost a quarter of his life, San Quentin would be his home.[6]

The prison was less than five years old. With very few jails and no state penitentiary in California during the first years of the gold rush, convicted state prisoners had been held in two prison brigs, one in San Francisco and one in Sacramento. In response to widespread demand for a state penitentiary, the California legislature authorized a private contractor, James Estell, to build a prison and lease out convict labor to local ranchers and businesses. In 1852 a prison brig was anchored at Point San Quentin in Marin County, where twenty acres had been purchased for a prison. The site was a spit of land jutting out into the bay. The point itself was a knoll, which soon became the prison graveyard and was known as Cemetery Hill. Just north of it the prisoners built a two-story cellblock made of large stones they cut from a nearby quarry. Finished early in 1854, it quickly became known as the "Stone Cellblock," or simply "the Stones," and housed three hundred convicts. At the time Tiburcio entered San Quentin, the prison was home to 512 convicts, of whom thirty-seven were Californios, seventy-four Mexicans, and thirteen Chilenos. Fully one-fourth of the prison population was Spanish-speaking, the vast majority of them convicted of livestock theft.[7]

Conditions in the privately run prison were abysmal. In order to maximize profit, the private contractor worked the largest number of convicts and employed the least number of guards possible. During Tiburcio's time, the principal profitable business was brick making, both for prison construction and for private sale. This required that many convicts work outside the prison, not only in the brickyard, but also in crews that cut firewood in the nearby forests and loaded brick for shipment on prison schooners. The prisoners were poorly clothed and food was meager, consisting of bread, beans, and a little meat. Mismanagement, corruption, and lack of discipline were common. The twenty guards, or freemen, were too few, underpaid, and often drunk on duty. Neither guards nor prisoners wore uniforms. To make up for the lack of freemen, trusted prisoners, or trusties, were armed with guns and assigned to guard duty; often they could not be distinguished from prison officers.[8]

By the time Vasquez arrived, a new contractor, John McCauley, had taken over San Quentin. Some of the worst abuses, such as the arming of trusties and guards' cohabitation with female prisoners, were ended. The prison had an outer wall, twenty-feet high and five hundred feet square, completed in December 1855, along with several new buildings. The Stone Cellblock was located at the south end of the prison. Adjacent to and just outside the east wall was the two-story guards' quarters; the main gate was on the first floor of this building. Entrance to the prison was through an outer gate in the guards' building, and then via a short corridor to the inside gate in the wall around the prison yard. There was only one other gate, on the west wall, which was used to move prisoners to and from the brickyard. Like the main entrance, it had double gates, one to enter the gatehouse, and a second in the prison wall. A short distance southwest of the prison was the estuary and the prison wharf, and just north of it, the brickyard.

San Quentin's guards were issued the Model 1841 U.S. Percussion Rifle, commonly known as the Mississippi Yager (or Jaeger), and a sidearm, either the .44 caliber Colt's Dragoon or the .36 caliber Colt's Navy revolver. On top of the prison wall were six small guardhouses. Outside the walls the prison was encircled by five guard towers constructed of prison-made brick. Post 1, located on the hill northeast of the prison, was equipped with a six-pound brass cannon, loaded with grape and canister shot. Three guards, armed with rifles and revolvers, were detailed to man the post. Post 2, located high on the hill north of the prison, was manned

West gate of San Quentin prison, as seen from the brickyard, 1872. A hand-operated brick press is in the foreground. (Author's collection)

by one sharpshooter. Post 3, on the hill just northwest of the prison, above the north brickyard, was equipped with a twelve-pound mountain howitzer, ostensibly manned by three freemen. Post 4, located on the east side of the prison between the bay and the main gate, was manned by a single guard, armed with rifle and six-shooter. Post 5, on a high bluff above the bay, just southwest of the prison and overlooking the prison wharf and the west brickyard, had a six-pound cannon, and was to be manned by three guards with rifles and revolvers. On most days, however, due to efforts by the prison lessees to cut costs, only one guard was on duty at each post. Three mounted guards patrolled the prison perimeter on horseback.[9]

Despite the physical improvements under McCauley, prison conditions remained primitive when Vasquez arrived. Far too many convicts were crowded into the Stone Cellblock. It was 180 feet long and 24 feet wide. The upper floor held forty-eight cells in two rows of twenty-four. Each cell was ten feet by six feet and intended to hold two prisoners, but now each held four. The lower floor had two large rooms. One was the turnkey's office, on the east side of the cellblock. The rest of the floor was taken up by the Long Room, a huge dormitory cell almost 150 feet long. Three hundred men were jammed inside it, sleeping in three-decker bunk beds placed so close one could not walk between them. No effort was made to separate old prisoners from young, violent from nonviolent; all were thrown together in a common mass. The result was that youthful prisoners, instead of being reformed, became steeped in the criminal arts.

A legislative committee inspected the prison a few months after Tiburcio's arrival, finding the convicts "in such tattered, torn, forbidding, and filthy condition that the commonest street beggars, sleeping by the wayside and begging their daily bread, would by comparison have the appearance of newly Parisian clad gentlemen." More than one hundred of the prisoners did not even have shoes; many of them wore gunnysacks and scraps of blankets tied around their feet. Their bedding consisted of a lumpy straw mattress and a lone threadbare blanket, often swarming with lice. The cells in the Stones were cramped, foul-smelling, inadequately ventilated, and windowless. Each had a sheet iron door with a small opening at the top to allow air inside. The four convicts in each cell shared a single slop bucket for a toilet. But the legislative committee found that the small, stench-filled cells were "by no means the worst feature of the prison":

> In the Long Room ... are turned loose like so many brute animals in a corral, to stay and sleep, the young, middle-aged and old; the boy of 15, perhaps his first offense, with upwards of 300 convicts, among whom are necessarily the vilest of the vile, thus rendering

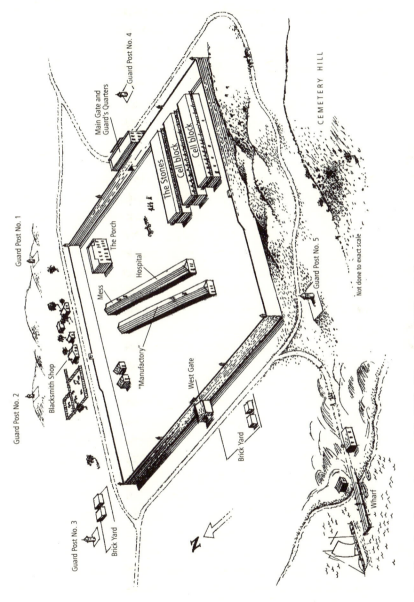

Guard Post No. 1

Guard Post No. 4

Main Gate and
Guard's Quarters

The Stones

Cell block

Cell block

CEMETERY HILL

The Porch

Hospital

Mess

Guard Post No. 5

Guard Post No. 2

Blacksmith Shop

"Manufactory"

West Gate

Not done to exact scale

Guard Post No. 3

Brick Yard

Brick Yard

Wharf

N

San Quentin prison as it appeared in 1859. Diagram by William B. Secrest.

77

reform and reformation seemingly impossible. . . . The manner of stowing away such a number in so small a space is accomplished by placing a row of standing bunks close to each other on either side of the room, with their heads to the wall, leaving an open space through the middle of the room; the bunks being one above the other, and into which the prisoners crawled from the end, the open space being so small that before they take their bunks it is with a great deal of difficulty you can make your way through the crowd; and the stench ensuing from the room when open in the morning will have to be imagined, as a description is impossible."[10]

Like many other convicts, Tiburcio was put to hard labor in the brick-yard. The convicts dug clay, loaded it onto carts, and hauled it to the brick molds. Water was brought in carts from a large holding tank near the north wall, then mixed with the clay. The wooden molds were filled with wet clay, then placed into a brick press. The prison had fifteen hand-operated brick presses and one steam-powered press, a recent invention. After the press compacted the clay inside the mold, the newly formed bricks were removed and hauled to a drying shed. Once they had dried, other convicts brought them to the kilns where they were baked into a finished product. The majority of the convicts in the brickyard were Hispanic or Indian, probably because many of them had prior experience in making adobe bricks. Other prisoners were assigned to gangs that chopped firewood in the nearby hills for the brick kilns.

Surplus bricks not needed for prison construction were shipped to market in San Francisco on the prison sloops *Pike County* and *Marin*. Construction was then underway on a second two-story brick cellblock, built next to the Stones, and by 1859 a third cellblock was finished. The three cellblocks were parallel to one another on the southeast corner of the prison grounds. At the same time several other large brick buildings were completed, all by convict labor. They included a kitchen, a dining hall, and a two-story hospital building, adjacent to each other, west of the main gate. The hospital, incongruously, had a dungeon in the basement, with fourteen "dark cells" for punishing prisoners who violated the rules. Between the hospital and the west wall was built a long manufactory building, where wagons, furniture, shoes, and other goods were made. The prison office, also completed in 1859, was located in the northeast corner of the yard, near the main gate, and was famously known as "the Porch" for its long veranda. The irony that he was helping build his own prison was certainly not lost on Tiburcio Vasquez.[11]

Brick making was hard, backbreaking work that Vasquez undoubtedly despised. Once a week he was allowed to bathe in an outdoor cold-water plunge, an often-filthy cesspool facetiously nicknamed "the Rose Bowl." Twice a day the prisoners were marched into the dining hall where they ate beans, stew, bread, and coffee at long, narrow tables. The prison had a small library and Vasquez, who enjoyed reading works in Spanish, may well have tackled its English-language books when he was not toiling in the brickyard. But several old convicts told Cora Older that Tiburcio spent his free time gambling with other prisoners. As one recalled, "Vasquez kept them all poor."[12]

Vasquez found in San Quentin many of the worst badmen on the Pacific Coast, among them members of the infamous Tom Bell gang. Soon more noted ruffians would join him: Henry Plummer, the corrupt outlaw-lawman who would later be lynched as a sheriff in Montana; pioneer stagecoach robbers Jim Driscoll and Ike McCollum; and "Longhair Sam" Brown, the notorious gold rush gunfighter. A boyhood compadre from Monterey, Ramón Rangel, was also there, serving a term for livestock theft. Yet, despite his youth, Vasquez was able to withstand the rigors of San Quentin. James Towle, later warden of San Quentin, when asked about Tiburcio's reputation in the prison during the early days, commented, "Vasquez stands well among the old prisoners. I cannot find on inquiry among them that he ever showed the 'white feather' here."[13]

The Spanish-speaking inmates, whether Californio, Indian, Mexican, or South American, tended to congregate together in San Quentin, connected by their common language and culture. The bilingual Vasquez, however, was able to associate with both fellow Hispanics and Anglos. In the brickyard he became friendly with Charles Horace Dade, known as the Duck Hunter, a brick molder by profession and a thief by avocation. Dade's expertise in making bricks was important to the prison officers, and he played a key role in prison construction, undoubtedly helping to run the steam-powered brick press. A favorite of the guards, he was made a trusty, given a shotgun, and allowed to leave the prison for days at a time to hunt ducks and other game for the prison mess. Those convicts not assigned to work details whiled away the days in idleness. Criminal friendships were made and cemented in San Quentin, and numerous gangs of highway robbers, burglars, cattle rustlers, and horse thieves were organized by ex-convicts who had met in the Stones. Recalled one early San Quentin convict, "At this time prisoners could go where they pleased inside the walls, and knots of two, three, four and even eight or ten could be seen talking together. Thus they would talk over their past life and future hopes and plans. Very few made good resolves. The young and old in crime alike looked to the future only as a period to commit fresh crimes in. They would coolly discuss plans of escape and calculate how many lives would be sacrificed in contemplated breaks."[14]

From the moment he stepped onto San Quentin's wharf, Tiburcio Vasquez's uppermost thoughts were of escape. Despite the outer wall, breaks were still commonplace. Between 1851 and 1861, 547 convicts broke out of San Quentin; only 219 were recaptured. Many prisoners simply ran away from wood-chopping duty in the Marin County hills. Others took part in mass breakouts. Surprisingly, convicts were not prosecuted in court for attempting to escape, nor were their terms increased. Instead they were punished by flogging, being put in irons, or being placed in a dark cell on a diet of bread and water. In the yard was the whipping post, nicknamed the Ladder. It was in the shape of a large cross, leaning at an angle toward the ground. The prisoner was tied to it hand and foot, and lashes were laid on with a rawhide whip. Typical punishments were ten "stripes," or lashes, for lying, twelve for stealing, eighteen for fighting, thirty for insubordination or for trying to break their cross chains, and fifty or sixty for attempting to escape. Lieutenant A. D. "Dorse" Moon was the official flogger during Tiburcio's term. Although Hispanics routinely suffered societal discrimination in that era, they appear to have been treated no worse than Anglo prisoners. One study of San Quentin found that Hispanic convicts received punishment proportionate to their percentage of the total prison population in the late 1850s.[15]

Two months after Tiburcio entered San Quentin an incident occurred that should have relieved him of any thought of escape. On November 4, 1857, thirty prisoners were unloading a cargo of wood from a schooner at the prison wharf. The boat started to push off, and the guard in Post 5 called on them repeatedly to come back. The convicts paid no heed, either because they intended to escape or because they could not hear him. The guard fired a load of grapeshot with his six-pounder, killing five convicts and wounding three. The prisoners claimed that they had been following the overseer's instructions and had not been trying to flee. Regardless of the consequences, many convicts continued attempting to escape.[16]

Tiburcio ached to get out of San Quentin, a desperation that was amplified by another family wedding. His favorite sister, María, had a short-lived first marriage, for her husband Mariano Serena soon died. On February 14, 1859, at Mission San Juan Bautista, she married Manuel Lara, a twenty-seven-year-old carpenter from Guaymas, Mexico. Manuel adopted María's eleven-year-old son, Jesús, and the couple would soon have children of their own. Tiburcio had known Manuel in San Juan and liked him, and perhaps the fact that he could not be at the wedding is what drew him into an escape plot. One of his prison compadres was Francisco "Acapulco" Lulio, a notorious bandit serving a fourteen-year term for a robbery in Amador County, who took his nickname from his hometown in Mexico. Another was Jesús Mendoza, an eighteen-year-old Californio vaquero serving a five-year term for horse theft in Los Angeles County. Lulio, a leader among the prisoners, took Vasquez, Mendoza, and forty-odd other Spanish-speaking inmates into his confidence to plan a break. They fashioned knives from tools stolen in the brickyard, carefully devised their plans, and waited for an opportune moment. It was later reported that their "plan of operations had been kept wholly secret from all those prisoners unacquainted with the Spanish language." On Saturday, June 25, 1859, Vasquez and three hundred fellow convicts were at their usual labor in the brickyard. At noon they were marched single file back into the prison for their midday meal, and at one o'clock they lined up to return to the brickyard. Led by the prison's carpenter and super-intendent of labor, George Lee, they filed out the west gate under the watchful eye of John Spell, the gatekeeper. When about 160 convicts had passed through, Lulio let out a wild yell and the conspirators pulled out their knives and rushed the guards. Vasquez later recalled, "Three or four of us prisoners made a rush for the carpenter, George Lee, and the gate-keeper, John Spell, and overpowered them. We got the keys, rushed out of the gate on the hill, and got away."[17]

Characteristically, Tiburcio made no mention of the bloodshed that quickly followed. The convicts slammed the gate shut, locked it, and threw away the keys, thus preventing the guards inside the walls from following them outside. The escapees, after capturing Lee and Spell at knifepoint, bound their hands. They held the two close, forcing the sharpshooters on the wall to hold their fire for fear of hitting the hostages. Then Lulio, Vasquez, and forty more convicts crossed the brickyard in the face of the cannons and headed west along Corte Madera Creek toward Mount Tamalpais.

In the meantime more than a hundred prisoners were outside the walls; many were short-termers who had no wish to escape. They rushed to and fro in the excitement, not certain what to do. Others fled around the wall to the main gate on the east side. Thinking they were trying to flee, the guards opened fire. The *San Francisco Bulletin* reported that while the convicts "who refused to run were outside the wall, a cannon was turned on them and, notwithstanding several of them fell on their knees, 'crossed' themselves and begged for life, it was discharged." One newspaper reported that one convict was killed and four wounded, another that five were killed and "many more" wounded. The prison log book, perhaps more accurate, showed one prisoner slain and seven wounded.[18]

One of the guards gave an account years later in which he admitted that "the rattled guards, thinking [the convicts] were striving to escape, opened fire." He claimed however that most of the convicts were shot while trying to capture one of the cannons: "Up the hill they charged in the face of the frowning gun with the courage worthy of better men. Their evident purpose was to reach the gun before the guard could discharge it, but the latter was 'on his job,' as the saying is, and before they were midway up the slope he touched the weapon off. With a flash of crimson flame the wedge of grape-shot hummed though the mass of desperate men and nearly half of them went down, either dead or maimed. Those who were not hit scattered in various directions."[19]

As gunfire rattled the brickyard, Acapulco Lulio, Tiburcio Vasquez, and the other convicts pressed on rapidly up Corte Madera Creek, jabbing their hostages with knives to keep them moving. They had gone one mile when they released John Spell, who was too winded to proceed any further. Two miles farther on, as the convicts neared a deep ravine at the foot of Mount Tamalpais after crossing the creek, a party of eight guards on horseback caught up with them. Acapulco Lulio was holding his knife to George Lee, and spotting the freemen, threatened to kill his hostage. One of the guards raised his shotgun and fired a blast of buckshot into Lulio's face, puncturing one eye. Lulio dropped, badly wounded. He

The main gate and guards' building at San Quentin prison, 1872. The door to the warden's office is at right. (Author's collection)

dragged Lee to the ground, slashing at him with his knife. Lee warded off the blows, but his hands were badly gashed. As the escapees fled, two convicts were shot dead and several more wounded. A bullet tore into Tiburcio's hand, but the wound proved to be minor.

Vasquez and his fellow convicts disappeared into the heavily wooded hills at the base of Mount Tamalpais. Marin County at that time was sparsely settled, and it was not difficult for the escapees to avoid the citizenry. News of the break was sent to San Rafael and also to San Francisco, where large broadsides were posted giving exaggerated accounts of hundreds of convicts escaping and many guards being murdered. Given San Quentin's reputation for mismanagement, these reports were widely believed. Large posses took to the field and eleven convicts were soon captured, several more were killed, and a number were shot and wounded.[20]

The San Francisco newspapers railed against the prison's management, calling for the privately run prison to be turned back over to state control. The *Bulletin's* editor termed San Quentin "a shame and disgrace to the state" that "outrages public decency." He claimed that the convicts were "half-famished, nearly naked young men, driven to desperation" by hunger and cold, and that they attempted to escape "in preference to dying by slow torture, from hunger, and being consumed by swarms of loathsome vermin." Yet several legislative committees, while highly critical of both the private lease system and the poor living conditions, nonetheless found that the convicts were amply fed and that ill treatment was reserved for prison troublemakers. In truth, conditions at San Quentin in the late 1850s were little worse than those in the rugged mining camps, where men struggled for survival in primitive conditions and were in frequent danger of injury or death due to accident or violence.[21]

Vasquez was too smart to stay long with the big group of escapees. Tiburcio knew the country well, and he and Jesús Mendoza quickly struck out on their own. Because prisoners wore civilian clothes (striped uniforms were not introduced at San Quentin until 1865), the pair was not recognized as escaped convicts. Vasquez later recalled, "I traveled on foot, with one companion, through Solano, Napa, and Sacramento Counties until we came to Jackson, Amador County." It was a grueling, 150-mile hike. Tiburcio never went to a new place without a reason, and he apparently had friends or relatives in Amador County whom he hoped would harbor him. Some years later, Sheriff Harry Morse noted in his diary that Vasquez sometimes stayed with a woman in Jackson named Ramona "Negrita" (Little Dark One). Perhaps it was because of Ramona that he went there.[22]

It took Vasquez and Mendoza more than two weeks to make the long trek to Jackson, and they arrived exhausted and unwilling to walk any

further. They did not stay long. On the night of July 13 they stole two
fine American horses belonging to J. F. Blythe, the town's Methodist
minister. The theft was discovered in the morning, and Amador County
Sheriff William J. Paugh set off in pursuit. By then Tiburcio and Mendoza had a fifty-mile head start, riding bareback through Mokelumne
Hill and out of the Sierra Nevada foothills to Stockton. From there they
continued southwest sixteen miles to Chamberlain's Ferry on the San
Joaquin River, heading for Tiburcio's old stomping grounds in Monterey
County. It was evening when they rode up to the tavern at Chamberlain's
Ferry. Two local cattlemen, Lorenzo Dow Stephens and his partner,
named Land, watched them approach. Stephens later recalled:

> We were sitting in the cool side of a porch of a road-side inn
> when two men rode up and called for dinner and they were riding
> bare-back. After they came out we questioned them pretty closely
> and they said that the horses belonged to their uncle and the
> reason they were riding bare-back was that their uncle had driven
> the horses up with a carriage and they were taking the horses
> back. They were two fine looking American horses and we well
> knew that it was almost a sure thing that a Spaniard was not the
> possessor of an American horse.
>
> We let them depart on their journey, but after they were gone
> we talked over the circumstances attending the situation and both
> came to the conclusion that they were riding stolen horses and
> we agreed that we would follow them up and take them. We
> overtook them after riding about a mile or so and commanded
> them to stop and go back to Stockton. At that they commenced
> pleading and said kill them, do anything but do not take them
> back to Stockton, which was about fifteen miles distant. We
> told them in Spanish, it was no use for them to make any fuss
> about it, they would have to go back and that ended it. By the
> way neither of us had any weapon of any kind, but they didn't
> know that.
>
> Just before we entered Stockton, we put the horses' necks
> together and tied the men's feet together under the horse's bellies,
> so we were sure they could not break away from us. As we were
> going up one of the principal streets, a man rushed out of a livery
> stable and hailed, or rather tried to hail us, but we only put spurs

to our horses the more and rushed them through to the jail, where I was well acquainted with the officers and told them to take care of them, which they did in short order. They hadn't much more than gotten them in jail, till here came a man just puffing and blowing and pretty mad too because we wouldn't stop. He proved to be the Sheriff of Amador County and was after these same horses and wanted the men turned over to him.

The next morning the prisoners were taken out and tried before a Justice of Peace, and they acknowledged being escaped convicts and had stolen the horses to get away on. They said they had tried on foot but thought they could make better headway on horse-back. They were sent back to San Quentin and the sheriff took the horses to their rightful owners and the only simple thing in the whole affair was, we never put in a claim for the reward which we were entitled to, fifty dollars each.[23]

Stephens failed to mention that he and Land objected strongly to Sheriff Paugh's demand that the prisoners be returned to Amador County. The cattlemen told the editor of the *San Joaquin Republican* that they refused to "journey to Jackson two or three times, at their own expense, to testify against them." Tiburcio and his compadre were brought into court and a Stockton judge ordered that they be held for a local trial. But a few days later a bench warrant from Amador County was delivered, and the Stockton officials relented. Vasquez and Mendoza were sent back to Jackson, where they were arraigned on grand larceny charges. Although the court record shows that neither of them had a lawyer, the district attorney appears to have offered them a plea bargain: one additional year in San Quentin. Vasquez and Mendoza thought it over and the next day both of them pled guilty. By August 17, less than two months after their escape, they were back in San Quentin.[24]

Tiburcio Vasquez was obscure enough that Stephens, when he wrote his account almost sixty years later, did not recall his name and had no knowledge that the young horse thief he had arrested would one day become the notorious bandit leader. The *San Francisco Alta California* published a short item announcing that Vasquez and Mendoza had been returned to San Quentin. Tiburcio's lack of celebrity was also evident by the brevity of the report and its misspelling of his name. The newspaper called him "Tebruzzo Baskes, alias Tiburcio Basquez." Its reporter added, "Of the forty escapees, fifteen have been recaptured, which leaves twenty-five still at large. The two Mexicans are at work again in the brickyard, and with the memory of the great peril they braved, will not be likely to attempt a similarly concerted escape." Vasquez would soon prove the newspaper wrong.[25]

Because the standard punishment for escaping was between fifty and sixty stripes, Vasquez and Mendoza would have been lashed to the Ladder and the strokes "well laid on" by Lieutenant Dorse Moon. In 1874, an elderly Californio claimed to have "heard it from good sources" that Vasquez was "severely lashed with a cowhide. . . . he received as many as one hundred and fifty lashes, and though he had fainted before the punishment was over, the keepers kept on whipping him till his life's blood streamed down from every part of his back, which they afterwards washed with salt water so as to prevent it from rotting." Tiburcio left no description of his ordeal, saying simply, "At San Quentin I was pretty roughly handled. The treatment was very rigorous. The discipline at that time was undergoing a reform." However, one convict provided an account of the Ladder a year later when punishment was handled by Captain Edward Vanderlip: "I got twenty lashes there with a four foot rawhide in the hands of a powerful man, Vanderlip, who seemed to delight in how deep he could sink the lash into a man's quivering flesh. Every blow laid open my flesh from six to fifteen inches." While Tiburcio recovered from the shredding, he nursed a bitter hatred for Lieutenant Moon.[26]

When he was well enough to work Tiburcio was returned to the brickyard. As additional punishment, when not working he was kept in a dark cell in the dungeon basement of the hospital building. Disheartened, he now turned to his mother for help. Guadalupe Vasquez was deeply shamed by Tiburcio's imprisonment. None of her other children had ever seen the inside of a calabozo. When A. S. Berreyesa, member of a prominent Californio family of Napa County, came to visit his inmate cousins, Dámaso and Nasario Berreyesa, Vasquez asked him to mail a letter to his mother. Tiburcio wrote to her of his escape from prison and said that he had been recaptured near her home, implying that he had been on his way to visit her when he had been captured. Guadalupe did not answer the letter, possibly because Berreyesa never mailed it or more likely, as Tiburcio suspected, because his mother was too angry with him to reply.[27]

As soon as he was released from the dungeon, he began making new escape plans. This time his fellow conspirators were Anglos, not Hispanics.

After the brickyard breakout the entire convict population had been locked in their cells and the prison thoroughly searched for weapons. Yet despite the guards' efforts, the new conspirators were able to fashion contraband daggers. It was not long before they put their plan into operation. On the afternoon of September 27, Vasquez was working on the prison wharf with a large crew of Anglo convicts, loading brick onto the *Bolinas,* a two-masted schooner. Lieutenant Moon was the overseer on the landing. Suddenly Vasquez and twenty of his co-conspirators seized Moon and rushed onto the *Bolinas.* Throwing the vessel's captain and first mate into the hold, they cut the moorings and hoisted the sails. Tiburcio now saw an opportunity to avenge himself on Moon. Yanking out his dagger, he rushed toward the guard, egged on by the prisoners on deck, who yelled, "Kill him! Kill the son of a bitch!"

Just as he reached the overseer, another convict, Charles Ryan, jumped between them and wrested away Tiburcio's knife. Moon had once befriended Ryan, a fact that now saved his life. Ryan squared off between the crowd and Moon. Brandishing the knife above his head, Ryan cried that he "would stick the first man who approached a step nearer to Moon." By this time the sails had filled and the schooner began slowly to move away from the wharf. The guards at Post 5, alerted by the commotion aboard the ship, swiveled the barrel of their six-pound cannon toward the ship. Without warning they opened fire with alternate charges of grape and canister shot. The first few charges missed the *Bolinas,* but the freemen quickly adjusted for range and a deadly barrage tore through the schooner. Several convicts held Dorse Moon in front of them, believing that the guards would hold their fire. But after the last break the guards had been ordered to disregard the safety of hostages, and they continued to rain down deadly fire with the six-pounder. Simultaneously riflemen in the gun post joined in, peppering the ship with their Mississippi Yagers.

Chunks of lead and exploding wood ripped across the vessel. One shot shattered Lieutenant Moon's left arm. Charles Ryan dragged him below, then piled lumber on him to protect him from the grapeshot that ripped through the hull. On deck, two escapees, A. B. Winchell and "Long John" Dixon, were instantly killed, and a third, Billy Burke, was mortally wounded. Six more convicts dropped in bloody heaps, riddled with shot and rifle balls. At the same time the large grapeshot tore through the masts and rigging, which fell crashing to the deck. Vasquez and the rest fled into the hold of the disabled ship. The cannoneers now held their fire, having put eight charges into the ship. The convicts quickly surrendered, and a dozen guards in whaleboats rowed out to the *Bolinas* and climbed aboard its blood-spattered deck. Vasquez was unscathed. The wounded were sent to the prison hospital, while Vasquez and eight others were flogged and fitted with heavy iron cross-chains. Despondent and demoralized by his unsuccessful attempts to get out of prison, Tiburcio once again turned to his mother for help.[28]

CHAPTER SIX

The Big Break

In the first part of October 1859, another of the Berreyesa family, S. T. Berreyesa, visited his cousins in San Quentin. Vasquez gave him a letter for delivery to Doña Guadalupe, the text of which would soon become public in a deadly way. Berreyesa, after leaving the prison, rode to the East Bay with two compadres. They stole several horses in Alameda County, then rode over the coastal hills to the tiny hamlet of Lafayette. Here, early in the morning of October 13, they pilfered three saddles, then headed east. The theft of the saddles was quickly discovered and a posse of armed citizens, six to eight strong, was soon in pursuit. The trail led across the hills through the San Ramon Valley near the settlement of Alamo, and then toward Mount Diablo. The posse caught up with the outlaws in their camp at the base of Mount Diablo. The thieves were quickly surrounded and ordered to surrender. Instead all three promptly broke for the brush. The possemen opened fire, wounding Berreyesa with a shot to the head. His two compadres surrendered, and the outlaws were brought into Walnut Creek.[1]

The posse carried Berreyesa into the Walnut Creek House, a hotel and tavern, where later that night he died from his head wound. In his pocket they found the letter from Tiburcio Vasquez, dated "Point San Quentin, Oct. 9, 1859," and addressed to "Señora Doña Guadalupe Cantúa, by the hand of S.T. Bsa [Berreyesa]." The letter, written in Spanish, read as follows:

Beloved Mother:

Perhaps you are not aware of the difficulties that I have to surmount and overcome every time I feel inclined to open my heart to you by the way of a few badly written lines; but I hope you will overlook the little faults and mistakes of your unfortunate son, and rather than to feel angry, to pity him.

A month ago I wrote to you and I sent the letter by A. S. Berreyesa, which gentleman was here visiting some cousins of his, and I am sure that he put it in the Express, as I requested him to do; but I have received no answer to the same yet. The contents of said letter was to give you information of an unfortunate affair into which I was led. I left this place during a riot, and was arrested a month after in the San Joaquin Pass, and very near to you, by a party of armed men, who took us (my friend and me) by surprise, and brought us back again here, and after two months of close, hard confinement in prison they put me again to hard work.

A party of Americans one day took possession of a small vessel, and I went with them, but by being unused to working a vessel, the guns and rifles from shore soon put our craft unmanageable; and out of fifteen men on board, three were shot [killed] on the spot, and five badly wounded; amongst the latter were one of the guards, whom we took with us. I came out without a scratch, although being like the rest, in the midst of the shot and the grape. Divine Providence watches over me. I therefore, now most earnestly beg you to come and see me, as I am overloaded with irons, and, without any cause, cruelly ill treated. I do not believe you will deny me this, and for me such a great favor; and believe that your son shall always live to acknowledge such an interesting event—that of seeing you.

Courage, mother! Do not lose your spirits for me. Your son was born to suffer, and the Supreme Being shall assist him in all this time of distress, until he may again go to serve his mother once more.

Be so kind as to give my humble respects to Don Norberto Gradillas, and tell him that I beg of him to bring you and accompany you here to see me. Tell him to remember that he is really and truly a man, and that true men are very scarce.

I am now in the road and way of true men—because I am following those who are worthy of imitating their virtues.

My salutes and compliments to the whole family—Brothers and all; also to my little cousin—see if she can also come to see me.

I am your son, who wishes you happiness.[2]

Although Tiburcio's letter was true in a general sense, some of his statements were false and others patently manipulative. His mother had plainly been angry with him, and the letter was intended to get her sympathy. It was printed in a number of California newspapers, not because of the notoriety of Vasquez, who was still an obscure figure, but because of its newsworthy content and the violent manner in which it came to light. Guadalupe Cantúa soon learned about her son's letter. She was no doubt horrified to learn of Tiburcio's attempts to escape from San Quentin and greatly distressed by the additional year added to his sentence. Determined to do something to help her wayward son, in late November 1860 she took a steamer to Los Angeles and met with a family friend, Juan María Sepúlveda, a member of a prominent and highly respected Los Angeles family. Sepúlveda had previously served a term as justice of the peace in Los Angeles, and he knew California Governor John G. Downey, who was also a Los Angeles pioneer. Guadalupe and Sepúlveda met with lawyer Ezra Drown, former district attorney of Los Angeles County, who had prosecuted Vasquez. On November 23, 1860, Drown wrote out a petition to Governor Downey:

> The undersigned residents and citizens of the County of Los Angeles respectfully represent unto your excellency that for several years previous to the conviction of Tiburcio Basques, they were acquainted with him, his conduct, and deportment in the vicinity in which he lived. He is now but a young man, and was convicted of Grand Larceny in this county in Nov. 1857 (it being his first offense) and was sentenced to five years imprisonment in the State's Prison. The undersigned, up to the time of the making of the accusation upon which he was convicted, ever knew him to be an industrious, sober and energetic young man and believe that it is only owing to the excitement which existed at and about the time of the conviction of said Basques, on account of the shortly previous murder of Sheriff

Barton & his party by a band of outlaws, the said Basques was sentenced to a much longer term of imprisonment than his youth, his first offense, and the crime demanded. The undersigned, believing that he has suffered sufficient imprisonment, and considering that his place of confinement with its associations can produce no salutary influence upon his morals, would respectfully ask that your executive clemency be extended toward him & as in duty bound your petitioners will ever pray it.[3]

Guadalupe circulated the petition among friends and relatives and soon gathered signatures of thirty-four Hispanics and ten Anglos, including those of Sepúlveda, Drown, and such prominent Angelenos as merchants Alexander Bell and Francisco Alvarado, rancheros Felipe Lugo and José Ramón Carrillo, and Los Angeles Mayor Damien Marchessault. Several of the grand jurors who had indicted Vasquez were also among the signers. On November 29, Guadalupe boarded a San Francisco–bound steamship, armed with the petition and a letter of introduction from Drown to Governor Downey: "The mother of Tiburcio Basques goes up today on the steamer with a petition numerously signed for the purpose of making application for the pardon of her son. I was the Dist Atty who prosecuted his case, and am satisfied that the matters represented in the petition are correct. I drew it up and if upon due consideration you think the views set forth in the petition are well expressed and you concur therein, I trust you will extend to the prisoner full pardon."[4]

On December 1, 1860, the *Los Angeles Star* published Juan María Sepúlveda's public notice of intent "to apply to the Governor of the State of California for the pardon of Tiburcio Vasquez." This was a legal requirement that gave the community an opportunity to object to the application. Although no objection was made, the governor failed to pardon Vasquez. The petitioners were clearly unaware that although Tiburcio's conviction in Los Angeles was his first, it was certainly not his first offense. Nor were they aware that he had been handed an extra year for horse theft in Amador County or that he had been involved in two bloody prison breaks. Some of these facts, at least, were made known to the governor, probably by officers at San Quentin, for the file was marked with a note that Vasquez had "escaped June 25, '59."[5]

Unable to get out of prison by legal means, Tiburcio quickly joined in a new plot formulated by Dámaso Berreyesa. Twenty-three years old, big and powerful, Berreyesa was a notorious outlaw. His large and prominent Californio family had suffered heavily at the hands of Anglos. Since the Mexican War, eight of them had been slain, engendering in the family a strong antipathy toward the newcomers. In 1859 Dámaso and his elder brother Nasario were sent to San Quentin from Napa County for horse theft. Nasario was well liked by his Californio and Anglo neighbors, and since the evidence against him was extremely flimsy, they successfully campaigned the governor for his pardon. But Dámaso was a hardcase and no effort was made to get him released. In San Quentin he pretended to be an obedient convict. One guard later recalled that he was "somewhat of a model prisoner—smooth, mild mannered, and attentive to his work. . . . and no one suspected him as the organizer of a plot to break jail."[6]

Dámaso's plan was simple. He and about thirty other Hispanic convicts, who had managed to fashion small knives, would jump the guards at a favorable moment and force their way out. Tiburcio's old Monterey friend, Ramón Rangel, who was serving a ten-year term for theft, and another compadre, Manuel Rojas, also took part. The most notorious of the plotters was Froilan Servin. As a member of the infamous Jack Powers–Pío Linares band, he had participated in several brutal robbery-murders in San Luis Obispo County in 1858. Servin was one of the few members of the gang to escape lynching by the Anglo and Californio vigilantes of San Luis Obispo.

The convicts saw their chance at two o'clock on the afternoon of January 16, 1861. Deputy Warden James C. Pennie, Lieutenant Moon, Turnkey John Davis, and a trusty were in the Porch, the prison office, located on the north side of the yard, about seventy feet from the main gate. They were chatting with Sutter County Sheriff S. E. Kennard, who had just delivered a prisoner. Kennard was unarmed, as prison rules required lawmen to hand over their guns at the outer guard's station. Just as the main gate was opened to allow a water cart to pass out, the convicts burst into the turnkey's office. Berreyesa first seized the trusty, but when the man howled that he was only a prisoner, the big outlaw let him go and grabbed Sheriff Kennard instead. While several desperadoes seized Deputy Warden Pennie, Lieutenant Moon, and Turnkey Davis, others quickly made a fruitless search of the office for weapons. Then, holding their knives to their hostages' throats, Vasquez and the rest marched them to the main gate. In a brief scuffle with several guards, they stabbed one in the shoulder and knocked another down, stomping him so severely he coughed up blood.

Vasquez, Berreyesa, Servin, Rangel, Rojas, and sixteen more made it outside before guards managed to slam the inner gate shut. Circling the wall, the convicts headed west toward Corte Madera Creek, clutching their hostages close. They had not gone far when Sheriff Kennard managed to pull loose from Berreyesa. Tearing off his heavy cloak, he threw it over the desperado's head and raced back toward the main gate. There the sheriff recovered his six-shooter and, with a posse of armed guards, rushed outside in pursuit. Dámaso Berreyesa seized Deputy Warden Pennie and held him close as the convicts continued toward the creek. They made it only a hundred yards before the guards caught up with them. When the freemen hesitated to open fire, Pennie bravely cried out, "Shoot, there! Shoot!"

Berreyesa, his knife at Pennie's throat, hissed at him to order the guards to hold their fire. Ignoring the threat, Pennie jerked his right arm loose and shook a clenched fist at his officers. "I tell you to shoot!" he yelled angrily. "Shoot or I'll discharge every last one of you!"

At that the guards and Sheriff Kennard opened a volley of fire with their pistols and Mississippi Yagers. Pennie was wounded in the arm. Dámaso Berreyesa dropped dead with a bullet in his brain. Two more convicts were killed instantly and another mortally wounded. Vasquez and the rest turned loose their hostages, Moon and Davis, and tried to run, but they didn't get far. All but Froilan Servin dropped in a veritable hail of whining lead. Vasquez, Rangel, Rojas, and eleven others were severely wounded. Two more escapees suffered minor gunshot wounds. Tiburcio and the other injured convicts were brought to the prison hospital where their wounds were dressed. Most of them, including Vasquez, were too badly hurt to receive any punishment. Two who were listed in the prison log as "slightly wounded" were released from the hospital three days later. The pair, along with Froilan Servin who somehow avoided being shot, were taken out into the yard. There, one after the other was tied to the Ladder and Lieutenant Moon administered sixty lashes each. As their screams of agony echoed through the hospital ward, just a few yards away, Tiburcio must have been thankful. His gunshot wound could not have been as painful as the flesh-shredding blows from Lieutenant Moon's whip. The prison doctor, Alfred Taliaferro, was kind and competent, and under his care Tiburcio soon recovered. Fortunately for him, the gun-powder used in the percussion firearms of that era was not as powerful as that in modern cartridges, and the wounds caused were often not fatal, provided the victim received prompt medical attention.[7]

Later that year the prison lease system ended and the state took control of San Quentin. California's lieutenant governor lived at the prison and was ex-officio warden, while the day-to-day management was handled by the deputy warden. Little else changed, however, as most guards were inexperienced political appointees and escapes were almost as frequent. By this time Tiburcio Vasquez was recognized as a leader among the convicts. His quick and creative mind, his ability to make friends of both races, and above all, his daring roles in three of the prison's biggest breaks, stamped him as a man to be reckoned with.

By July 1862, even though he had only a year left of his sentence, Tiburcio was helping plan yet another escape. This time it would be even bigger—one of the largest prison breaks in American history. The "Big Break" involved so many convicts it is impossible to determine Tiburcio's exact role. But according to an old convict interviewed in 1881, the leaders in the plot were Tiburcio Vasquez and Lewis Mahoney, a notorious horse thief. Other ringleaders included Jim Smith of the Tom Bell gang, the irrepressible Acapulco Lulio, Tiburcio's Monterey compadre Ramón Rangel, his fellow escapee Jesús Mendoza, and Jesús Villalobo, a murderer whose death sentence in Calaveras County had been commuted to life imprisonment. As their actions would reveal, the plan was carefully crafted. They plotted to seize firearms, put several of the cannons out of commission, and take an important hostage with them.[8]

Following the noonday meal on July 22, Vasquez and his fellow convicts filed out of the mess hall and toward the west gate, where they waited in line to go back to their labor in the brickyard. The gatekeeper, Robert Nixon, had counted 134 of them as they stepped outside into the brickyard. Suddenly a group of about seventeen, including Jim Smith and, presumably, Tiburcio, broke into a run. The guards poured a hail of lead after them but they paid no heed. Instead of making the usual flight toward Corte Madera Creek, they raced along the outer wall, then along the north wall, and back to the main gate on the east side. Vasquez and the others had learned important lessons from their prior escape attempts. They had no intention of simply running for the hills unarmed. They stormed the main gatehouse, breaking into the office of John Chellis, the warden and lieutenant governor. Chellis was as obese as he was cowardly, a pasty politician who was unfit to run a prison. As they dragged him outside, one yelled gleefully, "Now we've got you, Gov!"

At the same time the rest of the band attacked the outside guard, Cornelius Murphy, who put up a desperate fight despite being armed with nothing but his big padlock keys. The convicts forced Chellis to order Murphy to give up the keys, but the guard stubbornly refused, until he was finally beaten into submission. The prisoners then opened the outside wicket and rushed into the gatehouse. The big iron door to the yard was guarded by a single trusty, who was held at knifepoint while the convicts pried it open with an iron bar. Now the small group of ringleaders burst into the prison yard, yelling "Liberty!"

The escapees had actually broken back into the prison. The ensuing scene beggared description. Convicts, screaming like demons, poured out of the workshops, carrying axes, hatchets, hammers, knives, files, and anything else that could be used as a weapon. Two or three hundred, almost half the prison population, streamed out the main gate as the guards on the wall sent withering rifle and revolver fire into them. A large number fell wounded in bloody heaps. At the same time the small group of ringleaders burst into the armory and seized several pistols, but in their haste they overlooked a case full of sabers. The guards in several of the outside gun posts dropped their weapons and fled in terror. Convicts quickly seized their abandoned guns.

Isaac N. Quinn, a former lieutenant governor and now a private contractor in charge of the brickyard, was stunned to see the guards abandon Post 1 on the hill above the prison. He rushed up to the post and fired its cannon at the convicts fleeing out the main gate, but without effect. Now the ringleaders, holding Chellis hostage, headed out of the gatehouse, then slowly walked south and around the wall toward Post 5, on the bluff overlooking the prison wharf. This post was manned by Thomas Watson, who swung his cannon around and prepared to pull the firing lanyard. Chellis was not made of the same stern stuff as Deputy Warden Pennie. He shrieked in terror, "For God's sake, don't shoot!"

Watson, thinking quickly, rotated the big gun toward the water, fired its charge of grapeshot into the bay, and then disabled it by driving a spike into the touchhole. Just then a charging mob of escapees, led by the burly Jesús Villalobo, reached the top of the bluff and seized Watson. They had planned on turning the cannon and firing across the brickyard to disable the howitzer at Post 3 but were enraged to discover that the brass gun had been spiked. They beat Watson savagely, threw him off the steep bluff, then shoved the cannon and carriage after him. Watson, badly injured in the fall, barely missed being killed by the tumbling gun carriage.

The escapees and their hostage now moved past the west gate, where a hundred brickyard laborers, mostly short-termers, had refused to join in the break and voluntarily reentered the gatehouse. They were now locked in the corridor between the inner and outer gates. As the convicts passed through the brickyard toward Post 3, Chellis repeatedly waved his arms and called for the cannoneer to hold his fire. Ignoring that order, the guard aimed his gun at the edge of the crowd and jerked the lanyard. The grapeshot tore into the mass of men and many dropped. Quickly reloading, he fired again, and the band scattered. A large group of terrified escapees fled back to the main gate and surrendered. Another bunch, more intrepid, raced down to the boat landing where the prison sloop *Pike County* was moored. They cut the ropes with hatchets, raised the sails, and cast off into the bay. But the tide was low and they soon got stuck in the mud. By now Captain Edward Vanderlip had rallied the guards inside the prison, and they poured a deadly fire into the prison sloop. Three convicts were shot and fell overboard into the water; the rest surrendered.

The ringleaders, with the main band of about one hundred, kept Chellis in front of them as a shield and headed rapidly up the road that followed Corte Madera Creek, toward Mount Tamalpais. This band included Acapulco Lulio and Jesús Villalobo, and probably Vasquez also. It can be safely surmised that, given his prior escape experience, he did not join the group that boarded the *Pike County*. Chellis—hot, exhausted, overweight, and overwrought with fear—could not keep up, and the convicts dragged him along, occasionally pricking him with knives to keep him going. They stopped and looted three farmhouses. At one they found an unbroken stallion and ordered the lieutenant governor to mount him bareback. Chellis pleaded that he could not ride, and the convicts relented. After walking four miles they came to Ross Landing, located a few hundred yards north of the present-day Bon Air Road bridge in Kentfield. This was the uppermost navigable point on the creek, whence small sailing craft shipped lumber to San Francisco.

By now it was four o'clock, and a posse of freemen on horseback, led by Captain Vanderlip and Isaac Quinn, had caught up with the escapees. The guards were soon joined by a small posse from nearby San Rafael,

1722—San Rafael, Mount Tamalpais, from Ross' Landing.

Ross Landing, with Mount Tamalpais in the background, showing the scene of the gun-fight between guards and escaped prisoners. (Author's collection)

headed by Marin County Sheriff Val Doub. A terrified Chellis con-tinued to wave them off. The convicts now crossed the creek—which was, and still is, a muddy slough—hoping that the possemen could not get their horses across. Chellis, despite his continued protestations, was forced into the creek, which turned out to be only chest deep. After wading though, they rushed across open marshland for the foothills of Mount Tamalpais, several hundred yards distant. Reaching a high fence, the escapees made several efforts to hoist the corpulent Chellis over, then finally gave up and released him.

This was what the posse had been waiting for. The moment Chellis was freed, they opened fire from a distance of more than one hundred yards. A dozen convicts fell. Those convicts who were armed returned fire, but they quickly ran out of powder and shot. The prisoners ran for the brush. Sheriff Doub immediately sent a rider to San Rafael for reinforcements, and soon every man for miles around who could scare up a gun and a horse was on the scene. By dusk they had managed to capture forty-seven of the escapees, who were marched back to the prison that night. For the next several days volunteer posses scoured the Marin hills, bringing in a score of convicts, some of them badly wounded in the fight at Ross Landing. Exactly where and how Tiburcio Vasquez was retaken is unknown.[9]

In the end, ten convicts were slain and thirty wounded in one of America's biggest and bloodiest prison breaks. The prison hospital was packed. Recalled one convict, "For the next two weeks the groans and cries of the wounded and dying could be heard day and night." It was the last mass escape from San Quentin. A dozen guards were forced to resign, and security was greatly improved at the prison with the hiring of more guards. In 1864, the legislature passed a law providing for reduced sentences for good behavior, and the following year striped uniforms were adopted. Prison food and medical care were improved, and additional cells reduced overcrowding. These changes reduced breakout attempts drastically. Tiburcio's fourth escape attempt was also his last. He decided to serve out the final year of his sentence peaceably.[10]

Tiburcio Vasquez had changed greatly during his six years in San Quentin. Little more than a boy when he entered the prison, he had reached manhood behind its stony walls. He had formed many close friendships in prison, receiving an advanced education in the fine arts of lock picking, safe breaking, burglary, and highway robbery. The floggings and other harsh punishments he received had helped inflame his hatred for gringos. Yet at the same time, his close confinement with Anglo prisoners had led him to befriend several of them. Though he generally rejected American society, Tiburcio would make many Anglo friends—criminals and honest men alike—over the years. He had helped conceive, plan, and carry out four bloody prison breaks, showing little fear of guards, grapeshot, or the Ladder. Now, despite his soft-spoken and genteel ways and love of books, poetry, dance, and music, some of the toughest and most dangerous ruffians in California looked up to him as a leader, thus marking for the first time his emergence as a bandit chieftain. And finally, his repeated attempts to escape, in the face of great danger, spoke volumes of his ferocious appetite for life and for freedom.

CHAPTER SEVEN

Bandido

Tiburcio Vasquez was twenty-eight when he stepped into the warm sunshine of August 13, 1863, as a free man. In the east the Civil War was raging, but U.S. politics were unimportant to him. Disconnected by geography, language, and culture, he lived in a world far from events in mainstream America. Vasquez, wearing new civilian clothes, passed through the main gate and walked around Cemetery Hill to the wharf. After crossing the bay on the prison launch, he made his way south to Monterey County. Old Montereños described Tiburcio's return to Cora Older. She wrote that "among the younger people at Monterey there was general rejoicing because Tiburcio had come back. Americans were still foreigners to Spanish-Californians. Tiburcio Vasquez was one of their own people. They refused to speak the English language. Hatred inspired by the conquest was still keen. The fact that Vasquez had served a term in a hated gringo prison meant little to them."[1]

Most of Tiburcio's immediate family no longer lived in the town of Monterey. In 1855 his elder brother Antonio and his wife, Asunción, had moved to Rancho Buena Vista, owned by the Estrada family. Antonio, Asunción, and their brood lived in the Estrada adobe, on the west bank of the Salinas River opposite the present-day town of Spreckels. Antonio was a vaquero for the Estradas for nine years and reared five children on the Rancho Buena Vista. Frugal and hardworking, he eventually managed to save enough to buy a small plot of grazing land in Palo Colorado Canyon, located near the coast, some fifteen miles south of Monterey. He and Asunción also kept their adobe house on Hartnell Street until they sold it in 1861. Tiburcio's elder sister Concepción and her musician husband, Jesús Soto, had lived in their house next to the Vasquez adobe on Dutra Street for years, but by 1866 both were dead and Antonio was rearing their children.[2]

Tiburcio's mother had sold the family home in Monterey in the late 1850s and moved to San Juan Bautista (then known simply as San Juan), where she lived with her daughter María, son-in-law Manuel Lara, and their children. The family's plight was emblematic of most Californios. The Laras were poor and did not own the home they lived in. In 1860 the Laras and Doña Guadalupe each had personal property worth only one hundred dollars. Nearby lived Tiburcio's sister Manuela; her husband, Tomás Salgado; and four of their children. Manuela's husband worked in the pueblo as a carpenter and taught their teenage son, Adolfo, his trade. Concepción Espinosa, Claudio's teenage daughter, also lived with them. The Salgados, though poor, were honest and proud. Two years earlier, in 1861, their eldest daughter, nineteen-year-old Guadalupe, had married Ygnacio Villegas, a bright young man who had attended Santa Clara College, then studied law under James F. Breen in San Juan. But Villegas was soon forced to give up his studies to work on his family's four-thousand-acre ranch near Tres Pinos. He was ashamed that Tiburcio Vasquez was his wife's uncle and made no mention of the relationship when he described the bandido in his memoirs.[3]

On a horse borrowed or stolen, Vasquez rode from Monterey to Natividad and then up the San Juan grade across the Gabilan Mountains. As he descended the stage road, the sprawling expanse of the beautiful San Juan Valley unfolded before him, dominated by the adobe-tiled rooftops of the pueblo, now interspersed with the shingled roofs of Anglo homes. Beyond that, shimmering in the August sun, loomed the 3,500-foot-high crests of the Picachos of the Coast Range. The stage road wound its way down the foothills of the Gabilans and past the ancient redwood cross erected by the padres, standing like a lone sentinel on the hill just south of the pueblo. Mission bells pealed, calling the faithful to worship. But it was family and fandango halls, señoritas and gambling houses, that beckoned Tiburcio. His spurs jingled and gun leather creaked as he dismounted and walked down the boardwalk on Third Street. It was a joyous homecoming with his mother and sisters. Any lingering anger that Doña Guadalupe may have felt vanished at first sight of her beloved youngest son.

San Juan Bautista as Tiburcio Vasquez knew it in the 1860s and 1870s. (Author's collection)

Cora Older wrote that Doña Guadalupe relocated to San Juan because law officers were hounding Tiburcio in Monterey. Tiburcio himself recalled, "After I was released from San Quentin, I returned to the house of my parents, and endeavored to lead a peaceable and honest life. I was, however soon accused of being a confederate of . . . bandits. . . . I was again forced to become a fugitive from the law officers, and driven to desperation, left home and family, and commenced robbing whenever opportunity offered." Neither statement was true, for census records show that Doña Guadalupe had moved from Monterey by 1860, three years before Tiburcio's release from prison. Vasquez would often repeat the claim that he was "driven to" a life of banditry, once saying, "At the expiration of my time, I returned to Monterey County, and resided with my mother, voting in that county. The fact of my having been tried, convicted, and sentenced to the State Prison caused the people of the county to look upon me with suspicion. This treatment made my position particularly disagreeable. To escape from the persecution of enemies, I went to a remote part of the county and went to work on a ranch."[4]

Tiburcio hired on as a vaquero on Rancho Santa Ana, east of San Juan Bautista, owned by the prominent and wealthy Don Manuel Larios. He spent much of his spare time in town, where he stayed with the Laras and the Salgados. His mother, with funds from the sale of her Monterey house, purchased an adobe building on the west side of Third Street, between Polk and Mariposa streets. There she opened a little Spanish-Mexican restaurant, called simply La Fonda Mexicana. Doña Guadalupe—assisted by Manuela and María, and probably also by her granddaughter, Concepción Espinosa—made and served Spanish rice, tamales, enchiladas, and frijoles in the little cafe from 1863 to 1867. A large fire on November 1, 1867, destroyed it and the other buildings on this block. The current Taix Block building was erected in 1908 on the spot where the little restaurant stood. Doña Guadalupe, her daughters, and their families, although poor, were hardworking, honest, and well regarded in the little pueblo. Estolano Larios, who was a boy at the time, recalled Tiburcio's mother as "a highly respectable and well liked old lady."[5]

San Juan was still predominately Hispanic. The center of the pueblo was the plaza, dominated by the old mission. Diagonally across from it was the Plaza Hotel, one of the earliest in California. The mission, the hotel, and many other old buildings are still standing in San Juan, known as one of America's most historic old pueblos. A block south was the main business section, called Third Street by Anglos and Calle Principal by Californios. Fourth Street, known to Hispanics as "El Bronco" and to Anglos as "the waterfront," was the wild part of town and featured several saloons, gambling dens, fandango halls, and bordellos. It was a favorite haunt of Tiburcio Vasquez and other troublemakers. Recalled Isaac Mylar, who was fifteen in 1863, "The bandits would stay, during the day, in the upper story of the buildings along Fourth street, which was known as the 'waterfront,' and come out and prowl around the streets at night. We never said anything to them for fear of reprisals." The only one of these two-story adobes still standing is located at 203 Fourth Street. It was the home of George Castro, who divided his time between San Juan and his grazing land in Cantua Creek, high in the Coast Range, where he and Tiburcio would tangle later. Widely considered the most dangerous man in San Juan, Castro had a violent temper, was quarrelsome in the extreme, and killed a number of men in shooting and cutting scrapes. He and Tiburcio disliked each other intensely. George Castro was reputed to be the only man Vasquez feared.[6]

A visitor to San Juan in 1860 described its people as "native Californians of all classes, Frenchmen, patriotic Union-saving members from North and South, stock raisers with 'cattle on a thousand hills,' mule drivers, noisy, riotous whiskey-drinking, horse-killing vaqueros." The old ways of life were then still prevalent in San Juan. On Sundays an oak fence was set up around the plaza, where bull and bear fights would be staged. Other entertainments included cockfighting, horse racing, and, of course, gambling, which was always heavy at such events. Old-timers told Cora Older that on warm evenings, Tiburcio would ride into town after work, gathering with other young vaqueros at the Plaza Hotel, where bailes were held. A bevy of raven-tressed young beauties draped themselves over the upper balcony, among them Josefa Chavarría, Antonia Castro, Pilar Soto, Paciencia Soto, Carlota Cariega, Ignacia Soto, and Rosa Castro. The cool night breezes from the Pacific, drifting across the Gabilans, would carry the music of the fandango through the little pueblo, summoning the paisanos from their adobes to the gathering at the hotel. There Tiburcio never failed to charm the señoritas with his guitar playing, love of music and poetry, and skill as a dancer.[7]

Tiburcio's niece Concepción was a frequent visitor to the home of her natural mother, Dolores Espinosa, and stepfather, Francisco Chávez. The Chávez family lived in a low, crudely built adobe situated where there is now an abandoned gas station on the southeastern corner of the Alameda and the San Juan–Hollister Road, on the southern outskirts of town. Behind it was an orchard of fig and apricot trees. They had five children. The second eldest was Clodoveo Chávez, fourteen years old in 1863. Tiburcio was a frequent and welcome visitor, and young Clodoveo was particularly impressed with the dashing, well-dressed horseman who was his half sister's uncle. Just across the stage road from the Chávez family was the home of Rafael Hernández and his wife, Pilar. Hernández, like Chávez, was a sheepherder from New Mexico, and Pilar, a pretty, fair-haired woman, kept the most beautiful flower garden in San Juan, which she jealously guarded behind a white picket fence. They also had a flower of another kind: their thirteen-year-old daughter, Rita. Like her mother's garden, she would soon blossom into one of the most beautiful girls in San Juan, and also one of the wildest. The Hernández adobe is now gone, but the First and Last Chance Saloon, built by Pilar Hernández in 1897 next to her adobe, is still standing, converted into a residence. Tiburcio Vasquez became friendly with both Clodoveo and Rita.

A simple life as an honest vaquero in San Juan held little interest for Tiburcio Vasquez. Before long he was running with his second cousin Faustino Lorenzana, a dangerous cutthroat whose body was covered with knife and bullet scars. Faustino and several of his brothers were ruffians from Branciforte, the Californio settlement adjacent to Santa Cruz. Vasquez, Lorenzana, and their compadres engaged in stealing horses and cattle in Monterey and Santa Cruz counties. They drove them to Southern California for sale, then stole more livestock there and peddled them on their return north. Between raids they rusticated at the New Almaden, Guadalupe, and Enriquita quicksilver mines where, flush with coin, they drank and gambled freely.[8]

Situated in the mountainous country ten miles south of San Jose in Santa Clara County, the New Almaden was one of the world's richest quicksilver mines. Quicksilver, or mercury, was used in refining gold and silver ore and in making gunpowder. The New Almaden employed five hundred Mexican, Chileno, and Cornish miners, who lived in two separate camps of simple wood cabins. Cornish Camp was halfway up Mine Hill, and Mexican Camp was clustered at the top of the hill. Mexican Camp was a popular hideout for bandidos and fugitives, and its gambling dens and cantinas were the scene of frequent cutting and shooting scrapes. The Guadalupe Mine, two miles north of the New Almaden, although much less productive, also had a thriving camp populated by Hispanic miners. The Enriquita Mine, two miles southwest of New Almaden, was the smallest and least successful of the three. Like the others, its adjoining miners' camp was a rendezvous for the rough element. Tiburcio Vasquez became well known as a gambler and horse-race promoter at the Enriquita Mine. Abdon Leiva, a young Chileno miner who would later play an important role in Tiburcio's life, recalled that he first saw Vasquez at a horse race there in 1864. Tiburcio Vasquez would also soon become well known to Captain John H. Adams, the burly, rough-and-ready sheriff of Santa Clara County. Of his stay in the remote mining camps, Vasquez later said, "Even there my reputation followed me, and the shortcomings of others cast suspicion upon me, to the extent that an attempt was made to arrest me, which I successfully resisted. No blood was shed, and I escaped. . . . From this time I commenced my career as a highwayman."[9]

As usual Tiburcio's account is scarcely true. On the night of June 4, 1864, Vasquez and Faustino Lorenzana were playing cards in a cantina at the Enriquita Mine when the camp's Italian butcher, Joseph Pellegrini, wandered in, apparently flush with cash. At eleven that night someone—according to several accusations, Tiburcio and his cousin—followed Pellegrini to his shop, where he had an adjoining bedroom. As the butcher was getting ready for bed, the robbers broke the lock on his door and forced it open. Pellegrini seized a gun and fired at the bandits, but they managed to disarm him and, after a short but terrific struggle, one or both stabbed him to death. The intruders quickly swept four hundred dollars in cash from the till and slipped away in the darkness. The gunfire attracted miners to the house, and they found Pellegrini's bloody corpse on his bed. According to the *San Jose Mercury,* "He was stabbed through the heart, apparently with a large butcher knife, and otherwise cut in a shocking manner."

The room showed evidence of a violent struggle. The gunfire had caused the bandits to flee quickly, and one of the outlaws had left his hat behind. They also did not search Pellegrini's body, as his watch and forty dollars were found on his person. Word of the murder was sent to Sheriff Adams in San Jose. By morning, before a manhunt could be started, the camp was thrown into even more excitement when Julio Almanca, a one-armed saloonkeeper, shot and killed a ruffian named Juan José Rodríguez during a quarrel in his cantina. Almanca fled the camp. Undersheriff Richard B. Hall rode to Enriquita where he learned that "a gang of desperadoes were secreted and fortified in a defile in the mountains about six miles from the scene of the murders." While Hall led a posse in pursuit, Sheriff Adams and Dr. A. J. Cory, coroner of Santa Clara County, arrived at Enriquita to hold an inquest into the two killings.

Adams rounded up the witnesses, none of whom spoke English. He soon found the only man in camp who could speak both Spanish and English was Tiburcio Vasquez. The wily bandit knew that if he fled the camp, he would be immediately suspected of the killing. So instead he attended the inquest and actually interpreted the witnesses' testimony for Dr. Cory. Needless to say, nothing was learned, and the verdict was that Pellegrini was slain "by some person or persons unknown." Tiburcio knew better than to press his luck. No sooner had Sheriff Adams left camp than he and Lorenzana also rode off. Several days later the sheriff received a tip that Tiburcio and his cousin were the probable murderers, but since there was no definite evidence against them, they were never charged. Adams was not shy about accusing the pair, and in later years he repeatedly told newspaper reporters that Vasquez and Lorenzana were the killers. The sheriff was a fair man, not given to baseless accusations; he would later maintain that Tiburcio's notorious compadre, Juan Soto, was innocent of murder. Years later, when asked about the Pellegrini killing, Vasquez insisted, "I had nothing to do with it. I was unjustly accused and had to leave the country, and that is one of the many reasons that induced me to continue in the bad life I had commenced."[10]

Tiburcio fled back to Monterey County. There he associated with the notorious Arceo brothers, who lived on Rancho Pilarcitos, near the Salinas River east of Monterey. Of five brothers, three were desperadoes. The eldest, Fernando, was known to Anglos as "Cherry Pie" (probably a corruption of Chiripa, meaning "Lucky"). Next in line was José María, ironically nicknamed Obispo (the Bishop), which hardly fit his violent personality. The youngest was Manuel, called Chavo, or Kid. Vasquez was with Chavo Arceo when he pulled one of his first highway robberies. Tiburcio described it to George Beers, who no doubt added literary embellishments to his account:

It would be almost impossible for me to remember all the robberies I have committed. Among the first that comes to my memory is that of a Jew whom I robbed as he was crossing the Soledad [Salinas] River, on his way to San Juan. I left the adventurous

Israelite his pack and his horse, and satisfied myself with his pistol and his purse. The affair took place about as follows: I saw the Jew coming some distance off, and took my station in the brush by the roadside above. When I advanced upon him, the Jew drew his pistol. I told him he had mistaken my intention, and that I wanted to buy some of his goods. I took out some money wherewith to pay him. Satisfied that I was telling the truth, he unpacked his horse to exhibit his wares, and in an unguarded moment I succeeded in taking advantage of him and disarmed him. Then I obliged him to give up his money. I then mounted my horse, bade him a polite adios, and recommending him to ruminate over the mutability of human affairs, galloped away.[11]

Tiburcio's story was not entirely correct, and his actions were hardly polite. On November 23, 1864, Samuel Chatelaine, a French-Jewish watchmaker in San Juan Bautista, was on his way from San Juan to Monterey when he was accosted by Vasquez and Chavo Arceo. Chatelaine tried to resist the bandits, and they beat him savagely with their pistols, breaking one of his arms. They took forty-five dollars from him and fled on horseback. Chatelaine raced back into San Juan and raised the alarm. A posse started in pursuit and caught up with the two highwaymen. In a brief gunfight one of the bandits fell from his horse, wounded, but managed to remount and both bandits escaped. Chavo Arceo was recognized, but it was only later that Tiburcio's involvement came to light.[12]

While Vasquez dodged lawmen, his eldest brother, Antonio, labored at honest pursuits. By 1864 he had scraped together enough money to buy a 320-acre squatter's claim in Carmel Valley. There he built a crude house from wood shakes for his family. He raised a few head of cattle and planted crops. Antonio wasted nothing. For example, potatoes were then very expensive—seven dollars per hundred. Before any potatoes were prepared for supper, he cut out the eyes and planted them. His land was fertile and after years of hard labor, Antonio prospered. He constructed a new house and sent his brood, now seven, to the Carmelo School. Antonio María Vasquez was highly respected and served for a number of years as trustee of the Carmelo School District. A high peak overlooking his property, still known as Vasquez Knob, was named in his honor. Tiburcio made frequent visits to Antonio's rancho, and his brother lent him money and tried unsuccessfully for years to get him to reform.[13]

At about this time Vasquez had a romantic adventure that was widely reported after he achieved notoriety. As he was riding through the isolated country near Mount Diablo, in Contra Costa County, his horse stumbled and threw him violently to the ground, breaking his arm. A wealthy ranchero, owner of a nearby hacienda, witnessed the accident and helped Tiburcio to his home. There the ranchero and his beautiful young daughter, Anita, cared for the injured stranger. Vasquez told them that his name was Rafael Moreno and that he had recently come north from Mexico. As was his custom, Tiburcio took his alias from his extended family, in this case from his maternal aunt María Antonia Moreno.

It took Vasquez several weeks to regain his normal strength and health. By this time Anita had become fascinated with the charming young vaquero, whose courtly ways and love of music and poetry drew her to him. Eugene Sawyer, one of Tiburcio's early biographers, described Anita thus: "The girl was innocence personified; she had always lived at the ranch and knew scarcely anything of human nature, much less the caution of experience. It can scarcely be wondered that the bandit succeeded in winning her affections and overcoming her most virtuous scruples." One morning Anita and Tiburcio were missing. Her father was no fool and immediately suspected Vasquez. Mounting his fleetest horse, he started in pursuit and soon caught up with the lovers in the Livermore Valley, south of Mount Diablo. They were resting beneath a tree by the roadside. Vasquez leaped to his feet, but did not draw his pistol. Anita shrieked to her father, "If you kill him you must also kill me!"

Eugene Sawyer penned several versions of this encounter. In one, he wrote, "After some consideration the ranch owner said if Anita would return home her lover might go free. The girl consented and Vasquez shrugged his shoulders as father and daughter rode away." In a much earlier account, however, Sawyer said that the ranchero "shot Vasquez in the arm, causing the bandit to drop the girl and take safety in flight." Boyd Henderson, an early journalist who wrote extensively about Vasquez, also recorded this incident, concurring that Anita's father shot Tiburcio in the arm. But Henderson claimed that Vasquez had raped the girl: "Failing, with a pleasing address and the warmth of a reciprocal passion, to ruin her, he accomplished his evil design by brute force."

But Tiburcio seduced women—he didn't rape them—so the charge of rape was probably false.[14]

By mid-1865 Tiburcio was riding with Manuel Rojas, the jail-breaker whom he had known in San Quentin. In October Rojas—with young Juan Soto, a Spanish-speaking ex-convict named Alfonso M. Burnham (alias Fred Welch), and another bandit—attacked the ranch and trading post of Charles Garthwaite, located a mile west of Pleasanton in the Livermore Valley. Garthwaite's wife, Mary, was home alone, but she put up a stiff fight and shot and wounded Burnham. The bandits overpowered the plucky woman, tied her securely, and escaped with her jewelry, money, and six-gun. Burnham fled to San Francisco, where he was soon arrested for another offense. In jail, a fellow prisoner "peached" on him, and Harry Morse, sheriff of Alameda County, was notified. Morse brought Mrs. Garthwaite to the San Francisco city prison, and she promptly identified Burnham as one of the gang. Burnham, who refused to identify his compadres, was sentenced to eighteen months in San Quentin. Sheriff Morse subsequently learned that Manuel Rojas and Juan Soto were involved, but they could not be found. In retrospect, it is possible that the unidentified fourth bandit was Tiburcio Vasquez.[15]

Tiburcio made occasional visits to San Francisco, always dressed in the height of fashion. In the city's red light district, famously known as the Barbary Coast, he found easy women in its many bordellos and easy money in its gambling parlors. Barbary Coast rangers were the ruffians who frequented this tough neighborhood, which was vividly described by a contemporary observer:

> The Barbary Coast is the haunt of the low and the vile of every kind. The petty thief, the house burglar, the tramp, the whoremonger, lewd women, cutthroats, murderers, all are found here. Dance-halls and concert-saloons, where blear-eyed men and faded women drink vile liquor, smoke offensive tobacco, engage in vulgar conduct, sing obscene songs . . . are numerous. Low gambling houses, thronged with riot-loving rowdies, in all stages of intoxication, are there. Opium dens, where heathen Chinese and God-forsaken men and women are sprawled in miscellaneous confusion, disgustingly drowsy or completely overcome, are there. Licentiousness, debauchery, pollution, loathsome disease, insanity from dissipation, misery, poverty, wealth, profanity, blasphemy, and death, are there.[16]

One day in 1865 Vasquez dropped into the photographic studio of Wilbur F. Bayley at 620 Washington Street, two blocks south of the Barbary Coast, where he posed for a *carte-de-visite* image. Bayley, like all photographers of that era, stored the negative, and later sold carte-de-visite prints when Vasquez achieved national notoriety. This photograph, the earliest of him known, shows the thirty-year-old bandit leaning jauntily against a blanket-covered pedestal. He is wearing a hip-length gray wool coat with beaver collar, fancy velvet vest, watch, and high-heeled boots. In his hand is a flat-brimmed California hat. His trim and youthful appearance belies the rugged life he had led in prison and in the saddle. A far cry from the uncouth Barbary Coast rangers, Tiburcio looked every inch the gentleman, the image of a Californio caballero.

By year's end Vasquez had moved his operations north to Marin and Sonoma counties. As was his custom, Tiburcio stayed with members of his extended family in remote areas. In this case, he was the guest of his cousins, the Bojorques family. The patriarch, Hermenegildo's first cousin Bartolomé Bojorques, had been granted the Rancho Laguna de San Antonio, consisting of almost twenty-five thousand acres in west Marin County. By the time the aged Bojorques died in 1863, he had sold most of the rancho. When Tiburcio visited in 1865 it was but a thirty-acre tract with a dozen houses, occupied by Bojorques's numerous children and grandchildren. The little settlement, known to Anglos as Spanishtown, was on the west side of San Antonio Creek, about six miles southwest of Petaluma, near the present-day Laguna schoolhouse. Two of the Bojorques sons, Ángel and Pedro, were gamblers, and were undoubtedly pleased to keep company with a kindred spirit. The Bojorques family, especially the women and children, were surely charmed by Tiburcio's guitar playing, singing, dancing, and poetry. It is doubtful they knew that Tiburcio intended to make their little rancho his base for a series of brazen bandit raids. Tiburcio also undoubtedly spent time at the hacienda of his widowed cousin Guadalupe Vasquez on Mark West Creek, seven miles north of Santa Rosa. Vasquez—popular, gregarious, and full of life—was always a welcome visitor.[17]

Vasquez now organized a new band of robbers and stock thieves. According to an entry in Sheriff Harry Morse's diary, Tiburcio's compadres in the North Bay were Manuel Rojas, one Jesús Hilario, and a man Morse described as "Juan, 6 feet pimples," probably Juan Soto, who was six feet tall with a badly pockmarked face. From Spanishtown,

The earliest known image of Tiburcio Vasquez, showing him at age thirty. This is a carte-de-visite taken by San Francisco photographer Wilbur F. Bayley in 1865. (Author's collection)

Tiburcio and his compadres rode north on raids into Sonoma and Mendocino counties. As he later recalled, "I robbed stagecoaches, wagons, horses, houses, indiscriminately, carrying on my operations for the most part in daylight, sometimes however, visiting homes after dark." In this instance, Tiburcio did not exaggerate. His arrival at the little rancho on San Antonio Creek coincided with an epidemic of crime.[18]

Vasquez became a well-known figure in Petaluma, a bustling farm town of 1,500 where he posed as a sheepherder and called himself "José Mauricio." His nickname was "José Borrego," or "Sheep Joe" to the Anglos. But Petaluma's highly capable city marshal, James H. Knowles, was almost immediately suspicious of the expensively attired, immaculately groomed stranger. Knowles knew he was no sheepherder. Tiburcio's compadre, Manuel Rojas, was hiding out in Petaluma to avoid Sheriff Morse, who wanted him for the Garthwaite robbery. Acting on a tip from the Alameda lawman, Marshal Knowles arrested Rojas on the night of December 21 and lodged him in the town jail, in full irons. But before Sheriff Morse could pick him up, several of the outlaw's compadres, including perhaps Tiburcio, dug into the jail at night and took Rojas out, chains and all.[19]

In Petaluma Vasquez linked up with Charles Horace Dade, the notorious ex-convict whom he had known in San Quentin's brickyard. Despite his general distaste for gringos, Vasquez liked Dade, a burglar and bandit who had been accused of highway robbery in Solano and Marin counties as well as of the murder of a Chinese man near Folsom. Like Tiburcio, Dade enjoyed gambling and fast women. On June 17, 1866, Dade made a visit to Petaluma in royal style. Somewhere he obtained a large boat, which he sailed from San Francisco Bay up the Petaluma River. Anchoring it in the stream behind a bordello, Dade settled in for the night with one of the girls. His arrival created quite a stir in the little town; the editor of the *Petaluma Journal and Argus* commented that "Dade visited our city somewhat in the style of Com. Vanderbilt—in his own yacht!"

Marshal Knowles immediately obtained a warrant for Dade's arrest, charging him with burglarizing a store in Lakeville, a few miles downriver. After watching the brothel all night, in the morning, Knowles moved in and arrested Dade without incident. Concealed in Dade's pockets were a pistol, a black mask, and burglar's tools. The newspaper editor reported that Knowles had been assisted "by several of our prominent citizens—who do not wish to have their names mentioned in this connection." Evidently these helpful citizens were also patrons of the bagnio, hence their desire for anonymity. Knowles brought Dade into court, but when the witnesses against him failed to appear, the judge had no choice but to release him. The city marshal was disappointed but not discouraged.[20]

Dade, for his part, was not deterred by this close shave. He met up with Tiburcio Vasquez, and the two enjoyed the Fourth of July festivities in Petaluma. At eleven o'clock that night they continued their celebrations. While the townsfolk slumbered, the pair forced their way underneath a two-story building on Main Street. The upper floor held Ross's Photograph Gallery; on the ground floor was the Sargent & Barnes general store. Vasquez and Dade cut though the floor of the general store with an auger, then climbed inside. After looting the store, they made off with a large quantity of clothing and a fancy double-barreled rifle valued at the then-exorbitant price of sixty dollars. Marshal Knowles soon suspected the two, but lacking evidence he made no effort to arrest them.[21]

Dade departed for Napa, some twenty miles to the east. It is unknown whether Vasquez went with him, but perhaps he did, for Napa's red light district, known as Spanishtown, was "a city of refuge for all the murderers, thieves, escaped convicts, and prostitutes in the state," according to the local newspaper editor. On the night of July 20, 1866, Dade and an unidentified partner held up a teamster, Joseph Howell, at gunpoint near the Catholic church. The two wore masks, and one seized the team's lead horses and covered Howell with a pistol. They relieved him of a silver watch and a small amount of coin. Later that night the same bandits stopped and robbed two butchers of a watch and a few dollars. The following afternoon Dade was recognized as an ex-convict and arrested. He was carrying a bundle, which when searched, proved to contain a mask made from a black handkerchief with eyeholes cut out. Dade was held for trial and in September was convicted of robbery and sentenced to four years in San Quentin.[22]

During this period Tiburcio was also riding with Pedro Sais, the black-sheep son of a prominent Marin County ranchero. His father, Domingo Sais, was the grantee of the Rancho Cañada de Herrera, encompassing part of what is now San Anselmo and Fairfax. When Domingo Sais died in 1853, his land passed to his widow and six children. Pedro, the eldest, built a home on his section of the rancho, which is now Butterfield Road in the Sleepy Hollow section of San Anselmo. By the mid-1860s Pedro's rancho was, according to the *Marin County Journal,* "a rendezvous of horse

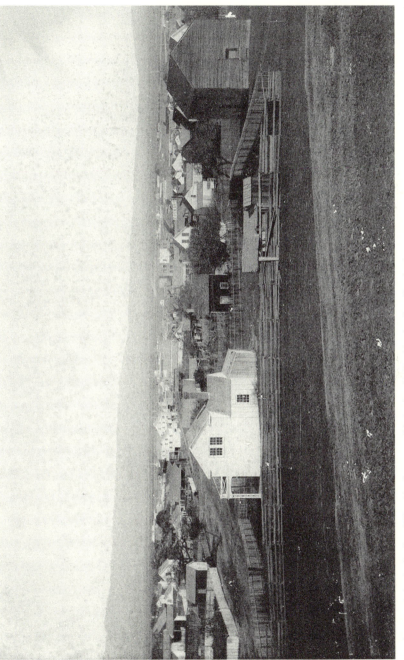

Petaluma as it looked when Tiburcio frequented it in the 1860s. (Author's collection)

117

thieves and discharged convicts of the Mexican persuasion." In late September 1866 Vasquez and Pedro Sais made off with a herd of sixty cattle from the ranch of John Walker, near Sebastopol, seventeen miles north of Petaluma. They drove the herd south to San Rafael, where they sold some of the cattle, then pressed on to San Pablo in Contra Costa County, where they sold the rest. Walker managed to trail the herd, and eventually recovered some forty head but was unable to capture the cattle rustlers. Marshal Knowles had better luck. On October 9 he arrested Pedro Sais in Petaluma. Sais was charged with grand larceny and released after posting a three-thousand-dollar bond. He apparently refused to name his accomplices.[23]

The arrests of Dade and Sais did little to discourage Tiburcio Vasquez. Marshal Knowles later learned that Vasquez was the leader of a gang that caused a veritable crime wave in Sonoma County. In late September burglars entered the house of Dr. John Rhodes, near Sebastopol, and stole a shotgun, a sword, forty-eight dollars in coin, and jewelry. On October 4 a youth named Nelson, while riding on horseback near Sebastopol, was held up by two Hispanic robbers who ordered him to "shell out," which he did to the tune of fifty dollars. Shortly after this a band of stock thieves stole twenty-five saddle horses and escaped north into Mendocino County. That was a mistake, for Deputy Sheriff Jeremiah M. "Doc" Standley soon got on their trail. Barely twenty-one years old, Standley was destined to become one of California's finest sheriffs. He and his posse trailed the thieves into Anderson Valley, in the mountains west of Ukiah. When they came in sight of the mounted outlaws, about a mile distant across a deep canyon, the fugitives abandoned the remuda of stolen horses and disappeared into the mountains. Standley was unable to capture the thieves but did return the stolen animals to their owners in Sonoma County.[24]

A week later one hundred head of cattle were rustled from the ranch of Winfield Wright on the Russian River. At the same time stock theft suddenly increased just to the south in Marin County. The *Marin County Journal* reported, "The business of stealing beef and dairy cattle has been carried on briskly in our neighborhood recently. Droves have come in from Sonoma County and elsewhere, and been readily disposed of to San Francisco dealers at liberal prices." Then, in a repeat of the Petaluma break-in, burglars entered the store of Kessing & Tupper in Santa Rosa, the county seat, on the night of October 16. They made off with three hundred dollars in dry goods and cash. On October 27 a band of six or eight robbers, believed to be the same ones Doc Standley had pursued, rode onto the ranch of Henry Carson near Healdsburg in the northern part of Sonoma County. They held up Carson and his ranch hands at gunpoint, then searched the house and galloped off with five hundred dollars in cash plus firearms and ammunition. Tiburcio Vasquez was probably involved in some, if not all, of these raids. An old tradition, dating to the nineteenth century, is that the Secret Pasture, situated in the hills six miles north of Sonoma and two miles east of Glen Ellen, was the spot where the Vasquez band hid stolen livestock.[25]

On the night of November 26, stock thieves stole a saddle and two horses in Petaluma. Next, on December 4, a daring nighttime burglary took place in the little hamlet of Bloomfield, sixteen miles west of Petaluma. Thieves entered the store of W. B. Wood, and for three hours worked on the safe with hammer and chisel. They finally cut a hole through the side of the safe and removed $200, but were unable to get the $2,000 held in the safe's upper compartment. Complained the editor of the *Petaluma Journal and Argus,* "This county is literally swarming with thieves, and the success with which they carry on their operations and elude detection is really alarming to law abiding citizens." Three days later, at midnight, a horse thief entered the stable of the George Watriss ranch north of the town of Sonoma. He had harnessed one horse and was bridling a second when one of the ranch hands was wakened by the noise. As the latter approached, the thief raced from the stable, and the ranch hand opened fire but missed. A few days later, on the night of December 11, burglars removed several bricks from the rear wall of the Levy store in Petaluma. Reaching inside, they lifted the bolt on the iron window shutters and climbed inside. They took $240 from the till and several hundred dollars in men's clothing.[26]

All the while Marshal Knowles had been quietly investigating the crime spree. His first break came when Charles Horace Dade, while in the Napa jail, made a confession, probably in return for leniency, in which he apparently identified Vasquez as his partner in the Sargent & Barnes store burglary. Dade gave Knowles extensive details of the gang's operations. Exactly how Knowles developed further evidence against Vasquez is unknown, but it seems clear that at least one more member of the band, probably Pedro Sais, turned informant. On the evening of December 17, Knowles arrested Vasquez, taking from him the valuable rifle he had stolen from Sargent & Barnes and also a burglar's skeleton key that could open a large variety of locks. The marshal lodged Tiburcio in the Sonoma County jail in Santa Rosa. Knowles was tight-lipped about how he had cracked the case. Reported the *Petaluma Journal and Argus,* "The strategy which our efficient Marshal has resorted to in order to discover these criminals, and obtain information of other robberies, is not proper to be made public at present. We will advise all persons who have been losing horses and cattle to communicate with him at once, as he has undoubtedly succeeded in exposing, if not effectually breaking up, the most persistent gang of robbers that ever infested this county."[27]

Vasquez was indicted on two charges: for breaking into the Sargent & Barnes store and for stealing the rifle. On January 11, 1867, he was tried and found guilty on the burglary charge. He then promptly pled guilty to the second charge of grand larceny, apparently in a plea bargain. Three days later he was sentenced to two years in prison on each count, the terms to run consecutively. An angry and embittered Vasquez told the county officers that he would kill Marshal Knowles on his release. Four days later Tiburcio found himself back inside the walls of San Quentin.[28]

CHAPTER EIGHT

In the Saddle with Juan Soto

Tiburcio discovered many changes in San Quentin. On entry, he was required to trade in his civilian clothes for a new striped woolen uniform. There was now a larger contingent of guards, the food was better, and the cells were less crowded. Security had greatly improved, and mass escapes were now unknown. The Goodwin Act, passed by the state legislature in 1864, awarded convicts credits for good behavior. For each year served, a prisoner received two months off his sentence. No fool, Vasquez realized that his best chance for early release was to keep his nose clean and to serve his time quietly. He made no effort to escape and earned good time credits, known as "coppers" to the convicts. One of Tiburcio's cousins told Cora Older that Doña Guadalupe visited her son in San Quentin, and was plunged into depression on seeing him in chains. She was sixty-three, then an advanced age, and returned to San Juan in a weakened state. She then went to a friend's home in Monterey, where she was so frail and broken she soon died. Whether or not this story is true, Guadalupe Vasquez did pass away in Monterey on May 19, 1869. There can be little doubt that when Tiburcio got the news it was the darkest day of his life.[1]

Despite his good behavior in prison, Vasquez was just biding his time. He found several old Monterey friends in the cellblocks. One was Ignacio Rangel, brother of Ramón Rangel, who had participated in two of Tiburcio's prison breaks. Another was the notorious desperado José María "Obispo" Arceo, serving thirty years for a murder on Rancho Pilarcitos. Also incarcerated were his bandit compadres Juan Soto and Manuel Rojas, as well as Rafael Mirabel, a robber, cattle thief, and old friend of Soto's. Vasquez made many new friends as well, among them Francisco Barcenas, a stock thief from the East Bay; Francisco "Pancho" Galindo, a hardcase from San Jose; and Abelardo Salazar, a slender Mexican silversmith who, though only twenty-two, was already serving his second theft-related prison term. Most notorious of all was Procopio Bustamante, a nephew of Joaquín Murrieta's known as "Red Dick" because of the blood he had spilled. In 1862, at age twenty, he had been the main suspect in the murder of John Rains, a well-known Southern California rancher. A few months later, with two other outlaws, he had robbed and murdered four people, including a woman and a boy, near the Livermore Valley. In July 1863 he was captured after shooting a constable in Alameda County. He could not be prosecuted for the killings as all the witnesses were dead, so he was sentenced to nine years for cattle theft. Tiburcio made plans to meet up with his San Quentin compadres after they were released. Beginning in 1869, all of them except for the thirty-year man, Obispo Arceo, were discharged. By the next spring Tiburcio eagerly looked forward to his freedom.

On the morning of June 4, 1870, Tiburcio Vasquez stepped out of the Stones for the last time. Crossing the yard in the early summer sunshine, he entered the commissary and exchanged his woolen prison stripes for civilian clothes. He beat his way to Spanishtown on San Antonio Creek in west Marin County, twenty-five miles northwest of the prison. There his Bojorques cousins welcomed him, offering food and shelter. Although Tiburcio was an ex-convict, first and foremost he was a paisano. Californio family ties were stronger than any qualms over his imprisonment. Tiburcio stayed with his relatives for two months and made a number of visits to Petaluma. There he encountered City Marshal James Knowles, who was well aware of the death threats Tiburcio had made four years earlier. Knowles, who had arrested numerous desperadoes, quietly told the bandido that it would give him "pleasure at any time to ward off his vengeance." The *Petaluma Journal and Argus* later reported that "the bandit concluded to indefinitely postpone his thirst for vengeance." Knowles kept a close eye on him, and Tiburcio managed to stay out of trouble in Petaluma.[2]

In August Vasquez rode south to his old haunts in Monterey County. With Doña Guadalupe gone, he had a bittersweet reunion with his surviving brothers and sisters, who were still loyal to him and could be counted on to provide a roof over his head. Antonio again tried to get

Tiburcio to mend his ways, but to no avail. Tiburcio's sister Manuela was still in San Juan, where her husband, Tomás Salgado, and eldest son, Adolfo, still eked out a poor but honest living as carpenters. The Salgado family still did not own their home and had but two hundred dollars in personal property. Manuela evidently strongly disapproved of her youngest brother's outlaw ways. But her three daughters—María, age fifteen; Genoveva, ten; and Eulalia, five—undoubtedly enjoyed visits from their guitar-playing, ballad-singing, and poetry-reading uncle. Nearby lived Tiburcio's favorite sister, María, her husband, Manuel Lara, and their three children. Jesús, María's natural son, was now twenty-one, and there were two daughters: Carlota, eight, and María, a newborn infant.[3]

San Juan then had a population of about twelve hundred, a modern schoolhouse, a dozen stores, three hotels, and four churches, in addition to the old mission. It also boasted seventeen saloons, and a number of brothels were located on Fourth Street. Just outside of town was a popular racetrack. For years San Juan had prospered from the trade brought by teamsters who hauled freight to and from the New Idria Mine. The town still retained much of its Californio culture and had, as a visitor observed in 1867, "a mixed Spanish and American population." In San Juan Tiburcio found many desperado compadres who had recently been released from San Quentin, among them Juan Soto, Francisco Barcenas, and Pancho Galindo. Other ruffians often drifted into the pueblo, including Juan Soto's friends Bartolo Sepúlveda and Rafael Mirabel; Fernando "Chiripa" Arceo and Manuel "Chavo" Arceo, both brothers of Obispo Arceo's; plus local desperadoes Manuel López and Guadalupe Olivas. Another was the rotund José Castro, of a prominent Californio family, who lived with Tiburcio's niece, Concepción Espinosa.[4]

Vasquez was especially close to Juan Soto, with whom he had ridden five years earlier. Soto, twenty-four, stood more than six feet tall and weighed two hundred pounds. Ill-tempered and with a ferocious countenance, he was a crack shot despite being badly cross-eyed. Juan Soto was widely known to lawmen as a daring highway robber. In 1867 he had engaged in a wild gun battle with a posse at the Guadalupe Mine. Vasquez admired Juan Soto, once calling him "a very brave man. He was a good man, too." This loose confederation of pillagers constituted the Vasquez band, which was never an organized gang. The widespread belief that gangs of bandits lived together in mountain camps, riding out only on robbing sorties, is a misconception. As Tiburcio himself once explained, "When I wanted a party of men I had no difficulty in finding the requisite number. The work done, the party disbanded, and each went his own way. I trusted no one. This plan of operation was the best, for the reason that the men, when not wanted by me, were engaged in their ordinary occupations, and were scattered over the country. No one suspicioned them."[5]

Although San Juan and Monterey had changed little, Vasquez must have been stunned by the changes he saw everywhere else, many of them triggered by the new railroad. The transcontinental railroad had been completed in 1869, and now that the Pacific Coast was no longer connected to the East only by a long sea journey or an arduous trek by covered wagon across the plains, new settlers were pouring into California. The Salinas and Pajaro valleys were especially attractive to the newcomers. East of Monterey, on the bank of the Salinas River, a new town had sprouted up, appropriately called Salinas. Just three years earlier there had been only a few buildings on the spot. Early in 1868 construction had begun on the Southern Pacific Railroad line south of San Jose; within a year the tracks extended to Gilroy. As the fertile Salinas Valley attracted wheat and barley growers and dairy farmers, the village of Salinas boomed. Tiburcio found it a bustling, modern town, with 150 brick and wood-frame buildings and a population of six hundred; in ten years the population would triple. By late 1872, with the arrival of the railroad, Salinas had eclipsed the Old Spanish Capital in economic and political prominence, and soon became the new county seat. Robert Louis Stevenson contrasted it with Hispanic Monterey, calling Salinas "a town of a purely American character."[6]

Not far from San Juan was another town that had not existed when Tiburcio entered San Quentin. Hollister was first laid out in 1868 on a site ten miles east of San Juan. Two years later the Southern Pacific Railroad completed a spur line from Gilroy, and the new town prospered, attracting a population of seven or eight hundred. The railroad brought gamblers and saloonkeepers, and Hollister soon became known as a "wide open" town. It quickly eclipsed San Juan as the commercial and political center of eastern Monterey County. Local residents began lobbying to form a new county, and early in 1874 San Benito County was carved out of the eastern portion of Monterey County. The decline of Monterey and San Juan, and their displacement by the American towns of Salinas and Hollister, encapsulated the cultural, political, and economic disenfranchisement of the Californios.[7]

Carte-de-visite photograph of Juan Soto, who was slain by Sheriff Harry Morse in 1871. (Author's collection)

In San Juan, Tiburcio found that one San Quentin compadre, Abelardo Salazar, had settled down, opening a cantina on the main street with a partner named Gonzáles and trying to go straight. Vasquez often stayed with Salazar, who became engaged to a very pretty young Californio, María "Pepita" García. (She was the daughter of Pedro García and his wife, Dolores Higuera, of San Juan.) Tiburcio was also attracted to Pepita, but another development had already caught his attention. In San Juan and Natividad, the rough element was abuzz with talk about a band of recently captured Anglo stage robbers. In June and July they had robbed three stagecoaches on the road south of Salinas. Detectives from San Francisco had worked up the case and three outlaws had just been arrested in Natividad. These events probably inspired Tiburcio to try his own hand at stage robbery, and he later said about this period, "I diligently robbed coaches, houses . . . nearly all the time."[8]

Fifteen miles east of San Juan and four miles west of Pacheco Pass was Bell's Station, a stage stop on the road that handled traffic to and from the San Joaquin Valley through the main pass of the Coast Range. At two o'clock in the morning of August 18, 1870, the stagecoach from Visalia to Gilroy left Bell's Station. It had proceeded west about two miles when a pair of masked freebooters halted it. One was armed with a shotgun, the other with a six-shooter. Ignoring the three passengers, they ordered the driver to throw out the Wells Fargo express box. After the stage went on, the bandits broke open the iron-strapped wooden chest and escaped with five hundred dollars in coin. Later the company's waybills and papers were discovered scattered at the scene, but no trace of the holdup men could be found. A month later, early on the morning of September 17, the scene was repeated. As the Gilroy-bound stage crossed through Pacheco Pass, it was halted by several masked highwaymen. They obtained four hundred dollars from the Wells Fargo box and vanished into the blackness. Because Tiburcio later admitted to robbing several stagecoaches in the Gilroy area, and as these were the only unsolved stage robberies in the region at that time, he and his band almost certainly took part in them.[9]

Tiburcio continued to make his headquarters at Salazar's saloon in San Juan. On a rain-whipped night in December, twenty-four-year-old Eugene Sawyer, later a reporter and popular author, was driving a small herd of cattle from Gilroy to Hollister. He recalled a chance encounter with Vasquez on Rancho Bolsa de San Felipe:

As I was riding along, wet to the skin, cold and dispirited, two Mexicans rode up from the direction of Hollister. They stopped to ask a few questions and one of them took from his pocket a black bottle and said that a few swigs from the contents would do me no harm. My opinion coincided with his, and I took a generous pull at the bottle and soon felt a generous warmth stealing over me. As I was about to hand back the bottle the Mexican said in fair English, "Keep it, we get some more soon." Then they rode off with a "buenos noches." Arrived at the outskirts of Hollister, I spoke of the meeting to the rancher at whose house I had stopped for the purpose of spending the night. "Why," said he, "the man who gave you the bottle was Tiburcio Vasquez. He was in town this afternoon and was in a dance house when the constable tried to arrest him. But Vasquez was too foxy, for he got away by donning the skirt and mantilla of a Mexican woman, one of the frequenters of the dance house."

Four years later, Sawyer would repeatedly interview Vasquez and write a short biography of his life. Sawyer recalled that after mentioning this incident to Vasquez, "He laughed and said that he was the man and that his companion was Jose Castro." Over the years, a number of stories were told of Vasquez escaping capture either by dressing in women's clothing or hiding under a woman's dress. Sawyer's account provides the basis for those legends.[10]

On the evening of January 10, 1871, Juan Soto and two other Californios cantered their mustangs up the old Stockton road, which led from San Jose north into the Livermore Valley. At Scott's Corners in Sunol Valley (at the present-day intersection of Interstate 680 and Vallecitos Road), they dismounted and hitched their horses in front of Thomas Scott's store and trading post. In the rooms behind the store were Scott; his wife and two young sons; his clerk, Otto Ludovisi; and two visitors. There was a knock at the front door, and Ludovisi got up from the fire and let a stranger inside. He was a Californio, booted and spurred, with a black beard and a dark, wide-brimmed hat. He bought a bottle of whiskey and left. Ten minutes later there was another knock at the door, and again Ludovisi opened it. This time all three Californios entered, their lower faces covered by bandannas, six-shooters in their hands.

"Get out of here!" Ludovisi shrieked in terror. "Get out of here!"

"Say nothing! Say nothing!" ordered one of the bandits. Then, without provocation, he raised his pistol and fired. The heavy pistol ball tore into Ludovisi's breast. He turned and staggered into the back room, then collapsed in a heap, dead. Thomas Scott and the others fled out the back door. The robbers sent several pistol shots flying after them, wounding one of the visitors in the hand. Throwing her arms around her boys, Mrs. Scott cried out, "For God's sake, don't shoot."

The bandits left her alone and turned to looting the store. Then they mounted up and galloped off with their paltry spoils: sixty-five dollars and a bundle of garments. This cold-blooded murder caused a public uproar, and Alameda County Sheriff Harry Morse was determined to bring the killers to justice. Sheriff Morse was one of the great lawmen of the Old West. In 1849, at age fourteen, he had joined the gold rush, signing on to the crew of a California-bound sailing ship. During the Civil War, he served as a volunteer militia officer and deputy provost marshal of Alameda County. In 1864 he took office as the elected sheriff of Alameda County, a position he held for fourteen years. The county's Livermore Valley was infested with dangerous bands of stock thieves and highwaymen, and the young sheriff embarked on a campaign to eliminate them. He had already captured numerous desperadoes in wide-ranging manhunts, and had killed one outlaw and wounded another in hair-raising gun battles.[11]

The bandidos had made a fatal blunder in committing a murder in Sheriff Morse's bailiwick. He and his deputies conducted an intensive investigation and learned that Juan Soto and Bartolo Sepúlveda had ridden through Sunol Valley the day before the raid. Morse believed they had been casing Scott's store. Morse also discovered the bundle of stolen clothing behind the adobe home of Sepúlveda's mother-in-law, in what is now Milpitas. The Alameda County grand jury indicted Juan Soto, Bartolo Sepúlveda, and his brother Miguel Sepúlveda for murder. It would later develop that Bartolo Sepúlveda was entirely innocent, as was Miguel, who was in jail in San Jose at the time of the murder. Although Juan Soto's partners in this crime are uncertain, Tiburcio Vasquez was soon suspected. Newspaper reports, probably based on information from local lawmen, later claimed that Vasquez's gang was responsible. Thomas Scott's family always believed that the third bandit was Vasquez. Since Tiburcio was then a close compadre of Juan Soto's, he is a likely suspect. Vasquez, however, denied he had been with Soto, insisting, "I never was

Otto Ludovisi, murdered by Juan Soto and other bandidos in the raid on Scott's store, January 10, 1871. Tiburcio Vasquez was a suspect in the crime. (Author's collection)

with him on any raid." What is certain is that Juan Soto and Bartolo Sepúlveda quickly learned they were wanted for the murder. They fled into the Coast Range high above San Juan, where they were soon riding with Tiburcio Vasquez.[12]

On March 1, Procopio Bustamante was released from San Quentin and headed for his old haunts in the Livermore Valley. He spent a month carousing in the bordellos and fandango halls of Little Mexico, now part of Livermore. Then Procopio stole a cow belonging to rancher John Arnett, which he delivered to a local *tapadera,* or fence, named Juan Camargo. Arnett trailed his missing beef to Camargo's adobe hut, and Camargo was arrested. That night a mob seized him from two deputies and strung him up until he confessed that Procopio had stolen the cow. By then Procopio had vanished, but Arnett feared that the notorious bandido would retaliate against him. He slept with a watchdog on guard and a Henry rifle at hand. A week later, on the night of April 10, Arnett was roused by the dog's howling. Seizing his rifle, he rushed outside in time to spot two riders driving off a herd of his cattle. Arnett opened fire, dropping one of their horses. The rider jumped onto the back of his partner's saddle and the pair thundered away. Sheriff Morse happened to be in Livermore with one of his deputies, Ralph Faville. After a quick search of Little Mexico, they headed for Alisal, now called Pleasanton. On the road they encountered Rafael Mirabel, a compadre of Juan Soto's then living in a jacal (mud-and-brush hut) in the nearby Arroyo Valle. The saddle-born Mirabel was uncharacteristically on foot. He told Morse that his mount had been stolen that night. Convinced that the cattle thieves were Procopio and the dismounted Mirabel, Sheriff Morse brought the latter to jail in San Leandro. But Arnett could not identify the men he had shot at, so the sheriff was forced to release him.[13]

Procopio fled south to San Juan. There, in Abelardo Salazar's saloon, he was happy to find Tiburcio Vasquez and other compadres from San Quentin. Impressed by Salazar's efforts to reform, Pepita García's parents consented to her marriage to the two-time ex-convict. Their beautiful fifteen-year-old daughter was wild and promiscuous, and they undoubtedly hoped that marriage would settle her down. On April 17 they celebrated the wedding at Mission San Juan Bautista. Although it is unknown whether any of Salazar's outlaw compadres attended the wedding, what is clear is that Tiburcio Vasquez, Francisco Barcenas, and Procopio all lusted after Pepita.

Just as wild was her friend Rita Miranda, the beautiful and vivacious daughter of Rafael and Pilar Hernández, who lived opposite Clodoveo Chávez and his family in San Juan. A contemporary called her "very pretty and rather flirtatious," a profound understatement. She had attracted the eye of Pedro Miranda, who during the Civil War had been a bugler in Company B, First Battalion, Native Cavalry, California Volunteers. The battalion, made up primarily of Californios and some Mexican

Bartolo Sepúlveda, compadre
of Tiburcio Vasquez and Juan
Soto. (Author's collection)

immigrants, was stationed at Camp Low in San Juan in 1864 when
Rita and Pedro married. But when the battalion rode to Arizona Territory in 1865, Rita refused to accompany him. After the war, Miranda
was discharged and he returned to his young wife in San Juan. By 1871
Rita Miranda was twenty-one, the mother of a five-year-old son, and
extremely dissatisfied with her domestic life. Vasquez, Procopio, and
Barcenas spent a great deal of time with Pepita and Rita at Salazar's
cantina. The two girls, though married, were flattered and excited by
the attention of these well-dressed, heavily armed men who always had
plenty of money to throw around.[14]

Contrary to western films and fiction, Hispanic outlaws in California
did not wear huge straw sombreros nor drape bandoleers of cartridges
across their shoulders. Such costumes were worn in Mexico after 1900.
California's bandidos did not sport "Mexican" clothing at all, for fancy
calzoneras (trousers) with buttons down the legs, embroidered vests, and

Rafael Mirabel, robber, cattle thief, and compadre of Juan Soto's. (Author's collection)

short-waisted bolero jackets were not readily available in California's general stores. Instead, they wore the same clothing as all working men— sturdy wool or canvas trousers, vests, and the ever-popular blue soldier's overcoats. Hispanics would often add a bit of cultural flair: a colorful scarf around the neck or sash about the waist. The outfit was completed by a pair of high-heeled riding boots and a California-style hat, with a low, flat crown, and a flat, stiff brim. Tiburcio, however, shunned such common clothing and dressed in the height of style. Sheriff Harry Morse wrote in his diary in 1872 that Vasquez wore a black coat trimmed with a beaver collar, black trousers, and a black velvet vest decorated with floral designs from which protruded an open-face pocket watch and silver chain.

Morse also noted the risks inherent in Tiburcio's profession: "Bullet mark in right breast, also in neck left side, also in arm."[15]

No self-respecting California badman—Tiburcio Vasquez included— would venture forth without pistol and bowie knife. While a Barbary Coast ranger in San Francisco might carry a small pocket revolver con- cealed from a police officer's scrutiny, California's horseback bandidos liked to carry the largest and most fearsome handguns available. Especially popular were the huge .44 caliber Colt's Dragoon model of 1848 and the 1860 Colt's Army, with barrels up to eight inches in length. Almost as well liked were the .36 caliber Colt's Navy and Remington's .44 and .36 caliber six-guns. Not only were they intimidating, these weapons had substantial range and knock-down power. Although metallic-cartridge firearms started to become common by the early 1870s, percussion (or cap-and-ball) revolvers were regularly carried in California until the 1880s. Because they often misfired, a bowie knife was worn as a backup weapon. A bandido often carried his knife in a bootleg, although Tiburcio gen- erally wore his under his arm or inside his vest, suspended by a leather thong attached to the scabbard. Vasquez at various times wielded a brace of Colt's Navys or a large Colt's Dragoon revolver. He also carried a sixteen-shot, lever-action Henry rifle, one of the first guns to shoot metal cartridges. The Henry rifle was superseded by the Winchester Models of 1866 and 1873, and Tiburcio carried a Winchester as soon as he could get his hands on one.

Although Vasquez was suspected of various robberies, no charges were pending against him and he was free to come and go as he pleased. San Juan's telegrapher, Wells Fargo agent, and local manager of the Coast Line Stage Company was twenty-four-year-old Frank Mauk. His office was in a corner of the old mission, and he slept with the other stage employees in a large room they called "the corral." In old age he recalled, "I had a sort of understanding with Vasquez. I had the company's business to take care of. It was my first consideration. And part of that business was the telegraph department. Vasquez and his partner, Red Dick, frequently sent telegrams from my office. And it was understood that if they let me alone and let my office alone I would give them the same consideration." Mauk described how his arrangement with Vasquez was made:

> I was sleeping in the corral then—the big room occupied by all the stage men. The adjoining room was occupied by Espiritu

Varios, of whom it is generous to say that she was a lady of easy virtue. Late one night I heard someone enter her room. And although they talked in whispers I thought that the visitor was Vasquez. I heard him ask who was in the next room—meaning the corral. She said, "Frankie is in there." The next day she came to the office to send a telegram and I questioned her about her visitor. At first she stoutly denied having had a visitor.

"Who was in that room?" I insisted.

"Nobody," said Espiritu, equally determined.

I kept at her until she confessed that Vasquez had been her visitor. And then I gave her a message to carry to her bandit friend. "You tell Vasquez," I said, "that if he will let me and my offices alone I will neither know nor care anything about him."

"Vasquez thinks you're a good boy," answered Espiritu, "and he will do what you say." I told her that was all right. Just tell Vasquez to hold up the stage or shoot up the town if he had to do it to keep happy—but to let me alone. And in return for his immunity for my company I would know nothing about him. He kept his part of the agreement and I kept mine.[16]

Soon after, on the evening of May 5, 1871, the Los Angeles–bound stage was halted by three masked road agents north of the Salinas River crossing at Soledad. They ordered the driver to throw down the Wells Fargo express box, which they broke open but found to contain no valuables, only letters and waybills. They did not rob the passengers, and before riding off, congenially offered their best wishes to Frank Mauk in San Juan. The three highwaymen were undoubtedly Tiburcio, Procopio, and either Juan Soto or Bartolo Sepúlveda. Wells Fargo soon offered a reward of one hundred dollars each for the bandits. Mauk recalled that Vasquez "robbed the stage, sending me word that he would not destroy the letters or way bills. . . . Someone asked him why he didn't leave a twenty dollar gold piece in the box for Frankie along with the way bills. But Vasquez laughed and said that he needed all the gold."[17]

To avoid capture, Tiburcio and his compadres rode into the mountains above San Juan to the Saucelito Valley, located at the foot of St. Mary's Peak, twelve miles south of Pacheco Pass and high in the Coast Range. To this day it is one of the most remote and inaccessible places in California. Nearby Juan Soto's uncle ran a small rancho. Five adobe homes were located in and near the Saucelito Valley. They were occupied by herders who lived a simple, pastoral life, far from Anglo civilization. They regularly harbored stock thieves and bandidos, who were often friends or relatives and could pay for their keep with stolen coin or pilfered livestock. Vasquez, Procopio, Juan Soto, and Bartolo Sepúlveda, as well as several lesser-known badmen including Ambrosio Gonzáles, who had escaped from jail in Santa Cruz, and Pío Ochoa, a ruffian and tapadera, were there. All made their headquarters at the Alvarado adobe, two miles south of the Saucelito Valley.

Procopio and Soto had much in common, which may help explain why they were not on good terms. Both were tall and physically powerful, headstrong and bad tempered, and natural leaders of men. Procopio was twenty-nine and Soto four years younger. Due to his bandit lineage as nephew of the legendary Joaquín Murrieta, Procopio was widely known in the Hispanic community, greatly feared by some and greatly admired by many more. Juan Soto was just as well known. His family had settled in the Santa Clara Valley several generations before. His bandit activities had made him prominent among Hispanics and lawmen. Juan Soto no doubt viewed the Mexican-born Procopio as an outsider, decidedly not a Californio. But Procopio's striking good looks made him a favorite of the señoritas, while Juan Soto's pockmarked face and badly crossed eyes gave him a countenance that inspired dread and was hardly attractive to the opposite sex. Thus, it was not surprising that a few days later, on May 9, Procopio and Soto quarreled for reasons unknown. "I was there," Vasquez later recalled. "Soto made Procopio go down into his boots. If Procopio had not left like a coward Soto would have killed him."[18]

Procopio, accompanied by Tiburcio, rode out of the bandit camp and headed for San Juan. It was a fortuitous decision. Unbeknownst to them, Santa Clara County Sheriff Nick Harris, having received a tip that Juan Soto was hiding out in the Saucelito Valley, was then leading a posse to raid it. He had invited his friend Harry Morse to join them. Following the Ludovisi murder, Sheriff Morse had made repeated rides into the Coast Range, unsuccessfully hunting for Juan Soto, so he jumped at the chance. The day before Tiburcio and Procopio left the Saucelito Valley, Morse and Harris had ridden out of San Jose at the head of a heavily armed, nine-man posse. They spent two days riding through the mountains in an effort to find the remote hideout. Finally, on the morning of May 10, the posse crossed a ridge adjacent to St. Mary's Peak and

Procopio Bustamante, nephew of Joaquín Murrieta and member of the Vasquez gang. (Author's collection)

looked down on several small adobes. Morse divided the posse, taking a former constable, Theodore Winchell, to the nearest adobe and sending Sheriff Harris and the rest of the posse to search the other houses. The closest adobe was at the northwest end of the Saucelito Valley and is still standing.[19]

Morse and Winchell rode up to a rock corral behind the adobe where a Mexican was working. Morse asked for a drink of water, and the man, unsuspecting, invited them into the adobe. As the sheriff stepped inside, he got the shock of his life. Juan Soto sat at a table directly in front of him, surrounded by male and female companions, including Bartolo Sepúlveda. When Morse pulled his Smith & Wesson six-gun and demanded, "¡Manos arriba!" (Hands up!) the burly outlaw sat motionless. Several times Morse ordered Winchell to handcuff Soto, but Winchell lost his nerve and fled outside, leaving the sheriff to fend for himself.

Two of Soto's band quickly seized Morse. At the same time the bandido leaped to his feet and struggled to draw his pistols, which were buttoned beneath his long soldier's overcoat. Sheriff Morse jerked his six-gun loose and fired; the bullet tore off Soto's hat. Morse broke free and ducked out the door with the enraged bandit, a revolver in each hand, close behind. As the sheriff raced around back of the adobe, Soto opened fire on him at close range. Morse dropped to the ground and the bullet passed harmlessly over his head. Morse fired back, then leaped to his feet and sprinted for his horse. Four times this happened: Soto fired, Morse dodged the bullet, and shot back. Each time Sheriff Harris, who was racing to Morse's aid, thought that his friend had been killed. Harry Morse's last shot struck Soto's pistol and rammed the barrel into the outlaw's face, stunning him.

While Soto rushed back into the adobe to rearm, Sheriff Morse reached his horse and grabbed his rifle, a Winchester Model 1866 carbine. Moments later Juan Soto and Bartolo Sepúlveda burst out of the adobe. They had switched coats and Sepúlveda had donned Soto's hat. Sheriff Harris leaped from his horse, Spencer rifle in hand, and took dead aim at the fleeing outlaw in the long blue soldier's overcoat. But the ruse did not fool Morse. He knocked up the barrel of Harris's gun, saving Bartolo Sepúlveda's life. Instead Morse turned his attention to Juan Soto. The bandit, with a five-shooter clutched in each fist and a third in his belt, raced toward his horse, which was hitched to a large oak tree west of the house. When the animal spooked, Soto turned and

Nick Harris, sheriff of Santa Clara County, about 1870. (Author's collection)

raced toward another horse that was picketed two hundred yards north. Morse called for the outlaw to surrender but Soto ignored the command. At a range of 150 yards Morse put a rifle ball through the desperado's right shoulder. Badly wounded and desperate to kill his pursuer and escape, Soto turned and charged headlong at Morse. Sheriff Harris fired once with his Spencer rifle but missed. As Soto closed to one hundred yards, Harry Morse fired again. The heavy slug tore off the top of the outlaw's head. Morse took eighty dollars in coin from Soto's pockets and gave it to an old woman to bury the body.

Sheriff Morse's ability to dodge Juan Soto's pistol fire at close range, and his deadly marksmanship in twice hitting an armed, running opponent at long range, did not escape the notice of the press. The gunfight, coupled with numerous other exploits, firmly established his reputation as the best-known peace officer and manhunter on the Pacific Coast. Harry Morse's duel to the death with Juan Soto remains California's most famous outlaw-lawman gunfight and is considered by historians to be one of the classic shootouts of the Old West. Sheriff John Adams later questioned Soto's involvement in the Ludovisi murder, saying that he was "a daring and fearless robber but no murderer." But Adams's claim is difficult to reconcile with the fact that Soto attempted to kill lawmen twice, first at the Guadalupe Mine in 1867 and again in his fatal duel with Harry Morse. Adams also was a bitter rival and frequent critic of the Alameda sheriff, and may have wanted to cast doubt on Morse's heroic exploits.[20]

Of the slaying of Juan Soto, Vasquez later recalled, "At the time he was killed I was in San Juan." By this time local newspapers had reported the recent stage robbery and the bandits' salutations to Frank Mauk. Sheriff Morse visited San Juan and looked up Mauk, who later recounted their meeting: "I had no information to give him. I told him of my strange agreement with Vasquez and he agreed with me that if I were ever to 'peach,' my life and the company's wouldn't be worth a cent."[21]

There seemed to be no end to the trouble that Tiburcio could find. His repeated narrow escapes emboldened him, making him more reckless. That daring and boldness heightened his appeal to women, leading to more violence. One day in mid-June 1871, Vasquez, Barcenas, and Procopio were visiting Abelardo Salazar's house. Francisco Barcenas, a thirty-one-year-old Californio, was short, stout, and wore fancy brocaded vests and expensive suits. Vasquez later claimed that Barcenas, not he, was infatuated with the newly married Pepita Salazar:

> Barcenas seemed to like the wife of Salazar, and after we left he told me he was going to get her away. I told him all right, it was none of my business. A few days afterwards, one night, I started for Salazar's house, and when within a few rods, I met Barcenas, who had come in from another direction. He went in the house and got the wife into the stable, then came and told me he wanted me to get her away for him. I consented, the woman wanted to go and so I took her away. We first went to the saloon of Salazar's partner, one Gonzáles, where Barcenas got the woman's clothes, by telling Gonzáles some lie. Barcenas took the woman to Natividad. I had nothing to do with her. . . .
>
> Some enemies of mine in San Juan went to him [Salazar] and told him that I was the one who had taken his wife away. He threatened to kill me on sight, and one night while walking in San Juan with one of my friends, we came upon Salazar. He stopped and said, "Vasquez, I want to speak to you." I said, "All right," for I had done nothing. He asked me if I took his wife away. I laughed in his face and told him no; that I would bring Gonzáles as a witness to that effect. Without saying a word—I was within two feet of him at the time—he drew a pistol and fired at me. The bullet struck me in the neck on the right side and came out below the shoulder. I was blinded by the powder, but ducked my head and fired at him several times, he returning the shots. I don't think I hit him.[22]

Tiburcio's account seems exculpatory, as was typical for him. Although there can be little doubt that Pepita went with him willingly, several contemporary reports held that Vasquez had abducted the girl, then tired of her and turned her over to Barcenas. According to brief accounts in two local newspapers, the incident took place on Friday night, June 16. First, Vasquez, Procopio, and another desperado took the girl, then Salazar shot it out with them. The newspapers erroneously reported that Vasquez was wounded so badly he soon died. Frank Mauk provided an account of the gunfight's conclusion. By this time he was boarding in the house of San Juan's leading merchant, Tom McMahon, who was a member of a vigilante group, the Pajaro Valley Protective Society, and a bitter enemy of Vasquez. Recalled Mauk,

> I was just getting ready to leave the office for home . . . [when] I heard a lot of shooting. . . . I hurried toward home fearing that some of that fusillade of shots might have harmed Tom or [his wife] Bella. . . . Not far from the house there was a big pepper tree. And just as I neared the tree a man stepped out and covered me with a gun. It was Tom, and his surprise was as great as mine. He had mistaken me for Vasquez and decided to lose no time in getting the drop. Tom and I stood talking under the pepper tree when we were joined by Abelardo Salazar, who came sauntering up as if nothing unusual had happened.
>
> Salazar said that the bombardment was directed against him, but he was quite uninjured. His coat alone had suffered. He wore one of the long, loose army overcoats which the early day Spaniards loved to wear. One button held it at the throat, but just now there was no button. One of Vasquez' shots had torn it away, and there was a bullet hole through the tail of the coat. Salazar, quite unmoved, smoked a cigarette and smiled as he related how the coat had dropped off when the button was shot away. He said that he felt sure he had winged the bandit. . . . Salazar expressed his profound regret that he hadn't killed Vasquez.[23]

Tiburcio later said, "I got away and was near death for many days afterwards. Salazar got out a warrant for me, but I was not arrested. I was not guilty of any crime towards him, as you will perceive." According to Cora Older, he was nursed back to health by his sister Manuela and Rita Miranda. Tiburcio, tough and resilient, was soon back in the saddle with his compadres. Pepita Salazar and Rita Miranda, who had abandoned her husband and child, were now with them. The gang reportedly hid out in a cave in the Gabilans, in another cave near Soledad, and on the rancho of Manuel López in the Santa Lucia Range west of Jolon. Tiburcio rarely stayed in one place more than a few days, constantly moving from one hideout to another. Monterey County lawmen made little attempt to arrest him on the warrant for assaulting Salazar. From time to time Vasquez made bold rides into Monterey to visit with friends and extended family. In 1879, Robert Louis Stevenson, who lived there

Abelardo Salazar, from a San Francisco police mug photograph taken about 1865. Tiburcio seduced Salazar's wife, Pepita García, and was in turn shot and wounded by Salazar. (Author's collection)

briefly but memorably, wrote that "Vasquez, the bandit . . . returned to his native Monterey, and was seen publicly in her streets and saloons, fearing no man."[24]

The Monterey County sheriff, Thomas Watson, known as Don Tomás, and his undersheriff, Jacob R. Leese, had both known Tiburcio since childhood. Watson, a year older than Vasquez, was the son of an English sailor who had settled in Monterey and married a Californio woman. His parents had been close friends of Hermenegildo and Doña Guadalupe, and Watson's mother, Mariana Escamilla, was Tiburcio's godmother. The sheriff's nephew, C. A. Canfield, later recalled, "Vasquez had the drop on Don Tomás several times, yet he always spared his life on this account." Canfield described an incident that was often talked of in Monterey: "Alonzo Allen and Don Tomás, as the Mexicans called him, were out collecting the county taxes in the southern part of the county. . . . They had reached the crossing in their buggy at the Salinas River where the willows grew thickly. Vasquez had read the papers and knew that the sheriff would come along that way with much money. Suspecting the intent of his gang to murder Allen and Watson, he sped his white horse and reached the spot in time to see his gang with arms already leveled to murder them as they would drive by. The gang was greeted thus by Vasquez: 'Stop, there. Whoever kills Don Tomás must also kill me. Down with those arms. Let him pass on.'"[25]

Perhaps Watson and Leese were sympathetic to Vasquez, or perhaps they simply weren't very capable lawmen. The laxity of Sheriff Watson and his deputy was amply illustrated by Daniel Martin, an early Montereyan, who recalled that "Watson was about to depart for Hollister, then a part of Monterey County, on urgent business, when he received word that Vasquez was at the Union Saloon in Monterey. Watson called his chief deputy, Jacob R. Leese, and ordered him to go at once to the Union Saloon and arrest Vasquez." When Leese stepped into the saloon, Vasquez was at the bar with several compadres. Spotting his boyhood amigo, Tiburcio called to him, "¿Cómo estás Jacobo? Venga a tomar un trago con nosotros." (How are you, Jacob? Come and have a drink with us.")

Leese obligingly complied, and the two engaged in friendly conversation over several drinks, with Tiburcio paying. When Leese offered to buy the next round, Vasquez replied, "No, no, Jake, I get my money easier than you. You save your money. Remember, you are an official and frequently

Jacob Leese in 1872 when he was undersheriff of Monterey County. A boyhood friend of Tiburcio's, he was half Californio and half Anglo. (Dennis T. Copeland collection)

thrown in contact with criminals and may be shot all to pieces and necessitate all the money you can scrape together to patch you up."

This remark had its intended effect, for Leese forgot all about arresting the highwayman. Vasquez said to him, "Jake, let's go down to old Simoneau's restaurant and get some supper." Leese complied, as Martin later recalled: "It was agreed and as they emerged into the street Vasquez suggested they take a back street and avoid detection, if possible, thus avoiding any embarrassment to either. So they arrived at the restaurant and ordered two porterhouse steaks, with all their trimmings, also wine, black coffee, and a brandy called Cognac. No doubt they enjoyed the meal. Vasquez paid the bill, and after bidding each other good morning they retired to their respective homes."

The next day Sheriff Watson arrived from Hollister with a prisoner. Seeing that the jail was empty and the front cell door was open, he called to Leese and asked, "Where did you put Vasquez?"

His deputy quickly retorted, "If you expect me to commit suicide by attempting to arrest that man, you are disappointed. Here is the warrant. Vasquez will be back in town in a few days and you can arrest him yourself."[26]

It is notable that no Monterey lawman ever captured Tiburcio Vasquez. On each occasion when he ventured far from his home county—to Los Angeles, to Amador, to Sonoma—he was arrested and sent to prison. But in Monterey, Tiburcio operated with impunity. Harry Morse, however, was made of sterner stuff than the Monterey officers. Apparently convinced that Vasquez was one of Ludovisi's killers, Morse was determined to track him down. He owed much of his success in bandit hunting to a judicious use of informants. One of them was Juan Soto's old partner, the Spanish-speaking Alfonso Burnham, alias Fred Welch. After Burnham's release from San Quentin in 1867 the sheriff had befriended the ex-convict, got him work, and helped him to reform. Now Morse called on Burnham to help capture Vasquez. Almost sixty years later the former outlaw gave a detailed account of how he infiltrated the Vasquez gang:

Vasquez, I knew, was frequenting a district around Sotoville, a little village in Monterey County.[27] I rode into Sotoville and sought out the restaurant. Dismounting in a dark angle formed by a wall at the back, I tied my horse and entered. Dinner was in full swing and I did not at once locate the man I sought. I was about to drop nonchalantly into a seat when I was hailed in the native tongue by the voice of Vasquez. I looked around quickly. Seated in a far corner of the room was a party of four Mexicans, two men, one of whom was Vasquez, and two women, their dinner spread before them. Vasquez was signaling me with a wine glass, trickling its contents over the table in his eagerness. I crossed the room and found myself the fifth member of a strange group, and although it was just the situation to further my plans, my heart beat faster because of the company.

The two senoritas were pretty young women of an ordinary Mexican type, but it was the second man I had to take into account. It was Procopio, nephew of Joaquin Murrieta, and a man of more than ordinary intelligence. I realized grimly that only my best acting and eternal vigilance would see me through. At all costs I must throw myself into the part.

There was no lack of conversational topics in those days and I managed to enter the talk with great gusto; besides, there was an undercurrent of hostility between the two men which aroused my interest. Procopio was six feet tall and an exceptionally hand-some man. His Castilian birth, too, set him above Vasquez and he was regarded with favor by the women. But he was a rene-gade and outlaw to the core of his being and had served several terms in prison.[28] There he had become an expert shoemaker and though he might easily have become an honest citizen when he left the prison, he immediately joined a band of highwaymen. At the time of our restaurant meeting he was hiding from the San Joaquin authorities. The senoritas had no scruples for themselves nor for their men, and Procopio rode the high wave of popularity.

Throughout the dinner the conversation took a rollicking vein, interrupted occasionally by an anxious glance I bethought me to throw over my shoulder. Jesting went on until the meal was ended, then sobering, I told them of my plight. I had killed a man in Marin and was a fugitive from justice. Vasquez's eyes narrowed. A look of cunning crossed his face and he leaned toward me. The friendship in his eyes was prompted not by kindliness but by selfish longing to outwit the law supposed to be after me. He grew ardent in his schemes to preserve my safety and defeat the despised law. He bestowed slaps on my shoulders and

Alfonso M. Burnham, the reformed Spanish-speaking desperado whom Sheriff Harry Morse had infiltrate the Vasquez gang. (Author's collection)

his own thighs without favoritism, hurling Spanish oaths liberally as he contemptuously spat upon the restaurant floor.

His scheme found favor as it was the one I had privately formed. I agreed to join the camp which was situated on a sheepherder's place about fifteen miles away. Under the cover of darkness we drove into the mountains and I became one of a band of the most desperate and notorious killers that has ever existed. I was to realize very soon the risk I was taking, for at the camp I saw enough to convince me that if the deception was suspected or even hinted at, they would stab me as readily as they made any of the many gestures of indulgence they permitted themselves.

The days in the camp were crowded with interest—interest made up of anxiety and expectation, excitement, and amazement. The group gave free rein to their chatter and unrestrainedly boasted of their vicious exploits. Plans for their future were openly discussed and in the scheming I was included as one who might be counted on for the lowest of their crimes. . . . I was forced to appear in sympathy with my hosts until I could get word to Morse, and the opportunity had not presented itself. Leaving the camp without some of the band was sure to excite suspicion and this I meant to avoid. Then one day it was casually suggested that supplies were running low and someone must go to Salinas for them. Pancho Barcenas proposed to go—who else? I was burning with eagerness, but somehow managed to be indifferent in my offer to accompany him. It was finally so arranged and he and I saddled our horses and headed for Salinas.

The deserted road gave me no hope of finding a way to communicate with my friends. Barcenas was one of the most desperate of the band and I was afraid I was as bad off with him as I had been at the camp. But Salinas provided me the opportunity I wanted by offering Barcenas many places to drink, and when he became overindulgent, I slipped away. I managed surreptitiously to get a message off to Morse, advising the sheriff as to the camp's location and its habitués.

As we drove back to the outlaw camp, I experienced an exhilaration over the outcome of this great experiment that I can still call up, even though it failed in its accomplishment. It was an elation that lasted through the succeeding days, filled though they were with anxious watching. Every sound during the long week carried the imagined alarm of a posse's approach. . . . I could not know that an emergency had called Morse from his office for several days and that the message failed to reach him.

Toward the end of the week Procopio and Vasquez drew pistols over a woman, and though neither of them was seriously injured, the affray led to the disruption of the camp. I was amazed at the fairness in the division of goods that followed. If there was any honor among these thieves it was the first display I had witnessed, but the loot was evenly apportioned among them, the band of stolen horses exactly distributed, and every member of the band drove off with a goodly number. . . .

Procopio added the woman of the dispute to his loot and they made ready to go to San Luis Obispo. Vasquez and Barcenas had "business" near Santa Cruz and left the camp without ceremony. My way lay along the route taken by Procopio and he rode beside me. I had given up hope of Morse's arrival and considered that my best move now was to make as full a report as possible. I accompanied Procopio as far as the Pleyto ranch where adios was said.[29]

Rancho Pleyto, now inundated by the San Antonio Reservoir, was located in the Coast Range in the southern part of Monterey County. The two "pretty young women" were undoubtedly Pepita Salazar and Rita Miranda. The girl taken south by Procopio was probably Pepita. Procopio apparently tired of her, for she was soon back in the company of Vasquez and Barcenas.

With the death of Juan Soto and the departure of Procopio, Tiburcio emerged as the leader of the loose-knit band of pillagers that became known as the Vasquez gang. As Frank Mauk recalled, "His banditry kept things pretty generally stirred up. One never knew just when or where he would make his next appearance." As his notoriety grew, Tiburcio reveled in his role of gentleman-bandit and lady-killer. Yet his veneer of fine clothes, gold watches, immaculate grooming, and charming demeanor of a caballero were in stark contrast to the hard-riding, fast-shooting desperado who stood San Juan on its ear. He exemplified the Mexican bandido, laughing and carefree but simultaneously menacing and deadly. That image would soon become part and parcel of the legend of Tiburcio Vasquez.[30]

CHAPTER NINE

Stagecoach Robber

Tiburcio Vasquez now moved his headquarters to the rancho of Pedro Regalado, located in Calera Canyon, a rugged gorge in the mountains about seven miles east of Monterey, and south of the road leading to Salinas. Regalado, forty-two, was a tough character who had once been jailed in Monterey for theft. His daughter, Ramona, had married the notorious Monterey gunfighter James Bushton.

Calera Canyon ran south, watered by a small creek. Heavily wooded, with green pasture in the creek bottom, it was walled in on the east side by cliffs and steep rock ridges, and on the west by high, craggy hills. It was a risky hideout, as Sheriff Thomas Watson's ranch was located in an adjacent canyon, the Corral de Tierra. Among the hardcases who drifted into the camp were Francisco Barcenas, Manuel López, Pancho Galindo, Fernando and Chavo Arceo, and from Santa Cruz, the Rodríguez brothers, Narciso and Gracia, as well as Pepita Salazar and Rita Miranda.[1]

Calera Canyon was also home to several Anglo settlers, including the Martin, Robinson, and Moore families. Daniel Martin, then a boy, recalled that several Hispanic families had moved to the canyon from the former notorious outlaw village in nearby Pilarcitos Canyon. Also in Calera Canyon was a Mexican named Agapito, who was a blacksmith and an expert spur and bit maker. On Tiburcio's arrival he was put to work making and repairing riding tackle for the band.

Daniel Martin later wrote of encounters with Tiburcio Vasquez when he was twelve: "This was in the early summer of 1871 and as it was my daily duty to drive cattle to the Calera Creek to water, I met and talked with Vasquez frequently, and when he learned that my native town was Monterey, that I had attended school in 'the Old Cuartel,' and that Doña Señora Catherine Cole (Mrs. Tom Cole), who had owned the Rancho San Carlos, or Potrero, in the Carmel valley, was my aunt and for whom he had worked, we became quite friendly, which allayed my feelings somewhat. Being as I spoke the Spanish language, it was easy to converse. Vasquez spoke [to me] very few words of English."[2]

Pepita Salazar's romantic dalliance with the outlaw gang was brief, for she soon died at the Regalado ranch. The circumstances of her death are not clear. In 1874, newspaper reporter Boyd Henderson wrote that Vasquez tired of the girl: "After a few months dalliance he presented her to Pancho Bacinos [Barcenas], one of his adherents, under whose brutal treatment she died." Old-timers in San Juan told Cora Older that Pepita had been in poor health and had died of a vague and undescribed illness. However, the most reliable account comes from Isabel Meadows, sister-in-law of gang member Manuel López. She said that the girl died at Regalado's place from a botched abortion. The Arceo boys' eldest sister, Francisca, known as Pancha, was a well-known midwife who lived in nearby Pilarcitos Canyon, so perhaps she performed the abortion.[3]

According to Cora Older, Francisco Barcenas and the Arceo brothers rode to the ranch house of Cayetano Lugo, located about ten miles south of Salinas. It was one of the few dwellings in the area. Lugo's stepson, Francisco Blanco, loaded tools and wood into a spring wagon and followed the outlaws to a camp in a nearby grove of oak trees. There he found Vasquez and Rita Miranda with the body of Pepita Salazar. Rita was crying and stroking the forehead of her dead friend. Blanco built a rude coffin and brought the body back to the Lugo ranch house, accompanied by the gang. The Lugo women laid out the body, prayed over her, and dressed the corpse in black. Finally, the gang rode off with Rita Miranda, while Francisco Blanco brought the body in his wagon to Abelardo Salazar in San Juan. Overcome with grief and rage, Salazar insisted that Vasquez had killed Pepita. He swore vengeance.[4]

If Vasquez felt any remorse over Pepita's death, he certainly did not spend much time mourning her, as he promptly returned to the Regalado ranch and began planning even more ambitious bandit raids. Tiburcio knew that Sheriff Harry Morse was hunting him. Perhaps he had learned that Morse had sent Alfonso Burnham to infiltrate his band. Now Morse asked Tom McMahon for help in locating Vasquez. Tiburcio later claimed that he had outwitted the Alameda lawman:

> Sheriff Harry Morse . . . desirous of capturing me, wrote to Tom McMahon, of San Juan Bautista, in Monterey County, who, through his native relations with the Creole (native Californian) population of that region could best serve him, to inform himself without delay in regard to my whereabouts and to notify him (Morse) with all possible dispatch. This coming to my ears, I determined to teach Tom a lesson, because in his position as merchant I thought he was traveling out of his way to injure me, who had always befriended him. Learning that Tom was going to Salinas to pay his taxes, I took occasion to stop him at a convenient point.
>
> "How are you, Tom?" said I.
>
> "Very well, friend Tiburcio," he replied.
>
> I then inquired if I had in any way done him any harm. He replied in the negative. I then informed him of what I had learned of his underhand dealing with Morse, and that I was prepared to repay him in his own way. Upon being called on to deliver, he handed over his coin and a fine improved Colt's revolver. I then informed him that I wanted a fine ring that ornamented his handsome hand. To this he rather objected, but on being informed that I would stand no nonsense, he made a virtue of necessity, and Tom and his ring parted company. I then told him that as I was no assassin, I would make him a present of his cowardly life, which he was by no means loathe to accept, with permission to jog on with his fine buggy and horse.[5]

Contrary to Tiburcio's story, he and McMahon were hardly on friendly terms, and he did not deliberately target the merchant, but instead encountered him by chance. On August 5, 1871, Vasquez and a compadre rode out of their hideout at the Regalado place on a robbing expedition. Passing through Salinas and Natividad, they turned their horses north on the stage road that crossed the Gabilan Mountains to San Juan Bautista. It was evening when the bandidos rode up behind Thomas McMahon's buggy. The twenty-nine-year-old merchant had attended a political meeting in Salinas and was on his way home to San Juan. As his buggy approached the summit he was overtaken by the two robbers. Speaking Spanish, they covered him with six-shooters and ordered him out. Then the outlaws tied and blindfolded him and relieved him of a pistol, a silver watch, a gold ring, fifty dollars in coin, and his blue sack overcoat. Hidden in McMahon's buggy was a shot sack holding five hundred dollars in gold, which the two bandidos overlooked. McMahon recognized Vasquez. Tiburcio and his compadre then continued on to a roadside inn, the Gabilan House. There, they held up the occupants at gunpoint and took all the money they could find. Pressing on toward San Juan, they encountered a Frenchman, Pierre Save, on the road. Before they could rob him too, he spurred his mount and escaped.[6]

Tom McMahon later heard that Vasquez was furious when he learned that he had missed the hidden sack of gold, declaring, "I will get that fellow for that!" McMahon was so worried by the threat that he started carrying a double-barreled shotgun with him on his daily trips between his home and store. He did not stop his efforts to have Vasquez arrested, however, and sought help from Tiburcio's enemy, Abelardo Salazar. Vasquez recalled, "Salazar went to Tom McMahon and stated that for $300 he would effect my capture. McMahon gave him the money, but Salazar, instead of hunting me, left immediately for Mexico, and I believe he has never returned." But Tiburcio denied ever seeking revenge against McMahon: "I have friends all over the southern country, and I have always been posted in regard to every move planned or directed against myself. Once I lay in a thicket near San Juan when McMahon passed with his sister. I could have shot him easily if I had wanted to."[7]

A few days later, early in the morning of August 8, Vasquez and one of his compadres ventured out again from their hiding place in Calera Canyon. First, they rode eight miles south along the Salinas River to Chualar. Two miles east of Chualar, on the Old Stage Road, they cantered up to the Deep Wells stagecoach station, run by J. S. Nance and his partner, Allen Foster. Nance later described what happened:

About daybreak I was aroused from sleep by a heavy rap at my door. I got up, dressed, and went to the door and found two horsemen. One said that he wanted a bottle of whiskey. I filled a bottle and gave him [it]. He put down a $20 piece and asked me to change it. I refused, saying I did not think I had sufficient change for it, but finally went and got my money, and found I had enough to do so. They then called for two boxes [of] sardines, and paid for them. While I was in the act of putting the money in the bag, they drew pistols, and presenting them at me, said "Lay down that money, and all other money that you have, or we will give you some of this."

Seeing there was no use to refuse, I complied with their request. They then compelled me to hold up my hands, while they "went through" my pockets, taking in all from me about $30. They then ordered me out of the house and made me hold up my hands while they mounted their horses, and riding off, ordered me back into the house. I had no firearms about the place to protect myself with, otherwise I should have made it warm for them. After a few moments they again came back to the door, remained two or three minutes, and rode up the road again, apparently looking for something. Mr. Foster had got up by this time, and seeing them, went out and asked what they wanted there, when they said that they had lost $60, and said, "Damn you. Leave, or we'll kill you."

Foster started toward the house, but in an instant they were in front of him with a pistol aimed, telling him to hold up his hands, while they took all the money he had in his pockets, amounting to about three dollars. They then rode off towards the Gabilan mountains.[8]

Two days later, Tiburcio pulled the most audacious stagecoach robbery that had taken place in California in years. Stage holdups were common and most were humdrum affairs, almost routine. One or two highwaymen would stop a coach on an upgrade, order the driver to throw out the Wells Fargo box, and order the stage on. Sometimes sleeping passengers were not even aware they had been held up. But this one was different, and Tiburcio later gave a dramatic account of it:

Having concluded to rob the stage between Gilroy and Pacheco, I took position with two men in a narrow lane, making an opening in the fence. I arrested all parties coming in either direction in advance of the arrival of the stage. Taking them under some oak trees, I tied their hands behind their backs. Finally, when the stage approached, I saw it was covered with a multitude. However, I determined to take the chances. The coachman obeyed my order to turn and drive through the opening in the fence and halt under the oak trees.

The passengers asked whether it was life or money that I wanted. I replied that I only wanted their money. One senorita in the coach had burst into tears, and taking off her watch, and a twenty dollar piece and some small coin from her pockets, tendered them to me. I politely told her to keep them. She begged me not to injure her husband. I asked her to point out her husband, which she did, and I made him take his seat alongside of her. The balance of the party were all tied, and some four hundred dollars taken from them. Then, telling them I was going to bring up the balance of my party, I galloped off with my men, having realized quite as well as I expected to. This adventure took place in broad daylight, and in a thickly settled neighborhood.

Four miles beyond where I left the stagecoach, on the main road, I met two parties in a spring wagon, father and son, whom I stopped in order to effect a forced loan, in which I succeeded to my own satisfaction and the great surprise of the people who were laboring in the nearby fields. Five miles further on we went to a house for water, and I asked the boys who were with me whether we should go to the mountains or strike across the country to intercept the stage from Gilroy to San Juan Bautista. They decided upon the latter plan. But people who had been robbed in the morning had already alarmed the country, and as we approached Gilroy, I saw parties coming who were sufficiently near to recognize us, and open fire upon us, whereupon we found it convenient to change our course and strike for the mountains, successfully eluding our pursuers, and making good our escape.[9]

The victims later gave a more complete and accurate account. The stagecoach had left the train depot in Gilroy shortly after noon on August 10. There was then no railroad to Southern California, and the stage line carried southbound passengers to Visalia in the southern San Joaquin Valley. The route skirted Soap Lake (now San Felipe Lake), then rose up into the Coast Range, through Pacheco Pass, dropped down into the San Joaquin Valley, then went south to Visalia. On this day Dennis Conroy was at the reins; eleven passengers were on board, most inside the stage, and a few riding next to the driver and on the dickey seat on top of the coach.

Vasquez, with Narciso Rodríguez and Francisco Barcenas, posted themselves on the stage road near where it skirts Soap Lake, about seven miles south of Gilroy. The spot, later known as Vasquez Canyon, is situated in Santa Clara County, half a mile west of the Monterey County line. The bandidos were splendidly mounted, well armed, and well dressed in expensive clothes and gold watches, but they did not bother to wear masks. They knocked down the roadside fence and got ready to detain any travelers on the highway. The outlaws first captured Shelby Moore, who was driving his buggy to a local political meeting. They tied and blindfolded him, took fifty-five dollars from his pockets, then drove his buggy through the broken fence and across the adjoining field, secreting it in a grove of oak trees at the mouth of a side canyon. Next was a boy on horseback, who was secured in the same way. He had only fifty cents in his pockets, so the bandits returned it to him.

By this time the stagecoach was approaching. The "whip," Conroy, heard someone shout an order to halt, "Halloa!" Conroy ignored the command and continued on. Several minutes later a mounted Californio raced past the stage, then suddenly whirled his horse in front of the coach. Flourishing a revolver, he yelled, "Halt!" At the same two more bandidos galloped up behind the coach. Conroy reined in his team. The outlaws directed him to drive through the fence to the oak grove, where the coach was halted next to the prostrate Shelby Moore. Then Narciso Rodríguez ordered the passengers in English, "Get out and shell out."

The driver and passengers alighted from the stagecoach and lined up. Only one passenger was a woman, Mrs. Murphy. She was traveling alone, perched on one of the seats on top of the stage. Young and quick-witted, Mrs. Murphy begged to be allowed to keep her seat. Rodríguez asked her, "Which one is your husband?"

She pointed to a passenger next to her, Orrin Simmons, and the outlaw replied, "All right."

The robbers ordered Simmons down from the coach, but allowed the woman to remain. Unknown to the bandits, the Wells Fargo express box was underneath her seat, partly hidden by her dress. With one foot, she carefully slid the box back until it was fully concealed. Meanwhile the rest of the passengers were securely bound, blindfolded, and stripped of valuables. From Simmons they took one hundred dollars and a gold watch, but his "wife" pleaded with them to leave them some money to pay for their meals on the trip to Visalia. The bandits returned three dollars to Simmons. Vasquez and his men pocketed their booty, several gold watches and about $650 in coin, and then swung into their saddles. Before riding off they ordered, "Don't move until we come back, or we'll murder every one of you!"

The road agents galloped out onto the road, but didn't get far. A teamster carrying a load of fence pickets was approaching, and the Vasquez bunch captured him as well, taking him and his wagon into the oak grove, where he was tied up with the rest. Then Tiburcio and his men rode back onto the highway and headed south toward Hollister. They soon encountered Andrew Wasson, a candidate for sheriff of Monterey County, and J. L. Griffith, who was running for district attorney. Both were canvassing the county for votes. At that time, most California sheriffs were not professional lawmen; many were either politicians or public-spirited citizens, with little or no training or experience in law enforcement. Few of them served more than a couple of two-year terms, hardly enough time to master a difficult and complex profession. Although years earlier Andrew Wasson had served one term as a Monterey deputy sheriff, he was notably inexperienced. Now, although aware that a band of young, well-dressed, well-armed, and well-mounted Californios had committed several robberies in the area just a few days earlier, he made no effort to follow or otherwise investigate the three young, well-dressed, well-armed, and well-mounted Californios. He and Griffith did get a good, close look at the three, and then the two aspiring law officers—in blissful ignorance, or perhaps cowardice—continued down the road on their election campaign. Tiburcio did not bother them.

Vasquez and his compadres soon encountered a farmer, Abram Grewell, about two hundred yards from his house, relieved him of six dollars, and continued south. Grewell raced home and grabbed his Henry rifle. Then he and a friend, Billy Brown, armed with an old Kentucky rifle, mounted up and started in pursuit of the gang. They caught up with the outlaws just north of Hollister. Tiburcio and his men flourished their pistols, then turned their mounts and raced east toward the mountains. Brown fired at them and missed. Grewell, working the lever on his Henry rifle, dropped the hammer some fifty times, but the weapon failed to discharge. He then realized that in his haste and excitement he had forgotten to load it. By this time Vasquez and his riders were long gone.

Meanwhile the stage passengers remained motionless in the August heat. Dennis Conroy pleaded with young Mrs. Murphy to get down from the coach and untie them. At first she refused, believing that the robbers would return, find the Wells Fargo box, and kill her for deceiving them. For an hour and a half they lay still, until Conroy finally persuaded her to loosen the rope that bound him. Conroy then untied the rest, and the stage raced back to Gilroy, where the alarm was raised.[10]

Sheriff Nick Harris led a large posse south from Gilroy after the road agents. Sheriff Harris believed that the bandits were Tiburcio Vasquez, Bartolo Sepúlveda, and Procopio Bustamante, assisted by Pancho Galindo and Francisco Barcenas whom the sheriff did not believe actually took part in the holdup. In fact, Procopio had already split with Vasquez, and Bartolo Sepúlveda, after his close call with the two sheriffs in the Saucelito Valley, had fled to the Cerro Gordo Mines near Lone Pine, east of the Sierra Nevada.

Grewell had last seen the three bandits heading into the mountains east of Hollister, so Harris and his men first searched the area from Santa Ana Mountain to Quien Sabe Creek, then crossed the Coast Range into the Saucelito Valley. Finding no trace of the outlaws, Sheriff Harris and his posse returned to Hollister, then rode west into the Gabilan Mountains. There they learned that on August 13 Vasquez had robbed a sheepherder named Patterson of $2.50, but had overlooked two hundred dollars hidden in his bootleg. Harris soon lost all track of the robbers, and returned to Santa Clara County empty-handed.[11]

By capturing a passenger-laden stagecoach and robbing numerous persons on a well-traveled highway in broad daylight, Tiburcio Vasquez created a public sensation. The holdup received prominent attention in the state's newspapers, for it was the most brazen stage robbery in California since the Civil War, when a band of Confederate guerrillas had robbed two coaches at Bullion Bend near Placerville. Two weeks after the Soap Lake robbery the San Leandro–based *Alameda County Gazette* published a long, detailed report about the band that was widely reprinted in California's newspapers. It was based on information provided by Sheriffs Morse and Harris. For the first time the operations of the gang and the connection among Vasquez, Bustamante, Soto, Sepúlveda, and Galindo were described. The article was reprinted without elaboration in the *Monterey Republican*. That it took two out-of-county sheriffs to explain this outlaw gang to the Anglo population of Monterey County

Francisco "Pancho" Galindo, one of the Vasquez gang in 1871. (Author's collection)

speaks volumes about the ineptitude of Sheriff Watson and his deputies. They simply didn't know what was going on in their own backyard.[12]

After robbing the stage, Tiburcio and his compadres rode back to Pedro Regalado's place. At least eight of the band were there, as was Rita Miranda. That night a number of the outlaws visited the ranch of a settler named Moore in Calera Canyon, knocking on the door and asking for coffee and food. Several more nights that week they came to Moore's place for food, and Moore later professed that he was "ignorant of their character." Moore's teenage son, Will, had a best friend, Jim Robinson, whose father ran a farm and ranch nearby, at the mouth of Calera Canyon. In 1916, Jim Robinson, then a deputy sheriff in Salinas, vividly recalled to Cora Older the arrival of Vasquez, with several of his men and Rita Miranda, at the Regalado ranch. Mrs. Older recorded Robinson's story:

> He was about fifteen. At the time he was not aware who Vasquez and his company were. They were strangers on horseback. . . . Robinson knew well the Regalado family, who were Spanish-Californians and neighbors of his own family. The Regalados gave a fandango for Vasquez and his company, and the Spanish dancers came from as far as Monterey to be present on that occasion.
>
> Mr. Robinson says that at the time children often talked of Vasquez. They always feared that he would appear, but they had great curiosity to see him. At the head of the canyon where Vasquez was in hiding lived an American family named Moore. Mr. Robinson's boyhood chum was Will Moore. The Moore boy often came to the Robinsons' in the evening to help little Jim do his chores. . . . One night he was walking down the canyon with little Jim Robinson when he said, "Jim, I have a new pistol. I'd like to use it to capture Vasquez."
>
> "Do you think that you could capture Vasquez?" asked little Jim, dubious, but greatly impressed by the boyish boast.
>
> "Of course," said the Moore boy, who was seventeen. He believed so much in his own courage that he took his pistol from his pocket. Just at that moment there appeared from the bushes three men who greeted them with guns. "Here is Tiburcio Vasquez," said the leader.
>
> Young Moore forgot that he had a pistol. Little Jim Robinson's Spanish saved the day. "Don't shoot us. We didn't mean it. Bill doesn't know how to shoot. Honest, we didn't mean it. We are friends of Mrs. Regalado. She'll tell you we don't know how to shoot."
>
> Vasquez and his friends pretended to doubt them. With great gravity the boys were led to Mrs. Regalado's house. Vasquez, with solemn demeanor, said to Mrs. Regalado that these boys had been threatening their lives [and] he didn't know whether to spare them or not. Mrs. Regalado told Vasquez, with a smile, that they were harmless, they were friends of hers, and even if they did threaten their lives she did not think they ought to be killed.

By this time, in spite of their fears, it dawned on the boys that Vasquez and his friends were laughing at them, that they were all snickering at the expense of the poor frightened lads whose wish to meet Vasquez had come true. With mock solemnity Vasquez warned them that they must never again threaten the life of Tiburcio Vasquez. The lads thought that they were lucky to escape with their lives.[13]

Vasquez himself recalled this visit to the Regalados' place: "I spent several days on a ranch, resting, amusing myself with dancing, etc., with the senoritas. Here I was attacked by Sheriff Tom Watson, and a party of fifteen men, who captured eight of my horses and outfit, including my arms. I escaped, of course, on foot. I struck into the mountains and lay perdu for more than a month, during which I succeeded in renewing my mount with the best of horses, saddles, etc."[14]

Indeed Vasquez did have a close call with Sheriff Watson's posse. So many persons came to know Vasquez was in the canyon that word soon reached the Monterey sheriff at his ranch in the Corral de Tierra. On the night of August 15, five days after the Soap Lake stage robbery, Watson organized an eleven-man posse to raid the canyon hideout. The posse included his undersheriff, Herbert Mills; his friend, Andrew Wasson, the candidate for sheriff; and several local ranchers, including Mike Noon, half brother of young Daniel Martin, and E. J. Robinson, father of Jim Robinson. It was four in the morning when the possemen picketed their horses and crept through the moonlight toward the Regalados' house. The posse's attempt at stealth was in vain, for immediately the howls of a pack of watchdogs echoed though the canyon. Sheriff Watson and his men raced forward and surrounded the house. Watson flung open the front door and inside found Regalado and Rita Miranda.[15]

The posse hurriedly searched the rancho and soon discovered a man and a boy in a haystack, feigning sleep. The pair turned out to be Regalado's son and his hired hand. Suddenly, the possemen heard someone running through the chaparral near the creek bed, farther up the canyon. Rushing forward, they stumbled upon the empty camp of the robbers. Blankets and provisions were scattered about; three stolen horses were picketed nearby, saddled and bridled. The coat taken from Tom McMahon was also found. The outlaws' blankets were still warm. Sheriff Watson and his men cautiously combed the heavy brush on both sides of the canyon, but no trace of the fugitives could be found. Watson questioned Rita Miranda, but she would say only, "They are well armed, each having a repeating rifle and two six-shooters."

No doubt she was telling the truth. Her statement had the desired effect, for the posse quickly lost interest in pursuing the desperadoes. Most of them returned home, while Sheriff Watson, Andrew Wasson, and several others stayed behind to guard the rancho in case the outlaws returned. The officers remained only one day, however, then rode back to Monterey, bringing Regalado, his son, and Rita Miranda with them for questioning. All three denied helping the gang commit robberies, and they were set free. Sheriff Watson and his posse had squandered an ideal opportunity to capture Tiburcio's band, who were on foot, without food, blankets, or provisions. Unlike Sheriff Morse, who had once spent weeks alone in the mountains hunting the gang, the Monterey posse spent less than two days searching for the outlaws before giving up. Some of them plainly feared a gun battle with the badmen. As posse member Mike Noon later confessed, "It was just as well that the raid had been 'tipped off' to Vasquez, thus avoiding, no doubt, a fierce encounter."[16]

Tiburcio and his men, including Francisco Barcenas and Narciso Rodríguez, remained hidden in the mountains until they were sure Sheriff Watson and his men had given up the chase. They quickly managed to steal or borrow fresh horses. Two days after the Calera Canyon raid a pair of bandidos was spotted a mile from Salinas, riding magnificent mounts and carrying rifles. One of the riders may have been Vasquez himself. He had already decided that Monterey County was too hot for him, and that Santa Cruz, where the Rodríguez brothers lived, would be safer. As Tiburcio recalled, "By this time all the parties that had been following me, with the exception of that led by an American assassin named Tarpia [Tarpy], had returned to their respective homes."[17]

Sheriff Watson was better positioned than any other lawman to capture Vasquez. Unlike officers who had only physical descriptions to go on, Watson knew Tiburcio personally. He knew his friends, his customs, his haunts, and his hideouts. Watson was very popular, had arrested a number of dangerous outlaws, and had presided over several legal hangings in Monterey. But he lacked the ability, or perhaps the motivation, to capture Tiburcio Vasquez. Now, having served as Monterey County sheriff for almost six years, Watson had lost interest in the office, and he was not running for reelection. Instead he threw his support behind his friend Andrew Wasson. In the election several weeks later Wasson won, despite his dismal performance as a budding lawman. Wasson would soon come under harsh criticism for his inept efforts to track down Tiburcio Vasquez.[18]

Sheriff Watson's ineffectiveness had helped create a law enforcement vacuum in Monterey County. Into that void rode a band of vigilantes led by the notorious Matt Tarpy, a thirty-five-year-old Irishman who owned a ranch near Watsonville. Tarpy was a dead shot, a fine horseman, and an expert tracker. His hatred of Hispanic and Indian thieves was matched only by his great courage and terrible temper. For years Matt Tarpy had been active in tracking down stock rustlers, and he had contempt for local lawmen, whom he considered incapable of protecting him and his neighbors from horse and cattle thieves. A year earlier Tarpy had organized the Pajaro Property Protective Society, a vigilante group that included many of the Anglo ranchers of Santa Cruz and Monterey counties.

By this time California had a long history of vigilantism. During the first years of the gold rush, California had few jails, no state prison, and little organized government or law enforcement. With few alternatives, the gold-seekers resorted to summary justice: captured thieves were banished, flogged, or branded, and killers were hanged. The example set in the mining camps was copied by the San Francisco Committee of Vigilance, first formed in 1851 and again in 1856, in response to widespread fear of crime and political corruption. After the gold rush, as society became more stable and law enforcement more consistent, vigilante hangings became less frequent. Yet weak and ineffective law enforcement, such as that seen in Monterey County, continued to be a principal cause of vigilantism. Although the San Francisco vigilantes were the most famous, they hanged only eight men. Far more criminals were lynched in lightly populated and poorly policed Monterey and Santa Cruz counties between 1850 and 1877.[19]

Matt Tarpy and his vigilantes, by using informants as well as third-degree techniques on captured suspects, compiled a list of wanted outlaws, including Tiburcio Vasquez, Faustino Lorenzana, Narciso and Gracia Rodríguez, Guadalupe Olivas, and the Rangel brothers from Monterey. While local newspapers launched journalistic attacks on his vigilante group, Matt Tarpy set out to rid the two counties of rustlers. During the next year his band lynched at least six stock thieves, all of them Hispanic.

After the Soap Lake holdup Tarpy and his men began an intensive manhunt for the Vasquez gang. Unlike the Monterey lawmen, Tarpy's riders were persistent and stayed in the field long after the sheriff's posses had quit. But in the end, they had no better luck finding the elusive Tiburcio Vasquez.[20]

CHAPTER TEN

Shootouts and Lynchings

After his escape from Sheriff Watson, Vasquez recalled, "I now turned my steps in the direction of the Gabilan mountains, and then passed through the large towns of Natividad, Salinas, and Watsonville to Santa Cruz, traveling only at night." Tiburcio was accompanied by Francisco Barcenas and Narciso Rodríguez. Santa Cruz had changed greatly from the tiny, sleepy pueblo where Tiburcio had raced horses during the gold rush. Now it was a bustling seaside town of 2,500 people, its streets dotted with hundreds of modern brick and wood-frame buildings. The town thrived on fishing and lumbering. Santa Cruz County boasted twenty-two lumber mills and nine shingle mills. Redwood cut from the massive forests in the Santa Cruz Mountains was used for constructing many buildings in San Francisco and other Bay Area communities. To Vasquez, most of the townsfolk were newcomers. Only his old Californio friends recognized him. He knew he would be well received by the Rodríguez and Lorenzana families, and also by his first cousin Manuel Vasquez, three years his senior. Manuel was a teamster who had moved from Monterey to Santa Cruz in 1865 and settled in a house on Bay Street, near the ocean. Manuel Vasquez was hardworking and well respected, and although he befriended his wayward cousin, he never took part in his crimes.[1]

Tiburcio first sought refuge with his Lorenzana cousins. His old compadre Faustino Lorenzana had been shot to death by lawmen in Santa Barbara County a year earlier. Faustino's brother, Matías, was happy to see him. The ranch of Matías Lorenzana, located in Blackburn Gulch off what is now Vine Hill Road, was in the mountains seven miles north of the Santa Cruz plaza. On a nearby ridge was the ranch owned by his brothers-in-law, the Rodríguez boys. Lorenzana's wife was their eldest sister, María Concepción Rodríguez. The Lorenzana and Rodríguez ranches were remote and Tiburcio felt safe there. But this sanctuary did not last long, as Vasquez later explained:

> I remained at Santa Cruz some days unrecognized, when my presence became known to L.T. Roberts [Robert Liddell], the marshal. One night early, as I was riding through town with one of my companions, a resident of the place, Roberts emerged from a house to halt us. I was on the opposite side of my comrade, when Roberts sang out, "Halt!"
>
> Reining my horse back, and wheeling toward him, I sang out, "Never!"
>
> Simultaneously we exchanged shots. His bullet struck me under the right armpit, passing out back near the spine. Mine struck him in one of the legs. My companion and myself succeeded in gaining a secure hiding place in the mountains, where my wound—at first exceedingly painful—soon healed, and I was once more ready for business.[2]

Tiburcio's account was customarily brief and lacking in any details that would show him in a bad light. The facts are that on the night of September 10, 1871, Vasquez, along with Francisco Barcenas and Gracia Rodríguez, flush with loot from their robbery spree, rode into Santa Cruz, looking for entertainment. It was midnight when they cantered up to Tom Cramer's bordello on the corner of Sand Lane (now called Ocean Street) and Water Street at the outskirts of town. They dismounted and loudly called to the proprietress, Paulina Florini, known as Madam Pauline, for admittance. The three were drunk and rowdy, and Madam Pauline refused to let them inside. Vasquez and his two compadres were enraged. Yanking out their six-shooters, they fired half a dozen shots into the house, shattering all the windows and sending the occupants scampering for cover. One pistol ball crashed through a window and struck Madam Pauline below the breast. Fortunately, she was wearing a corset that had a rigid metal or bone busk in the front. The bullet struck the busk and glanced off harmlessly. Two male customers received minor gunshot wounds.

Tiburcio and his men swung into their saddles and crossed the shallow San Lorenzo River toward the lower plaza. There were several more brothels near the plaza, and the desperadoes may have hoped for a better welcome there. Officer Robert Liddell, patrolling the west side of the San Lorenzo River, ran across the ford where the Water Street bridge is now located. He found Madam Pauline's house "completely riddled by bullets." Liddell was a veteran officer, unafraid of badmen. Five years before, unknown assassins had ambushed him in the river bottom, after first digging a grave for him in the sand. In a sharp gunfight, Liddell had put them to flight. From Madam Pauline the lawman obtained a description of the three assailants and the direction of their escape. Liddell headed after them on foot, crossing back over the river into town. When he came to the lower plaza, now the intersection of Mission, Pacific, Water, and Front streets, he spotted three riders approaching. Even in the darkness he could tell, from their easy grace in the saddle, that they were Californios. Liddell yelled out, "Halt!"

At that, Vasquez, Barcenas, and Rodríguez unholstered their six-guns and opened up with a terrific barrage of pistol fire. Liddell didn't flinch. In an instant his own revolver was in hand, muzzle flaming. As the outlaws' pistol balls thudded into the wall of the Flatiron Building behind him, Liddell stood his ground, firing as quickly as he could thumb the hammer. Suddenly, a bandit's bullet ripped into Liddell's thigh. As the lawman went down, he squeezed off a final shot that tore into Tiburcio's right side and lodged in his back. The robber reeled in the saddle, and was almost unhorsed. Vasquez managed to right himself, and the three bandidos then spurred their animals at full speed down Front Street, firing wildly left and right as they went. Their bullets crashed into the Santa Cruz House hotel, a "hurdy-gurdy" dance hall, and several other buildings lining the street. Perhaps their reckless shooting was simply a result of drunken excitement, or perhaps it expressed their violent contempt for the Anglos who had cluttered the pueblo with their modern buildings and their alien culture. But Vasquez, bleeding profusely, had no such motive. Having received his second serious gunshot wound in less than three months, he merely wanted to escape and get help.

As Liddell sprawled in the dusty street, a hotelkeeper rushed out and carried him into the Pacific Ocean House. His wound was in the fleshy

The lower plaza in Santa Cruz, scene of the 1871 gunfight between Tiburcio Vasquez and police officer Robert Liddell. The Santa Cruz House is at left, with the Flatiron Building in the center. (William B. Secrest collection)

part of the thigh, and proved not to be dangerous. Liddell quickly recovered and returned to his duties. The two wounded customers of the bullet-riddled bagnio proved to be prominent citizens of Santa Cruz. They were forced to leave town to recover from what their wives would describe as "rheumatism." For many years thereafter the bullet holes in the brick face of the Flatiron Building could plainly be seen, much to the delight of small boys. As one of them recalled years later, "We never missed an opportunity to point out the famous bullet holes to a new boy in town."[3]

Tiburcio and his comrades rode back up Branciforte Avenue to the Lorenzana ranch on Vine Hill. Matías's wife, Concepción, dressed his wound and put him to bed. Word of the shootout spread like wildfire and by daylight lawmen and volunteers were hunting the desperadoes. Certain that his house would soon be searched, Matías Lorenzana moved the wounded brigand to a ravine not far from his barn. His brothers-in-law, Narciso and Gracia Rodríguez, knew that they would also be suspected, so they camped with Vasquez and Francisco Barcenas in the ravine. They kept their horses saddled, although Tiburcio was in no condition to ride. Their efforts to hide proved futile. On the night of September 13, three days after the shootout in the plaza, Undersheriff Charlie Lincoln got a tip from Matt Tarpy's vigilante group that some "suspicious looking characters" had been seen near Matías Lorenzana's place.

Charlie Lincoln, an energetic young lawman who had previously served one term as "the boy sheriff" of Santa Cruz County, was eager to capture the desperadoes who had shot Bob Liddell. Securing the assistance of Charles Haynes, Bill Dickerman, and Bob Majors, he rode out to the Lorenzana place at midnight. Majors, the son of a Tennessee mountain man and his Californio wife, both early settlers of Santa Cruz, was a *bravo* and a dead shot. The little posse surrounded the house, then rousted Matías and Concepción and their children from bed. They searched the house from top to bottom but found no trace of the outlaws. In a nearby thicket the possemen discovered three horses, saddled and worn out. Leaving Haynes to guard the house, Lincoln led the others up Blackburn Gulch in a fruitless hunt. When they returned, Haynes told Undersheriff Lincoln that the Lorenzanas' young son Jesús had gone toward the barn, where he had pretended to be talking to the horses. Haynes suspected that he had been speaking to someone inside the barn.

Lincoln posted his men around the perimeter of the barn and entered alone to search it. Six-gun in hand, he went cautiously through the stable but found nothing. He then climbed a thirty-foot ladder to the hayloft. The loft had a low roof, so Lincoln shoved his pistol into his belt and began crawling forward on his hands and knees in the darkness, probing the hay. Suddenly he touched a man's arm. Lincoln had time to see an elaborately patterned velvet vest under the hay just before Francisco Barcenas abruptly bolted upright, a six-shooter in his fist. The young lawman sprang back and reached for his own pistol. To his horror, it was not there, having fallen into the straw. Without hesitating, Lincoln leaped from the loft and dropped to the ground, landing heavily but uninjured. Majors and Haynes rushed into the barn as Barcenas also jumped from the loft. Lincoln yelled, "Shoot, boys! He's coming!"

Barcenas hit the ground with a thud, then sprang to his feet. Lincoln was between the outlaw and the possemen, who held their fire for fear of hitting the officer. Barcenas raised his pistol and fired at Majors but missed. Lincoln rushed for the door, and just as he reached it a second bullet from the bandit's six-gun tore past him. Haynes swung up his weapon, a double-barreled percussion shotgun, and pulled the triggers. Both percussion caps failed to explode. By this time Bob Majors had got his own six-shooter into play. He fired and the ball struck Barcenas full in the mouth. The desperado staggered back and fired again, missing Haynes by two inches. Majors thumbed the hammer and squeezed off a second round, which ripped into Barcenas's head, just below the right eye. The badman dropped to the ground, still trying to recock his revolver, when Bob Majors put a final bullet into him. Francisco Barcenas died instantly.

Lincoln and his posse rode back into Santa Cruz with Matías Lorenzana, the dead bandit's body, the three captured horses, and three riding rigs. In hopes that the dead outlaw would be identified, his corpse was put on display on a board slab in front of the county jail. A large number of townsfolk filed by, and several recognized the dead man. Undersheriff Lincoln also had photographs taken of the body to aid in identification. Newspapers initially reported that the dead outlaw was Procopio, but he was soon properly identified as Francisco Barcenas.[4]

Later that day a warrant charging Tiburcio Vasquez and Narciso Rodríguez with the Soap Lake stage robbery was telegraphed from Monterey and Narciso was quickly placed under arrest. But Vasquez was nowhere to be found. At the first sound of gunfire in the Lorenzana barn, Narciso and Gracia Rodríguez had helped him out of the brushy ravine to the house of Juan Pérez. A tough Californio who ran a fandango hall and bullring by the San Lorenzo River, Pérez was a noted knife fighter with a strong antipathy for Anglos. Happy to help the wounded bandido, Pérez made a bed of straw in his wagon, loaded Vasquez onto it, covered him with hay, and headed out of town unnoticed. He drove Tiburcio south to Watsonville, then east to Hollister, and finally to the New Idria area, a trip of more than one hundred miles. Tiburcio undoubtedly was cared for by his favorite sister, María, in the Vallecitos, and her neighbor, Agustín Hernández, on Griswold Creek.[5]

Tiburcio was soon moved to a remote hideout in Cantua Canyon, south of New Idria. While he struggled to recover from his breast wound, his compadres in Santa Cruz were having trials of their own. Narciso

Rodríguez was lodged in the Monterey jail, under the mistaken belief that the stage robbery had occurred in Monterey County. Matías Lorenzana was kept in the Santa Cruz jail on a charge of harboring the outlaws. No doubt he was terrified, for six years earlier his nephew Pedro Lorenzana had been taken from the same jail by vigilantes and lynched for participating in a murder. Matías spent a week in the lockup. Then, at one o'clock in the morning of September 21, the jailer was wakened by a voice calling, "Wilson, get up. Here is a prisoner."

He opened the jail door and stepped outside, where he was confronted by a crowd of ten to fifteen men, with white neckerchiefs covering their faces. According to later accounts, Undersheriff Charlie Lincoln was part of the mob, as was Matt Tarpy. They seized the jailer, stuffed a handkerchief into his mouth to silence him, and relieved him of the cell keys. While two of the mob kept him secure, the rest entered the jail and dragged Lorenzana outside. The vigilantes took Wilson to the room he shared with his wife, returned the jail keys, and disappeared into the night with the prisoner. They took Lorenzana to his rancho on Vine Hill, where they strung him up on a rope suspended from a tree limb. It was later reported that Charlie Lincoln hoisted him up in an unsuccessful effort to make him reveal what he knew about the outlaw gang. Lorenzana's friend and neighbor, a black ex-slave named Dave Boffman, then interfered by stepping forward and cutting Matías down before he died. But still Lorenzana refused to talk. Finally Matt Tarpy and the others tied him to a tree, stripped off his shirt, and laid on forty lashes with a bullwhip. At that point, according to the *Santa Cruz Sentinel,* "he was turned loose with the admonition to go and sin no more."[6]

The Rodríguez brothers were treated more humanely. On September 29 Narciso was brought to trial in Monterey for robbing the stagecoach driver, Dennis Conroy, at Soap Lake. This happened despite the fact that Sheriff Nick Harris had advised Monterey authorities that the holdup had taken place in Santa Clara County. Conroy identified him as one of the robbers, and Andrew Wasson swore that he was one of the riders who passed him soon afterward. Narciso's parents and an Anglo friend testified that he was at the family home the day of the robbery. The jury did not believe them, and young Rodríguez was sentenced to five years in San Quentin. By this time Sheriff Nick Harris had determined that Bartolo Sepúlveda had nothing to do with the Soap Lake robbery. He now believed that one of the bandits was Gracia Rodríguez, who was picked up in a brothel in Mayfield, now part of Palo Alto. He was charged with five separate counts of robbing passengers on the stage. But at his preliminary hearing two days later, the witnesses could not identify him and the judge dismissed the case. Santa Clara authorities still wanted their pound of flesh from Narciso Rodríguez. In November the grand jury indicted him and Vasquez for the holdup. Six months later he was brought from prison to stand trial in San Jose for robbing passenger Orrin Simmons. The jury deliberated just five minutes before finding Narciso guilty, and the judge sent him back to San Quentin with an additional three years tacked on to his sentence.[7]

Meanwhile Tiburcio was slowly recovering at his Cantua hideout. It was two months before he could get on a horse. He said later, "I was shot through the body, the ball striking me in the right side below the nipple and ranging diagonally, lodged in the back under the left shoulder. It has never been extracted. . . . I was laid up in the Cantua Canyon a long time with the wound." Fortunately for him, the bullet had not hit any vital organs. While he recuperated Vasquez had time to think over his predicament. He had been publicly identified as a stagecoach robber, and another warrant had been issued for his arrest. This had caused great embarrassment to his brothers and sisters, all of whom were honest and upstanding citizens in Monterey County. Tiburcio decided to escape to Mexico, but he needed money for the trip. So when he could again ride, he may have started planning yet another stage robbery.

He rode to San Juan, stopping at the Larios home near Tres Pinos, now called Paicines, twelve miles south of Hollister. The only occupants were María Larios, widow of the prominent Don Manuel Larios, and her sixteen-year-old son, Estolano, who had been educated at the Franciscan College in Santa Barbara. Estolano was reading a Spanish-language edition of the classic novel *Paul and Virginia* when, just before dark, he was startled by the clattering of a horse's hooves in the creek bed. A heavily armed stranger on a large gray appeared in front of the house and greeted them amiably. "I am very hungry," he said in Spanish. "Could I get a bite to eat?"

María Larios never turned a hungry man away from her door, and she invited him to dismount and step inside. The rider led his horse behind the house and tied it out of sight, concealed by an oak tree. Stepping inside, he took a chair, then picked up Estolano's novel and read while María prepared the meal. After supper he said, "I have to keep hidden.

The officers are after me. An officer in Santa Cruz tried to arrest me. I considered myself innocent of any crime and I resisted him. He took a shot at me. The bullet struck me above the collar bone and bored through my left shoulder. I returned the shot and downed the officer. Being on horseback at the time, I got away."

Mother and son exchanged looks and asked, "Aren't you the outlaw, Tiburcio Vasquez?" The stranger replied proudly that indeed he was. Estolano, who had never seen a bullet wound, eagerly asked for a look. Tiburcio removed a large red neckerchief and showed him the wound, which still had not fully healed. Estolano Larios never forgot his meeting with the bandit chieftain.[8]

Soon after, on November 13, 1871, three masked road agents held up the stage from Visalia near the Mountain House in Pacheco Pass. It was close to the spot where Vasquez had robbed the other two coaches a year before. After looting the Wells Fargo express box, which the driver said was "well filled with treasure," the highwaymen escaped. If in fact Tiburcio robbed this stage, either he quickly spent his share of the booty, or it was not enough to pay for a trip to Mexico.[9]

Still searching for funds, he rode to Carmel Valley and called on his brother Antonio. Antonio, ever loyal to Tiburcio, was deeply concerned about his wayward brother and overcome with pity on seeing his frail frame and ugly gunshot wound. By this time Antonio, through hard work and industry, had prospered. His cattle and crops provided a comfortable income that fully supported his wife and seven children. Don Antonio's personal estate was worth $6,000, and though not rich, he was comfortable by the standards of the day. According to George Beers, Antonio gave Tiburcio five hundred dollars "on the bandit's solemn promise to never return to California. Vasquez professed regret that he had brought sorrow on his relatives, who were living respectable lives, and vowed that he would never return to the State." Tiburcio never admitted that he had been helped by his brother; he said merely, "As soon as I was able I went to Mexico, where I remained for three months."[10]

Now flush with cash, Tiburcio took a Mexico-bound coastal steamer to the port of Guaymas. He didn't stay long and by early February was back in San Francisco. The excuse he later gave to his brother Antonio was that soon after arriving in Mexico he was inducted into the Mexican army. He sought help from the American consul at Guaymas, who obtained his release on the grounds that he was an American citizen. The consul, Tiburcio claimed, told him that he "had best leave the country at once and return to California," as he was "liable to be conscripted at any time." Vasquez recalled, "I came back by steamer to San Francisco. Procopio was there then. I immediately left for the lower country, and a short time afterwards Procopio was arrested in the city by Sheriff Morse. . . . I knew the officers wanted me, and San Francisco was no place for me to stay in." His choice to leave the city was indeed a wise one. San Francisco police detectives had been tipped off, probably by a prostitute, that his compadre Procopio had been frequenting a brothel on Morton Street, now called Maiden Lane.[11]

On February 9 the chief of police telegraphed the news to Sheriff Harry Morse in Oakland. Within hours Morse and a deputy had crossed the bay by ferry, bringing a warrant for Procopio's arrest on the charge of stealing John Arnett's cow. The Alameda lawmen, with two police detectives, watched the brothel all night, but Procopio failed to appear. The next afternoon they learned that Procopio had been inside the whole time. While Morse covered the back door, the rest of the little posse stepped to the front entrance. Through a window, the sheriff spotted Procopio eating at a table and watching the front door. As he slipped in through the rear, the other officers barged through the front door. The bandido leaped to his feet and reached for his pocketed pistol. But Morse was on him in an instant. The muscular sheriff seized him by the throat and rammed the barrel of his six-gun into the outlaw's ear. "Put up your hands, Procopio," Morse said quietly. "You're my man."

The desperado had no chance to resist. The arrest of one of California's most notorious bandidos in its most populous city created a sensation, and was even given prominent coverage in newspapers in New York and other eastern cities. Readers were treated to colorful accounts of Procopio's violent career and familial connection to Joaquín Murrieta. E. Z. C. Judson, better known as Ned Buntline, America's most famous dime novelist and the man who had "discovered" Buffalo Bill Cody, promptly authored a blood-and-thunder account, *Red Dick, The Tiger of California*. Procopio was soon brought to trial, convicted of grand larceny, and sentenced to seven years in San Quentin. The irony of this sentence was not lost on the public, as one newspaper editor commented: "There is no doubt but this man has been guilty of all the crimes on the calendar, from petit larceny to murder, and it seems absurd that the only charge that could be made to stick against him should be that of stealing a $75 cow."[12]

Procopio's capture had little effect on Vasquez. He returned to the mountains south of Hollister and made his headquarters at the home of his niece, Concepción Espinosa. Because Doña Guadalupe had raised them together and she was only eight years his junior, she was more like a younger sister than a niece to Tiburcio. Now twenty-eight, she had suffered all her life from the social stigma of her illegitimate birth. But she was good looking and men enjoyed her company. Concepción had married and borne a seven-year-old daughter. But when she and her husband separated, her ensuing poverty forced her to work as a prostitute in Hollister. Then she began living with José Castro, the son of a prominent family that had owned the Rancho San Andres near Watsonville. When the rancho was lost, Castro, like many Californios, came to the remote mountains to claim free government land. He was twenty-eight and exceedingly heavy. He and Concepción owned 160 acres on the San Benito River about thirty miles south of Hollister, as well as a nearby mining claim. Near Pine Rock, several miles north of San Benito, where the stage road crossed their claim, they had a small wood-frame house that doubled as a roadside saloon.[13]

Concepción's half brother Clodoveo Chávez was now twenty-two, big and muscular, standing six feet tall and weighing two hundred pounds. Although not related to Tiburcio by blood, Chávez called him *tío* (uncle). Chávez was a frequent visitor to Castro's saloon and began spending his free time with Vasquez. At that time Chávez was working for Estanislao Hernández, wealthy owner of the huge Rancho Quien Sabe in the mountains east of Hollister. Hernández, a highly respected ranchero, heard rumors that young Chávez was associating with Vasquez and tried in vain to persuade him to stay away from the bandit chief. But Clodoveo idolized Tiburcio and was eager to accompany him on a robbing expedition. Vasquez told him that he first needed armament and a proper riding rig. Tiburcio knew where he could get outfitted without raising suspicions. The previous July the railroad into Hollister had been completed, and the long trip to San Francisco was now easy. Young Chávez, probably for the first time in his life, took the train north through Gilroy and San Jose to San Francisco. There the young vaquero bought a saddle, a bridle, and a pair of six-shooters. Within a few days he was back in Hollister, ready to ride with Tiburcio Vasquez.[14]

The severed head of Clodoveo Chávez, Tiburcio's right-hand man. After Chávez was killed in Arizona in 1875, his head was removed and returned to California for identification. (William B. Secrest collection)

It was second week of April 1872 when Tiburcio and his protégé crossed the Coast Range into the San Joaquin Valley. Vasquez planned to rob the Visalia stage near Kingston, hoping it would be carrying riches from the mines in Inyo County. The old stage road ran west from Visalia to Kingston, where a ferry crossed the Kings River, and then proceeded north to Pacheco Pass. The two bandits made camp north of Kingston and waited for the stage. Vasquez later told George Beers that he and Chávez "overslept three consecutive nights," and the coach passed them while they were slumbering. The pair decided to return to New Idria. It was two o'clock on the afternoon of April 15 when they spotted two men walking along the road in the distance. They were E. A. Bedell and his unnamed partner, who were on their way from the mines at Lone Pine to San Francisco. After spending the night at Kingston, the two miners decided that rather than taking the stage to Gilroy, they would walk north to the Central Pacific railhead, located at the recently completed railroad bridge across the San Joaquin River, north of what would soon become the important town of Fresno.

They had hiked twenty-five miles across the plains and were thirsty and worn out by the time Vasquez and Chávez rode up. Tiburcio wore a black hat, black pants, and a black cloak with a cape, and according to the two miners, "spoke broken English." Chávez wore a dark felt hat, gray pants, and a soldier's overcoat, and "spoke English almost fluently." Each was armed with three six-guns. Bedell's partner asked the two Californios for a drink of water, but they refused. After asking directions to the railroad bridge, the miners proceeded on. Soon, however, they noticed that one of the horsemen was following them at a distance. Half an hour passed, when suddenly the other rider joined him and the two raced their horses up the stage road. Bedell and his partner stepped out of the road to let them pass, but the outlaws abruptly pulled up their horses and covered them with pistols.

"Fall down on your faces and deliver," they ordered. The two miners obeyed immediately, and the bandits tied their hands behind their backs. Vasquez and his compadre took from the pair a hundred dollars, a pistol, a piece of gold bullion, and two penknives. The bandits marched their captives several hundred yards from the road and grilled them separately about the time the stage left Kingston, the number of passengers, and whether it carried any treasure. The two miners were then brought back to the road and forced to lie facedown in the dirt. A driving rain began to fall as the bandits and their captives waited by the road for two hours for the Visalia stagecoach to arrive. As darkness approached, Vasquez concluded that he had again missed the stage and decided to abandon his plans. The two prisoners were untied and ordered to march in the opposite direction, while Vasquez and Chávez headed west toward Panoche Pass and the New Idria Mine.

While Vasquez and Chávez quickly spent their stolen money in the cantinas at New Idria, Bedell and his partner almost perished on the plains. The San Joaquin Valley was then still very sparsely inhabited, with only a handful of ranches and tiny settlements between Visalia and Stockton. The miners pressed on in the dark, but soon wandered off the road, became hopelessly lost, and staggered on through the night without food or water. In the morning Bedell and his partner stumbled into a miner's camp, where they got directions to the railroad, fifty miles distant. They finally reached Stockton that night. The two were exhausted, starving, dehydrated, and barely able to stand, having walked more than seventy-five miles in two days. They made their way to the riverboat landing and managed to borrow enough money to pay their passage to San Francisco. The story of their ordeal was published in at least one newspaper, but Tiburcio's role did not become known until two years later.[15]

Vasquez still wanted to make a big haul in a stagecoach holdup. Within a few days he and Chávez were back at José Castro's saloon. Vasquez explained to Castro his plan to rob the stage that ran from Hollister to the Picacho Mine, near New Idria, and asked for his assistance. But José Castro was no bandit. He was a property owner and a saloonkeeper, and he refused to participate. According to Eugene Sawyer, "Vasquez taunted him with cowardice, when Castro drew a pistol, and the light of Tiburcio Vasquez would have then and there been extinguished, had not the cap of the pistol snapped without igniting the powder." A desperate struggle between the two broke out. Castro was a big, heavyset man, and Vasquez no doubt needed the help of the muscular young Chávez to overpower him. "A reconciliation took place," explained Sawyer, probably brought about by the intervention of Concepción. Although Castro refused to take part in the actual holdup, he agreed to try to find out what treasure the stage would be carrying.

On April 19, 1872, José Castro rode into Hollister and began nosing around. He sought out several stockmen who were visiting town from the mountainous area around New Idria. One was Upton S. Matthis, a well-to-do stock raiser who lived in the Peach Tree Valley and knew Tiburcio Vasquez. Another was a mountain rancher named Doc Garner. Castro learned that Matthis was carrying a large amount of coin. Tiburcio's reluctant accomplice asked Garner several times when he was going back to his ranch in the mountains, and Garner told him that he would be leaving on the next day's stage to New Idria. When Garner asked Castro when he would be returning home, the saloonkeeper replied, "In three or four days."

But early the next morning, before the New Idria stage departed, Castro mounted his horse and raced out of town at breakneck speed. After he left, the stage bound for the Picacho Mine rolled out, followed by Upton Matthis on horseback. José Castro rode so hard that his horse gave out some distance before he reached his saloon at midday. Castro turned the animal loose and hurried up the road on foot. He passed a rancher, "Dutch John" Niesen, who was slowly driving a four-horse team and wagon up the road. Castro rushed into his saloon, where Tiburcio and Clodoveo were waiting. He quickly told Vasquez that Niesen would soon be coming up the road, followed by the stagecoach, and that Upton Matthis would also be passing by. Vasquez and Chávez mounted their horses and headed north on the river road.

The stage road, known as the river route, followed the narrow San Benito River, which is really more of a creek, crossing it frequently. The spot Tiburcio chose for the holdup was the ford where the stage road crossed the shallow streambed, seven miles north of the village of San Benito and a short distance north of Castro's saloon. Here a large sand-stone outcropping, some fifty feet high and three hundred feet long, jutted out next to the river. At its base was a huge oak tree, behind which the outlaws took cover and waited. Each was armed with a six-shooter and a Henry rifle. Soon the heavy wagon of Dutch John could be heard clattering up the road. Vasquez and Chávez donned masks, and as the wagon slowed to cross the rocky streambed, they stepped out and ordered its driver down from his wagon at gunpoint. The robbers took Dutch John and his wagon behind the rock outcropping. Just as they had done five days before, they forced the teamster to lie facedown and then tied his hands behind him. They looted his pockets of twenty-six dollars and held him while they waited for the stage.

It was four o'clock when the coach rattled into sight. George Chick was at the reins, and his passengers were Doc Garner, William Billings, and newlyweds Allen and Belle Leonard. They had been married just five days before and were on their way to their new home in San Benito, where Leonard ran the general store. As Chick slowed to make the crossing, the outlaws halted his coach and forced the passengers out. They were marched up the streambed a short distance, where they were surprised to see Dutch John tied up on the ground next to his wagon and team. The bandits bound the driver and passengers, and put them facedown next to Dutch John. Their pickings were slim indeed. From Chick the bandits took a watch and seven dollars, from Billings a gold watch and twenty-five dollars, and from Doc Garner twenty-one dollars and a new suit of clothes he was carrying. Vasquez then untied Doc Garner, took him back to the stage, and ordered him to break open the trunks and valises and cut open the mailbag. Vasquez and Chávez scattered the contents all over the road but found no valuables. They even broke open the young bride's trunk, but it held nothing but her clothes. After retying Garner, Tiburcio and his compadre mounted their horses and headed back down the road in the direction of Hollister. They had gone a short distance when

Scene of the San Benito stage robbery in 1872, today known as Robbers' Roost. Tiburcio hid behind the large oak tree at its base and robbed the coach a few feet distant, where the old stage road crosses the San Benito River. (Photo by Ray Iddings)

they came upon two young men, George Saul and a youth named Eding, whom they also bound and robbed. From Eding they got just two dollars. Angered, the bandits cursed the youths and told Saul, "You are not worth going through."

Vasquez and Chávez continued north on the road for two miles, and at the spot where Willow Creek empties into the San Benito River they encountered Upton Matthis and another horseman, Charles Pierce, who owned a ranch near San Benito. Matthis was the one Vasquez was looking for. Again, he and Chávez bound both travelers on the roadside, and from Matthis they took $784, but Pierce's pockets were empty. During the robbery, Tiburcio's mask slipped, and Matthis immediately recognized him. Tiburcio seemed unconcerned, and told Matthis, "I could easily escape capture." The two highwaymen then remounted and galloped up the road. Two miles before they reached Tres Pinos they left the road, headed west into the Gabilan Mountains, and disappeared. The spot just south of Cornwell's Crossing where the holdup took place was christened Robbery Gulch, and today is known as Robbers' Roost.[16]

The stage passengers soon managed to get loose. Chick whipped up his team, rushing toward San Benito to raise the alarm. Soon they passed José Castro's saloon. A local farmer, J. Warren Matthews, recorded the events in his diary: "When the stage reached Castro's they found him digging post holes. This looked very suspicious for Joe is very lazy." Soon the other robbery victims arrived in San Benito and exchanged stories about Castro's suspicious behavior in Hollister. It became evident that José Castro had had something to do with the holdups. News of the brazen robberies quickly spread, creating a sensation in eastern Monterey County. Wrote Matthews, "Very great excitement prevails on the river tonight. A number of threats have been expressed against Jose Castro who they think is at the bottom of the affair." The next day, Constable Wilson McCool of Tres Pinos Township obtained a warrant for Castro's arrest and brought him before the local justice of the peace for arraignment. Castro was ordered held for a preliminary hearing. McCool took the prisoner to the ranch of Edward J. Breen, a prominent farmer and survivor of the Donner Party, which was located about two miles from the holdup scene. That night he was placed under guard by McCool, Deputy Constable Lyman Modie, and William Billings, one of the passengers who had been robbed. The following afternoon, April 22, Castro asked McCool to find Edward C. Tully, a lawyer and rancher in the Bitterwater

Valley. While McCool rode off in search of the attorney, Modie and Billings guarded the prisoner in the Breen ranch house.

Shortly after midnight, as the two guards were warming themselves by the fire, the front door was kicked in and a band of eight or nine armed men burst into the house. The guards were ordered to raise their hands, and one of the mob quickly disarmed them. Each of the mob wore a sack mask, with only the eyes visible, and shrouds made from large barley sacks over their clothing. All the talking was done by a single man, whose voice they did not recognize. Lyman Modie was ordered to tie Castro's hands and blindfold him. The vigilantes then stepped outside with their prisoner, telling Modie and Billings to remain inside for an hour and a half, on pain of death. At first light the two guards searched for their erstwhile prisoner. They found him hanging from a large willow tree about three hundred yards from the Breen house. Modie immediately notified the justice of the peace, then rounded up a coroner's jury. One of the jurymen was J. Warren Matthews, who noted in his diary: "Upon repairing to the spot we found the body still dangling in the air. The rope used in hanging him was a very small one, about half inch I think, and well worn. I would not have believed it would have held up the weight of so heavy a man as Castro. Joe's face, eyes and mouth looked natural like and not distorted as I would have supposed. His wrists were tied in front of him and his feet were very close to the ground. We could move his head from side to side very easily and as his other joints were very stiff we concluded that his neck was broken."[17]

The coroner's jury found that the hanging had been "perpetrated by parties to us unknown." Who lynched José Castro? One of the prime suspects is Matt Tarpy, for the crime bore all the earmarks of the summary executions carried out by his vigilante group. The victim had been removed from confinement at night by a small group of masked men and quickly strung up, something Tarpy had done at least half a dozen times. Matt Tarpy had led numerous manhunts in the mountainous country south of Hollister. While lynchings of stage robbers were exceedingly rare in California, Tarpy had made a specialty of lynching Hispanic thieves. Although during the gold rush robbers were sometimes lynched due to a lack of secure jails to hold them, by the 1870s vigilantes hanged men for murder, not robbery. Matt Tarpy, on hearing that Vasquez had robbed another stagecoach, had ample time—two days—to ride to the scene from his ranch near Watsonville and organize a lynch mob. Lastly, Tiburcio

Vasquez was high on Tarpy's blacklist, and as we have seen, Vasquez was acutely aware that Tarpy wanted to capture him.

There are other suspects in the Castro hanging as well. Years later, during the investigation of the 1885 murder of Dr. A. W. Powers in the same area, public accusations were made that some of the same vigilantes who plotted to kill Dr. Powers had also lynched José Castro. The leaders of the 1885 mob were John Prewett, a local rancher, and his brother-in-law, Andrew Irwin. Although no link between the two crimes was ever proven, it is possible that Matt Tarpy acted in concert with Prewett, Irwin, and others to lynch José Castro.[18]

Vasquez always maintained that José Castro had no involvement in the holdups, declaring, "José Castro was an innocent man. He was caught and hanged by the vigilantes for the robbery, but he had nothing to do with it whatever. He is dead now, and I speak the truth and do justice to him. I was the man who planned and executed the robberies. I had one assistant, a young man, but I cannot give you his name. . . . He [Castro] kept a saloon on the San Benito a short distance from the place where the stage was stopped. His wife was Concepción Espinosa, who is a distant relation of mine. I used to happen into the saloon once in a while. In fact I was there immediately preceding the robbery, and I suppose that the people suspected [Castro] for these reasons. But not only was he innocent of taking an active part, but he knew nothing whatever about the matter beforehand."[19]

Vasquez later admitted to George Beers that it was Clodoveo Chávez who had assisted him in the robberies. But it is plainly untrue that José Castro was not involved; the evidence against him is especially compelling. Tiburcio also falsely identified Concepción as a "distant relation." There can be little doubt that he lied to protect his niece. He had already brought tragedy and grief into her life, and now she had to live with the stigma of being connected to a lynched criminal. But neither Concepción nor José Castro's family blamed Tiburcio for his role in Castro's death. For them, blame lay squarely on the gringos who had hanged him.

CHAPTER ELEVEN

Ride the High Country

The lynching of José Castro rattled Tiburcio Vasquez to the core. For the first time he had visited violence and death upon a member of his own family. At the same time Vasquez had a wholesome dread of Matt Tarpy and his vigilantes, who had no intention of bringing him in alive. Tiburcio decided to disappear until the excitement died down, and for more than a year he committed no known robberies. He spent most of that period, sometimes alone and sometimes with compadres, riding the high country south of Hollister. His range was and still is exceedingly remote: the Pinnacles, Panoche Valley, Hernandez Valley, the New Idria Mine, Cantua Canyon, and countless isolated gorges and creek bottoms high in the Coast Range. Many more people lived in this remote area in the 1870s than today because settlers, both Anglo and Hispanic, could claim free government land. Many of them—especially Californios and Mexicans—were impoverished, and these mountains, lush in the winter but harsh and dry in the summer, offered a new start. From the late 1850s on, large numbers of Californios from Monterey and Santa Cruz counties, having lost their valuable lands in the Salinas and Pajaro river valleys, relocated to homestead claims high in the Coast Range.

Many others sought work in the New Idria Mine. Situated sixty-five tortuous miles south of San Juan, New Idria, discovered in 1854, was one of the largest quicksilver mines in North America. The mine headquarters, post office, shops, church, school, and furnaces were located in a deep bowl, surrounded by 4,500-foot peaks and ridges. The slopes and ridges 2,000 feet above were honeycombed with tunnels. In the early 1870s it employed some seven hundred men, primarily Californio, Mexican, and Chileno. Many were skilled miners, while others were woodcutters who provided fuel for the furnaces. They lived with their families in two villages of wooden shacks. Mexican Camp was situated on a two-acre flat some two thousand feet above and south of the bowl, and a one-mile trip from mine headquarters by foot or donkey over rough mountainside trails. A mile southwest of the bowl, perched precariously on a sloping ridge, was Chileno Camp. Both were favorite haunts of Tiburcio Vasquez for their saloons, gambling halls, and bordellos. And if he had to escape, a trail from New Idria to Cantua Canyon ran east along the east fork of San Carlos Creek and over the high ridge to the headwaters of Cantua Creek where there was a small settlement of adobes, occupied by herders. Cantua Creek (known as "the Cantua") was sacred ground for California outlaws, for the spot where it empties into the San Joaquin plain is where Joaquín Murrieta was slain in 1853. And the creek itself was first explored by José de Guadalupe Cantúa, Tiburcio's great-uncle.

East of New Idria and the Cantua, located along the west side of the San Joaquin Valley, were a number of small, isolated Hispanic settlements, mostly clusters of adobe houses and brush huts. They would be of utmost importance to Tiburcio Vasquez and his band. Many of them had been ancient Indian villages that over the years, through emigration and intermarriage, had become primarily Californio and Mexican. There, peones eked out a precarious living, tilling the arid land and raising a few head of sheep and cattle. These settlements, now vanished, also served as watering places along El Camino Viejo a Los Ángeles (the Old Road to Los Angeles), known to Anglos as the Los Angeles Trail. It ran south from the Livermore Valley along the base of the Coast Range on the west side of the San Joaquin Valley, then through Tejon Pass into Southern California. The old trail wandered lazily from one *aguaje,* or watering hole, to another, over hills and arroyos, and through tule swamps and barren alkali desert. From El Camino Viejo, smaller trails led high into the Coast Range along a number of creeks: Little Panoche, Big Panoche, Cantua, Alcalde, Jacalitos, and Zapato Chino. Beginning in the gold rush, these lonely, isolated pueblos became favorite hideouts for fugitives and thieves.

Northeast of New Idria, located on a spur of El Camino Viejo, were the two largest and most notorious settlements: Pueblo de las Juntas (The Junctions) and Rancho de los Californios, known to Anglos as California

Blacksmith shop and miners' houses at New Idria, Tiburcio's favorite hideout. (Author's collection)

Ranch. Las Juntas was located on the west bank of the San Joaquin River, at its confluence with Fresno Slough, about three miles northeast of present-day Mendota. One of the oldest communities in Fresno County, it boasted some 250 Hispanic settlers in the early 1870s. Like the other pueblos, it consisted of a cluster of mud-and-brush jacales with tule-thatched roofs and was served by a general store and saloon built of rough-hewn lumber, with board-and-batten construction. The isolation of Las Juntas made it an ideal hideout for bandits, both Anglo and Hispanic, and it was the scene of many shooting and cutting scrapes.

Twelve miles east, on the south bank of the San Joaquin River north of the present-day town of Kerman, was Rancho de los Californios. It was located on the stage road that crossed the valley from Pacheco Pass to Millerton. On either side of the road were many adobes and mud-covered brush huts. This settlement also had a substantial saloon and general store, owned by Pedro Aguirre. Just north of the pueblo was a large section of land called Chidester's Island, cut off by two channels of the San Joaquin River and covered with an almost impenetrable thicket of underbrush and willows. There, in the mid-1860s, Anglo and Hispanic outlaws had built a stockade made of logs that had drifted downstream from the Sierra Nevada. Its log cabins were surrounded by an outer wall twelve feet high, made from upright timbers partly buried in the ground. By the early 1870s Rancho de los Californios had a population of about three hundred, greater than that of the county seat at Millerton. Although most of the settlers in Las Juntas and Rancho de los Californios lived quiet, pastoral existences, the large numbers of hardcases who drifted in and out of these communities made them the most notorious and lawless in the San Joaquin Valley. The Hispanic settlers, some through friendship and some through fear, kept secret the comings and goings of the outlaws.[1]

The next settlement south on the meandering Camino Viejo was Poso Chane, a tiny village of a dozen small jacales situated where three creeks—Jacalitos, Los Gatos, and Alcalde (now Warthan)—flowed into a marshy lowlands six miles east of the present-day town of Coalinga. Its name meant "watering hole of the Chane Indians." In those years it was a verdant oasis in the arid alkali plain, but by 1900 the marsh had gone dry and now nothing is left. Southernmost on El Camino Viejo was the little pueblo of San Emigdio, a lush, garden-like spot where a grove of poplar and cottonwood trees shaded the adobe huts of Hispanics and Indians whose gardens were watered by tiny streams that branched in every direction. During the 1870s it was home to about 150 people, with some thirty adobe houses, a small church, a store, and two grave-yards. It was situated near the mouth of San Emigdio Canyon in Kern County, about fifteen miles west of what is now the Grapevine exit on Interstate 5. Today nothing remains of any of these settlements.[2]

Within a few weeks after José Castro's lynching, Tiburcio and Clodoveo rode south to Poso Chane. It was a picturesque spot, lush with willow trees, tules, and large numbers of birds and wildlife. Its most prominent settler was Narciso Higuera, who had settled there with his family in 1854. Higuera herded horses and cattle and lived in a two-room jacal constructed of mud and brush, situated on Jacalitos Creek a mile and a half upstream from Poso Chane. Higuera was friendly with both Tiburcio and Procopio, and Vasquez enjoyed his hospitality as they rested, basking in the warm spring weather at the edge of the alkali plains.[3]

After a twenty-day respite in Poso Chane, Tiburcio and Clodoveo rode south toward San Emigdio. From there they swung east, crossing the Tehachapi Mountains to Elizabeth Lake, an oasis on the edge of the Mojave Desert, forty miles due north of Los Angeles. A few miles away, in Leonis (now Leona) Valley, lived Tiburcio's brother Chico, who worked for the well-known rancher Francisco "Chico" López. Chico Vasquez, who was highly respected and had served as the township's justice of the peace, had seen very little of Tiburcio over the years. Chico reintroduced Tiburcio to his wife, María, now thirty-six, and their six children. The eldest, Felicita, was sixteen, and the youngest, only a year old. Tiburcio was using an alias—Ricardo Cantúa—and Francisco kept his brother's identity secret, even to his own children, which was to prove a serious mistake.

Through Chico's connections, Tiburcio met many area rancheros. None knew who he was, except for Jim Hefner, who ran a stage stop at Elizabeth Lake. A forty-seven-year-old blacksmith, Hefner was married to Margarita Ruiz, twenty-three, who was reportedly related to the Vasquez family. Near the stage road Hefner had erected two single-story frame houses with high-pitched roofs, connected by a patio or breeze-way. One served as a stage station and rooming house, the other as their home, where Vasquez was always welcome. A few hundred yards from Elizabeth Lake was the crude board saloon run by August de Bert, a hard-drinking French Canadian. His real name was reportedly August Ferlin, and he was commonly known as the "humpbacked Frenchman." De Bert and Vasquez became good friends. Tiburcio probably did not

Jim Hefner's house and stagecoach stop at Elizabeth Lake, a favorite hideout of Tiburcio Vasquez. (Charles Miller collection)

exaggerate when he later claimed that he was "the most popular man in the neighborhood, taking part in all the amusements of the people."[4]

From Elizabeth Lake, Tiburcio made a number of visits to Los Angeles. To avoid raising suspicion, he often went unarmed. In the Spanish-speaking section, called Sonoratown, were many monte halls, fandango houses, and saloons, where Vasquez was in his element. His favorite woman there was a Mexican prostitute known as La Coneja, The Rabbit. Vasquez later recalled that he befriended Eulogio Celis, son of a prominent ranchero of the San Fernando Valley. One day Celis had to ride from Los Angeles to San Fernando, and Tiburcio lent him a pistol for self-protection. Vasquez saw the irony in that, for he later laughingly recalled that Celis had no idea he was an outlaw.[5]

Chico's wife, María, had a nineteen-year-old cousin, José Jesús López, who would later serve for many years as majordomo of the enormous Rancho El Tejon. His father owned a stagecoach stop, general store, and saloon called Lopez Station, now covered by the Upper Van Norman Reservoir in the city of San Fernando. This spot was about halfway between Los Angeles and Elizabeth Lake, and Tiburcio stopped there frequently. Young López vividly recalled Tiburcio during his visit that spring: "He had a good saddle and riding rig, carried the best of Colt revolvers, and had a fine watch and chain. Always, he wore a fine black broadcloth cape, I believe for the purpose of enabling him to draw a knife or his revolver unnoticed. . . . He represented himself to be Don Ricardo Cantua, using his mother's maiden name as a surname. . . . He dressed well, wearing a good black felt-brimmed hat, the broadcloth cape, a good suit of clothes, and well polished boots." López recalled that Tiburcio spent a week at the station, playing poker in the saloon, before he rode off. It would be two years before the López family learned who their guest really was.[6]

After several months in Los Angeles County, Vasquez and Chávez, their funds running low, headed back north along El Camino Viejo to their old stomping grounds in the mountains near the New Idria Mine. Fifteen miles south of New Idria, in Griswold Canyon, lived Tiburcio's old friend Agustín Hernández, brother of Domingo Hernández, the notorious bandit and killer who had been lynched in Santa Cruz in 1852. Agustín Hernández had settled with his wife, Natividad, and seven children, some of them young adults, on a homestead claim about five miles south of Panoche on the New Idria Road. His small, two-room wood-frame house and stable, which are no longer standing, stood on a terrace above Griswold Creek. A spring still flows into the creek at this point, providing a year-round source of water, even when the creek is dry in the summer. Here the canyon walls rise one thousand feet, and behind the house grew a large acacia tree, with a five-acre fruit orchard and vegetable garden just south of it. Hernández grazed twenty head of cattle on the nearby hills, and had fenced twenty-five acres along the creek where he grew wheat, barley, and hay. The household furnishings were sparse: a wood stove, two beds, a little furniture, a table, and chairs. The children slept on the floor. They were poor but self-sufficient. Agustín Hernández's little ranch and mode of life were similar to those of most of the mountain homesteaders, both Anglo and Hispanic. It is little wonder that they welcomed a friendly bandit like Tiburcio, who was willing to pay in coin for food and shelter.[7]

Just north of Griswold Canyon was Panoche Valley, about ten miles long and two miles wide, surrounded by high rolling hills and rocky peaks. Here lived Joaquín Castro, father of the lynched José Castro, with another son, Juan. Like Concepción Espinosa, he did not blame Vasquez for his son's death. Tiburcio visited Castro's place often, and Clodoveo Chávez moved in with him, probably working for room and board. A few miles south of Griswold Canyon was a small valley, the Vallecitos. Here Tiburcio's sister María and her husband, Manuel Lara, had relocated from San Juan. Tiburcio's niece Concepción moved to New Idria and the nearby San Carlos Mine, where she got by as a prostitute. A short distance west lived Tiburcio's good friend Lorenzo Vasquez. Although widely believed to be Tiburcio's cousin, Lorenzo was no relation. Fifty-two and an emigrant from Mexico, Lorenzo Vásquez owned a 160-acre homestead at Sweetwater Spring on the Hernandez Road, a location to this day known as Lorenzo Vasquez Canyon. He built a frame house and barn where he lived with wife, Paula, brother, Loreto, and two adopted children. Tiburcio was always a welcome visitor at these homes. He seldom stayed more than a day or two, drifting from one place to another. He supported himself by gambling at New Idria and by occasional theft of sheep or cattle. He reportedly made a raid in nearby Peach Tree Valley and ran off a band of stock belonging to cattle baron Henry Miller.[8]

Tiburcio began to look for new riders to replace his old compadres who had been killed or imprisoned, recruiting from the young vaqueros and miners of Monterey, San Benito, and Fresno counties. In New Idria he found his first cousin from Gilroy, Teodoro Moreno, twenty-eight years old, tall and slender, as well as Romulo Gonzáles, a Mexican woodchopper. He was later joined by August de Bert, who wanted to try his hand as a highwayman. Tiburcio sometimes recruited youths by promising them excitement and easy money. But on at least one occasion he did the opposite. In 1873, a teenaged Victor Gardenas was working as a vaquero on the ranch of Jesús Sotelo near Soledad. Despite his youth he possessed physical size, strength, and skill with horses and firearms. Gardenas recalled, "When I was fourteen years old the Vasquez gang came to the Sotelo ranch and they urged me to join their group. I hesitated, knowing their reputation. They talked with me for about an hour with Vasquez astride his horse a short distance away. Finally Vasquez rode up and told his men to leave me alone. He then gave me the advice I shall never forget when he said, 'My child, it is very wise of you to not follow our gang, because this is a sad life. Sometimes you don't eat or sleep, always waiting for the enemy to overcome you.'"[9]

New Idria remained his favorite hideout, a place he felt safe. William H. Brewer, who visited New Idria some years before, described its isolation: "I can hardly conceive a place with fewer of the comforts of life than these mines have—a community by itself . . . separated from the rest of the world by desert mountains, a fearfully hot climate where the temperature for months together ranges from 90° to 110°F, where all the necessities of life have to be brought from a great distance in wagons in the hot sun. As might be expected, little besides the bare necessities of life is seen, and if any luxuries come in, it is only at an extravagant price."[10]

New Idria was so remote that the closest lawman was a day's ride away. Bandits and fugitives were generally tolerated there as long as they caused no trouble. When they did commit a serious offense, a message would be sent by stagecoach for a deputy sheriff to come from Hollister to investigate. Of Tiburcio's sojourn in New Idria, Eugene Sawyer wrote:

> In the hills he was comparatively safe. White settlers were scarce, and the native Californian population, almost to a man, aided and befriended him, principally through fear. He was known to have appeared openly at the New Idria Mine on several occasions. The law abiding people in that section were prevented from doing anything toward bringing the bandit to justice through fear of the consequences. It is very probable that the Mexicans there would have backed Vasquez against any attempt at arrest. One superintendent, from motives of policy, permitted Vasquez to come to the mine without molestation, as long as he committed no depredations there. And it is a fact that Vasquez never troubled the miners, or even cast a covetous eye on any of their horses. Several bold attempts to capture the bandit at the mine were made by Sheriff Adams of Santa Clara County, but on every occasion, in spite of disguise and the utmost secrecy, so Vasquez says, he was apprised of the officer's movements and design before half of each journey was made.[11]

Like Sheriff Adams, Monterey County lawmen made several ineffective efforts to capture Vasquez at New Idria. But Tiburcio had so many friends among the Spanish-speaking population, and among some of the Anglo settlers, that he easily evaded capture. On one occasion a three-man posse rode into New Idria looking for the bandit chieftain, acting on a tip from a convict who had known him in San Quentin. They sought out mine superintendent John W. C. Maxwell, who stated that he did not know Tiburcio's whereabouts. After a fruitless three-hour search, they headed back toward Hollister. Vasquez watched them ride off from his

New Idria Mine headquarters as it looked in Tiburcio's day. (Author's collection)

hiding place in a small cabin on San Carlos Creek, which ran through the mine property. That night the posse camped in the Panoche Valley, on the road to Hollister. When they awoke in the morning, their horses were gone. Tiburcio later gave his version of this affair to Eugene Sawyer, adding with a chuckle, "Smart boys. I saw them all the time they were looking for me, and when they left I made up my mind to play a trick on them, and I am sure they knew where their horses went to."[12]

Maxwell was the superintendent of New Idria for many years. He and his assistant Thomas N. Williams, a Cornish mining engineer, had an awkward, uneasy relationship with the Vasquez gang. They had an informal agreement to allow the band to stay provided they did not steal mine property. Maxwell had a number of encounters with the bandit chieftain. Once Vasquez visited him several days after a robbery in the San Joaquin Valley to ask for a newspaper account of the incident. On another occasion a member of the gang got drunk and insulted Maxwell, who drew a pistol and ordered the desperado out of the camp. As the outlaw rode off, Maxwell fired a shot over his head to hasten his departure. The following day, an angry Vasquez called on Maxwell and told him, "My men have orders to raise no disturbance in this camp. If any of them do cause any trouble, notify me and I will deal with them, but do not shoot them." After an angry exchange of words with Maxwell, Vasquez stormed out with a final vow:"If you had killed him I would not have left an Americano alive in Idria."[13]

D. F. McPhail, a merchant and teamster from Tres Pinos, had a contract to haul grain from Hollister to New Idria. One night his team was stolen, and he reported the theft to Maxwell. The superintendent sent for one of Tiburcio's men, and demanded, "What do you mean by running off these horses? You have violated your agreement, and you get them back here immediately." The bandido retorted that the horses belonged to McPhail, not to the mining company. Maxwell, however, insisted that the animals were used on mine business and were protected property. He demanded, "You tell Vasquez I will give him until noon tomorrow to bring back those horses." The next morning McPhail had his team back. Obviously, Tiburcio was far more interested in having a safe hideout and Maxwell's grudging cooperation than a team of draft horses.[14]

Jeremiah J. Croxon, who was sheriff of San Benito County from 1898 to 1934, recalled an encounter with Tiburcio Vasquez in 1873, when he was about sixteen. Croxon's parents had settled at New Idria, and one night a saloonkeeper, Manuel Gonzáles, invited the youth to a fandango in Mexican Camp. As they approached the dance hall, a Mexican sentry demanded of Gonzáles, "Who is that you have with you?" Gonzáles vouched for young Croxon and they were allowed to proceed, but were quickly stopped by three more Mexicans, and Gonzáles told them that the Anglo youth was "all right." Croxon enjoyed the fandango, but he suspected something was wrong, and when there was a break in the music he asked Gonzáles if Tiburcio Vasquez was present. "There he is, right there," Gonzáles replied. "He just danced that set with you."

A frightened Croxon told the saloonkeeper he wanted to leave, but Gonzáles assured him that he was safe. Croxon then joined in *el jarabe tapatío,* the Mexican hat dance. At the end of el jarabe it was the custom for the crowd to toss money at the feet of the most graceful dancers. A silver dollar was thrown in front of the young señorita who had danced with Croxon, but it rolled through a crack in the floor. Not about to let that much money get away, the youth rushed outside and crawled under the building to retrieve the coin. As he groped his way in the dark, his hands fell upon a small stack of firearms that had been secreted under the building. Evidently they belonged to the Vasquez band, for at the same time a menacing voice hissed at him in the darkness, "Atrás!" [Go back!] Jere Croxon never got the silver dollar and never saw Tiburcio Vasquez again.[15]

Another of Tiburcio's mountain hideouts, according to an old tradition, was a large talus cave in what is now Pinnacles National Monument. A popular tourist spot in the 1920s and '30s when it was called Vasquez Cave, today it is known as the Bear Gulch Cave. Given that Tiburcio had many friends nearby who were willing to shelter him, it seems improbable that he would live in a cave. However, the Vasquez Cave tradition dates to the nineteenth century, so perhaps he did use this hideout from time to time. There is no doubt that Tiburcio frequented the Pinnacles region. One day Henry Melendy, who owned a nearby ranch at the north end of Bear Valley, was searching for stray stock when he came across Vasquez and his band camped out at Willow Spring, just north of the Pinnacles. Several of the outlaws were barbecuing a beef, while others engaged in target practice.[16]

Clodoveo Chávez was particularly friendly with Henry Melendy and his family. He was a frequent visitor to the Melendy ranch, often while Henry's young wife, Deborah Shell Melendy, was home alone with her three small children, whom he seemed to enjoy entertaining. No doubt the friendship had begun before he had turned outlaw. On one occasion Deborah was hanging the laundry when a hungry Chávez rode up in time for the midday meal. At Deborah's request, Chávez watched her baby while she went inside and prepared lunch. She and her family considered Vasquez and his men "kind-hearted, genial fellows, never giving them trouble. Especially is this true of Chaves [sic] who was . . . always gentlemanly and courteous, kind and sociable." For more than a century the Melendy family would consistently recall the jarring image of the ferocious outlaw cradling Deborah's infant.[17]

But Deborah's younger sister had a different experience with Tiburcio Vasquez. Susan Shell, eighteen years old and unmarried in 1872, was a pretty, slender girl whose stunning good looks are proven in a carte-de-visite photograph owned by her descendants. She had a reckless, perhaps even fearless, streak and could ride bareback standing up. Susan lived with her mother, stepfather, and siblings on the Bacon ranch, located near the Pinnacles. One day she was carrying a full bucket of water from the well to the ranch house when Vasquez rode up. She recognized him immediately. He asked for a drink of water, and Susan filled the dipper and handed it to him. Tiburcio reached down for it without dismounting, but instead of taking the dipper, he gently stroked her under the chin. Offended by the unwanted attention, she dashed the ladle of water into his face. The surprised Tiburcio grinned broadly at her. Wiping his wet face with the back of his hand, he tipped his hat, then wheeled his horse and started off. When Susan rushed into the house she discovered her brother, John Shell, twenty-two, and her half brother, Oliver Bacon, fifteen, with their guns trained on Vasquez through a window. They had watched the whole scene. As Susan's granddaughter recalled years later, "Had he shown one movement of harm to their sister, the brothers would have shot him."[18]

Susan always scoffed at the idea that Vasquez sought shelter in caves or other outdoor hideouts, because he could obtain support from local ranchers. She recalled that "he and his outlaw men rode horseback to the different ranches to obtain what they needed. It was usually food, sometimes livestock, they took [and] didn't pay for what they took. . . . The ranches were far from each other and far from any legal protection. The ranchers knew who the bandits were and avoided actual confrontation with Tiburcio and his outlaw men."[19]

Many of Susan's neighbors viewed Vasquez more positively. One early Bear Valley resident recalled that Tiburcio was "a genial, light hearted character [and] a good conversationalist," adding "that Vasquez was a most affable person all the pioneers . . . fully agreed. I suppose that was why he could roam the country in such an open manner." Other pioneers insisted that Tiburcio routinely paid for food and shelter. One morning, mounted on a big palomino horse, he and a compadre rode onto John Prater's place near Tres Pinos. They stepped into the kitchen, and without doffing their hats, sat down and consumed a plentiful breakfast cooked by Prater's wife, Charlotte. As the bandit chief got up to leave, he put a silver dollar on the table and said simply, "Bueno, adiós."[20]

Vasquez and members of his band stopped frequently at the place of T. H. "Hugh" French, who owned a squatter's claim near Lone Tree, in the mountains northeast of Hollister. Although later in life French became a wealthy land baron, during the early 1870s he lived in a primitive mountain cabin made of brushwood, raising a few head of cattle. In old age he recalled that he had been "well acquainted with Tiburcio Vasquez . . . and as a matter of 'safety first,' kept on good terms with him." Vasquez and members of his band often visited French's place, sometimes sleeping

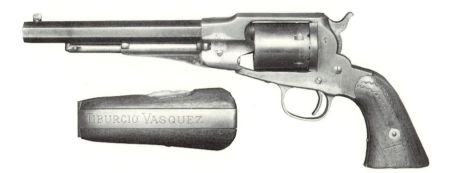

This revolver, a .36 Caliber Remington Navy, serial no. 40280, converted to fire metallic cartridges circa 1870, bears the bandit chieftain's name in a very old inscription on the backstrap. (Author's collection)

in his cabin and cooking their meals in his fireplace. They always brought their own provisions and although they usually feasted on stolen beef, they never harmed French nor drove off any of his cattle.[21]

Of all the Anglo settlers, none was as close to Tiburcio Vasquez as the Tully family. Edward C. Tully was a prominent, forty-seven-year-old rancher from Tennessee who settled in the Bitterwater Valley in 1861. He spoke Spanish and had lived in Mexico, where he married Guadalupe de Álvarez. Also a lawyer, he served several terms in the California legislature. Because his wife was Mexican, Ed Tully was close to the Hispanic community and was highly respected by both Anglos and Californios. He first encountered Vasquez when the outlaw sent word that he would like to meet him. Tully replied, "I'd rather not, but if he treats me kindly I'll not bother him." Tully's grandson later recalled, "Vasquez hated gringos but as my grandmother was born in Mexico he did not molest us. Once some Tully sheep were stolen. . . . . Not long after they were all back on the ranch—Vasquez had ordered it so, we heard, because he recognized the heart brand of the Tullys."[22]

Tiburcio's cousin and fellow gang member Teodoro Moreno worked off and on for Ed Tully as a sheepshearer and wool tier. But Vasquez's own visits to the Tully ranch were mostly of a nocturnal nature. From time to time, the Tully children would be awakened by an awful commotion in the middle of the night, with a great deal of stomping of hooves and neighing of horses in the corral. The children would bound out of bed and head for the door, but were stopped by their father who, with a finger to his lips, would caution them in Spanish, "Be quiet and go back to bed!" In the morning they would rush down to the corral and to their amazement not a Tully horse would be in sight. In their place was a whole string of horses the children had never seen before. A month or two would pass, then the whole process would be repeated—first midnight noise and commotion in the corral, then at daybreak all of the Tully horses would be back in the corral and the strange animals gone. The children later learned from their parents that the nocturnal visits had been from Tiburcio Vasquez and his band, borrowing fresh horses.[23]

Ed Tully's brother-in-law, Francisco de Álvarez, had a sheep ranch nearby. Francisco's son later recalled Tiburcio's visits. "My father knew him quite well. Vasquez would come to Dad's sheep camp and ask for a meal. Dad would say, 'Come on in and eat but then you'll have to leave.'" On one occasion, Vasquez bought some saddle horses from Álvarez. The sheepman kept Tiburcio's letters of sale as a memento, but apparently felt remorse over his dealings with the bandit—the money he received was undoubtedly stolen—and burned the letters before his death in 1923.[24]

Joaquín Bolado also experienced Tiburcio's need for fresh horses. Bolado was a prosperous Spaniard who purchased part of the Rancho Santa Ana in 1867 and built a home northeast of Tres Pinos. From time to time Vasquez stayed on his property, near present-day Bolado Park. On Tiburcio's trips into the mountains, he would occasionally leave a jaded horse with Joaquín Bolado in exchange for a fresh mount.[25]

Not all the mountain settlers welcomed Tiburcio's visits. Henry and Sarah Akers Chambers settled in the Hernandez Valley in 1869 at a ranch not far from that of Lorenzo Vásquez. In 1873 Tiburcio Vasquez, accompanied by several Portuguese drovers, herded a band of sheep across their ranch. Their then-teenage son James vividly recalled the incident many years later:

> When a boy of fifteen, I first met Tiburcio Vasquez. He was piloting some Portuguese through Hernandez Valley with their sheep which were grazing along the edge of our range. Vasquez said he was going to feed off a certain mountain, part of which was on our range, so my father asked some of the neighbors to help drive the sheep and see that they did not trespass. Mr. Short, Mr. Button, and two of his oldest boys, Ival and Ira, father, and myself composed the crowd.

Occasionally Vasquez would say, "Leave them sheep alone." Father told him that we would when we got them away from there and not before. We drove over as far as the ranch belonging to Lorenzo Vasquez, a cousin [sic] of Tiburcio Vasquez. There we got in below and headed them off and held them there for awhile, so finally they decided to take the road toward Hollister. That was the last we saw of Vasquez for some time.

One day I had been on the mountain looking for cattle, and I decided to go to Lorenzo's place. It happened that Tiburcio was there and about ready to leave, so I rode along with him a distance of three or four miles. He said he was going to Vallecitos, which was on my road home. He was very talkative and used very good English. He was about thirty-five years of age, rather good looking, seemed intelligent, and did not have the appearance of a desperado at all. His voice was like that of a woman.[26]

Henry Chambers's brother-in-law was Anderson Akers, a Kentuckian and a veteran of the Mexican War. He too was a stock raiser in the Hernandez Valley. Once Akers was on his way home after selling a herd of cattle in Hollister. He had not gone far past the village of San Benito when he was stopped by Tiburcio Vasquez and several of his men. Akers was unshaven and wearing ragged clothes, and the long trip had left him dirty and unkempt.

"Where you going, old man?" they asked.

"Oh, up the river," was the answer.

"Where'd you get these fine-looking horses?" inquired one, as he examined Akers's team.

"Belongs to my wife. No good 'cept pulling wagons," Anderson replied.

"Got any money or valuables?" asked another, looking over the poorly dressed rancher doubtfully.

"Do I look like I got anything?" answered Anderson. At that, Vasquez and his men roared with laughter. They rode off, with a parting comment that they should probably give some money to the impoverished-looking Akers. The stockman breathed a sigh of relief, for a small sack of gold coin, the proceeds from the cattle sale, was concealed under the floorboards of his wagon.[27]

Tiburcio, always the ladies' man, was particularly drawn to ranchos with unattached young women. James McGrury, an early rancher in

Bear Valley, wrote that Vasquez was "quite at home" in the area near Tres Pinos, where "there were several senoritas living. . . . Black Hill, three miles to the south of Tres Pinos, was another locality where the outlaw called regularly when passing through. Here also resided several Spanish damsels ready to greet him with a smile." Tiburcio was friendly with Ben Williams, an old hunter and trapper who settled on isolated Lewis Creek, south of Hernandez Valley, and had several pretty daughters. One of them, Julia, married their neighbor Guadalupe Olivas, a member of the Vasquez gang, in about 1872. A younger daughter, Millie, was twelve that year, and in old age remembered Tiburcio's many visits to their ranch. "I knew Vasquez the bandit. He was very polite when he came to our house. He never killed anyone as far as I know. . . . None of his gang would stop, just him. We never asked any questions."[28]

Tiburcio, of course, did not restrict his attentions to single women. According to newspaperman Boyd Henderson, he had several paramours in northern Los Angeles County. Beers said that one was "a married woman now living on the Placeritas; her husband is so notably an admirer of Vasquez as not to object to the liaison. She is a slovenly, unattractive woman, about thirty years old. On the Llano Verde there lives a volup-tuously formed young woman who is now and has been for some time the recipient of Vasquez's impure love." One of Tiburcio's lovers, whose identity is unknown, bore him a son named Rodolfo. Like his other reputed son, Luis Tarango, nothing is known about this child.[29]

Tiburcio's cousin José Antonio Águila once recalled a visit from the bandido in 1872 at his place on Orestimba Creek in the Coast Range. Said Águila, "Vasquez visited with me for about three days. We talked over all his troubles and I persuaded him to promise me he would not go on the road again. Then he borrowed twenty dollars from me. He confessed to me all his misdeeds and I believe he told me everything. Vasquez was that way. He would repent, make a clean breast of everything and make all kinds of resolutions; but the first fat-looking purse, or good-looking senorita he saw would break them all."[30]

CHAPTER TWELVE

"I'm a Ranger, By God!"

In a small adobe in the Vallecitos, a few miles north of New Idria and not far from the home of Tiburcio's favorite sister María Lara, lived twenty-four-year-old Rosario Leiva. Descended from the proud and prominent Alviso family of the Santa Clara Valley, Rosario had cast her lot in life with a poor laboring man, Abdon Leiva. They had been married for seven years, and had a six-year-old boy and two small daughters. A Chileno, age twenty-seven, Abdon Leiva ran a few head of cattle, grew some crops, and worked off and on at the New Idria Mine to support his family. To make ends meet, Leiva sold his produce at New Idria and may have rustled livestock from time to time. At the beginning of 1873 Tiburcio Vasquez was in the Vallecitos, no doubt staying with María. With him was Teodoro Moreno, his first cousin. Moreno and Abdon Leiva had been close friends for years, and on January 8, 1873, Tiburcio and his cousin rode over to the Leiva place. The bandido received a warm welcome, especially from Rosario. Youthful, vivacious, and sensual, she would change his life forever.

Abdon Leiva knew Vasquez by reputation and had first seen him nine years earlier at a horse race at the Enriquita mines. He recalled, "Teodoro Moreno first introduced me to Vasquez in the Vallecitos Valley in January 1873. I was then living in that vicinity with my wife, Rosario. Vasquez told me that he was glad to find a place where he could stop and rest occasionally; that he had no place—the world was his home. A few days afterwards August de Bert, the hump backed Frenchman, came to my house, and then

Vasquez proposed to make the raid on Firebaugh's Ferry. He said that on the last day of February Henry Miller would have $30,000 there to pay off his men—sheep-herders, cattle drovers, etc.—and it was his intention to steal it."[1]

Abdon balked at this bold plan, but his wife was fascinated. Rosario was high-spirited, graceful, and a noted dancer, with sparkling brown eyes and a lustrous shock of raven hair. George Beers, who met her, said, "She was by no means a beauty, being rather short in stature, inclined to embonpoint [plumpness], and badly pock-marked. She was vivacious in disposition, however, generous and rather romantic, and fond of adventure." She also loved men. Rosario saw Tiburcio Vasquez as their savior from a life of poverty, and she convinced her reluctant husband to take part. As Leiva recalled, "I never would have gone with Vasquez but for her importunities. She kept urging me and was very mad when I twice backed out."[2]

The intended victim, Henry Miller, was California's great cattle baron. With his partner, Charles Lux, he owned 800,000 acres, 80,000 cattle, and 100,000 sheep. Miller and Lux, ruthless and rapacious in their quest for land, acquired the better part of fifteen ranchos and epitomized the greedy land sharks who preyed on Californios. It was commonly said that one could ride through California from Mexico to Oregon and never leave land owned by Miller and Lux. Tiburcio's claim that Henry Miller would have a $30,000 payroll at Firebaugh's was a gross exaggeration, however. In 1873 Miller employed no more than a few dozen vaqueros and borregueros in the San Joaquin. They earned forty to fifty dollars per month each, so his monthly payroll was at most a few thousand dollars. Vasquez himself later admitted, "I heard that Henry Miller would be there on a certain day with several thousand dollars to pay his herders."[3]

Firebaugh's Ferry was an ideal spot for a robbery. An isolated stagecoach stop on the route from Gilroy to Visalia, it was situated on the San Joaquin River at what is now the town of Firebaugh. At that time there was no railroad in the San Joaquin Valley south of what is now Fresno, and the west side of the valley was very sparsely settled. There were few telegraph lines and communication was slow. George L. Hoffman operated the ferry across the San Joaquin River, as well as a steamboat landing, as the spot was near the upper navigable reach of the river. A few hundred feet from the ferry was his hotel and store. Hoffman also acted as postmaster and Wells Fargo agent. His hotel was a big, two-story building—the store, dining room, and express office were downstairs with the lodgings upstairs.

Abdon Leiva of the Vasquez gang. Tiburcio seduced Leiva's wife, Rosario. (Author's collection)

Firebaugh's Ferry, robbed by the Vasquez band on February 26, 1873. The hotel, store, and express office were in the building on the right; the barn for the stagecoach horses is at the left. (William B. Secrest collection)

At seven o'clock on the evening of February 26, 1873, Tiburcio Vasquez, Clodoveo Chávez, August de Bert, Teodoro Moreno, and Abdon Leiva rode up to Firebaugh's and hitched their horses in front of the hotel. All but Tiburcio wore masks. The hotel's seven guests, relaxing and smoking in front of the fire, were startled when the bandits stepped inside, armed to the teeth. Vasquez ordered them to hold up their hands, and they were lined up on the floor and bound with rope. One was a Mexican named Parroda. One of the bandidos recognized Parroda as a man who had once befriended him, and told him he would not be robbed. Another of the victims, Wash Allen, was robbed of twenty-seven dollars.

The bandits were so quiet that they did not disturb the owner, Hoffman, who was eating supper in the dining room. When Hoffman finished his meal he stepped into the main room and found himself looking down the barrel of a large revolver. He was holding his wife's watch in his hands, and Tiburcio took it from him. Vasquez later recalled: "We laid hands on whatever article of value we saw. I took a watch away from a man they called the captain [Hoffman]. His wife saw me, and coming up, threw her arms around my neck and begged me to return the watch; that her husband had given it to her during her courtship, and she couldn't bear to part with it. I gave it to her, and then she said, 'Come with me.' I followed her into another room, and from behind the chimney she took out another watch and gave it to me. The captain said, 'You haven't got a bad heart after all.'"[4]

Vasquez then ordered Hoffman to open the safe, from which the robbers took $350. After looting the store of a hundred dollars worth of clothing, the outlaws helped themselves to whiskey and cigars. They lounged about the saloon, smoking and drinking while awaiting the Gilroy stage. Before long a loud rattling announced coach's arrival.

Dennis Conroy, the same "whip" the gang had robbed at Soap Lake a year and a half earlier, was at the ribbons when the bandits swarmed out of the hotel and surrounded his stagecoach. They ordered Conroy down at gunpoint, took him into the hotel, and bound him with the rest. Conroy recognized Vasquez as one of the Soap Lake stage robbers. The driver's testimony had sent Narciso Rodríguez to San Quentin, and seeing Vasquez, he feared the outlaws would kill him in revenge. Tiburcio seemed to remember the stage driver also, for he looked closely at him several times then asked Hoffman who he was. Hoffman, remembering Conroy's role in the previous robbery, told Vasquez that the reinsman "had just arrived in the state, and that the regular driver being sick, he had been driving in his stead." Vasquez accepted the explanation, much to Conroy's relief. After taking twenty dollars from Conroy, the outlaws broke open the stagecoach's Wells Fargo box and looted it of a sack of coin. Henry Miller's payroll was not there. Tiburcio then made a short speech, declaring that they "were outlaws, and could only work at night, while their victims could work in the daytime, and so raise money for them."

Vasquez and his men mounted their horses and galloped off into the darkness, riding hard into the Coast Range, toward New Idria. Late that night in the Panoche Valley they raided a sheepherders' camp. The sheepmen had no money, so the outlaws forced them to cook dinner, which they devoured, then continued on their ride back to Abdon Leiva's place in Vallecitos. For Rosario Leiva, the booty was a small fortune, and one can only imagine her thrill when the bandidos divided it.

The next morning the gang split up. Leiva recalled, "Vasquez and de Bert immediately left for Elizabeth Lake and I went about my work as usual, so as not to arouse suspicion. Moreno went to Lorenzo Vasquez's house in Hernandez Valley and got a place to shear sheep. De Bert and Vasquez, on their way south, passed through Peach Tree Valley and stole several horses and five head of cattle."[5]

It was a two-hundred-mile ride south to Elizabeth Lake, where Tiburcio no doubt stayed with Jim Hefner. He soon decided to visit his elder brother Chico, who three months before had moved his family from nearby Leona Valley to the mines in Soledad Canyon. While his brother went to work at the Soledad mines, Tiburcio spent time with Chico's wife, María, and their children. Felicita, now seventeen and attending school, was especially attracted to the charming, well-dressed stranger who seemed so comfortable with her family. José Jesús López later described her as beautiful, "a tall, graceful girl, fair complexioned, and with dark hair and eyes," and declared, "I . . . was very much in love with Felicita." Tiburcio, for his part, had much more than a familial interest in his niece. Recalled López, "Always Tiburcio was glad to be in company of a pretty girl, so he made it a regular practice to go riding with Felicita. She was a fine horsewoman, and rode a beautiful black saddle animal. She did not know that Tiburcio was her uncle. Tiburcio got Felicita in the family way, and skipped the country." Boyd Henderson later wrote about this affair in the *San Francisco Chronicle.* He reported that Chico's daughter knew she was Tiburcio's niece and had been "taught to look with pride upon the achievements of her uncle" before Vasquez "succeeded in effecting her ruin." Henderson's claims are improbable, for Chico Vasquez took no pride in his brother's criminal career, and it is unlikely that Felicita, a naive and innocent schoolgirl, would knowingly have had sexual relations with her own uncle.[6]

Tiburcio's dalliance with Felicita took place in March 1873. Vasquez, contrary to López's implication, could not have known that his niece was pregnant because he left Soledad Canyon within a month and rode north to the Cantua Creek region. When Felicita's condition became evident a few months later, Chico was enraged and vowed to kill Tiburcio on sight. But by that time the bandit chieftain had had his own brush with death. On April 12, 1873, he had a gunfight with his old enemy George Castro in the Cantua, and several newspapers reported that Vasquez had been killed. Declared the editor of the *Fresno Expositor,* "There is much rejoicing at the death of this desperado." But like that of Mark Twain, the news of Tiburcio's demise was greatly exaggerated. Vasquez had no wish to tangle further with Castro, who was one of the deadliest gunmen on the Pacific Coast. He left the Cantua and by April 17 was spotted in nearby Warthan Canyon. Castro probably soon returned to his big adobe house in San Juan, for a few weeks later Tiburcio came back to the Cantua area. There he probably learned of the death of his old foe Matt Tarpy in Monterey. A few weeks earlier, the vigilante had shot and killed a woman in a land dispute. On Dutra Street, directly in front of Tiburcio's childhood adobe, a mob had overpowered the incompetent sheriff, Andrew Wasson, and bound him hand and foot. They broke into the Monterey jail, dragged Tarpy out, and lynched him. And it was a

Californio who draped the noose around his neck. The delicious irony could not have been lost on Vasquez.[7]

By this time Abdon Leiva had moved to Cantua Creek where he acquired, perhaps with his share of the loot from the Firebaugh raid, an adobe house on a small plot. Leiva later recalled, "In May, Vasquez came back to my house. He made several trips to the San Joaquin, looking out for a good opening, always returning to my house. My wife seemed to like him very much, but I suspected nothing wrong." Like many women before her, Rosario was fascinated by her husband's charming compadre, who was totally unlike the rough, uneducated miners and vaqueros who lived in the mountains. Before long they were engaged in a secret, passionate affair, and Rosario became pregnant, most likely by Tiburcio. Now two of Tiburcio's women were with child at the same time.[8]

On May 14, Vasquez, Leiva, and another of the band, probably Chávez, were on a cattle-stealing foray on the San Joaquin River, twenty miles from Firebaugh's Ferry. As they drove off fifteen head of Henry Miller's cattle, they were spotted by one of his vaqueros, Rafael Ponzo. The outlaws saw him approaching from a distance, so they stopped and waited. As Ponzo rode up they saw that his horse carried Miller's brand. Drawing their guns, the three surrounded him and took him prisoner. Ponzo and Leiva knew each other. The bandidos took Ponzo with them, drove the cattle west into the Coast Range, then camped for the night on the trail into Panoche Valley. They told Ponzo they intended to kill him to keep him from identifying them. While two of the band guarded Ponzo, the other herded the cattle. The cows soon became so scattered that one of the guards had to help the herder. Ponzo saw his chance, leaped onto his horse, and raced for his life. The three outlaws charged after him, six-guns flaming. One bullet ripped through the brim of Ponzo's hat, within an inch of his ear, another tore through his coat and under his left arm, and a third grazed his stomach. But Ponzo's mount was a good one, and he managed to outrun his pursuers. He soon reported his narrow escape, but out of fear and prudence, kept Leiva's identity to himself. Tiburcio Vasquez later denied any involvement, blaming the whole affair on Abdon Leiva.[9]

One day Leiva rode into New Idria, where he got into a quarrel, pulled his gun, and shot a bystander by accident. He fled the camp, but angry miners threatened to go out to his place, about five miles distant, and lynch him. Although they never carried out their threats, Leiva was frightened. By June he was in more trouble. Tiburcio later claimed that

Leiva plotted to acquire the land of his neighbors, Vidal Castro and Florencio Vallesteros, by threatening to kill them if they didn't vacate. When they countered that they would have Leiva and Vasquez arrested for cattle theft, Abdon proposed that he and Tiburcio kill them both. Said Vasquez, "I replied that I would not submit to any proposition of that nature because I already had a bad name as a robber and I did not want to have the stain of an assassin." From that time on, the once-honest Leiva lived in constant fear of arrest. Vasquez preyed on his fears and manipulated him into staying with the gang.[10]

Vasquez, Chávez, and de Bert soon made a scouting trip into the San Joaquin Valley. On July 2, 1873, about eight miles south of Watson's Ferry and due west of Fresno, they came across two sheepmen, named Bacon and Wilson, traveling in a wagon. Covering them with pistols, the freebooters blindfolded the pair and searched them, taking twenty-three dollars, Wilson's coat, and Bacon's silver watch. As Vasquez and his men started off, Wilson told them that "it was hardly fair to leave them without a dollar, but they should give back enough to bear their necessary expenses to Visalia." Tiburcio asked how much that would cost, and Wilson replied, "Five dollars would do." At that, Vasquez magnanimously returned half that amount.[11]

August de Bert had had enough of a brigand's life, and he soon returned to his little saloon at Elizabeth Lake. Tiburcio quickly replaced him with a diminutive, twenty-six-year-old laborer named Blas Bicuna. Now, as Abdon Leiva recalled, Vasquez planned his most ambitious holdup yet: "Vasquez proposed to rob the pay-car of the Southern Pacific Railroad on the 1st of August. The place selected for the work was the curve just beyond the Twenty-One Mile House, between San Jose and Gilroy. The track was to be torn up and the train thrown off, after which the plundering was to take place. I objected, and at last flatly refused to go along. My wife urged me to take a hand. She extolled Vasquez's bravery and said I ought not to be afraid to go where he would lead. I wouldn't budge, and the band for this work was made up of Vasquez, Moreno, Chávez and Bicuna. The latter was a young Mexican whom Vasquez had picked up near the New Idria a few days before."[12]

On the first of each month the railroad company sent a pay-car south from San Francisco to pay its employees along the line. The place Vasquez had chosen for the holdup was known as the "divide," a mile south of

Blas Bicuna, a member of the Vasquez gang. This photo was taken when he entered San Quentin for a 1903 murder. (Courtesy of California State Archives)

the Twenty-One Mile House, where the railroad bridge crossed Llagas Creek. His inspiration for the plan is evident. Just before this, on July 21, bandits led by Jesse James had derailed a train near Adair, Iowa, killing the engineer and robbing the express. The affair had created national headlines, and Vasquez, an inveterate newspaper reader, certainly knew of the holdup, one of the earliest in the West.

Tiburcio planned to pull off California's first train robbery. However, as Abdon Leiva explained, "The party started out, but at Gilroy Vasquez learned that Dolores Larios of San Juan had given the railway officials information of the plot, and an attempt to carry it out would be attended with great danger. Vasquez resolved not to return from this trip empty-handed, and so the robbery of the Twenty-One Mile House was determined upon." How José Dolores Larios got wind of the plot is unknown, but as one of numerous sons of the prominent ranchero Manuel Larios, he was well connected and likely heard rumors.[13]

Vasquez, greatly disappointed, led his men north from Gilroy to the Twenty-One Mile House, a hotel, tavern, and stage stop situated twenty-one miles south of San Jose on the road to Monterey. The spot is now at the northwest corner of the intersection of Monterey Highway and Tennant Avenue in Morgan Hill. Tiburcio believed that owner William Tennant would have a large amount of money on hand. But unknown to the bandits, Tennant was gone, visiting his family in England. Half a mile from the stage stop the bandidos came upon a horseman on the road. They robbed him of six dollars, then bound his hands and feet and threw him over a fence, where he was not discovered until daylight. It was eight o'clock on the evening of July 30, 1873, when Vasquez and his men cantered up to Tennant's hotel.

The Twenty-One Mile House was a large, white, two-story wood-frame building with a long covered porch in front. Next to it was a water tank; a large oak tree stood between the house and the highway. The bandidos watered their horses, then tied them to the oak, known ever after as the Vasquez Tree. While Clodoveo Chávez stood guard outside, Vasquez, Moreno, and Bicuna entered the hotel. None bothered to wear masks, but Moreno wrapped a muffler around his lower face. Inside the saloon were barkeep Newton Finley; Archie McAlister, the young brother-in-law of the absent owner; John Horne, a farmhand; and a traveling salesman named Perkins. While Moreno stood in the doorway with a Henry rifle, Vasquez and Bicuna, pistols drawn, stepped into the barroom.

"Get down on the floor," Vasquez ordered in English. Perkins initially thought it was a practical joke, but it quickly became clear that the robbers were deadly serious. The outlaws tied the four hand and foot and relieved them of their watches, coin, and two shotguns. The bandidos demanded to know where the cash was kept. When no one would answer, one of the desperadoes seized young Archie McAlister and began poking and thrusting a knife blade into his ribs. Finally Finley agreed to tell, and the bandits untied his feet. He led them to a trunk where $160 was hidden. Then Vasquez and his men stepped up to the bar and treated themselves to drinks all around. With eight hundred dollars in loot, including the watches and other valuables, the bandidos retreated toward their horses. Tiburcio, invoking the slang term for Barbary Coast thieves, called back with a parting shot in English: "I'm a ranger, by God!"

After the band had galloped off, the Chinese cook who lived behind the hotel discovered the bound victims and untied them. Horne and

Perkins mounted up and raced north toward San Jose to spread the alarm. Santa Clara County Sheriff John H. Adams and his deputy, Adolph Sellman, initiated an unsuccessful hunt for the brigands. Sheriff Adams believed that the bandits were the same who had raided Firebaugh's Ferry, and quickly identified Tiburcio Vasquez as the leader. One local newspaper called the robbery "the coolest and most impudent ever perpetrated in Santa Clara County"; another pointed out that "next to that at Firebaugh's Ferry . . . this is the boldest robbery which has occurred in this vicinity in a long time."[14]

Tiburcio and several of the band slipped into Hollister to spend their loot. The town's red-light district, located in the area around Fourth and San Benito streets, was called Whiskey Row. Vasquez visited a señorita in a bordello at the corner of Third and San Benito streets, later known as the Helvetia Hotel. He left long before daybreak. Emboldened by how easily he could enter town and spurred on by his romantic urges, Tiburcio made several more visits, staying longer each time, until he finally drank too much and ended up sleeping with the woman until daylight. He went into the barroom and engaged in a game of casino with one of the señoritas. City Marshal Orson Lyon got wind of the outlaw's presence, and summoning a four-man posse, started for the brothel. But Vasquez was alert and saw them coming. He slipped out the back door, mounted his horse, and rode out of Hollister unmolested.[15]

Now Tiburcio and his men vanished. As Abdon Leiva recalled, "Vasquez and Bicuna returned to the Cantua; Moreno and Chávez stayed about Gilroy and Hollister for about a week, and while the sheriff's officers were looking for them. Then Moreno went to Lorenzo Vasquez's and Chávez left for the San Joaquin." Leiva described the difficulties facing Sheriff Adams: "Without knowing the fact, the officers passed places where some of the bandits were concealed a score of times. Every movement, however, of the officers was known to the bandits. . . . They knew when Adams and Sellman started for Hollister, when they arrived in San Benito, when they stopped, what they were after, and when they returned to San Jose. . . . The Mexicans living in the hills thereabouts are nearly all confederates of Vasquez, or so afraid of the bandits as to prevent them from giving any information that would lead to their capture."[16]

Unlike his Midwestern counterpart Jesse James, Tiburcio Vasquez never committed a daylight bank robbery or held up a railroad train. He confined his raids to remote stores and taverns, stagecoaches, and travelers on isolated byways. There were very few banks or railroads in the areas Vasquez roamed, limiting his opportunities. In 1871, between San Jose and Los Angeles there were only seven banks: three in San Jose, one in Santa Cruz, one in Snelling (Merced County), and two in Los Angeles. There was then no north-south railroad, only a handful of short lines. And Vasquez was no fool. A daring daylight bank robbery was sure to be resisted by the citizenry and result in someone being wounded or killed. He recognized that pursuit was less persistent if he confined himself to robbery without murder. By raiding in remote locations, he rarely met resistance and avoided bloodshed. This necessarily limited his spoils, as his targets generally had little of value. However, a little money went a long way in that cash-poor era. It has been estimated that in the mid-1860s, there was less than fourteen dollars of currency and coin in circulation for every man, woman, and child in America. By the mid-1870s that number had increased to only about twenty-one dollars per person. The prices of hard goods reflected this: a saddle cost ten dollars, a Colt's revolver twelve, and a good horse fifty to one hundred. As Vasquez himself once said, "I made but little money by my exploits." He had a second motive besides greed. George Beers said that Tiburcio "throughout his eventful career has been actuated principally by cupidity and an inordinate vanity, which impelled him to desperate adventures for the sake of notoriety, as much as for gain."[17] Yet the bandido would soon become, like Jesse James, a subject of national notoriety, for Tiburcio's greatest bandit raids were about to begin.

CHAPTER THIRTEEN

The Tres Pinos Tragedy

Abdon Leiva had been in a constant state of apprehension over the threats of lynching, and he decided to sell his ranch and leave for Arizona or Mexico. But now he needed money for the trip south. On August 13, 1873, two weeks after the Twenty-One Mile House robbery, Abdon and Rosario Leiva hosted a fiesta at their house in Cantua Canyon. Among the guests were Tiburcio Vasquez, Clodoveo Chávez, Teodoro Moreno, and Joaquín Castro. As they lounged under the shade of a nearby tree, Tiburcio suggested that they undertake another robbing expedition. His plan was to hold up the stage that left Hollister for New Idria every Tuesday, then rob Snyder's store at Tres Pinos, south of Hollister. That evening Romulo Gonzáles rode up, and quickly agreed to join them. Abdon Leiva recalled, "I did not want to go on this raid. I did not like the business, but my wife insisted and finally I consented." He explained that Vasquez "told me if he put me in trouble he would get me out of it, as he had a good many friends in the county."[1]

Clodoveo Chávez was then living with Joaquín Castro in Panoche Valley. Leiva discussed the robbery plan with Rosario and Joaquín Castro. Before the raid, Leiva's family would go south, and the outlaws, after robbing Tres Pinos, would meet them at San Emigdio, the isolated pueblo at the south end of El Camino Viejo. Then they would continue on to the border. Joaquín Castro agreed to drive Leiva's family south in exchange for a portion of the loot. Castro's motives were both money and hatred of the gringos who had lynched his son, José. A few days after the fiesta

Tiburcio rode out of the mountains to scout the Tres Pinos store. On about August 19 he boldly rode into Hollister, arriving at two in the morning. He spent several hours in a brothel before fleeing when local officers again got wind of him.[2]

For the next ten days Abdon Leiva made plans to leave, unaware that Tiburcio's real motive was to separate him from his wife. Leiva sold his Cantua ranch cheaply. On the morning of August 24 the gang left Leiva's adobe for the last time. Leiva and Chávez led his family eighteen miles out of the mountains through Cantua Canyon to the San Joaquin Valley. Joaquín Castro drove Rosario and her children in Abdon's wagon, while Castro's younger son, Juan, herded Leiva's livestock. When they reached El Camino Viejo, the party separated, with the Castros taking Rosario and her children south to San Emigdio.

Leiva and Chávez rode back into the mountains to Martinez Spring, just north of Joaquin Rocks. There they met Vasquez, Moreno, and Gonzáles, and the five outlaws headed north, passing Leiva's adobe on Cantua Creek. Near midnight they reached the house of Tiburcio's sister María, in the Vallecitos; after a short visit, they continued on to the nearby ranch of Agustín Hernández, located five miles south of Panoche on the New Idria Road. There, having ridden some seventy miles, they spent the night, first telling Hernández about their robbery plans. The following day, in two separate groups to avoid attention, the five outlaws rode twelve miles down the road toward Hollister, meeting late that night at the Gómez ranch. They continued on through the darkness, stopping at a roadside saloon where Vasquez bought a bottle of whiskey. At daybreak on August 26, they reached Grogan's Spring on Tres Pinos Creek a mile from the store, where they watered their horses and made camp on the hill above. Exhausted from hard riding and little sleep, they spent the day resting and napping. Recalled Leiva,

> We stayed there until about five o'clock in the evening. . . . Vasquez said the time had come, and we began to clean our arms. He cleaned his rifle and pistol and we cleaned our pistols. After they were all ready we fixed our horses. Vasquez told us several times what we should do. He told me to go ahead, as I was going to leave the country. He told me and Gonzáles, "You go ahead and see what is in the store and me and Chávez will stay back and rob the New Idria stage. You two go ahead and we will take the creek

down and take the Hollister road, and from there we will go straight to the store, and you and Gonzáles wait til we get there."

He had a [Henry] rifle, a fifteen-shooter, and a large Navy revolver, with cartridges and a knife, one of those steel knives made by blacksmiths. He carried his rifle on the saddle with the muzzle down, his revolver on the right side, and his knife in his left breast. Chávez had a [Colt's] Dragoon revolver and a double barreled shotgun and an old revolver; Gonzáles had a Dragoon revolver like Chávez's. Moreno had the same kind of a revolver with a white handle. I had one of Colt's small revolvers.[3]

Abdon Leiva and Romulo Gonzáles rode toward the store, while Tiburcio Vasquez, Clodoveo Chávez, and Teodoro Moreno stationed themselves near the road to halt the stagecoach. Leiva and Gonzáles had not gone far when the New Idria–bound stage approached, having dropped off the mail and newspapers at Snyder's store in Tres Pinos. Leiva saw that the passengers on top of the stage included the assistant superintendent of the New Idria Mine, Thomas Williams, and his family, and he ducked behind a passing wagon so that he would not be recognized. As the stage approached Tiburcio's ambush, the bandit leader also spotted Williams on board. Explained Leiva later, "As Vasquez did not want to rob him, the stage was allowed to go on unmolested." Tiburcio himself later said that Williams had always treated him "like a gentleman."[4]

By this time Leiva and Gonzáles had reached the store, located twelve miles south of Hollister. Tres Pinos, named for three stunted pine trees on the creek, is now called Paicines. It was a tiny cluster of buildings situated on the Hollister–San Benito road. There the Hollister road forks, the east fork proceeding south through the Panoche Valley to the New Idria Mine, and the west fork, or river road, also going south, through San Benito and Hernandez Valley to the Picacho Mine, with a range of mountains separating the two routes. Andrew Snyder's general store stood on the east side of the Hollister–San Benito road; next to it on the north was Snyder's two-story hotel, which he had leased to Leander Davison.[5] Snyder kept two rooms in the hotel for himself and his family. Behind the hotel was a large barn that served as a feed and livery stable. Just north of the hotel, across the New Idria Road, stood a saddlery and blacksmith shop. In the center of the stage road, directly fronting the hotel, was a windmill tower and water trough for stock. Like many roadside stores in California, Snyder's also served as a saloon, stage stop, and post office. There were a number of farmhouses nearby, and some forty people lived in the area of the little settlement.[6]

Leiva and Gonzáles dismounted in front of Snyder's and stepped inside. The store had two counters, one on either side, with storerooms in the rear. A dozen patrons were present, most of whom had dropped by to pick up their letters and newspapers. The youthful clerk, John Utzerath, was busy sorting the mail. Leiva said to him, "Let us have some drinks."

Utzerath replied that they had no hard liquor, only beer, so Abdon Leiva paid for two glasses. Gonzáles quickly downed his and called for another. Leiva later recalled, "Gonzáles used to get drunk whenever he had a chance." Leiva bought two cigars and convinced Gonzáles to smoke instead of drink. It was fifteen minutes later, and all but a few of the customers had cleared out, when Teodoro Moreno dismounted and stepped inside. As at the Twenty-One Mile House, Tiburcio's cousin had a muffler covering his face. Without ceremony he jerked his six-shooter and commanded, "Lie down!"

At the same time Leiva and Gonzáles pulled out their pistols. The three quickly began hog-tying Andrew Snyder, John Utzerath, and the two remaining customers—Lewis C. Smith, the local blacksmith, and a young man named Henry Murray. Those who attempted to raise their heads were pistol-whipped into submission. Utzerath had known Moreno well when they both lived in Peach Tree Valley, and despite the bandit's mask, recognized him from his voice and mannerisms. At that point Tiburcio Vasquez and Clodoveo Chávez rode up to the front of the store, leading a pack mule. The bandit leader's failed train robbery plan, his paltry spoils from the Twenty-One Mile House robbery, and now his decision to let the stagecoach pass, made him determined that the raid on Snyder's store would be a success. Dismounting, Tiburcio stepped into the doorway. He was distinctively attired in a large, sleeveless cloak with red flannel lining and clutched a Henry rifle in his hand. He called out to his men, "Are you through?" Receiving a negative reply, Vasquez ordered, "One of you fellows come out."

Romulo Gonzáles stepped outside, leaving Leiva and Moreno to finish tying the victims and placing grain sacks over their heads. From the porch of the store, Vasquez spotted more people than he had expected. A number of men and two women were walking in and out of the hotel next door, several young boys were in the yard between the store and the

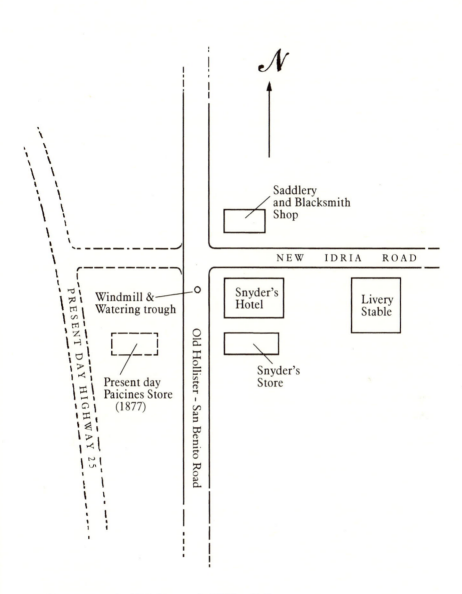

Tres Pinos as it was in 1873. Diagram by William B. Secrest.

stable, and a teamster was approaching in the distance on the Hollister road. At the same time a Portuguese sheepherder named Bernard Bahury, having driven his flock into a nearby field, was walking toward the hotel, where he intended to spend the night. As he passed in front of the store, Romulo Gonzáles yelled at him, "Halt and lie down!"[7]

Bahury did not speak English and failed to understand the order. According to Andrew Snyder, Bahury recognized some of the outlaws. He panicked and fled around the back of the store, with Gonzáles in pursuit. Bahury circled the store, running back toward the road through the empty lot between the store and the hotel. As Gonzáles turned the corner behind the store, he spotted Bahury near the front, scaling a picket fence that separated the lot from the road. He fired twice with his Colt's Dragoon and a heavy .44 caliber ball struck Bahury in the mouth, knocking out his front teeth. Desperately wounded, the sheepherder staggered onto the front porch of the store. As he did so, Teodoro Moreno raised his Dragoon revolver and shot Bahury in the chest, just below the neck, killing him. At that, Gonzáles stepped onto the porch and growled in English, "I guess you will lay still now, damn you."

In the meantime Chávez spotted a fifteen-year-old boy, one of the sons of the blacksmith Lewis Smith, near the stable. Chávez ordered him to lie down, and when he didn't act quickly enough, struck him over the head with his shotgun. Chávez then brought the boy into the store, where he was bound with the rest. By this time the teamster George Redford had pulled up in front of the hotel with a load of fence pickets from Hollister. He was deaf and oblivious to the robbery and the shooting. As he climbed down from his wagon, Vasquez and Moreno approached and ordered him onto the ground. Seeing their guns and not understanding the order, Redford fled for the protection of the barn, with Vasquez in pursuit. The bandit chieftain opened fire with his Henry rifle. His first shot killed an old horse in a stall near the barn door. As Redford entered the door, Vasquez fired again. The .44 caliber slug tore through Redford's back and he plunged into the straw, instantly killed.

By now the little settlement was in an uproar. Inside the hotel were Louis Scherer, the Tres Pinos saddler; hotelkeeper Leander Davison with his wife, Elizabeth, and her brother, Ebenezer Burton; plus Andrew Snyder's wife, Lucilla, and her sister-in-law, Elizabeth Moore. Several of them saw the killing of Redford. Louis Scherer rushed out of the rear of the hotel toward the saddlery and blacksmith shop across the road, intending, as he later said, "to defend all I could." Vasquez, rifle in hand, spotted him running from the hotel. Scherer, seeing that the bandit was about to cut him off, turned and fled back into the rear door of the hotel. Glancing behind, he saw Vasquez rushing toward the front door of the hotel. Scherer raced toward the front room, accompanied by Leander

Andrew Snyder's feed and livery stable at Tres Pinos (now Paicines). George Redford died just inside the barn door. (Author's collection)

Davison, his wife, and her brother. The front door was open, and as they reached it Abdon Leiva suddenly appeared in front of the hotel, pistol in hand. "Keep in the house and you won't be hurt," he warned. "Keep in. Go in!" At that, both Burton and Scherer yelled to the Davisons, "Shut the door!"

Husband and wife each took hold of the doorknob and started to pull the door shut. Davison was to the right of the door and his wife to the left; Scherer and Burton were just behind them. At that moment Tiburcio Vasquez came around the corner. Swinging up his rifle, he fired a single shot that ripped through the door at an angle and shattered Davison's heart. He fell backward into his wife and died in her arms.

Vasquez, unfazed by his killing of two men, was determined that nothing would thwart the robbery. He spotted a youth attempting to flee on foot down the Hollister road. He ordered Leiva, "Go and bring that boy back."

Leiva leaped into his saddle and raced after the boy, catching up with him a quarter mile distant, near Tres Pinos Creek. He was a ten-year-old son of Lewis Smith's. The frightened youth tried to turn over his money, two dollars. Leiva told him to keep it and brought him back to the store, where he had the boy lie down next to his father. By this time

Tiburcio had returned to the store, where he told Snyder and the rest, "Boys, I am sorry to treat you this way. But if I should try to make my living by honest work and the people should find out who I am, they would hang me inside of a week. The only way I have to make a living is robbing other people, and as long as you have money I am going to have my share."

The outlaws searched those in the store, taking their watches, jewelry, and cash. Tiburcio then demanded, "Who is the boss?" and Leiva pointed out Snyder, who later recalled: "He told me he didn't want to hurt me, that he wanted my money and that if I didn't give it up he would kill me." Vasquez and Leiva then marched Snyder, his hands tied behind him, to the front door of the hotel. Ignoring the bloody corpse of Leander Davison and the hysterical screaming of his widow, Vasquez ordered Mrs. Snyder to bring out their money. She told him, "I am willing to give everything I have got, but don't hurt anybody."

Leiva replied, "For my part I won't hurt anyone."

She went upstairs and pulled out a bureau drawer with some $220 in silver coin, plus gold dust in a deerskin poke. The drawer was too heavy for her, so she slid it down the steps. Then she and Elizabeth Moore handed it to the bandits. The robbers took Snyder back to the store and put him back on the floor with the others. At this point, a wagon pulled up, driven by John Haley, a teamster from Hollister. The outlaws swarmed out of the store, and at gunpoint ordered, "Git down. Git, you son of a bitch."

"Boys, if you think to scare me you've got the wrong man," answered Haley.

Vasquez and Moreno climbed onto the wagon box and hauled Haley out. The teamster began yelling for Andrew Snyder, but the outlaws tied him to one of the wagon wheels and took four dollars from his pockets. Reentering the store, the gang ransacked it, taking clothing and other goods. Several of the band exchanged their trail-worn clothes for new coats, vests, trousers, and boots. Vasquez attired himself in a brand-new suit and black hat. Said Andrew Snyder, "They tied my hands so tight, my arms were swollen up to my shoulders. I spoke to Vasquez several times about it. It became very painful to me. He finally came and examined it and said it was too tight and loosened it up. I thanked him for it as I was in great misery."

While Chávez stood guard outside the store, the robbers tapped a keg of beer and helped themselves to a leisurely meal of crackers, cheese, canned oysters, and sardines. Bellies full, they began loading booty and provisions onto the pack mule. By now it was half past eight o'clock, and the robbers had been in Tres Pinos for two and a half hours. Leiva recalled, "Vasquez was then walking up and down, telling us to hurry up and get away." Tiburcio sent Leiva and Chávez into the stable to take all the horses. As the bandidos stepped inside, they saw the body of George Redford facedown near the first stall, and Chávez remarked, "My uncle killed this man."[8]

They took eight horses, two of them saddled, then mounted their own mustangs and headed up San Benito Creek at a fast clip, driving the extra mounts before them. The men in Snyder's store managed to get loose. John Utzerath ran on foot to a nearby farm, borrowed a horse, then raced twelve miles into Hollister to raise the alarm. By morning some two hundred people had gathered at the scene of the tragedy. In Hollister the news was sent out over the telegraph wire. Accounts of the raid, dubbed "the Tres Pinos Tragedy," created great excitement and were published in newspapers throughout the state. Californians were used to deadly violence and often excused it, provided that it took place in mutual combat or private quarrels. But the killing of innocent people in their homes, especially a husband slain in his wife's arms, was beyond the pale. A typical editorial comment came from the *Los Angeles Star:* "This is one of the most terrible events that has transpired in our state since the bloody raids of the terrible Joaquin Murrieta." The Tres Pinos Tragedy had netted the gang only $2,200 in loot, but quickly gained Tiburcio Vasquez statewide, then national, notoriety. Governor Newton Booth promptly offered a reward of one thousand dollars for the capture of one or all of the killers.[9]

The morning after the raid, John H. Adams, sheriff of Santa Clara County, was in Gilroy, campaigning for reelection on the following week's ballot. As he was passing the hotel, the telegraph operator called him inside and told him the news. Adams instantly abandoned his campaigning. Although he had no obligation to respond to a crime in a different and distant county, his only thought was to pursue the killers. Sheriff Adams was one of California's finest lawmen, and he knew Tiburcio Vasquez well.[10]

Adams ordered the telegrapher to send a wire to Sheriff Andrew Wasson in Salinas, then rushed to the railroad depot. In fifteen minutes the sheriff was aboard a southbound freight train, and by ten o'clock he was in Hollister. Adams was shocked to discover that no pursuit of the

THE BANDITTI.

Further Particulars of the Tragedy at Tres Pinos.

A Chronicle Reporter at the Scene of the Massacre.

A Concise Statement by Two of the Men Who Were In Snyder's Store.

The Three Men Murdered By Vasquez Alone.

FEARS OF FURTHER DEPREDATION

The Course Taken by the Bandits in their Flight.

The Country Aroused and a Swarm of Pursuers Out.

ONE PARTY CLOSE UPON THE MURDERERS' TRAIL.

An Inquest Upon the Bodies of the Victims,

A Sketch of the Red-Handed Outlaw's Career.

[SPECIAL DISPATCHE TO THE CHRONICLE.]

HOLLISTER, August 28.—The principal topic of conversation in town is the daring robbery and murder committed at Snyder's store at Tres Pinos on Tuesday evening by Tiburcio Vasquez and his gang of cut-

to-day in Hollister, his funeral being largely attended. Redford and the Portuguese were buried to-day at the school-house on the Tres Pinos.

FEARS OF FURTHER DEPREDATIONS.

Since dispatching the above I have learned that Vasquez and his gang, in the forenoon preceding the raid upon Snyder's, stole five horses and a mule in the Panoche Valley. It is feared that the New Idria stage will be the next object of their attack. Adams and Wasson, two of the best officers in the State, may spoil their plans, however, and the citizens here are waiting in great suspense for intelligence from them.

LATER NEWS.

R. M. Matthews of San Benito has just arrived in town and reports that Sheriffs Adams and Wasson and party camped last night at Stone's ranch, twenty miles south of Hollister, and that Vasquez and his gang had only half a day's start of them. The officers were confident of coming upon their game by to-night. Vasquez has a sister living in Hernandez valley, and the probabilities are that he will take a short rest there, which will give the officers a still better start on them. By all accounts, Vasquez (who was recognized, he wearing no mask) fired all the shots and acted throughout in the most heartless and ruthless manner. If he is caught, I am satisfied, from public opinion that no jury will ever act upon his case.

The Infamous Career of Vasquez.

His record is black with infamy, and he is well called the "Dick Turpin of California." He was born in Monterey, and is now about 35 years of age. He attended the public schools, was a fine scholar, and now speaks good English, and writes an excellent hand. His parents were of the lowest class, and at 14 years of age he was regarded as a Hoodlum of the ultra caste.

HIS FIRST EXPLOIT

Was the murder of the Constable of Monterey Township in 1852, when he was not quite 15 years of age. He was in a dance house and became infatuated by liquor, and the efforts of the Constable, who was called in, resulted in the murder. Vasquez fled, but was captured, tried and sentenced to ten years confinement in the State Penitentiary. When he was released he returned to his old habits.

MORE CRIMES.

He first robbed a fish peddler two miles below San Joaquin. He was pursued by the officers, but managed to elude them and shortly afterward went to the New Almaden mines, in Santa Clara county, where he murdered an Italian butcher. He was captured and afterwards convicted of the crime and sentenced to the State Prison for a term of two or three years. He served out his time and his hungry soul thirsted for more blood and rapine. Wandering around Mount Diablo he fell in with a Mexican rancher who was the possessor of a lovely daughter named Anita. He fell in love with Anita and fearing that the stern parent would not favor the suit, he abducted the girl. A short distance from the ranch he was met by the old man, who shot Vasquez in the arm, causing the bandit to drop the girl and take safety in flight. The next we hear of Vasquez is at San Juan, where he again became

A VICTIM TO THE WILES OF CUPID.

A daughter of Pedro Garcia was abducted by him. Tiring of the girl soon after, he delivered her over to the tender mercy of Panocho Barcillos, who shortly before had become a partner of Vasquez. This brings our history down to 1865, and at this time Tomaso Redondo alias Procopio, the noted outlaw and an old compadre of Vasquez, met the latter. A band was formed, with Procopio and Vasquez as leaders, and a magnificent programme of plunder and outlawry was mapped out. The murder of the Frenchman at Pleasanton is supposed to have been committed by this combination, being preceded and succeeded by some

DARING ROBBERIES

In Santa Clara and Monterey counties. Sheriff Morse started out on their trail, and near Panoche, in this county, came upon them. He killed Juan outlaws had been started. Wild rumors had increased the size of the gang to twenty, all heavily armed with rifles and revolvers, and the people of Hollister were busy organizing bands of men to guard the town from attack. The veteran manhunter was stunned by their foolishness. He knew that robber bands rarely numbered more than half a dozen, and that the killers were now fleeing into the mountains, not preparing to raid the town. He quickly met with Hollister's leading citizens and tried to raise a posse, but the townsfolk were too afraid to join up.

In western fiction and film, a sheriff recruits a posse of brave volunteers simply by walking into a saloon and deputizing every man present; within minutes they are heavily armed and in the saddle. But in reality, a shortage of good horseflesh, modern repeating rifles, and courage were common problems. Sheriff Adams was outraged by the reluctance and cowardice of the people of Hollister. By noon he had managed to get only two volunteers. A town meeting was held at two o'clock, but despite cajoling, no one else would join. Allen Leonard, the San Benito storekeeper who had been held up by Vasquez at Robbers' Roost, told the crowd, "You are cowards if you will not go. I will go alone, and not wait til the sheriffs come along." He promised to have horses ready for the posse by the time they reached his store in San Benito.

Earlier that morning, Sheriff Wasson had ridden on horseback from his Monterey home to the new county seat at Salinas. On reaching his office, he got Sheriff Adams's telegram, and immediately started for Hollister, arriving there at three o'clock. By five the two sheriffs had managed to recruit six volunteers, most of them armed only with pistols. Seven valuable hours had been wasted. Adams deeply regretted that he had not pushed on alone after the gang as soon as he arrived in Hollister. But he was determined to capture the killers. The posse headed south for Tres Pinos. Tiburcio Vasquez was about to endure his longest ride and his toughest manhunt.[11]

CHAPTER FOURTEEN

Pursuit and Betrayal

After riding out of Tres Pinos, Vasquez pushed his men and horses hard all night. Fifteen miles up the road, Tiburcio's horse gave out, and he exchanged it for one of the stolen mounts. Chávez's mustang broke down next, and he mounted a stolen horse. By daybreak they had traveled forty miles and reached the ranch of Lorenzo Vasquez, just north of Hernandez Valley. At the house were Lorenzo's brother, Loreto Vasquez, and two friends, Pedro Hernández and Manuel Cortez. The bandidos devoured the breakfast cooked by Lorenzo's wife, Paula. Then, with Lorenzo Vasquez and Pedro Hernández, they went behind the stable to divide the spoils. "We took all the money we had taken out and laid it on a coat and there it was divided," recalled Leiva. Tiburcio claimed two valuable watches, and sold one to Romulo Gonzáles for ten dollars. Said Leiva, "Vasquez said he took the jewelry because he was a lost man and did not care who saw it with him. . . . He said that he had done more than any of the party—he had shot two men." The bandits gave a few dollars each to Lorenzo Vasquez and the others as payment for their help. Lorenzo in turn presented Moreno with a fresh horse, and then told the band, "You had better leave as the stage will soon be here."[1]

The outlaws shook hands with Lorenzo and the rest. Moreno threw his arms around his compadre Leiva and said, "Good-bye. We may not see each other again as you are going to leave the country." Moreno, confident that he had not been recognized, left the band and rode to the nearby ranch of Ed Tully in Bitterwater Valley where he hired on to shear sheep. The rest of the band headed south to meet Rosario Leiva and Joaquín Castro in San Emigdio. Said Leiva, "We . . . went up the creek in a tight gallop til we got to the wagon road. When we passed a house we went slow."

On the ride south, Abdon Leiva was filled with remorse. Although no saint, he was not a hardened desperado and had never expected any bloodshed at Tres Pinos. As he later explained, "I . . . didn't think there would be any shooting, as I had been out with Vasquez before and no blood was shed." He had become accustomed to a quiet, married existence, was not used to a rough life in the saddle, and had no stomach for murder. His trifling share of the spoils had been two coats, a pair of pants, some merino cloth, and less than a hundred dollars in cash. For that he had given up his home and become a fugitive. Leiva also had begun to suspect that Vasquez was having an affair with his wife; he later said that a friend had warned him about it. As much as he now wanted to leave the band, he had no choice but to flee with them. With Tiburcio riding far ahead, the gang rode down Alcalde Creek, in Pleasant Valley, meeting up at Narciso Higuera's ranch near Poso Chane. Romulo Gonzáles liked hard drinking but not hard riding, and he was having trouble keeping up. After a short rest, the fugitives headed south to Zapato Chino Creek. Here Leiva angrily confronted Vasquez, accusing him of improper attentions to Rosario. In a heated exchange, the bandit chief denied it. From there the gang made a hard, eighty-mile ride south along El Camino Viejo to Buena Vista Lake. This ride was too much for Romulo Gonzáles. Neither he nor his jaded horse could go any farther, and the gang left him at the lake.

Vasquez, Chávez, and Leiva continued south some fifteen miles to San Emigdio Canyon. There Abdon found Rosario and his three children with Joaquín and Juan Castro in one of the adobe houses. Instead of accusing Rosario of infidelity, Leiva kept his misgivings to himself. In nearby Tecuya Creek canyon the outlaws rustled three steers from the herd of the Rancho El Tejon. After butchering them, they hauled the hindquarters back to San Emigdio in Leiva's wagon. Vasquez and Chávez had two of the stolen horses shod by San Emigdio's blacksmith and at nightfall they rode south toward Tejon Pass. Leiva stayed behind, spending the night with his family and the Castros. In the morning Abdon paid Joaquín Castro with two horses and a saddle, and Castro and his son started back north to New Idria. Leiva, after loading his wagon, headed south to meet Chávez in Tejon Pass. From Tejon the little band skirted the Tehachapi Mountains and the edge of the Mojave Desert, reaching Jim Hefner's remote stage station at Elizabeth Lake two days later. There they found Vasquez waiting for them. Tiburcio's plan was to separate Rosario from her husband and children and escape with her to Mexico.[2]

In the meantime Sheriff Adams's little posse finally headed out of Hollister, reaching Tres Pinos at dusk. They found the settlement in a state of terror. Elizabeth Davison was bedridden and inconsolable at the loss of her husband. A neighbor noted in his diary that she was "expected to die of grief." A grateful Andrew Snyder fed the posse dinner, and two more volunteers joined. One of them was George W. Chick, the stage driver whom Vasquez had robbed the previous year. Chick had recently been elected constable of San Benito Township. Soon a mail rider cantered in. On learning about the murders, he told the sheriffs that he had seen "quite a lot of horses" at Lorenzo Vasquez's place the previous morning: "two large ones necked together besides four horses with saddles on and very sweaty." This was a solid clue and Adams was more impatient than ever to start on the trail. It was dark when the posse rode out of Tres Pinos, twenty-four hours behind the killers. They rode hard through the blackness, picking up one more volunteer on the way, and reached Allen Leonard's store in San Benito at 2:00 A.M. Instead of being ready with fresh horses as he had promised, Leonard was asleep. Recalled one of the posse, "When we first asked him, 'Are you going?' he replied, 'Yes,' and promised to get some saddle horses right away. We waited and waited for this noble hero, but we finally found out that he felt sick at the stomach, and at last he backed clean out and said he would not go." Another of the manhunters reported that Leonard "even refused to lend a rifle to one of the party, who . . . were thoroughly disgusted at his conduct and false promises of assistance."[3]

Sheriff Adams rousted two blacksmiths and had their horses reshod. The San Benito ranchers had much more nerve than the Hollister townsmen, and four more volunteers now joined the band. One was young John Shell, who a year earlier had Tiburcio in his gun sight while the bandit flirted with his pretty sister, Susan. At daylight they started up the wagon road along the San Benito River, and a fifteen-mile ride brought them to the summit, from which they dropped down into Lorenzo Vasquez Canyon. At the eastern end of the canyon was Sweetwater Spring; a short flume led from the spring to Vasquez's cabin, near the road. The posse questioned Lorenzo Vasquez closely. He denied any knowledge of

Captain John H. Adams, the rough-and-ready sheriff of Santa Clara County. (Author's collection)

the gang but said that the previous morning, at daybreak, a band of horse-man had passed by and had fed their animals on a flat meadow below his house. One of the possemen later grumbled, "This man would probably have told more if he had a rope around his neck, and been jerked off the ground a few times." But Sheriff Adams would allow no brutality, and they rode on, following the road east through Hernandez Valley.[4]

Soon they lost the trail, and spent several hours resting in Hernandez Valley. After a search they found the tracks of horses leading south, and followed them until nightfall, continuing in the same direction until they reached Lewis Creek canyon. The posse rode up to Abe Lewis's ranch late that night, and learned that Vasquez and his band had passed there the previous afternoon. Lewis fed the exhausted manhunters a venison dinner. After tying their horses to a fence near a haystack, they spread their blankets on the straw and quickly fell asleep. The possemen were jittery, as one of them recalled: "All went well til two A.M. when one of the horses at our feet got foul on his rope and commenced to pull back. One of our party said, 'Whoa, whoa.' At that signal up jumped three or four and cried out, 'Whoa! Whoa! Whoa!' One man tried to jump the fence. Failing in that, he tried to get over the stack, and several who thought the robbers were amongst us, took hold of their guns and got ready for a fight. It was a pretty rich scare, and caused lots of laughter afterwards."[5]

Seven minutes later they were in the saddle, riding slowly through the darkness, feeling their way through the brush-choked canyon of Lewis Creek. At daybreak they stumbled across five Mexicans and an Indian sleeping under some trees, but they proved to be herders, not bandits. The posse continued south through Pleasant Valley to Albion Baker's sheep ranch at the mouth of Alcalde Creek, arriving at 11:00 A.M. on August 29, three days after the murders. Here they made a brief stop to feed both horses and men. Sheriff Adams's horse and several others were so exhausted that they would not eat. He borrowed a fresh mount and the posse started out onto the San Joaquin plains. The August heat was like an open furnace and water was scarce. The manhunters followed fresh horse tracks south to Carey Creek, where they lost the trail. Fanning out, they cut the bandits' sign in Zapato Chino Creek, but again lost the track. Their best clue came from a youth they encountered, who described a man who was undoubtedly Vasquez: "He said he saw a high toned Spaniard dressed in new clothes, having a Henry rifle and two six-shooters." Adams led the posse back north where they reined up in front of the jacal of

Andrew Wasson, the incompetent
sheriff of Monterey County.
(Author's collection)

Narciso Higuera, near Poso Chane. They questioned Higuera closely, as
one of the posse recalled: "He denied seeing anything of the band almost
before he was asked. He commenced saying, "No, no," before the questions were finished."[6]

Sheriff Adams was convinced that the killers were about thirty-five
miles ahead of them, heading toward Los Angeles County or the Mexican border. He decided to cross the San Joaquin Valley to Fresno, seventy
miles distant, where there was a telegraph station, and alert the officers
in Southern California. From Fresno Adams intended to proceed by train
and stage to Bakersfield and try to cut off the outlaws' flight southward.
At age fifty-three, he was twenty years older than Sheriff Wasson but possessed the strength, energy, and endurance of a much younger man. But
Wasson now announced that he could no longer pursue the gang. He
insisted that he had to get back to Monterey to complete his political
campaign, as the election was just five days off. Adams was stunned. He
too was running for reelection, but he gave no thought to turning back.
For him no election was more important than capturing the worst outlaw
gang since the days of Joaquín Murrieta.[7]

By now many of the posse's mounts were completely spent. The sheriffs agreed that Constable Chick would take over command of the posse, begin a hunt for fresh horses, and then proceed south. Neither Adams nor Wasson knew the trail to Fresno, so they paid Narciso Higuera fifty dollars to guide them. They started at eight o'clock that night, and had not eaten since their meal at Baker's ranch that morning. Higuera missed the trail, or perhaps intentionally misled the two sheriffs, and the three got lost in a tule marsh near Tulare Lake. Unable to ride safely and with no dry ground anywhere, they were forced to spend the night catnapping in their saddles. At daybreak they worked their way out of the slough, and that afternoon, August 30, finally arrived in Fresno, half-dead from dehydration and heat exhaustion. While Wasson boarded a special train for home, Adams wired news of the bandits' flight and caught up on much-needed sleep. The next day, by train and stagecoach, he traveled forty-five miles south to Visalia. In the morning he got word that a party of suspicious riders had been spotted between Tipton and Tulare. Adams pursued this band and caught up with them, only to find that they were honest vaqueros. He boarded a southbound train, arriving in Bakersfield that evening, September 1. In the meantime Constable Chick had been unable to find fresh horses, so he and the balance of the posse rode back home.[8]

After meeting with Sheriff Adams, local officers in Bakersfield first made a raid on Panama, a tiny adobe pueblo three miles south of town. They found that neither Vasquez nor his band had been there. The next morning Adams started out with Kern County Deputy Sheriff Joe Short and a posseman named White to search San Emigdio. While crossing the lower San Joaquin Valley near Buena Vista Lake, they encountered an old Mexican driving a herd of horses. Among them was a mule, worn out from days of hard driving, that matched the description of the pack mule the gang had brought to Tres Pinos. The viejo said that he had found the mule on the west side of Tulare Lake, where he had also seen the tracks of a band of horses. Since this was on the route that the outlaws must have taken from Poso Chane, Adams knew he was on the right trail. The three lawmen pressed on at a rapid gait and found fresh horse tracks on the west side of the lake, leading toward San Emigdio. They soon spotted a horse picketed in a grove of willow trees a quarter mile from the trail and, riding to it, discovered a Mexican lying down next to a brush fence. He claimed to have come from the Livermore Valley, in Alameda County, and remarked, "You are after Vasquez, I suppose?"

"No," replied Sheriff Adams. "We are only looking after stock."

The man said he had heard that the gang had passed that way, and was afraid of them. He was using a sack for a pillow, and Adams searched it, finding a brand-new coat, vest, and trousers. The Mexican explained that they were his Sunday clothes that he wore at Livermore and New Idria. Adams had been told at Tres Pinos that the outlaws, when putting on the new clothes, had left their old outfits behind. In addition to knowing Vasquez personally, the sheriff had obtained good descriptions of most of the band, and this rider did not fit them. Adams carefully considered whether to arrest the Mexican as a suspect. But he had no specific evidence against him and would have to take him fifteen miles back to the nearest jail, in Bakersfield. Adams was loath to do that, as he was certain that he was hot on the outlaws' trail. Sheriff Adams let the man go and pushed on toward San Emigdio. It was the biggest blunder of his professional career. The Mexican was Romulo Gonzáles. He promptly fled and was never recaptured.[9]

The sheriff's posse followed the tracks that night to San Emigdio and found that the outlaws had been there two days before, and had had their horses shod before heading south. At four o'clock the next morning Adams, Short, and White started again, following the trail south to Hudson's Station, later known as Rose's Station, a mile from the mouth of Tejon Canyon near what is now Grapevine. There the driver of the Los Angeles stage told them he had seen a man with a herd of horses camped near Delano's Station in San Francisquito Canyon, six miles south of Jim Hefner's stagecoach stop at Elizabeth Lake. By this time White was completely exhausted from the hard riding and could go no farther. At Hudson's Station Adams and Deputy Short recruited the latter's brother John plus an old mountaineer, David McKenzie, and a one-legged vaquero named Young. The makeshift posse pushed on to Fort Tejon, in the Tejon Pass, where there was a telegraph station. Sheriff Adams wired William R. "Billy" Rowland, Los Angeles County's half-Anglo, half-Hispanic sheriff, that the band was fleeing toward the Mojave Desert, and asked him to send a posse east to the Elizabeth Lake area. The bilingual Rowland was popular with both Anglos and Hispanics and took his duties seriously.[10]

The next day, September 4, a well-armed posse rode out of Los Angeles. Its members were three Anglos—Pete Gabriel, Henry M. Mitchell, and "Babe" Crowell—and three Californios—José Redona, Esteban Sánchez, and Ramón Benítez. Pete Gabriel and Henry Mitchell were deputy sheriffs;

the others were volunteers. They arrived at the toll gate in Cajon Pass and set up a watch for Vasquez, as they knew he would have to go through the pass if he wanted to escape south to Baja California. The same morning Sheriff Rowland boarded a northbound stage, intending to meet up with Sheriff Adams on the road to Tejon Pass.[11]

Sheriff Adams directed Deputy Short to continue south to Elizabeth Lake, and then boarded a Los Angeles–bound stagecoach. His plan was to meet up with Sheriff Rowland and attempt to cut off the outlaws from the south, while Deputy Short's posse pushed forward from the north, trapping the bandits between the two groups of lawmen. In those years the route into Southern California did not follow the path of today's Interstate 5 or even the old Ridge Route over the Tehachapi Mountains. Instead, the stage road took a circuitous route east at Gorman and followed the edge of the Mojave Desert to Elizabeth Lake. From there it went south through San Francisquito Canyon, then into the San Fernando Valley to Los Angeles.

At the last station before reaching Elizabeth Lake, Adams learned that Tiburcio Vasquez had eaten dinner there the night before. Later that morning, September 4, Adams's stage reached Jim Hefner's station near Elizabeth Lake. While the driver watered his team, the sheriff stepped inside and questioned Hefner. The station keeper falsely denied any knowledge of Vasquez, but after close questioning by Sheriff Adams, admitted that a wagon had passed by the day before. The description Hefner provided matched Abdon Leiva's wagon. Sheriff Adams considered waiting at Hefner's for Short and the posse, but he did not trust Hefner and believed it was not safe to stay there alone. He reboarded the coach and continued south six miles to Delano's Station, a large adobe house and stage stop in San Francisquito Canyon, where he waited impatiently for the rest of his posse.[12]

The sheriff's suspicions were well founded, for the gang had left Jim Hefner's house just the day before, having spent two nights there. One of the band, probably Chávez, had camped with the herd of horses nearby at Delano's Station. Abdon Leiva had remained with Tiburcio. Rosario's pregnancy was not yet apparent. Leiva had no definite proof that she had been unfaithful, and he was still trying to devise a way to get her and his children away from Vasquez. After leaving Hefner's, the little band headed south to the rancho of Francisco "Chico" López in Leona Valley, seven miles southeast of Elizabeth Lake. Chico López was one of the oldest and best-known settlers in the region. In fact, Elizabeth Lake had earlier been known to Californios as La Laguna de Chico López. López was a friend and sometime employer of Tiburcio's brother Chico. He welcomed the robber chief and allowed his band to spend two nights there and rest.[13]

The next morning, September 6, they started again, Leiva driving Rosario and the children in his wagon, and Vasquez and Chávez herding some twenty horses behind them. A twenty-mile trip brought them to the mouth of Little Rock Creek, which drained the towering seven-thousand-foot peaks of the San Gabriel Mountains to the south. The creek was dry in the summer, and the sandy streambed made an ideal road for the wagon. Two miles up the canyon they made camp, near what is now the site of the Little Rock Reservoir dam. Here they put the horses out to graze, butchered a stolen beef, dug a waterhole in the sand, and built a campfire. But Vasquez did not feel safe there, and the next morning they pushed another two miles up the canyon, as Leiva later said, "as far as the wagon would ride." At the spot where Santiago Canyon enters the main gorge they veered right up the narrow Santiago Canyon a short distance. Here they made a second camp.

Now Vasquez instructed Abdon Leiva to return to Elizabeth Lake and buy provisions. Leiva finally saw a chance to test his wife's faithfulness. He drove off alone in his wagon, telling Tiburcio he would be back by midnight. Instead of going to Hefner's, Leiva went to a ranch that was much closer and returned to the camp at four in the afternoon. After getting down from the wagon, he recalled, "I went up the creek in the soft sand to the camp, and found Vasquez and my wife lying together." Enraged, he pulled his six-gun, but before he could use it Chávez threw down on him, exclaiming, "If you shoot Vasquez I will blow your brains out."

"All right," Leiva responded, lowering his six-gun. But to Tiburcio he warned, "Be sure, I will kill you if I have a chance."

A penitent Vasquez answered, "You have a right. I have been a traitor to you."

Leiva later recalled, "I told him I would not go with him another minute—that I would get away from there, and if I could ever do him any harm I would do it."

Neither Vasquez nor Chávez suspected what Leiva intended to do, or they undoubtedly would have killed him on the spot. Instead, Vasquez allowed Leiva to stay in the canyon all night unmolested, and in the morning Abdon left camp with Rosario and his children. Tiburcio made no attempt to stop them, undoubtedly fearing that if he killed Leiva, he would lose Rosario. Abdon drove his family north on the old stage road to Llano Verde (now Green Valley), just south of Elizabeth Lake. There they stopped to rest at a teamster's house. Leiva did not want to lose his family, but he was filled with shame and anger. It had become clear to him that Rosario was in love with Vasquez, though he did not know that she was pregnant. Leaving two trunks containing some of the property stolen from Snyder's store, he put Rosario and the children back into the wagon and returned to Hefner's. There he drove his wagon and team into the corral, borrowed a saddle horse from Jim Hefner, and headed toward Los Angeles, leaving Rosario and the children behind. Abdon Leiva was determined to turn himself in and seek vengeance on Tiburcio Vasquez. He rode hard through San Francisquito Canyon to Lyon's Station, a stage stop located in what is now Newhall, where he met William W. Jenkins, a former Los Angeles constable, and surrendered to him. Leiva's ride would have momentous consequences for the bandit chieftain.[14]

Meanwhile Sheriff Adams was closing in on the killers. At Delano's Station he learned that the riders with the herd of horses and the wagon had turned off the stage road and headed back toward the rancho of Chico López in Leona Valley. Adams borrowed a buggy and drove back toward Hefner's. Within a few miles he met the Short brothers with McKenzie and Young, who had been strung out along the road to avoid attracting attention. The possemen held a quick council and Adams recommended that they immediately raid Chico López's place. McKenzie and Young, however, believed that Vasquez had a large gang and insisted on waiting for Sheriff Rowland and reinforcements. But when the evening stage from Los Angeles arrived, Rowland was not aboard. This time Sheriff Adams's instincts were correct, for it later developed that Vasquez was at Chico López's rancho that very day, September 4. After spending the night at Delano's Station, posseman Young found a Californio friend who had seen Vasquez several days before. The bandit chief had confided to him that he was waiting for a woman whom he planned on taking to Mexico by crossing Cajon Pass near San Bernardino. But by now Young, the one-legged vaquero, had had enough of manhunting. He left the posse and headed back to his home in Kern County.

Sheriff Adams recognized that he was now close behind the gang. While his little posse headed south to guard Cajon Pass, Adams made a hard, three-hour, thirty-mile ride through San Francisquito Canyon to the nearest telegraph office, at Lyon's Station. He sent a wire to the Los Angeles sheriff and received a prompt reply that Rowland was already on the northbound stage. Adams pressed on southward to Lopez Station, in what is now San Fernando, where he met Sheriff Rowland. They immediately headed back into Los Angeles, where they wasted no time in getting fresh horses and starting for Cajon Pass late that night. They rode through the darkness, catching up with Rowland's men at George Martin's ranch, a stagecoach station ten miles from San Bernardino, at the mouth of Cajon Pass, near present-day Devore.

Sheriff Adams had ridden 130 miles without rest. He badly needed sleep, but at 1:00 A.M. a Paiute Indian rider arrived with a message from the Short brothers and McKenzie. They had obtained positive information that Vasquez was camped in Little Rock Creek canyon. Immediately Rowland and Adams, with their full posse and the Indian as a guide, mounted up and rode thirty-five miles north to Big Rock Creek canyon, where they made camp at midday on September 6. Sheriff Adams sent out scouts in an effort to find Vasquez, but they returned empty-handed. That night they rode out in all directions, vainly looking from high ridges for the light of campfires. In the morning, September 7, they pushed on northwest eleven miles to the mouth of Little Rock Creek canyon, located about eight miles southeast of the present-day city of Palmdale. There they met Deputy Short's little posse, which had trailed Leiva's wagon south from Elizabeth Lake. At the mouth of the canyon the posse discovered the tracks of the wagon and a herd of horses, and followed them several miles up the dry, sandy creek bed. At this point they found that the wagon tracks now led back out of the canyon. The officers held a parley, and Sheriff Rowland suggested that they follow the wagon tracks. Sheriff Adams and Deputy Short were the only members of the posse who believed that they should press on into the canyon, Adams pointing out that horses' hoofprints appeared to continue into the rocky gorge.

While Rowland led his posse back down the creek bed after the wagon, Adams and Short started on alone up the canyon. They quickly saw that the horse tracks had not turned back with the wagon, and Deputy Short raced after Rowland to tell him the horses were still in the canyon. Now the entire eleven-man posse was urging their mounts up the sandy creek bed. They soon came upon the ashes of a recent campfire near the present Little Rock Reservoir dam. Nearby a waterhole had been dug in the sand

and hanging from the limbs of a tree were three-quarters of a butchered beef, left to dry in the sun. Near the waterhole was the head and hide of the steer. Little Rock Creek canyon at this point opens up into a wide valley, almost a mile and a half long. The sandy creek bed (now covered by Little Rock Reservoir) was about two hundred yards wide. On the west bank an elevated ridge, twenty feet above the creek, extends south for more than a mile. Today it is the site of a paved access road and campgrounds. As Adams and his men spread out in the sandy streambed, looking for sign, Deputy Short suddenly spotted a rider on a large sorrel horse emerge from a clump of cedar trees on the ridge above. It was Clodoveo Chávez. Short yelled out, "There's a man!"

Chávez put spurs to his horse, bent over his saddle, and raced south along the ridge. Sheriff Adams quickly drew a bead with his Henry rifle and squeezed the trigger. The .44 caliber slug grazed the outlaw's cheek. The possemen whipped and spurred their jaded horses through the sandy creek bed. Gunfire crackled as the other officers got their rifles into action. Chávez paid no heed, but urged his horse into a dead run along the ridge, weaving in and out of the rocks and underbrush. Every time his bobbing horse came into view the lawmen fired. But Chávez had the freshest mount, and he pulled away from his pursuers. Suddenly, his horse stumbled, almost throwing him to the ground, but the outlaw recovered. Reaching the far end of the ridge, he spurred his mount down the steep bank and emerged onto the creek bed, two hundred yards in front of the posse. Here the canyon narrows for some three hundred yards through a right-hand bend to the confluence of Little Rock Creek and Santiago Canyon. The canyon walls are steep, with Santiago Canyon branching off to the right, southwesterly, its streambed dry and flat. Chávez had disappeared, and the officers found numerous fresh tracks in the sandy beds of both canyons.

Unbeknownst to the posse, Tiburcio Vasquez was still camped in Santiago Canyon, not far from its junction with Little Rock Creek. He heard the gunfire and rode down to the confluence, where he met Chávez in full retreat. The pair fled up Little Rock Creek. Tiburcio later recalled,

> We knew that the officers were close behind us and we pushed rapidly up the canyon. We halted in some underbrush around a turn in the road and near a high point that commanded a view of the road below. I saw Adams coming ahead and the others

behind. I heard him urge them to come on. For a moment I hesitated as to whether I should kill him or not. He was within easy range and I could have dropped him on the first shot. Then I thought that it would only make matters worse for me, and so I fired over his head several times, after I had shouted to Chávez to get the horses ready. I meant to keep the officers back until Chávez had the horses on hand, when I intended to fly. As I left the point I heard Adams say, 'Come on! We can get them!' If the men followed Adams they might have caught us.[15]

Tiburcio's account was reasonably accurate. The lawmen, after quickly searching the mouth of Santiago Canyon, continued half a mile up Little Rock Creek, with Mitchell in the lead. Behind him were Adams, Deputy Short, Rowland, and Sánchez. The rest of the posse, horses jaded from the hard pursuit, lagged behind. Near the present spot of Basin Campground, where a high bluff juts out over the canyon, Deputy Mitchell heard the sound of falling rock and glanced up. At the same time the loud blast of a Henry rifle echoed in the narrow canyon and a bullet whined past his head. High on the bluff, gunsmoke wafted from behind a boulder. Tiburcio Vasquez, prone with his rifle barrel resting on the rock, levered another round and fired again. The bullet plowed into the sandy bank six feet from Mitchell, who wheeled his horse and raced for cover. Meanwhile, Adams and Rowland leaped from their horses. The former opened a barrage of fire with his own Henry rifle, but the distance was two hundred yards and he could not get a clear shot at Vasquez. Tiburcio had the high ground, and he kept the officers pinned down with constant rifle fire. Sheriff Adams scrambled up the high bank until he was level with Vasquez. From there he opened up again on the outlaw, and Tiburcio's return fire suddenly stopped.

Adams yelled for the others to join him in charging the outlaws' position. But Mitchell called back that he and Rowland wanted the rest of the posse to join them. Mitchell then jumped onto his horse and raced back down the canyon. Adams was furious. He was but two hundred yards away from a band of killers he had pursued for more than five hundred miles. Yelling back that he would "go it alone," he scrambled back down the bluff, leaped into the saddle, and charged forward. Spurring his mount to the top of the bluff, he found that the outlaws had fled. Adams made a quick search and spotted two horses picketed on a nearby ridge. By this

Los Angeles County Deputy Sheriff Henry M. Mitchell, who played a prominent role in the manhunt for Tiburcio Vasquez. (Sven Crongeyer collection)

time he had been joined by Rowland, Short, and Sánchez. They spread out and found nine more horses, including five of those stolen at Tres Pinos. Soon Mitchell rode up with the rest of the posse, and they pushed three miles up the canyon, sending scouts into the surrounding hills. They discovered another ten saddle horses that Vasquez had abandoned. When the outlaws' tracks vanished into the mountainside brush, the lawmen decided to go back and follow the wagon's trail. First they searched Santiago Canyon and found the robbers' camp. Here was another horse, already saddled with one of the rigs stolen from Tres Pinos, as well as a pair of pants and a coat from Snyder's store, fresh beef hung to dry, coffee, sugar, and a bottle of whiskey. The posse had eaten almost nothing in two days, so they devoured the beef, and probably the whiskey as well.[16]

Sheriff Adams gathered all of the captured stock and other items, being astute enough to know that they would be important evidence if the outlaws were captured. Now the posse set off following the tracks of Abdon Leiva's wagon. They followed the sign all night and at noon reached the teamster's cabin in Green Valley. The manhunters surrounded it but found only "old men, women, and children." The teamster admitted that Leiva had been there and showed the sheriffs the two trunks, which were found to contain clothing and jewelry taken from Snyder's store. Sheriff Rowland detailed Pete Gabriel and two other possemen to guard the house in case Vasquez appeared. It was night when the rest of the posse pressed on after the wagon tracks, which they followed to Jim Hefner's, arriving at 3:00 A.M. Leiva's wagon and horses were in the corral. The lawmen demanded to know if Leiva was there, and Hefner said he had left that evening for Los Angeles to give himself up. When asked about Rosario, he replied that Tiburcio Vasquez had arrived two hours earlier and ridden off with her.

The sheriffs were dumbfounded. In a feat of extraordinary daring, Vasquez had skirted the stage road, crossed the hills, and arrived at Hefner's before the posse. Rosario and her three children were asleep when he arrived. Although there is no doubt that she went with her lover willingly, she later, in an attempt to protect her reputation, claimed to have been abducted:

> About the middle of the night Vasquez came to the house. The first intimation I had that he was about was when he put his hand on my shoulder and awakened me. I was lying in bed. He had one hand on my shoulder and in the other he held a pistol, which was cocked and pointed towards me. He told me to get up quick and go with him, or he would blow my brains out. I asked him what I could do with my children. He said he didn't care anything about them. I didn't get up the first time he told me to, and he came back to the bed again, cocked his pistol, and said if I didn't jump out of bed he would kill me. I was afraid he would do it and so I got up. He ordered me to get on my clothes and go with him as soon as possible. I was crying all the time I was dressing. He put me up on his horse and got on behind me.[17]

Tiburcio later described how he had outwitted the sheriffs: "I took Leiva's wife behind me on my horse, and started back in the direction I knew Rowland and Adams and their party would be coming, knowing that I could hear them approaching on their horses. I did so, and as they drew near I turned aside from the road. The sheriffs and their posse passed on." Rosario detailed their flight from the officers: "We met Chávez that day in the mountains. [We] hid in the brush all day and dared not go out, as they knew that the officers were looking for them. We had nothing to eat that day, and not until late the following day, when Vasquez found a young calf and killed it. He brought part of the meat into camp, which we ate without even salt to put on it. All the time I was with them the only bed we had consisted of one pair of blankets and his saddle blankets."[18]

The two sheriffs were chagrined to learn that they had so narrowly missed Vasquez. They demanded that Jim Hefner explain himself, and the station keeper claimed that he had acted in fear of Vasquez and his band. Rowland and Adams were after bigger game and they elected not to arrest Hefner. The lawmen now exchanged their worn-out mounts for those they had seized from Vasquez. While Rowland took the other horses to Delano's Station to feed them, Adams and the rest trailed Tiburcio's tracks southwest to Chico López's ranch in Leona Valley. They found only women and girls in the adobe, so the exhausted man-hunters rode back to Delano's to meet Rowland and get some food and sleep. There they were surprised to find Bill Jenkins with Abdon Leiva in tow. The former constable had sent a telegram to Sheriff Rowland in Los Angeles, and had received a prompt reply advising him to go back up San Francisquito Canyon toward Elizabeth Lake, where the sheriff might be found.

Adams and Rowland were overjoyed at their luck. Sheriff Adams, in particular, knew that his relentless and exhausting manhunt had not been in vain. He and Rowland had no authority to offer Leiva immunity, but they told him that if he cooperated they would recommend leniency. Leiva thereupon made a full confession, providing complete descriptions of the entire gang. He told the sheriffs that Vasquez had slain Redford and Davison. He said that Teodoro Moreno had killed Bernard Bahury and could be found at Ed Tully's sheep ranch with Guadalupe Olivas. Adams was chagrined to learn from him that the Mexican he had let go near Buena Vista Lake was none other than Romulo Gonzáles. Leiva said that Gonzáles and Blas Bicuna could probably be found at the New Idria Mine. He even revealed that Tiburcio had sent his brother Chico a watch he had taken in the Twenty-One Mile House holdup, in an apparent effort to make amends. Armed with this information, Sheriff Adams boarded a

Delano's Station in San Francisquito Canyon. Here Abdon Leiva surrendered to Sheriffs Adams and Rowland. (Author's collection)

northbound stagecoach on the night of September 9, intending to track down the gang members in the north.[19]

Sheriff Rowland now divided his men into three groups to search for Vasquez. He returned Leiva's gun and sent the Chileno with his under-sheriff Albert Johnston and another deputy on a fruitless, weeklong search of Tiburcio's haunts between Elizabeth Lake and Tehachapi. They managed to recover five stolen horses but could find no trace of the fugitives. Meanwhile Sheriff Rowland returned to Jim Hefner's, bundled Leiva's children into his wagon, and brought them into Los Angeles. Leiva, on his return with the rest of the posse, was locked up in the county jail and his three children were placed in the care of Adolfo Celis, one of Rowland's deputies.[20]

Sheriff Rowland's men continued to hunt for Vasquez, Chávez, and Rosario in the San Gabriel Mountains. Rosario had quickly learned that an outlaw's existence was anything but the romantic life of which she had fantasized. She described her ordeal:

One night while we were in the mountains, Vasquez thought he heard the officers whistling to each other, and started up, saying, "That's the officers exchanging signals." The sound came closer and he seized his rifle. Presently, out of the brush, only a short distance from where they were lying, sprang a large California lion. It was a bright moonlight night, and he could be plainly seen. Vasquez fired quickly, and the lion fell dead with a bullet through his heart. The sound which had been taken for a whistle was made by this animal.[21] I think that we were about eight days on the mountain, during which time we had nothing but meat to eat. I was crying a great deal of the time, and Vasquez used to get very angry with me for it. My health was also getting very bad on account of the exposure and bad treatment. Vasquez then took me to another mountain on the other side of the valley. I had been pregnant for three or four months before this time, and was therefore unable to undergo such hardship and ill treatment. On the 22nd of September I was prostrated with a miscarriage. Late in the afternoon of that day, Vasquez and Chávez rode off and left me, sick, helpless, and alone, in these mountains. Vasquez said, "You can get out of here the best way you can with God's help."[22]

Rosario claimed that she had been cared for by a local Mexican, and stayed with his family for more than six weeks until she was well enough to travel, when he bought her a train ticket so that she could return to her parents' home near San Jose. This portion of Rosario's story was untrue. There was then no railroad from Southern California, and she was neither ill treated nor abandoned by Tiburcio. She later admitted, under oath, that she had stayed with Vasquez for two months, until November. As Tiburcio recalled, "I provided for all her wants while she was with me." He arranged for friends to give her shelter and care while he was busy dodging manhunters. But Sheriff Rowland and his men had no luck in finding Vasquez.[23]

Sheriff Adams, first by stagecoach to Bakersfield and then by train, reached San Jose on the night of September 10. Although completely exhausted, he was elated to discover that he had been reelected. The public recognized that Adams had no obligation to pursue the killers; the crime was not even committed in his bailiwick. Yet he had not only conducted one of the most determined manhunts of the Old West, he had come close to capturing the whole gang and had recovered important evidence connecting Tiburcio Vasquez to the Tres Pinos murders. Adams learned that Sheriff Wasson, in contrast, had been heavily criticized for

quitting the manhunt and had been defeated at the polls. As a correspondent from Hollister noted, "Nine out of ten . . . in this community
condemn Wasson . . . for his lack of pluck, his lack of endurance, and his
lack of perseverance." Eugene Sawyer later pointed out, "His turning
back instead of going on was the mistake of his life." Adams soon discovered that other Monterey County lawmen were just as inept as Wasson.
Shortly after he had left Hollister in pursuit of the gang, a posse from
that town, instead of tracking the real killers, had ridden to San Benito
and placed Tiburcio's brother Claudio under arrest. Claudio had been
imprisoned in Hollister but was soon released, guilty of nothing except
being the bandit's brother.[24]

The next day a reenergized Adams telegraphed the now-lame-duck
Sheriff Wasson to meet him in Hollister, where they recruited Constable George Chick and Deputy Sheriff Orson Lyon on the twelfth.
Adams explained to them the details of Abdon Leiva's confession: Teodoro
Moreno was one of the killers and could be found at Ed Tully's sheep
ranch, along with gang member Guadalupe Olivas. Romulo Gonzáles had
likely returned to the New Idria Mine, where Leiva thought he could be
found with Blas Bicuna. Because Adams now knew Gonzáles by sight,
and Lyon and Chick were acquainted with Moreno, he sent the latter
two after Tiburcio's cousin.

Then he and Wasson rode to Tres Pinos, where Adams displayed part
of the stolen property. It was immediately identified by Andrew Snyder
and some of the other victims. From here they made the long ride to New
Idria by buggy, driving all night on the twelfth. At 2:00 A.M. they were
slowly climbing a hill less than a mile from Idria when three shadowy
figures stepped out of the moonlit blackness. One of them caught the
team's bridles and another ordered, "Shell out!" Wasson was holding the
reins, but Adams swung up his Henry rifle and took close aim at the
man holding the team. Just as he was about to squeeze the trigger, the
robber moved around the horses and with his partners stepped toward
the side of the buggy. They found themselves staring down the barrels
of Adams's rifle and Wasson's seven-shooter. The three road agents fled
into the darkness. The sheriffs did not pursue them for fear that an alarm
would be raised and their real quarry would escape. But it was too late.
When the lawmen arrived at the mines, they learned that Gonzáles and
Bicuna had fled half an hour before. The sheriffs returned to Hollister
empty-handed.

Chick and Lyon had much better success. They found Teodoro Moreno, armed with a six-gun and busy shearing sheep on the Tully ranch in Bitterwater Valley. Having no idea that he was suspected of the Tres Pinos raid, he quietly submitted to arrest. The two lawmen picked up Guadalupe Olivas at a nearby ranch and brought their prisoners into Hollister, where they turned them over to Sheriffs Adams and Wasson. The captured outlaws were taken to Salinas and locked up in the Monterey County jail.[25]

Sheriff Wasson took a steamer to Los Angeles and returned with Abdon Leiva, lodging him in the Salinas jail on September 26. The next morning he was brought into court to testify at the preliminary examination of Moreno and Olivas on the charge of murder at Tres Pinos. The purpose of the hearing was to determine whether there was probable cause to hold the prisoners for trial. Moreno was represented by Bob Tully, cousin of Ed Tully, a former judge and the first lawyer in Gilroy. The courtroom was packed with spectators—many of them Hispanic—and a number of newspaper reporters. Lorenzo Vasquez was also there, having made the long trip to Salinas to testify for Moreno. Leiva impressed observers by his frank and forthcoming demeanor. He appeared eager to testify against Tiburcio but reluctant to implicate his friends, primarily Moreno and Lorenzo Vasquez, and broke into tears when he testified against them.

Leiva explained in great detail the planning of the raid and the robbery of the store. He described how Moreno had shot and killed Bernard Bahury on the front porch of Snyder's store and how Lorenzo Vasquez had aided the gang in their flight. He testified at length about their escape to Southern California and his discovery that Rosario was Tiburcio's lover. Leiva was then questioned at length by attorney Tully. A reporter who attended the trial wrote, "The cross examination failed to shake the testimony of the witness on a single point, and all who heard him were convinced that he told nothing but the plain unvarnished truth." Strangely, however, Leiva said nothing about Vasquez killing anyone at Tres Pinos. Instead he recalled that after Moreno killed the sheepherder "Vasquez told me to mount a horse and pursue a boy who had fled toward the creek. What transpired during the time I was overtaking the boy I don't know. . . . Vasquez told me that two other men had been killed. I saw one dead man in the stable when I went to loose the horses. I did not see any others that were killed."[26]

Abdon Leiva had repeatedly told his captors that Vasquez had killed Davison and Redford at Tres Pinos, and his admissions were published in the newspapers. He later told reporters that he had not told "the whole story of the Tres Pinos tragedy" when he testified in the Moreno case. The reason why he now failed to implicate Vasquez can be guessed. He evidently believed that, by holding back his testimony against Vasquez, he could negotiate a better deal for himself in the event the chieftain was captured. He would be able to offer evidence that could send the bandit chieftain to the gallows, which he hoped would give him his freedom. From his simplistic viewpoint, he did not consider that such inconsistent testimony might damage his credibility. In the end, Leiva's decision would benefit him greatly. The fact that he was at least omitting important facts, and at worst committing perjury, was ignored by the prosecution.[27]

Abdon Leiva was on the stand all day and into the evening. At eight o'clock Sheriff Adams took the witness stand and described his hunt for the killers, his recovery of the stolen property, and the surrender of Leiva. Sheriff Wasson then testified to the same facts. The prosecution called no other witnesses, nor did Tully for the defense. Tully, after first making an unsuccessful motion that the case against Moreno be dismissed for lack of evidence, then asked that Moreno be released on bail. That too was denied. The judge found probable cause that Moreno had killed Bahury, but ordered Olivas released as there was no evidence to connect him with the Tres Pinos raid.

Sheriff Adams promptly arrested him on a charge of robbing the Twenty-One Mile House. However, Leiva assured Adams that Olivas had not taken part in that holdup, and two days later Adams released him. In the meantime, however, Lorenzo Vasquez was surprised to find himself under arrest and charged as an accessory to the Tres Pinos murders. The following Saturday, October 4, his preliminary examination took place in the same courtroom in Salinas. Like Moreno he was represented by Bob Tully. Sheriffs Adams and Wasson testified that Lorenzo had denied any knowledge of the band stopping at his place. For the defense, Ed Tully and his brother-in-law, Francisco de Álvarez, testified that Vasquez had always borne a good reputation and that he had told them he had only helped the gang out of fear. Although Lorenzo Vasquez was held to answer, the charges were later dropped, apparently on his promise to testify against Moreno.[28]

In the meantime Tiburcio had remained holed up in the San Gabriel Mountains near the rancho of Chico López. Through López, Jim Hefner, and other friends he obtained newspapers and probably learned that a woodcut engraving of his portrait had been published prominently in the *San Francisco Chronicle,* California's leading daily newspaper, three days after the Tres Pinos murders. The portrait accompanied the first detailed account of his career, written by Eugene Sawyer. The enterprising Sawyer had obtained from a Gilroy constable a copy of the carte-de-visite photograph taken of Vasquez in San Francisco some eight years before, and a wood engraving was made from it. Newspapers of the 1870s seldom had illustrations, and the publication of pictures of criminals was rare. Now for the first time Tiburcio's image was widely circulated to the public. However, he had changed considerably over the years. He had gained weight, his face was fuller and darkly tanned, and he wore a full beard. Tiburcio correctly guessed that few would recognize him from the *Chronicle*'s engraving. He decided to raise a new band and head back north to his stomping grounds in the Coast Range.[29]

Vasquez sent Clodoveo Chávez into Los Angeles to pick up supplies, news, and recruits. Chávez rode to the adobe of Georgios "Greek George" Caralambo, situated eight miles northwest of Los Angeles in what is now West Hollywood. Greek George was a tough character who had come to the United States as a camel herder in the army's ill-fated experimental use of camels in the southwestern deserts. A close friend of Vasquez's, Greek George was married to a Californio woman, Cornelia López. Tiburcio had an eye for Cornelia's attractive twenty-eight-year-old sister, Modesta, and had been a frequent visitor to the Caralambos' home. Chávez left his rifle and horse at Greek George's and walked into Los Angeles, armed only with a pistol and bowie knife. In Sonoratown he found Ysidro Padilla, a dangerous bandit who had been tried twice in the famous Medina murder case, the brutal execution-style killing of five men during a store robbery near Stockton in 1869. In his first trial, Padilla had been convicted of murder and sentenced to hang with his partner, Jesús Tejada. His conviction was overturned by the California Supreme Court. When he was retried in 1872, important witnesses were gone, and he was acquitted. Padilla, undaunted by his narrow escape from the noose, readily accepted Chávez's invitation to join the gang.[30]

Clodoveo Chávez spent two days in Sonoratown, where he learned that Sheriff Rowland's posses had given up the chase. He and Padilla

The notorious Ysidro (Isador) Padilla, about 1870. While riding with Vasquez, he took part in the Kingston raid and the Repetto robbery. (Author's collection)

agreed to leave separately and meet at Greek George's. Before heading out of town, Chávez knocked down a pedestrian and robbed him of ninety dollars in coin and a fine gold watch. He and Padilla laid low at Greek George's for two days, paying the Greek well for his hospitality. Then they rode northeast through San Francisquito Canyon to Chico López's rancho. They soon met up with Vasquez and Rosario, who were hidden in the nearby hills. By now Rosario had recovered from her miscarriage. Vasquez was highly impatient, as he had expected Chávez back much sooner. But the bandit chief was mollified by the appearance of the new recruit, and he gave Padilla a hearty welcome. That night the three outlaws discussed Tiburcio's plan to ride back north and make a series of daring raids in the San Joaquin Valley. Vasquez was distressed to learn that Teodoro Moreno had been arrested and quickly developed a wild scheme to break his cousin out of the Salinas jail. Tiburcio believed that one of his Cantúa cousins, Francisco Gómez, a dangerous outlaw and horse thief, might be willing to help. He sent Padilla to Panama, the tiny Mexican settlement near Bakersfield, to find Gómez and invite him to join the gang at the New Idria Mine.

Then Vasquez, Chávez, and Rosario headed north on horseback. After sending Chávez into Poso Chane to look for recruits, the three continued on to Cantua Canyon, where they arrived on October 17. While Tiburcio and Rosario stayed out of sight, Chávez had a long talk with a Mexican friend and two Americans, giving them a detailed description of the fight at Rock Creek. He told them that two bullets had grazed his right side and one had nicked his head. He said that he and Vasquez had planned on fleeing to Mexico, but every avenue of escape south was guarded, and now they were returning Rosario to her family and friends in Santa Clara County. The next day the three continued on toward New Idria. Now Vasquez rode in cautiously alone, while Chávez and Rosario lagged behind. He was elated to receive a joyous reception from many of the miners. Tiburcio described in detail the story of his flight and claimed that Abdon Leiva, on seeing him in bed with Rosario, had killed her. By this time his stealing of Leiva's wife was widely known and had been published extensively in the newspapers. Leiva had many friends in Idria, and Vasquez no doubt told this yarn to keep them from turning against him.

Vasquez, Chávez, and Rosario stayed near the mines for two or three days, probably at Agustín Hernández's place on Griswold Creek or at the home of Tiburcio's sister María in nearby Vallecitos. They were joined by Blas Bicuna, Ysidro Padilla, and Francisco Gómez. Tiburcio was too cautious to stay in one spot for more than a few days at a time. They rode north to a sheep camp in Cañada Verde in the mountains east of Hollister. Now Vasquez sent Blas Bicuna, who was a stranger in Monterey County, to take a message and money to Teodoro Moreno in the Salinas jail. Following Tiburcio's directions, Bicuna rode into Salinas at night and stopped at the house of a Mexican prostitute. The next day she visited the county jail, bringing Moreno the cash and Vasquez's offer to help him escape. Tiburcio's cousin was grateful for the money, but he wanted no part in a jailbreak. He told the woman that he doubted it would succeed, and it would only leave him worse off than he already was. When Bicuna returned to the mountain hideout, Vasquez was disappointed but accepted Moreno's decision. Later Vasquez asked Bicuna to secretly visit San Jose, where Abdon Leiva was being held, and through some women friends of Tiburcio's, to deliver poisoned food to him in jail. Bicuna thought it over for a day or two, and finally responded that he was too afraid of Sheriff Adams to set foot in San Jose. Vasquez then approached Francisco Gómez, whose answer was an emphatic "No!"[31]

Gómez's decision was a wise one. Sheriff Adams had already been tipped off by several informants that the band had been seen in Cantua and Idria, and Sheriff Wasson had learned from another informant that Vasquez planned to rescue Moreno from the Salinas calaboose and had even obtained diagrams of the jail. On October 24 Sheriff Adams was in Salinas when he got word that Vasquez and Chávez would pass through Hollister that night. He and Wasson armed themselves and made a hard ride over the Gabilans to Hollister, but they could find no trace of the outlaws. Soon Adams got a tip that Vasquez was at the sheep camp in the Cañada Verde in the mountains east of Hollister. By this time Adams had apparently had enough of Sheriff Wasson. He recruited John Phelps, a friend and reporter for the *San Francisco Chronicle,* and on October 28 they left San Jose to hunt the outlaws. The two spent a week scouring a hundred-mile radius around the Cañada Verde and the Quien Sabe Valley. They found that Vasquez had been there, but as usual, could not find him, as Adams explained, "on account of the friendly feelings entertained by the mountaineers, all of whom are Californians [Californios]."[32]

Tiburcio, in turn, learned that his nemesis was again on his trail. He fled south to a hideout in the canyon of Zapato Chino Creek. He left Rosario behind, probably in the care of his sister María, or perhaps with some other friend in the Panoche Valley. Now, in his hideout near Poso Chane, Tiburcio began planning a grand series of bandit raids that would propel him into folklore.

CHAPTER FIFTEEN

Raiders of the San Joaquin

The San Joaquin Valley sprawls across the heart of California, three hundred miles long, from the Sacramento River delta in the north to the Tehachapi Mountains in the south, and from the Coast Range east to the Sierra Nevada. Its vastness, more than fifteen thousand square miles, dwarfs some New England states. The east side of the valley is lush, watered by countless rivers and streams that drain the snow-capped Sierra Nevada. The west side is dry, its alkali plains broken only by tumbleweeds and scattered arroyos. The great valley is immense, monotonously flat, and except in winter, insufferably hot. Its remote harshness perfectly suited Tiburcio Vasquez and his band. Besides Las Juntas, Rancho de los Californios, and Poso Chane, there were other Hispanic settlements where he was safe, among them Spanishtown in the northern part of Visalia, La Libertad near the Kings River, and Panama, just south of Bakersfield.

On November 4, Clodoveo Chávez and another desperado, Anastacio Androtio, were camped at a jacal on Carey Creek in the Cholame Valley, high in the Coast Range. Chávez came across an old Mexican borreguero, who foolishly revealed that he had just been paid $230 in coin. Chávez invited the unsuspecting sheepherder to their hut and furnished him with food and provisions. When he left, Chávez and Androtio followed and ambushed him in Cholame Valley. They shot him three times, then emptied the dead man's pockets. After unsuccessfully trying to cut off his head to prevent the body from being identified, Chávez sliced open the Mexican's forehead and pulled the facial skin down over his mouth. The two killers then dragged the corpse into a ravine and covered it with brush. Chávez gave Androtio a twenty-five-dollar gold note and $3.50 in coin, keeping the rest of the booty for himself.

The area was well settled and a Mexican herder, attracted by the gunfire, saw the cutthroats hiding the body. He raced to Carey Creek and raised the alarm. Soon a posse of Anglos and Hispanics, led by a rancher named Jackson, was in pursuit. Chávez had a fine saddle animal and managed to escape. But Anastacio Androtio was thrown attempting to mount his horse, and the animal ran off, leaving him on foot. He hid in the brush, but the posse captured him the following day. According to his captors, "He made a full confession of the whole affair, and said that he wished to be hung, as he was tired of life." Androtio blamed the crime on Chávez. The Hispanic posse members wanted to lynch him on the spot, but the Anglos persuaded them to wait until another party of American ranchers arrived and a vigilante trial could be held. Soon a group of forty-two herders and ranchers had gathered and an informal hearing began. Androtio was found guilty of the murder and sentenced to be hanged immediately. A rope thrown over a cottonwood tree on Carey Creek served as his gallows, and Anastacio Androtio was quickly strung up.[1]

Clodoveo Chávez returned to the hideout on Zapato Chino Creek. The gang decided to scatter. While Vasquez and some of the band went north, Francisco Gómez had already ridden more than one hundred miles south into Kern County. Gómez lived with a Native American woman in an Indian *ranchería* on Tunis Creek, north of Tejon Pass, and he figured there he would be safe. No sooner did Gómez get there however than he was taking part in a murder. A compadre of his, a Mexican *curandero* (folk healer) in Tehachapi, had been asked to treat a sick Mexican. The curandero gave him a dose of medicine, and he died almost immediately. The poisoning was reportedly part of a scheme by the curandero and Gómez to acquire the dead man's remuda of horses. The victim's friends swore out a murder warrant for the curandero and Gómez. Tehachapi Constable William S. Mettler promptly arrested the curandero and began hunting for Francisco Gómez. Two days later, on November 6, Constable Mettler, with two possemen, Charles Russell and a man named Glenn, encountered Gómez with three other desperadoes on the road between Tehachapi and Tunis Creek. Mettler rode up and told Gómez he had a warrant for him.

Gómez replied, "I will go anywhere you want me to."

At that, Russell cautioned Mettler, "We had better disarm him"

Constable Mettler and Glenn rode close to Gómez and asked him for his pistol.

"Here it is. Take it," the desperado replied.

Mettler wrapped the reins around his saddletree. Before he could dismount, Gómez pointed the weapon at Mettler and said again, "Here, take it," as he cocked the hammer and fired. The ball tore through Mettler's left arm and shattered his heart. As the officer fell dead from his horse, Gómez emptied his pistol at Russell and Glenn. Russell put spurs to his mount and fled, but Glenn was made of sterner stuff. Jerking his revolver, Glenn advanced on the killer, six-gun flaming. Gómez ducked for cover behind his horse and was saved when a loose percussion cap jammed the cylinder of Glenn's pistol. As Glenn tried frantically to pry it loose, Gómez leaped to Mettler's body, yanked his six-shooter from its holster, and opened fire again on Glenn. The defenseless posseman had no choice but to jump back into the saddle and flee in a hail of bullets. Gómez then calmly removed the saddle from Mettler's horse and rode off with his compadres, leading the officer's mount behind them. Two posses spent three fruitless weeks hunting him.[2]

In Panoche Valley Vasquez rejoined Rosario, who by this time was completely disenchanted with outlaw life. Often in tears, she missed her children and was despondent over her miscarriage. Vasquez began planning a new raid, as he later said, "for money to send her back to her parents' house." One of Tiburcio's fresh recruits was Ignacio Rangel, a notorious young bandido from Monterey and younger brother of Ramón Rangel, Tiburcio's San Quentin compadre. He had known the Rangel brothers in Monterey, and had renewed his acquaintance with Ignacio in San Quentin, where he had been a prisoner from 1866 to 1869. Ignacio Rangel had worked as a vaquero in Fresno County and probably suggested to Tiburcio that the gang rob Jones' Store in the Sierra Nevada foothills. Jones' Store was similar to the hotel-stores at the Twenty-One Mile House and Firebaugh's Ferry. Owned by James R. Jones, it was situated on the north bank of the San Joaquin River, two miles downstream from Millerton (then the Fresno County seat) and opposite the present-day town of Friant. It consisted of a large, two-story hotel and a single-level store, fifty feet in front of the hotel. Here Jones also operated a ferry across the San Joaquin River. Once it had been an important location for travel and trade, but a year earlier the railroad had reached Fresno and the new town boomed. Many Millerton residents pulled up stakes and settled in

Fresno, leaving the Jones place as one of the few stores in the Millerton area. The once-bustling settlement at Jones' Ferry had now become somewhat deserted, and was an ideal target for robbers.

At six o'clock on the evening of November 10, 1873, Tiburcio Vasquez and six compadres rode toward the store: Ignacio Rangel, Clodoveo Chávez, and four other riders who were never identified. The outlaws rode in from the north, and as they reached the high bluff overlooking the river, they encountered a lone horseman, John Hoxie. Believing that the band was a group of borregueros, Hoxie conversed with them for a short while, then rode on. Vasquez and his men rode down to the store, dismounted in the darkness, and surrounded it. Inside, ten men were clustered around two tables, smoking and playing cards. The tables were in the center of a large room, with store counters on either side. The clerk, Smith Norris, was tending the store while owner Jim Jones read a newspaper inside the nearby hotel. Suddenly, the front and back doors were thrust open simultaneously. Tiburcio and his men burst inside, six-shooters drawn, and commanded, "Hands up!"

The card players, surprised and unarmed, cursed loudly as they were ordered to lie prone on the floor. One of them, a colorful ranch manager named John Bugg, had known Ignacio Rangel as a local vaquero. Although the bandits were masked, Bugg instantly recognized Rangel as the man holding a pistol to his head. Enraged, Bugg cursed him, saying in Spanish, "You God-damned black son of a bitch. If I had my six-shooter I'd show you damned quick whether I'd lie down or not!" Recalled one of the rancher's friends, "Fifty years after, Bugg was still mad." Tiburcio Vasquez then ordered the card players to "lie down and keep quiet at the peril of life." They were bound with rope and their pockets emptied of coin and valuables. Then the clerk was forced to open the safe, which was looted of cash. Vasquez then told his men to help themselves to any clothing and riding gear they wanted. They went through the stock, and each man took a suit of clothes, a new saddle, spurs, bridle, and rope, plus several firearms and all the ammunition he could find. Meanwhile the supper bell rang at the hotel, and when no one responded, Jones sent his Chinese cook to the store. He was captured and tied up with the rest. Vasquez and his band spent a leisurely hour and a half in the store, with one bandit posted outside to watch their horses. Finally they mounted up and rode off toward the west with their loot, valued at $1,000, draped from their saddle horns.[3]

In the meantime the Chinese cook managed to free himself and untie the others. So quietly had the robbery proceeded that Jones, in the hotel, had no idea what had taken place. One of the card players mounted a horse and raced to Millerton for help. Fresno County Sheriff J. Scott Ashman immediately began raising a posse. At daybreak he headed out of town with nine heavily armed and well-mounted men. They first rode to Jones' Store, where the furious John Bugg and another volunteer joined them. Sheriff Ashman and his posse then followed the bandits' tracks out of the foothills to Borden Station, located on the rail line four miles south of Madera. Here the hoofprints of a large band of horses, which had passed through earlier, obliterated the fugitives' trail. Certain that the outlaws were part of Vasquez's gang and were headed toward the Coast Range, Sheriff Ashman decided to ride west to Firebaugh's Ferry. They arrived at the hotel at dusk, where George Hoffman, still smarting from the raid eight months before, greeted them warmly and provided food for the men and their horses. The posse bedded down for the night in the hotel, and in the morning made a hard ride south to the mouth of Cantua Creek, where they spent the night with a Basque sheepherder. In the morning they continued south and searched the country near Poso Chane. The next day they rode into the Coast Range, searching every jacal they came across.

At a settlement near the headwaters of Cantua Creek the possemen met Tiburcio's favorite sister, María Lara. She and Manuel still lived in the Vallecitos, about five miles northwest of New Idria and a few miles south of Agustín Hernández's house on Griswold Creek. María, ever loyal to Tiburcio, was not happy to see the posse. John Bugg later recalled that she "derided them, saying there was no rope to hang her brother, and with truculent scorn defied them to find him, and advised them to go home." Bugg added that "it was afterward discovered that Vasquez was hidden in a rough side canyon not far distant."[4]

Sheriff Ashman and his posse continued on to the headwaters of Martinez Creek, near Joaquin Rocks, arriving at nightfall. There they found the adobe of Mariana, the best-known resident in the Cantua Creek country, who for many years had claimed to be Joaquín Murrieta's widow. Sheriff Ashman and his posse found Mariana living with a Mexican named Linares. Mariana welcomed the Anglo officers and prepared a meal of tortillas, *tasajo* (beef jerky), and hot coffee. The posse spent the night at Mariana's place, and in the morning Linares led them south over rough trails to the little settlement of Alcalde, in the hills west of what is now Coalinga. By now it was clear that the bandidos had vanished, and Sheriff Ashman led his weary posse toward home. They made a two-day ride back north, stopping at Rancho de los Californios, which they searched without success. The possemen finally arrived back in Millerton on November 20, having spent ten fruitless days in the saddle.[5]

Tiburcio had left Rosario with friends, as he said, "in the hills at a sheep ranch," probably in Panoche Valley. He returned to the sheep camp immediately after the raid, gave Rosario money, and had one of his men, probably Chávez, take her to the train station in Hollister. Two days afterward, on the night of November 12, Rosario arrived at the home of Jim Gould, a family friend who owned a farm in Milpitas, just north of San Jose. The next day Sheriff Adams learned she was there, and with a *San Francisco Chronicle* reporter—probably his friend John Phelps—visited Rosario. "She is below the medium height," the journalist wrote, "rather light for a Mexican, and her face is badly marked by smallpox. She is said to have been a beautiful girl and a famous ballroom belle among her country people. Traces of beauty still remain. In animated conversation her face lights up and her black eyes fairly sparkle." To Sheriff Adams Rosario denied any knowledge of the Tres Pinos raid, and claimed that Vasquez had abducted her from Jim Hefner's house and had abandoned her in the mountains after two weeks.[6]

By now Teodoro Moreno's trial date was rapidly approaching. The Monterey prosecutor had been eager to get a second witness who could corroborate Abdon Leiva's testimony against Moreno. Sheriff Adams knew that Rosario was his best bet and he obtained a subpoena for her. He found Rosario staying at her grandfather's home in Alviso. At first she refused to cooperate, still claiming she knew nothing about the Tres Pinos murders, but Adams explained that Abdon had turned state's evidence and would be treated leniently. Rosario was desperate to see her children and hopeful that she could reconcile with her husband, so she finally relented. On November 23 Sheriff Adams took Rosario and her mother to see Abdon in the Salinas jail. There the two had a tearful reunion, and Rosario tried to persuade Abdon that Vasquez had carried her off by force. He seemed mollified and replied that he held no ill will against her. Finally Rosario, after being assured that her cooperation would help win her husband's release, agreed to testify. Leiva, however, mistrusted his wife: "She said that she had been forced to be untrue to me, and wanted to make up, and immediately afterwards she tried to persuade me not to testify against Moreno." Rosario was obviously conflicted. She still held strong feelings for Tiburcio, but in the end they were outweighed by her desire to get back her husband and especially, her children.[7]

The next morning Moreno's trial began before District Court Judge David Belden in Salinas. After 105 potential jurors were examined, a jury of eleven Anglos and one Californio was chosen. The courtroom was packed with Moreno's friends and relatives. For the first time, friends and family of Tiburcio Vasquez would be called to testify in court. Abdon Leiva began the testimony, repeating the story he had told during the preliminary hearing. He was humiliated by his wife's infidelity, and again broke into tears when he described it to the jury. Then Rosario took the stand during the evening session. She confirmed her husband's story, explaining how the Tres Pinos robbery was planned at her house and detailing the escape south to Los Angeles County. She denied having a sexual relationship with Tiburcio, saying, "My husband never caught me in bed with Tiburcio Vasquez, nor did he catch me lying on the ground with him."

Now Lorenzo Vasquez was called as a prosecution witness. He was too wily to implicate himself in the gang's wrongdoing. He admitted that Vasquez and three of the band had appeared at his place the morning after the murders, and that his wife had cooked them breakfast. He denied receiving any of the loot, saying, "If these men divided money at my place, I didn't see it." He claimed that Moreno showed up half an hour later and did not say "anything about the Tres Pinos robbery. . . . Tiburcio was the only one who spoke anything about the robbery, and that was said in the presence of myself and my wife." He denied receiving stolen property, but admitted that Romulo Gonzáles had left a bundle of clothing, adding, "They also gave me a few rings and cheap trinkets." His testimony seemed carefully crafted to implicate everyone in the band except Moreno. Lorenzo's wife, Paula, testified next, telling essentially the same story. She claimed that Moreno was not present when Lorenzo was given "some finger rings, three necklaces, three pocket knives, and a coat." She claimed that she had acted in fear of the band, saying, "I was too frightened to remember anything."

Fred Taylor, a well-known settler in nearby Hernandez Valley, provided damaging testimony against Moreno. The morning after the raid he had been raking hay in a field on the Button family ranch near the stage road when he saw four mounted men with pack animals pass by. A few hours later Taylor rode three miles north to visit Lorenzo Vasquez. He was surprised to see his friend Teodoro Moreno there. "It was the first I had seen of him for some time. I asked him where he had been, and what he had been doing. He said he had been sick and confined there in Lorenzo's house for the past month. When I asked him why he had not sent for or informed me, he made no answer, but gave an evasive reply and changed the subject."

Andrew Snyder's clerk, John Utzerath, then testified that he had known Teodoro Moreno since the previous April and identified him positively, despite the muffler he wore around his face during the robbery. "His size, actions, voice and general appearance were those of Teodoro Moreno," he said. "I thought it was him that night, and so remarked at the time." Andrew Snyder was called to the stand and described the raid in detail. He swore that the only member of the band he could identify was Abdon Leiva. Louis Scherer, Elizabeth Davison, and Lewis Smith also described the raid at Tres Pinos and gave descriptions of the robbers. Of these three, only Smith was able to partially identify the lanky Moreno. During the testimony, wrote one newspaperman, "Moreno has presented a calm, unruffled front, taking great interest in the developments as they progress, but giving no outward sign of nervousness or excitement, seldom speaking to his counsel, and taking no notice of any of the throng of spectators of all classes who surround him."

After the prosecution rested, Bob Tully's first defense witness was Manuel Lara. He admitted that he was Tiburcio's brother-in-law and attempted to provide an alibi for Moreno. He said that Vasquez, with Abdon Leiva, Clodoveo Chávez, and Romulo Gonzáles, had come to his house one Sunday night in August, and that Moreno had not been with them. On cross-examination, however, he was unable to state the date of the visit nor the date of the Tres Pinos raid. He testified that he had heard about the murders a week later from people at the New Idria Mine. He said he had known Tiburcio about fifteen or sixteen years, but his credibility was seriously damaged when he stated, "I did not know what business Vasquez was engaged in; never asked him."

Bob Tully's next witness didn't fare any better. By any measure, Tiburcio's niece Concepción Espinosa was a tragic figure. Born out of wedlock and raised by Doña Guadalupe, she had lived most of her life in poverty. Her lover José Castro had been lynched, and at times she had eked out a precarious living as a prostitute. Her difficult life made her look much older than her thirty years; a reporter at the trial described her as "fair, fat, and about forty." She testified through an interpreter that on August 26, the day of the raid, she was living with her eight-year-old daughter at the San Carlos Mine, a few miles south of New Idria. Concepción said that Teodoro Moreno came to visit her and spent the night, making it impossible for him to have been present at Tres Pinos. On cross-examination she admitted that he "was in the habit of visiting my house frequently" and that she had "known Moreno for the past thirteen or fourteen years." She said, "I am married, but do not live with my husband" and admitted that she had lived with José Castro at the time he was lynched. Concepción said that she had moved from San Carlos to the Laras' home in the Vallecitos, and from there to Hollister. She admitted that she "lived permanently in Hollister in former years, in a saloon," but vehemently denied being a prostitute: "I never lived in a house of prostitution in Hollister, nor kept a house of that kind." Tiburcio's niece tried to downplay her connection to Vasquez and his family, falsely insisting, "I am not related to Tiburcio Vasquez. I was raised from infancy by a woman named Vasquez. I was an orphan. I am not an intimate friend of Tiburcio Vasquez. I have never been much in his company. The last time I spoke to him was ten years ago. I am positive I have not spoken to him within that time."

Now Teodoro Moreno took the stand on his own behalf. He denied taking part in the raid, saying he had spent that night with Concepción Espinosa, leaving her house at 3:00 A.M. because he was unwell and wanted to make the ride before it got hot. He arrived at Lorenzo Vasquez's place at 6:30, and Tiburcio, Leiva, Chávez, and Gonzáles were just sitting down to breakfast when he arrived. Moreno said he ate with them, and after the gang left, rode to Ed Tully's ranch on Bitterwater Creek to shear sheep. He insisted that Abdon and Rosario had lied when they testified that he had participated in planning the Tres Pinos raid. He did admit, "I am first cousin to Tiburcio Vasquez," one of his few truthful statements. In response to cross-examination, he claimed, "I am not an intimate friend of Tiburcio Vasquez. I have seen him but three times in the past three years. I saw him last on the 10th day of August last, at a Mexican camp."[8]

Moreno's testimony closed the defense case. The prosecution introduced four witnesses to impeach Concepción Espinosa: Andrew Snyder, John Utzerath, Fred Taylor, and Constable George Chick. All asserted that she "bore a bad reputation in the community for honor, truth, and integrity." Then the lawyers gave closing arguments. Reported the *Salinas*

Index, "Mr. Tully has had a very difficult case to contend with, both on account of the nature of the testimony and the popular prejudice against Moreno." At 10:00 P.M. on November 27 the case was submitted to the jury. They deliberated an hour before finding Teodoro Moreno guilty of second degree murder. Bob Tully's able defense had saved him from the gallows. The next morning Judge Belden sentenced him to life in prison. The shadow of Tiburcio Vasquez loomed large in the courtroom. Judge Belden, in delivering the sentence, told him, "It is shown that you were the friend, the companion, and the associate of Tiburcio Vasquez, the red handed outlaw, whose connection with the present murder is as well established as his other numberless crimes are notorious and unquestioned. That you should associate yourself with this wretch's crimes as you confessedly did with his companionship is, in my judgment, no small circumstance against you."[9]

Large crowds, both friendly and hostile to Moreno, had gathered around the jail. To avoid trouble, Sheriff Wasson brought Moreno directly to the train station, and he was quickly taken to San Quentin. Teodoro Moreno's trial had lasted three days, about average for a California murder trial in that era. The evidence was clear that he had shot and killed Bernard Bahury in cold blood. Such offenses, especially when committed during a robbery, almost always resulted in a conviction of first degree murder and death by hanging. But here the jurors, for reasons that are not entirely clear, spared his life. Perhaps they felt that Vasquez was the instigator and Moreno merely a follower; perhaps they were reluctant to send him to the gallows based largely on the testimony of a fellow bandit. Or perhaps the jury's lone Californio, Rafael Pombert—who like his brother Juan had grown up in Monterey and knew the Vasquez family well—convinced the others to spare Teodoro Moreno's life.

Tiburcio gleaned no lesson from his cousin's fate. By late December he was at Rancho de los Californios, making his headquarters in the log stockade on Chidester's Island. Now he began planning the biggest raid of his career: to sack an entire town. With him were his loyal compadres Clodoveo Chávez, Francisco Gómez, Ignacio Rangel, Ysidro Padilla, Manuel López, and Blas Bicuna. He had no trouble finding new recruits among the desperadoes who hung around Rancho de los Californios. One of them was an impressionable, seventeen-year-old vaquero, Procella Anamantoria, whose true name was probably Refugio Monteros. Another new recruit was Ramón Molina, a dangerous cutthroat with a face savagely scarred from knife fights. A local sheepshearer named Ramón also joined, as did a fugitive Mexican named Márquez, who had fled Visalia a few weeks before. On December 4 Márquez had shot and killed a fellow Mexican in Spanishtown, the Hispanic part of Visalia, in a fight over a woman.[10]

On Christmas Day 1873, Tiburcio spent the holiday in the log stockade while a portion of the gang saddled their horses and headed south. On the highway south of Visalia, three of them stopped a teamster named McCloud and robbed him of seventy-five dollars. They rode boldly through Visalia, unsuspected, and headed west to Cross Creek, where they robbed another man of a large sum of money. They continued on to await Vasquez at La Libertad, a little Hispanic settlement on the Kings River (now called Riverdale), where a handful of families lived in dugouts and tule-thatched huts.[11]

Early the following morning Tiburcio Vasquez with six of his band rode out of Rancho de los Californios. At five o'clock they cantered up to a switching station on the railroad, fifteen miles south of Fresno. Although it would later grow into the town of Selma, at that time it consisted of several small wood-frame shacks near the railroad tracks. A Chinese work crew occupied several of the sheds, and in another slept Pat Reardon, a tough Irish section boss. The bandidos awakened Reardon and demanded that he cook breakfast for them, but the groggy Irishman refused. One of the robbers produced a whip, and Reardon was flogged savagely and left for dead. The freebooters, still hungry, mounted their horses and rode south six miles to the ranch of Wilson Livermore, located two and a half miles west of the present-day town of Kingsburg. Livermore's daughter, Florence, then thirteen, later described their arrival:

> My mother and I were home alone as my father was away working. It was about six o'clock in the morning when the Vasquez band came and asked for something to eat; they said they would be satisfied if they could only get a cup of coffee. They had just come from Selma where the section boss, Pat Reardon, had refused to give them anything. He had been severely beaten, but naturally we did not know anything about this until they had left. My mother used good judgment and treated them in the best possible manner. We prepared coffee and a fresh batch of biscuits and also gave them fresh cream and butter. They seemed very much pleased. Upon leaving they asked us how much we

Ramón Molina, who took part in the Kingston raid. This photograph was taken in 1897 when he entered Folsom Prison on a manslaughter charge. (Courtesy of California State Archives)

charged and my mother said "Nothing." They insisted on paying, so my mother said they could give us fifty cents; thereupon Vasquez gave her a big silver dollar. They all thanked us and treated us very nicely. There were seven of them. They all got on their horses, which were very fine animals, tipped their hats to us, and left.[12]

Tiburcio and his men continued to La Libertad, where they met the rest of the gang. Vasquez now had a dozen desperadoes under his command, including Chávez, Gómez, Rangel, Anamantoria, Molina, Padilla, López, Bicuna, Márquez, the sheepshearer Ramón, and two others whose names were never learned. Vasquez now set forth on his most daring raid. He later recalled, "After sending Leiva's wife home I went on to Kings River, in Tulare County, where with a party of eight men besides myself I captured and tied up thirty-five men. There were two stores and a hotel in the place. I had time to plunder only one of the stores as the citizens aroused themselves and began to fight. The numbers were unequal and I retired. I got eight hundred dollars and considerable jewelry by this raid." As was customary with Tiburcio's accounts, his story was not entirely correct.[13]

Kingston was a small settlement on the south bank of the Kings River, across from the present-day town of Laton. It had its origins as a stop on the old Butterfield stage route, and a ferry enabled coaches and travelers to cross the river. By 1873 the ferry had been replaced by a brand-new toll bridge, operated by Oliver H. Bliss. The town's main street ran parallel to the steep bank of the Kings River. Just east of the ferry stood a small cluster of buildings. To the east stood the Pioneer Store, owned by two Jewish merchants, Elias Jacob and Louis Einstein. Adjacent to it was Simon Sweet's general store, and next door to that was Reichert's Hotel. Kingston also boasted two saloons, a blacksmith shop, and a scattering of small houses. Near the bridge was a barn, used to keep the horses for the stagecoach line. There was also a livery stable, run by John W. Sutherland, Kingston's most prominent resident, who owned fourteen thousand acres of ranchland on either side of the river. Today nothing remains, except a historical marker in Kingston-Laton Park.[14]

At seven o'clock that night, December 26, the band, ten to twelve strong, rode up to a point near the bridge on the north bank of the Kings River. Vasquez had his compadres hide their horses in a heavy thicket, leaving one man in charge of the animals. Most of the band wore masks, but Tiburcio did not. According to one report, he was heavily armed, carrying four Navy revolvers. The rest, armed with rifles and six-shooters, followed Vasquez across the toll bridge on foot, hoping to surprise the townsfolk. The first man they encountered was the bridge owner, Oliver Bliss. He was seized, thrown to the ground, bound hand and foot, and his pockets pilfered of nine dollars. Bliss complained of neck pain, and one of the robbers, evidently more kind-hearted than whoever had horsewhipped

Kingston, showing Jacob & Einstein's Pioneer Store on the left and, to its right, Reichert's Hotel. Simon Sweet's general store, located between the two buildings, is not visible. Standing, second from left, is Oliver H. Bliss; fifth from left, leaning against the post, is Lance Gilroy. (William B. Secrest collection)

Pat Reardon, retrieved a blanket from a nearby wagon, folded it into a pillow, and put it under his head.

Now the band split up into several smaller groups. One of them stopped three citizens, John Potts, Pres Bozeman, and Milt Woods, near the stable and ordered them to lie down. Potts and Bozeman did so immediately, but Woods refused, declaring that it would ruin his good Christmas clothes. The bandits, surprisingly accommodating, marched him toward the hotel while other robbers hogtied Potts and Bozeman, binding their hands and one bent leg together behind their backs. From Bozeman they took $180. In the meantime sentries had been placed in front of the two general stores and the hotel, and two parties of outlaws simultaneously entered the Pioneer Store and Reichert's Hotel.

Vasquez and one group marched Milt Woods into the hotel's saloon, where a dozen men were startled by the loud command, "Down!" Vasquez told them that "he had no desire to hurt anyone and did not want any of his own men hurt, and that if any of his men should be killed or

wounded he would kill them and burn the town." The bandits quickly
tied the men with rope and rifled their pockets of watches and coin.
Meanwhile Vasquez and Chávez stepped into the hotel's sitting room,
where they encountered guest Ed Douglas and ordered him to get on
the floor. He refused, but a heavy blow from Chávez's six-gun brought
him to terms. Tiburcio relieved him of his money and his pocket watch.
Douglas begged the outlaw chieftain not to take the watch, as it was a
gift from his late father. Reichert made the same request, and Vasquez
gave back a watch to each man. Later they realized that he had returned
the wrong watches.

At the same time Blas Bicuna burst into the hotel dining room, where
Lance Gilroy, a twenty-four-year-old clerk in the Pioneer Store, was fin-
ishing his dinner. The waitress, hotelkeeper Reichert's daughter, screamed
in terror at the sight of the pistol-wielding stranger and fled the room.
Gilroy, startled by her yell and thinking Bicuna was a drunken loafer
who had insulted the girl, seized a chair and felled the diminutive ruffian.
Francisco Gómez heard the commotion and rushed into the dining room.
He quickly pistol-whipped Gilroy into submission with the barrel of his
heavy Colt's Dragoon. The only man in the hotel who was not robbed
was the black cook, who fled out the back door and rushed to warn
John Sutherland.

In the meantime another bunch of bandidos entered the Pioneer Store.
The outlaws ordered the clerk, Ed Erlanger, to get down on the floor, but
he fled out the back and dashed into the rear of Simon Sweet's store next
door, yelling, "The robbers have come!" A customer, George Butz, later
recalled, "Louis Elsasser and I were in Sweet's store and the proprietor was
there also in a room asleep. The lights were immediately extinguished and
the doors locked. Mr. Sweet asked what was up and when told that Vasquez and his band were in town, instructed the clerk to light the lamps
again and stated that he was not afraid of Vasquez or anyone else."[15]

Sweet then poked his head outside the front door. One of the bandidos
seized him by the hair and yanked him onto the boardwalk. While Sweet
was dragged next door into the Pioneer Store, his clerk blew out the lights
and relocked the front door. By now Vasquez had finished looting the
hotel, and he turned his attention to the Pioneer Store. Tiburcio learned
that Louis Einstein had said he did not have a key to the safe, that it had
been carried off by the clerk Erlanger. Vasquez told the storekeeper that he
knew there was another key to the safe, and threatened to "blow his brains

out" if he didn't produce it. At this point Tiburcio's men brought in the other clerk, the battered Lance Gilroy, who also had a key, and forced him to open the safe. They looted it of eight hundred dollars. By this time another dozen victims had been tied up and robbed in the Pioneer Store. One of the outlaws tried to pry a ring from Simon Sweet's finger, but he pleaded with him not to take it because it was a present from his wife. The bandit relented. While the victims lay helpless on the floor, a small dog happily went from man to man, licking their faces and ears. Several later grumbled that this "was the most annoying part of the entire affair."

Now Vasquez turned his attention to Sweet's general store, where Ramón, the sheepshearer, stood guard. Tiburcio marched Simon Sweet and Ed Erlanger to the front door, and Sweet called out to the men inside to light the store lamps and not to shoot. They complied and the brigands stepped inside and looted the till and the safe. Fortunately for Sweet, the day before he had sent $3,000 in cash to Visalia, so the robbers got only twenty-five dollars. Everyone in the store except George Butz was tied. When Butz pulled out his purse, a masked robber said, "We don't want any of your money, George." Butz furtively slipped the purse into a pile of blankets. He never learned who the friendly bandit was.

Meanwhile the black cook had managed to locate John Sutherland. The rancher grabbed his Henry rifle and rounded up three townsmen. Sutherland and the trio, armed with revolvers, quickly took up positions behind the steep riverbank directly across from the stores and hotel. By the light from Sweet's store, Sutherland got a good view of Ramón standing guard on the boardwalk. Taking careful aim, he squeezed the trigger and the bullet ripped into Ramón, causing a deadly wound. The bandit fell against the doorway, and gasped in Spanish to his compadres, "I am shot!"

At this, Vasquez ordered his men, "Vamos!" He and his band rushed outside, and as they did, Sutherland's little posse opened up with a barrage of rifle and pistol fire. Vasquez and his men made a run for the bridge, six-guns blazing, helping the wounded Ramón along with them. The posse had the advantage because they were behind cover and stationary whereas the bandits were in the open, illuminated by the lamps in the buildings, and firing as they ran. The outlaws, unsure in the dark where the gunfire was coming from, shot wildly to the left and right as they raced toward the bridge. At the same time their horse sentry opened fire on the posse from across the river. The bandidos dashed across the bridge and Sutherland and a townsman followed, shooting as they went. As the outlaws leaped into their saddles, a ball struck Clodoveo Chávez in the right leg above the knee. Tiburcio's cousin, Francisco Gómez, was slightly wounded in the neck. Procella Anamantoria, the youngest of the band, was unwilling to face the gauntlet of fire, and instead of crossing the bridge, fled down the river on foot. By now the posse's guns were empty and the pillagers vanished into the blackness. Sutherland and his men had fired some forty shots at them.[16]

Vasquez and his band had left thirty-five men tied up in Kingston. Despite the violence and Tiburcio's threats to kill the townsfolk, he had been overheard telling his men not to take any lives, saying they "had already done quite enough in that way." With some $2,500 in cash and jewelry in their saddlebags, the freebooters rode eight miles west along the Kings River to La Libertad. There the wounds of Ramón, Chávez, and Gómez were treated and the booty was divided. Then the band split up. Ramón headed north to Rancho de los Californios, where he could be cared for by friends. But his wound proved fatal and he died soon after he got there. Francisco Gómez volunteered to take Clodoveo Chávez to Poso Chane, where the two could rest and recover. Vasquez and five of the band, including Ysidro Padilla and Blas Bicuna, rode south toward the Kern River near Bakersfield. The balance soon returned to their usual occupations as vaqueros and borregueros.

In the meantime the citizens of Kingston waited for dawn to pursue the bandits. At first light they found blood on the toll bridge. John Sutherland, with two local men, rode west along the Kings River. Four miles downstream they discovered young Procella Anamantoria hiding in the brush. He swore that he worked at a nearby sheep camp, but when he was taken there the borregueros did not know him. His stories were so conflicting that Sutherland decided to bring him into Kingston, where he was identified as one of the bandits. The youth finally admitted to being with the gang, but claimed that he had been on his way to Kingston to buy some new clothes when the outlaws robbed him and forced him to accompany them on the raid. He claimed that all he did was to stand guard at the hotel, and insisted that he did not know the names of any of the bandits. Anamantoria was brought to the Fresno County jail in Millerton to stand trial.[17]

News of the bold raid spread like wildfire across the San Joaquin Valley and ignited a frenzy of excitement. Within a few days posses from Millerton, Fresno, Visalia, and Bakersfield were in the field. Isolated herders and

Kingston at the time of the raid. The gang crossed the Kings River on the new bridge at right. Center, facing the river and left to right, are Jacob & Einstein's Pioneer Store, Simon Sweet's general store, and Reichert's Hotel. The gunfight took place between the riverbank and the stores. (William B. Secrest collection)

farmers formed vigilante organizations for self-protection. Newspapers in Fresno, Visalia, and Bakersfield told their readers to expect attacks on their towns, while men stockpiled guns and patrolled the streets in anticipation of another raid. A sheepherder came into Visalia with a wild yarn that was widely published: Vasquez and his gang had entered his camp, ordered him to cook a meal, and then forced him to eat first to make certain the food was not poisoned. He claimed that "there were some ten Americans in the gang, all of whom were stoutly built and had sandy complexions. The rest were Spaniards." Valley newspapers published more wild rumors: two bandits had been lynched near Kingston; the gang was committing wholesale robbery at Whitesbridge on the San Joaquin River; Vasquez was seen simultaneously at points all over the San Joaquin. Although in western films and novels, outlaw gangs routinely raid and sack entire towns, this happened only once in the far West: at Kingston. Thus, settlers in the San Joaquin Valley were understandably shaken to the core. At the same time, however, the leading newspapers in distant San Francisco—the *Alta, Bulletin, Call, Chronicle,* and *Examiner*—ran only brief wire service accounts of the Kingston foray. The story, and the danger posed by the band, were plainly much more significant to settlers in the San Joaquin than to San Franciscans.[18]

Tiburcio had little trouble keeping out of the way of manhunters, as he later recalled with a dose of conceit: "I went . . . to a small settlement named Panama on the Kern River where myself and my party had a carouse for three days, dancing, love making, etc. El Capitan Vasquez was quite a favorite with the senoritas. It was well known to the citizens of Bakersfield which is only two or three miles from Panama, that I was there, and the arrangement was made for my capture but the attempt was not made until I had been gone for twenty-four hours. Then they came and searched the house in which I was supposed to be concealed."[19]

Panama was a small Mexican settlement situated on a branch of the Kern River about three miles south of Bakersfield. It had several cantinas and fandango houses. Vasquez later gave George Beers additional details of his visit to the little pueblo. He and his band arrived on the Kern River, across from Panama, and waited for nightfall. They crossed the river, and entered the settlement quietly, one at a time. The bandits were flush with booty and spent it freely, drinking and whoring. But Ysidro Padilla apparently thought it was too dangerous to stay there. On December 29 he and several of the band headed north toward Visalia. By this time the railroad had been completed through Tulare and the bandidos followed the tracks on horseback. Later that day, a northbound passenger train passed the outlaws as they rode leisurely along the rails. Several passengers were from Stockton, and they immediately recognized Padilla, who was notorious there for having been tried twice in the Medina murder case. When the train arrived in Stockton the news was quickly sent over the wires, but still the Vasquez gang could not be found.[20]

Tiburcio's recklessness seemed to know no bounds. On Sunday morning, January 4, elements of the gang did in fact raid an important town. Visalia, with a population of about one thousand, was then the largest San Joaquin Valley settlement south of Stockton. A number of the bandidos rode into Spanishtown in the northern part of Visalia. While most of the townsfolk were attending church, three Mexican desperadoes broke into the house of a widow, tied her up, and took sixteen dollars in coin. A family member in her backyard spotted them and cried out, "Robbers!" Soon worshipers were pouring out of the churches and a posse of armed citizens rushed into Spanishtown. The bandits, not wishing a reprise of their bloody escape from Kingston, fled with the posse in short-lived pursuit. In their haste, the robbers left behind some sixty pieces of rope, pre-cut into short lengths for binding their victims. The citizens recognized one of them, the killer Márquez, who had fled town a month before. This incursion was so bold it seems probable that Vasquez led it, and given the large amount of rope—enough to tie sixty people—it is likely that far more than three bandits were involved.[21]

Tiburcio Vasquez finally decided to exercise caution, and he and the band rode north to Rancho de los Californios. The brigands hid out in the log stockade in the dense willow thicket on Chidester's Island in the San Joaquin River, just north of the little pueblo. Here they remained concealed for two weeks. At night they would ride into the settlement and throw twenty-dollar gold pieces on the bar of Pedro Aguirre's saloon. Aguirre was terrified of the bandidos. Early in January a band of Anglo vigilantes from Kingston rode into Rancho de los Californios. After questioning settlers in the little pueblo, they became convinced that an old Mexican knew "more than he would tell of the late raid." Interrogation proved fruitless, so the vigilantes draped a noose around his neck and hoisted him up. The gasping viejo quickly changed his mind, and when he was let down, led the vigilantes to a fresh burial site. They dug it up and found the body of Ramón, the mortally wounded sheepshearer. The vigilantes rode back to Kingston, not knowing that the rest of the band was hiding nearby.[22]

Tiburcio's raids had exacerbated racial tensions. Other bands of vigilantes scoured the Hispanic settlements along El Camino Viejo, terrifying Californios and Mexicans. On the morning of January 15, a Mexican was found hanging from a tree near Kingston. He was identified as one of the gang, and it was claimed that he had taken part in the Firebaugh's Ferry raid and had tied down and robbed one of the victims, Wash Allen. The lynched man's name and his actual involvement with the gang, if any, are unknown. Rancho de los Californios and Las Juntas were raided several times by both legitimate posses of lawmen and bands of vigilantes. On January 12, a mob of some thirty Anglos entered Rancho de los Californios and ordered its residents to pack up and leave within eight days. Saloonkeeper Pedro Aguirre, fearful of both Hispanic bandits and Anglo vigilantes, took his family away and did not return for months. Later that day a committee of ten terrified Mexicans rode into Millerton and through an interpreter declared that they were "peaceable, inoffensive citizens" and demanded the protection of the sheriff. The county officials told them that they could best protect themselves by turning in any bandits who sought refuge in the settlement. Although this answer apparently satisfied some of the group, others who were Mexican citizens wrote letters to the Mexican consul in San Francisco, protesting their treatment. The Mexican consul in turn complained to Governor Newton Booth, who telegraphed a warning to Sheriff Ashman: "I understand from the Mexican Consul that the Mexican settlers at Las Juntas and Rancho California . . . are threatened with violence and their lives are in danger. You are required to protect them."[23]

The party of Mexicans returned to Rancho de los Californios. By now Vasquez and the rest of the band had wisely fled back into the Coast Range. Only Ignacio Rangel was foolish enough to linger behind. He was feared in the little settlement, not only for his connection with the gang, but also for shooting a Mexican and wounding him so badly his leg had to be amputated. On January 19, several members of the little committee of Mexicans seized Rangel, bound him with rope, and turned him in to the county jail in Millerton as one of the Kingston raiders. Rangel was held for trial, along with Procella Anamantoria. Ignacio Rangel pled guilty to robbery, admitting that he was "one of those fellows at Kingston . . . but did not go into the houses with the rest of them," and had only "attended to the horses." Since he was an ex-convict, the judge sentenced him to a stiff term of ten years in San Quentin. A similar fate awaited young Procella Anamantoria. He also pled guilty to robbery and received a six-year sentence.[24]

Countless rumors had lawmen and volunteer posses constantly in the field, running down false leads. The wild yarn that Tiburcio's band now included ten Anglos predictably resulted in a fiasco. On January 30, a rancher named John Funk spotted what he believed was the gang, camped near several jacales at the mouth of Tunis Creek, twenty miles west of Tehachapi. Funk rode into Tehachapi to report that the gang included Vasquez and Francisco Gómez and was "composed of ten Spaniards and ten white men." While the settlers in Tehachapi began raising a large posse, a rider was sent on a hard, forty-mile ride into Bakersfield with a message for Kern County Sheriff William H. Coons, requesting that he send a posse to the opposite end of the canyon to trap the outlaws. Sheriff Coons and his deputy, Joseph Short, quickly raised a force of twenty riders. It was dark when they headed south.

The Tehachapi posse of thirty-one men had already departed. They were especially eager to capture Francisco Gómez, as his victim, Constable Mettler, had been highly popular. At daybreak the two posses converged on Tunis Creek canyon in a pincer movement. It was the largest and best-organized effort yet made to capture the Vasquez gang. The Tehachapi men first raided the jacales, but no bandits were to be found. They then headed into the canyon, and within thirty minutes met Sheriff Coons's men, riding down from the opposite end. The possemen were hugely disappointed, and later learned that the initial report was false. The men Funk had seen were merely vaqueros.[25]

Tiburcio Vasquez later told George Beers that he had not been anywhere near the canyon. After leaving Rancho de los Californios, he and Blas Bicuna had ridden to Poso Chane. There they found Clodoveo Chávez and Francisco Gómez. Chávez was almost fully recovered from his leg wound. Leaving Gómez and Bicuna, Vasquez took Chávez with him and rode south to Elizabeth Lake. He spent several weeks with Jim Hefner and also with friends in Soledad Canyon. Tiburcio made a point of staying away from Chico's place, as his brother had threatened to kill him. Then he and Chávez, now back to full health, made a long ride north across the Mojave Desert to Lone Pine in Inyo County.

In the mountains to the southeast were the Cerro Gordo silver mines, discovered by Mexican prospectors in 1865. Mortimer W. Belshaw, a San Francisco mining engineer, had bought one of the most important mines, built a smelter, and constructed a toll road into Cerro Gordo. Between 1868 and 1875 some $13 million in silver and lead bullion was hauled to Los Angeles, helping spur an economic and real estate boom that quickly transformed the sleepy adobe pueblo into an American city. Several thousand miners labored in the Cerro Gordo mines, many of them Mexicans and Californios, and Vasquez no doubt felt safe among them. Clodoveo Chávez was particularly impressed with the boom camp and the wealth that was being extracted from the mines. Before long, the miners would have reason to remember the young bandido.

From Cerro Gordo, Tiburcio headed thirty miles south to the Hispanic mining camp of Coso. The sheriff of Inyo County soon learned from a Mexican miner that Vasquez had spent several days there, accompanied by "eight or nine men. . . . He went there for supplies but found none and went quietly off." It was the last week of February when Vasquez and Chávez rode south alone. On the evening of February 23, 1874, they made camp at the base of a huge rock monolith situated one mile southwest of the Coyote Holes stage station. From this towering butte Vasquez could see for miles in each direction and had a ready view of travelers and freight teams as they crawled along the desert floor. To this day it is known as Robbers' Roost. Tiburcio intended to rob the stage from the Cerro Gordo Mines when it stopped at the Coyote Holes station. The stage stop, operated by Freeman Raymond and his wife, was situated at the intersection of two important roads, one heading south to Los Angeles and the other west through Walker Pass to Bakersfield. The site was a mile and a half west of the spot where Highways 14 and 178 meet, now called Freeman's Junction.[26]

The next morning, February 24, an overnight lodger left Coyote Holes in search of his stray stock. When he stumbled upon the outlaws' camp at Robbers' Roost, they took him prisoner and bound him securely. By now Vasquez was so brazen he made no effort to hide his identity. He told the man his name and declared that he "intended to rob the station and both the up and down stages." After ascertaining the time the first stage would arrive, the two robbers took the man with them to Coyote Holes. On the way, they encountered Freeman Raymond, whom they also seized and tied. Leaving their two captives on a hill overlooking the stage station, Vasquez and Chávez rode to a small rise above the station, pulled out their Henry rifles, and fired fifteen to twenty shots into the wood-frame building. While Chávez covered him from the ridge, Tiburcio rode to within twenty yards of the station and called out, "Come out, everyone, or I will burn the house!"

At that, Mrs. Raymond stepped to the front door, and the bandido announced, "I am Tiburcio Vasquez. Tell everyone to come out. I will not injure them if they obey. It is the position only that I want. I am going to rob the stage when it arrives."

Mrs. Raymond ducked back inside. She and the half dozen men in the building held a quick parley. Their only weapons were an unloaded shotgun, a Henry rifle with no cartridges, and an antiquated pepperbox revolver. Convinced that Vasquez had a large gang with him, they elected to surrender. Tiburcio had them file out and sit down while Chávez guarded them. When he walked over to search the barn, he encountered W. M. Shore, known as "Old Tex," who was drunk and ornery. Shore demanded, "What the hell is up?"

Robbers' Roost, where Vasquez and Chavez made camp before robbing the Coyote Holes stage station in 1874. (Courtesy of Tom Schweich)

Tiburcio ordered him to put up his hands. Instead Old Tex jerked his revolver, but he did not have time to use it. Vasquez, pistol in hand, took careful aim and shot Shore in the thigh. Standing over Old Tex, the bandit told him that his name was Tiburcio Vasquez, and that he could kill him if he wanted to. He added, "Next time I order, you obey!"

Now Shore, Mrs. Raymond, and the others were marched to a small hill a quarter mile distant, where they could not be seen from the stage road. Vasquez ordered them to remain there on pain of death. Then he and Chávez went back to Coyote Holes to patiently await the stagecoach from Los Angeles. Two hours later, at about three in the afternoon, the coach hauled up to the station. The two bandits, with guns drawn, stepped toward the stage. Two passengers, Fessenden and Craig, were inside, while Belshaw, the wealthy owner of the Cerro Gordo Mines, sat on top next to the "whip," Davis. Vasquez ordered the driver, "Stop! Tell the passengers to come out!"

Davis did so, and the passengers were forced to sit in the sand while they were searched for valuables. From Craig Vasquez took five dollars, then

Coyote Holes stagecoach station, robbed by Tiburcio Vasquez and Clodoveo Chávez on February 23, 1874. (William B. Secrest collection)

told him to take off a new pair of gloves. Craig answered that he "needed to keep his own hands warm."

"Very well," Vasquez replied. "I'll buy 'em of you. I'll give you two dollars for 'em."

Craig relented and exchanged his own two dollars for his gloves. Next, Fessenden handed over forty dollars in gold coin and a small telescope. Taking his cue from Craig, Fessenden asked Tiburcio to return the spyglass. "No, no," the outlaw responded. "I have looked a long time for such an instrument, and have particular use for it."

From Belshaw Vasquez took twenty dollars and a fancy silver watch. He searched the mine owner's carpetbag and pulled out a new pair of handmade boots. Belshaw later said that he regretted "the loss of them more than all the rest." Chávez then marched the three passengers to a nearby hill and ordered them to remain still. After Chávez returned to the station, the passengers saw the group from Coyote Hills on the opposite hill and thought they were part of the bandit gang. Although neither group was restrained in any way, they were too terrified to move.

Now Tiburcio told the driver to unhitch his team and fetch the Wells Fargo express box from the stagecoach boot. The robbers gave the driver an iron bar, which he used to pry open the hasp. Vasquez was chagrined to find that the strongbox contained only law books and $10,000 in mining stocks, which he angrily scattered into the wind. At that point two of Belshaw's heavy teams, which hauled freight from Los Angeles to Cerro Gordo, pulled up. Vasquez later explained, "I had to be paid some way for my trouble, so I went through the station men." Tiburcio "took in" the two teamsters and marched them to the hill to join Belshaw's group. By this time it was 6:00 P.M. and Vasquez selected six of the best horses from the stable. Then he and Chávez leisurely rode off to the south, with the horses in between them. Although the two outlaws had robbed sixteen persons, they had secured only a few hundred dollars in coin. The passengers, except for "Old Tex," were unharmed, and later declared that they "were treated with great urbanity and gentleness" and that "Vasquez was very friendly and communicative." Tiburcio and Chávez rode south at a steady gait through the barren Mojave Desert, changing mounts as needed. Vasquez had decided to return to Los Angeles County. It was one of the most momentous decisions of his life, for his old nemesis Harry Morse would soon be on his trail.[27]

The raids in the San Joaquin Valley, following on the heels of the Tres Pinos tragedy, made Tiburcio Vasquez a household name. The *Little Rock Republican,* harkening back to the days of English highwaymen, called him the "Dick Turpin of California."

The *Chicago Inter Ocean* told its readers, "This desperate robber has for years been the terror of the Pacific Coast. His exploits and career rival those of the bandits of any age." The *New York Times* described Tiburcio's "characteristically bold and daring outrages" and explained his elusiveness: "Since the time of the murder at Tres Pinos there have been a thousand reports as to Vasquez' whereabouts. At one time he was seen in Virginia City. The next day an eminently 'reliable' citizen saw him near San Diego. Then a steamer from Mexico would bring intelligence that he was spending his ill-gotten coin in Guaymas."[28]

For years Vasquez had roamed a broad swath of country, from the redwood forests of Mendocino and the fog-swept hills of Sonoma to the Mojave Desert and semitropical Los Angeles. His sociable nature and charming personality had made him a host of friends. Now his notoriety popularized him with Hispanics who knew him only by reputation. Californios and Mexicans increasingly idolized Vasquez. As the *San Francisco Chronicle* reported in March 1874, "Outlaw as he is, among the native Californians he is considered a veritable hero, whose lawless deeds are worthy subjects for emulation." Tiburcio reveled in the notoriety. His ego was enormous, and he began to call himself "El Capitán" and "Chief of the Mexicans." To disenfranchised Hispanics, he was now a full-fledged folk hero. And that in his own lifetime.[29]

CHAPTER SIXTEEN

Harry Morse Tries His Hand

In response to the daring raids of Tiburcio Vasquez, the day after New Year's legislators from the San Joaquin Valley met with Governor Newton Booth in Sacramento to demand that the state take action against the "Vasquez banditti," as the gang was now popularly called. Within a week the legislature passed an act appropriating $15,000 to finance a manhunt for Vasquez and his men. Of this sum, $5,000 was to pay for a special posse to track down the band, and a heavy reward was offered: $3,000 for Vasquez alive, $2,000 dead. Lastly, Governor Booth appointed Sheriff Harry Morse to lead the posse after Vasquez. This was the first state police action in California since the short-lived California Rangers were organized in 1853 to track down Joaquín Murrieta.[1]

Sheriffs Harry N. Morse and John H. Adams both aspired to lead the manhunt, but Governor Booth appointed Morse alone. The Alameda sheriff had thoroughly proved himself to be the best bandido hunter on the Pacific Coast. He was a dead shot, could ride like a vaquero, spoke Spanish, and had captured scores of dangerous cattle thieves and highway robbers. In the years to come, as the West's most prominent private detective, he would handle countless sensational cases: the capture of Black Bart, America's most prolific stagecoach robber; the long battle against municipal corruption in San Francisco and Oakland; the Selby Smelter Robbery, one of America's biggest thefts; and the poisoning death of Stanford University founder Jane Stanford in 1905.

Harry Morse hand-picked an eight-man posse of seasoned manhunters, including Tom Cunningham, the energetic and highly capable sheriff of San Joaquin County, and Ambrose Calderwood, former sheriff of Santa Cruz County. Calderwood was partly blind in one eye, having been stabbed repeatedly in a desperate fight with Tiburcio's cousin Faustino Lorenzana. Their guide and scout was Ramón Romero, a vaquero and reformed outlaw whom Morse had known for years. Sheriff Morse also allowed a correspondent for the *San Francisco Chronicle,* A. B. "Boyd" Henderson, to ride with them, a decision that would prove particularly unwise.[2]

Morse spent almost two months preparing for the manhunt. He planned to set off in early spring, when rain-swollen streams in the Coast Range would have subsided and the grass would be high enough to feed their horses. He hired a Mexican informant who lived in the Cantua to act as a spy. While Morse quietly went about his preparations, newspapers published highly sensational accounts of Vasquez. Reported the *San Francisco Chronicle* on March 5, "Rumors of the movements, daring deeds, and whereabouts of the red-handed outlaw have almost daily, of late, been telegraphed from the lower counties of this State. Every stage robbery and lawless deed committed within a range of a hundred miles . . . was at once credited to Vasquez." Within days the *Chronicle* published the most outrageous report of all: Vasquez, disguised as a woman, had fled San Francisco a day earlier on the Pacific Mail steamship *Constitution,* bound for Mexico. To his credit, the *Chronicle's* writer soon tracked down the Alameda sheriff at his home in Oakland, reporting, "Morse expressed his disbelief in the most positive terms."[3]

Soon the sheriff was ready to start, and on March 13 the posse members met at Firebaugh's Ferry, where cattle baron Henry Miller lent them a remuda of horses. A heavy, four-horse wagon was loaded with food, gear, and ammunition, and the little party set off into the Coast Range on what would be the longest manhunt of nineteenth-century California. Before they were done, they would spend sixty-one days in the saddle and cover more than 2,700 miles. Boyd Henderson later described how their ride began:

Camping on the San Joaquin, near the ferry, that night, we started at daybreak the next morning, March 14th, for the Cantua Canyon, where we expected to meet our Mexican guide. Making an easy ride of but 24 miles, we camped on the Little Panoche, a

Harry N. Morse, sheriff of Alameda County at the time of the Vasquez manhunt. (Author's collection)

point memorable to us as giving us our first idea of how brackish water can be and yet be drinkable. The next day, the wagon going over the plain and the party across the hills, we reached Cantua Canyon, the wagon at its mouth and the horsemen about eight miles up the creek. We had today our first experience of mountain trails, and at the end of the march, while we were mutually commiserating one another, could anyone have foreseen the trails we had yet to encounter and ride over in a two months' service, our trip might have ended there. But unfortunately there was no "gift of second sight" in the company, and believing that the morrow would bring us very near "the hour and the man," we pitched our tent by the creek, stationed the guards, and slept. The mysterious disappearance of the Spaniard whom Morse had purchased to betray Vasquez totally deranged his plans. This man's fate is yet a dark mystery. Whether he was murdered by the men whose betrayal he contemplated, or conscientious scruples restrained him, can only be determined by time, if at all. After a thorough search of the Cantua Canyon, Morse proceeded to Zapato Chino [Creek] where he pitched his camp and from which point we scoured all of the adjacent country.[4]

Morse and his men posed alternately as surveyors or sheep buyers. Henderson described their method of searching: "We would leave the supply wagon in a secure place, and with sufficient provisions and one blanket for each man, would scout for a week, and then return to camp, and after a brief respite, again start out in another direction." They quickly learned that finding Vasquez would be no simple task, as Henderson explained: "Morse believed it would be an easy matter to find Vasquez if he could only induce the Mexican settlers in this region to disclose his lurking place. He therefore offered to them a reward of $1,000, in addition to the entire sum offered by the state, if they would simply furnish him information that would bring him in sight of Vasquez; but . . . there is a sort of glamour about the character and career of Vasquez in the eyes of the Mexican settlers and they all, with one accord, professed to have no knowledge of the bandit's whereabouts and declined to furnish any information concerning him. Vasquez's Mexican friends will not betray him, and his friends number most of the Mexicans in this region, who all admire the doughty robber in greater or less degree."[5]

San Joaquin County Sheriff Tom Cunningham, Harry Morse's right-hand man. (Author's collection)

On March 18, while scouring the country near Poso Chane, Sheriff Cunningham arrested John Robb, an Anglo desperado from Monterey and a friend of Vasquez's. The lawmen kept Robb prisoner for five days, a course of action they took with a number of suspicious persons they encountered during the hunt. He was held with Nicolás Ruiz, who was arrested a few days later by Ramón Romero as a suspect in the Kingston raid. At night the two prisoners were handcuffed to a wagon wheel. Within a few days Ruiz's wife came into camp to seek her husband's release. Since there was no evidence against either of them, both were set free.[6]

The day after Robb was arrested, Morse, Cunningham, and Henderson rode out of camp in search of Mariana, the self-proclaimed widow of Joaquín Murrieta. Sheriff Morse and his men located her south of her usual haunts, in a sheepherder's tent on Kettleman's Plains, in what is now Kings County. Henderson later gave a vivid description of their meeting with Mariana:

> Joaquin's widow, now forty-three years old, is a woman of medium height, and though rather stout, is of finely developed proportions. Despite her age, her loose mode of life, her present fondness for aguardiente, and a scar extending across her face, from nose to ear, she is not by any means a homely or repulsive-looking woman. Her lips still retain their fine curves and her teeth are a marvel of perfect preservation. It required no very strong draughts on the imagination to believe that twenty years ago she possessed a figure which was a model of grace, and that then, arrayed in the brilliant-hued garments her husband admired, with her magnificent eyes, either sparkling at the daring deeds of her protector or looking with defiance at his hunters, she was the woman of rare beauty and witchery who could maintain her supremacy in the robber's ardent affections, even after his discovery of her infidelity to himself. Then, too, more in harmony with her appearance was her soft, musical name, Mariana Murrieta. . . .
>
> Scarcely less than her tongue do her eyes, head, and gracefully shrugged shoulders assist to convey her ideas, while under the exciting influence of her stories, her swinging arms, and her small feet stamping the earth, she gives strong emphasis to her assertions. All her life she has been associated with cattle thieves, highway robbers, and murderers.[7]

Mariana La Loca, who claimed to be the widow of Joaquín Murrieta. She did not think much of Tiburcio Vasquez. (William B. Secrest collection)

In the 1880s she would acquire notoriety as a prophetess and would be nicknamed "Mariana La Loca"—Crazy Mariana. She knew Tiburcio Vasquez well, wrote Henderson: "Mariana is fond of drawing comparisons between Joaquín and Vasquez, greatly to the disadvantage of the latter, whom she considers but a petty thief." Mariana told Morse that Clodoveo Chávez had been at the sheep camp on January 1 with a bad wound in his right leg. With him was a tall, dark Mexican who had been wounded in the neck in the Kingston raid. (That was Tiburcio's cousin, Francisco Gómez.) Leaving Mariana's camp, Morse and his men turned their horses toward Cholame, in the mountains, which had the only post office in that section of the Coast Range. There, on March 21, Morse made his first report to Governor Booth. His letter contained many errors of fact and illustrated the difficulty in getting accurate information about the gang. He wrote that Chávez "must be some where in these canyons as he has not been able to ride since his wound." In fact, Chávez had quickly recovered and was then with Vasquez in Los Angeles County. The sheriff incorrectly identified gang member Manuel López as the robber who had been shot in the neck at Kingston. Morse opined, wrongly, "I think that Tom Heffernan, one of the escapees from Nevada State Prison about three years ago is the man who done the robbery at Coyote Holes and claimed to be Vasquez." But the sheriff did get one thing right: "It is going to be hard work to find Vasquez, he has so many friends among the Mexicans, they hide him and feed him, and lie to the officers."[8]

Sheriff Morse and his men spent the next week searching Jacalitos Creek, just north of Zapato Chino Creek. They discovered several herds of stolen horses and cattle, but the thieves fled into the mountains on sight of the posse. The vaqueros and borregueros they met were most unhelpful, and if they gave any information at all it was usually false. As a result the officers were kept busy tracking down many false trails. Boyd Henderson reported:

> But little could be learned from the native Californians of the lower counties. Most of these people, while professing an utter ignorance of the designs or locality of the bandit chief and his desperate associates, and a desire that they might be overtaken and brought to summary punishment, yet developed a certain instinctive sympathy with the outlaws, particularly the chief, whom they

regard as a brave man, and of whom they stand in no fear, inasmuch as he is not wont to trouble settlers, either Mexican or American, but confines his depredations mainly to travelers and to the more thickly populated settlements.

Some of the native women, especially, show an almost undisguised admiration for Vasquez, who is to them a sort of hero; and even among the American settlers we have found some who were disposed to shrug their shoulders and say that they knew nothing of Vasquez and did not expect him to trouble them, as he had always treated them well, paying for everything he got from them, and being rather a generous sort of fellow than an arbitrary rascal, so far as their intercourse with him had served to develop his character. One free-spoken Irish woman, being interrogated, boldly uttered her conviction that Vasquez is a good-looking, brave fellow, "a man sure, worth a hundred of the paltry divils about this part of the country," and cheerfully added, "If I was a widow I'd marry him tomorrow."[9]

Tiburcio's popularity among Californios and Mexicans was in part due to their admiration of his courage and daring, for many had begun to see him as a symbol of resistance to a society that had oppressed them. His popularity was also partly a result of the personal friendships he had made with so many of the mountain paisanos. Explained Henderson:

He is very liberal with the Mexican families he visits. They say of him that he always pays generously for the food and shelter furnished himself and men, and that it is a common practice with him, upon calling at houses where inmates are unable, through poverty, to supply him with the desired refreshments, to give them a ten or twenty dollar gold piece. It is needless to say that all of these people are his attached friends, offer him the shelter of their houses when he is pursued, and tell the officers the most prodigious lies without any compunction.

A popular fallacy about this bandit is that he has constantly about him a regularly organized band of men, with whom he travels from place to place, now robbing this stage, then sacking that town, and now hiding away in some canyon or rocky fastness.

He has no band, or gang, unless the entire Mexican population (with but few exceptions) of the mountain regions of Fresno, Kern, Tulare, Monterey, and Los Angeles counties can be called such.[10]

At the end of March Harry Morse at last received a piece of reliable information: Manuel López could be found in the vicinity of Mission San Antonio de Padua, across the Coast Range in western Monterey County, seventy miles distant by horseback. López had formerly lived in the Panoche Valley, but had moved his wife and four children to a small rancho in the Santa Lucia Range west of Jolon in southern Monterey County. According to Sheriff Morse, López had committed three murders; Boyd Henderson put the number at six. Said Henderson in a dispatch, "From the well known desperate character of the man, no attempt had hitherto been made to arrest him, and in the absence of any reward for his apprehension, no party could be found willing to undertake the work." As López was one of the most dangerous of the Vasquez band, Morse was eager to capture him.

On the night of March 28, Morse and his posse rode into the settlement at San Antonio, not far from López's home in Jolon. Posing as surveyors, they stopped to ask directions at the ranch house of Pedro García, then started on toward Jolon. The officers found that not all the mountain paisanos were enamored of Vasquez. "Immediately upon our departure," recalled Henderson, "the whole family, including two lovely young ladies, fled precipitately to the woods where they remained concealed until the next day. They believed us to be Vasquez and his band, and their actions in the premises tell more significantly than can any words of the terror inspired by the bandit, even among people of his own nationality."[11]

The posse spent several days searching for López in the Santa Lucia Range, finally learning the approximate location of his house. Pushing their horses to the limit, they crossed the summit, wading though snow three feet deep and reaching the coast the following day, April 1. Recalled Henderson, "Although furnished with a plot of the trail leading to the house of López, the western slope of the mountain range was so checkered with trails that our map was absolutely worthless, and nothing remained to be done but to institute a systematic hunt for our objective point. From noon of the day of our arrival on the coast until the evening of the following day, in which time we had nothing to eat but a single cracker apiece and two small boxes of sardines for the whole party of eight men, we searched most thoroughly the hills and small valleys which make up that territory, without success, although in the afternoon of the second day we could hear plainly the shouts of the men whom we suspected."[12]

The possemen could hear López and his two vaqueros calling to each other a mile distant, but the hills and canyons were so steep they could not find them before dark. They made camp, and at daylight surrounded López's house and searched it. Only his wife, Augusta, and their children were present. She told Sheriff Morse that López had left the day before with his vaqueros for San Antonio with fifteen head of cattle. The posse started in pursuit but López, knowing the trails, had ridden through the night and was far ahead of them. Morse and three others, with the freshest horses, pushed on far ahead, and a few miles outside of Jolon caught up with López's vaqueros and the herd of cattle. They said that López had gone up a side canyon to search for five cattle that had strayed. Leaving one man in charge of the vaqueros, Morse and the others galloped after López. But, as Henderson related, they "unfortunately were seen by López before they were within rifle shot and he, suspecting their intentions, clapped spurs to his horse" and escaped.

Henderson summed up the futile manhunt: "The remarkable feature of this affair is the drive made by López, who in about twelve hours not only drove a herd of cattle forty miles, twelve of which were over a bad mountain trail, but in fifty-five miles and thirty hours increased their number from fifteen to twenty-five. In this fruitless search and chase the party suffered more inconvenience and discomforts than in any other time they were out. The chilliness of the nights spent in the mountains, from which their only protection was their single woolen and Fort Yuma blankets, the scarcity of food, and the effects of contact with some poisonous weeds [poison oak], all combine to make it a trip long to be remembered by the participants."[13]

Unfazed by their failure to capture Manuel López, Morse's posse recrossed the Coast Range to Kettleman's Plains. They had ridden more than one thousand miles, had been in the saddle for twenty-seven days, and had thoroughly scoured all of Vasquez's known haunts from Monterey south to Kern County. Morse became convinced that the elusive bandit chief was south of the Tehachapi Mountains. On April 8, the possemen headed south, searching the country as they went, and arrived four days later at Hudson's Station, later known as Rose's Station, a mile from the mouth of Tejon Canyon near what is now Grapevine. Here Morse penned a rueful report to Governor Booth:

> This is our thirty-first day in the saddle and no Vasquez. Myself and party arrived at this stage station, which is 8 miles from Fort Tejon, this evening after a hard ride of 45 miles, tired and hungry. We start at daylight to skirmish through the canyons south of here, and thence by the Mohave desert to Elizabeth Lake. I have been following up rumors of Vasquez' whereabouts from the New Idria Mines through to the coast in Monterey Co. and back again through all the canyons southerly to this place. Have been in the saddle every day sleeping out from our wagon with only one blanket and about half the time without eating. Our greatest trouble is in getting fresh horses, every new lot of horses are grass fed, and they don't stand our riding very long. I shall stay out 30 days longer. Please telegraph me at Fort Tejon if this meets with your approval.[14]

Morse's hunch that Vasquez was in Southern California was correct. But he was about to make the biggest blunder of his long and eventful career.

CHAPTER SEVENTEEN

Manhunt in Los Angeles

After robbing Coyote Holes station, Tiburcio Vasquez and Clodoveo Chávez rode steadily south on the desert trail toward Los Angeles. They had no trouble covering one hundred miles in two days, arriving in Soledad Canyon on February 26. A new toll road through Soledad Canyon provided the shortest route from the Mojave Desert to Los Angeles and had largely replaced the old road through San Francisquito Canyon to the north. Between the settlement of Soledad (now called Ravenna) and Mill Station, about four miles south of present-day Acton, the two bandidos stopped the stagecoach from Los Angeles. After tying up the passengers, they went through their pockets and the express box, taking three hundred dollars. When one of them complained about lying on the cold ground, Vasquez said, "I'll sell you my coat. You can have it for eight dollars."

Tiburcio handed over the coat, then searched the passenger for payment, taking more than the eight dollars he had bargained for. Next Vasquez turned his attention to another passenger, a Mexican blacksmith who worked for freighting magnate Remi Nadeau. Tiburcio told him, "I don't want anything from you. I know you, and where you work. We only intend to collect from Americans."

Then he and Chávez mounted up and rode toward Soledad. Encountering one of Nadeau's teamsters, they robbed him of a twenty-dollar gold piece and a pocketknife. It was dark when they rode into Soledad. The pair brazenly entered Sam Harper's stable and took a wagon and six horses, then left unmolested. News of the robbery did not reach Los

Angeles until three days later. Sheriff Billy Rowland apparently made no effort to investigate, as the editor of the *Los Angeles Express* complained that it was a "disgrace to our State that the peace and safety . . . should be disturbed by these brigands, while the authorities look on with indifference."[1]

After the Soledad stage robbery Vasquez and several of his men remained hidden in Soledad Canyon and the Elizabeth Lake area. An old tradition holds that one of his principal hideouts was a desolate area just west of Soledad Canyon, studded with massive sandstone rock outcroppings. Among the spectacular rock formations, reaching 150 feet in height, are small canyons and passageways that could easily hide man and horse, and small caves for shelter. Known to this day as Vasquez Rocks, it is now a Los Angeles County park. On March 18 a miner returning to Los Angeles from Panamint was passing though Soledad Canyon when he encountered Vasquez and a dozen of his compadres. The miner knew Tiburcio and exchanged greetings with him, learning that he had been camped in the canyon for several days. The following night a suspicious man who matched the description of Vasquez was spotted near the Pico House (still standing at 430 North Main Street), just off the Los Angeles plaza. The police quickly searched the area but the stranger had vanished. It was later reported that at this time Tiburcio made a number of visits to Sonoratown, the Mexican section of Los Angeles. He was harbored by several friends on his visits there. One was Mariano G. Santa Cruz, a merchant and cockfight promoter who had a *tienda* located on Upper Main Street, just north of the plaza. Another was the Mexican prostitute La Coneja. Tiburcio reportedly stayed with her for a week or two in March. Sheriff Rowland had her house watched, but Vasquez did not return.[2]

Los Angeles County was then in the midst of an economic boom. In 1870 the county had a population of fifteen thousand, and the city six thousand; both numbers would double in the next decade. The growth was fueled in large part by wealth from the Cerro Gordo Mines, California's greatest silver rush. Silver and lead bullion were hauled by mule team from Cerro Gordo across the Mojave Desert to the Los Angeles port at San Pedro. The mules needed barley, and an influx of new farmers into Los Angeles County helped provide it. The Anglo population exploded, and real estate developers laid out new townsites in what would become the burgeoning young city's suburbs. The Los Angeles that Tiburcio

The massive sandstone outcroppings of Vasquez Rocks, Tiburcio's hideout in western Los Angeles County. (Author's collection)

Vasquez saw in 1874 was rapidly evolving from its days as a Mexican pueblo. And for Angelenos, both Anglo and Hispanic, Vasquez served as a dramatic and violent symbol of resistance to that change.

By this time Tiburcio had become emboldened by his skill in eluding pursuers. He regularly read the newspapers and found that his name was fast becoming a household word, not only in California, but throughout the country. Calling himself "El Capitán," he concocted a wild scheme to steal enough money to arm, mount, and equip two hundred men. He planned to divide them into three companies under his command, then sack the principal towns in Southern California. Vasquez boasted, "With the arms and provisions I could have purchased with fifty or sixty thousand dollars, I could raise a force with which I could revolutionize California." Yet his goals were so vague that when reporter George Beers later asked him what his plans were after the raids, he said that he "intended to leave the state." The reality was that Vasquez had no soldiers under his command, just a motley band of horse thieves and highway robbers with no political or social agenda and no military ability to implement it. And in all his robberies combined he never stole even close to $60,000.[3]

Tiburcio was not long in Los Angeles County when he learned that his niece Felicita had given birth to his child. It was a boy, named Alfredo Vasquez. Later known as Fred, he would be raised by Chico and María as one of their own children, and to his dying day he insisted that Tiburcio was his uncle. Probably he did not know the truth. Chico was so humiliated he left his job in the Soledad Mines and moved his family back to Leona Valley, southeast of Elizabeth Lake. There he worked as a vaquero and majordomo for Chico López, the biggest ranchero in the valley. One night Tiburcio rode up to his house, tied his horse near the fence, and crept to the bedroom window. In Spanish, he called out to Chico, "Get up. It is I, your brother Tiburcio. Get up and come out here." Chico had never wanted to see his brother again, but he did step outside. As José Jesús López related,

> Tiburcio got down on his knees and begged Francisco's forgiveness. He told Francisco that he knew he had brought disgrace on him and had ruined his family. He took out his revolver and, holding it by the muzzle, offered it to Francisco, telling him, "There is an eight thousand dollar reward for me. Someone is going to collect it. You kill me and get the reward to use in raising my child."
>
> Francisco was overcome. He had sworn to kill Tiburcio, but when the opportunity presented itself, he could not do it. Finally he pointed into the distance and told Tiburcio to go and never to come near him again, saying that he would care for the child himself. Tiburcio left.[4]

Vasquez boldly rode through northern Los Angeles County, seemingly unafraid of capture. One of his most brazen encounters took place at the end of March. While riding along Verdugo Canyon in the present-day city of Glendale, not far from Big Tujunga Canyon, he came across Mike Madigan, a county tax collector. Madigan later reported that he recognized Vasquez from his description and that Tiburcio made no effort to hide his identity. Madigan, an eccentric Irishman, claimed that he had no fear of the bandit, and they rode along for several hours, chatting good-naturedly. As they were about to go their separate ways, Tiburcio handed him two dollars for the poll tax, saying, "Don Miguel, let it not be said that Vasquez would seek to evade a miserable poll tax imposed by a government which has so high an appreciation of his value as to offer $15,000 for his head. Here, let my mite be contributed to maintain so good and liberal an administration." Madigan wrote out a receipt for the money and handed it to the desperado. When this incident was reported in the Los Angeles newspapers a few days later, it was met with hoots of derision and widespread skepticism. But indeed it happened, though, as we shall see, perhaps not exactly as Madigan described.[5]

At the end of March Vasquez moved his headquarters to the adobe of Greek George. It was approximately situated at what is now Melrose Place in West Hollywood. The house was ideal for a hideout. It was surrounded on three sides by a dense thicket of wild mustard, growing five to seven feet high. Looking south, Vasquez had a clear view for miles across the plain that stretched toward Los Angeles. Nearby was a spring in a grove of willows, where the gang could hide and water their horses. Just north was a high ridge, now called the Hollywood Hills, bisected by canyon trails leading to the San Fernando Valley and providing quick escape routes. Between the house and the hills was a little-used wagon road running east-west and roughly paralleling today's Santa Monica Boulevard. The house consisted of a one-story adobe with two bedrooms, and on the south wall was a wood-frame addition that served as the dining and living room. Attached to that was a wood lean-to that held the kitchen. When Tiburcio stayed at the adobe he apparently shared the bed of Greek George's comely sister-in-law, Modesta López. Other times he, Clodoveo Chávez, Francisco Gómez, and Ysidro Padilla camped in the nearby willow grove. In the morning Modesta would cook for the band. Greek George's, wife, Cornelia, was pregnant and confined to her bed, and Modesta cared for her and their eight-year-old son, George. Tiburcio found time to recruit an eighteen-year-old Mexican sheepherder, Librado Corona, who like many youths before him, was eager to follow the bandit chieftain. Vasquez sent young Corona, who had no criminal record and was unknown to lawmen, into the countryside to scout the ranchos for a profitable haul. The youth returned a few days later and reported that a wealthy Italian sheep rancher, Alessandro Repetto, had sold his wool crop and had much cash on hand. A year earlier Corona had worked for Repetto, and he knew the rancho well.[6]

Alessandro Repetto was in his mid-fifties, a former surgeon in the Italian navy who had joined the gold rush in 1849. Like most gold-seekers, he found real wealth not in mining but in agriculture. Settling in Los Angeles

County, he raised sheep and goats and practiced medicine until he was able to acquire a thirty-five-thousand-acre portion of the Lugo rancho. His hilltop home was the adobe built by José del Carmen Lugo. No longer standing, it was located on what is now South Garfield Avenue, near El Repetto Drive in Monterey Park. The Italian was exceedingly rotund, weighing more than three hundred pounds. A notorious miser, Repetto never married, but lived for a time with an Indian woman with whom he had a son out of wedlock. In 1874, he lived with his young nephew, Stefano Repetto, and several ranch hands.[7]

On April 14, 1874, Vasquez, with Chávez, Corona, Padilla, and Gómez, left Greek George's place and rode northeast toward the San Gabriel Mountains. Evidence of rapid settlement was everywhere. The outlaws crossed the railroad line, which had recently been built north from Los Angeles into the San Fernando Valley and would eventually connect Northern and Southern California. From here they rode farther east to the lands of the San Gabriel Orange Grove Association, a four-thousand-acre tract being developed by settlers from Indiana. In a precursor of the agricultural boom soon to come, they had built a large reservoir, dug wells, laid pipes, and planted orchards and vineyards. The settlement would soon become Pasadena. Vasquez and his gang made camp that night in the bottoms of the Arroyo Seco, on the Orange Grove Association land. "I camped at the Piedra Gorda [Fat Rock] at the head of the Arroyo Seco," Tiburcio said. Now called Eagle Rock, it is a huge sandstone on the north side of the Ventura Freeway at North Figueroa Street. According to local lore, the band camped in a cave in the rock. Tiburcio, who was not familiar with that section of the San Gabriel Mountains, hired a Mexican guide to lead them across the mountains to Soledad Canyon after the raid. The next day Vasquez and Corona rode south to Mission San Gabriel, and from there continued south four miles to Repetto's adobe. Tiburcio described what took place:

> In pursuance of the plan I had adopted, I went to a sheep herder employed on the place and asked him if he had seen a brown horse which I had lost. [I] enquired if Repetto was at home, took a look at all the surroundings, and told the man I had to go to the Old Mission on some important business, that if he would catch my horse I would give him $10 or $15. I then returned by a roundabout way to my companions on the Arroyo Seco. As

soon as it was dark I returned with my men to the neighborhood of Repetto's and camped within a few rods of the house. The next morning about breakfast time we wrapped our guns [rifles] in our blankets, retaining only our pistols, and I went toward the house, where I met the sheep herder and commenced talking about business. [I] asked him if Repetto wanted herders or shearers, how many sheep could he shear in a day, etc., speaking in a loud tone in order to let Repetto hear us and throw him off his guard.

I had left my men behind a small fence, and being told that he was at home, I entered the house to see if I could bring the *patron* to terms without killing him. I found him at home, and told him I was an expert sheep shearer and asked him if he wished to employ any shearers; told him that my friends, the gentlemen who were waiting out by the fence, were also good shearers and wanted work. All were invited in, and as they entered surrounded Repetto. I then told him that I wanted money. At this he commenced hollering, when I had him securely tied and told him to give me what money he had in the house. He handed me eighty dollars. I told him that that would not do, that I knew all about his affairs; that he had sold nearly $10,000 worth of sheep lately, and that he must have plenty of money buried about the place somewhere. Repetto then protested that he had paid out nearly all the money he had received in the purchase of land, that he had the receipts to show for it.

I told him that I could read and write and understand accounts; that if he produced his books and receipts and they balanced according to his statements, I would excuse him. He produced the books, and after examining them carefully I became convinced that he had told very nearly the truth. I then expressed my regrets for the trouble I had put him to, and offered to compromise. I told him I was in need of money, and that if he would accommodate me with a small sum I would repay him in thirty days, with interest at 1½% per month. He kindly consented to do so, and sent a messenger to the bank in Los Angeles for the money, being first warned that in the event of treachery or betrayal his life would pay the forfeit. The messenger returned, not without exciting the suspicions of the authorities, who, as it is well known, endeavored at that time to effect my capture but failed.[8]

As was customary with Tiburcio, his story was neither entirely accurate nor complete. Although Repetto trusted Corona, he was immediately suspicious of Vasquez. The bandit's fine clothes and uncalloused hands showed that he was no sheepshearer, and Repetto told him so. Vasquez smiled and readily admitted that he was a robber. He demanded $10,000, but Repetto insisted that he had only eighty dollars in the house, and that his money was in the Temple & Workman Bank in Los Angeles. This was a first for Tiburcio, as banks were virtually unknown in the remote areas where he normally ranged. So he and his men tied Repetto to an olive tree in the yard and told him they would hang him unless he paid a ransom of eight hundred dollars. When Repetto finally relented, the desperadoes untied him and took him back into the house. While the Italian's terrified nephew, Stefano, looked on, Repetto wrote out a check for eight hundred dollars and instructed the youth to take it to Los Angeles and return with the cash. Before the boy left, Vasquez warned him not to give any alarm, or they would kill his uncle. The gang then searched the adobe, taking Repetto's shotgun and a spyglass. From Repetto's sheepherder they took twenty-nine dollars; they found another hired man sick in bed, and relieved him of his shotgun and five dollars.

Stefano made a quick ride into town and presented the check to banker Francis Temple for payment. But the youth was so nervous that Temple became suspicious. He locked the boy in an office and ran one block to the courthouse. The banker soon returned with Undersheriff Albert Johnston, who closely questioned the boy. When he quickly broke into tears and told the whole story, Johnston sensed immediately that he was telling the truth. Johnston and Sheriff Rowland hurriedly raised a posse and requisitioned horses from the town's livery stables. One of his volunteers was Justo Chávez, former police chief of Baja California, who was living in Los Angeles at the time. Rowland was certain that Vasquez would flee toward the mountains, so he sent a five-man posse north toward Big Tujunga Canyon to cut off any escape route into the San Gabriel Mountains. Led by Deputy Sheriffs Henry Mitchell and J. M. Baldwin, it included Constable Sam Bryant, Justo Chávez, and volunteer Tom Vincent. Undersheriff Johnston was detailed to ride alone to El Monte, a settlement of Texans near San Gabriel, to raise a second posse. Rowland himself headed directly toward Repetto's ranch, accompanied by two of the best lawmen in Southern California, Los Angeles Chief of Police B. F. "Frank" Hartley and police detective Emil Harris. A saloonkeeper friend, Walter E.

Rogers, plus José Redona, Esteban Sánchez, and Ramón Benítez, the three Californios who had accompanied Rowland in the Rock Creek manhunt, also rode along.[9]

In the meantime Stefano Repetto begged piteously for Temple to release him from the locked bank office. He insisted that if Vasquez saw the posse coming they would kill his uncle. Francis Temple was an exceedingly kind man. He and his father-in-law and partner, Los Angeles pioneer William Workman, had lent money to anyone in need, often without proper collateral. A year later their bank would fail, leaving both men ruined and Workman dead from suicide. Now Temple, worried that he might be the cause of Repetto's death, gave the boy five hundred dollars in gold and let him go. The youth leaped into the saddle and cut across city lots, riding so fast he arrived back at the ranch a full mile ahead of Rowland's posse. He rushed inside the adobe and threw the bag of coin onto the table. Vasquez and his men had cooked themselves a hearty breakfast, while Padilla was stationed outside as a lookout, using Repetto's spyglass. No sooner had Tiburcio picked up the sack of gold than Padilla yelled out that a band of riders was approaching.

"A caballo!" ("Mount up!") Vasquez shouted. In an instant the outlaws were in the saddle and racing across the hilly terrain toward the San Gabriels. Sheriff Rowland's common livery plugs were no match for the bandidos' California mustangs. Tiburcio slowed his men so as to keep a half-mile distance between them and the posse. As soon as the lawmen got close to rifle range, he and his band spurred their mounts to keep their distance. When they reached the Arroyo Seco on the Orange Grove Association tract, they spotted a freight wagon on the road ahead. The outlaws charged at full speed several hundred yards to increase the distance between themselves and the posse, and surrounded the wagon. It was driven by expressman John Osborne, who was delivering a load of water pipes to the new reservoir. With him were Charley Miles, supervisor of the Los Angeles Water Company, and two workers, Pat Cone and Jack Rhodes.

While Corona covered them with a Henry rifle, Vasquez ordered, "Hand out your money!"

Charley Miles, thinking it was a joke, laughed and replied that he "didn't have a cent." Vasquez, seeing his gold watch chain, demanded, "Then I'll take that watch!"

Miles was carrying a fancy gold English hunting lever watch worth three hundred dollars, and when he was slow about pulling it out, Tiburcio

Sheriff William "Billy" Rowland, who led the manhunt for Vasquez in Los Angeles County. (Author's collection)

barked, "Hurry up! Don't you see those damned sons of bitches coming yonder? I'm Vasquez, and they're after me!"

At that moment, Sheriff Rowland and his posse could be seen cresting a hill a thousand yards off. Osborne handed over a seventy-dollar gold watch, and Rhodes a few dollars in change. Vasquez and his men galloped off toward the mountains, and soon encountered a youth named Strickland, whom they relieved of fifteen dollars. Tiburcio and his compadres rode hard and quickly outdistanced the posse. Not since the days of Joaquín Murrieta, when that outlaw and his gang had robbed a band of miners in full sight of a galloping posse, had a California bandit been so bold as to hold up victims in plain view of pursuing lawmen.[10]

Sheriff Rowland and his men pursued the gang to the mouth of the Arroyo Seco, whence the robbers had started up Moore's trail, a narrow, treacherous path that ascended the San Gabriel Mountains north toward Big Tujunga Canyon. Unbeknownst to Vasquez, the trail had a dead end, for its builder, Captain Moore, had run out of money and could not complete the route into Big Tujunga. At the entrance to the Arroyo Seco, Rowland met Deputy Sheriff Mitchell's posse, which had circled around the base of the mountains and failed to meet the outlaws. By this time many of their horses were completely worn out. Billy Rowland and part of the posse headed back to Los Angeles for fresh mounts. Deputy Sheriffs Mitchell and Baldwin, Chief Hartley, Detective Emil Harris, Constable Bryant, and possemen W. E. Rogers and Tom Vincent were well mounted and they continued up Moore's trail into the mountains. They were one mile behind the outlaws.

Here Vasquez had expected to meet his guide, but the man failed to appear and the gang was forced to head up a trail none of them knew. Tiburcio later told George Beers that he blamed himself for "not previously exploring the trail." The path was narrow, tortuous, and steep, as it clung to the rim of the Arroyo Seco gorge. Finally, the outlaws had to dismount and proceed on foot, leading their horses. They stopped to rest at the forks of the Arroyo Seco, three miles up the trail at the junction of Dark Canyon and Arroyo Seco, near the present Oakwilde campground. Here Clodoveo Chávez proposed they set up an ambush and attack the posse as they came up the trail. Vasquez would have none of it, telling the gang that they would have "half the people in the state hunting them" and that if they were captured they would be lynched on the spot.[11]

The band continued on, but soon it was so dark they were in danger of falling off a cliff. The robbers made camp for the night, after eating meat and bread they had brought from Repetto's. The posse could not proceed safely either, so they camped a mile below the outlaws. Tiburcio later told George Beers that his biggest fear was that Sheriff Rowland would send posses into Little Tujunga and Big Tujunga canyons to cut them off. At first light the outlaws started off quickly to avoid such a trap. Five miles up the trail they reached a large mesa, now called Grizzly Flat, on the divide that separates the Arroyo Seco and Big Tujunga watersheds. Here they were shocked to discover that the trail abruptly stopped. Below Grizzly Flat was very steep terrain, with deep gulches and cliffs choked with dense manzanita and scrub oak that led to Big Tujunga Canyon, one mile distant. The canyon was so deep, more than a thousand feet, that it was virtually impassable. Vasquez realized that they were trapped and had no choice but to find a way down into Big Tujunga.

He sent Padilla down the trail to keep a lookout for the posse, and directed Chávez to beat a path through the brush. Clodoveo, big and muscular, broke through the prickly manzanita, leading his horse behind him. Vasquez, Corona, and Gómez followed close behind, and were soon joined by Padilla. It took them three hours to descend only a few hundred yards. By noon the heat was upon them, and they were out of water and food. At three o'clock they spotted one of the possemen on the ridge above, but so dense and high was the chaparral that they could not be seen. Below them ran a narrow, deep gulch, known to this day as Vasquez Creek, which, unknown to the bandidos, drops steeply through a series of waterfalls·to Big Tujunga Canyon. Tiburcio ordered Padilla to find out if they could get their horses down it. He returned half an hour later and reported that it was barely possible, but the horses might make it. Chávez led on horseback, and the others followed on foot, leading their animals. Chávez's skittish mount picked its way down the steep bank on a path less than a foot wide. The outlaw made it fifty feet down when his horse balked. He dug his spurs into its flanks, the animal sprang forward, and suddenly plunged downward. Chávez leaped out of the saddle as the horse tumbled head over tail a hundred feet to its death at the bottom of the gulch. Its rider plunged down the abyss after his mount, but landed on a rocky ledge, lost his balance, and then dropped twenty feet down to a jutting rock, where he landed safely.

The rest of the band followed gingerly on foot. It took them an hour to get their horses to the narrow creek bed, where they found Chávez waiting for them. Chávez had explored the creek bed, and he told Vasquez that they were trapped. Less than a hundred feet downstream was a twenty-foot waterfall. Both sides of the gulch were solid walls of rock, and the gorge was choked with dead trees and boulders. It was getting dark and Tiburcio knew they had no time to lose. Taking only their guns, and leaving horses, saddles, and spurs in Vasquez Creek, they scaled the opposite side of the gorge, worked their way past the falls, then crawled and scrambled down the boulder-strewn mountainside to Big Tujunga Canyon. From here they walked four miles to the mouth of the canyon, then another four miles north to the mouth of Little Tujunga Canyon. There lived a Californio, Fructuoso Avaria, who fed them a hearty meal. The robbers made camp for the night three hundred yards from his house. In the morning, April 17, Vasquez borrowed a horse from Avaria and rode four miles to Mission San Fernando. Two years before he had enjoyed the hospitality of local Californios and had earned the friendship of the prominent López family and of Eulogio Celis, one of the community's most notable men. Now he needed their help.

The ancient mission was the private home of General Andrés Pico, the old Californio soldier and hero of the Mexican War. Pico's home was one of the social centers of the San Fernando Valley, and in the Californio custom, visitors were always welcome. The general entertained his guests with frequent fiestas, balls, hunting parties, and horseback rides. Seventeen years earlier, Pico had led posses of Californios after the Juan Flores bandit gang, summarily lynching two of them. It speaks volumes for Tiburcio's popularity and gregariousness that even the old warrior and bandit hunter welcomed him. He spent three days loitering about Pico's San Fernando home. By this time the posses had given up the hunt and returned to Los Angeles. On April 20 a prominent guest arrived, former state senator Charles Maclay, who was then arranging the purchase of fifty-seven thousand acres in San Fernando Valley and would soon lay out the townsite of the city of San Fernando. Tiburcio rode up to the mission and greeted Maclay with a genial "buenos días." Then he stepped inside and shared a drink with Andrés Pico and an unsuspecting Maclay. Soon after, a Mexican woman told Maclay that the visitor was Tiburcio Vasquez. The dumbfounded Maclay later reported, "Most of the Mexicans about the locality seemed to know him and treat him with consideration." That evening Maclay noticed that Pico was very particular about locking the bedroom doors. Maclay asked if the stranger really was Vasquez, and the old hacendado answered that he "needn't be afraid, Vasquez wouldn't hurt anybody about there." Tiburcio spent a restful night in one of the bedrooms.[12]

The next day Maclay visited Los Angeles on business and while there reported his story to former sheriff James F. Burns, who in turn notified Billy Rowland. The sheriff knew that Harry Morse and his posse were camped at Lyon's Station, just ten miles north of San Fernando, and that there was a telegraph station there. He tried to send a message, but by that time it was 11:00 P.M. and the telegraph office was closed. Then Rowland and his posse started on horseback toward the old mission. In the morning, when the office reopened, Burns wired a message to Morse, as related by Boyd Henderson in a telegraphic dispatch to the *Chronicle:*

This morning, our horses being fresh, we were about starting out on a hard day's ride, when at half past eight o'clock Morse received important news from Los Angeles, which served to point out the direction which should be taken with more certainty. The dispatch stated that Vasquez was known to have been at the San Fernando Mission at noon yesterday, that he was believed to be still in that locality, and that a pursuing party headed by Sheriff Rowland had started to San Fernando at eleven o'clock last night, intending to ride hard throughout the night and make a determined effort to intercept the bandit and foil his evident purpose of escaping southward.

Morse at once gave orders to mount and be off toward San Fernando. Unfortunately we went astray, through imperfect knowledge of the present condition of the country, by our making a blunder in the route taken. Passing through the Placeritas [Placerita Canyon], we followed the old trail toward Little Tujunga Canyon, which would have shortened the distance eighteen miles if we could have got through. But we found ourselves brought to a dead stop in the bottom of the canyon, which had been blockaded with stones by a waterspout to such a degree that our further progress was rendered utterly impossible. We were therefore compelled to retrace our steps and return to this point.

We are unable to account for Sheriff Rowland's failure to promptly inform Morse last night of the presence of Vasquez at San Fernando. Had he sent us immediate notice and notified us of the impassability of the canyon, if that fact was known to him, we could probably have taken such steps as would have insured the capture of Vasquez.[13]

Harry Morse's decision to allow Henderson to send such dispatches to the *San Francisco Chronicle* was unwise, as it enabled Vasquez and his supporters to know where the posse was. So too was the unwarranted criticism of Rowland. However, the *Chronicle* had succeeded in scooping all the newspapers. Journals in Los Angeles, San Jose, and Salinas, which had significant Spanish-speaking populations, reported on the Vasquez story without resort to racist commentary or ethnic stereotypes. The *Chronicle,* with a statewide readership, was less restrained. It headlined its sensational report on the Repetto raid "The Gory Greaser," and racial stereotypes permeated some, though not all, of its reporting. Vasquez's story was now national news, mesmerizing readers from coast to coast. The *Chronicle* sent to Los Angeles its ace reporter George Beers, a close friend of Sheriff Morse's. Beers, a rugged Civil War veteran, lost no time in joining up with Sheriff Rowland's posses. The San Francisco daily's coverage was vastly superior to that of the local newspapers. In a fit of jealousy, J. M. Bassett, editor of the *Los Angeles Herald,* went so far as to claim that the *Chronicle* had no correspondent with Morse's posse and that Henderson's reports were "all sensation and bosh, containing but little sense and no truth."[14]

The Repetto robbery and resulting manhunt, taking place so close to Los Angeles, created intense excitement among the citizens, both Anglo and Hispanic. When the *Los Angeles Express* accused the Hispanic community of harboring Vasquez, the editors of *La Crónica,* the city's Spanish-language newspaper, responded that only a few families in remote areas were helping the bandido. Fearing a resurgence of the racial violence, Hispanic banditry, and Anglo vigilantism that had embroiled Los Angeles in the 1850s, *La Crónica* called on its readers to cooperate with the authorities: "The capture of Vasquez is now a real necessity for our state. . . . The effort to free society of this danger should be unanimous."[15]

Soon the *Los Angeles Express,* in a lengthy editorial, voiced public fears that "Vasquez is capable of conceiving and executing even more dangerous

George Beers, the
newspaperman who
played a prominent role
in the manhunt and later
wrote a biography of
Tiburcio Vasquez.
(Author's collection)

undertakings," warning that with "twenty-five or thirty resolute men, armed with Henry and Spencer rifles" he could raid the town and rob its banks and jewelry stores. The editor cautioned citizens "to be prepared for such an attack" and demanded that "a well armed band of men" be "prepared to welcome the robbers with a hospitable reception." In response, the *Herald* scoffed at the danger of a raid, pointing out that "the chances against his doing so are about a million to one" and that there was no "occasion to fear the appearance of Vasquez in our streets." A few days later the *Express* dismissed a rumor that Vasquez had attended a ball in Sonoratown and afterward, with several compadres, had created a disturbance at a bordello. Its editor commented, "But it is the fashion now to make the famous bandit the scapegoat for every extraordinary proceeding of a daring and criminal nature."[16]

The fear of a raid on Los Angeles was widespread. On May 7, Phineas Banning, prominent Los Angeles businessman and brigadier general of the National Guard, sent a telegram to Governor Booth: "I consider this city in great danger of being attacked by desperadoes and murderers and earnestly and respectfully request that you will send me arms immediately for its protection." Within days his request was echoed by some of the city's most prominent men, including former governor John G. Downey, financier Isaias W. Hellman, banker Francis Temple, and state senator C. W. Bush. By letter to the governor, Senator Bush detailed the Anglos' fear of Vasquez: "A large proportion of our people are Spanish, who are nearly all in sympathy with him. They furnish all the information he requires, and they have such confidence in him as a leader, because of his daring and successful operations, that he could raise a body of two or three hundred men any time in this part of the state. He has boasted that he intends to make a big haul at this place. . . . The upper part of this city is nearly all Spanish, who harbor him, and consider it an honor to do so. He could send his men, by detachments, into this part of the city and by a bold dash rob all of our banks and get away before a sufficient force of citizens could be gotten together to prevent it."[17]

Such fears were not entirely unwarranted. Vasquez later admitted that he had conceived a daring plan to rob one of the two banks in Los Angeles. He said he would first send a decoy into town to give Sheriff Rowland a false report of his whereabouts. As soon as Rowland left with most of the city's lawmen, Vasquez and his band would quickly ride in, hold up the bank, and escape before Rowland could return.[18]

While working on this plan, Tiburcio was quietly holed up at Greek George's. One night he attended a dance at Judge John G. Nichols's granary in Nichols Canyon, which ran due north into what is now the Hollywood Hills. The mouth of the canyon was a mile northeast of Greek George's place. As was the custom, everyone from the nearby ranches, both Anglo and Hispanic, was welcome at the dance. One guest was twenty-one-year-old Eugenio Rafael Plummer, whose family home was located two miles northeast of Greek George's and is now called Plummer Park. Plummer's mother was half Hispanic and he spoke Spanish fluently. He was widely known in the Californio community and acted as an interpreter in the Los Angeles courts. Years later Plummer vividly recalled Tiburcio Vasquez, and his story illustrated not only how the bandido obtained aid for his gang, but how reckless he had become. Plummer related that between dances a short, dark man came up to him and said, "I understand you can read a newspaper?"

"Sí, señor," Plummer replied.

"Greek George" Caralambo in old age. He betrayed Tiburcio Vasquez for a share of the reward. (Author's collection)

"What do the periódicos say about Tiburcio Vasquez?"

"Oh, a great deal that is true, I suppose, and just as much that isn't."

"Sí, sí, es verdad." [Yes, yes, that's true.]

After some casual talk the stranger told Plummer, referring to their conversation, "This is all confidential."

"In that case, señor," Plummer replied, "Perhaps you will give me your confidence. What's your name?"

"Señor Tiburcio Vasquez, at your service."

Later in the evening Vasquez asked Plummer to step outside for a private chat. He had evidently made inquiries about young Plummer, and said, "You have a good reputation. You've helped a lot of Mexicanos. Will you do me a favor, amigo?"

Vasquez then gave Plummer fifty dollars and asked him to buy ten pairs of boots and a supply of food and bring them to Greek George's house. He was to leave the boots at Greek George's and take the provisions to the gang's hideout in Big Tujunga Canyon. A day or two later Plummer packed his saddlebags and rode into Big Tujunga, following Tiburcio's directions. Vasquez had been watching for him, came down the heavily thicketed mountainside, and led him to a cave hideout, which Plummer called "a filthy, miserable den you'd never think men could exist in." Plummer gave Tiburcio the supplies and after a short talk said to him, "By the way, señor, a couple of my horses have been missing for some time—a jet black with the Vicente Váldez brand and a dappled gray branded with the Domínguez mark."

"Oh yes," Vasquez admitted. "I think I've seen them. You'll get them back."

A few days later the horses mysteriously reappeared in the Plummer family pasture. Plummer later explained why he agreed to help Vasquez: "I knew about this fellow's crimes and felt like turning him over to the authorities, but it would have spoiled the faith that a lot of the Spanish-speaking people had in me—people that needed my help now and then, in the courts and out. . . . I realized too that some of these bandits and their followers weren't much worse in their way than some of the land sharks and lawyers were in theirs." Plummer's desire to get back his family's horses was undoubtedly another motive.[19]

In the meantime Sheriff Morse was hunting Vasquez relentlessly. On the morning of April 23, he and his men searched Placerita Canyon and in the afternoon met Sheriff Rowland's posse at San Fernando. From Rowland they learned that the gang's horses had been found, starving and trapped in Vasquez Creek, and had been saved after a difficult rescue. Before they separated the two sheriffs agreed to coordinate their efforts the next day. But Morse suspected that Billy Rowland was not fully cooperating with them, as Boyd Henderson explained: "Our information as to the movements of Rowland have been meager, unfortunately. We have not received the details of his operations, which would have enabled us to guide our course so as to fully cover the points not reached by him. . . . We had expected that Rowland would reach our camp this morning; but after waiting two hours in vain for him, Morse concluded to push ahead and we proceeded up the Little Tujunga, carefully keeping a lookout around and ahead."

In Little Tujunga Canyon, Morse's posse located the spot where the gang had camped after their escape from the Los Angeles officers. Said

Henderson, "We found but little to indicate their recent presence. There were lying on the ground the broken shells of a couple of eggs and the remains of a torn-up shirt which indicated the desperate, perhaps wounded, condition of the hunted wretches." Visiting the nearby home of Fructuoso Avaria, Morse learned that Sheriff Rowland had arrested and released him the previous day. Explained Henderson, "Vasquez has little, if anything, to fear from those of his countrymen who are scattered through this region. . . . Fructuoso . . . professed utter ignorance as to the movements of the fugitives, the utmost enlightenment that could be obtained from him being contained in the all-meaning words, so constantly in the Californian's mouth, 'Quien sabe?'"[20]

Boyd Henderson's harsh criticism of Rowland soon circulated in Los Angeles in late editions of the *Chronicle*. An angry Rowland assured the *Chronicle*'s readers that he had tried to telegraph Morse and had instructed his deputies to cooperate with him. Rowland's political enemies spread rumors that, due to his Hispanic ethnicity, he sympathized with Vasquez and had been lax in hunting him. For Harry Morse, this public censure of the Los Angeles sheriff would prove to be a major tactical blunder. After one more day of fruitless hunting, Sheriff Morse became convinced that Vasquez had returned to his old haunts in the Coast Range. He and his men had been in the saddle for six weeks, and they were exhausted and frustrated. Many of his possemen had pressing business at home, so Morse decided to head back, searching as they went. They rode north and stopped at Fort Tejon on April 27. Here the sheriff received an electrifying piece of information: Tiburcio Vasquez was hiding out at Greek George's adobe.[21]

CHAPTER EIGHTEEN

Dead or Alive

Felicita Vasquez's family was scandalized when she gave birth to Tiburcio's child. Felicita's mother, María Villa, was furious with Tiburcio and made her feelings known to her extended Californio clan. She was related to the huge family of Los Angeles pioneer Claudio López, whose great-grandson was José Jesús López, the youthful vaquero who loved Felicita. Young López despised Vasquez, saying, "I consider him one of the most disgraceful rascals and degenerate scamps among the native Californios. Tiburcio Vasquez was a man of no principle at all. When he was not robbing some honest, hard-working person, he was busy seducing some wife or a young girl, not sparing even his own niece. Much has been said of Tiburcio's hatred for los Americanos, and of his supposed preying on them as a justified retaliation. Nothing could be farther from the truth. His treatment of his own people was just as miserable and unscrupulous as it could be."[1]

López's feelings were shared by his father and also by his cousin Cornelia López, Greek George's wife. Her sister Modesta, with whom Vasquez had a sexual relationship, was furious when she learned that Felicita had borne Tiburcio's child, and her feelings multiplied when Los Angeles newspapers reported rumors that Tiburcio had visited the prostitute La Coneja. Soon it became rumored among the extended López family that Vasquez was hiding out at Greek George's place on Rancho La Brea. José Jesús López recalled that when his father learned that, he notified the authorities, perhaps Harry Morse. The Alameda sheriff never revealed the

name of his informant, but it was undoubtedly a member of the López
clan. Sheriff Morse promptly boarded the evening stage for Los Angeles,
leaving Tom Cunningham and the rest of his posse in Fort Tejon. Although
it was a long, 110-mile ride, Morse considered it a professional courtesy
that Sheriff Rowland be in on the capture. Sheriff Morse arrived in town
the next day. As it was widely believed that Vasquez had spies keeping
an eye on Rowland, Morse sent word for the sheriff to meet him at the
Los Angeles Real Estate Agency. There the Alameda sheriff revealed his
information and suggested that he, Rowland, Cunningham, and one Los
Angeles officer attempt the capture. But Billy Rowland was unimpressed.
He told Morse that the story was a "sell" and that the informant "knew
nothing about Vasquez."[2]

Morse was greatly disappointed, but he trusted Rowland. The popular Los Angeles sheriff had been born in the county, his mother was
Hispanic, he spoke Spanish fluently, and he was a prominent member of
the Californio community. He would certainly know which informants
were reliable. A discouraged Morse left Los Angeles, rejoined his posse,
and rode north—a miscalculation that he would forever regret. Sheriff
Rowland owed no loyalty to Harry Morse, an interloper from Northern
California whose correspondent, Henderson, had publicly criticized
him. Rowland later insisted that he did not use Morse's tip. To George
Beers he "denied emphatically that the information brought by Morse
located Vasquez anywhere near the La Brea ranch, or assisted in any way
toward finding him." Nonetheless, no sooner had Morse boarded the
northbound stage than Rowland sent one of his deputies, D. K. Smith,
to keep watch on Greek George's place. Deputy Sheriff Henry Mitchell
and partner Charley Knowlton owned a bee ranch in Nichols Canyon, and
Smith made his headquarters there. From an adjacent ridge Deputy Smith
could observe Greek George's adobe on the plain below. A newcomer to
Los Angeles, Smith was little known in the community, and his mission was
not suspected by Vasquez or his friends. From Mitchell's bee ranch Smith
kept up the surveillance for two weeks, and soon spotted several horsemen
visiting the house whom he believed to be Vasquez and his band.[3]

Greek George's house was situated such that an approaching posse
from Los Angeles could be seen a long way off. Rowland knew that he
needed inside information for the capture to be successful. He secretly
approached Greek George and offered him a share of the $3,000 reward.
The Greek was not interested in such a small payment and denied any

knowledge of Vasquez. On May 8, Governor Booth, under political pressure, increased the reward for Vasquez's capture: $6,000 dead or $8,000 alive. This was exactly what Sheriff Rowland needed. He approached Greek George again, offering him a share of the larger reward for his cooperation. Greek George apparently talked the matter over with his wife and sister-in-law. Despite fears of being murdered by the gang for their betrayal, they agreed. Their motives seem to have been mixed: partly the increased reward and partly family loyalty. On May 13, 1874, Greek George rode into Los Angeles and told Rowland that Vasquez would be at his house the next morning. At eight o'clock that night Deputy Smith rode in and reported that several of the band were camped near the house.[4]

Billy Rowland wasted no time. He sent word for a group of his trusted deputies and fellow lawmen, those who had most consistently hunted Vasquez, to meet him at the law office of his deputy, Henry M. Mitchell, who was also a practicing attorney. They were Undersheriff Albert Johnston; Deputy Sheriffs Henry Mitchell, Walter Rogers, and D. K. Smith; Los Angeles Chief of Police Frank Hartley; Detective Emil Harris; Constable Sam Bryant; and reporter George Beers. Rowland had intended to lead the posse, but now he changed his mind, for he was convinced that Tiburcio had spies watching his every movement. He instructed the men to meet after midnight at John Jones's corral at the corner of Spring and Fifth streets on the southern outskirts of town, each taking a different route and arriving at a different time. Their horses were taken to the corral surreptitiously, and their guns were boxed up and brought in by express wagon. At 2:00 A.M. the posse headed silently out of town. Emil Harris later recounted the events:

> After riding all night very cautiously and slowly, for it was exceedingly dark and foggy, and we were obliged to make long detours around farm houses to avoid rousing dogs, we reached Nichols Canyon in the gray of the morning, and proceeded up about half a mile past Charley Knowlton's bee ranch, where we halted. There is a trail leading up the mountainside from Knowlton's place, and from the top of the mesa observations could be taken of the valley.
>
> Johnston requested me to remain in camp with most of the party, while he took Mitchell and Smith and went up on the mountain for the purpose of ascertaining with field glasses what

the situation was at Greek George's. In due time I sent Sam Bryant up to their lookout, and he came back and reported that while it was still quite foggy and dark, a gray horse had been seen tied to a fence, leading them to believe that Chávez was there, too, as he always rode an animal of that color. Bryant, Hartley, and Beers then went down to Knowlton's for breakfast, and while they were away, about 10 o'clock, a two-horse wood wagon came along driven by a couple of young Mexicans, aged respectively about 18 and 24 years.

I had instructions from Johnston to permit nobody to pass in either direction, so emerged from behind a tree and ordered them to halt, which they did in a reluctant way after considerable expostulation. They eventually laid down in the bottom of the wagon, which was empty, and went to sleep, while I stood guard over them. About 11:30 A.M. Bryant, Hartley, and Beers returned from Knowlton's and I asked Bryant to go up and learn what Johnston had discovered. Leaving Hartley and Beers in charge of the two Mexicans, Rogers and I went to Knowlton's for breakfast, which consisted of black coffee and bread hard enough to knock down tenpins with, but I think we enjoyed the repast more than if we had dined at the Van Nuys or Angelus.

In the meantime the fog had lifted materially, and a man was seen to leave the Greek George house on a gray horse. Thinking it might be Chávez, Mitchell and Smith gave chase, while Johnston and Bryant returned to our camp, and sent word for me to come immediately, as we were about to start. Johnston, Rogers, Hartley, Beers, and myself, besides the younger of the two Mexican boys, then laid down in the bed of the wagon, at Johnson's suggestion, while Bryant, who was rather dark and resembled a Mexican at a distance, got up on the seat with the driver to prevent any treachery. We were completely concealed from view by the side-boards of the wagon, and were as closely packed as sardines. The driver was ordered to proceed to a point near Greek George's house, and not to attempt to betray our presence in any manner, either by word or sign, under penalty of death.

Johnston, Bryant, Rogers, Hartley, and Beers were armed with double barreled, muzzle loading shotguns loaded with buckshot, while I had an old style sixteen shot Henry rifle.[5] All of us carried

Los Angeles Chief of Police B. F. "Frank" Hartley, one of the leaders of the posse that captured Tiburcio Vasquez. This photo was taken in the 1890s when he was captain of the guard at Yuma prison. (Author's collection)

revolvers in addition—powder and ball, of the Colt's navy pattern.
When within one hundred yards of the house we stopped the
wagon and all jumped out and threw themselves face downwards
on the ground, while the wagon turned and was driven rapidly
back in the direction of Nichols Canyon. As soon as we saw the
coast was clear, we arose in a body and made a dash for the house.
My intention was to kill Vasquez's horse in the event of his
coming out and trying to escape in that way. The house was
constructed in the form of an L. I ran to the northeast corner
of the structure, followed by Johnston, Bryant, and Rogers, while
Hartley and Beers took up a position in a mustard patch on the
southwest side of the building.

I looked through an open door into the living room and beheld
a young woman of rather comely appearance with some plates
in her arms, in the act of waiting upon a man seated at the table,
who was in his shirt sleeves and wore overalls.[6] Both had their
backs toward me. I turned and beckoned our men to close in.
The woman's attention seemed to have been attracted in some
way, and she made haste to close the door, but I rushed up and
thrust my gun between it and the sill and forced it open. As I
entered the room the man had arisen hurriedly and made a break
for a small window, and was partially through when I raised my
rifle quickly, without taking deliberate aim, and fired. The ball
struck him in the fleshy part of his left arm underneath, entered
his body immediately over his heart, ran around under the skin
and came out at his right breast, making a superficial wound. I
did not know this at the time, however, as he bled profusely. He
plunged through the window, and I turned and hurried around
the house to head him off, when I saw Johnston, Bryant, and
Rogers outside, and one of them—either Johnston or Bryant—
fired at him as he was making for his horse.

At this juncture Hartley also fired upon him at close range
with both barrels of his gun, but when captured only two buckshot were found to have struck him, one having lodged in the
back of his head and the other in his right arm.[7] I thereupon
leveled my rifle at him, when he turned and threw up his hands,
exclaiming, "Don't shoot! I give up!"

When I reached him he was covered with blood and I took him by the arm and led him toward an enclosure, at the same time asking him why he ran. He replied that he was afraid we wanted to kill everybody in sight. At that time none of us knew it was Vasquez, but I told him we were hunting for criminals, and the fact of his trying to get away had led us to assume that he was some guilty party. Upon being asked his name he replied, "Alejandro Martínez." I had in my possession a photograph taken of Vasquez when he was about twenty-five years of age. Upon referring to it, I immediately saw the resemblance, and said, "Yes, Alejandro Martínez sometimes, and sometimes something else."

"Oh, no," was his answer. "I came here to shear sheep."

By this time we had reached the enclosure, where Johnston, Bryant, and Rogers were, and I said, "Boys, I think we have got the chief." I told him to sit down in the enclosure until the whole of us were together, when Beers was placed over him as a guard, while the rest of us returned to search the house, as we had been led to believe from our information that he would be accompanied by four others, comprising his entire gang. Johnston, Hartley, and Rogers stood guard outside, while I proceeded to investigate matters on the inside of the house.

At this time a young Mexican [Librado Corona] emerged with an infant in his arms, followed by the Mexican woman whom we had first observed, and she implored us not to kill the man. We assured her it was not our intention to harm anybody if we could avoid it, and endeavored in other ways to calm her fears, whereupon she took the baby from him, and we handcuffed him to a post, telling Beers to keep a close watch upon both prisoners. We then continued our search, and by the side of the chair at the table . . . was found a long bladed Bowie knife sticking in the floor. The wife of Greek George had only recently been confined, and underneath her bed we resurrected a vest, in one of the pockets of which was a stop watch which I at once recognized as having been taken from Charley Miles in the Arroyo Seco affair. In the room from whence the man had come with the baby we found six revolvers, two Winchester rifles of the model of 1873, then considered the best weapon

Emil Harris, Los Angeles police detective and one of the captors of Tiburcio Vasquez. (William B. Secrest collection)

made, and a Spencer seven-shooter [rifle], besides another dangerous looking knife and some saddles, bridles, etc.

We afterwards found out that Greek George's premises were one of the regular headquarters for the gang. Upon searching Vasquez we found a silver watch chain belonging to John Osborne, which was likewise one of the proceeds of the Miles holdup in the Arroyo Seco. Then I said, "Now, I am certain we have got the chief. Your name is Tiburcio Vasquez."

For a moment he hesitated, but finally made a clean breast of it in the following language, "Yes, once I was a gentleman, but now I am guilty."

I then inquired, "Are you hurt very badly?"

"Yes," was his reply. "I think I am."

"Do you think you will die?"

"Yes, I think I shall."

At our suggestion the young woman brought a basin of water and we dressed his wounds as well as possible under the circumstances. Then I inquired if he wished to make any statement in view of his probable death, and he asked, "Who is your captain?"

I referred him to Undersheriff Johnston, and he requested the latter to bring a small memorandum book from one of the pockets of his coat. I got the book, and upon opening it found clippings from the Los Angeles papers of the day previous, giving detailed accounts of our movements. I handed it to Johnston, and Vasquez continued, "I have two children living in Monterey, although I am not married."

We then adjourned to Judge Thompson's place, near by, and procured an old spring wagon, and with two mules for a team, started to town with our prisoners. In the meantime we had secured our saddle horses from Knowlton's, which we all mounted, except Hartley, who rode Vasquez's horse, and ranged ourselves upon either side of the wagon. Before starting, however, I took a flask of whiskey from my saddlebags and offered Vasquez a drink. He responded, "I like to drink with brave men, and you are all brave, like myself."

About three miles from town Mitchell and Smith overtook us with their captive, who afterward proved to be some innocent party, and placed him in charge of our posse. Mitchell then rode

Greek George's adobe, scene of Tiburcio Vasquez's capture. (Author's collection)

on ahead to apprise Sheriff Rowland of the capture, and the news spread like wildfire, so that when we arrived at First and Spring Streets, which was then the outskirts of the business portion of Los Angeles, we were met by an immense concourse of people, rendering it necessary for some of us to ride on ahead and clear a pathway for the vehicle. We reached the county jail between four and five o'clock in the afternoon. It was then located on North Spring Street.

The city council was in session, but it adjourned in a very undignified way, and all the city fathers came piling through the windows to get a glimpse of the famous bandit. Sheriff Rowland was in waiting with a corps of physicians, and Vasquez's wounds were attended to at once.[8]

Two physicians came to the jail to treat Vasquez. As he was undressed, he asked the doctors not to tear his shirt, remarking that its front had been embroidered for him by a señorita. They removed buckshot from Tiburcio's arms, right leg, chest, and neck. Observers were impressed at how stoically he bore the pain. Although all his injuries were serious, inch-deep flesh wounds, the doctors pronounced that he would soon recover. Just then Charley Miles stepped into the jail, took one look at the prisoner, and cried out, "That's him! That's Vasquez! That's the fellow." Thereupon Frank Hartley handed Miles his gold pocket watch. Tiburcio, looking up from his bed, commented, "It belongs to him now." Earlier, Vasquez had asked Hartley's name, and now the police chief asked Tiburcio why he had wanted to know. The outlaw replied, "Usted es un hombre valiente lo mismo que yo." [You are a brave man the same as I.][9]

Among Tiburcio's effects were found photographs of his two young children and a lock of hair, bound in silk ribbon. He also had the receipt for the poll tax he had paid Mike Madigan. Tiburcio's name had been written by Madigan in a very tremulous hand, which was explained when Vasquez asked one of his guards, "Who is that little Irishman—the poll tax collector?"

"Mike Madigan," replied the guard. "Would you like to see him?"

"No, but he is a funny little fellow," Vasquez responded, and then gave his own version of the affair, which was undoubtedly more truthful than Madigan's: "I was riding alone in the Canyon de los Verdugos when I met him driving in a buggy. He asked in a very important manner whether I had paid my poll tax. I said no, and he asked if I would pay it then. I answered that I would, for I was a good citizen, and always paid my taxes. He drew a book and pencil from his pocket, and swelling up like a turkey cock inquired my name. When I said Tiburcio Vasquez, his hand shook so that he could hardly write the receipt. I paid him the two dollars, and without saying good-bye he whipped up his horse, and kept whipping as far as I could see him."[10]

The posse had brought in Tiburcio's beautiful white horse. It turned out to have been stolen a year before from Volney E. Howard, a prominent Los Angeles attorney and politician. They also recovered another mount, four hundred rounds of ammunition, and two very fancy saddles and bridles. The possemen kept the guns and other items as trophies, Emil Harris taking one rifle and Tiburcio's knife and scabbard. After the bandido's wounds had been treated, one of the officers produced a bottle of whiskey and offered him a drink. Reported the editor of the *Los Angeles Express,* "He cheerfully accepted, and gave a toast to the President of the United States, and expressed a strong and eloquent desire that nothing would occur to mar the relations of harmony existing between our country and Mexico."[11]

Tiburcio Vasquez's bowie knife and scabbard, taken from him by Emil Harris at the time of his capture. (Author's collection)

Later that evening Vasquez called Billy Rowland to his cell, and telling the sheriff that he knew he had been betrayed, begged for the name of the informer. Rowland was noncommittal and went to great lengths to conceal Greek George's complicity. He arrested and jailed the Greek as an accessory to the Repetto robbery in order to cover up his involvement in the capture. Greek George was quickly released on bail, the case was continued until the next term of court, and the charges were eventually dismissed. Rowland never publicly revealed Greek George's role, and for a number of years his involvement was a well-kept secret. Over time, however, other lawmen talked, and eventually Greek George's role in the capture became public. In 1892 U.S. Marshal George Gard, a former Los Angeles police chief and county sheriff, told newspaper readers that Greek George "gave Vasquez away." When the informer died in 1913, the *Los Angeles Times* reported what was by then well known: "Greek George won local fame by his assistance rendered Sheriff William Rowland in capturing the famous bandit, Vasquez." It was reported that Rowland paid Greek George one-fourth of the $8,000 reward, the balance of which was divided among his captors.[12]

The man Deputy Mitchell had arrested was a Californio named Reales. He was lodged in jail with young Librado Corona but was released when he proved to be an honest vaquero from El Tejon who had nothing to do with the gang. Tiburcio later said that two of his men, probably Padilla and Chávez, were in Los Angeles at the time of his arrest, and that Francisco Gómez was on a ranch fifteen miles away.[13]

The capture created a public sensation when reported in newspapers throughout the United States. Crowds flocked to the jail to see the noted outlaw. Sheriff Rowland allowed one and all to visit Vasquez in his cell. Although the bandido was wounded, Rowland kept leg irons on him, with a long chain connecting his shackles to the bars on his cell window. Women, in particular, were drawn to see him. Reported George Beers, "Among the callers were quite a number of first class ladies, all of whom were evidently charmed with the prisoner's excessive politeness. . . . Some of the ladies went so far in their admiration of the famous bandit as to present him rare bouquets and shower upon him their sweetest smiles." Beers noted that "to everyone who called on him, Vasquez was polite, and conversed freely in regard to his career, making no attempt to deny the numerous robberies he had planned and executed; but always asserting that he had never in the course of his career found it necessary to kill." Los Angeles merchant Harris Newmark recalled, "Everybody who could, visited him and I was no exception. I was disgusted, however, when I found Vasquez's cell filled with flowers, sent by some white women of Los Angeles who had been carried away by the picturesque career of the bandido; but Sheriff Rowland soon stopped all such foolish exuberance."[14]

Newspapermen, aware that their readers were hungry for information about the elusive bandit, flocked to his cell. They found him in bed and weak from his wounds. Expecting to meet an uncouth ruffian, they were surprised to find a well-groomed, articulate man who was genteel, sociable, and talkative. Wrote one, "Lying upon his pallet, a price set upon his head, an outlaw and an outcast, he received us and a number of other visitors with an ease and grace and elegance which would have done no discredit to any gentleman in the land." J. M. Bassett, editor of the *Los Angeles Herald,* interviewed Vasquez and gave his eager readers a pen portrait: "In appearance he is anything but the ferocious, red-handed brigand his reputation has given him. He is a man of ordinary stature, with a well knit, wiry figure. He does not weigh over 140 or 150 pounds. His complexion is much lighter than the ordinary Mexican. His features are clear cut, with an intelligent expression. His eyes are rather large, and a light grey or blue in color. His forehead is high, and his head well shaped.

In manner he is frank and earnest, with no disposition to make himself a hero. His general demeanor is that of a quiet, inoffensive man, and but for his calm, steady eye, which stamps him as a man of great determination and firmness, no one would take him for the terrible Tiburcio Vasquez."[15]

Basset added, "He understands English very well, but speaks it imperfectly." Perhaps due to fatigue, Vasquez chose to converse in his native tongue. In the course of the lengthy interview, with Sheriff Rowland acting as interpreter, Basset asked him, "Do you think a woman had anything to do with your capture or in placing the officers on your track?" Tiburcio, never suspecting Modesta's complicity, responded with a laugh, "No. I never trusted one with information that could harm me." Vasquez was shrewd enough to use the interview to gain sympathy, and gave a revisionist version of the motivation for his career: "I have been persecuted and driven from point to point, from year to year. The white men heaped wrong upon me in Monterey, and the officers hounded me until I was driven from an honest calling in Mendocino County." Vasquez described the Tres Pinos tragedy, claiming that when he arrived on the scene with Chávez, the shooting was all over. He declared that Abdon Leiva had killed Bahury and Redford, and that Romulo Gonzáles had slain Davison.[16]

Flattered by the attention, Tiburcio gave interviews to George Beers, *Los Angeles Star* editor Ben C. Truman, and *La Crónica* editors E. F. Teodoli and Pastor Celis. The interviews with Beers and Truman took place in English, and both found him able to speak it comfortably. For the first time in print he provided detailed information about his life and exploits, much of it true, some of it deliberately vague, and some manifestly false. He uniformly denied ever killing anyone, always blaming any deaths on other desperadoes in his band. Yet Tiburcio was loyal to his compadres, and in recounting his raids, was careful to lay blame on men who were dead or had escaped to Mexico. Some of them, such as Clodoveo Chávez and Teodoro Moreno, he claimed were innocent of murder. Of the Tres Pinos Tragedy, he told editor Truman, "I told them not to use any violence, as when I arrived I would be the judge, and if anybody had to be shot I would do the shooting. When I arrived there with Chávez, however, I found three men dead, and was told that two of them were killed by Leiva and one by another of the party called Romano [Romulo]."[17]

To Bassett, Vasquez boasted, "I knew every movement Morse made. I have been around his camp night after night, but have never been near enough to Morse to recognize him and should not know him if I met him on the road. I do not know Sheriff Cunningham of San Joaquin County. I know Sheriff Adams of Santa Clara County. He is a brave man. I could have killed him several times. I never had Morse in a sure place." He also claimed to have had several chances to kill Sheriff Rowland, adding, "He has taken more chances than any of them. The pursuit after the Repetto robbery was very close. Rowland passed within ten yards of me as I lay in the brush after abandoning my horses in Tujunga Canyon. I had by my side two Henry rifles and two revolvers." Yet Vasquez was mistaken, for it was Deputy Mitchell who had pursued him toward Big Tujunga Canyon.[18]

The editors of *La Crónica,* echoing the views of California's educated, upper-class Spanish-speaking populace, were effusive in their praise of Los Angeles's Hispanic sheriff: "It took the astuteness, perseverance, and tactics of Rowland to catch him." Pointing out that Rowland had spent his own funds to finance the manhunt, they wrote that "a public servant who sacrifices his own purse for the public good is not found every day of the week." Regarding the political allegations that Rowland sympathized with Vasquez, they countered, "It was believed by some that he would not succeed in catching Vasquez . . . because of the Spanish blood in his veins. . . . He did succeed and it was not for the reward that was offered, but rather to vindicate his character, that our noble sheriff went into debt to stage this hunt with true tactics and zeal, even using Greek George as a tool." *La Crónica's* editors did not conceal their pride in Rowland: "We must feel a debt of gratitude to the men who captured him and especially to the noble sheriff who with skill and admirable preparation worthy of praise has accomplished the great enterprise."[19]

California's leading photography firm, Bradley & Rulofson of San Francisco, sent a telegram to George Beers advising that if Vasquez would provide them with a negative, they would have cabinet card images printed for the public, and Tiburcio would receive 25 percent of the profits. Vasquez agreed, and on the afternoon of May 18 Los Angeles photographer Valentin Wolfenstein was called to the jail. Tiburcio was strong enough to get out of bed and walk slowly but painfully to a shady spot behind the jail. He sat in a chair while Wolfenstein set up his heavy camera. Two photographs were taken, and one, a bust view, remains the best-known image of Tiburcio Vasquez. The next day, when Beers asked Wolfenstein for the negatives, he refused to hand them over, and instead began printing photographs and selling them himself at twenty-five cents each. He gave nothing to Vasquez, and even had the photographs copyrighted. Within a week, Wolfenstein left on a visit to his old home in Sweden, taking a steamer to San Francisco to connect with the overland railroad. He was confronted there by one of the owners of the Bradley & Rulofson gallery, who promptly gave him a sound thrashing. "This manner of settling the case seemed to please Tiburcio highly, and he wants to shake hands with the San Francisco artist," reported one newsman.[20]

The great courtesy Vasquez showed to his many visitors drew comment. When Alessandro Repetto visited on May 18, *Los Angeles Star* editor Truman was present and described the scene: "No two Hidalgos meeting in 'the Alhambra's halls' could have been more scrupulously observant of all the forms of etiquette." After the usual salutations, the Italian said, "I have called, signor, to say that, so far as I am concerned, you can settle that little account with God Almighty. I have no hard feelings against you, none whatever."

Vasquez thanked Repetto profusely and began to offer repayment, when Repetto interrupted him: "I do not expect to be repaid. I gave it to you to save further trouble, but I beg of you, if you ever resume operations, not to repeat your visit to my house."

At that, Tiburcio replied, "Ah, señor, if I am so unfortunate as to suffer conviction and am compelled to undergo a short term of imprisonment, I will take the earliest opportunity to reimburse you." Placing his hand over his heart, Vasquez added, "Señor Repetto, yo soy un caballero, con el corazón de un caballero." [I am a cavalier, with the heart of a cavalier.]

As the sheepman-physician turned to leave he said, "Signor Vasquez, that young man Librado Corona who accompanied you, worked for me a year ago, and I cured him of a very disagreeable complaint. I think it was decidedly ungrateful of him to bring you to my house."[21]

The following afternoon Tiburcio had a surprise visitor. Chico Vasquez had heard of his capture and took pity on his wounded brother. Their relationship was still strained, for as George Beers reported, "the interview lasted but a moment. The two men exchanged only the ordinary courtesies of friends." Notably, Chico was not accompanied by María, Felicita, nor Tiburcio's infant son, Alfredo. Although Chico was willing to reconcile with his brother, María would never forgive him.[22]

To satisfy the public's insatiable interest, Ben Truman worked feverishly on the first biography of the captured outlaw. With a speed that would put modern true crime publishers to shame, on May 20, six days after the

Tiburcio Vasquez, photographed behind the Los Angeles jail on May 18, 1874, by Valentin Wolfenstein. The frontispiece image was taken at the same time. (California State Library collection)

capture, he offered for sale *The Life, Adventures, and Capture of Tiburcio Vasquez, The Great California Bandit and Murderer.* Written in English and Spanish, forty-four pages in length, it consisted primarily of news articles that had been published in the *Star* and *Herald.* Although eight thousand copies were printed for the San Francisco market, they sold out quickly. Dramatists also cashed in on Tiburcio's story. Samuel Piercy of the Merced Theater quickly penned a short play, "The Capture of Vasquez." According to the *Los Angeles Express,* "Some of the most striking events of the bandit's career have been woven together for representation. A feature of this production will be Mr. Piercy's personation of the bandit." Greatly flattered, Tiburcio lent his garments to the actor and allowed him to study his personality and voice so as to better impersonate him on stage. The play debuted on May 23, much to the amusement of Angelenos, but had a very short run.[23]

Tiburcio had now recovered enough to travel. The following afternoon Sheriff Rowland, Undersheriff Johnston, and Deputy Walter Rogers quietly loaded their prisoner into a carriage and brought him to the railroad depot just in time to catch the train to San Pedro, the Los Angeles port. Tiburcio was loaded down with handcuffs and leg irons, but Rowland acted so quickly and secretly that fewer than twenty people knew the infamous bandido was leaving. The three officers took him on board the coastal steamer *Senator,* which quickly set off north for San Francisco. From there he was to be taken by train to Salinas to stand trial for the Tres Pinos murders.[24]

Tiburcio Vasquez's quiet and inconspicuous departure from Los Angeles contrasted greatly with the way Angelenos would celebrate his memory. Although he had spent a total of only a few years in Southern California, he would always be thought of as a Southern California bandido. The Southland never forgot him.

CHAPTER NINETEEN

The Murder Trial

Winds, violent seas, and strong currents made for a slow, three-day trip to San Francisco. Tiburcio was seasick much of the time. When the *Senator* stopped at San Buenaventura (now Ventura), large crowds came to the wharf to see the noted bandido, including several who had known him during his sojourn there in 1856. At Monterey bad weather prevented a landing at the wharf. Sheriff Rowland, hearing a rumor that a lynch mob was waiting for Vasquez, ordered that the ship anchor in the stream. Although the threat was unfounded, Rowland was taking no chances. He was well aware that a year earlier Tiburcio's nemesis Matt Tarpy had been hanged by a Monterey lynch mob. According to an improbable report in the *San Francisco Alta California,* Rowland handed Vasquez a six-shooter and said, "If the worst is reached, defend yourself. We will defend you on deck." A small boat was sent ashore from the steamer, bearing a letter Tiburcio had written to his family. Finally, on the morning of May 27, the *Senator* arrived in San Francisco. Several hundred people gathered at the wharf to catch a glimpse of its infamous cargo. Chief of Police Theodore Cockrill and twenty-five officers were on hand to preserve order.[1]

Word spread quickly, and a huge crowd gathered as Vasquez was lodged in the city prison. After breakfast Chief Cockrill, with Rowland, Johnston, and several policemen as guards, took him in a hack to Bradley & Rulofson's photographic gallery at 429 Montgomery Street. Tiburcio wanted not only to complete his agreement with that firm, but undoubtedly also to congratulate the photographer who had thrashed Wolfenstein. Four images were taken of the outlaw, two standing, and two seated. These were later printed on cabinet cards and sold to the public, with Tiburcio presumably receiving his share of the proceeds, which would help pay his lawyers. By this time more than a thousand excited onlookers had gathered outside the gallery. After the officers shoved their way through the crowd, Vasquez was soon back in the city prison.

He was interviewed in his cell by a reporter for the *San Francisco Bulletin,* who found him lying on his cot, still weak from his wounds. Vasquez had no trouble conversing with him in English, and the journalist commented, "There is nothing particularly striking in his features, and he would hardly be taken for the blood-thirsty villain which he has proved himself to be." In the course of a long interview, Tiburcio denied ever shooting anyone. The surprised newspaperman retorted, "Now, Vasquez, you don't really mean to say that you never shot a man in your life?"

"Yes, I do," he replied. "I never shot a man."

"Did you like your robber life?"

"No, not at all. Of course, a man would not like to be hunted all the time like a dog."

"Why did you live such a life, then? Wasn't it your own choice?"

"No, I was obliged to," Vasquez responded quickly.

"What do you mean by that?"

"I mean that when I settled down anywhere and tried to get a living, they came and drove me out. They wouldn't give me any peace."

"Who are 'they'?"

"Why, the Americans—the officers."

"If you behaved yourself they wouldn't meddle with you, would they?"

"Oh, yes, they would. That didn't make any difference."

Despite his previous denial of ever shooting anyone, in the next breath he admitted wounding Santa Cruz police officer Robert Liddell. A moment later Mortimer Belshaw, whose main offices were in San Francisco, appeared at the cell door, and asked Vasquez in Spanish what he had done with the silver pocket watch he had taken from him at Coyote Holes. Belshaw wanted the watch so badly he offered to pay for its return. Wrote the *Bulletin*'s man, "Vasquez seemed a good deal pleased at this reminiscence, and replied that he did not know where the watch was, but thought that Chávez had it." That ended the interview, with

Tiburcio Vasquez. One of four images taken by Bradley & Rulofson in San Francisco, May 27, 1874. (Robert G. McCubbin collection)

the reporter concluding, "His manner is such that one cannot place a particle of confidence in what he says."[2]

Harry Morse also visited Vasquez in jail, and Tiburcio now vehemently denied ever stating that he had full knowledge of the sheriff's movements. A reporter for the *San Francisco Call* interviewed him briefly, and wrote, "He speaks the English language with sufficient fluency to be well understood. Whenever any questions were asked him, to which he did not desire to give a direct answer, he evaded them by answering in Spanish." The crowd outside had been clamoring to see the noted brigand, and Chief Cockrill asked Vasquez if he objected.

"Let them come in," he replied quickly. "Charge them half a dollar apiece, and give me half."

When Cockrill declined, Tiburcio said, "Well, all right. Let them in."

Cockrill had his officers admit them, six at a time. A long line formed, and each was allowed a brief glimpse of the outlaw in his cell. A number were sympathetic, and one reportedly handed Tiburcio sixty dollars to help pay his lawyers. Another offered him cigarettes but he politely declined. A policeman prodded them along: "Take a peep, gentlemen, and pass on. That'll do, now, no speaking to the prisoner, it's not allowed."[3]

The next morning Sheriff John Adams, with Monterey's new sheriff, James B. Smith, took Vasquez by train to Salinas. All along the route crowds gathered to catch a glimpse of the prisoner, but they were disappointed, as the two officers kept him under close watch in the express car. He was lodged in the Salinas jail under heavy guard. Three thousand people, many of them Hispanic, thronged to the calaboose to see him. A San Francisco reporter described the scene: "Mexicans and [native] Californians by scores come into town every day to get a glimpse at their beloved hero. Many sit down by the side of the jail and put up piteous appeals for this fiend; and it is safe to say that nine-tenths of the Californians sympathize with the noted cut-throat."[4]

A few days later Tiburcio received a letter from Felipe Fierro, a Chileno who published a Spanish-language newspaper in San Francisco. He recommended that Vasquez hire Charles Ben Darwin, a prominent San Francisco trial lawyer who had previously served as a judge in Washington Territory, had lived in South America, and spoke Spanish fluently. On June 2, Tiburcio wrote to Darwin, and four days later the lawyer met Vasquez in the Salinas jail. Tiburcio was pleased and impressed with Darwin, and the same day engaged him as counsel. The two became very friendly and

Tiburcio Vasquez. Another of the four images taken by Bradley & Rulofson in San Francisco, May 27, 1874. (Robert G. McCubbin collection)

began a regular correspondence in Spanish. Darwin lent Tiburcio several popular Spanish-language novels, including *Don Quixote de la Mancha, Guzmán de Alfarache,* and *Amalia.* Reading them helped pass the time, and Vasquez thanked Darwin profusely.[5]

While Tiburcio was being held in Salinas, Abdon Leiva was a model prisoner in the San Jose jail. During daylight hours the inmates were allowed out of their cells, and they congregated on the second floor. On the afternoon of June 17, Abdon Leiva and a fellow prisoner, Tom Jones, alias Tom McGuire, were playing a game of casino. Jones was a dangerous ruffian serving thirty days for disturbing the peace. When Jones won twenty-five cents, Leiva accused him of cheating and refused to pay. Jones tried to goad him into a fight, but Leiva went downstairs. Jones followed and, picking up a heavy board from one of the bunks, savagely attacked Leiva. He struck him three heavy blows to the head, and Leiva collapsed unconscious, bleeding profusely from one ear. Jones was about to finish him off with another blow when he was stopped by the prisoners, who later heard him say "he wished he had killed the greaser." Leiva was badly injured but recovered. His assailant was charged with attempted murder. According to the *San Jose Patriot,* it was rumored that "Jones was hired by friends of Vasquez to get into the jail and get away with Leiva so that [he] could not testify against Vasquez." The truth was never ascertained.[6]

Tiburcio soon hired a second attorney, Bob Tully, who had defended Teodoro Moreno. On July 20 he appeared with his lawyers in Salinas before Judge David Belden of the district court, which included Monterey and Santa Clara counties. The district attorney moved that the case be transferred to San Benito County because the crimes were committed there. San Benito was a new county, having been carved out of the eastern part of Monterey County. Because neither the Hollister nor Salinas jail was considered to be secure, Judge Belden ordered that Vasquez be moved to the Santa Clara County jail. In a final affront to the officers of Monterey County, who had been so inept in hunting Vasquez, they now were deemed incapable of safeguarding him.[7]

The same day the bandido arrived by train in San Jose, heavily ironed, an ignoble return to the town his grandfather had helped found. The tiny adobe pueblo had mushroomed into a bustling young city of ten thousand, with hundreds of modern brick buildings and wood-frame houses. Tiburcio was ushered into a cell in Sheriff Adams's new jail, directly behind the courthouse. Completed in 1871 at a cost of $60,000, it was considered the strongest county jail in California: a large, three-story building of brick and granite, its thick walls reinforced with iron bars in the center. The roof was made of sheet iron layered with brick. On the first floor was the jailer's office. The second and third floors each had a row of cells in the middle, separated by a hallway, while a large corridor ran around the perimeter of the floor, between the cells and the outside walls. The jail no longer exists but the courthouse, completed in 1868, still stands, beautifully restored, facing St. James Park.[8]

A local reporter who visited Tiburcio in the jailer's office noted, "He has entirely recovered from his wounds, and was looking well." When asked what he thought his chances in court were, the outlaw replied, "Quién sabe? I am not guilty of murder, and don't see how I can be convicted." Of his new lodgings, Vasquez remarked, "I was well treated at Salinas, but it is a larger and better place here, and I am satisfied." And when asked how he felt about Abdon Leiva, he replied, "I feel friendly. I could shake him by the hand and willingly bury all our grudges." At that, Sheriff Adams brought his former compadre into the jailer's office. The reporter noted that Leiva "looked coldly and steadfastly at his enemy. There was an awkward pause, and then Vasquez held out his hand. Leiva took it mechanically, gave it one shake, and turned away."

Sheriff Adams asked Tiburcio, "Do you want to talk to Leiva?"

Vasquez replied, "No, that's all I want. I only wanted to see him."

Then Adams asked Leiva, "Do you want to say anything to Vasquez?"

The former bandit quickly responded, "No. I have nothing to say to him." As Leiva later explained, "I shook hands with him . . . but my feelings toward him have not changed."[9]

A few days later, the same reporter visited Vasquez and interviewed him at length about his criminal career. When he asked Vasquez to give an account of the Tres Pinos raid, the bandit refused, saying, "I am to be tried for that and I shall say nothing until I speak in court." Presumably Vasquez had been instructed by his lawyers not to talk about the case. The reporter insisted, "I don't want you to say anything that you have not already stated to others. You told J. M Bassett, editor of the *Los Angeles Herald,* that Leiva and Gonzáles were the murderers, and that you and Chávez did not arrive on the scene until after the shots had been fired. That statement has appeared in print."

"I have never stated anything of the kind," Tiburcio snapped. "I have told no one about the Tres Pinos raid." That was clearly a falsehood, for

Tiburcio Vasquez. Another of the four images taken by Bradley & Rulofson in San Francisco, May 27, 1874. (Author's collection)

he had made this claim to both Bassett and Ben Truman of the *Los Angeles Star.* Vasquez had told so many lies he could not keep his stories straight. The reporter concluded, "He is cunning, audacious, vain, and egotistical, and has none of Leiva's frankness and apparent honesty."[10]

Just as in Salinas, people flocked to the jail to see the celebrity prisoner. On July 21, Tiburcio had 470 visitors, including 20 to 30 women. Three days later there were 673 more, 93 of them female. Within a week the number was more than 1,700. So great was the public demand to see Vasquez that Sheriff Adams was forced to set aside Tuesdays and Fridays as visiting days. One of the visitors was, as the *San Jose Patriot* reported, a "female relative," probably his favorite sister, María, who "'took on' at a terrible rate, and it required three men to tear her from the arms of the bandit when her time was up." Another visitor was the sheepman Bacon, whom Vasquez and Chávez had robbed a year earlier on the San Joaquin plains. Bacon was surprised to see that Tiburcio's cell was decorated with a large selection of fresh flowers, all left by what he termed "chivalrous ladies" earlier that day. Bacon asked Vasquez for his silver watch back, but the bandido replied he did not have it. Bacon's watch turned out to be among the stolen property in the trunks captured from the Vasquez gang at Green Valley. It was later returned to him by Sheriff Adams.[11]

Meanwhile, young Librado Corona was tried in Los Angeles for his part in the robberies of Alessandro Repetto and Charles Miles. His defense was that Vasquez had forced him to take part in the holdups. In a declaration prepared for the youth's trial, Tiburcio scoffed at his story: "I knew Librado Corona about two months. I met him first in the Tejon. For two or three weeks he had been with me around the place where I was arrested. He had been in my employ. He came to me of his own accord and said he would do anything I asked. We went to rob Repetto and Corona went as a member of the gang. He was the only one of us Repetto knew or recognized . . . I never threatened him. All his acts were of his own accord." The jury did not believe Corona's story either, for he was convicted and sentenced to seven years in San Quentin.[12]

Tiburcio's lawyers were concerned that he could not get a fair trial in Hollister because the murder victims had many friends in San Benito County. They also worried that he might be lynched there. The attorneys moved for a change of venue to San Jose. On August 3 Judge Belden granted the request, ruling that "great prejudice does exist in this County of San Benito against said Vasques [sic], and that he cannot have a fair and impartial trial in said county, and that there is danger of personal violence to said Vasques." On September 7, Tiburcio appeared with his attorneys, Darwin and Tully, before Judge Belden. When asked, "Do you plead guilty or not guilty?" he replied in a firm voice, "I am not guilty. I never shed human blood in my life." He pled not guilty to each indictment against him: the murders of Bernard Bahury, Leander Davison, and George Redford; assault with intent to kill Abelardo Salazar; and robbery of Thomas McMahon. The prosecuting attorney stipulated, however, that Vasquez would be tried only on the charge of killing Davison. Tiburcio's lawyers asked for a continuance because only three of the thirteen defense witnesses they had subpoenaed had actually been served. The attorneys claimed that one, Luciano Carranza, would testify that Abdon Leiva had admitted killing two of the victims at Tres Pinos, but that Carranza was then "absent on a mining expedition." Judge Belden agreed to continue the trial until January 5, 1875.[13]

Now Tiburcio received an offer of aid from an unexpected quarter. Charles G. Johnston, a Los Angeles lawyer and brother of Undersheriff Albert Johnston, wrote to George Beers and offered to help defend Vasquez without charge. Johnston wrote that "knowing as well as I do the impositions practiced upon the native Californians whereby their property and almost all else sacred to them have been wrested from their hands and otherwise despoiled, I believe there exists a moral tho' not a legal justification of the acts to which Tiburcio Vasquez confesses guilt." Johnston astutely pointed out that "as the brother of his captor," his presence would incite sympathy among the jurors, and asked Beers to deliver the letter to Vasquez. Eventually, his letter ended up in the hands of Darwin, who foolishly declined Johnston's offer.[14]

Tiburcio had given his lawyers the names of more than twenty witnesses whom he wished to call in his defense. Most of them were scattered in the remote country between Hollister and Los Angeles. Darwin had subpoenas issued for them, but apparently took no further steps to locate them other than delivering the subpoenas to local officers for service. In mid-November, at Tiburcio's request, his old friend Ed Tully visited him in jail and agreed to assist his cousin Bob Tully and Ben Darwin. Vasquez was worried that the trial date was approaching but very few witnesses had been obtained. Ed Tully, as a lawyer and longtime rancher, knew the people and the mountain country. He wrote to Darwin, offering to help track down the witnesses, but for reasons that are unclear, his offer was apparently not accepted.[15]

Darwin needed a copy of the transcript of testimony in the Teodoro Moreno trial so that he could impeach the prosecution witnesses if they testified differently in the Vasquez trial. He wrote to Attorney General John Love requesting a copy of the transcript, but Love never sent it. Under modern discovery laws, prosecutors are required to provide all such evidence to the defense, and if they withhold evidence a new trial is granted. But such laws did not exist in 1875 and Love had no legal obligation to comply. Darwin then contacted the Monterey court clerk and was told that he could purchase a copy of the transcript for ten dollars. Much of Tiburcio's contact with Darwin was by correspondence, and he wanted to meet personally with the San Francisco lawyer. When Darwin wrote to him, asking for ten dollars for the transcript, Vasquez responded, "I withhold the ten dollars . . . until you come in person. Thus I expect you as soon as possible." Darwin, plainly angered, did not respond. The trial was looming and Tiburcio became alarmed. On December 18 he wrote again to Darwin: "I wish to make clear to you that I am in the greatest danger. . . . I await your goodness to do me the honor to come." But Darwin did not come. This petty dispute would have profound consequences for Tiburcio Vasquez.[16]

During the long hours in his cell, Tiburcio's thoughts turned to his family. He made a public announcement that the Teodoro Moreno who was sent to San Quentin was not the same man who accompanied him on the Tres Pinos raid. It was a pathetic and patently false attempt to save his cousin. He was also concerned about the welfare of his two small children. He wrote a short letter to his natural son Rodolfo, "a mi idolatrado hijo, el día de su cumpleaños" (to my idolized son, on his birthday). It was evidently never delivered and ended up with a collection of mementos kept by one of his jailers. The letter was filled with love and affection. Who the boy's mother was, where they lived, and what became of him, no one knows. In 1884, it was reported that a young son of Tiburcio's "is now living in Hollister, and is the principal attraction of a tamale factory." Perhaps he was Rodolfo, or perhaps yet another illegitimate son. Tiburcio searched for a way to provide a little money for Rodolfo and for Alfredo, his son with Felicita. In November, newspapers reported that Vasquez intended to bring a lawsuit against the members of Rowland's posse for "the recovery of sundry rifles, revolvers, saddles, bowie-knives, reatas, saddle blankets, etc." that they had seized from him. He claimed he and his compadres had bought them legally in Los Angeles. But no lawsuit was filed, and the items were kept as relics by the lawmen, with the apparent single exception of an obsolete, cap-and-ball Colt's Dragoon revolver, which was returned to his sister María.[17]

As his trial approached, Vasquez was in good spirits. He firmly believed that because Moreno had not been hanged, he wouldn't be either. He had several visits from George Beers, who by this time had developed a degree of sympathy for him. Beers later wrote, "At San Jose I was permitted to spend several days alone with him, while writing a biographical sketch for a New York publishing house, and I had a good opportunity to study his character. In many respects he was a remarkable man. He told me that he was thoroughly disgusted with the life he had led, and he had no respect, not the slightest, for the class of men from whom he selected his assistants when he planned a robbery. His original boyish idea was that he could incite a revolution among the Spanish-speaking population, and recover Southern California from the United States."[18]

On January 4, 1875, the day before the trial was to begin, Ben Darwin stunned his co-counsel, Bob Tully, by telling him he was dropping out of the case because of Tiburcio's "dereliction" in paying him. Tully managed to convince Darwin that he had an ethical duty to stay on, and the San Francisco lawyer relented. But the next morning Darwin met with Judge Belden and told him he was withdrawing as Tiburcio's counsel. Even though Belden had the power to order Darwin to remain on the case, the judge allowed him to depart. Darwin promptly boarded a train for San Francisco, taking with him important legal papers, including the subpoenas and most significantly, the transcript of testimony from the Moreno trial. It was a serious blow to Tiburcio's defense.

When court opened, a crowd of more than two hundred, many of them Californios, flooded into the cavernous second-floor courtroom. Every seat in the auditorium and the gallery above was taken, and spectators filled the aisles and lined the walls. More than fifty women, some of them well dressed señoras and señoritas, filled the front seats. Tiburcio's sister, María, took a seat in one corner of the upper gallery, with her four-year-old daughter, Mary, on her lap. Sheriffs Tom Cunningham and Billy Rowland were there, and one observer noted that "San Jose and San Francisco reporters were as thick as bob-tailed bees in summer time." The acoustics in the courtroom were so bad that reporters were provided with small tables and allowed to sit almost at the foot of the witness stand. The prosecuting lawyers were California Attorney General John L. Love, San Benito County District Attorney N. C. Briggs, and his deputy William E. Lovett. At the last moment Bob Tully managed to recruit two local attorneys, W. H. Collins and J. A. Moultrie, to assist him in the defense.[19]

When the case was called, Tully moved for a ten-day continuance due to the sudden absence of Darwin as lead counsel, which prejudiced his ability to properly defend Vasquez. After hearing arguments from both sides, Judge Belden ruled that the case had been continued once before, and that since Tully had ably defended Teodoro Moreno on the same facts, he was fully informed of the case. Belden then instructed the clerk to call the names of jurors. Tully leaned toward Vasquez, who looked at him anxiously and asked, "Well?" The lawyer replied, "It's no go. We've got to go to trial." Tiburcio turned pale, but said nothing.

A panel of seventy-five jurors was called, and two days were spent in examining them. Many were excused for having formed prior opinions of Tiburcio's guilt. The courtroom was packed throughout, as a reporter noted: "The gallery was filled with ladies, representing the elite and respect-ability of the city. . . . Vasquez seemed pleased at the sight of the large crowd in the court room, but his glances were unblushingly concentrated upon the ladies in the gallery." Finally twelve jurors were chosen, and after District Attorney Briggs made his opening statement, he called Abdon Leiva as the first witness. Leiva testified in detail about his involvement with the gang and the planning and execution of the robbery at Tres Pinos. He described how Gonzáles and Moreno had shot Bernard Bahury, and swore that Vasquez had slain George Redford and Leander Davison. He told how Vasquez had stolen his wife, and freely admitted that he hated the bandit leader and would do anything to hurt him.

On cross-examination, Bob Tully tried vainly to impeach Leiva by pointing out that in the Moreno trial he testified that the only killing he saw was that of Moreno shooting Bahury, and that Leiva had left to chase Lewis Smith's son when the other murders took place. Tully demanded, "Did you see Davison killed?"

"Yes, sir," Leiva replied. "I know Moreno shot the man on the porch. I didn't say I only knew that. I didn't state anything about Vasquez in the Moreno trial, about his killing anybody. I was not asked. I heard and saw the shooting."

Tiburcio Vasquez. Last of the four images taken by Bradley & Rulofson in San Francisco, May 27, 1874. (William B. Secrest collection)

"Wasn't you asked if you saw Vasquez and Chávez kill anybody and you said no?" Tully persisted.

"If the question was asked, I surely said yes. But I don't know if I was asked the question. . . . Davison was killed about six minutes after the man was killed by Moreno."

Because Ben Darwin had decamped with the Moreno trial transcript, it was impossible for Tully to properly impeach Leiva with his prior testimony. The Chileno was on the stand for the better part of two days, but Tully could not shake his story. In the meantime, Rosario Leiva had been subpoenaed as a prosecution witness, but failed to appear. She had not given up trying to reconcile with her husband, but Abdon was not interested: "After Moreno had been convicted and I was removed to San Jose, she came to see me. And after Vasquez had been captured she wanted me to swear falsely and try and clear Vasquez. She is a traitor, and has no influence over me whatever." Judge Belden issued a warrant for Rosario. That day Deputy Sheriff Adolph Sellman arrested her and brought the reluctant witness into court.[20]

A reporter described Rosario as "an ordinary looking Mexican woman, neatly dressed and somewhat conspicuous from having a huge braid of brown hair woven in and out among her own shining tresses." Through an interpreter, Rosario explained how Vasquez had planned the Tres Pinos robbery at her house in Cantua Canyon, and detailed the flight southward, the gunfight with Sheriff Adams's posse as related to her by Tiburcio, and her alleged kidnapping by the bandido. She said that she had been with Vasquez and Chávez for two months in the mountains. Sheriff Adams next took the stand and described at length his long manhunt for the outlaws, the shootout in Little Rock Creek canyon, and his recovery of the property stolen from Snyder's store. He brought into court much of the loot, providing crucial corroboration of Abdon Leiva's account. But the most damning testimony came from the witnesses to the killings at Tres Pinos. Andrew Snyder, John Utzerath, and L. C. Smith all detailed the robbery and identified Vasquez as the leader. Although Snyder had testified at Teodoro Moreno's trial that the only bandit he could identify was Abdon Leiva, he now changed his story. He declared, "Vasquez had been pointed out to me as a bad man before this. I was told to look out for him. . . . I had seen Vasquez at different times for two years prior." Snyder claimed that Tiburcio and a compadre had once visited his store, bought food and some items of clothing, paid for them, and rode off. His testimony was plainly false, but Bob Tully, without the Moreno trial transcript, could not challenge it. Snyder's motive for lying was simple. His wife had been terrorized by the raid and refused to stay in Tres Pinos, so Snyder had been forced to sell his store and hotel. His bitterness over the murders and his financial loss overcame his duty to tell the truth.[21]

Because their heads had been covered by grain sacks, Snyder, Utzerath, and Smith were unable to state who had committed the murders. But Louis Scherer testified that Vasquez had killed both Redford and Davison. Ebenezer Burton testified that he had seen the small man with the cloak—Vasquez—chasing Redford toward the stable just before he was shot. And he swore that the man with the cloak killed his brother-in-law, Davison. Lucilla Snyder and her sister-in-law, Elizabeth Moore, both identified Vasquez as the robber wearing the cloak, but admitted that they did not see who had shot Davison.[22]

The trial lasted five days, about average for a murder case in that era. On Friday, January 8, Vasquez entered the courtroom with a relaxed smile, telling a reporter he had "passed the night well, sleeping long and soundly." The attendance that day was much smaller, and Tiburcio, after looking around, was visibly disappointed. Calling to the bailiff, he asked, "No ladies?" When the response was no, his smile turned into a frown. Later in the morning the courtroom began to fill, and at the sight of women spectators, Tiburcio's smile returned. Each day his ever-loyal sister María took a seat in the gallery, her daughter in her lap, gently rocking to and fro while listening intently to the testimony. The district attorney's witnesses completed their testimony the next day, and the prosecution rested.

Now it was Bob Tully's turn, but he had very little to work with. He called Joaquín Castro, who detailed his actions in helping the gang flee. He provided no testimony that helped Vasquez. This left Tiburcio with little choice but to take the stand in his own defense. His lawyers unwisely had him testify through an interpreter, leaving the impression that he could not understand English. He surprised the jury by answering some questions without waiting for them to be translated into Spanish, and responding to others in English, causing some to believe that he and his lawyers were trying to dupe them. Tiburcio's testimony directly contradicted his oft-repeated claim that the murders took place before he arrived at Snyder's store:

I was at Leiva's place in the Cantua on the 24th of August. Leiva told me, in the presence of Chávez, that he wanted to please me in this robbing expedition, and he wanted to know our opinion about it as to whether we would assent to it or not. This was at the exact time when the agreement was made to rob, but not to kill. I and Chávez told Leiva that we would go in; that he, Leiva, was the captain. Gonzáles and Moreno were brought in and induced to join. Afterwards the five of us went under a tree and conversed. We came to the conclusion to rob the Tres Pinos store. An agreement was made that no blood was to be shed, and no woman violated. Under these conditions we departed.

We arrived on the top of the hill . . . on the 26th. We left there at 4:30 o'clock. Leiva said he would go ahead with his pistol concealed in his breast, and that Gonzáles would follow—that the rest should stay behind about an hour, hiding themselves. Leiva further added that if he didn't appear in an hour we should come up to the store. That would be the signal that everything was all right. Moreno left before this to see that Gonzáles did not get drunk. I followed with Chávez up to a lane leading to the store. When I arrived in front of the hotel I saw some ladies. I thought it was a private residence and passed by. We got down from our horses. Just as I stepped on the porch, Leiva, Moreno, and Gonzáles stepped out of the store. I stepped in the door. They told me all the men were tied. Before I went in I left my rifle outside near Moreno.

Leiva went out of the rear of the store toward the yard. I saw persons tied in the store. When I turned around I saw persons coming up and down, and I was afraid they would create an alarm. I went towards the well and Gonzáles went towards the stable. As I went towards the well I heard a shot coming from the stable. I didn't see who fired. On turning round I heard a shot fired at the corner of the store on the edge of the fence. Then I went to the store again. I saw that Leiva had hold of a man by the shoulder. Moreno was following behind. Leiva threw the man face downwards. I told Leiva that was not right. We had not come for that purpose.

Then I went back to the well. I heard Gonzáles's voice near the stable. At that moment a boy rode out on horseback. Leiva got on his horse and said he would bring him back dead or alive. I was going towards the well when I heard someone say, "Stop. Lie down." I heard a shot towards the stable. I don't know who fired. Chávez was then standing on one side of the front door of the hotel. Moreno was keeping guard at the store. I cried that someone was coming down the road in order to get them all together. Someone opened the door at the hotel. Gonzáles told him to stop. The man shut the door and then the shot was fired by Gonzáles. I did not see whether the man was killed or not. I told Gonzáles to quit that, and took the rifle from him. Leiva was not present when the second shot was fired.

I saw a team coming up. I went towards the wagon and told the teamster [John Haley] to come down. The teamster resisted somewhat, but finally complied and came down. A short time afterwards I saw Leiva coming back. Another wagon was coming at the same time. I took the driver down, assisted by Moreno. At that moment Leiva arrived with the boy. I told the party that they had done wrong, and now all of us would be pursued. That I had no idea such a thing would happen. It had never to me before in my life. That now I was in for it with the rest.

I told the owner of the store that I wanted his money, not his life. Leiva went with me to get the money. I took Snyder to a door of the residence and spoke to some lady, and told her to bring the money in the house. She brought the money and Leiva received it. I took Snyder back to the store and left him there. I did not kill any human being on that occasion. I am innocent of killing anyone since I was born. I did not shoot anyone at Tres Pinos. There was no necessity for shooting.[23]

After Tiburcio stepped down from the witness stand, Tully called Sheriff Adams in an effort to impeach Abdon Leiva. In response to questioning, Adams testified, "Leiva never stated to me that he saw Vasquez shoot Davison. He said that Vasquez shot two persons." With that, the defense abruptly rested. Closing arguments were scheduled for the next morning, when once again the courtroom was packed. A reporter noted, "Vasquez appeared self-possessed as usual." N. C. Briggs gave the prosecution's closing argument. He recounted the testimony and pointed out what was by then obvious: "The defendant is guilty by his own confession, for he says he was there and also that he aided and abetted in the conspiracy to rob and pillage." Bob Tully then addressed the jury, speaking simply and making the only plea he could. He begged the jury to spare Vasquez and give him life imprisonment. Tully was followed by his co-counsel W. H. Collins, a noted orator. In the overwrought, bombastic style so popular in that era, Collins made a long, rambling address that wandered from Aaron Burr to the North Star to Genesis to Mary Magdalen. Hoping to persuade the jury to exercise mercy, he argued that the witnesses who said that Vasquez had shot Davison were mistaken. In his closing argument Attorney General Love pointed out that the witnesses had testified that the "little man with the black cloak" was Vasquez, and that Vasquez was the man who had shot Davison. "If you believe he is wrongfully accused, for God's sake let him go," Love pleaded. "But if you believe he is guilty, punish him so that others may be deterred from his example."

At that, many of the spectators broke into applause. Judge Belden then instructed the jury on the law regarding first degree murder, accomplice testimony, and reasonable doubt. Most important was his correct instruction regarding murder committed during robbery: "It is no defense to a party associated with others in and engaged in a robbery that he did not propose or intend to take life in its perpetration, or that he forbade his associates to kill, or that he disapproved or regretted that any person was thus slain by his associates. If the homicide in question was committed by one of his associates engaged in the robbery in furtherance of their common purpose to rob, he is as accountable as though his own hand had intentionally given the fatal blow, and is guilty of murder in the first degree."[24]

The jury retired at five o'clock and deliberated for three hours. On the first ballot, they voted unanimously to convict Vasquez of first degree murder. On the second ballot the jurors voted for the penalty: ten for hanging, two for life imprisonment. After further deliberations, they held a third and final ballot, and this time they all voted for death. When Judge Belden and the lawyers filed back into the packed courtroom, Belden, concerned about the prior applause, told the crowd that anyone who applauded would immediately be arrested. Then the jury filed out and Belden ordered that Vasquez be brought in. There was dead silence when the bandido entered. A reporter noted, "He had evidently guessed the result, for his face wore a deadly pallor and he glanced nervously from right to left. . . . As he took his seat several of the officers spoke to him, but though looking directly at them he failed to show that he either saw or heard them." After briefly reviewing the verdict, Judge Belden handed it to the clerk to be read aloud: "We the jury empanelled to try this case find the defendant guilty of murder in the first degree and assign the death penalty." Judge Belden announced that he would pass sentence two weeks later, on January 23.[25]

Vasquez accepted the verdict stoically. Two days later a local reporter who visited him in his cell noted, "We found him in good spirits. The old smile had returned. He was engaged in reading a Spanish novel when we came in, but threw it aside upon seeing us." When asked how he felt, the irrepressible outlaw replied, "Oh, first rate. I am all right."

"Then you don't expect to be hanged?"

"No, no. I will get another trial."

"Upon what grounds?"

"We shall show that it was impossible for that man Scherer to have seen the man who shot Davison from the position he described himself to be in, behind the door. I'd be willing to swing if I had killed one of those men at Tres Pinos. I did not kill anyone, and I want to live. Gonzáles killed Davison."

The reporter crossed the jail to Abdon Leiva's cell for a brief interview. The former bandit felt fully vindicated by the verdict. "I told the truth. I have as great a feeling against Chávez as I have against Vasquez, and I swore that Chávez did not fire a single shot. If I had wanted to lie I could have made Chávez a murderer as well as Vasquez." Of the Moreno case, Leiva said, "At his trial I was the only witness who swore positively that Moreno was at Tres Pinos. His friends tried to prove an alibi by swearing that he was eighty miles from there at the time. Now what I had testified about him has been proved to be true, for at Vasquez's trial, Vasquez himself comes to the stand and swears that Moreno was there, and that he came to the store precisely as described by me."[26]

On January 23 Tiburcio and his lawyers appeared before Judge Belden for sentencing. The judge, known as a florid orator, gave a long and damning indictment of Tiburcio's career: "The motive of your life . . . is one unbroken record of lawlessness . . . a career of outrage, pillage and murder. . . . For years, in this section of the State plagued by your presence, outrages known to be yours, crimes self aroused, made your name the synonym for all that was wicked and infamous. . . . What hidden crimes, what secret deeds of violence, unseen and unrecognized by men, may stain your hands and burden your conscience, yourself can alone know. This was your accepted career—that of a robber." Of the Tres Pinos victims, he declared, "Helpless, unarmed, and unresisting, you slew them in the mere wantonness of butchery, and with the corpses at your feet you gathered the paltry spoils of your four-fold crime and fled to the mountains." He minimized Vasquez's popularity among Hispanics: "The appeals you have made to your countrymen for aid in your present distress have met a response becoming them and befitting you. Shocked at your atrocities, they have neither aided you to escape the punishment merited, nor pretended the sympathy you have sought to invoke." Belden finished with the classic language required by law: "The judgment is death. That you be taken hence, and securely kept by the sheriff of Santa Clara County, until Friday, the 19th day of March, 1875. That upon that day, between the hours of nine o'clock that morning and four in the afternoon, you be by him hanged by the neck until you are dead. And may the Lord have mercy on your soul."[27]

Vasquez was dispassionate. He had been prepared for the sentence. He later said that after Ben Darwin abandoned his case, "everything [had] gone wrong." Now he placed his hope in an appeal to the California Supreme Court and in a new governor. Newton Booth had been elected to the U.S. Senate, and upon his resignation Lieutenant Governor Romualdo Pacheco would become governor of California. Vasquez hoped that Pacheco, a Californio, would commute his sentence to life imprisonment. A few days later an effort to aid him came from another quarter. Three letters, written in Spanish and purportedly signed by Clodoveo Chávez, were dropped into the Wells Fargo letter box in Hollister. One letter was addressed to "the people of Hollister," another to Sheriff Adams, and the third to a party in San Jose. Substantially the same, the letters claimed that Chávez had returned from Mexico to seek revenge if Vasquez was hanged. Proclaimed its author, "It was I who was at the head of the affair at Tres Pinos. . . . Vasquez was certainly our captain, but on account of Abdon I neglected the orders that Vasquez had imposed on us." The letter concluded that if Tiburcio was not freed, "then you will have to suffer as in the times of Joaquin Murieta—the just with the unjust alike will be reached by my revenge." Although San Benito County Sheriff Benjamin Ross and many people in Hollister believed the threat was real, the letters were variously signed "Cleovaro Chavez," "Clorobello Charbez," and "Cloreovara Chavez." One can safely assume that Chávez was not the author, for Clodoveo, who could read and write, surely knew his own name.[28]

Did Tiburcio Vasquez receive a fair trial? Under modern case law, he did not. The last-minute withdrawal of his chief counsel, and his departure with the transcript of the Teodoro Moreno trial, prevented his other lawyers from being able to properly impeach the witnesses. This was fundamentally unfair and today would result in a reversal and a new trial. The stringent modern rules regarding ineffective assistance of counsel did not exist in 1875, however. The issue was not even raised when Tiburcio's lawyers appealed his conviction to the California Supreme Court. Yet, even if the case had been retried, with or without Darwin, Vasquez would surely have been convicted. Whether or not he physically pulled the trigger at Tres Pinos was wholly immaterial. Vasquez planned and took part in an armed robbery that left three innocent victims dead. Under the law then and now, all of the participants were thus equally guilty of first degree murder.

Tiburcio's own conflicting statements cast a pall of suspicion upon his claim that he killed no one at Tres Pinos. In his interview with Ben Truman of the *Los Angeles Star* shortly after his capture, he claimed that when he arrived on the scene with Chávez, the shooting was all over. He blamed two of the killings on Abdon Leiva and one on Romulo Gonzáles. On the same day he repeated his claim in an interview with J. M Bassett, editor of the *Los Angeles Herald,* saying that Leiva had killed Bahury and Redford, and Gonzáles had slain Davison. Soon after he told the editor of the *San Jose Patriot* that "Leiva killed two" of the victims. Several months after that he told a reporter for the *Oakland Tribune* that Abdon Leiva and Romulo Gonzáles "committed the murders two hours before my arrival." At the trial, he admitted being present when the murders were committed, but the only man he accused was Gonzáles. He claimed that Leiva was not there when Redford and Davison were slain. Not long after the trial, he changed his story yet again, telling a *San Jose Mercury* reporter that Leiva had killed one victim at Tres Pinos. His shifting and conflicting accounts are not those of an innocent man.[29]

CHAPTER TWENTY

To Die Game

Tiburcio's first cousin Agustina Rosa Vasquez, who lived in nearby Santa Clara, visited him frequently in jail. She was married to Guadalupe Bee, the half-Californio son of Harry Bee, a colorful Englishman who had settled in California in 1830. Agustina's first husband had been Encarnación García, brother of Anastacio García. Accompanying her were her twenty-three-year-old son, also named Encarnación García, who idolized Tiburcio, and her pretty daughters, Genoveva, age twenty-eight, and Esiquia, twenty. Tiburcio was greatly pleased by their visits, and wrote poetry for the two señoritas, some of which has survived. To Esiquia he presented a beautiful poem, which translated into English read:

> With truest love I worshiped you
> When you, so lovely, were at my side
> My soul with true devotion adores
> You, most beloved idol.
>
> Separated now from you, lost and alone
> Sadly my lamentations become my pastime.
> My only memory is the beloved idol
> The only object of my lonely contemplations.
>
> I cry out and beg you to stand by me,
> Sharing my burdens and bitterness.

> I deeply believe that you hear me
> During my moments of madness.
> Even though we are far apart
> Constant beats my loving heart,
> And I embrace with these humble hands,
> You, the angel, my love, the very reason for my existence.[1]

Tiburcio's poetry illustrated not only his literate intellect, his romantic nature, and his passion for beautiful women, but also his loneliness and despair. On a visit in January, just before his trial, he presented Agustina and her daughters with a long *corrido,* or ballad, titled "The Vasquez Romance." Corridos, then becoming popular in the northern Mexican frontier, were an outgrowth of the eighteenth-century Spanish romance. The lyrics were often a narrative, with a moral, about a famous criminal or folk hero. Tiburcio's corrido was autobiographical, reflecting his awareness of his fame and notoriety, as well as the fate awaiting him. Translated, it read in part:

> It is in the year 1875, today, the Americans say,
> That Tiburcio Vasquez is the leader of all the Mexicans.
> The tyrants are saying that he will have to be hanged,
> For crimes committed in several counties.
> In Los Angeles, it is true, Vasquez lost his head, and the police
>   took him.
> No longer will he roam the desert.
> For he was ruined by confidence he misplaced,
> For with great tyranny a woman betrayed him. . . .
> The robberies and damage he has caused to many, he himself
>   has confessed.
> But he has never killed anyone, for Vasquez was not an assassin.[2]

Vasquez now evidently recognized that Modesta López had betrayed him. He had once said that he loved women but did not trust them with his secrets. It must have been plain to him that his uncontrolled romantic urges had been his downfall.

Soon he received a special visitor, Wilbur Wright, a local photographer, who took two photographs of him, one of his bust and one of him

Tiburcio Vasquez, taken by San Jose photographer Wilbur Wright. One of the last two images taken of the bandit chieftain. (Author's collection)

standing. These were printed as carte-de-visite-sized images. Wright later recalled, "Vasquez, near as he was to death, enjoyed posing."[3]

Tiburcio's appeal, pending before the California Supreme Court, was based on his attorneys' arguments that one of the jurors had been biased and that several of Judge Belden's jury instructions were erroneous. In that era long appellate court delays were unknown, and death penalty reviews were prompt. On March 10 the court issued its ruling, rejecting his lawyers' arguments and upholding his conviction. Rumors now spread that Clodoveo Chávez would lead an attack on the jail to rescue Vasquez. On March 17, when several parties of vaqueros were spotted on the road from Gilroy, a wild story quickly spread that five hundred armed Mexicans had gathered outside town. Although Sheriff Adams scoffed at these yarns, he placed a strong guard on the jail, which was surrounded by a twenty-foot-high brick wall. He put three bloodhounds in the jail yard at night in case an intruder tried to scale the wall.[4]

Tiburcio's lawyers had petitioned the new Californio governor, Romualdo Pacheco, to commute his sentence to life imprisonment, or at least to grant him a temporary reprieve. But Pacheco was no friend of bandidos. Born into a prominent family, he been instrumental in breaking up the Jack Powers–Pío Linares bandit gang in San Luis Obispo County in 1858. On March 16 Governor Pacheco wired his response to Tiburcio's attorney W. H. Collins in San Jose: "I am unable to perceive any good reason for intervening between Vasquez and his sentence, nor is there any feature of the case that can with propriety be invoked to delay the vindication of the law. A plea for mercy is always strong and persuasive; but the quality is not genuine of that mercy which prolongs misery when there remains no hope. I profess to be humane, but true humanity does not require his reprieve, which could only afford him a few more days of suffering." At the same time, Ygnacio Sepulveda, Volney Howard, and other prominent Angelenos, fearing an outbreak of racial violence, had also wired the governor for a reprieve. Pacheco's response was the same: "I have already officially refused to reprieve Vasquez, after a careful examination of his case. . . . I do not think any danger that may exist from the gang could be avoided or lessened by a postponement of the execution. There would be the same condition of affairs at the end of the delay, and for these reasons I must decline to interfere." A reprieve had been Tiburcio's last hope. On hearing the news, he vowed to die "as a man and a Californian." Said George Beers, "In the saloons about town the principal topic of conversation was Vasquez's courage, and—to the discredit of human nature—bets were offered and taken as to whether the bandit would die 'game.'"[5]

The next day Tiburcio was visited by María and Manuel Lara and two of their young daughters. Deputy Sheriff Adolph Sellman was present and described the heartrending scene: "All parties broke down with emotion and their conversation was intermingled with sobs and exclamations of grief and intense anguish." For several days Catholic priests had called at the jail, but Vasquez had steadfastly refused to see them. As a condemned man he could not receive a Catholic burial unless he confessed his sins to a priest and received absolution. María was able to persuade her brother to see Father Lorenzo Serda, a Spanish priest who was assistant pastor of St. Patrick's Church. To Father Serda, Tiburcio made a full confession and was administered the last rites, clearing the way for him to be buried in the Mission Santa Clara cemetery.[6]

That night Tiburcio was visited by Sheriff Adams, Undersheriff Theodore Winchell, and George Beers, who sat in chairs in the corridor outside his cell. (Winchell was the same man who had lost his nerve and failed Harry Morse in the gunfight with Juan Soto.) At first they found him in good spirits, and he eagerly rehashed with Beers the details of his capture. But in his typical revisionist style, Tiburcio now claimed that when he was shot he cried out, "Shoot, you cowards, shoot!" Then he and Adams compared stories on the gunfight in Rock Creek Canyon, and found that their accounts tallied exactly. He vehemently denied that Abdon Leiva had found him in bed with Rosario. When asked if he wanted to see Leiva one last time, he angrily replied, "I do not wish to see him. Why should I? What good would it do me or him? He would only embrace the opportunity to insult me, and I do not wish to be annoyed. I am ready to see everybody else, and shall die like a man." Referring to the reward that had been offered, he turned bitter and told Beers, "Well, you remember when you shot me, you took me round the corner of the house and attended my wounds. Well, that care was taken to save the $2,000." He insisted that the Winchester Model 1873 rifles taken from him at Greek George's were not stolen but had been purchased new in Los Angeles.[7]

Tiburcio's thoughts turned next to Teodoro Moreno, and he declared, "I assure you that he is innocent of murder. He is well known as a hard

Tiburcio Vasquez, taken at the same time as the previous photograph. This image has not previously been published. (Author's collection)

working, good man. The only crimes I ever knew him to commit were with me at Firebaugh's Ferry and Tres Pinos. I assert as a dying man that the man found dead near the door of Snyder's store [Bahury] was killed by Abdon Leiva. The two others were killed by Gonzales." When one of the party remarked that he believed in the "immortality of the soul," Tiburcio replied, "I hope your opinion is correct, for in that case, on Friday, I shall see my old sweethearts together."

Tiburcio's mood now turned reflective, and he told Sheriff Adams that he wished to make a speech from the gallows. The sheriff persuaded him to make a written statement instead, saying that Father Serda had suggested doing so. Tiburcio agreed, and pressing his hand to his brow, said, "Let me think a minute." Then, after Beers pulled out his notebook, he dictated a long statement in Spanish, with Winchell translating, entitled, "To the Fathers and Mothers of Children." Vasquez said in part, "I wish the children throughout the world, who may read the incidents of my life, to take warning in time of the example before them of me, and to realize the force of the saying, 'The way of the transgressor is hard,' the truth of which is now being verified to me." He asked for "pardon from each and every one who I have in any way injured" as well as from "the Great Father whose laws I have so ruthlessly trampled upon." Tiburcio concluded by thanking Sheriff Adams and his deputies for their kindness to him, adding, "I thank my brothers for their brotherly love extended to me during all the time of my troubles, and to my darling and devoted sisters I render inexpressible thanks. . . . Farewell brothers! Farewell, sisters dear! The end has come!" Tiburcio had abandoned all pretense and excuses for his career of banditry.[8]

At the suggestion of Sheriff Adams, Vasquez now dictated a warning, "To My Former Associates." He declared, "You must well know that I, who could, had I been so disposed, have disclosed to the authorities and to the world the perpetrators of many atrocious crimes, might thus have saved my own life." He again denied ever committing a murder, but admitted that "common sense compels me to realize the justness of the law which holds me responsible for the innocent lives lost in the prosecution of my unlawful calling of robbery." Referring to threats made by some of his band to kill his captors or the members of his jury, he concluded, "By the course threatened you could do me no earthly good, but only bring yourselves in the end to my own fate. Take warning, then, by my fate, and change your course of life while you may."[9]

The interview lasted well past midnight. Finally, rising from his chair, Vasquez said with a yawn, "I have one last request to make of you, Mr. Adams."

"What is that, Tiburcio?" asked the sheriff.

"It is that when I am taken upon the scaffold to meet my doom that you give me a glass of wine and one of the best cigars that can be obtained in San Jose. I want to die with the taste of wine and tobacco on my lips."[10]

Vasquez slept soundly, awaking early and asking for breakfast. In the morning Tiburcio had a tearful reunion with his family. Present were his brothers Claudio, Chico, and Antonio; Antonio's eldest two daughters, eighteen-year-old Amada and fifteen-year-old Lucy; Vasquez's sisters Manuela and María; the latter's husband Manuel Lara; Agustina Vasquez Bee with daughters Esiquia and Genoveva; and Father Serda. Perhaps it was not surprising that his brother Chico came all the way from Los Angeles County. Although it is doubtful that he had fully forgiven Tiburcio, family loyalty compelled him to see his brother for the last time. Tiburcio, in another effort to provide for Felicita's son, asked for a notary public to come to the jail, and he signed a power of attorney authorizing Chico to make a claim against Sheriff Rowland for the guns and other gear confiscated when he was captured.[11]

Santa Clara County had not seen a legal execution since 1863 and did not have a gallows. To save money, Sheriff Adams borrowed a scaffold from Sacramento County Sheriff Hugh M. La Rue upon which he had hanged two killers, Filomena Cotta and Domingo Estrada, a month earlier. It had also served as the gallows for the notorious thief and killer Charles Mortimer, in 1873. The gibbet was dismantled and shipped to San Jose, and that morning two carpenters began erecting it in one corner of the jail yard, next to the jail door. Built of pine, it was ten feet square, with the platform ten feet above the ground. Eight feet higher was a large beam, from which the noose was suspended. The double trapdoors were four feet square, and held in place by two wooden posts secured by an iron bolt. To the bolt was attached a cord, which ran across a pulley to the rear of the scaffold where a heavy weight was attached. The weight was held in place by another cord. When that cord was cut, the weight dropped, jerking open the bolt and causing the trapdoors to plunge downward.[12]

While the macabre rattling of the carpenters' tools echoed through the jail yard, a San Francisco reporter visited Vasquez in his cell. Tiburcio extended his hand in greeting and remarked, "I am glad to see you, but have really nothing to say. I have already prepared a statement of all that I wish to communicate to the public. That statement I would like very much to have published in every paper in California."

After some conversation, in which he shifted nervously in his chair, Vasquez remarked, "It is very cold outside, is it not? I have to keep fires here to keep warm, but after tomorrow I shall not need any."

"How do you feel in regard to your fate?" the reporter asked.

Vasquez responded with a shrug, "I am pretty well, but in a rather unpleasant situation." He laughed hollowly.

"I suppose you are prepared to meet your doom?"

"You shall see me die like a man. I am innocent of murder, and am not afraid to die."[13]

That day more than a thousand spectators visited the jail yard to inspect the gallows. At the same time, a long line of people filed into the jail to catch a glimpse of the noted outlaw through the wicket of his cell. In the evening, after praying with Father Serda, Tiburcio was visited by Sheriff Adams, two reporters, and several lawmen, including his old nemesis, Petaluma City Marshal Jim Knowles. They found him in better spirits, seated in a chair in the corridor outside his cell, puffing on a cigar. He stood up and greeted them warmly. When asked how he felt, Tiburcio replied, "Oh, very well. I have just eaten a good supper to make me feel strong, you know," and he smiled broadly. "I am in very good health and eat well. I was up very late with the sheriff and the reporter last night, and am a little fatigued, that's all."

Earlier Tiburcio had asked to see his coffin. Sheriff Adams told him it was now outside and asked if he wanted it brought in. "Why yes, certainly," Vasquez replied. "Bring it in. I want to look at it. That's what I told you."

The undertakers carried it into the jail corridor. The outlaw was pleased and said, "It's away up." Then he remarked that he thought it might be too small, and began measuring it with his hands. The undertaker responded, "Vasquez, it is large enough. I knew your height, and the coffin is five feet eight inches long on the bottom."

To that, Tiburcio replied, "Well, it's a nice one, ain't it? Can't you open it?"

The lid was lifted, and after examining the satin lining and cushions, he said laughingly, "I can sleep forever quietly in that." As an afterthought he asked, "Well, how much are you going to charge me for it?" When he was told that it had been paid for by his family and Captain Adams, he turned to the sheriff and thanked him for his kindness. Just then he noted a large, inscribed silver cross on the lid, and with the aid of a candle, he stooped over to read it: "Tiburcio Vasquez, died March 19th, 1875. Aged 39 years."

Vasquez looked up and said with a chuckle, "That's correct." Then, stroking the lid with his hand, he repeated, "It's a very nice one."

When the casket was removed, Tiburcio and his visitors again took their chairs, and one of them told him he was "very plucky, and had genuine nerve, as few men could go through the scene." Tiburcio quietly answered, "I can't help it, and may as well be that way."[14]

Tiburcio asked Undersheriff Winchell about the arrangements for his funeral, saying that he "did not want to be buried in an ugly or lonely spot, but in the middle of a graveyard where he would have plenty of company." After some casual chatting with his visitors, Vasquez remarked again that he had been up too late the previous night and wanted to retire. Captain Adams had detailed two jailers on a suicide watch: E. J. "Seeley" Shaw and Willie Adams, the sheriff's twenty-two-year-old son. Bidding them "buenos noches," Tiburcio went to bed at nine o'clock and dozed restlessly for an hour. Then he got up, calling to young Adams, "Willie, please bring me a cigar." He smoked in silence, gazing into the fireplace, and finally said to his guards, "Come, let us talk. This stillness is oppressive. I cannot sleep, and I don't want to remain silent. Talk to me."

After some idle conversation he exclaimed, "I have been a bad man, but I am not a murderer. It would have been better that I had been killed when captured than to suffer death in the disgraceful manner that I must. For myself I do not care, but my family and friends are disgraced through my death. If I had been guilty of murder, I would not have been fool enough to have returned to this country after having made my escape into Mexico. But death advances and I must meet him boldly. I will show you how a brave man can die. I am not afraid. You will see that I am a brave man."[15]

After smoking the cheroot and taking a glass of wine, Vasquez said to Shaw, who had done him many small favors, "Here, you have been kind to me. Take this. It's all that I have left," and handed the jailer a silver match case. At two o'clock he threw himself on his bed, without undressing. He was still unable to sleep, and soon arose and walked the corridor, smoking another cigar. He finally fell asleep at 4:00 A.M. According to a report in the San Francisco press, Vasquez had also said to young Adams, "Hell, I can't sleep. Let's talk," and "Willie, I *would* like to make a speech on the scaffold, but that damned priest won't let me. It's hard to die without saying a word." Willie Adams later denied that Vasquez had made either statement, and added that he "was not heard to utter an oath during the entire time of his incarceration."[16]

Tiburcio's last day dawned bright and clear. He awoke at sunrise, and after a light breakfast, met with Father Serda in prayer. At eight o'clock some thirty grief-stricken relatives and friends, including his attorney Bob Tully, were allowed to visit, shake his hand, and say good-bye. María, his brother Antonio, and his cousins and nieces stayed with him until a quarter past eleven. Their final reunion was an emotional one, and for the first time Tiburcio's brave front collapsed. Reported the *San Jose Mercury,* "Vasquez broke down and wept as one in great agony." But when Tiburcio's family left, his usual calm demeanor returned.[17]

The hanging was scheduled for 1:30 P.M. Sheriff Adams, as was then the custom, had three hundred invitation cards printed and presented them to prominent citizens, fellow lawmen, newspaper correspondents, and Tiburcio's relatives. It was the most important and most publicized execution in the history of the Pacific Coast. Reporters from every leading newspaper in the state were present, as were correspondents for many East Coast journals. A woman reporter even traveled from Canada. She was given permission to watch from the roof of the jail, where chairs had been placed for spectators. Public interest in attending the hanging was huge. Reported one San Jose newspaper, with only mild exaggeration, "If all were admitted who ask, it would take a coliseum to hold them." Several trainloads of passengers had arrived, most hoping to see the execution, and all the hotels were filled to capacity. Many businesses closed their doors so that their employees might watch it. Some forty or fifty peace officers were present from throughout Northern California, including a number of the men who had hunted Vasquez: Harry Morse, Nick Harris, Jim Knowles, Andrew Wasson, and Orson Lyon. Also present were such noted lawmen as Ben K. Thorn, sheriff of Calaveras County, James B. Hume, chief of detectives for Wells Fargo, and Samuel Deal, chief of detectives for the Central Pacific Railroad. Two officers had traveled from Nevada, and one, the famed Sheriff Seth Bullock, from Montana.[18]

By late morning a huge crowd had gathered in front of the courthouse, unaware that invitations were required. Many became angry on

Invitation to the hanging of Tiburcio Vasquez. (Cliff Kennedy collection)

being denied admittance, as one reporter noted: "Hundreds, including many women, were standing without, eagerly gazing at the jail walls and abusing themselves and everybody else because they could not witness the hanging." The jail yard quickly filled with ticket holders. The jail roof was also crowded with spectators, while others, including several women, leaned out the second-story windows of the courthouse. Some scaled nearby fences, trees, and rooftops, but few could see the gallows. One adventurous soul even risked his neck by climbing a windmill that afforded a good view of the yard.[19]

Just before noon Sheriff Adams brought Vasquez a new pair of black trousers. He stepped into his cell to put them on, and returned with a smile on his face. "Too tight, Captain, but as I shan't wear them long it don't make much difference." At a quarter past twelve Tiburcio asked permission to bid farewell to the deputy sheriffs and reporters present. Standing in the corridor, with Father Serda at his side, he shook hands with an earnest "good-bye" to each one. Then he was served his last meal: roast beef, claret, pudding, and pound cake. He ate only the cake and sipped the wine. Wrote one of the newspapermen, "Although he had slept very little the previous night, his self command never deserted him for a moment, and while everybody around him was nervous and excited the little bandit smoked his cigar and sipped his claret with an air of perfect composure."[20]

An hour later, at a quarter past one, Sheriff Adams read the death warrant. Vasquez sat stoically in a chair, holding rosary beads and listening attentively, surrounded by officers and reporters. When Adams was done, Tiburcio nodded, handed Winchell a slip of paper, and said, "There is my answer." It read, "I am prepared to die and I hope that God will have mercy on my soul."

"That is your answer, is it?" asked Adams.

"Yes, sir," replied Vasquez in a firm voice. He then stood, picked up the wine glass, and drank a little. He started to put it down but Winchell encouraged him to drink the whole glass, saying it might make things easier, and Tiburcio did so. Now jailer Harmon Curtis led the way toward the gallows. Behind him walked Vasquez with Father Serda at his side, followed by Adams, Winchell, and other officers. The jail door opened almost at the foot of the scaffold, and Vasquez showed no nervousness as he quickly climbed the stairs to the platform. As he took his position on the trap, the densely packed crowd was deathly quiet. Next to him stood Adams, Winchell, Sellman, Sheriff La Rue, Sheriff Morse, Sheriff Ben Thorn, San Benito County Sheriff Ben Ross, Santa Cruz County Sheriff Bob Orton, and former sheriffs Nick Harris and Andrew Wasson. Father Serda then asked the assembled crowd to join in saying the Lord's Prayer. Most of the men present doffed their hats to recite the prayer. Tiburcio then removed his coat, collar, and necktie and handed them, and the rosary beads, to Sheriff Adams. While Winchell and Sellman pinioned his arms and legs with leather straps, Father Serda prayed in Spanish, with Tiburcio answering each prayer aloud.

Winchell placed the rope around his neck. It was the same one that had been used to hang Filomena Cotta a month before. The large knot was placed under the left ear, so that the force of the drop would cause the neck to snap to the right, breaking the vertebrae and spinal cord and causing a quick death. Sheriff Adams had carefully measured the drop based on Tiburcio's weight, so as to avoid a slow and painful death by strangulation. Such botched executions were a great embarrassment to sheriffs. When Winchell drew the knot too tightly, Vasquez quietly told him, "Loosen it a little, please." The officer did so, and then a white shroud was draped across Tiburcio's shoulders. Just before the black hood

The gallows upon which Tiburcio Vasquez was hanged. (Courtesy of San Jose Public Library)

was dropped over his head, he gave a "wild and startled look," according to a witness, and gasped his last word: "Pronto!"

Sheriff Adams gave the signal and the cord was cut. Tiburcio Vasquez plunged through the trapdoors with a heavy thud, his neck snapped cleanly by the fall. A woman shrieked in terror from a courthouse window and two men in the yard fainted in their tracks. As the body hung motionless, three doctors stepped forward to measure the pulse. After eight minutes the pulse stopped, and the physicians pronounced him dead. Sheriff Adams allowed the body to hang another fifteen minutes, after which it was cut down and placed in the coffin. As the crowd melted away, journalists rushed to the telegraph office to file their reports. They uniformly commented on the courage with which Tiburcio Vasquez had faced death. The *New York Tribune* reported, "The coolness he displayed throughout his imprisonment did not desert him, but he maintained his fortitude to the last." Wrote the correspondent for the *New York Times,* "The bold, dashing, and handsome caballero died the death of a dog. He carried himself with lightness and jolly recklessness to the scaffold. . . . And so, with mingled tragedy and melodrama, the thief and murderer came to an end."[21]

At two o'clock the casket was loaded into a hearse, then driven to the Santa Clara house of Agustina Vasquez Bee, three miles north of San Jose. That night a wake was held in the Bee home. It was a simple two-story wood frame house located on the southwest corner of Washington and Harrison streets. Tiburcio's brother Antonio did not attend. He had been so overcome with grief that he had suffered a stroke and was bedridden. Many curious people thronged to the house to get a final glimpse of the noted outlaw, among them George Beers, accompanied by Undersheriff Winchell. Beers found "the body of the dead criminal lying in state, as though he had died a martyr in some glorious cause":

> The house was a modest little cottage in a pleasant portion of the town, neatly kept, and the grounds made pleasant and inviting by shrubbery and flowers, which grow so prolifically in that climate. The body was neatly laid out on a raised platform covered with black cloth, near the center of the room. The body was neatly dressed. The arms peacefully folded across the breast and holding a crucifix. The countenance looked perfectly natural, exhibiting none of the hideous distortions characteristic of cases of hanging or strangulation. It presented the appearance of one peacefully sleeping. Roman candles were burned in silver candlesticks placed at intervals around the body.
>
> The female relatives of the dead bandit were seated about the room gazing mournfully and silently at the remains, while the male relatives and friends were gliding spectre-like through the

Relics of the hanging of Tiburcio Vasquez: his tie, rosary beads, and piece of the hangman's rope. (California State Library collection)

various apartments, occasionally stopping a few moments to gaze at the dead, and then passing out to converse in solemn groups, or wandering about dejectedly alone.[22]

The next morning the body was brought to Mission Santa Clara for a high mass. Then the casket was returned to the Bee home, where once again a large crowd of visitors came. There Tiburcio Vasquez lay in rest until two o'clock, when the coffin was brought to the mission cemetery and buried in a plot on the west side of the grounds. A large wooden cross, some ten or twelve feet high, was placed to mark the site. Nearby was the grave of his father, who had been buried there seventeen years before.

Soon rumors began to circulate that Tiburcio's body would be stolen by ghouls so that the head could be cut off and exhibited like that of Joaquín Murrieta. Night after night his sister María, almost crazed by worry and

The house of Tiburcio's cousin, Agustina Vasquez Bee, located on the corner of Washington and Harrison streets in Santa Clara, where the wake for Tiburcio Vasquez was held. (Author's collection)

grief, jealously guarded the grave, until she collapsed from exhaustion. Finally, to comfort her and allay fears that the body had already been decapitated, cousin Encarnación García agreed to exhume the body. On April 29 he led a group of thirty, including eight relatives and several reporters and constables, to the cemetery and dug up the grave. The coffin lid was opened and María was greatly relieved to see that although the body had quickly decomposed, it had not been disturbed. The corpse was reinterred. Over time the large wooden cross decayed into dust. For many years thereafter the grave was marked only by a solitary palm tree. Finally, in 1930, a new granite marker was erected, with a simple inscription: "Tiburcio Vasquez, 1835–1875. Rest in Peace." To this day fresh flowers are placed on the grave by admirers.[23]

By then most of the Vasquez band was gone. Drinking pure alcohol in San Quentin had killed Narciso Rodríguez in 1873. Francisco Gómez was slain in the Serna rebellion in Mexico in 1875. The same year Clodoveo Chávez was shot dead resisting arrest in Arizona; his head was cut off and returned to California for identification. Ysidro Padilla died of natural causes in San Quentin in 1877, as did Pancho Galindo in the

Santa Clara County jail three years later. Rafael Mirabel was stabbed to death in Los Gatos by Tiburcio's cousin Encarnación García in 1883; a lynch mob promptly strung up García. Fernando Arceo was shot dead at the New Almaden Mine in 1887; his killer was legally hanged. Teodoro Moreno died of throat cancer in 1888, still behind San Quentin's iron bars. Agustín Hernández breathed his last at his home on Griswold Creek in the early 1890s, and Procopio Bustamante was slain in Mexico about 1894. Ramón Molina's days ended in Folsom Prison in 1902. Lorenzo Vasquez died in Hollister in 1907, Jim Hefner in Los Angeles County in 1908, and Greek George in Whittier in 1913. Rosario Leiva succumbed to a lung infection at the Guadalupe Mine in 1900. Abdon Leiva, who had divorced Rosario, passed away in peaceful respectability in Sacramento in 1916, surrounded by his family, as did the fully reformed Bartolo Sepúlveda in San Jose ten years later. Obispo Arceo served twenty years in San Quentin, then lived quietly in Hollister until 1926 when infirmity claimed him at age eighty-four. Ninety-seven-year-old Alfonso Burnham died in San Francisco in 1936, denying to the end that he had once been a notorious outlaw. He was the last of the Vasquez gang.

A century before Tiburcio's hanging, José Tiburcio Vasquez had been one of the founders of San Jose. Now, in that very pueblo, taken and transformed by the gringo, his grandson died in infamy. It was an ignominious and ironic fate for a proud family whose story was in many ways the story of early California. And for many of the faded, propertied class of Californios, the ricos and rancheros, it was the nadir, for now the most famous paisano was not Governor Romualdo Pacheco, of whom they were immensely proud, but instead an infamous bandido. For many more Californios and Mexicans, however, especially the impoverished vaqueros, peones, and campesinos, Tiburcio's death was not, as he believed, shameful. Instead they saw him as a potent symbol of resistance against the gringos who had stolen their legacy and reduced them to second-class citizens in their own land.

Now that Tiburcio Vasquez was safely in the grave, most Anglos thought that he would soon be forgotten. They were wrong.

Epilogue

Buried Treasure, Social Banditry, and Other Myths

In 1993, the Santa Clarita School Board in Los Angeles County voted unanimously to name its new high school in Agua Dulce after Tiburcio Vasquez. Earlier, in a local contest to christen the school, Vasquez was the overwhelming choice. The decision created an immediate storm of controversy, bringing to the forefront the issue of whether Tiburcio Vasquez was a hero or a villain. As an editorialist for the *Los Angeles Times* commented, "Mention Vasquez, Joaquin Murieta or Gregorio Cortez of Texas to history buffs of the Old West and you will be duly informed that these were 'bad hombres,' outlaws or, at best, colorful folkloric characters. But many Chicanos, Latinos and progressive biographers see these figures in a different light: as avengers, natives of formerly Mexican territory who resisted the Yankee invasion."[1]

This was not the first time Vasquez had been so honored. In 1971 the nonprofit Tiburcio Vasquez Health Center was established in southern Alameda County. Even before that, in 1964, Vasquez Rocks County Park was created, perhaps the only public park named after an American outlaw. In the early 1920s the weird geological formations of Vasquez Rocks were a popular destination for motorcar tourists and treasure hunters from Los Angeles. By that time the rocks had already been discovered by Hollywood filmmakers. The first motion picture made there was a 1920 silent film starring Harry Carey. Thereafter Vasquez Rocks became one of the most popular film locations in the United States. It served as the backdrop for countless movies, including *The Arizonian* (1935), *Adventures of Marco*

Polo (1937), *Gunga Din* (1939), *The Charge of the Light Brigade* (1936), *Law and Order* (1942), *Flame of Araby* (1951), *Blazing Saddles* (1974), and *The Flintstones* (1994). Television shows such as *Gunsmoke, Bonanza, Zorro,* and *Star Trek* were frequently filmed there. Even before the first motion picture was made at Vasquez Rocks, a silent movie about Tiburcio was released. Entitled *Vasquez of the Pinnacles,* it was filmed on location in 1919 at the Pinnacles, Paicines, and Hollister, and released locally in California.[2]

Tiburcio Vasquez's fame grew exponentially in the years after his death. Books, magazine articles, and newspaper features about him were published. Landmarks and creeks were named after him. Mexican balladeers sang corridos about his exploits, and he took his place alongside such outlaw folk heroes as Joaquín Murrieta, Juan Cortina, and Gregorio Cortez. No sooner was he buried than a new and even more potent Vasquez came to life: a mythical bandido who robbed, fought, loved, and buried treasure throughout California. Fictitious yarns of his hidden loot were legion. One said that he and his gang robbed a stagecoach between Tejon Pass and Antelope Valley. Before escaping in a hail of gunfire, they buried the treasure box. He allegedly also concealed booty near an old Indian village at Castle Rock and near West Chilao and at Las Juntas. He hid a five-hundred-pound silver ingot in Vasquez Rocks. He buried a cache of gold coins in "Coehody Pass," a nonexistent location. He left a treasure trove in Lone Tree Prairie in the Santa Cruz Mountains. He concealed loot from a stage robbery under a huge sandstone rock near Calabasas. He buried loot on Stevens Creek in San Jose. Although not a whit of evidence supports any of these stories, people wanted desperately to believe them.[3]

In 1892 a tree house was found hidden in a clump of redwoods in Isbel Grove, near Santa Cruz. Because of reports that "Mexican men and women frequently passed among the trees," it was immediately identified as Tiburcio's hideout. Treasure hunters descended on the grove, vainly churning up the ferns and wildflowers with spades and shovels. Four years later, when a herder found a rusty Colt's percussion revolver in a cave in Kern County, it was promptly proclaimed to be Tiburcio's. In 1912, newspapers reported that a banker from Mexico, armed with a treasure map, had uncovered a chest filled with $75,000 in silver and gold buried by Vasquez on a mountain ridge in San Benito County. Given that in his entire life Tiburcio never stole even close to that sum, the story can be dismissed as a wild rumor. In 1913, while tearing down an old adobe house in Los Gatos, workers discovered a casket of twenty-dollar gold pieces worth one thousand dollars. The cache, as well as an old shot-gun found in the house, were, of course, immediately attributed to Vasquez. Alessandro Repetto's adobe was a favorite site for treasure seekers. So many believed that Vasquez buried loot there that its walls were weakened by constant digging in the 1920s. Finally heavy rains brought it down in 1927. How the bandit would have had time to bury treasure while Rowland's posse was in close pursuit was never considered. In 1920 a Jolon rancher found two old cap-and-ball revolvers in a nearby cave; of course, they were Tiburcio's, as several newspapers enthusiastically reported. In 1932 treasure hunters descended upon the Pinnacles, on the theory that since Tiburcio hid out there, he must have buried booty there. In 1934 a San Jose contractor claimed to have a map, prepared by Vasquez, showing where he had buried a metal chest full of loot on a ranch near Hollister. The story came to naught when the ranch owner refused to let treasure hunters dig up his property.[4]

In 1954 the wild stories of Tiburcio's buried treasure precipitated tragedy. A Los Angeles machinist, Ronald M. Fuller, became convinced that Vasquez had stolen three chests of gold in a stagecoach robbery between the San Fernando Valley and Ventura. He believed Tiburcio had buried the gold near Santa Susana, in Ventura County, at a spot marked by a boulder shaped like a lizard's head. Fuller began hunting for the trea-sure in 1946, and an eight-year search brought him to what he thought was the site. With the help of two friends and a supply of dynamite, he dug and blasted a fifty-five-foot vertical shaft under the boulder. On July 6, 1954, the three were working in the shaft when they were overcome by dynamite fumes. Fuller's two friends managed to scramble to safety, but he fell from a ledge to the bottom of the pit, dead. Fuller had claimed to have "read extensively of the life of the Mexican bandit," but if that were true, he would have known that Vasquez had never robbed a stage-coach in that area, had never stolen chests of gold, and certainly would not have buried the loot. He would have spent it. And that, of course, is the fatal flaw in all such buried treasure yarns.[5]

Tales of hidden treasure represent only a small part of the Vasquez legends. Many claimed they had known him, seen him, or been robbed by him. Anything done by a Spanish-speaking bandit in California was later attributed to either Joaquín Murrieta or Tiburcio Vasquez. How such stories developed is best illustrated by a popular tale which held that cattle baron Henry Miller visited Vasquez in jail and paid thousands of dollars for his legal defense. The basis for this story is factual. On May 31, 1874, Miller, on a trip to Salinas, did visit the bandido in jail. A correspondent for the *San Francisco Bulletin* reported that Tiburcio's "piteous appeals caused Mr. Miller to give him $20 in gold coin." As the story was retold over the years, twenty dollars grew to thousands.[6]

Countless blowhards and barroom braggarts claimed to have met Vasquez, befriended him, or ridden with his gang. In later years a number of people alleged that they had either been eyewitnesses to the Tres Pinos killings or had seen and talked with Vasquez on his way to or from the raid. None of these claimants testified in court, and none of their yarns is true. A Salinas old-timer named Jesús Vasquez convinced gullible people that he was Tiburcio's brother. When he died in 1925 at age ninety-three, newspapers eagerly published his bogus claim. In 1935, statewide newspapers gave prominent coverage to an old boaster who died in Hanford claiming to have been a friend of Tiburcio's. But thirteen years earlier an authentic compadre of Vasquez's had died in that very town. Blas Bicuna had served two terms in San Quentin, one for murder, and later lived quietly in Hanford under his own name. No one there knew his past. When he died in the Kings County Hospital in 1922, one of the last of the Vasquez riders, not a word was published in the press. He died as he wanted, in obscurity, his reckless outlaw past thoroughly forgotten.[7]

An enthusiastic and oft-quoted writer about Tiburcio Vasquez was Will Thrall (1873–1963), a popular Los Angeles explorer, chronicler, historian, and protector of the San Gabriel Mountains. Unfortunately, some of the Vasquez "history" he compiled was patently false. Thrall, in an effort to demonstrate a strong Southland connection with the bandit leader, claimed, "The last three years of Vasquez operations were, with two notable exceptions, almost entirely in Southern California." That, of course, is wildly incorrect, as Tiburcio spent only a few months in 1873 and 1874 in Los Angeles County. Thrall created a busy life for Vasquez in the San Gabriels. He had him running a gold-mining operation in Big Tujunga Canyon and building an *arrastra* for crushing ore. He claimed that Vasquez hid out in Dunsmore Canyon in the San Gabriels and at an Indian village north of Castle Rock, near Chatsworth. He created an extensive horse-theft ring, in which Vasquez stole animals from the U.S. government at Yuma, Arizona, drove them to Chilao, in the San Gabriels, and sold them in the San Fernando Valley. Why the U.S. government would have herds of horses in Yuma he did not explain. Nor is there any contemporary evidence that Vasquez ever set foot in Chilao. What is known is that the only time he fled into the San Gabriels, following the Repetto robbery, he needed a guide to lead his band. When the guide failed to appear, Vasquez got thoroughly lost and was almost trapped. This is not indicative of a man who had spent years living in the San Gabriel Mountains. Oddly, Thrall does not even mention two Los Angeles County locations that Tiburcio actually visited—Vasquez Creek and Piedra Gorda, now known as Eagle Rock. He seems to have compiled folk tales and legends and failed to adequately consult contemporary published accounts, of which there are many. Thrall's fictions have been widely accepted, and tourists to this day visit Chilao to see Tiburcio's hideout.[8]

The influential author Carey McWilliams (1905–80) was another promulgator of false information about Tiburcio Vasquez. In his popular book *North from Mexico* (1948), he devotes several frequently cited pages to California's Hispanic bandits. Unfortunately, almost every statement he makes about them is erroneous. He provides a list of bandidos, including Vasquez, Joaquín Murrieta, Juan Flores, Procopio Bustamante, and Juan Soto, claiming that "not a few of these men had fought on the side of Mexico in the war of 1846." In fact, none did so; most were children during the war. He writes, "Many of the outlaw bands, in fact, contained a hundred or more men and were well organized for guerrilla fighting," a claim which is simply preposterous. Every single fact Williams cites in an oft-quoted paragraph on Los Angeles vigilantes is wrong. Despite the errors, which could have been uncovered with a modicum of research, numerous historians have followed him uncritically, thus propagating his fallacious history.[9]

But the biggest myth of all is that Tiburcio Vasquez was a so-called social bandit. The social bandit concept was developed by the British Marxist historian Eric Hobsbawm in an attempt to define and explain certain movements of peasant brigandage in Europe, India, Asia, and the Americas from the Middle Ages until modern times. Writes Hobsbawm, "Social banditry, a universal and virtually unchanging phenomenon, is little more than endemic peasant protest against oppression and poverty, a cry for vengeance on the rich and the oppressors, a vague dream of some curb upon them, a righting of individual wrongs." Hobsbawm sees it as a social movement, primarily rural in nature. "The point about social bandits is that they are peasant outlaws whom the lord and state regard as criminals, but who remain within peasant society, and are considered by their people as heroes, as champions, avengers, fighters for justice, perhaps even leaders of liberation, and in any case as men to be admired, helped, and supported." Hobsbawm's concept has been widely accepted and uncritically followed by several generations of historians.[10]

Numerous scholars have identified Tiburcio Vasquez as a social bandit.[11] Writing of Vasquez, proponents of this concept declare, "In actuality, many Chicanos, seen as bandits through Anglo-American eyes, were not lawbreakers. They were instead victims of the Anglo-American invasion. . . . Their actions were those of men who refused to submit to this invasion. . . . The Chicano social bandits . . . can be described as victims of injustice. They were forced into a life that was outside of the newly imposed Anglo-American law; theirs was a banditry in the form of retribution and for the purpose of survival."[12]

Shortly after his capture, Vasquez told J. M. Bassett, editor of the *Los Angeles Herald,* "With the arms and provisions I could have purchased with fifty or sixty thousand dollars, I could raise a force with which I could revolutionize California." Historians have often cited this quotation to support the conclusion that Vasquez was a social bandit or revolutionary, and at first blush it does so. However, Tiburcio's self-aggrandizing declaration is hardly dispositive of the issue. A year later, bravely facing death, Vasquez changed his tune. He asked for pardon "from each and every one whom I have in any way injured" and from "the Great Father whose laws I have so ruthlessly trampled upon." He denied ever having personally killed anyone but added, "Common sense compels me to realize the justness of the law which holds me responsible for the innocent lives lost in the prosecution of my unlawful calling of robbery." At the moment of truth, Vasquez made no claim of being a revolutionary and offered no excuses for his lengthy criminal career.

Vasquez never took any steps to carry out a revolt against the Anglo majority. His raids were for plunder and profit, not principle. But could he have led or incited a rebellion of Spanish-speaking people in California? The answer can be found in events that took place a decade earlier, during the Civil War. Large numbers of white Southerners had come west in the gold rush, many settling in Los Angeles County. The biggest concentration of the state's Secessionists was in Southern California. Many prominent Californios also supported the South, believing that a Confederate government in California could restore their lost power. At least one Unionist newspaper charged that one-third of the Spanish-speaking people of Los Angeles were Southern sympathizers.[13] An alarmed federal government stationed troops in Southern California and anti-sedition laws were strictly enforced. California gold and Nevada silver were hugely important in funding the war effort, and it was imperative that the state not fall into Confederate hands. Although there was scattered sectarian violence during the war, no rebellion ever materialized on the Pacific Coast. If Californios, with the support of a large segment of the Anglo population in the Civil War, could not mount a revolt, then Tiburcio Vasquez with his small band of highway robbers surely could not have done so.

Vasquez did not rob from the rich and give to the poor, nor did he ever claim to have done so. He did pay for meals and shelter, a prudent course that bought him protection. During the Firebaugh's Ferry raid he returned Mrs. Hoffman's watch, but then took almost everything else of value that she and her husband owned, hardly the act of a Robin Hood. On occasion, he did steal from the rich. He took Wells Fargo's express boxes in several stage holdups, planned the failed robbery of cattle baron Henry Miller, and held up the prosperous merchant Thomas McMahon. He held for ransom the wealthy doctor and ranchero Alessandro Repetto, poor thanks for the medical treatment the Italian had earlier given to gang member Librado Corona. However, most of the people Vasquez robbed were working men: travelers, stage passengers, storekeepers, and by his own account, even a wandering Jewish peddler. After the San Benito stage robbery in 1872, Vasquez held up a boy named Eding, taking a measly two dollars. In Sonoma County he committed many burglaries and nighttime thefts. Finally, he was convicted of breaking into the Sargent & Barnes store in Petaluma—the act of a petty burglar and sneak thief, not that of a rebel or a revolutionary. His accomplice was not a fellow Hispanic avenger, but the Anglo burglar and highway robber Charles Horace Dade.

At times Vasquez victimized his own people: he resisted arrest with Anastacio García when the latter killed the Californio hero Joaquín de la Torre. He stole horses from a fellow Hispanic, Luis Francisco, in 1857, and seven of the seventeen grand jurors who indicted him for that offense were Spanish-surnamed. He planned to murder the vaquero Rafael Ponzo because the latter was a witness to a crime, and fired at him when he fled the outlaws' camp. He had personal enemies among the Californios and in

1873 narrowly escaped being killed by his bitter foe George Castro. He took Pepita Salazar from her husband and certainly bore some responsibility for her death, and later absconded with Rosario Leiva as well. He seduced and impregnated his own niece, and fathered and neglected several other illegitimate children. He caused his family, especially his mother, untold grief and heartache, and was a severe financial burden on his brother Antonio. In the end it was fellow Californios who, ignoring his folk hero status, turned him in for money because of Tiburcio's treachery to his brother's family. And, lest we forget, Sheriff Rowland, the lawman who organized his final capture, was half Hispanic.

The characterization of Tiburcio Vasquez as a social bandit and rebel is wildly simplistic, ignores the layers of complexities of the man and his times, and does no justice to either the real man or the truth. But the weaknesses of Hobsbawm's social bandit concept go far deeper than its inapplicability to Tiburcio Vasquez. In recent years numerous scholars have reexamined the concept, severely and justly criticizing it.[14]

The fatal defect in Hobsbawm's concept is that a social bandit must both be perceived by the public to be a rebel or a Robin Hood and, in fact, be such. Hobsbawm writes that "in one sense banditry is a rather primitive form of organized social protest." Hobsbawm describes the noble robber, or Robin Hood, model of social banditry in detail: he is the victim of injustice, he rights wrongs, he takes from the rich and gives to the poor, he kills only in self-defense. Hobsbawm contends that "the facts largely confirm the image" and that "genuine Robin Hoods have been known," but fails to offer any proof for his conclusions. Hobsbawm believes that bandits "will almost certainly try to conform to the Robin Hood stereotype in some respects," that is, they will do good to gain public sympathy.[15]

Hobsbawm's view is naively romantic. He fails to recognize that the outlaw hero is, as numerous authorities have pointed out, a creature of folklore, not history. His good deeds, his care for the poor, and his fine character are all aspects of myth rather than of reality.[16] The social bandit is simply, as one historian has explained, "a stereotyped figment of imagination rather than a creature of recorded history."[17] The social bandits identified by Hobsbawm and other writers are no more than folk heroes dressed in analytical garb.

Hobsbawm claims that social banditry took place in preindustrial societies, such as in medieval England, but no longer exists in "developed" countries.[18] Yet the reason for this is not that there really were social bandits in primitive or pastoral communities, but rather that they were created by ancient storytellers, minstrels, and balladeers who wove myth and fact together to produce outlaw folk heroes. On the frontiers of Mexico and the U.S. Southwest, Spanish-speaking people sang corridos about them. Such Robin Hood characters appear frequently in ballads and legends of the past not because they actually existed, but because modern methods of communication and recording of news and history did not exist. This void was filled in by folklore. Common criminals were adorned with heroic traits so as to make them fit the popular concept of the outlaw hero. Modern outlaw heroes are rarely encountered because mass communication quickly uncovers the truth about notorious criminals and their crimes, and the truth about criminals is rarely pretty.

Hobsbawm's theory that crime is perpetrated by criminals who want to perform good by stealing or killing, or that thieves may steal from the rich to give to the poor, would surprise most authorities in the fields of criminology, sociology, psychology, psychiatry, and criminal jurisprudence. On the American frontier, social banditry was neither a cause of crime nor a social movement. No historian has yet introduced evidence to show a movement of the rural western poor to engage in a primitive revolt against the rich or the oppressors.[19]

The causes of crime on the frontier, as today, were exceedingly complex and ranged from the societal to the personal. The societal causes are manifold and may never be fully understood. Relevant factors include income; education; religion; death and divorce rates; employment opportunity; political and social unrest; ethnic composition; religious, racial, or economic discrimination; and mobility versus stability of the community. Humans by nature tend to have consistent emotions from generation to generation and from century to century. Thus, the common personal causes of crime—greed, lust, despair, anger, jealousy, family dysfunction, mental illness—do not and will not change. These are basic human conditions, consistent since the dawn of humankind. Social banditry is not one of them. Robbery and theft are acts of moral turpitude and dishonesty, not of nobility or benevolence. Humans might kill to do good, but they rarely steal to do good.

So if Tiburcio Vasquez was not a social bandit, what was he? First and foremost, he was a Californio. He had immense pride in his ethnicity, his culture, his customs, and his language. This identity was so important to him that at the end he vowed to die "as a man and a Californian." As much as his Californio ancestors had disliked and distrusted their Mexican rulers and longed for independence, Vasquez never forgot his close cultural connection to old Mexico and frequently expressed resentment toward the Anglos who had annexed California. After his capture in Los Angeles, he toasted the president of the United States and "expressed a strong and eloquent desire that nothing would occur to mar the relations of harmony existing between our country and Mexico." But his ultimate loyalty was to California, not Mexico. By his own account, the one time he went to Mexico, in 1871, he was inducted into the Mexican army. But instead of using this as an opportunity to start a new life or to do his patriotic duty, he fled back to California to resume his career of outlawry. He was no Mexican patriot.

Vasquez was a true gentleman-bandit—good-natured, personable, charming, handsome, well dressed, educated, cultured, and well read. Such contradictions were inherent in his personality. As a youth he was gentle, almost feminine, with a love of music and poetry. But despite that genteel, cultured exterior and a small, almost frail build, he was tough as nails. He was shot and wounded six separate times: by San Quentin guards in two prison breaks, by the Livermore Valley ranchero, by Abelardo Salazar, by Robert Liddell, and by the Los Angeles posse that captured him. In each instance his hardy constitution allowed a quick recovery. He possessed great daring, physical stamina, and courage. He could withstand extreme hardships, exposure, cold, and hunger. He could live off the land, eating wild game or stolen cattle. His horsemanship, like that of most Californios, was excellent; he could ride more than sixty miles in a day. In an era when all men knew how to handle firearms, Vasquez was noted as a dead shot.

He knew California north and south, from Mendocino to Los Angeles: five hundred miles of trails, streams, forests, and mountains. Throughout that country he enjoyed the hospitality of countless friends and family. His great charisma and magnetism made him immensely likeable. Even prominent Anglos like Ed Tully befriended him. A natural leader, Vasquez was loyal and generous to his supporters. After his capture, he steadfastly refused to give information about his compadres who were still at large. At the same time, Vasquez took advantage of his friends. He persuaded José Castro to help him in a stage robbery, for which Castro paid with his life. He acted treacherously toward his compadres Abelardo Salazar and Abdon Leiva by stealing their wives, and toward his brother Chico

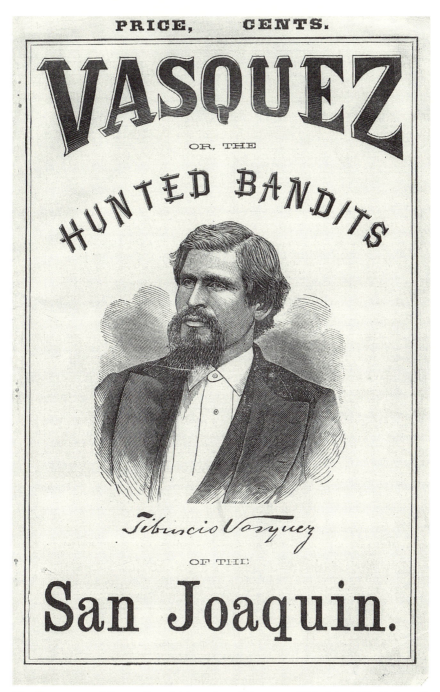

The front cover of George Beers's biography of Vasquez, published in 1875. (Robert G. McCubbin collection)

by seducing his own niece. An overwhelming passion for women was one of the driving forces in his life. His romances were legion. His literate intellect, romantic nature, and rakish reputation were a magnet for the opposite sex, offset by his lifelong inability to commit himself to any one woman. For Vasquez, females were playthings, and once he became bored, he moved on to another conquest. His dalliances with married women were foolish in the extreme. His affair with Pepita Salazar earned him a bullet in the chest, and that with Rosario Leiva got him the noose. His extreme recklessness and risk taking showed a type of narcissism bordering on the sociopathic.

By personality and nature Vasquez was a robber. His sense of entitlement led him to take whatever he wanted: horses, cattle, money, women, human life. As George Beers pointed out, Vasquez was vain and egotistical in the extreme. Recall the line from the corrido he wrote for his cousin Esiquia García: "Tiburcio Vasquez is the leader of all the Mexicans." At the time he wrote it, the Californio Romualdo Pacheco was governor of California. Yet Vasquez knew that among many of the Spanish-speaking poor and disenfranchised, he was certainly viewed as, if not a leader, then at least a folk hero, for they could identify better with him than with a rico like Governor Pacheco. Vasquez reveled in that notoriety, and in jail and at his trial he was immensely pleased by the large numbers of women who came to see him.

His life was one of extraordinary drama and adventure. He was not the creation of dime novelists, for his reputation was based on real exploits. By 1874 his status as a folk hero among Hispanics was so great that even the old bandit hunter Andrés Pico gave him shelter. As Boyd Henderson learned during Sheriff Morse's manhunt, "Some of the native women, especially, show an almost undisguised admiration for Vasquez, who is to them a sort of hero; and even among the American settlers we have found some who were disposed to shrug their shoulders and say that . . . he had always treated them well." For the most part, Vasquez made a point of targeting Anglos and not Hispanics. During the Soledad stage robbery in 1874 he would not take money from a Mexican passenger, telling him, "We only intend to collect from Americans."

Fully aware of his folk hero status, Vasquez burnished it by persistently claiming that he had never killed a man. It is true that he was not the bloodthirsty fiend the press so often portrayed him as, for as a general rule he did try to avoid killing people. His raids were, without exception, for plunder and not for rape or murder, and it is significant that he often tied up his victims to avoid violence. However, Vasquez was involved, one way or another, in at least nine murders: those of William Hardmount, Isaac Wall, Thomas Williamson, Joaquín de la Torre, Charles Layton, Joseph Pellegrini, Bernard Bahury, George Redford, and Leander Davison. It is possible, as he insisted, that others who were with him killed these victims. But Vasquez also tried to kill Lieutenant Moon at San Quentin. He shot and wounded Abelardo Salazar, Robert Liddell, and W. M. Shore. He took part in gunfights with Sheriff Adams's posse in Little Rock Creek canyon and with John Sutherland's posse during the Kingston raid. He repeatedly showed a reckless disregard for human life. He robbed miners E. A. Bedell and his partner, and callously left them without water on the San Joaquin plains where they almost perished. He and Chavo Arceo pistol-whipped Samuel Chatelaine so badly they broke his arm. He endangered innocent people by firing into occupied dwellings: at Santa Cruz, where the madam Paulina Florini and two of her customers were wounded; at Tres Pinos, where he shot through the door of Snyder's Hotel, killing Leander Davison; and at Coyote Holes, where he and Chávez riddled the stage station with rifle balls. His murder of Davison was by far the most brutal crime of his career, as the hotelkeeper literally died in his wife's arms. Vasquez helped plan and carry out four prison breaks that resulted in the deaths of twenty convicts. For twenty years Tiburcio Vasquez led a consistently violent life, and his repeated claim that he never killed rings hollow.

Among the Hispanic community, opinion was divided about Tiburcio Vasquez. As much as he was lionized by the lower economic classes, educated Hispanics saw him as a common criminal. The editors of *La Crónica* reflected the opinion of the upper classes in condemning him as an "endless menace" and "the man who has had the longest reign of terror on our community," and in heaping praise on his captors.[20] Even within his own family there were differing opinions. His sister Manuela and her family were deeply shamed by his conduct. When she died in Soledad in 1907 at age eighty-five, her obituary proudly mentioned that her grandson was the town's postmaster but made no mention that her brother was the famous bandit. In contrast, Tiburcio's sister María Lara was loyal to him—even proud of his exploits—and so were her children. When María's youngest daughter, Mary, died in Gilroy in 1936, her obituary appeared prominently on the first page of the local newspaper, headlined, "Vasquez'

Last Niece, Gilroy Woman, Passes in San Jose." Mary's pride in her notorious uncle, his career, and her mother's efforts to aid and protect him were described in detail.[21]

Vasquez was neither unfairly prosecuted nor singled out because of his ethnicity. Although his murder trial, under modern law, was unfair, the evidence against him was overwhelming. The punishment he received was typical for that era, for robbers who killed innocent victims were consistently sentenced to death. At the same time, several members and supporters of his band were never criminally prosecuted. They included Joaquín Castro, Lorenzo Vasquez, Agustín Hernández, August de Bert, Guadalupe Olivas, Blas Bicuna, and Manuel López, all of whom were publicly identified as having either participated in various robberies or aided and abetted the gang. Given the public outcry, it is surprising that little or no effort was made to bring them to justice. Only Lorenzo Vasquez and Guadalupe Olivas were arrested, and the charges against them were quickly dropped. Undoubtedly, the expense of bringing these men to trial was a major consideration to local counties. Nonetheless, the fact that they were not punished indicates that California's criminal justice system was not as biased as many scholars have argued. For it would certainly seem odd that, if the justice system was primarily driven by racism, these men would be allowed to go free.

There is no question that Vasquez, like all Hispanics in frontier California, suffered from racial prejudice to varying degrees. Scholars have generally identified this as the cause of his bandit career. However, Tiburcio's case was not that simple. For most of his youth, Californios were in power in Monterey. Even after the American conquest and through the mid-1850s, when Tiburcio reached adulthood, Californios, by virtue of their sheer numbers, retained a significant degree of political, social, and economic control in Monterey County.[22] Anglos did not begin to dominate until mid-decade, by which time Vasquez was already an outlaw and had fled the county. Although his uncle had been slain by Americans in the Mexican War, he never blamed his banditry on that. Instead, he complained that Americans had beat and abused him, shoving him aside at fandangos and "monopolizing the dance and the women." The explanation he offered for his crimes was that of a blow to his manhood and an affront to his personal honor—that Hispanic women were claimed by Anglo men instead of him—rather than an appeal to racial, political, or economic injustice.

The Monterey of his youth was a wide-open town where drinking, gambling, whoring, fighting, and robbing were commonplace. Tiburcio Vasquez made a conscious choice to participate in that life. His brothers and sisters chose different paths. Antonio managed by hard work to acquire land and prosper as a farmer. He was highly respected by both Anglos and Hispanics, served as trustee of the local school district, and died on his Carmel Valley farm in 1887. His seven children harbored no ill will toward Anglos: four daughters and one son married them. Tiburcio's brother Chico lived honorably, raised a large family, and was the highly respected majordomo for Chico López. His integrity was such that he served for a time as a justice of the peace in Los Angeles County. His brother Claudio, who lived in obscurity and never married, was also an honest man. His sister Manuela was a devoted mother who saw her children married into respectable families. The only crime committed by Tiburcio's favorite sister, María, was her undying loyalty to him. She too was a devoted mother who, despite a life of poverty, raised a stable family. Although Tiburcio had a close relationship with his mother, it was Manuela and María who supported her in old age, not him. The fact that Tiburcio's siblings—who were raised in the same era, in the same community, and in the same household—did not become criminals demonstrates that his outlaw career was a voluntary choice and refutes any claim that he was forced into a life of banditry.[23]

Antonio, Chico, Manuela, and María Vasquez, unlike their notorious brother, left a wholly different kind of legacy: their countless progeny in California. Antonio María Vasquez alone has scores of living descendants, employed in every occupation imaginable. His grandson Fred Vasquez served with extreme courage as a tank crewman in World War I. Badly wounded in the Meuse-Argonne offensive, he was awarded the Distinguished Service Cross, the second highest military decoration of the U.S. Army. He returned home to San Jose a hero, but died from complications of his wounds in 1922. Another grandson, Ernest R. McAnaney, born in 1906, was also a local hero, serving as police chief of Pacific Grove for many years until his retirement in 1966. He was the leader of McAnaney's Navy, a volunteer search-and-rescue group that saved many lives in treacherous coastal waters. Over time the Vasquez family—once marginalized because of their ethnicity and cursed by the notoriety of Tiburcio's criminal career—has become part of mainstream American society.[24]

In the end, Tiburcio Vasquez—like Jesse James, Billy the Kid, Butch Cassidy, and other outlaw folk heroes—will forever ride through our collective imaginations as the laughing, romantic bandido, seducing young women, robbing the Anglos, outwitting sheriffs, and escaping on horseback into the mountains. While a portion of his power and potency lies in that mythical image, the real Vasquez made an indelible mark on his world. In an era when most Hispanics were largely disenfranchised, often deprived of basic civil liberties, and able to obtain only the most menial labor, rightly or wrongly he came to symbolize their struggle for social justice. When people are oppressed, they will grasp at anything that gives them hope. Californios and Mexicans needed a man they could hold up as an avenger who acted out their collective desire to resist a society that had marginalized them. In death his legend grew even larger, and to many Hispanic Americans Tiburcio Vasquez remains a powerful symbol of their ongoing struggle for ethnic, social, political, and economic equality.

So was he a Robin Hood who stole from the rich and gave to the poor, a great revolutionary, a guerrilla, a freedom fighter battling to protect the rights of America's Spanish-speaking people? Of course not. But generations of Hispanics have believed he was, and that is what makes him significant. For in the microcosm of his turbulent life can be seen the larger effects of racism, intolerance, and social injustice that plague our nation to this day. That is the lesson and legacy of Tiburcio Vasquez, a corrido of dust and dreams.

Appendix

They Rode with Tiburcio Vasquez

The story of Tiburcio Vasquez necessarily encompasses the lives of many desperadoes who rode with him over the years, as well as hangers-on who materially assisted him. Here I present short biographical sketches of several of these individuals. Many are obscure and little is known about them, as they were secretive and frequently illiterate; none left memoirs or correspondence for historians to study. Accordingly, I have gleaned details of their lives mostly from old newspaper accounts, court files, genealogical data, and prison records. Some members of the band were exceedingly obscure, and all that is known is their participation in certain crimes or their violent deaths. Only those gang members for whom I have been able to learn something substantive are included in this appendix.

PROCELLA ANAMANTORIA

Born in California, Anamantoria was a seventeen-year-old vaquero when he took part in the 1873 Kingston raid. He was quickly captured and sent to prison for six years. In both court and prison records he is identified as Procella Anamantoria, which is undoubtedly an alias as it is not a Spanish name. He was identified by Sheriff Morse, George Beers, and others as Refugio Monteros or Montejos, one of which was perhaps his correct name. A newspaperman who interviewed him in prison wrote, "Anamantoria is handsome in form, and has a face feminine in its delicacy. His dark eyes are large and lustrous and fringed with long lashes, and there is manifest sadness in his presence. . . . The youth admits that he rode on the highway with Vasquez, and says that the bandit ensnared him with false promises and rosy pictures of glory." He was released from San Quentin in 1878. The balance of his life is lost to history.[1]

THE ARCEO BROTHERS

Fernando Arceo, born in 1839; José María Arceo, born in 1841; and Manuel Arceo, born in 1845, were the sons of Felipe Arceo and María del Carmen Arroyo. Their last name was often misspelled Arseo, Arcia, and Asero. They grew up with seven brothers and sisters on Rancho Pilarcitos on the Salinas River east of Monterey. Their father was a rough character who was punished in 1831 for killing a man. The Arceo boys were friends of Tiburcio Vasquez's. Fernando was a gambler, known to Anglos as "Cherry Pie," probably a corruption of Chiripa (Lucky). José María was called "Obispo" (Bishop), an appellation that had clung to him, for unknown reasons, since boyhood. Manuel Arceo was nicknamed "Chavo" (Kid). On November 23, 1864, Vasquez and Chavo Arceo robbed and beat Samuel Chatelaine, near San Juan. On April 7, 1866, at a fiesta in the family adobe, Obispo Arceo shot and killed a black youth named John Scott. He was sentenced to hang, but the governor commuted his sentence to thirty years. The eldest brother, Laureano, an honest and industrious man, was mistaken for a horse thief and shot dead near Monterey on October 11, 1866. Fernando and Chavo Arceo joined Vasquez in Calera Canyon in 1871 and were present when Pepita García died. On February 22, 1887, Fernando Arceo got into a drunken quarrel with José Ramírez and Juan Prado at a dance at the New Almaden Mine and was shot to death. Obispo Arceo was released from San Quentin in 1886. He lived quietly in Hollister and died in the San Benito County Hospital on February 3, 1926, aged eighty-four.[2]

FRANCISCO "PANCHO" BARCENAS

José Francisco Barcenas was born March 14, 1840, in what is now Pinole (Contra Costa County), the son of José Guadalupe Barcenas and María Teodora Soto. His father soon died, and his mother married Desiderio Briones in 1843. In 1865, Francisco Barcenas, with Jesús and Desiderio

Briones, probably his half brothers, and Juan Alvarez, were unfortunate enough to steal a cow belonging to the undersheriff of Contra Costa County. The four were arrested in the Briones house in Martinez; Barcenas was found hiding under the floor. He was convicted of two counts of grand larceny and sentenced to six years in San Quentin, where he met Tiburcio Vasquez. Barcenas was released on March 23, 1870, and later joined up with Vasquez. Francisco Barcenas took part in the "abduction" of Pepita García de Salazar, the Soap Lake stage robbery, and the gunfight with Santa Cruz police officer Robert Liddell. On September 14, 1871, he was shot dead by Santa Cruz lawmen while resisting arrest.[3]

BLAS BICUNA

Standing just five foot one, Blas Bicuna was born in Mexico about 1847. His last name was variously spelled Becuna and Vicuna. He was recruited by Vasquez at the New Idria Mine in 1873 and took part in the Twenty-One Mile House robbery and the Kingston raid. Although Bicuna was publicly identified, he was never charged with these crimes. In 1877 he got into a quarrel in a Ventura saloon and beat a man with a club. Convicted of assault with a deadly weapon, he was sentenced to two years in San Quentin. On his release he returned to Ventura County, where he worked as a laborer for many years, keeping his nose clean. By 1903 he was working at the Bald Eagle Ranch, five miles north of Modesto in Stanislaus County, when he got into a brawl with a drunken worker and stabbed the man to death. Blas Bicuna was convicted of second-degree murder and handed a fifteen-year term in San Quentin. He served out his time and returned to the San Joaquin Valley. In December 1921, suffering from tuberculosis, he was admitted to Kings County Hospital in Hanford, where he died on April 19, 1922.[4]

ALFONSO M. BURNHAM

Alfonso Mason Burnham was born in Massachusetts in 1939, the son of Simon P. Burnham, a master mariner and state senator. The elder Burnham brought his family to California in 1849, where he bought a large rancho, was elected assessor of San Francisco, and served as a district court judge prior to his death in 1859. Alfonso grew up on the family rancho, working as a vaquero with Californio youths and learning to speak Spanish fluently.

After his father's death he fell in with Hispanic bandidos. In 1862, with Manuel Rojas and Antonio "Red Antone" Valacca, he was suspected of killing a party of Chinese miners near Oroville. He was known by his alias of Fred Welch, or among the Californios, as Don Federico. The next year he was sent to San Quentin for two years on a larceny charge. On his release in 1865 Burnham joined up with Juan Soto, Manuel Rojas, and Tiburcio Vasquez, taking part in the Garthwaite robbery in Alameda County, and was returned to San Quentin by Sheriff Harry Morse. He served a year, then Morse found him a job, helped him reform, and sent him as an informant to rejoin the Vasquez gang in 1871. Harry Morse arrested Burnham one final time in 1878, for horse theft. He avoided a prison term and evidently changed his ways; during the 1890s he appears to have worked as a private detective for the Morse Detective Agency. In old age he provided two magazine accounts of his adventures with bandits, but never revealed that he had been a notorious outlaw himself. Alfonso Burnham died in San Francisco on July 17, 1936, at age ninety-seven.[5]

TOMÁS PROCOPIO BUSTAMANTE

Tomás Procopio Bustamante, alias Procopio Murrieta, alias Tomás Redondo, was born circa 1842 to Tomás Bustamante and Vicenta Murrieta of Hermosillo, Sonora, Mexico. His mother was the sister of Joaquín Murrieta. Procopio's father, a stagecoach driver, was killed by Indians in 1852. Vicenta later brought her son to California and married Francisco Valenzuela. They reportedly lived in an adobe in Niles Canyon in southern Alameda County, but Procopio did not get along with his stepfather.

By the time Procopio reached adulthood he was tall, handsome, and fast following in his notorious uncle's footsteps. He was a prime suspect in the murder of John Rains, owner of Rancho Cucamonga in San Bernardino County, on November 17, 1862. On January 29, 1863, Procopio and two other desperadoes robbed and killed rancher Aaron Golding and his wife, son, and vaquero in Corral Hollow, east of the Livermore Valley. On July 9, 1863, he shot and wounded a constable at Alvarado (now part of Union City) who was trying to arrest him for cattle theft. He was captured and sentenced to nine years in San Quentin. With time off for good behavior, he was released on March 1, 1871. Procopio soon joined up with Vasquez, and was identified as the leader of the gang by a number of newspapers that year. On February 10, 1872, Sheriff Harry Morse captured him in a

San Francisco brothel. Convicted of cattle theft, Procopio received a seven-year term in San Quentin. Released, with time credits for good behavior, on June 6, 1877, he soon stole cattle in Alameda County, then fled south. On November 12, 1877, he led a band that held up a general store in Grangeville, Tulare County. A month later, on December 16, he led a dozen men into Caliente in the Tehachapis, robbing the express office, hotel, and stores. Six of the robbers were captured on the Rancho El Tejon and jailed in Bakersfield. On the night of December 21 a mob broke into the jail, gave the prisoners a summary trial, and lynched them all. Five days later, Procopio and the remnants of his gang held up and robbed a general store in Hanford. A posse of five citizens tracked them west across the San Joaquin Valley to the jacal of Narciso Higuera, near Poso Chane. Procopio shot and killed posseman Sol Gladden and fled to Mexico.

During the early 1880s he operated along the Arizona-Mexico border. In 1882 newspapers claimed that he killed an actor in a brothel in Hermosillo. On February 6, 1884, he married Juanita Armida Bernal in Hermosillo. They had two daughters, Margarita, born about 1886, and María, born in 1891. The circumstances of Procopio's death are uncertain, but he is reported to have been slain near Hermosillo in 1894.[6]

"GREEK GEORGE" CARALAMBO

Born Georgios Caralambo (also spelled Xaralampo) in Smyrna (now Izmir), Turkey, in about 1829, Greek George came to the United States with several others as a camel driver for the army in an ill-fated experiment to use dromedaries in the southwestern deserts. The Americans dubbed him "Greek George." He was stationed with the camels at Fort Tejon in 1859–60 and also served as a camel dispatch rider to Fort Yuma, Arizona. He saw extensive service and was once wounded by an Apache arrow. In 1864 the camel experiment ended and the animals were sold.

Greek George spoke Spanish fluently and in about 1865 he married a thirty-year-old widow, María Cornelia López, member of a prominent Californio family. She had lost her first husband, José Hermenegildo Oliveras, in 1852 when she was only seventeen. Cornelia gave birth to a son, George, in 1866. A year later Greek George became a naturalized citizen and took the name George Allen. By 1874 Greek George was living in an adobe house on Rancho La Brea, located near what is now the tony, two-block Melrose Place in West Hollywood. He was a good friend of

Tiburcio Vasquez's, and his twenty-eight-year-old sister-in-law Modesta López, who also lived in the adobe, was one of the bandit's lovers.

Greek George betrayed Vasquez for the reward and perhaps out of loyalty to the López family, and Modesta betrayed him out of jealousy over his infidelities. For some years his role in Vasquez's capture was a well-kept secret, as Sheriff Rowland consistently refused to name his informant, but it eventually became common knowledge. In 1882 Greek George was constable of La Ballona Township. His famous adobe was still standing in 1888, but by 1892 all that was left was one crumbling corner. In 1885 he settled on a homestead claim in what is now Runyon Canyon in the Hollywood Hills. He built a house and stable, planted an orchard and crops, and lived there with his wife and two children; the land patent was issued to him in 1892. In 1900 Greek George married a second time, to Concepción Vejar. Charles F. Lummis, who met him in 1903, said that "he had forgotten all his Greek, and had learned no English. He spoke only Spanish."

According to Eugene R. Plummer, Greek George lost his property to "land sharks" and moved to what is now the Hollywood Bowl, on land he later sold to Plummer. This led to the oft-repeated fable that Vasquez was captured in the Hollywood Bowl. There is also no truth to the claim that he was the same Greek George who assassinated Alfred C. Bent, son of New Mexico Governor Charles Bent, in 1865; that Greek George committed suicide at Bajada, New Mexico. Greek George Allen died in Whittier, California, on September 2, 1913. His grave is in Founder's Memorial Park in Whittier, California, and is a State Historical Landmark.[7]

JOSÉ CASTRO

José Apolinario Castro was descended from an old Californio family. His grandfather José Joaquín Castro settled in Branciforte in 1799; in 1833 he was granted the thirteen-thousand-acre Rancho San Andrés near what would become Watsonville. José's father, Joaquín Castro, born in 1821, lived most of his life on the rancho but seems to have lost much of his property by the early 1870s and relocated to New Idria. He married Eusebia Valencia. José Castro was their eldest son, born in Branciforte and baptized at Mission Santa Cruz on July 23, 1843. The family's large adobe home is still standing at 184 Old Adobe Road in Watsonville. José Castro lived with but was not married to Tiburcio's niece, Concepción Espinosa (the illegitimate daughter of Tiburcio's elder brother Claudio by Dolores Espinosa, mother of Clodoveo Chávez). José and Concepción lived on the San Benito River about twenty-five miles south of Hollister, where he owned a roadside saloon and a nearby mine. His saloon was a hangout for Tiburcio Vasquez. José Castro was lynched on April 23, 1872, for his involvement in the San Benito stage robbery (although he was not actually one of the perpetrators). His father, Joaquín Castro, was present when the Tres Pinos robbery was planned. In 1873 Clodoveo Chávez lived with Joaquín Castro in Panoche Valley. Joaquín and another son, Juan, helped the Vasquez gang escape after the Tres Pinos Tragedy by driving Abdon Leiva's wagon and livestock to San Emigdio. Although their involvement was made public, neither Joaquín nor Juan Castro was ever prosecuted for their role in the Tres Pinos raid.[8]

CLODOVEO CHÁVEZ

Luis Clodoveo de la Trinidad Chávez was born on August 4, 1849, in San Juan Bautista. He was the son of Francisco Chávez and María Dolores Carmen Espinosa (mother of Concepción Espinosa), who were married in Monterey in the 1845 triple wedding along with Tiburcio's elder sister María Concepción. Francisco Chávez and Dolores Espinosa settled in San Juan Bautista and reared four sons and one daughter. Clodoveo was their second eldest. Clodoveo Chávez grew into a big, muscular youth, standing six feet tall and weighing two hundred pounds.

After Tiburcio's capture, Chávez led the remnants of the Vasquez gang. The governor offered a $2,000 reward for his arrest. In January 1875 he appeared at the head of a band of desperadoes in the Cerro Gordo mines east of the Sierra Nevada. One of his seven men was Cruz López, a daring bandit who reportedly had been involved with the Vasquez gang before. On January 31 the gang robbed the isolated general store of William Scodie, near Walker Pass. On February 9 they stopped and robbed the mining magnate Victor Beaudry.

On the day Tiburcio was hanged, March 19, 1875, the grief-stricken Chávez made a reckless visit to Hollister. To old friends he spoke of Vasquez on the gallows and mourned his death. When word got out, he escaped into the mountains. At a sheepherder's camp he bewailed the hanging of Vasquez and threatened to "cut the throat of every American they met." By March 24 he had returned to the eastern Sierra, where he and his gang robbed the Little Lake stage station. Three days later Chávez and two of his band held up the Granite Springs stage station on the Panamint road near Coso. As they left, Chávez remarked to the station master, "Adiós. You catch me, maybe." Two days after that they robbed the Borax Lake station south of Panamint. These raids caused great excitement in the Inyo mining camps, but large posses could not find the bandidos. On April 13 the body of an Indian who had been robbed and murdered by the gang was found. The following night the gang pulled one of its boldest raids, robbing the tollhouse on the Yellow Grade road only a mile below Cerro Gordo.

On April 20, in a running gunfight with a detachment of soldiers from Camp Independence, one of the gang was mortally wounded. Eight days later they held up and robbed the Cerro Gordo stage on the Yellow Grade Road about two miles below the town. On May 4, Cruz López and another gang member, José María Guerro, robbed a stage at Panamint Junction, about five miles north of Coyote Holes. López and Guerro rode into the Sierra Nevada where, on May 16, Guerro was slain when they attempted to rob Prewett Station in Chimney Meadow.

By now Chávez and most of the band had already headed south into the Mojave Desert. On May 11, a week before Guerro was killed, Chávez and several compadres robbed Cottonwood Station, on the Mojave River about five miles north of Helendale. Chávez fled south into Baja California. By September he drifted north into Arizona where he hired on at the ranch of N. G. Baker on the Gila River, located near the present-day town of Tacna. There he was recognized by Luis Raggio, a boyhood enemy from San Juan. On November 25, 1875, Raggio and two other ranch hands, Clark Colvig and Harry Roberts, attempted to arrest Clodoveo. The bandit leader ran for his gun but was brought down by a fatal load of buckshot. Echoing the fate of Joaquín Murrieta, Chávez's head was cut off by an army doctor at Fort Yuma and placed in a five-gallon can filled with alcohol. The head was returned to San Juan and identified by numerous people who knew Chávez, and the $2,000 state reward was paid to Raggio, Colvig, and Roberts.

The remainder of the Chávez gang, led by Cruz López, loitered about the border town of Tecate, Mexico. On December 4, 1875, they made the fatal mistake of raiding the tiny settlement of Campo, situated just north of the border and fifty miles east of San Diego. Campo's store, mill, and other enterprises were owned by a hard-bitten pair of brothers, Silas and Luman Gaskill. In a wild gun battle with the bandidos, both Gaskill brothers were seriously wounded, but not before they killed two of the gang. The Gaskills wounded three others, including Cruz López who was shot in the neck. Two of the wounded men were captured and strung up by a lynch mob. Cruz López fled to Mexico, where he died a year later from his neck wound.[9]

LIBRADO CORONA

Born in Mexico about 1856, Librado Corona was eighteen when he met Vasquez at Rancho El Tejon in March 1874. He participated in the Repetto raid, having worked for Alessandro Repetto a year before. Captured with Vasquez at Greek George's adobe, he was tried and convicted of robbery on July 24, 1874. Judge H. K. S. O'Melveny sentenced the youth to five years for the Repetto robbery and an additional two years for his part in the Charley Miles holdup. Judge O'Melveny took into consideration both his youth and the fact that he did not try to flee Greek George's house, saying that if Corona were an experienced criminal, he would have given him a much longer term. Librado Corona served five years in San Quentin, and with credits for good behavior, was released in 1879. He worked as a teamster in Stanislaus County and died in San Benito County on August 28, 1909.[10]

CHARLES HORACE DADE

Charles Horace Dade, alias "the Duck Hunter," was born in Louisiana in 1827. A brick molder by profession, he came to California in the gold rush. An inveterate thief, he was sent to San Quentin for three years in 1857 for a grand larceny in San Francisco. There, he and Vasquez became friends while laboring in the prison brickyard. After his release he was suspected of highway robbery in Solano and Marin counties as well as of the murder of a Chinese man near Folsom. Dade and Vasquez met up again in Petaluma in 1866 and together burglarized the Sargent & Barnes store. Soon thereafter, Dade was arrested for robbery in Napa and sentenced to four years in San Quentin. With credits for good behavior, he was released in 1870. Less than a month after his release he burglarized a butcher shop in Sonoma. Jim Knowles, city marshal of Petaluma, quickly cracked the case and Dade was soon back in San Quentin. He made an unsuccessful attempt to escape in 1871. Discharged in 1875, a year later he was returned to prison on a burglary charge from Alameda County. In 1880 he applied for a pardon, alleging that he was "an old man and a cripple." Despite his long record, his sentence was commuted in 1881. This was his last term in San Quentin. His final years are unknown.[11]

AUGUST DE BERT

According to Los Angeles Sheriff Billy Rowland, August de Bert's true name was August Ferlin and he lived at Elizabeth Lake. He was French Canadian and suffered from a deformity of the back; Abdon Leiva called him the "humpbacked Frenchman." De Bert was undoubtedly the French Canadian who ran a crude board saloon a hundred yards from Elizabeth Lake and who was visited by the French traveler Edmond Leuba in February 1874. Said Leuba, "The principal occupation of this good man consisted of selling whiskey. His customers must have been singularly rare, because his tavern was off the road, and I think the Canadian was his own main customer." De Bert took part in the Firebaugh's Ferry raid and the holdup of the two sheep men Bacon and Wilson in Fresno County, both in 1873. Despite Leiva's confession, which implicated de Bert in these raids, he was never arrested nor prosecuted. In August 1874 he was still at Elizabeth Lake, where Billy Rowland served him with a subpoena as a witness at Tiburcio's trial. He soon fled to Mexico and never appeared to testify. M. F. Hoyle, editor of the *Hollister Free Lance,* incorrectly identified de Bert as "a hunchbacked Frenchman named Jean," and stated erroneously that Vasquez had killed him because he talked too much. A Los Angeles saloonkeeper of the 1890s named August Ferlin was probably the same man; if so, he died in Los Angeles on December 7, 1896, at age seventy.[12]

FRANCISCO "PANCHO" GALINDO

Descended from an old Californio family, Francisco Galindo was born in 1843 in what would become Santa Clara County. In 1861 he was sent to San Quentin to serve a one-year term for grand larceny. In 1863, with two compadres—one of them the noted bandido Francisco Soto—he stole a herd of twenty-two horses and mules near San Jose, but the three outlaws were captured near Pacheco Pass. For this offense he was sent back to San Quentin for three years. On his release Galindo joined up with

Juan Soto. In April 1867 he and Soto stole a one-hundred-dollar horse from local rancher Gordon Chase. Deputy Sheriff Robert H. McIlroy attempted to arrest the pair at the Guadalupe Mine, but they escaped after a sharp gunfight. Galindo was later captured, indicted with Juan Soto, and sentenced to a scant six months in San Quentin. After his release he rejoined Juan Soto and Tiburcio Vasquez. According to Sheriffs Harry Morse and Nick Harris, Galindo was riding with Tiburcio's band at the time of the Soap Lake stagecoach robbery in 1871, but did not actually take part in the holdup. In January 1880 he was arrested for stealing cattle from Juana Uridias, a wealthy widow who owned a rancho near Milpitas. He died of typhoid fever on August 6, 1880, while lodged in the Santa Clara County jail awaiting trial.[13]

ANASTACIO GARCÍA

Born José Matías Anastacio de Jesús García, Anastacio was baptized in Monterey on February 22, 1824. He was the sixth of eleven children born to José Julián García and María Paula Garibay, both from pioneer Monterey families. In later years his father went insane and was known in Monterey as "Crazy Julián," as he often wandered about the pueblo naked. Anastacio's younger brother Encarnación wed Agustina Rosa Vasquez, a first cousin of Tiburcio's, in 1844. Anastacio García married Guadalupe Flavia Vasquez, a second cousin of Tiburcio's, on November 1, 1847. She gave birth to twin sons less than a month before their wedding. They had four children, two boys and two girls. Although his elder brother José Antonio fought against U.S. forces at the Battle of Natividad, Anastacio was a close friend of Henry Cocks and sided with the Americans during the Mexican War. In November 1847 he testified before the alcalde of Monterey that Gabriel de la Torre was fomenting rebellion among certain Californios and had asked García to join in an attack on the Americans. Anastacio had refused, saying that he "had suffered enough already from his countrymen." In 1848 he petitioned the alcalde of Monterey for a plot of land for himself, two of his brothers, and his mother, on the Rancho El Tucho. By 1850 he owned sixty acres on El Tucho, with an adobe house on the banks of the Salinas River. Two of his brothers, José Antonio and Encarnación, lived nearby. Anastacio García served as constable for Henry Cocks when Cocks was justice of the peace of Salinas Township, and was a member of Cocks's posse when they gunned down Claudio Feliz and his gang in 1852. After starting Tiburcio Vasquez on his career of crime and taking a prominent part in the Roach-Belcher feud, Anastacio García was lynched in the Monterey jail on February 16, 1857.[14]

ENCARNACIÓN GARCÍA

Encarnación García was the son of Anastacio García's brother Encarnación and Agustina Rosa Vasquez. He was Tiburcio's first cousin once removed and was a friend and admirer of Vasquez, but not an active member of the gang. Encarnación García was born about 1852 on Rancho El Tucho. His father died soon afterwards, and his mother moved with her three children to San Jose where they lived with her mother, Petra Vasquez. His mother later married Guadalupe Bee, son of San Jose pioneer Harry Bee. Encarnación García was living with his mother and stepfather at their house in Santa Clara at the time Vasquez was hanged. His sisters, Genoveva and Esiquia, were favorites of Vasquez, who wrote them letters and poetry while he was in jail. Tiburcio's funeral was held at their Santa Clara home. At the request of Tiburcio's sister María, Encarnación dug up the grave to make sure the body had not been desecrated. In 1883 García was working as a ranch hand in Los Gatos and living with a married woman, the sister-in-law of the notorious desperado Rafael Mirabel. Encarnación became enraged when Mirabel and his wife, Juliana Robles, persuaded the woman to return to her husband. On June 17, 1883, the two men quarreled in the barroom of a Los Gatos hotel, and García stabbed Mirabel to death. He was locked up in the flimsy town jail, but within an hour a lynch mob broke in and hanged him from the bridge over Los Gatos Creek.[15]

FAUSTINO GARCÍA

Like his older brother Anastacio, Faustino García was a compadre of Vasquez's. Born José Faustino de Jesús García, he was baptized in Monterey on November 14, 1830. In 1853 Faustino García was fined a hundred dollars for assault and resisting arrest in Monterey. He joined the Juan Flores–Pancho Daniel band in Los Angeles in 1856, and although publicly identified, was never brought to trial. In 1863 he married an eighteen-year-old Monterey girl, María de Soto. In 1865 he engaged in a drunken brawl with Gracia Martínez, who was married to one of his sisters. García stabbed Martínez in the face and was sent to San Quentin for five years. On his release he returned to Monterey County where he lived to age eighty-one, dying on March 17, 1912.[16]

FRANCISCO GÓMEZ

Francisco Gómez, alias Francisco Gamas, alias Pancho Cantúa, was a maternal cousin of Tiburcio Vasquez's. He was born in California circa 1843, and evidently his father was a Gómez and his mother a Cantúa. Gómez lived with an Indian woman on Tunis Creek near Rancho El Tejon. On November 6, 1873, he shot and killed Tehachapi Constable William S. Mettler, who was trying to arrest him for murder. He took part in the Kingston raid where he was slightly wounded in the neck. He stayed with the gang and was in Los Angeles County at the time Vasquez was captured. According to José Jesús López, Francisco Gómez fled to Mexico where he joined the forces of Francisco Serna in his 1875 rebellion against the governor of Sonora. López stated that Gómez was slain while fighting as a captain of Serna's rebels.[17]

ROMULO GONZÁLES

Very little is known about Romulo Gonzáles. He worked as a wood-chopper at the New Idria Mine. He was about twenty-nine years old when Vasquez recruited him at New Idria in 1873, just before the Tres Pinos raid. There he shot and killed Bernard Bahury. According to George Beers, he spoke "fair English" and therefore may have been a Californio. In an 1874 interview, Vasquez said, "Gonzáles is now in Sonora, Mexico, or was the last time I heard of him." His fate is unknown.[18]

JIM HEFNER

Although he was not a criminal or a member of the gang, Jim Hefner (sometimes incorrectly spelled Heffner) was a friend of Tiburcio's and often harbored him. He was born in Posey, Indiana, on February 3, 1826, and later came to California where he was a blacksmith in the mining camp of Havilah, in Kern County. A widower, he also worked as a teamster, hauling freight between the Inyo County mines. In January 1865 he took part in a punitive expedition against Indians on the Owens River, saving three young Paiutes from a massacre. In the mid-1860s he met young Margarita Ruiz, whose widowed mother, Nieves Ruiz, had brought her seven young children to Elizabeth Lake to escape a smallpox epidemic in Los Angeles. According to family tradition, Margarita's family was related to the Vasquez family. The Ruiz family lived in a brush jacal on the bank of the lake, and Doña Nieves earned a living by serving meals to the many teamsters passing by. One of them was Jim Hefner, and in 1867 he married seventeen-year-old Margarita. Near the stage road he erected two houses that served as their home and stagecoach stop. The place became known as Hefner's Station. The couple raised twelve children at Elizabeth Lake. Jim Hefner claimed that he had harbored Vasquez out of fear, which was certainly untrue. However, he did cooperate with Sheriffs Adams and Rowland, which may have saved him from being prosecuted as an accomplice of the gang. Jim Hefner died in Los Angeles County on March 8, 1908.[19]

AGUSTÍN HERNÁNDEZ

Agustín Juan Hernández was born in Monterey on August 28, 1821. He was a younger brother of the notorious bandit Domingo Hernández, who was lynched at Santa Cruz in 1852. According to Bancroft, several of their nine brothers and sisters were criminals. As early as 1841 Agustín was punished for theft by the alcalde of Branciforte. He married María Natividad Feliz of Santa Barbara in 1844, and they reared seven children. Agustín first settled in the Panoche Valley about 1853, then moved to the Hernandez Valley, which was named after him. In 1862, during litigation over the famous McGarrahan mining claim, he testified that he had settled on property belonging to Vicente P. Gómez (Tiburcio's teacher) in the Panoche Valley. Gómez transferred his claim, which included the New Idria Mine, to William McGarrahan. In a famous court case, Hernández's testimony, along with McGarrahan's claim, were ultimately rejected by the courts as fraudulent. In 1867 Agustín Hernández settled on Griswold Creek, five miles south of Panoche on the New Idria Road. His home became a favorite stopping place for Tiburcio Vasquez, who had undoubtedly known Hernández since his youth in Monterey. Natividad either died or divorced him, for some time after 1880 he married Rufina Alviso, with whom he had five more children. Agustín Hernández died between 1891 and 1895, still residing on Griswold Creek.[20]

ABDON LEIVA

José Abdon Leiva was born in Chile on August 12, 1845. His parents brought him to California when he was seven years old, during the gold rush. A herder, he married Rosario Feliz in Santa Clara on October 2, 1865, in a civil ceremony. They were later married by a Catholic priest at the New Idria Mine. Rosario Feliz was probably the daughter of José Luis Feliz and Ana María de Jesús Escolástica Alviso, who were married at Mission Santa Clara in 1845; Rosario was born about 1848. Abdon and Rosario had a son, Frank, a daughter, Lena, and another daughter, name unknown. He worked as a miner at New Almaden and New Idria. At his wife's urging, Leiva took part in the Firebaugh's Ferry and Tres Pinos raids. Tiburcio's love affair with Rosario proved to be his undoing. After testifying against Teodoro Moreno and Vasquez, Abdon Leiva was released from jail in April 1875. He divorced Rosario and moved with his three children to Sacramento, where his brother, Joseph E. Leiva, lived.

He started a new life as a reformed man, hardworking and responsible, and to conceal his connection with the Vasquez gang, went by the Americanized name Joseph A. Leiva. His brother got him a job at the Sacramento Planing Mill, where he worked for many years. For a time in the 1890s the brothers operated a grocery store and saloon, but by 1905 Abdon Leiva was shop foreman for the Sacramento Transportation Co., which operated numerous steamboats and barges on the Sacramento River. This position of responsibility in a large and important business was a far cry from his days as a bandido. In about 1889 he married twenty-year-old Clotilda Imgerten (1869–1945), who was half Chileno and half German. They had three sons—Joseph Abdon, born in 1891, Hipólito in 1894, and John in 1898—and one daughter, Beatrice, who was born in 1901.

After the divorce Rosario Leiva moved to the Guadalupe and Almaden mines where, in 1885, she married José Martínez, who was thirteen years her junior. Abdon Leiva was a strict father, evidently fearing that his daughters might end up like his ex-wife. In 1887 one of his daughters ran away from home, and he followed her to Rosario's place in Almaden and brought her back to Sacramento. Rosario Leiva reportedly spent her final days working in a rag shop in San Jose. She died of pulmonary gangrene, a severe lung infection, at the Guadalupe Mine on September 17, 1900, and is buried in the Mission Santa Clara cemetery. Abdon Leiva died in peaceful obscurity in Sacramento on May 14, 1916, at the age of seventy, survived by a close-knit family: his wife, five of his children, his brother, and five nephews and nieces.[21]

MANUEL LÓPEZ

Born in Mexico in 1829, Manuel López settled in Monterey County and married Augusta Peralta, a half sister of Isabel Meadows's, circa 1860. They raised seven children, living first in the Vallecitos, then moving to the Jolon area, in southern Monterey County, in 1870. Sheriff Harry Morse described López as "six feet tall . . . looks as though he had consumption." Morse accused him of killing one man in Marysville in 1861 and later of killing another near Downieville. Morse also noted that in 1871 López "killed Pancho, an Indian, at San Luis Obispo," evidently Francisco Guerra, who was found murdered there on August 24, 1871. Manuel López associated with Tiburcio Vasquez as early as 1871, and took part in the Kingston raid in 1873. Harry Morse's posse pursued him unsuccessfully the following year. By late 1874 he was riding with Clodoveo Chávez in the Coast Range. As far as is known, López was never brought to justice. In 1880, the census enumerator found him at his home near Jolon, living with his wife and children. He apparently reformed, and in 1888 became a naturalized citizen by order of the Monterey County Superior Court. His final years are unknown.[22]

THE LORENZANA BROTHERS

Faustino de Jesús Lorenzana was born January 15, 1835, at the old Californio settlement of Branciforte in what is now Santa Cruz. He was the ninth child of Macedonio Lorenzana and María Romualda Vasquez, who was a granddaughter of Juan Atanasio Vasquez. Faustino was therefore a second cousin of Tiburcio Vasquez's. His father was a reputable man and served as alcalde for several years in the 1840s. In 1859 Faustino was arrested for assault with a deadly weapon. He managed to break jail, was recaptured, then secured his freedom through the efforts of an able lawyer. After he and Tiburcio murdered Joseph Pellegrini at the Enriquita Mine, Faustino laid low for a time in Branciforte. On February 11, 1865, Faustino; his eighteen-year-old nephew, Pedro Lorenzana; and a compadre, José Rodríguez, one of the notorious Rodríguez brothers of Branciforte, shot and killed Jack Sloan near Santa Cruz. Pedro Lorenzana and José Rodríguez were soon arrested, but Faustino fled with an eight-hundred-dollar price on his head. In June Pedro Lorenzana was taken from the Santa Cruz jail and lynched. It was a foolish move by the vigilantes, for he had agreed to testify against his compadres and was the only witness who could identify them. José Rodríguez was then acquitted for lack of evidence.

In the fall of 1865 Santa Cruz County Sheriff Ambrose Calderwood attempted to arrest Faustino, who was holed up in a cabin on the ranch of his elder brother Matías. In a desperate hand-to-hand struggle, Faustino repeatedly stabbed the lawman, who managed to shoot and wound his assailant. The following year a new sheriff, Albert Jones, trailed Lorenzana and attempted to arrest him. Instead, the outlaw captured the sheriff, taking his horse and pistol but letting the lawman walk back to Santa Cruz. In 1869, while on a horse-stealing expedition near Alviso, he attempted to abduct a rancher's wife, Mrs. John O'Hara. He lassoed her with his reata and rode off, dragging her behind his horse. O'Hara heard his wife's screams for help, pursued them on horseback, and shot Faustino in the breast. The desperado fled and soon recovered from his wound. On August 29, 1870, a posse caught up with Lorenzana near Santa Barbara. He drew two pistols and fought ferociously, but he finally dropped, riddled with bullets. The lawmen found that Faustino had been shot six times. His body was covered with old scars from knife and gunshot wounds, a testament to the dangerous, violent life he had led.

Several of Faustino's brothers also ran afoul of the law. The oldest, José de Jesús Lorenzana, was arrested twice on assault charges. Facundo was arrested for grand larceny and assault, and Juan served a six-year term in San Quentin for an 1862 murder. Matías Lorenzana (1827–1915) married the sister of the Rodríguez boys and harbored members of the Vasquez gang. In 1871 he was strung up—but not killed—by Matt Tarpy and his vigilantes.[23]

RAFAEL MIRABEL

Born in New Mexico in 1833, Rafael Mirabel came to California in the gold rush, then landed in San Quentin in 1856 for a grand larceny committed in Yuba County. He served five years under the alias Raphael Menavara. Released in 1861, Mirabel settled in the San Jose area. On September 19, 1866, storekeeper Frank Johnson was murdered in Natividad.

Mirabel and a compadre were spotted leaving the scene, heavily armed. They were trailed and arrested, and Mirabel was booked into the Monterey County jail. He was quickly released for lack of evidence. A desperado named Juan Valenzuela was later convicted and hanged for this crime. By this time Mirabel was riding with Juan Soto, Francisco "Pancho" Galindo, and Abelardo Salazar. In 1867 he robbed an express wagon in Santa Clara County and was sentenced to eighteen months in San Quentin. On his release he settled in the Arroyo Valle in the mountains of southern Alameda County, and was soon riding with Vasquez and Soto. In 1872 Sheriff Morse suspected him of stealing cattle with Procopio Bustamante; he was arrested but soon released.

Rafael Mirabel's later life was repeatedly marked by violence and tragedy. In 1877 he was living near Los Gatos with Juliana Robles, whom he later married. On January 13, Mirabel and the woman's son, Bruno Ulloa, quarreled with Charles Parr and W. A. Johnson in front of a Los Gatos saloon. Johnson dragged Mirabel from his saddle and began beating him. Ulloa tried to come to Mirabel's aid, but Charles Parr struck him with several rocks. Ulloa pulled his pistol and shot Parr dead, for which he was sentenced to ten years in San Quentin. In 1882, in Mirabel's house near Los Gatos, a twelve-year-old boy found a stolen revolver under his bed. While playing with the gun, the boy accidentally shot and killed Mirabel's five-year-old son. On June 17, 1883, Rafael Mirabel quarreled with Tiburcio's cousin Encarnación García in the barroom of a Los Gatos hotel. García stabbed Mirabel to death, for which he was promptly strung up by a lynch mob.[24]

RITA MIRANDA

Born Rita Hernández about 1850, she was the only daughter of Rafael and Pilar Hernández of San Juan. Pilar Hernández was very light-complected and attractive, and her daughter grew into a beautiful girl. In 1864 Rita married Pedro Miranda, a bugler in Company B, First Battalion, Native Cavalry, California Volunteers, which was stationed at Camp Low in San Juan during the Civil War. When the battalion rode to Arizona Territory in 1865, Rita refused to accompany him. After the war, Miranda was discharged and returned to his young wife in San Juan. At a rowdy wedding celebration in San Juan in 1866, Pedro Miranda was accidentally shot, but recovered. The same year their son, Rafael, was born. Rita was wild and flirtatious. In 1871 she and her good friend María "Pepita" García, wife of Abelardo Salazar, left their husbands and ran off with the Vasquez gang. Rita's father, Rafael Hernández, died in 1893 at the age of seventy-three. Four years later Pilar Hernández had her nephew, Quentin Miranda, build the First and Last Chance Saloon next to her adobe home. For stage passengers crossing the Gabilans from Salinas, it was the first saloon as they entered town, and the last as they left. It still stands, remodeled into a private residence, at the intersection of the Alameda and San Juan–Hollister roads. Rita Miranda later remarried. In 1936 she was still alive, living with a daughter in Santa Cruz.[25]

RAMÓN MOLINA

Born in Mexico about 1845, Molina was a vaquero in the San Joaquin Valley when he joined the Vasquez band, taking part in the Kingston raid in 1873. That notoriety spawned many tales in the Hispanic community. One was that Vasquez expelled him from the gang because he was "too bloodthirsty." Another was that "he was reputed to have killed twenty-six men in his career of outlawry." In September 1892 Molina shot and killed a young man, Juan Parra, during a drunken quarrel in Cantua Canyon. He fled, but five years later was captured in San Luis Obispo County. He was returned to Fresno, where a reporter saw evidence of his violent life: "there is hardly a part of his body that is not scarred by ugly gashes of knife or other cutting and stabbing instruments." Molina claimed self-defense but was convicted of manslaughter and sentenced to ten years in Folsom Prison. He died there on January 18, 1902, at age fifty-seven.[26]

TEODORO MORENO

A first cousin of Tiburcio Vasquez's, Teodoro Moreno was the son of José Teodoro Moreno, a Mexican who arrived in California in 1829 and was majordomo of the Rancho Laguna Seca in the southern part of what would become Santa Clara County. His mother was María Antonia Cantúa, the younger sister of Tiburcio's mother. The Morenos were married in 1839 and had numerous children. Teodoro, born in 1844, was raised on the Rancho Laguna Seca. His father died when he was ten, leaving the family penniless. "From the time of his father's death until about his 21st year, Theodore was a steady and industrious young fellow, and out of his earnings contributed to the support of his mother," said Albert Warthen, a Gilroy butcher for whom Moreno worked. When Moreno's mother went to live with her eldest son, Juan, in Los Banos across the Pacheco Pass, Teodoro stayed behind in Gilroy. He drank, gambled, and raised trouble in town. Warthen wrote that Moreno "began to indulge in dissipation, and gradually went from bad to worse until finally . . . he became associated at odd times with the Vasquez gang, and was with Vasquez at the Tres Pinos affair. . . . I believe that he was with Vasquez only a few months, and I believe moreover, from my knowledge of the man (he worked for me off and on during all the years I knew him) that his complicity in the atrocities of the Vasquez gang was brought about by the evil associations formed during the few years he was addicted to habits of dissipation, and there was nothing inherently bad in the nature and disposition of the young man—but the contrary." Moreno also worked at the Enriquita Mine, where he met Abdon Leiva long before they joined the Vasquez band. Moreno later introduced Leiva to Tiburcio. Frank F. Latta, relying on confused oral history, reported that Teodoro Moreno murdered a woman, Nocha Morales, in the Californio settlement of Las Juntas. In fact, this incident took place in June 1877, when Teodoro was in prison; a woman named Morales was killed at Las Juntas by Fernando Moreno, who received a life term in San Quentin. Teodoro Moreno was sentenced to life imprisonment for his part in the Tres Pinos murders. On November 7, 1876, he led an attempt to escape, for which he received twenty-five lashes on The Ladder. In 1883 an effort was made to have his sentence commuted to twenty years. The district attorney and five of the jurors who convicted him signed the application, but it was denied. Teodoro Moreno died of throat cancer, still in prison, on November 9, 1888.[27]

GUADALUPE OLIVAS

A Californio, Guadalupe Olivas was a hanger-on of the Vasquez band. Born about 1842, he was a neighbor of Edward Tully's and settled on a claim on the north fork of Lewis Creek in the late 1860s. In 1870 he was notorious enough to be placed on a blacklist by Matt Tarpy's vigilante group, the Pajaro Property Protective Society. He was named, incorrectly, as a suspect in the 1872 San Benito stage robbery. About 1872 he married twenty-two-year-old Julia Williams, daughter of Ben Williams, a local hunter and trapper. They had nine children, the first born in 1874, the last in 1895. Abdon Leiva implicated Olivas as a member of the gang, and he was arrested as a suspect in the Twenty-One Mile House holdup. Sheriff Adams decided that he was not guilty and soon let him go. When asked about Olivas, Vasquez told a reporter that he did not deserve his bad reputation. Ed Tully's son Gene remembered Olivas's visits to his boyhood home when he listened wide-eyed to his tales of Tiburcio Vasquez. Tully recalled, "Olivas was a chain smoker. When one cigarette was about half burned, he would begin to roll another, then with the short butt, he would light the fresh one—then flip the snipe into the fireplace." Guadalupe Olivas died between 1895 and 1900.[28]

YSIDRO PADILLA

Widely known to lawmen as Isador Padilla, he was born in Mexico about 1847 and came to California as a boy. He grew up in Marysville and in the early 1860s lived in Stockton with a Mexican named Alvarez. In Marysville he was well known as a petty criminal to the town's crack police officer, Henry L. McCoy. He first came into prominence as one of the suspects in the infamous Medina murder case. On September 9, 1869, Padilla, Jesús Tejada, and Antonio García robbed Frank Medina's store in the Sierra foothills west of Stockton. In one of the worst mass murders of the California frontier, Medina and four other men were bound, shot in the head, and dumped in a ditch. Padilla and Antonio García were soon arrested, and Jesús Tejada was tracked down by Sheriff Harry Morse. Padilla and Tejada were convicted of murder and sentenced to hang. Their convictions were overturned by the California Supreme Court due to legal errors by the trial judge. Jesús Tejada died in his jail cell while awaiting retrial. In his second trial Padilla was acquitted because important witnesses had moved away and could not be located. Released from jail in May 1872, he reportedly tracked down and killed a fellow desperado, Francisco Soto, who was a witness against him. He joined the Vasquez band the following year and took part in the Kingston raid and the Repetto robbery. He next formed his own outlaw band with such noted bandits as Joaquín Olivera, Ramón Ruiz and Antonio "Red Antone" Valacca. In 1874 and 1875 they robbed stagecoaches and Chinese mining camps until the band was broken up by posses led by

Sheriff Ben K. Thorn of Calaveras County and Sheriff Tom Cunningham of San Joaquin. A true desperado, Padilla was sentenced to twenty years and died in San Quentin on May 7, 1877.[29]

THE RANGEL BROTHERS

The Rangels were friends of the Vasquez family in Monterey. The last name was often misspelled Rankel, Ranquel, or Renguele. Juan José Rangel, a convicted criminal from Mexico, was exiled to California in 1829. Given his freedom in 1834, he married María de la Paz Espindola two years later in Monterey. Their first son, Roman, later known as Ramón, was born two months before their marriage. In all, the couple had twelve children. Three of them became desperadoes: Ramón, the eldest; Abran, born in 1846; and José Ignacio, born November 20, 1847. Their father was stabbed to death in Monterey in 1851. Ramón Rangel was an old compadre of Tiburcio's. In 1852 he was tried for attempting to murder the notorious desperado George Bushton; the result was a hung jury. He was sent to San Quentin for grand larceny in 1856, escaped, and was returned to serve out his term. He was sent back to prison in 1860 for ten years on two more charges of grand larceny. Ramón Rangel took part in the Berreyesa escape at San Quentin in 1861 and the Big Break in 1862.

Ramón's younger brother Ignacio served a three-year term in San Quentin, 1866–69, for grand larceny. In 1870 Ignacio and his brother Abran were placed on a blacklist by Matt Tarpy's Pajaro Property Protective Society. Prior to joining the Vasquez gang in 1873, Ignacio shot a Mexican at Rancho de los Californios, resulting in amputation of the victim's leg. Ignacio Rangel took part in the Jones' Store and Kingston raids, and was captured by settlers of Rancho de los Californios. Sentenced to ten years in San Quentin, he was interviewed by a newspaperman shortly after his arrival at the prison. Rangel greatly admired Vasquez: the reporter wrote that he was "prodigal in his praise of the bandit's accomplishments." Despite his involvement in an escape plot in 1876, Rangel's sentence was later commuted and he was released from prison in 1878. His two terms in prison and his association with the Vasquez band gave him a great deal of notoriety. He returned to Fresno County and apparently worked as a vaquero in the Coast Range near New Idria. In 1888 Rangel got into a brawl with a fellow ruffian, Juan Bautista, who pulled a knife on him. Both were arrested but escaped serious punishment. In

1891, in a Fresno saloon, he quarreled with Joe López and Alvino Romero and opened fire with his revolver. López ducked his shots and Rangel was arrested for assault with intent to murder, but managed to escape a state prison term. His fate is unknown.[30]

THE RODRÍGUEZ BROTHERS

Close friends with Tiburcio Vasquez and neighbors of the Lorenzanas, the Rodríguez brothers were the sons of Facundo Rodríguez and Guadalupe Robles of Branciforte (now part of Santa Cruz). Their brother-in-law was Matías Lorenzana. José Rodríguez was the eldest, born in 1847. On February 11, 1865, José Rodríguez and Faustino Lorenzana shot and killed Jack Sloan near Santa Cruz. When the main witness against him was lynched, José Rodríguez was acquitted for lack of evidence. The following year he stabbed an Indian in a brawl in a Santa Cruz bordello and received a two-year prison term. Soon after his release in 1868, he and two compadres were spotted in the mining town of Columbia by Calaveras County Sheriff Ben K. Thorn, who recognized them as highway robbers and horse thieves from Santa Cruz. The three bandidos were armed, well-mounted, and elegantly dressed. They put up a stiff fight, and José Rodríguez was shot in the side by Thorn's deputy and overpowered. José received a four-year term in San Quentin. After his release in 1872 he supported himself as a gambler and pimp. On November 10, 1879, he was shot dead in a quarrel in Mayfield, now part of Palo Alto.

José Narciso Rodríguez was next in age, born in Santa Cruz on October 26, 1850. A hardcase like his brothers, in January 1871 he was involved in a shooting and cutting scrape with a half-dozen Californios in Santa Cruz. He escaped with a mere thirty-dollar fine. In August he took part in the Soap Lake stage holdup, for which he was sentenced to eight years in prison. At San Quentin he frequently violated the prison rules and tried to avoid hard labor. To feign illness he obtained from the prison hospital steward a dose of pure alcohol, which he hoped would make him sick enough to be released from work. Instead, the dose was fatal, and he died in San Quentin on July 20, 1873.

The youngest brother was Gracia Rodríguez, born about 1851. A teamster by occupation, he rode with Tiburcio Vasquez and Francisco Barcenas, was accused of the Soap Lake stage robbery, and took part in the gunfight with Officer Liddell in Santa Cruz in 1871. Gracia was never punished for the shootout. He was arrested for the Soap Lake robbery and released for lack of evidence. But he did not live long to enjoy his freedom. On September 28, 1872, he was shot to death by a fellow ruffian, Miguel Soto, at Whiskey Hill, near Watsonville. His first name is also spelled "Garcia" in early newspapers and court records, but "Gracia" is probably correct, as García is a surname, not a given name.[31]

MANUEL ROJAS

Born in Mexico in 1835, Manuel Rojas was in Calaveras County in 1857 when he was sentenced to an eight-year term on five counts of grand larceny. He and Vasquez became compadres in prison. Rojas broke out in 1858, was recaptured a year later by the Santa Clara County sheriff, and was returned to prison. In 1861 he and Vasquez took part in the Berreyesa prison break, in which both were severely wounded. Released in April 1865, he robbed the Garthwaite ranch and trading post near Pleasanton six months later, with Juan Soto, Alfonso Burnham, and a third bandit, possibly Vasquez. In December Rojas was captured and jailed in Petaluma, but his compadres broke him out. He was finally arrested by Marysville police in 1867, again broke jail, but was promptly recaptured. Rojas was sent to Alameda County where he was charged with the Garthwaite robbery. Rojas pled guilty to a reduced charge of burglary and was sentenced to thirteen months in San Quentin. Upon his release in 1868 he disappeared from the public record.[32]

PEDRO SAIS

Pedro Sais (also spelled Saez) was born in 1832, the black-sheep son of soldier and ranchero Domingo Sais, grantee of the Rancho Cañada de Herrera in Marin County. Pedro's home, located on a portion of the rancho in what is now San Anselmo, was a rendezvous for stock thieves. In 1866 Tiburcio Vasquez and Pedro Sais stole a herd of cattle from a ranch near Sebastopol. Petaluma City Marshal Jim Knowles arrested Sais, who was charged with grand larceny but later released. According to a friend, "He was a physically fine specimen of the native Californian, robust and healthy" who "possessed the stately courtesy of manner" and was a "resplendent swell that dazzled the early gringo settlers of San Rafael." In 1870 the census taker found him living on his rancho with his wife,

Manuela, and six children. He was reasonably well to do, with $2,000 in personal property and real property worth $30,000. In later years Pedro reformed and enjoyed telling listeners and newspaper reporters about the early days in Mexican California. When he died on March 13, 1892, the San Rafael newspaper gave him a long and laudatory obituary, making no mention of his criminal career nor of his connection with Tiburcio Vasquez.[33]

ABELARDO SALAZAR

Born in Hermosillo, Sonora, Mexico, in 1845, Abelardo Salazar was the son of Francisco Salazar and Merced Villegas. A silversmith, he had emigrated to California by the early 1860s and soon fell into a life of crime. In 1865 Abelardo Salazar was arrested in San Francisco under the name of Fernando López, convicted of burglary, and sentenced to two years in San Quentin. There he met Tiburcio Vasquez. Released in February 1867, he joined up with Juan Soto and Rafael Mirabel in Santa Clara County. Less than four months later he stole a horse, saddle, and bridle from Gustave Brohasky. This landed him in San Quentin for another two-year term. Upon his release he settled in San Juan Bautista where he ran a saloon with a man named Gonzáles, associating with Vasquez and other members of his band. On April 17, 1871, Abelardo Salazar married fifteen-year-old María "Pepita" García, the daughter of Pedro García and Dolores Higuera, residents of San Juan. Vasquez and Francisco Barcenas persuaded Pepita to run off with them. This resulted in a gunfight between Salazar and Vasquez on June 16, 1871, in which Tiburcio was dangerously wounded. According to numerous contemporary accounts, Pepita soon died, possibly of a botched abortion. Vasquez claimed that Thomas McMahon later gave Abelardo Salazar three hundred dollars to turn him in, but instead Salazar fled to Mexico with the money. His fate is unknown.[34]

BARTOLO SEPÚLVEDA

Bartolo Sepúlveda was born in what is now Milpitas in August 1839, the son of Juan Bautista Sepúlveda and María Francisca Pacheco. He had seven brothers and five sisters. Like his brothers, he was an expert vaquero, horse breaker, and rope maker. Bartolo and two of his younger brothers,

Miguel and Nicolás, became lawbreakers. Bartolo married María de los Ángeles Alviso, the youngest daughter of a prominent Californio family that owned the Rancho Milpitas. Her family gave them thirty-five acres to farm, and there they raised five children. Bartolo Sepúlveda was well liked by his Anglo and Californio neighbors, but he had a fondness for gambling and drinking that did not sit well with his proper wife. When he was arrested several times for cattle theft, the couple separated.

In 1869 he drifted into Mexico, worked as a vaquero in Sonora, then returned to the Santa Clara Valley in July 1870. Sepúlveda and Juan Soto, just released from San Quentin, enjoyed drinking and playing pool at the Auzerais House, a popular San Jose hotel. In November 1870 he was jailed in San Jose for cattle theft but was tried and acquitted. He was charged along with his brother Miguel and Juan Soto for the murder of Otto Ludovisi in the raid on Scott's store in January 1871, and was present at the gunfight in the Saucelito Valley in May when Sheriff Harry Morse killed Soto. After Sepúlveda was identified as one of the Vasquez gang at the time of the Soap Lake stage robbery, he fled to the mining region near Lone Pine in Inyo County. In March 1873 he surrendered to Sheriff Morse, hoping to prove his innocence of the Ludovisi murder. Instead he was convicted and sentenced to death. Granted a new trial, he was convicted again but given a life term. His wife and family came to his aid and, with the assistance of former sheriff Nick Harris, proved his innocence. Bartolo Sepúlveda was pardoned in 1885 and returned to his family a reformed man. He became a respected citizen, working as a vaquero. In old age he was an expert maker of horsehair bridles, and was known as "San Jose's oldest native son." His wife died in 1920, and he followed her in 1926 at age eighty-seven, surrounded by his children and grandchildren.[35]

JUAN SOTO

One of the most notorious of California outlaws, Juan Soto was a grandson of the pioneer Ignacio Soto who came to California with Anza in 1776. He was born Juan Bautista Soto on February 2, 1846, to José Francisco Soto and María Carmen Flores, and was reared on Rancho Milpitas in Santa Clara County. Bartolo Sepúlveda and his brothers were neighbors and boyhood friends of Soto's. Banditry ran in his family's blood; his maternal uncle Sebastián Flores was a noted brigand and member of the Francisco García band of robbers in the 1850s. In 1860 the fourteen-year-old Juan Soto was working as a vaquero on the large ranch of Daniel C. Murphy near Gilroy. By age nineteen he had graduated to highway robbery. On May 4, 1865, with Francisco Salazar and Jesús Sánchez, he robbed a traveler on the road between San Jose and the New Almaden Mine. Although Soto was arrested and indicted, the case was never brought to trial and he went unpunished. In October Soto, with Alfonso Burnham, Manuel Rojas, and another bandit, possibly Vasquez, robbed the Garthwaite ranch and trading post near Pleasanton. By the next year Soto was riding with Tiburcio Vasquez, Francisco "Pancho" Galindo, Rafael Mirabel, and Abelardo Salazar. According to Undersheriff Richard B. Hall, Soto committed numerous highway robberies on the road between San Jose and the New Almaden Mine. In April 1867 he and Pancho Galindo stole a one-hundred-dollar horse. When Deputy Sheriff Robert H. McIlroy attempted to arrest them at the Guadalupe Mine, they escaped after a sharp gunfight. When Soto was captured, his old amigo Bartolo Sepúlveda posted the five-hundred-dollar bail. Juan Soto was convicted of grand larceny and sent to San Quentin for one year. On his release, he was returned to San Jose for trial on a charge of assault with a deadly weapon on Deputy McIlroy. This landed him another two-year term, and he was released on August 27, 1870. He then rejoined Vasquez, Bartolo Sepúlveda, and other bandidos. On January 10, 1871, Juan Soto and two other desperadoes robbed Scott's store in Sunol Valley, killing the clerk, Otto Ludovisi. On May 10, 1871, in the Saucelito Valley, he was shot to death by Sheriff Harry Morse in one of the most famous gun duels of the Old West. Soto's San Jose compadres were enraged by his killing and threatened to get even with the possemen. Two months later the house of Theodore Winchell was burned to the ground. Winchell, his wife, and his children barely escaped with their lives. Winchell believed that Soto's friends had set the fire.[36]

LORENZO VASQUEZ

Lorenzo Vasquez was a Mexican, and contrary to popular belief, was not related to Tiburcio Vasquez. He was, however, a close friend of Tiburcio's, and his little rancho was a favorite hiding place of the Vasquez gang. Lorenzo Vasquez was born in Mexico in 1825 and appears to have come to California during the gold rush. In 1872 he homesteaded a 160-acre plot at Sweetwater Spring on the Hernandez Road, built a house and barn, and lived there for many years. The spot is located at the south end of Lorenzo Vasquez Canyon. In about 1870 he married an Indian woman, Paula Ochoa, and adopted her two children. His brother Loreto lived with them. The morning after the Tres Pinos raid, Vasquez and his band stopped at Lorenzo's place. Lorenzo's wife cooked them breakfast and the band divided the booty behind his barn. They gave Lorenzo and his wife a small share of the loot as payment. He was later arrested as an accessory to the Tres Pinos murders, but the charges were dismissed. He worked successfully to reform and to escape his notoriety. In 1881 a newspaper correspondent who visited his ranch called him "a peaceable citizen, surrounded by evidence of thrift and industry." In 1891 Judge James F. Breen of Hollister found that he had "behaved as a man of good moral character" and granted his application for U.S. citizenship. His wife died in January 1898. Four months later Lorenzo Vasquez sold his homestead and moved to Hollister, where he died on September 7, 1907, at the age of eighty-two.[37]

CHARLES W. WEEKS

Charles Weeks is a conundrum. A native of New York City, he was a twenty-one-year-old gasfitter when he enlisted in the U.S. Army at Fort Schuyler in 1866. He soon deserted and apparently came to California. He reenlisted in the First Cavalry in 1872 in Nevada but again quickly deserted. In 1873 he rejoined his unit, but deserted again in January 1874. Within a few weeks he again surrendered at Camp Halleck, Nevada, and made a long, rambling confession in which he claimed to have been a member of the Vasquez gang. He said he was born near San Francisco in 1847, a claim which is certainly false. He confessed to killing a man named Fisher in the Peach Tree Valley in 1869. In fact, the murdered body of a German named Fisher was found on his Peach Tree Valley ranch on January 10, 1869. Weeks claimed that he later joined the Vasquez band and took part in the robberies at Soap Lake, Firebaugh's Ferry, and the Twenty-One Mile House. He said he was with the gang when the Tres Pinos raid was planned but was too sick to participate, and that he fled south with the gang and was present at the gunfight in Little Rock Creek Canyon. He also provided a detailed list of alleged gang members, most of whom do not appear in the historical record. None of his stories has been confirmed. It is certain that he did not take part in the Soap Lake stage robbery. After making his confession he was held in the military prison on Alcatraz Island but was released in July 1874. If in fact Weeks had taken part in these crimes, one would expect that at least he would have been brought to San Jose or Hollister for further investigation, but that never happened. However, there were undoubtedly many gang members who were never identified, and perhaps Charles Weeks was one of them. His fate is unknown.[38]

Notes

PREFACE AND ACKNOWLEDGMENTS

1. Starr, *California,* 1.

2. *Chicago Tribune,* March 20, 1875; *New York Times,* April 26, 1874. I exclude the Texas border rebel Juan Nepomuceno Cortina here, as he was a military and political figure, not a bandit.

3. A comment on Joaquín Murrieta is appropriate. This most noted of bandidos continues to bedevil historians. Joseph Henry Jackson, in his very popular *Bad Company* (1949), erroneously claimed that Murrieta was a mythical character who never existed. His ill-informed opinion, based on the most superficial of research, discouraged work on the real Murrieta for years. Frank F. Latta's *Joaquín Murrieta and His Horse Gangs* (1980) contains valuable documents and newspaper accounts, but the majority of his book is based on the recollections of old-timers who were not even alive during Murrieta's time. His main informant, Avelino Martínez, claimed to have been a member of Joaquín's gang, but his credibility is highly dubious. In a 1935 newspaper interview, Martínez never mentioned being part of the gang, but said that he had once met Murrieta in 1877, twenty-four years after the bandit's death. Historian Susan Lee Johnson devoted a chapter to Joaquín Murrieta in *Roaring Camp.* To the extent that she accepts myth and uncritically follows the spurious oral traditions compiled by Latta, Johnson's account of Joaquín is unreliable. In recent years a number of self-published paperbacks about Murrieta have appeared, based largely on Latta's folklore. They have little if any value as history. For factual accounts of Joaquín Murrieta, see Secrest's biography of Harry Love, *Man from the Rio Grande;* Thornton, *Searching for Joaquín;* Varley, *Legend of Joaquín Murrieta;* and Boessenecker, *Gold Dust and Gunsmoke,* chap. 5.

4. All three books are rare and have been reprinted, two of them in fairly available editions. Sawyer's book was reissued by Biobooks in 1944 with a foreword by Joseph A. Sullivan, and Beers's was republished by Talisman Press in 1960 as *The California Outlaw: Tiburcio Vasquez,* edited by Robert Greenwood. The latter two editions are cited herein.

CHAPTER ONE

1. The literature on the Anza expedition is considerable. See Bolton, *Anza's California Expeditions;* Garcés, *On the Trail of a Spanish Pioneer;* Bancroft, *History of California,* 1:257–92; and Langellier and Rosen, *Presidio de San Francisco.*

2. The town of San Juan would not officially be called San Juan Bautista until 1905, when the post office name was changed.

3. Winther, "Story of San Jose."

4. Bancroft, *History of California,* 1:311–13; Winther, "Story of San Jose"; Northrop, *Spanish-Mexican Families of Early California,* 2:315–17; Campbell, "First Californios." Hermenegildo Vasquez is sometimes referred to in the Spanish-Mexican colonial records as Ermenegildo, Esmeregildo, or Heregildo Vasquez.

5. Northrop, *Spanish-Mexican Families of Early California,* 2:42, 316.

6. Langum, "Sin, Sex, and Separation in Mexican California"; idem., *Law and Community on the Mexican California Frontier,* 239–40.

7. As set forth in the mission records, the siblings of Tiburcio Vasquez were as follows: Fernando de Jesús Vasquez, born May 30, 1821, died June 19, 1821; Manuela Norberta Vasquez, born June 6, 1822; José Miguel Pedro "Claudio" Vasquez, born February 18, 1824; Antonio María Vasquez, born May 10, 1826; María Concepción Vasquez, born February 6, 1828; Francisco Pablo Miguel de la Soledad "Chico" Vasquez, born March 31, 1830; José Joaquín Vasquez, born March 19, 1832, died February 21, 1841; María Antonia Anacleta Vasquez, born July 12, 1833; and María Josefa Cecilia Vasquez, born November 28, 1837, died in childhood (Mutnick, *Some Alta California Pioneers and Descendants,* 3:1197).

8. "Padrón del vendario del Rancho de San Isidro, 1833," Archives of Monterey, vol. 7, pp. 701–702, Monterey Public Library.

9. Rolle, *California: A History,* 112–15; Walton, *Storied Land,* 66, 79.

10. Rolle, *California: A History,* 114–15, 135–37.

11. On the size of Californio families, see Miranda, "Hispano Mexican Childrearing Practices in Pre-American Santa Barbara."

12. Shay, "Fandangos and Bailes."

13. Deed from Luis Placencia to Guadalupe Cantúa, November 17, 1834, in "Solares de Monterey," Deed Books, California History Room, Monterey Public Library. This deed, located by historian Dennis Copeland, leaves no doubt that this house was the birthplace and boyhood home of Tiburcio Vasquez. The original adobe quarters are unchanged from the 1830s. Today, visitors are few and the historical significance of the Vasquez adobe is little known. In fact, numerous published accounts state that this house was owned by Dolores Vasquez, "sister of Tiburcio," which is entirely incorrect, as Tiburcio did not have a sister named Dolores and the owner of the adobe was clearly Tiburcio's mother.

14. Mission San Carlos [Carmel–Monterey] Baptism Book II, no. 5569, Diocese of Monterey Archives (hereinafter cited as Mission Carmel records, which contain vital records for both the Carmel and Monterey churches). Since the 1950s, a number of researchers and genealogists have unsuccessfully sought the baptismal record of Tiburcio Vasquez. Monterey historian Dennis Copeland located the handwritten record cited herein, which is difficult to decipher and appears to record Tiburcio's name as possibly either "Leoncio" or (less likely) "Tevurcio." The parents are clearly listed as Hermenegildo Vasquez and Guadalupe Cantúa. Since Guadalupe could not have given birth to another child in 1835, this is plainly the birth record of Tiburcio Vasquez. Mr. Copeland also pointed out to me that August 11 was highly doubtful as Tiburcio's actual birth date, because this was his saint's day. Several accounts,

some attributed to Vasquez, give his birth date as August 11, 1837, or August 11, 1839, both of which are incorrect. The fact that Tiburcio was born in 1835 is confirmed by his age as reported in the U.S. censuses of 1850 and 1860 as well as the California state census of 1852. Lastly, after Vasquez attained notoriety, it was reported that Mariana Escamilla, mother of Sheriff Tom Watson, was Tiburcio's godmother, which is confirmed by this baptismal record.

15. Truman, *Life, Adventures, and Capture of Tiburcio Vasquez,* 25; Miller, *Juan Alvarado, Governor of California,* 7, 32, 74, 182; Bancroft, *California Pastoral,* 404.

16. Bancroft, *History of California,* 4:650–51.

17. Land Case 330 SD, Lands, San Juan Bautista, Bancroft Library; Expediente 159, Land Grant Records, Spanish and Mexican Archives. Translations, vol. 8, pp. 34ff., California State Archives.

18. Larkin, *Larkin Papers,* 1:264, 272, 291–93; [H]ermenegildo Vasques to Manuel Larios, Monterey, August 14, 1840, Mexican Archives of Monterey County, Oficios, vol. 9, p. 995. Translation courtesy of Phil Valdez, Jr., and Dennis Copeland.

19. Dennis Copeland to author, September 27, 2007; Shay, "Fandangos and Bailes," 107.

20. Mission Carmel baptismal record no. 4465, María Cánula Concepción Espinosa, baptized July 16, 1843; Mission Carmel marriage record no. 1186, Francisco Cháves to María Dolores Carmen Espinosa; Census Population Schedules, 1850, Monterey Township, p. 112.

21. 1852 California State Census, Monterey, p. 233; Census Population Schedules, 1860, Monterey, p. 7; Truman, *Life, Adventures, and Capture of Tiburcio Vasquez,* 14. José Jesús de la Cruz Vasquez was baptized July 7, 1847. Mission Carmel baptism record no. 4784.

CHAPTER TWO

1. Guinn, *History and Biographical Record,* 1:280.

2. On crime in Mexican California, see Mullen, *Dangerous Strangers,* 31; Langum, *Law and Community on the Mexican California Frontier,* chap. 3; Bancroft, *History of California,* 2:537–38; idem., *California Pastoral,* 682–83. A creek and a beach in San Mateo County are named after Pomponio.

3. Rolle, *California: A History,* 161–64; Nunis, *Trials of Isaac Graham,* 21–30. For Governor Alvarado, see Miller, *Juan Alvarado, Governor of California.*

4. Rolle, *California: A History,* 165–68; Miller, *Juan Alvarado, Governor of California,* chap. 5.

5. Phillips, *Indians and Intruders in Central California,* 114–16, 135–36, 139. For two Monterey-area murder cases of the early 1840s see Bancroft, *History of California,* 4:653–54, 686; idem, *California Pastoral,* 589–90; and Langum, *Law and Community on the Mexican California Frontier,* 64–65, 81–82.

6. Beers, *California Outlaw,* 74.

7. *San Francisco Call,* February 16, 1920.

8. Gay, *Calle de Alvarado,* 66–67; Clark, *Monterey County Place Names,* 599.

9. Bancroft, *History of California,* 4:653–54; idem, *California Pastoral,* 590–91, 610; Langum, *Law and Community on the Mexican California Frontier,* 83–84.

10. Guinn, *History and Biographical Record,* 2:285. Leese was the son of the prominent American merchant Jacob P. Leese; his mother was Rosalia Vallejo, sister of General Mariano Vallejo.

11. Beers, *California Outlaw,* 74; *San Francisco Call,* February 17, 1920; Bancroft, *Pioneer Register and Index,* 782; *Monterey Democrat,* August 13, 1871; Northrop, *Spanish-Mexican Families of Early California,* 2:207, 3:164.

12. Bjorgan, "Berryessa Family," p. 2, San Mateo County Museum.

13. *San Francisco Call,* February 17, 1920; Bancroft, *Pioneer Register and Index,* 740, 759; Miller, *Juan Alvarado, Governor of California,* 67. Examples of Vasquez's writing and poetry can be found in several public and private collections in California.

14. Bancroft, *History of California,* 4:298–314.

15. Ibid., 5:165–68, 174–77; Harlow, *California Conquered,* 108–109; Egan, *Frémont,* 354–58. José Manuel Candido Cantúa, born in 1814, was one of Guadalupe's eleven brothers and sisters. Northrop, *Spanish-Mexican Families of Early California,* 2:41–43.

16. Colton, *Deck and Port,* 390.

17. Bancroft, *History of California,* 5:363–72; Harlow, *California Conquered,* 195–97; Egan, *Frémont,* 380–84. Juan Ignacio Cantúa was the son of Vicente Cantúa, the uncle of Tiburcio's mother. José Antonio García was the brother of Anastacio García. Northrop, *Spanish-Mexican Families of Early California,* 2:97–98. Some accounts incorrectly state that José Antonio García was killed; Thomas O. Larkin reported that the dead man was actually a José García from South America.

18. *San Francisco Chronicle,* May 16, 1874.

19. Rolle, *California: A History,* 205–208.

20. On troublemakers from the New York Volunteers, see Boessenecker, *Gold Dust and Gunsmoke,* 3–4, 15, 24–26, 45, 103, 311.

21. *New York Weekly Tribune,* September 23, 1848; Rolle, *California: A History,* 215.

22. Susana Bryant Dakin, *Scotch Paisano,* 164.

23. Pitt, *Decline of the Californios,* chap. 6; Cleland, *Cattle on a Thousand Hills,* 111–16.

24. Cora Older, "Vasquez the Outlaw," *San Francisco Call,* February 21, 1920. Cora Baggerly Older (1875–1968) was the wife of muckraking San Francisco newspaper editor Fremont Older. In 1916 she conducted valuable interviews with old-timers in Monterey and San Benito counties as research for a biography of Vasquez, which was published as a long serial in the *San Jose News* from May 6 to August 13, 1918, the *San Francisco Call* from February 6 to May 22, 1920, and once again in the *San Jose News,* commencing on March 7, 1927. As was customary in that era, her account contains fictional dialogue and dramatizations. Unfortunately, her comprehensive diaries at the Bancroft Library do not contain her interview notes. In 1930 she submitted a manuscript on the life of Vasquez to the Coward-McCann publishing house in New York. It was rejected, with an editor commenting, "It was a rather clumsy and sentimental biography, and very likely will never be published" (Jesse Carmack to Walter Noble Burns, April 14, 1931, Special Collections, University of Arizona, Tucson). In 1964, in a flagrant case of plagiarism, one Dominga L. Cervantes Hoffer published Mrs. Older's newspaper serial almost verbatim in a crude paperback book, *Tiburcio Vasquez, the Bandit* (Puyallup, Wash.: Historic Memories Press, 1964), of which she claimed to be the author, giving no credit to Mrs. Older.

25. Truman, *Life, Adventures, and Capture of Tiburcio Vasquez,* 23; Beers, *California Outlaw,* 87.

26. On Anglo-Hispanic conflict in the gold rush, see Boessenecker, *Gold Dust and Gunsmoke,* chaps. 3–6; Standart, "Sonora Migration to California"; Pitt, *Decline of the Californios,* chaps. 3 and 4.

27. Northrop, *Spanish-Mexican Families of Early California,* 2:29; 1850 Census Population Schedules, Monterey City, p. 112; 1860 Census Population Schedules, Los Angeles City, p. 391; Dennis Copeland to author, July 24, 2006.

CHAPTER THREE

1. Guinn, *History and Biographical Record,* 1:280. On homicide rates in Monterey and other California communities of the 1850s, see Boessenecker, *Gold Dust and Gunsmoke,* 321–26; and Mullen, *Dangerous Strangers,* 1–2, 31.

2. Bancroft, *Popular Tribunals,* 1:292–93.

3. Ibid., 1:292–93, 435–36, 450, 474–75; Williams, *Papers of the San Francisco Committee of Vigilance,* 235–36, 456; Monterey County Jail Register, 1850–72, California History Room Archives, Monterey Public Library, prisoners nos. 43–47. Ironically, Andrew Randall would be slain in an unrelated murder in San Francisco in 1856 by Joseph Hetherington, an associate of "English Jim" Stuart. Hetherington was hanged by the San Francisco vigilantes for this crime.

4. Boessenecker, *Gold Dust and Gunsmoke,* 63–64, 84–85, 126, 131; Camarillo, *Chicanos in a Changing Society,* 20–21; Bancroft, *California Pastoral,* 650; Northrop, *Spanish-Mexican Families of Early California,* 2:207, 316; Dennis Copeland to author, July 12, 2005; Mutnick, *Some Alta California Pioneers and Descendants,* 3:1629 (family of José Tiburcio Vasquez and Ana María Bojorques), and 1648 (family of María Petra Vasquez).

5. Bancroft, *California Pastoral,* 684–85; Northrop, *Spanish-Mexican Families of Early California,* 3:400; *San Francisco Bulletin,* May 8, 1872.

6. Serrano, "Recuerdos históricos," Bancroft Library; Mexican Archives of Monterey, vol. 14, sheet 627; *Monterey Herald,* April 20, 1959; Bancroft, *California Pastoral,* 685.

7. Bancroft, *History of California,* 5:18; Bancroft, *California Pastoral,* 684–85; Bancroft Dictations: Agustín Escobar.

8. *San Francisco Alta California,* April 21, 1851; Williams, *Papers of the San Francisco Committee of Vigilance,* 239, 241; Monterey Jail Register, prisoner nos. 60–64.

9. *San Francisco Alta California,* March 21, April 9, and June 3, 1851; *Stockton Times,* April 12, 1851; Bancroft, *History of California,* 3:200.

10. *San Francisco Alta California,* July 12 and August 16, 1851.

11. Boessenecker, *Gold Dust and Gunsmoke,* 84–85; *Los Angeles Star,* May 12, 1860.

12. Northrop, *Spanish-Mexican Families of Early California,* 2:98; Mutnick, *Some Alta California Pioneers and Descendants,* 3:1629, 1648; Assessment List of Property in the County of Monterey, Year 1850, pp. 24, 56, California History Room, Monterey Public Library; *Santa Cruz Sentinel,* February 28, 1857; Bancroft, *California Pastoral,* 688. Tiburcio and María Guadalupe Flavia Vasquez shared the same great-grandfather, Juan Atanasio Vasquez, and therefore were second cousins.

13. *New York Times,* April 26, 1874; *San Jose Patriot,* March 18, 1875.

14. *Santa Cruz Sentinel,* September 16, 1885.

15. *People v. Alexander Ramos; People v. Alejandro Ramos;* Monterey Jail Register, prisoner no. 83, Alex Ramos.

16. Northrop, *Spanish-Mexican Families of Early California,* 2:122; Bancroft, *Popular Tribunals,* 1:476–77; *San Francisco Alta California,* September 14, 1850; San Jose Pueblo Index, 1842–43, transcript courtesy of Patsy Ludwig.

17. *San Francisco Alta California,* July 25, 26, 28, 1852; *Los Angeles Star,* August 7, 1852.

18. Boessenecker, *Badge and Buckshot,* 82–84.

19. Account of Daniel Martin, nephew of Catherine Cole, in the *Salinas Daily Post,* January 6, 1934; John P. Harrington Field Notes (1935), Reel 63, p. 135, Reel 71, pp. 226–28, Reel 75, p. 400, National Archives; *Monterey Herald,* July 20, 1926; Mission Carmel Death Register, María Cano Tarango, April 16, 1901; Census Population Schedules, 1870, Almaden Township, p. 14, and 1900, Monterey Township, p. 18; genealogical notes of Patsy Ludwig. Isabel Meadows was the last fluent speaker of the Rumsien language. She helped the noted Smithsonian Institution ethnologist John P. Harrington in his research during the 1930s.

20. Guinn, *History and Biographical Record,* 1:285; Assessment List of Taxable Property for the County of Monterey, 1850; Book of Deeds, A, pp. 287, 290; City Assessor's Book, 1851–52, vol.

2, section 2; William Pyburn Papers, Series 1; Dennis Copeland to author, October 11, 2004, January 10, 2005; Gay, *Calle de Alvarado,* 43.

21. *San Francisco Chronicle,* May 16, 1874; *San Francisco Bulletin,* May 15, 1874; *San Jose Patriot,* July 25, 1874; Truman, *Life, Adventures, and Capture of Tiburcio Vasquez,* 26; Northrop, *Spanish-Mexican Families of Early California,* 2:97–98.

22. Gay, *Calle de Alvarado,* 43. This account was based on Gay's interview in the 1930s with an eighty-nine-year-old Montereño. On competition for Californio women, see Moreno, "Here the Society Is United."

23. Truman, *Life, Adventures, and Capture of Tiburcio Vasquez,* 14–15.

24. Memoir of Donald McAnaney, collection of Elayne Silva Reyna, San Juan Bautista; *Salinas Californian,* April 5, 1869; *San Jose Patriot,* March 19, 1875.

25. *San Francisco Chronicle,* February 22, 1874; Beers, *California Outlaw,* 144–47.

26. *San Jose Patriot,* July 25, 1874; Beers, *California Outlaw,* 87. Concepción "Chona" García was another of Anastacio's sisters.

27. *San Francisco Herald,* November 18, 1855; *San Jose Telegraph,* September 14, 1854; *San Francisco Call,* February 23, 1920; Guinn, *History and Biographical Record,* 1:285–86; Beers, *California Outlaw,* 83–84; California State Census of 1852, Monterey County, p. 221. The wounded bystander was James Patridge, a local blacksmith.

28. *Salinas Index,* October 9, 1873; Beers, *California Outlaw,* 86–87; Higuera left behind a nine-year-old son, Juan. By 1865 Juan Higuera was, like his father before him, an outlaw, wanted for horse theft and for shooting a deputy sheriff in Santa Clara County. Captured near Monterey after a gunfight with a posse, he suffered the same fate as his father (*Monterey Gazette,* May 19, 1865).

29. Beers, *California Outlaw,* 85; *San Francisco Call,* March 1, 1920; *San Jose Patriot,* July 21, 1874. Leiva, as we shall see, was not an unbiased source.

30. Guinn, *History and Biographical Record,* 1:286.

31. On Hispanic incarceration rates, see McKanna, "Ethnics and San Quentin Prison Registers," and "Crime and Punishment." On the disproportionate incidence of Hispanic violent crime, see Mullen, *Dangerous Strangers,* chap. 3. On disparate treatment of Hispanic defendants in San Diego, San Luis Obispo, and Tuolumne counties, see L. Parker, "Superior Court Treatment of Ethnics." On machismo, see Gutmann, *Romance of Democracy,* 32–36.

CHAPTER FOUR

1. *San Francisco Alta California,* September 30, 1854.

2. Hoover, Rensch, and Rensch, *Historic Spots in California,* 196; Northrop, *Spanish-Mexican Families of Early California,* 1:141, 2:315–16, 3:109. María Águila was the daughter of Hermenegildo's eldest sister, María Ignacia Remigia Vasquez. The Feliz adobe is no longer standing. George Beers provides a long account involving the abduction of a girl, Anita, by Vasquez, García, and Juan Soto and her rescue by three Americans, after the killing of Constable Hardmount. This yarn appears in Beers, *California Outlaw,* 89–154; the editor correctly labels it fiction (p. 18). Juan Soto was only nine years old in 1855, when these events allegedly took place.

3. *Los Angeles Daily Star,* May 16, 1874; Truman, *Life, Adventures, and Capture of Tiburcio Vasquez,* 26.

4. Guadalupe was the daughter of Felipe Vasquez, an elder brother of Hermenegildo's.

5. Fitzgerald, "California Bandit," 740. Fitzgerald, like a number of other early writers, mistakenly claimed that Tiburcio Vasquez was a member of Joaquín Murrieta's band.

6. Carlo M. DeFerrari, preeminent historian of Tuolumne County, was unable to find any contemporary report of Tiburcio Vasquez in Sonora (DeFerrari to author, December 16, 2002). A John Davis was found murdered near Sonora, believed to have been shot by Indians (*Sonora Union Democrat*, August 5, 1854). O. P. Fitzgerald arrived in Sonora in the spring of 1855, after Davis's death (ibid., May 12, 1855). On the Rancheria Tragedy, see Boessenecker, *Gold Dust and Gunsmoke*, 52–58; and Secrest, *California Badmen*, 64–83.

7. *Watsonville Pajaronian*, January 2, 1879; *Santa Cruz Surf*, December 31, 1901; P. Parker, "Roach-Belcher Feud," 19–21. An excellent account of the legal fight over the Sánchez estate is William Crane Roddy, *Sanchez File* (1995).

8. P. Parker, "Roach-Belcher Feud," 20.

9. For a sketch of the life of Bill Byrnes, see Secrest, *Lawmen and Desperadoes*, 70–75.

10. *San Jose Telegraph*, March 22, 1855; *San Jose Semi-Weekly Tribune*, March 20, 1855.

11. *Santa Cruz Sentinel*, February 28, 1857; Clark, *Monterey County Place Names*, 10. Anglos commonly misspelled García's first name as Anastasio or Anastasia, hence the place-name Anastasia Canyon.

12. *Monterey Sentinel*, October 6, 1855; *San Francisco Call*, February 24, 1920.

13. *Salinas Index*, October 9, 1873.

14. *Monterey Sentinel*, November 17, 1855; *San Francisco Herald*, November 21, 1855; *Los Angeles Star*, November 24, 1855; *Hollister Advance*, October 11, 1873.

15. *Los Angeles Star*, November 24, 1855; *Watsonville Pajaronian*, January 2, 1879; *Monterey Sentinel*, November 17, 1855; *Salinas Index*, October 9, 1873.

16. *San Francisco Herald*, November 18, 21, 1855; *Monterey Sentinel*, November 17, 24, 1855; *Santa Cruz Sentinel*, May 12, 1877; *San Francisco Call*, March 1, 1920.

17. *San Francisco Herald*, November 18, 1855.

18. *San Francisco Herald*, November 21, 1855; *Santa Cruz Sentinel*, May 12, 1877.

19. On Manuel Poli (1819–56) and Ysidro Obiols (1821–97) see Escandon, "Dr. M.A.R. de Poli and the Escandon Family," Ventura County Museum; *Santa Barbara Gazette*, September 11, 1856; Sheridan, *History of Ventura County* 1:153–54, 391; Edwin M. Sheridan, Historical Writings, vol. 2, p. 84, Ventura County Museum. For María's marriage, see Casamientos, entry no. 1300, Mission San Juan Bautista records.

20. P. Parker, "Roach-Belcher Feud," 21–22, 26–27; Harrell, *Sánchez Treasure*, 168; Monterey County Jail Register, prisoner no. 236, Thomas H. Munk.

21. *San Francisco Herald*, June 21, 1856.

22. Boessenecker, *Gold Dust and Gunsmoke*, 195.

23. Ibid.

24. On Henry Plummer and vigilantism in Montana, see Allen, *Decent, Orderly Lynching*. For the Lincoln County War, see Utley, *High Noon in Lincoln*; Nolan, *Lincoln County War;* and Jacobsen, *Such Men as Billy the Kid*. On the Earp-Clanton feud and the cowboy troubles in southern Arizona, see Tefertiller, *Wyatt Earp;* and Shillingberg, *Tombstone, A.T.*

CHAPTER FIVE

1. *San Jose Patriot*, May 19, 1874; Truman, *Life, Adventures, and Capture of Tiburcio Vasquez*, 26; Sawyer, *Life and Career of Tiburcio Vasquez*, 5. Eugene T. Sawyer (1846–1924) was a newspaperman in San Francisco and San Jose. In the 1890s he became a popular dime novel author, and wrote many of the Nick Carter and Diamond Dick stories. In preparing his Vasquez book, Sawyer said that he "interviewed old schoolmates and acquaintances of Vasquez, living in various portions of Monterey County," as well as many of the robber's victims. He also conducted interviews with Vasquez while the bandit was in jail in

San Jose (*San Jose Mercury Herald,* October 30, 1924; *Los Angeles Times,* July 21, 1929). Chico's daughter, María Pascuala Felicita Vasquez, was baptized at Mission San Buenaventura on September 2, 1856 (Dennis Copeland to author, April 19, 2008).

2. Land Claim No. 30, U.S. District Court, Hermenegildo Vasquez, Bancroft Library; Northrop, *Spanish-Mexican Families of Early California,* 2:316; Dennis Copeland to author, January 4, 2006.

3. *San Jose Patriot,* July 25, 1874, March 18, 20, 1875; Sawyer, *Life and Career of Tiburcio Vasquez,* 5–6. Vasquez identified his codefendant as "Jesús Soto," which may be the basis for the fictional chapters of George Beers's biography, in which he claims that Juan Soto met Tiburcio Vasquez in 1855 and that the pair had various criminal adventures before 1857.

4. *People v. Tiburcio Basquez; People v. Juan, an Indian, and Jose, an Indian;* San Quentin Inmate Register, convict. no. 1216, Juan, an Indian, California State Archives; *Los Angeles Star,* July 25, August 15, 1857; Newmark, *Sixty Years in Southern California,* 49.

5. Boessenecker, *Gold Dust and Gunsmoke,* 64–66, 117–33; Spitzzeri, "On a Case-by-Case Basis." Numerous writers have claimed that Hispanics did not receive due process in the early courts of Los Angeles. Spitzzeri's study directly refutes that premise.

6. *San Francisco Bulletin,* August 26, 1857; San Quentin Prison Register, inmate no. 1217, California State Archives.

7. Boessenecker, *Gold Dust and Gunsmoke,* 273–76; *San Francisco Alta California,* January 25, 1852; McAfee, "San Quentin"; *San Francisco Bulletin,* February 3, 1858. Cemetery Hill was leveled by convict labor to make space for exercise yards and a huge cell building, the South Block, which was completed in 1913.

8. McKanna, "San Quentin," 47; idem, "Origins of San Quentin," 49–50.

9. *Report of the Joint Committee on State Prison Affairs; Annual Report of the Board of State Prison Directors for the Year 1858;* Lamott, *Chronicles of San Quentin,* 79–80.

10. *Report of the Joint Committee on State Prison Affairs. Appendix to Senate Journals of the Ninth Session of the Legislature of the State of California* (1858).

11. Lamott, *Chronicles of San Quentin,* chap. 2. Although it is generally believed that none of the prison buildings from the 1850s still exists, in fact, a stone cell building bearing the stonecutter's date of 1859, and an even older stone armory with a dungeon in the basement, are still standing, as are two brick buildings from the same period.

12. *San Francisco Call,* March 5, 1920.

13. Beers, *California Outlaw,* 164. "Showing the white feather" was formerly a popular term for cowardice.

14. Governor's Pardon Papers, file no. 2748, Charles Horace Dade; *San Francisco Bulletin,* January 19, 1871; Mortimer, *Life and Career of Charles Mortimer,* 53.

15. McKanna, "Crime and Punishment," 7–8. Although McKanna states that fifty lashes was the standard punishment for attempted escape, the number recorded in prison logs for the instances described herein is sixty.

16. *San Francisco Bulletin,* November 9, 1857; *Los Angeles Star,* November 28, 1857.

17. Casamientos, entry no. 1331 [1617], Mission San Juan Bautista records; *San Francisco Alta California,* June 27, 1859; *San Francisco Bulletin,* May 15, 1874; San Quentin Prison Register, no. 1133, Jesús Mendoza.

18. San Quentin Prison Log Book, June 25, 1859; Lamott, *Chronicles of San Quentin,* 72; *San Francisco Alta California,* June 27, 1859; *San Francisco Bulletin,* June 27, 29, 1859.

19. *San Francisco Chronicle,* August 9, 1903.

20. *San Francisco Alta California,* June 27, 1859; *San Francisco Bulletin,* June 27, 1859; *San Francisco California Police Gazette,* July 2, 1859; *San Jose Patriot,* July 27, 1874; Sawyer, *Life and Career of Tiburcio Vasquez,* 6.

21. *San Francisco Bulletin,* June 29, 1859; *San Francisco Alta California,* June 30, 1859.

22. *San Francisco Bulletin,* May 15, 1874; Henry N. Morse, diary, 1871–72, author's collection.

23. Stephens, *Life Sketches of a Jayhawker of '49,* 46–47; *Stockton San Joaquin Republican,* July 15, 16, 1859; *San Jose Mercury,* March 20, 1875.

24. *People v. Jesus Mindosa* [sic] *and Tebruzzo Baskes* [sic]; *Stockton San Joaquin Republican,* July 22, 1859.

25. *San Francisco Weekly Alta California,* August 20, 1859.

26. Cerruti, *Ramblings in California,* 96; Beers, *California Outlaw,* 163; Mortimer, *Life and Career of Charles Mortimer,* 53.

27. *Sacramento Union,* October 26, 1859.

28. San Quentin Daily Log, September 27, 1859; *San Francisco Bulletin,* September 28, 1859; *San Francisco Alta California,* September 28, 29, 1859; *San Francisco Herald,* September 28, 29, 1859; *San Francisco California Police Gazette,* October 8, 1859; *Sacramento Union,* September 29, 30, 1859. John Simms, the prison superintendent, reported that "a Mexican" had tried to kill Lieutenant Moon. Since the daily log shows Vasquez was the only Hispanic there, it is evident that he was the assailant.

CHAPTER SIX

1. *Sacramento Union,* October 15, 1859; *Nevada City Democrat,* October 19, 1859.

2. *San Francisco Alta California,* October 24, 1859; *Sacramento Union,* October 26, 1859; Munro-Fraser, *History of Contra Costa County,* 344–45. Norberto Gradillas was a cigar maker in San Juan Bautista (Census Population Schedules, 1860, Monterey County, San Juan Township, p. 378).

3. Application for Pardon, Tiburcio Basques [*sic*], Governor's Pardon Papers.

4. Ibid.

5. Ibid.

6. Boessenecker, *Gold Dust and Gunsmoke,* 68–69; Governor's Pardon Papers, Nazareno [*sic*] Berreyesa, File No. 1334; *San Francisco Chronicle,* August 9, 1903. Nasario Berreyesa, born in 1835, and Dámaso Berreyesa, born in 1837, were the sons of Nasario Antonio Berreyesa, the original settler of the valley now inundated by the incorrectly spelled Lake Berryessa.

7. San Quentin Prison Daily Log, January 16, 1861; *San Francisco Alta California,* January 17, 18, 1861; *San Francisco Bulletin,* January 17, 1861; *San Francisco Chronicle,* August 9, 1903.

8. *San Francisco Call,* June 5, 1881. On Jesús Villalobo (phonetically spelled Bealoba in contemporary accounts), see Boessenecker, *Badge and Buckshot,* 71–72.

9. *San Francisco Alta California,* July 23, 24, 26, 1862; *San Francisco Bulletin,* July 23, 24, 25, 1862; *Marin County Journal,* July 26, August 2, 23, 1862; *San Francisco Call,* June 5, 1881; *San Francisco Chronicle,* October 20, 1907; Mortimer, *Life and Career of Charles Mortimer,* 54; Lamott, *Chronicles of San Quentin,* 82–93.

10. Mortimer, *Life and Career of Charles Mortimer,* 54.

CHAPTER SEVEN

1. *San Francisco Call,* March 8, 1920.

2. Guinn, *History and Biographical Record,* 2:657–58; Howard, *Adobes and Indian Middens of Monterey County,* 2:1. Jesús Soto died a widower on December 9, 1866 (Dennis Copeland to author, November 4, 2007).

3. Census Population Schedules, 1860 and 1870, Monterey County, San Juan Township; Shumate, *Boyhood Days,* 1–7, 44.

4. *San Francisco Call,* March 8, 1920; Truman, *Life, Adventures, and Capture of Tiburcio Vasquez,* 15; Beers, *California Outlaw,* 164–65. Tiburcio also stated, erroneously, that in 1863 he was accused of being a confederate of the noted bandits Juan Soto and Procopio. In fact, Procopio entered San Quentin in 1863, and Vasquez did not join him until Procopio was released in 1871. Vasquez did not ride with Juan Soto until 1865, two years later.

5. Shumate, *Boyhood Days,* 6–12; *San Francisco Alta California,* November 2, 1867; *San Francisco Call,* March 8, 1920; Census Population Schedules, San Juan Township, Monterey County, 1870, household nos. 47 and 330; memoir of Estolano Larios, San Juan Bautista Public Library. Estolano Larios (1855–1941), son of prominent ranchero Manuel Larios, dictated his memoirs of San Juan Bautista to historian Ralph Milliken in the 1930s.

6. Isaac Mylar, *Early Days at the Mission San Juan Bautista* (1929), p. 48, 66.

7. *San Francisco Bulletin,* January 31, 1860; *San Francisco Call,* March 9, 1920. The building at 203 Fourth Street is now owned by the Native Daughters of the Golden West.

8. Reader, *Charole,* 5–6. Faustino Lorenzana and Tiburcio Vasquez were both great-grandsons of Juan Atanasio Vasquez. Faustino's mother, María Romualda Vasquez, was first cousin to Tiburcio's father, Hermenegildo.

9. *San Jose Patriot,* January 6, 1875; Beers, *California Outlaw,* 164–65.

10. *San Jose Mercury,* June 9, 1864, March 20, 1875; *San Jose Patriot,* June 8, July 25, 1874; *San Francisco Bulletin,* January 6, 1875; Beers, *California Outlaw,* 166; Sawyer, *Life and Career of Tiburcio Vasquez,* 7–8; Reader, *Charole,* 6–7; Guinn, *History and Biographical Record,* 1:286. In 1887, Undersheriff Hall, using the pseudonym "Rambler," wrote several colorful accounts for the *San Francisco Post* about his exploits in hunting such early California outlaws as Juan Soto and Captain Rufus Ingram's Confederate guerrillas. His story of Tiburcio Vasquez (*Post,* June 18, 1887), which includes a short account of the Italian butcher's murder, is simply copied from the booklets of Beers and Sawyer, and unfortunately tells nothing of Hall's unique experiences in hunting the Vasquez band.

11. *San Francisco Chronicle,* May 18, 1874; Beers, *California Outlaw,* 165. George Beers recorded this statement during his Los Angeles interviews with Vasquez. He insisted that it was "an honest and correct translation."

12. *San Francisco Bulletin,* November 23, 1864; *Monterey Gazette,* November 25, 1864; memoir of Estolano Larios, vol. 1, p. 32. The newspapers identified the victim as Mr. Shotwell.

13. Guinn, *History and Biographical Record of Monterey and San Benito Counties and History of the State of California,* 2:657–58. Vasquez Knob, elevation 2,136 feet, is just west of Carmel Valley village. Contrary to popular belief, it was not named for Tiburcio. Clark, *Monterey County Place Names,* 588–89.

14. Eugene Sawyer first recorded this incident in the *San Francisco Chronicle,* August 29, 1873; next in *Life and Career of Tiburcio Vasquez,* 8–9; then in "Californian Duval," 37; and finally in his *History of Santa Clara County,* 164. Slightly different versions appear in the *San Jose Daily Mercury,* March 21, 1875, and in Hoyle, *Crimes and Career of Tiburcio Vasquez,* 3. Boyd Henderson's account is in the *San Francisco Chronicle,* May 15, 1874. The *San Francisco Bulletin,* January 6, 1875, gave yet another version but commented, "The people residing about Mount Diablo never heard of this incident until it [recently] appeared in print, and do not take any stock in it." A check of the *Alameda County Gazette* for the years 1864 through 1866 failed to reveal any news stories about this incident. However, the account appeared so often and with so many details that it is credible. Vasquez denied the story, telling a reporter in 1875 that he "had never heard it before." The reporter did not believe him, writing, "It has generally been believed to be true, and may be notwithstanding his denial" (*San Jose Mercury,* March 18, 1875). Eugene Sawyer said that Vasquez himself told him about the incident (*San Francisco Call,* March 12, 1920).

15. Boessenecker, *Lawman*, 51, 86, 86–87.

16. Benjamin Estelle Lloyd, as quoted in Asbury, *Barbary Coast*, 101.

17. Northrop, *Spanish-Mexican Families of Early California*, 1:78–82; *Petaluma Journal and Argus*, February 24, 1874; Munro-Fraser, *History of Marin County*, 313. Bartolomé Bojorques (also spelled Bojorquez) was the son of Pedro Bojorques; the latter was a brother of Tiburcio's grandmother, María Ana Bojorques de Vasquez.

18. *Los Angeles Star*, May 16, 1874; Morse diary, 1866. Morse listed Vasquez by a misspelled nickname, "José Mauraucio alias Borajo."

19. *Petaluma Journal and Argus*, December 21, 1865; *Marysville Daily Appeal*, September 21, 1867; *Alameda County Gazette*, May 18, 1871.

20. *Petaluma Journal and Argus*, June 21, 28, 1866; San Quentin Prison Register, Charles Horace Dade, convict nos. 1132, 3347, 4525, and 7004.

21. *Petaluma Journal and Argus*, July 5, 1866; December 20, 1866; *People v. Tiburcio Vasquez* (1867); *People v. Tiburcio Basques* (1866).

22. *Napa Register*, July 28, September 15, 1866; San Quentin Prison Register, Charles Horace Dade, convict no. 3347. Spanishtown was situated on the east side of the Napa River.

23. *Marin County Journal*, February 3, 1872; *Petaluma Journal and Argus*, October 4, 11, 1866; *People v. Pedro Sais*.

24. *Ukiah Mendocino Herald*, October 5, 1866; *Petaluma Journal and Argus*, October 11, 1866; *Santa Rosa Sonoma Democrat*, October 13, 1866. On Doc Standley see Boessenecker, *Badge and Buckshot*, chap. 4.

25. *Santa Rosa Sonoma Democrat*, October 13, 1866; *Petaluma Journal and Argus*, October 11, November 8, 1866. Jack London mentions the Secret Pasture in two of his Sonoma-based short stories.

26. *Petaluma Journal and Argus*, December 13, 1866; *Santa Rosa Sonoma Democrat*, December 15, 1866. George Watriss was a wealthy rancher and part owner of the Rancho Agua Caliente (Murphy, *People of the Pueblo*, 184–85).

27. *Petaluma Journal and Argus*, December 20, 1866.

28. *People v. Tiburcio Vasquez* (1867); *Petaluma Journal and Argus*, January 17, 1867, September 5, 1873; *Santa Rosa Sonoma Democrat*, January 19, 1867.

CHAPTER EIGHT

1. *San Francisco Call*, March 13, 1920; "Monterey difuntos," p. 515, Monterey Public Library.

2. *Petaluma Journal and Argus*, September 5, 1873, February 24, 1874.

3. U.S. Census Population Schedules, San Juan Township, 1870, p. 32, and Paicines Township, 1880, p. 9.

4. *San Francisco Bulletin*, May 15, 1867.

5. *San Jose Patriot*, May 28, 1874; Truman, *Life, Adventures, and Capture of Tiburcio Vasquez*, 29.

6. Stevenson, *Across the Plains*, 30.

7. In 1947 Hollister was the scene of the so-called Cyclists' Raid, which inspired the 1953 Marlon Brando film, *The Wild One*.

8. Truman, *Life, Adventures, and Capture of Tiburcio Vasquez*, 41; *San Francisco Chronicle*, May 15, 1874.

9. *Gilroy Advocate*, August 20, September 24, 1870; *Visalia Weekly Delta*, August 24, 1870; *Salinas Index*, October 2, 1873.

10. All quotations from *San Jose News,* April 21, 1919.

11. Boessenecker, *Lawman,* 151–54.

12. Ibid., 151–56, 184–94; *San Jose Patriot,* July 27, 1874. An account written by Eugene Sawyer, published in the *San Francisco Chronicle* on August 29, 1873, and another, penned by George Beers or Boyd Henderson in the *San Francisco Chronicle* of May 15, 1874, reported that Vasquez was suspected of the Ludovisi murder. Since these journalists were friends of Sheriffs Morse and Adams, they may have received their information from them.

13. Boessenecker, *Lawman,* 157–59.

14. *San Francisco Call,* March 15, 1920; memoir of Estolano Larios, 1:237; Census Population Schedules, 1860, Monterey County, San Juan Township, household 707; ibid., 1870, p. 55.

15. Morse diary, 1871–72. The author has examined several hundred mug photographs of California Hispanic criminals taken between 1857 and 1900, and not one shows a man wearing Mexican-style clothing.

16. *San Jose News,* July 10, 11, 1922.

17. *Monterey Republican,* May 11, 1871; *Monterey Democrat,* May 13, 1871; *Salinas Standard,* May 13, 1871; *San Jose News,* July 11, 1922.

18. *San Jose Patriot,* May 19, 28, 1874.

19. Nicholas R. Harris (1836–1902) served as Santa Clara County sheriff in 1870–72 and 1876–80. From 1888 to 1898 he was a U.S. Secret Service agent in San Francisco and broke up numerous gangs of counterfeiters.

20. Boessenecker, *Lawman,* 159–69, 193.

21. *San Jose News,* July 11, 1922.

22. *San Jose Patriot,* July 25, 1874.

23. *Monterey Republican,* June 22, 1871; *Castroville Argus,* June 24, 1871; *San Francisco Chronicle,* May 15, 1874; *San Jose News,* July 10, 1922. Mauk's memory failed him in one detail: he stated that he believed Vasquez was not wounded in the gunfight.

24. *San Jose Patriot,* July 25, 1874; Robert Louis Stevenson, "Old Pacific Capital," first published in *Fraser's Magazine,* then in *Across the Plains,* 30. In 1880 Stevenson wrote that Vasquez's visits took place "only four or five years ago," placing them in 1874–75, which was impossible. Tiburcio's Monterey visits would have occurred well before the Tres Pinos Tragedy in 1873.

25. *San Jose Patriot,* July 25, 1874; Canfield's account is in the *Santa Cruz Sentinel,* September 11, 1910. Thomas Watson (1834–1910) was the son of James Watson and Mariana Escamilla. He was a cattleman and butcher and served as sheriff in 1866–72. Garbled versions of this story appear in the *San Francisco Call,* April 17, 1910, *San Francisco Chronicle,* August 9, 1914, and the *Monterey Beacon,* February 2, 1935.

26. Dialogue abstracted from Daniel Martin's diary, Monterey County Historical Society.

27. Sotoville is now part of the city of Salinas.

28. In fact, Procopio had served only one term in prison at this point, and he was of Mexican, not Spanish, birth.

29. Burnham, "I Knew Vasquez," 60–61, 71. In his account Burnham neglected to reveal that he himself had been a notorious outlaw.

30. *San Jose News,* July 10, 1922.

CHAPTER NINE

1. Monterey County Jail Register, inmate no. 281, Pedro Regalado. His full name was Pedro Regalado Valenzuela, and he was born in Los Angeles in 1829 (Dennis Copeland to author, July 23, 2007).

2. *Salinas Daily Post,* January 6, 1934.

3. *San Francisco Chronicle,* May 15, 1874; *San Francisco Call,* March 18, 1920; Harrington Field Notes (1934), Reel 75, p. 94.

4. *San Francisco Call,* March 19, 20, 1920. For the ranch of Cayetano Lugo, see *Gonzales Tribune,* March 19, 1925.

5. *San Francisco Chronicle,* May 18, 1874; Tiburcio's statement is from Beers, *California Outlaw,* 165–66. One suspects that Beers embellished Tiburcio's language, but he insisted that it was "an honest and correct translation."

6. *Monterey Democrat,* August 12, 19, 1871; *Monterey Republican,* August 10, 1871; *Castroville Argus,* August 12, 1871; *Hollister Central Californian,* August 9, 1871; *Salinas Standard,* August 12, 1871; *Watsonville Pajaronian,* August 17, 1871; Hoyle, *Crimes and Career of Tiburcio Vasquez,* 8. The old stage road from Salinas to San Juan was located just south of the present paved road.

7. Hoyle, *Crimes and Career of Tiburcio Vasquez,* 4; Sawyer, *Life and Career of Tiburcio Vasquez,* 13; *San Jose Patriot,* July 25, 1874. Thomas McMahon assisted his father in running a general merchandise store in San Juan. He and his sister Catherine, married, respectively, Isabella Breen and her brother, James F. Breen, who as children had survived the Donner Party ordeal in the winter of 1846–47. Breen would become a prominent judge in San Benito County. Thomas McMahon died in 1902 at the age of sixty. *Hollister Free Lance,* October 3, 1902.

8. *Salinas Standard,* August 12, 1871.

9. Beers, *California Outlaw,* 174–75.

10. *San Francisco Bulletin,* August 19, 28, October 7, 1871; *Gilroy Advocate,* August 12, 1871; *Castroville Argus,* August 19, 1871; *Monterey Democrat,* August 19, 1871; *Monterey Republican,* August 17, 1871; *Hollister Central Californian,* August 16, 1871; *Visalia Weekly Delta,* August 17, 1871; *Castroville Argus,* June 1, 1872; Hoyle, *Crimes and Career of Tiburcio Vasquez,* 8. According to the passengers' testimony in the trial of Narciso Rodríguez, it was Rodríguez who gave most of the orders during the robbery (*San Jose Mercury,* May 29, 1872).

11. *Hollister Central Californian,* August 16, 1871; *San Francisco Bulletin,* August 28, 1871.

12. *Monterey Republican,* August 31, 1871; *San Francisco Bulletin,* August 28, 1871. On the Bullion Bend robbery of 1864, see Boessenecker, *Badge and Buckshot,* chap. 6.

13. *Monterey Democrat,* August 19, 1871; *San Jose News,* June 11, 1918.

14. Beers, *California Outlaw,* 175.

15. The other members of the posse were John Hunter, W. L. Carpenter, M. L. Houk, J. H. Roche, Peter Conroy, J. Peters, and C. Hickey.

16. *Monterey Republican,* August 17, 1871; *Monterey Democrat,* August 19, 1871; *Salinas Standard,* August 19, 1871; *Salinas Daily Post,* January 6, 1934.

17. Beers, *California Outlaw,* 175.

18. On Thomas Watson and Andrew Wasson see Martinez, *Sheriffs of Monterey County,* 9–10.

19. On the development of vigilantism in California, see Boessenecker, *Gold Dust and Gunsmoke,* chap. 3. On the San Francisco Committee of Vigilance, see Boessenecker, *Against the Vigilantes,* 10–36.

20. On Matt Tarpy, see Reader, *Brief History of the Pajaro Property Protective Society,* and Boessenecker, *Gold Dust and Gunsmoke,* 41–43.

CHAPTER TEN

1. Beers, *California Outlaw,* 175; *Santa Cruz Sentinel,* December 12, 1951. Manuel Vasquez was a son of Tiburcio's uncle José Felipe Vasquez.

2. Beers, *California Outlaw,* 175–76.

3. *Santa Cruz Sentinel,* September 16, 1871, August 21, 1938, April 4, 1948; *Monterey Republican,* September 14, 1871; Koch, *Santa Cruz County,* 189, 221; Reader, *Harlots and Whorehouses,* 18–19; idem, "After the Soap Lake Stage Robbery," unpublished ms. The Flat-iron Building was damaged in the 1989 earthquake and was later demolished (Phil Reader to author, May 17, 2006).

4. *Santa Cruz Sentinel,* September 16, 1871; *San Francisco Bulletin,* September 15, 1871; Reader, "After the Soap Lake Stage Robbery;" Koch, *Santa Cruz County,* 148, 221. Robert H. Majors was the son of Joseph Ladd Majors, a trapper who settled in Santa Cruz, where he married María Castro in 1839. Bob Majors served for a time as a Santa Cruz police officer and managed local bitumen mines. In an 1890 saloon dispute he shot and killed his assailant, but was mortally wounded and died eleven months later from his wounds.

5. *Santa Cruz Sentinel,* September 16, 1871; *San Francisco Bulletin,* September 15, 1871; Reader, "After the Soap Lake Stage Robbery;" Koch, *Santa Cruz County,* 148, 221; Phil Reader to author, April 4, 2005. Most sources claim that the badly wounded Vasquez rode into the mountains alone, which was an impossible feat and ignores the help he received from his Santa Cruz friends. The two-story adobe and adjacent bullring owned by Juan Pérez were located where the Santa Cruz County Government Center is now.

6. *Santa Cruz Sentinel,* September 23, 1871; Reader, "After the Soap Lake Stage Rob-bery"; "Nigger Dave Boffman," University of California, Santa Cruz Library.

7. *Monterey Republican,* October 5, 1871; *Salinas Democrat,* October 7, 1871; *San Jose Morning Guide,* September 28, 29, October 3, 1871; *Santa Clara Argus,* December 2, 1871; *San Jose Mercury,* May 29, June 2, 1872.

8. Milliken, *California Dons,* 231–32.

9. *Gilroy Advocate,* November 18, 1871; *Watsonville Pajaronian,* November 16, 1871.

10. Beers, *California Outlaw,* 176; *San Jose Daily Patriot,* July 25, 1874; 1870 Census Pop-ulation Schedules, Monterey Township, pp. 4–5.

11. *San Jose Daily Patriot,* July 25, 1874; Beers, *California Outlaw,* 176. George Beers claimed that Vasquez and Procopio went to Mexico together, but they had already fallen out. Vasquez himself said he went alone.

12. Boessenecker, *Lawman,* 175–80.

13. Kimbro, *Historic Structure Report for Rancho San Andres,* 21, 34–41.

14. *San Jose Mercury,* December 2, 1875; Beers, *California Outlaw,* 177.

15. *San Francisco Call,* April 25, 1872; Beers, *California Outlaw,* 177.

16. Joseph Warren Matthews, diary, April 20, 1872, Bancroft Library; *Salinas Democrat,* April 27, 1872; *Salinas Index,* May 2, 1872; *Hollister Advance,* May 17, 1873; *Hollister Free Lance,* April 2, 1964; *San Jose Mercury,* April 25, 1872; Amelia Taylor, "Historical Piece on San Benito County," collection of Dan Schmidt; Sawyer, *Life and Career of Tiburcio Vasquez,* 16–17; Beers, *California Outlaw,* 177; Kimbro, *Historic Structure Report for Rancho San Andres,* 34–41.

17. J. Warren Matthews, diary, April 23, 1872; *Salinas Democrat,* May 4, 1872.

18. *San Francisco Post,* November 2, 1885; Reader, *Brief History of the Pajaro Property Pro-tective Society.*

19. *San Jose Patriot,* July 25, 27, 1874.

CHAPTER ELEVEN

1. *Tulare Daily Times,* February 2, 1932; *Memorial and Biographical History of the Counties of Fresno, Tulare and Kern,* 320–21. The last buildings standing at Rancho de los Californios burned in 1930.

2. Poso Chane (pronounced "Sha-nay") is often misspelled, with several variations. A housing development in Coalinga is even named Posa Chanet, which has no meaning in any language.

3. U.S. Census Population Schedules, 1880, Fresno Township, p. 274-A. In 1877 Procopio shot it out with a pursuing posse at the Higueras' jacal, killing Sol Gladden before he escaped (see Secrest, *Dangerous Trails,* 123–27).

4. Corinne Stasinos, Hefner family genealogical notes; Margarita Ruiz Hefner to editor of *Lancaster Ledger Gazette,* Palmdale Public Library; Beers, *California Outlaw,* 177–78.

5. Truman, *Life, Adventures, and Capture of Tiburcio Vasquez,* 40. Eulogio Celis became editor of *La Crónica,* the Spanish-language newspaper of Los Angeles.

6. Latta, *Saga of Rancho El Tejon,* 236.

7. Homestead Claim file no. 9634, Agustín Hernández, National Archives. Hernández's ranch was located at Township 16 S, Range 10 E, Section 24.

8. Sawyer, *Life and Career of Tiburcio Vasquez,* 17.

9. *Fresno Bee,* June 13, 1934.

10. Brewer, *Up and Down California,* 143.

11. Sawyer, *Life and Career of Tiburcio Vasquez,* 15–16.

12. Hoyle, *Crimes and Career of Tiburcio Vasquez,* 9; Sawyer, *Life and Career of Tiburcio Vasquez,* 16.

13. Hoyle, *Crimes and Career of Tiburcio Vasquez,* 24. Thomas N. Williams (1839–1904) later became superintendent at New Idria for years (*Hollister Free Lance,* September 23, 1904).

14. Hoyle, *Crimes and Career of Tiburcio Vasquez,* 25.

15. Ibid., 25.

16. Miser, *Pinnacles Story,* 12–14; Johnson and Cordone, *Pinnacles Guide,* 7–9; *San Francisco Examiner,* May 4, 1919; *San Francisco Chronicle,* April 24, 1932; McGrury, "Glimpses into the Days of Tiburcio Vasquez," Deborah Melendy Norman collection.

17. Barrows and Ingersoll, *Memorial and Biographical History of the Coast Counties,* 149; Pierce, *East of the Gabilans,* 138; Oberg, *Administrative History of Pinnacles National Monument,* 23; Deborah Melendy Norman to author, July 24, 2005.

18. Hinman, "The Trail Back," Deborah Melendy Norman collection; Pierce, *East of the Gabilans,* 138.

19. Hinman, "Did Tiburcio Vasquez Really Hide?" Deborah Melendy Norman collection.

20. McGrury, "Glimpses into the Days of Tiburcio Vasquez"; Frusetta, *Beyond the Pinnacles,* 54.

21. *Hollister Free Lance,* Supplement, May 1916; Deborah Melendy Norman to author, August 24, 2005.

22. Edgar Raymond Tully recollections, collection of Dan Schmidt; Barrows and Ingersoll, *Memorial and Biographical History of the Coast Counties,* 431–33.

23. Russell, "Tully Family of Bitterwater," collection of Dan Schmidt.

24. George de Álvarez recollections, collection of Dan Schmidt.

25. Pierce, *East of the Gabilans,* 123; McGrury, "Glimpses into the Days of Tiburcio Vasquez."

26. Chambers, "Experience with Tiburcio Vasquez," William B. Secrest collection. William Short and A. T. D. Button lived near the Chambers family in the Hernandez Valley, according to the 1870 census. In 1873 Ival Button was seventeen years old, and Ira was fifteen. Deborah Melendy Norman to author, September 15, 2005.

27. Hull, "And Then There Were Three Thousand," collection of Dan Schmidt; Deborah Melendy Norman to author, September 15, 2005.

28. McGrury, "Glimpses into the Days of Tiburcio Vasquez"; Steglich, "Salt of the Earth," collection of Dan Schmidt.

29. *San Francisco Chronicle,* May 15, 1874.

30. Latta, *Black Gold in the Joaquin,* 56.

CHAPTER TWELVE

1. *San Francisco Chronicle,* November 15, 1873, May 24, 1874.

2. Beers, *California Outlaw,* 180.

3. *San Jose Patriot,* July 21, 27, 1874.

4. Ibid., July 27, 1874.

5. *San Francisco Call,* February 28, 1873; *San Francisco Chronicle,* March 3, 1873, May 24, 1874; *Fresno Expositor,* March 5, 12, 1873; *San Francisco Bulletin,* November 25, 1873; Beers, *California Outlaw,* 178–79; Sawyer, *Life and Career of Tiburcio Vasquez,* 19–20.

6. Latta, *Saga of Rancho El Tejon,* 234–35; *San Francisco Chronicle,* May 15, 1874; *San Francisco Call,* May 15, 1874.

7. *Fresno Expositor,* April 23, 1873; *San Jose Mercury,* April 24, 1873; Boessenecker, *Gold Dust and Gunsmoke,* 43.

8. *San Francisco Chronicle,* May 24, 1874. Leiva's house had reportedly been the home of Mariana La Loca, who claimed to be the widow of Joaquín Murrieta.

9. *Hollister Advance,* May 24, 1873; Tiburcio Vasquez to Genoveva García, October 11, 1874, Huntington Library. Vasquez claimed he had not been present, but he described it in great detail in a letter he later wrote to his cousin, Genoveva García, for delivery to his attorney, Charles B. Darwin.

10. Beers, *California Outlaw,* 180; Tiburcio Vasquez to Genoveva García, October 11, 1874, Huntington Library.

11. Sawyer, *Life and Career of Tiburcio Vasquez,* 18–19; *Visalia Weekly Delta,* July 10, 1873; *Fresno Expositor,* July 16, 1873. Vasquez later claimed that Leiva but not de Bert took part in this holdup.

12. *San Francisco Chronicle,* May 24, 1874.

13. Ibid.

14. *San Jose Patriot,* August 1, 1873; *San Jose Weekly Mercury,* August 7, 1873; *Gilroy Advocate,* August 2, 1873; *Hollister Advance,* August 2, 1873; *San Francisco Chronicle,* August 3, 1873, May 24, 1874; *San Jose Pioneer,* February 18, 1882; *San Francisco Call,* April 3, 1920; "The 21 Mile House and Vasquez, the Bandit," Morgan Hill Public Library. The Twenty-One Mile House was torn down in 1917. The Vasquez Tree was still standing in 1968, but fell down sometime later (*San Jose Mercury-News,* October 6, 1968). A state historical monument now marks the spot. In true California fashion, the site is now a shopping mall. In later years this robbery gave rise to many absurd but widely believed yarns, such as that Vasquez had robbed the Twenty-One Mile House "many times," often visited there, and used it as a hideout. See, e.g., *Oakland Tribune,* August 2, 1942, and various undated newspaper clippings in the Tennant Family/Twenty-One Mile House file, Morgan Hill Public Library.

15. *San Francisco Chronicle,* August 29, 1873; Sawyer, *Life and Career of Tiburcio Vasquez,* 17–18; Hoyle, *Crimes and Career of Tiburcio Vasquez,* 9, 13.

16. *San Francisco Chronicle,* May 24, 1874; *San Francisco Bulletin,* December 6, 1873.

17. *Pacific Coast Business Directory;* Truman, *Life, Adventures, and Capture of Tiburcio Vasquez,* 15; Stiles, *Jesse James,* 170, 315; Beers, *California Outlaw,* 74.

CHAPTER THIRTEEN

1. *San Francisco Chronicle,* May 24, 1874; *San Jose Patriot,* January 7, 1875.
2. *San Francisco Chronicle,* August 29, 1873.
3. *San Jose Mercury,* January 7, 1875.
4. *San Francisco Chronicle,* May 24, 1874; Sawyer, *Life and Career of Tiburcio Vasquez,* 24.
5. In all prior accounts Davison's name is misspelled Davidson. A wheelwright, he was born in Nova Scotia in 1831, married Elizabeth Burton in 1858, came to California in 1869, and settled in Tres Pinos in 1872 (Deborah Melendy Norman to author, September 17, 2004).
6. Much confusion exists about the layout of old Tres Pinos. Contrary to popular belief, the present-day store is not the one robbed by Vasquez. Snyder's original store and hotel on the east side of the old north-south stage road to Hollister were destroyed by fire in 1876 (*Hollister Advance,* September 23, 1876). The following year, the current store was built on the west side of the road, opposite its previous location. The hotel was rebuilt on its original site, and burned down in 1919. The highway through Paicines continued to follow the old stage route until the flood of 1938, when the San Benito River and Tres Pinos Creek washed out a portion of it. The present highway, State Route 25, was built a few hundred feet to the west of the old road, so that it passed the rear of the store instead of the front. The owner converted the back of the store into an entrance facing the newly routed highway and built an addition onto the old façade, which is now the rear of the store. That is how it stands today. The spot where the murders took place is now a vineyard directly behind the current store. The route of the old stage road can still be seen running north-south between the rear of the store and the vineyard.
7. In most accounts, Bernard Bahury is incorrectly identified as Bernal Bihury or Berhuri, neither of which is a Portuguese name.
8. This account of the Tres Pinos Tragedy is based primarily on the testimony of the witnesses at Vasquez's murder trial, from a copy of the trial testimony in the author's collection.
9. *San Francisco Chronicle,* August 28, 1873; *Los Angeles Star,* September 10, 1873.
10. John Hicks Adams (1820–78) served as a captain of volunteers during the Mexican War, joined the gold rush in 1849, and served several terms as sheriff in San Jose. He had played a leading role in breaking up a band of Confederate guerrillas that had terrorized parts of California during the Civil War. He served as sheriff of Santa Clara County in 1864–70 and 1872–76. He was slain by Mexican bandits while serving as a deputy U.S. marshal in Arizona Territory. On California's Confederate guerrillas, see Boessenecker, *Badge and Buckshot,* chap. 6.
11. The Hollister volunteers were Henry Smith, Otho Jones, Frank A. Rounds, Robert Ransfield, Frederick Beach, and George M. Noble. At Tres Pinos and San Benito they were joined by Constable George Chick, Bolivar Smith, James W. Mills, John Shell, and Louis L. Land, making a total of thirteen (*San Jose Weekly Mercury,* September 18, 1873). The San Francisco newspapers erroneously reported that Harry Morse led a posse into the San Joaquin Valley after the Tres Pinos killers. In fact, the Alameda sheriff stayed out of the hunt, fearing that he would be accused of grandstanding in the midst of his own reelection campaign (*Alameda County Gazette,* September 6, 1873).

CHAPTER FOURTEEN

1. *Salinas Index,* October 2, 1874; *People v. Tiburcio Vasquez* (1875), District Court case files.
2. The preceding account is from the copy of Vasquez trial testimony in author's collection; Sawyer, *Life and Career of Tiburcio Vasquez,* 28–30; Beers, *California Outlaw,* 184–85; Latta, *Saga of Rancho El Tejon,* 225–27.

3. *Gilroy Advocate,* September 6, 1873; *Hollister Advance,* September 13, 1873; J. Warren Matthews diary, August 28, 29, 1873.

4. *Hollister Advance,* September 13, 1873; *Salinas Index,* October 9, 1873; Beers, *California Outlaw,* 188.

5. *Hollister Advance,* September 13, 1873.

6. Ibid.

7. *San Jose Weekly Mercury,* September 18, 1873.

8. *Visalia Weekly Delta,* September 11, October 2, 1873; Beers, *California Outlaw,* 189–90.

9. Trial testimony of John H. Adams, in author's collection; *Visalia Weekly Delta,* October 2, 1873; Beers, *California Outlaw,* 190–91; Sawyer, *Life and Career of Tiburcio Vasquez,* 33–35.

10. Rowland was the son of frontiersman John Rowland and María Encarnación Martínez of New Mexico. He was born November 11, 1846, on his parents' rancho in what is now La Puente in Los Angeles County. Educated at Santa Clara College, he served as sheriff in 1872–76 and again in 1880–82. When oil was discovered on Rancho La Puente he became wealthy. Rowland died in Los Angeles on February 2, 1926 (*Los Angeles Times,* February 3, 1926); Crongeyer, *Sixgun Sound,* 142–43, 167–68.

11. Pete Gabriel later had a long career as a lawman in Arizona, and is best remembered for his 1888 gunfight at Globe in which he killed his former deputy, Joe Phy. Henry M. Mitchell (1846–90) was sheriff of Los Angeles County from 1878 to 1880 and undersheriff from 1887 to 1890.

12. Delano's, a stop on the old Butterfield stage route, was first known as Gordon's Station and then as Widow Smith's. Built by Major Gordon about 1857, it is often misidentified as "Major Gorman's station."

13. Chico López was also, ironically, the father-in-law of Los Angeles City Marshal William C. Warren, who was killed in an 1870 gunfight, and the grandfather of Eugene Biscailuz, the highly popular sheriff of Los Angeles County who served longer than any other man (1932–58).

14. *Los Angeles Daily Star,* September 11, 12, 1873; *San Francisco Call,* September 11, 1873; *San Francisco Bulletin,* September 11, 1873; Beers, *California Outlaw,* 185–87, 197. Jenkins, as a young officer in 1856, had rashly shot a Californio, igniting a race riot in Los Angeles (Boessenecker, *Gold Dust and Gunsmoke,* 66–67).

15. *San Jose Daily Patriot,* July 27, 1874.

16. Trial testimony of Sheriff John H. Adams; *Los Angeles Star,* September 12, 1873; *San Jose Weekly Mercury,* September 18, 1873; *Visalia Weekly Delta,* October 2, 1873; *San Francisco Bulletin,* September 10, 1873; *San Francisco Call,* September 11, 1873; Beers, *California Outlaw,* 187–97.

17. *San Francisco Chronicle,* November 15, 1873.

18. *Los Angeles Star,* May 16, 1874; *San Francisco Chronicle,* November 15, 1873.

19. *Los Angeles Star,* September 11, 1873.

20. Beers, *California Outlaw,* 197–98; *San Francisco Call,* September 17, 1873; *San Francisco Chronicle,* January 8, 1875; *Bakersfield Southern Californian,* September 11, 1873.

21. A mountain lion makes a shrill, piercing whistle as an alarm when it is treed or cornered; a female uses this whistle to signal her cubs.

22. *San Francisco Chronicle,* November 15, 1873.

23. *Los Angeles Star,* May 16, 1874.

24. *Gilroy Advance,* September 6, 1873; *San Jose Patriot,* September 1, 1873; *San Jose News,* April 21, 1919.

25. *San Jose Weekly Mercury,* September 18, 1873; *Salinas Index,* September 18, 1873; *Visalia Weekly Delta,* October 3, 1873; *San Francisco Call,* September 17, 1873; Sawyer, *Life and Career of Tiburcio Vasquez,* 40–41.

26. *San Francisco Call,* September 28, 1873; *Salinas Index,* October 2, 1873; *Castroville Argus,* October 4, 1873. On Pleasant B. "Bob" Tully see Munro-Fraser, *History of Santa Clara County,* 633.

27. *Los Angeles Star,* September 11, 1873; *San Francisco Chronicle,* September 18, 1873; *San Jose Weekly Mercury,* September 18, 1873.

28. *Salinas Index,* October 9, 1873.

29. *San Francisco Chronicle,* August 29, 1873; *San Jose News,* April 21, 1919.

30. On the Medina murder case, see Boessenecker, *Lawman,* 130–31, 148–49.

31. *Hollister Enterprise,* October 25, 1873; *Salinas Index,* October 30, 1873: Beers, *California Outlaw,* 205–208.

32. *San Jose Weekly Mercury,* November 6, 1873. John Phelps (1843–80) was the son-in-law of District Court Judge Craven P. Hester of San Jose (Millard, *History of the San Francisco Bay Region,* 3:215–16).

CHAPTER FIFTEEN

1. *San Jose Weekly Mercury,* November 20, 1873; *San Francisco Call,* November 15, 1873; *San Francisco Bulletin,* November 19, 1873; *San Luis Obispo Tribune,* November 15, 1873; *Hollister Advance,* November 15, 22, 1873; *Fresno Expositor,* November 19, 1873; Sawyer, *Life and Career of Tiburcio Vasquez,* 42–44.

2. *Bakersfield Southern Californian,* November 13, 20, December 4, 1873; *Kern County Weekly Courier,* December 6, 1873; *Havilah Miner,* November 15, 29, 1873; Latta, *Saga of Rancho El Tejon,* 233–34.

3. *Fresno Expositor,* November 12, 1873; *San Francisco Call,* November 14, 15, 1873; Winchell, *History of Fresno County and the San Joaquin Valley,* 94–95.

4. Winchell, *History of Fresno County and the San Joaquin Valley,* 95.

5. *Fresno Expositor,* November 26, 1873; Winchell, *History of Fresno County and the San Joaquin Valley,* 95–96; Wood, *Mariana La Loca.* Mariana's claims were widely accepted in the Hispanic community. It is possible, perhaps even probable, that she was the young New Mexican woman Ana Benítez, sometimes referred to as María Ana Benítez, who had been Joaquín Murrieta's lover in Los Angeles in 1852 when he was suspected of killing General Joshua Bean. On Ana Benítez, see Boessenecker, *Gold Dust and Gunsmoke,* 80, 85–86.

6. *San Francisco Chronicle,* November 15, 1873.

7. *San Francisco Bulletin,* November 25, 1873; *San Jose Patriot,* July 21, 1874.

8. The preceding account is all from a copy of trial testimony in the author's collection.

9. *Salinas Index,* November 27, December 4, 1873; *Hollister Advance,* November 29, 1873.

10. *Visalia Weekly Delta,* December 11, 1873; *Tulare Daily Times,* February 2, 1932.

11. *Visalia Delta,* January 1, 1873.

12. Smith, *Garden of the Sun,* 455–56.

13. *Los Angeles Star,* May 16, 1874.

14. *Hanford Sentinel,* May 16, 1973; *Memorial and Biographical History of the Counties of Fresno, Tulare and Kern,* 431, 750–51; Vandor, *History of Fresno County,* 1:725.

15. Kathleen E. Small, *History of Tulare County,* 1:380.

16. *Visalia Delta,* January 1, 8, 1874; *Los Angeles Evening Express,* December 29, 1873; *Bakersfield Southern Californian,* January 1, 1874; *Kern County Weekly Courier,* January 3, 1873; Secrest, "Kingston Raid!"; Beers, *California Outlaw,* 208–11; Small, *History of Tulare County,* 1:379–81; Winchell, *History of Fresno County and the San Joaquin Valley,* 96–97; Vandor, *History of Fresno County,* 1:173–74.

17. Senate Bill 183 (1878), California State Archives; *Visalia Delta,* January 1, 8, 1874; Beers, *California Outlaw,* 211.

18. *Visalia Delta,* January 15, 29, 1874; *Fresno Expositor,* January 21, 1874.

19. *Los Angeles Star,* May 16, 1874.

20. *Fresno Expositor,* January 7, 1874; Beers, *California Outlaw,* 212; Bailey, *Kern County Place Names,* 21.

21. *Visalia Delta,* January 8, 1874.

22. *Fresno Expositor,* January 14, 1874; Winchell, *History of Fresno County and the San Joaquin Valley,* 97.

23. *San Francisco Chronicle,* January 21, 24, 1874. *Fresno Expositor,* January 21, 28, 1874; *Tulare Daily Times,* February 2, 1932.

24. *Fresno Expositor,* January 21, February 4, 11, 1874; *People v. Procella Anamantoria* in Senate Bill 183 (1878).

25. *San Francisco Chronicle,* February 7, 1874; *Visalia Delta,* February 5, 1874; *Los Angeles Express,* February 10, 21, 1874; Beers, *California Outlaw,* 214–15.

26. During the nineteenth century, Robbers' Roost was also called Vasquez Rocks (*Los Angeles Times,* April 15, 1897).

27. *Independence Inyo Independent,* February 28, March 7, 1874; *San Francisco Call,* March 8, 1874; *San Francisco Chronicle,* February 28, 1874; *Kern County Weekly Courier,* February 28, 1874; *Los Angeles Express,* February 28, March 3, 7, 1874; *Los Angeles Herald,* February 28, March 3, 1874; *Los Angeles Star,* March 1, 1874; *Oakland Tribune,* September 21, 1874; Beers, *California Outlaw,* 215–17; Edwards, *Freeman's,* 17–29. Both Beers and Edwards incorrectly give the robbery date as February 25. Oliver Roberts, a noted desert character, falsely claimed to have witnessed the robbery from a nearby hill. Although his account is often credited as factual, it most certainly is not. Roberts's fictitious story is in Walter, *Great Understander,* 184–86. "Old Tex" Shore, identified as M. P. Shore or W. P. Shore in some accounts, was a colorful frontiersman. He later settled in Panamint, where he reportedly turned down an offer of $1,000 for his life story (*Panamint News,* March 20, 1875).

28. *Little Rock Republican,* October 8, 1873; *Chicago Inter Ocean,* May 22, 1874; *New York Times,* March 28, April 26, 1874.

29. *San Francisco Chronicle,* March 7, 1874.

CHAPTER SIXTEEN

1. Boessenecker, *Lawman,* 196–97.

2. On Harry Morse and the hunt for Vasquez, see Boessenecker, *Lawman,* chap. 13.

3. *San Francisco Chronicle,* March 5, 7, 1874.

4. Ibid., May 15, 1874.

5. Ibid., April 23, 1874.

6. Ibid., April 20, 1874; Beers, *California Outlaw,* 225–26, 230.

7. *San Francisco Chronicle,* May 17, 1874.

8. H. N. Morse to Governor Newton Booth, March 21, 1874, Tiburcio Vasquez Reward File, California State Archives.

9. *San Francisco Chronicle,* April 20, 1874.

10. Ibid., May 15, 1874.

11. Ibid., May 18, 1874.

12. Ibid.

13. Ibid.

14. H. N. Morse to Newton Booth, April 12, 1874, Tiburcio Vasquez Reward File.

CHAPTER SEVENTEEN

1. *Los Angeles Express,* March 2, 1874; *San Francisco Chronicle,* March 4, 1874; *Inyo Independent,* March 14, 1874.

2. *Hollister Enterprise,* April 4, 1874; *Los Angeles Herald,* March 21, April 18, 1874; *Los Angeles Express,* April 18, 1874; *San Francisco Chronicle,* April 18, 1874; Newmark, *Sixty Years in Southern California,* 458.

3. Beers, *California Outlaw,* 232; Truman, *Life, Adventures, and Capture of Tiburcio Vasquez,* 29.

4. Latta, *Saga of Rancho El Tejon,* 235–36. The amount of the reward at this time was actually $3,000.

5. *Los Angeles Express,* March 31, 1874; *Los Angeles Herald,* April 1, 24, 1874.

6. *Los Angeles Star,* May 19, 1874; Beers, *California Outlaw,* 232–33.

7. The ruins of the Repetto adobe melted away in heavy rains in 1927 (*Los Angeles Times,* April 28, 1927, September 28, 1952).

8. *Los Angeles Star,* May 16, 1874.

9. Justo Chávez was a noted bandit hunter. In 1871, as chief of the Mexican Frontier Police, he led the posse that tracked down and killed the notorious murderer Stephen Samsbury, alias "Buckskin Bill," alias "Six-toed Pete." Albert J. Johnston, born in New York state in 1832, settled in Los Angeles in about 1870, and served as undersheriff for Billy Rowland from 1872 to 1876. He later returned to Canajoharie, New York, where he died in 1887 (*Los Angeles Times,* June 5, 1887). Frank Hartley was later a lawman in Arizona, where he spelled his last name Hartlee.

10. *Los Angeles Star,* April 17, 28, 1874; *Los Angeles Express,* April 16, 17, 1874; *Los Angeles Times,* April 28, 1927; *San Francisco Bulletin,* April 17, 1874; *San Francisco Chronicle,* April 18, 1874; Beers, *California Outlaw,* 236–40; Newmark, *Sixty Years in Southern California,* 454. According to Will Thrall, the Miles holdup took place near Sheep Corral Spring, which is now in Pasadena's Brookside Park.

11. Beers, *California Outlaw,* 242.

12. *San Francisco Chronicle,* April 23, May 15, 1874; Keffer, *History of San Fernando Valley,* 55.

13. *San Francisco Chronicle,* April 23, 1874.

14. *San Francisco Chronicle,* April 18, 1874; *Los Angeles Times,* December 29, 1889; *Los Angeles Herald,* May 9, 1874.

15. Quoted in Griswold del Castillo, *Los Angeles Barrio,* 114. On violence in 1850s Los Angeles, see Boessenecker, *Gold Dust and Gunsmoke,* 58–68, 79–86, 117–33, 250–54, 285–86, 323.

16. *Los Angeles Express,* May 7, 11, 1874; *Los Angeles Herald,* May 9, 1874.

17. Phineas Banning to Newton Booth, May 7, 8, 13, 1874, and C. W. Bush to Newton Booth, May 10, 1874, in Tiburcio Vasquez Reward File, California State Archives.

18. Truman, *Life, Adventures, and Capture of Tiburcio Vasquez,* 42–43.

19. Buschlen, *Senor Plummer,* 102–108. Eugenio Rafael Plummer (1852–1943) later became a much-beloved Los Angeles patriarch and "the best storyteller in town" (*Los Angeles Times,*

May 20, 1943). His former home, Plummer Park, is located at 7377 Santa Monica Boulevard, in West Hollywood.

20. *San Francisco Chronicle,* April 25, 1874.

21. Ibid., April 27, 1874; Boessenecker, *Lawman,* 206.

CHAPTER EIGHTEEN

1. Latta, *Saga of Rancho El Tejon,* 236.

2. Beers, *California Outlaw,* 257; Boessenecker, *Lawman,* 206–207.

3. *Los Angeles Herald,* May 15, 1874; *Los Angeles Times,* December 29, 1889; Boessenecker, *Lawman,* 206–207, 210.

4. Reward notice of Governor Newton Booth, May 8, 1874, Tiburcio Vasquez Reward File, California State Archives; *Los Angeles Herald,* May 9, 1874.

5. In fact, George Beers carried a Henry rifle, not a shotgun.

6. The woman was Modesta López. Greek George's wife, Cornelia, had just given birth and was confined to her bed. By "overalls" Harris means trousers; bib overalls were not used until after 1900.

7. In fact, six buckshot fired by Hartley and one rifle bullet fired by Beers struck Vasquez. There is some question as to whether Harris actually hit Vasquez at all. Beers said Harris's bullet struck the wall. In a public dispute between Emil Harris and ex-sheriff George Gard during an 1892 political campaign, Gard argued persuasively that Harris's shot had in fact missed Vasquez (*Los Angeles Express,* August 16, 23, 27, September 1, 1892).

8. *Los Angeles Herald,* August 3, 1902.

9. *Los Angeles Express,* May 15, 1874; *Los Angeles Star,* May 15, 1874; Truman, *Life, Adventures, and Capture of Tiburcio Vasquez,* 39.

10. *Los Angeles Express,* May 15, 1874; Bancroft, *History of California,* 7:205.

11. *Los Angeles Express,* May 15, 1874; *Los Angeles Herald,* May 15, 1874; *Los Angeles Times,* December 29, 1889. Emil Harris kept the knife, a New England–made bowie with a six-inch blade, for forty-six years, then gave it to western author E. A. Brininstool in 1920. It was acquired by Jack Reynolds in 1950, who sold it to a prominent Los Angeles collector in 1959. It is now in the author's collection.

12. *San Francisco Bulletin,* May 15, 1874; *Los Angeles Star,* May 19, 20, June 7, 16, 1874; *Los Angeles Herald,* May 15, 19, 1874; *Los Angeles Express,* May 21, 28, June 18, 1874, August 16, 1892; *Los Angeles Times,* December 29, 1889, September 3, 1913.

13. *Los Angeles Express,* May 21, 1874; *Oakland Tribune,* September 21, 1874.

14. *San Francisco Chronicle,* May 19, 1874; Beers, *California Outlaw,* 269–70; Newmark, *Sixty Years in Southern California,* 458.

15. *Los Angeles Star,* May 15, 1874; *Los Angeles Herald,* May 16, 1874.

16. *Los Angeles Herald,* May 16, 1874.

17. *Los Angeles Star,* May 16, 1874.

18. *Los Angeles Herald,* May 16, 1874.

19. *La Crónica,* May 16, 23, 1874.

20. *Los Angeles Star,* May 21, 1874; *Oakland Tribune,* September 21, 1874.

21. *Los Angeles Star,* May 19, 1874. Truman asserted, "We have in no respect exaggerated the character of the interview."

22. *San Francisco Chronicle,* May 20, 1874.

23. *Los Angeles Express,* May 23, 1874; *Los Angeles Star,* May 23, 26, 1874.

24. *Los Angeles Herald,* May 24, 1874.

CHAPTER NINETEEN

1. *San Francisco Alta California,* May 29, 1874; *Los Angeles Star,* May 24, 1874; *Los Angeles Herald,* May 24, 1874; *San Francisco Chronicle,* May 28, 1874; *Ventura Signal,* May 30, 1874; Sheridan, *History of Ventura County,* 158.

2. *San Francisco Bulletin,* May 27, 1874.

3. *San Francisco Call,* May 28, 1874; *San Francisco Alta California,* May 28, 1874.

4. *San Jose Patriot,* May 28, 1874; *Los Angeles Herald,* May 29, 1874; *Monterey Herald,* May 30, 1874; *Hollister Advance,* June 20, 1874; *Napa Register,* June 4, 1874.

5. Tiburcio Vasquez to Felipe Fierro, June 2, 1874; Tiburcio Vasquez, attorney engagement agreement, June 6, 1874; Tiburcio Vasquez to C. B. Darwin, July 25, September 11, November 11, 1874, all in Huntington Library.

6. *San Jose Patriot,* June 19, 24, 1874. Tom Jones (whose aliases were McGuire, McGrath, and Tim Murphy) was sent to San Quentin three years later for killing a man in San Francisco. In prison he stabbed to death the notorious stage robber Elisha W. "Bigfoot" Andrus on August 6, 1879, and was hanged for the murder a year later, on August 6, 1880 (*San Francisco Bulletin,* August 6, 1880; Boessenecker, *Badge and Buckshot,* 53).

7. *San Jose Mercury,* July 21, 1874; *Castroville Argus,* July 25, 1874.

8. This was the jail attacked by a huge mob that lynched the Brooke Hart kidnappers in 1933. Later deemed antiquated and insecure, it was demolished in 1958.

9. *San Jose Patriot,* July 20, 21, 1874; *Los Angeles Express,* July 25, 1874.

10. *San Jose Patriot,* July 27, 1874.

11. *San Jose Mercury,* July 22, 1874; *San Jose Patriot,* July 25, August 1, 1874, January 9, 1875; *Oakland Tribune,* July 25, 1874; *Kern County Weekly Courier,* October 10, 1874.

12. *Los Angeles Express,* June 18, July 25, 1874; *Los Angeles Star,* July 31, 1874; Crongeyer, *Sixgun Sound,* 159.

13. Order Granting Motion for Change of Venue, August 3, 1874, *People v. Tiburcio Vasquez,* Santa Clara County Clerk; *San Jose Patriot,* September 7, 1874; *Los Angeles Express,* September 11, 1874; *Los Angeles Star,* September 11, 1874; *Hollister Enterprise,* September 12, 1874.

14. Charles G. Johnston to George A. Beers, September 25, 1874, Huntington Library.

15. Edward C. Tully to Charles Ben Darwin, November 30, 1874, Huntington Library.

16. Charles B. Darwin to John L. Love, August 4, 1874; Tiburcio Vasquez to C. B. Darwin, November 11, December 18, 1874. Huntington Library; *San Francisco Bulletin,* December 17, 1874.

17. *San Jose Mercury,* September 2, 1874; *Los Angeles Star,* November 21, 1874; *Fresno Republican,* April 12, 1884. Tiburcio's pistol, a .44 caliber Colt's Second Model Dragoon revolver, serial no. 9381, manufactured in 1850 or 1851, taken by the posse, was returned to his sister, María Lara. It then passed to her youngest daughter, María, who later lived in Gilroy under her married name Mary Gonzáles. She outlived three husbands and died as Mary Mayo in Gilroy in 1935. A friend of the then Mary Gonzáles made a gift of the historic gun in 1920 to Henry Hecker (1861–1947), a prominent Gilroy merchant who served on the Santa Clara County Board of Supervisors from 1916 to 1945. Hecker donated the revolver to the California Historical Society in 1941. It was deaccessioned in 1988 when the cash-strapped society sold its gun collection, and is now in the author's collection.

18. *San Jose Mercury,* January 28, 1875; *Los Angeles Times,* December 29, 1889.

19. *San Francisco Bulletin,* January 7, 1875.

20. *San Jose Patriot,* July 21, 1874; Affidavit of A. Sellman, January 6, 1875, in *People v. Tiburcio Vasquez,* Santa Clara County Clerk.

21. *San Francisco Bulletin,* January 8, 1875.

22. From copy of trial testimony in author's collection.

23. Ibid.

24. Ibid.

25. Ibid.; *Los Angeles Express,* January 11, 1875.

26. *San Jose Patriot,* January 11, 1875.

27. Beers, *California Outlaw,* 280–82.

28. *San Francisco Chronicle,* March 18, 1875; *San Jose Mercury,* January 29, February 12, 1875; *San Jose Patriot,* January 28, 1875; *Hollister Enterprise,* January 30, 1875; *Alameda County Gazette,* January 30, 1875; Beers, *California Outlaw,* 282–83; Secrest, "Return of Chavez," 10.

29. *Los Angeles Star,* May 16, 1874; the *Herald* interview is in the *San Francisco Bulletin,* May 16, 1874; *San Jose Patriot,* May 28, 1874; *Oakland Tribune,* September 21, 1874; *San Jose Mercury,* March 19, 1875.

CHAPTER TWENTY

1. From the Spanish text in Sawyer, *Life and Career of Tiburcio Vasquez,* 1; *San Jose Mercury,* December 20, 1937.

2. This ballad and a second poem to Esiquia were translated and published in the *San Jose Mercury,* December 20, 1937. Esiquia García (1854–1936) had saved them, and her husband, Charles Francisco Alva, showed them to the *Mercury.* On the evolution of the Spanish romance into the Mexican border corrido in the mid-nineteenth century, see Paredes, *With His Pistol in His Hand,* chap. 5.

3. *San Jose News,* October 15, 1917.

4. *People v. Tiburcio Vasquez* (1875) 49 Cal. 560–63; *San Francisco Chronicle,* March 18, 1875; *Chicago Tribune,* March 20, 1875.

5. *San Francisco Chronicle,* March 18, 1875; Beers, *California Outlaw,* 284, 292. On Romualdo Pacheco as a bandit hunter, see Boessenecker, *Gold Dust and Gunsmoke,* 116.

6. *San Francisco Chronicle,* March 18, 1875. On Father Serda, see Baker, *Past & Present of Alameda County,* 48.

7. *San Jose Patriot,* March 13, 1875; Beers, *California Outlaw,* 284–85.

8. *San Francisco Bulletin,* March 19, 1875; Sawyer, *Life and Career of Tiburcio Vasquez,* 85; Beers, *California Outlaw,* 286–87.

9. Beers, *California Outlaw,* 287–88.

10. *San Francisco Post,* March 19, 1875.

11. Ibid.; *Chicago Tribune,* March 20, 1875; Tiburcio Vasquez, Power of Attorney, March 18, 1875, Huntington Library; Harrington Field Notes (1934), Reel 73, p. 240.

12. *San Jose Patriot,* March 13, 1875; Beers, *California Outlaw,* 288–89. The scaffold was subsequently used to hang Troy Dye in Sacramento in 1879 and Joseph Jewell in San Jose in 1883 (*San Francisco Bulletin,* November 30, 1883).

13. *San Francisco Post,* March 19, 1875.

14. *San Jose Patriot,* March 19, 1875.

15. *San Francisco Post,* March 19, 1875.

16. *San Francisco Chronicle,* March 20, 1875; *San Jose Mercury,* March 21, 1875; *Chicago Tribune,* March 20, 1875.

17. *San Jose Mercury,* March 21, 1875; *San Jose Weekly Mercury,* March 24, 1875.

18. *San Jose Mercury,* March 17, 19, 1875. Bullock had arrested a defaulter in San Francisco on March 14 and apparently decided to stay a few days to see the hanging (*San Francisco Alta California,* March 15, 1875).

19. *San Jose Mercury,* March 20, 1875.

20. *San Francisco Chronicle,* March 20, 1875.

21. *San Jose Mercury,* March 21, 1875; *San Francisco Chronicle,* March 20, 1875; *New York Tribune,* March 20, 1875; *New York Times,* April 5, 1875.

22. Beers, *California Outlaw,* 295.

23. *San Jose Patriot,* March 20, 1875; *San Jose Mercury,* March 21, 1875; *San Francisco Bulletin,* April 29, 1875; *Los Angeles Express,* April 30, 1875. San Jose's city historian, the late Clyde Arbuckle, told the author that in 1930 Cora Older pressured the parish priest into erecting the new monument. Mr. Arbuckle suspected that Mrs. Older had paid for it. The late Albert Shumate, noted California historian and friend of the author, once questioned Mrs. Older about this. She became very embarrassed and insisted she had no idea who had paid for the headstone, leaving Dr. Shumate convinced of the opposite.

EPILOGUE

1. *Los Angeles Times,* April 3, 17, May 24, 1993. Agua Dulce, located fifty-five miles north of Los Angeles, is the site of Vasquez Rocks.

2. *San Jose Mercury Herald,* May 15, 1919, *Gilroy Dispatch,* August 5, 2006. On the history of filmmaking at Vasquez Rocks, see Wanamaker, "Vasquez Rocks."

3. *San Jose News,* April 25, 1917; *Los Angeles Times,* April 25, 1926, October 21, 1928; *Oakland Tribune,* October 19, 1934. For Vasquez treasure yarns, see Penfield, *Guide to Treasure in California,* and Jameson, *Buried Treasures of California.* There are creeks named for Vasquez in San Benito, San Luis Obispo, and Los Angeles counties.

4. *San Francisco Examiner,* April 17, 1892, April 15, 1913; *Bakersfield Daily Californian,* June 5, 1896; *Philadelphia Inquirer,* October 1, 1912; *San Jose Mercury,* April 14, 1913; *Los Angeles Times,* November 21, 1920, April 28, 1927, July 22, 1934; *San Francisco Chronicle,* November 14, 1920, April 24, 1932.

5. *Los Angeles Times,* July 7, 1954.

6. Newmark, *Sixty Years in Southern California,* 458; *Napa Register,* June 4, 1874.

7. *Salinas Index Journal,* October 24, 1925; *Soledad Bee,* October 30, 1925; *Los Angeles Times,* May 7, 1935; death certificate, Blas Bicuna, author's collection.

8. Thrall, "Haunts and Hideouts of Tiburcio Vasquez," and "Vasquez, the Bandit."

9. McWilliams, *North from Mexico,* 129–31.

10. Hobsbawm, *Primitive Rebels,* 5; idem, *Bandits* (1969 ed.), 13.

11. See, for example, Griswold del Castillo, *Los Angeles Barrio,* 109–10; Mirandé and Enríquez, *Chicana,* 71–72; Acuña, *Occupied America,* 113; Burciaga, "Tiburcio Vasquez, a Chicano Perspective"; Monroy, *Thrown among Strangers,* 215–16; Sánchez, *Telling Identities,* 293–94; Gutiérrez, *Walls and Mirrors,* 35; Buhle and Georgakas, *Immigrant Left in the United States,* 13; Suchlicki, *Mexico,* 171; Vigil, *From Indians to Chicanos,* 157; Meier and Gutiérrez, *Encyclopedia of the Mexican American Civil Rights Movement,* 243; Walton, *Storied Land,* 130; Glenn, *Unequal Freedom,* 174; Carrigan, "Lynching of Persons of Mexican Origin"; Ochoa and Ochoa, *Latino Los Angeles,* 15; Navarro, *Mexicano Political Experience in Occupied Aztlan,* 105–106; Akers Chacón and Davis, *No One Is Illegal,* 23.

12. Castillo and Camarillo, *Furia y muerte,* 2.

13. Pitt, *Decline of the Californios,* 229–41.

14. Numerous critiques of the social bandit concept are compiled and summarized in Slatta, "Eric J. Hobsbawm's Social Bandit." The concept is deconstructed and debunked by Stiles in *Jesse James,* 382–92. For additional criticisms, see Blok, "Peasant and the Brigand";

McKanna, "Banditry in California"; Boessenecker, "California Bandidos"; Thornton, *Searching for Joaquín,* 141–45; and Mullen, *Dangerous Strangers,* 38–39. In the most recent edition of *Bandits* (2000), Hobsbawm acknowledges and accepts some of the earlier criticism but otherwise defends his social bandit concept.

15. Hobsbawm, *Primitive Rebels,* 13, 19; idem, *Bandits* (1969), 34–36.

16. Steckmesser, "Robin Hood and the American Outlaw," 353–54; Slotkin, *Gunfighter Nation,* 128.

17. Prassel, *Great American Outlaw,* 114.

18. Hobsbawm, *Bandits* (1982 ed.), 152.

19. An exhaustive study of the history of American crime and criminal justice, with a comprehensive survey of scholarship, is Friedman, *Crime and Punishment in American History.* Not surprisingly, it contains no reference to social banditry.

20. *La Crónica,* May 16, 1874.

21. *Salinas Daily Index,* December 13, 1907; *Gilroy Advocate,* June 14, 1935.

22. Walton, *Storied Land,* 121–27.

23. *Estate of Antonio M. Vasquez; Salinas Californian,* April 5, 1969.

24. *San Jose News,* January 2, 1919; *San Jose Mercury Herald,* December 3, 1922; Beatriz C. Wing to author, March 16, 17, 18, 2006.

APPENDIX

1. *San Francisco Bulletin,* March 17, 1874; San Quentin Prison Register, inmate no. 5911, Procella Anamantoria; Beers, *California Outlaw,* 211.

2. Mutnick, *Some Alta California Pioneers and Descendants,* 1:127, 128; California State Census, 1852, p. 246; Genealogical information from Dennis Copeland to author, February 11, 2007; Bancroft, *History of California,* 3:673; *Monterey Gazette,* August 10, October 12, 1866; *San Jose News,* March 3, June 13, 1887; *San Francisco Bulletin,* December 2, 1887; San Quentin Prison Register, inmate no. 3685, Obispo Arceo; Death Certificate of Obispo Arceo, courtesy of Sheila Lee Prader.

3. *Martinez Contra Costa Gazette,* January 14, 1865; San Quentin Prison Register, inmate no. 2966, Francisco Barcenas; genealogical research notes of Phil Reader, Santa Cruz, Calif.

4. San Quentin Prison Register, inmate no. 7649, Blas Bicuna; *Modesto News,* November 20, December 10, 12, 14, 19, 1903; death certificate, Blas Bicuna, author's collection.

5. Boessenecker, *Lawman,* 51, 99–102, 174, 322, 326.

6. Ibid., 30–37, 157–60, 173–81; Secrest, *Dangerous Trails,* chap. 3; Delfina Colby (great-granddaughter of Procopio Bustamante) to author, December 22, 2006.

7. U.S. Census Population Schedules, 1870, Los Angeles Township, pp. 39–40; Homestead Application No. 6292, National Archives; Howard Bryan to author, August 1, 2005; *Santa Fe Weekly Gazette,* December 23, 1865; *Los Angeles Times,* December 2, 1882, December 11, 1888, February 6, 1892, September 3, 1913, October 28, 1923, January 29, 1956; Patsis, "Go West Greek George"; Northrop, *Spanish Mexican Families of Early California,* 3:48, 259; Buschlen, *Senor Plummer,* 158–59; Thrapp, *Encyclopedia of Frontier Biography,* 1:225.

8. Northrop, *Spanish Mexican Families of Early California,* 2:48–51; Kimbro, *Historic Structure Report for Rancho San Andres,* 21, 34–41; Dennis Copeland to author, May 1, 2005.

9. Mission San Juan Bautista baptismal register II, p. 96v, no. 4876, courtesy Sheila Lee Prader; Frank F. Latta, "Death of Chavez," California State University at Fresno Library; Secrest, "Return of Chavez," 7; Guinn, *History of California,* 1299–1300; Pourade, *Glory Years,* 129–38. Clodoveo Chávez has undoubtedly the most misspelled name of any American outlaw. His

first name is frequently and incorrectly given as Cleovaro, and also as Clodovio, Cleobello, Clovobello, Clodero, and Crudorado, none of which are Spanish names. The name Clodoveo is Spanish for Clovis (A.D. 466–511), the first king of the Franks.

10. *Los Angeles Express,* June 18, July 25, 1874; *Los Angeles Star,* July 31, 1874; San Quentin Prison Register, convict no. 6104, Librado Corona; California Death Index, 1905–39, p. 2218.

11. *Petaluma Argus,* June 21, 1866; *Russian River Flag,* March 3, 1870; *San Francisco Bulletin,* January 19, 1871; San Quentin Prison Register, inmate nos. 1132, 3347, 4525, 7004, Charles Horace Dade; Governor's Pardon Papers, file no. 2748, California State Archives.

12. Hoyle, *Crimes and Career of Tiburcio Vasquez,* 5–6; Affidavit of William R. Rowland, August 24, 1874, in *People v. Tiburcio Vasquez,* Santa Clara County Clerk; *San Francisco Chronicle,* May 24, 1874; *Los Angeles Times,* April 20, 1893, May 4, 1894; Chickering, "Bandits, Borax and Bears"; Schulz, *Los Angeles County Deaths.*

13. San Quentin Prison Register, inmate nos. 2280, 2642, and 3977, Francisco Galindo; Santa Clara County Clerk, *People v. Juan Soto and Pancho Galindo,* case nos. 1311 and 1312; *San Jose Times,* June 12, August 6, 1880.

14. Northrop, *Spanish Mexican Families of Early California,* 2:97–98; Libro de casamientos, Monterey, November 1, 1847; Oficios, vol. 13, pp. 1217–18; vol. 14, pp. 395–96, Mexican Archives of Monterey County; Padrón de familias del cuartel (Monterey, 1833).

15. *San Francisco Call,* June 18, 19, 1883; *San Jose News,* December 13, 1917, April 2, 1918.

16. Northrop, *Spanish Mexican Families of Early California,* 2:98; Boessenecker, *Gold Dust and Gunsmoke,* 117, 129; *Monterey Gazette,* January 27, March 2, 1865; San Quentin Prison Register, inmate no. 2960, Faustino García.

17. *Havilah Miner,* November 29, 1873; Latta, *Saga of Rancho El Tejon,* 234.

18. Beers, *California Outlaw,* 190–91; *Oakland Tribune,* September 21, 1874.

19. Corinne Stasinos, Hefner family genealogical notes; Margarita Ruiz Hefner to editor of *Lancaster Ledger Gazette,* May 25, 1915, Palmdale Public Library; Corinne Stasinos to author, April 30, 2007; Latta, *Saga of Rancho El Tejon,* 170; Chalfant, *Story of Inyo,* 222–24.

20. Census Population Schedules, 1870, Fresno County, Millerton; Criminal Case No. 1894, Agustín Hernández, vol. 10, Mexican Archives of Monterey County (1841), Monterey Public Library; 1870 Census Population Schedules, Fresno County, Township No. 1; Homestead Application No. 9634, Agustín Hernández, National Archives; Northrop, *Spanish-Mexican Families,* 3:400; McGarrahan, *History of the McGarrahan Claim,* 237–38;. Langum, *Law and Community on the Mexican-California Frontier,* 60; Bancroft, *California Pastoral,* 686–87; Deborah Melendy Norman to author, July 28, September 7, 8, 2005.

21. *San Jose Patriot,* January 6, 1875; *San Francisco Chronicle,* January 7, 1875; *San Francisco Alta California,* April 26, 1875; *San Jose News,* September 19, 1900; *Sacramento Union,* May 15, 1916; Census Population Schedules, Sacramento, 1900, p. 159, 1910, p. 4788; Census Population Schedules, 1920, Los Angeles, p. 4299; Index Register of Deaths in Santa Clara County, 1873–1905, Santa Clara County Recorder's Office; Record Book No. 1, p. 80, Rosana [*sic*] Martínez, Mission Santa Clara Cemetery; Deborah Melendy Norman to author, November 27, 2005, November 1, 2007; Ron Lerch to author, September 18, 2007.

22. Morse diary, 1872; Census Population Schedules, 1870, Fresno County, Monterey Co., 1870, and San Antonio Township, Monterey County, 1880; Angel, *History of San Luis Obispo County,* 311; *Great Register of Monterey County, 1890,* Monterey Public Library; *San Luis Obispo Standard,* August 26, 1871.

23. Reader, *Charole;* genealogical notes of Phil Reader; Mutnick, *Some Alta California Pioneers and Descendants,* 2:638–40; *Santa Barbara Times,* September 3, 1870.

24. San Quentin Prison Register, inmate no. 891, Raphael Menavara, and no. 3694, Rafael Mirabel; *Monterey Gazette,* September 21, 1866, November 21, 1867; *San Jose Mercury,* January 18, 1877, July 30, 1882, June 19, 1883; Boessenecker, *Lawman,* 98, 158–59.

25. Memoir of Estolano Larios, 1:237; Census Population Schedules, 1860, Monterey County, San Juan Township, household 707; Census Population Schedules, 1870, Monterey County, San Juan Township, p. 55; *Monterey Gazette,* June 1, 1866; *Hollister Free Lance,* August 23, 1895; *San Francisco Chronicle,* November 23, 1902.

26. Folsom Prison Register, inmate no. 4091, Ramón Molina; *Fresno Expositor,* September 28, 29, 1892, May 4, 1897; *San Francisco Bulletin,* May 4, 1897; Secrest, "Riders with Vasquez," 25, 57.

27. Albert Warthen to Governor George Stoneman, July 10, 1883, Governor's Pardon Papers, file no. 4007, California State Archives; San Quentin Prison Register, inmate no. 5800, Teodoro Moreno, and inmate no. 7879, Fernando Moreno; *Oakland Tribune,* March 23, 1876; *San Francisco Chronicle,* November 16, 1876; *Visalia Delta,* June 25, 1877; *Los Angeles Times,* November 13, 1888.

28. *San Jose Mercury,* April 25, 1872; *San Jose Patriot,* March 18, 1875; *Hollister Advance,* July 5, 1963; Deborah Melendy Norman to author, September 20, 2005, October 21, 2006.

29. *Stockton Daily Independent,* May 12, 1871; *Los Angeles Express,* January 13, 1874; Boessenecker, *Badge and Buckshot,* 110–12; idem, *Lawman,* 130–31, 148–49.

30. Census Population Schedules, Monterey County, 1850, p. 108; California State Census, 1852, Monterey County, p. 254; San Quentin Prison Register, inmate no. 831, Ramón Rangal; no. 1834, Ramón Rankell; no. 3389, José Ignacio Renguile; and no. 5888, Ignacio Rankel; abstract of Monterey marriage and baptism records for Rangel family, courtesy of Dennis Copeland; *San Francisco Bulletin,* May 15, 1874; *San Francisco Chronicle,* November 16, 1876; *Fresno Expositor,* July 17, 26, 1888, September 21, 1891; Secrest, "Riders with Vasquez," 24.

31. San Quentin Prison Register, inmates no. 3390 and 4017, José Rodríguez; no. 5011 Narciso Rodríguez; *San Jose Mercury,* November 27, 1879; *Santa Cruz Sentinel,* January 28, 1871, July 26, November 10, 1873; Reader, *Charole;* Boessenecker, *Badge and Buckshot,* 74–75.

32. San Quentin Prison Register, inmate nos. 1185 and 3644, Manuel Rojas; *Petaluma Journal and Argus,* December 21, 1865; *Marysville Daily Appeal,* September 21, 1867; *Alameda County Gazette,* May 18, 1871; Boessenecker, *Lawman,* 51, 86–87.

33. Pedro Sais biographical file, Marin History Museum, San Rafael, Calif.; *Marin County Journal,* February 3, 1872; *Marin County Tocsin,* March 19, 1892; Northrop, *Spanish Mexican Families of Early California,* 1:294.

34. Marriage record of Abelardo Salazar and María García, April 17, 1871, Mission San Juan Bautista records; San Quentin Prison Register, inmate no. 3035, Fernando López; inmate no. 3692, Abelardo Salisar; *People v. Abelardo Salazar; San Francisco Chronicle,* May 15, 1874; *San Jose Patriot,* July 25, 1874.

35. *Santa Clara Argus,* November 19, 26, December 3, 1870; *San Jose News,* December 19, 1917, September 7, 1920; Northrop, *Spanish Mexican Families of Early California,* 1:324–26; Boessenecker, *Lawman,* 39, 151–56, 184–95.

36. Mission Santa Clara baptismal record, Juan Bautista Soto, Santa Clara University Archives; *San Francisco Bulletin,* July 3, 1871; Boessenecker, *Lawman,* 39–40, 98–99, 151–56, 159–69.

37. Homestead Application No. 7046, Lorenzo Vasquez, National Archives; U.S. Census Population Schedules, San Benito Township, 1880, 1900; Deborah Melendy Norman to author,

June 5, 2006; *Hollister Pacific Coast,* April 2, 1881; *Hollister Free Lance,* March 11, 1898; Frusetta, *Beyond the Pinnacles,* 48.

38. *Register of Enlistments in the United States Army,* vol. 64, p. 288, Charles W. Weeks, National Archives; Confession of Charles W. Weeks, February 5, 1874, Tiburcio Vasquez Reward File, California State Archives; *San Francisco Bulletin,* January 15, 1869; *Virginia City Territorial Enterprise,* February 4, 1874; *San Jose Weekly Mercury,* February 19, 1874.

Bibliography

ARCHIVES AND UNPUBLISHED MATERIALS

Bancroft Library

Agustín Escobar. Dictations, May 9, 1877.
Joseph Warren Matthews. Diary, 1872.
Florencio Serrano, "Recuerdos históricos."
Hermenegildo Vasquez. Land Claim No. 30. U.S. District Court.
Hermenegildo Vasquez. Land Case 330 SD, Lands, San Juan Bautista.

John Boessenecker Collection

Death certificate, Blas Bicuna.
Henry N. Morse. Diaries, 1866–72.

California Historical Society

California State Census of 1852, Monterey County.
Daughters of the American Revolution. *Early California Wills,* vol. 3.

California State Archives

Governor's Pardon Papers.
Folsom Prison Inmate Register.
San Quentin Prison Daily Log Books.
San Quentin Prison Inmate Register.
Senate Bill 183 (1878). Affidavits in Relation to Procella Anamantoria, one of the Vasquez Band.
Stockton State Hospital, Commitment Registers.

Hermenegildo Vasquez. Expediente 159, Land Grant Records, Spanish and Mexican Archives. Translations, vol. 8.
Tiburcio Vasquez Reward File.

California State University at Fresno Library

Frank F. Latta. "The Death of Chavez," unpublished ms., H. G. Schutt Collection.

Correspondence

Howard Bryan to author, August 1, 2005.
Delfina Colby to author, December 22, 2006.
Dennis Copeland to author, October 11, 2004; January 10, May 1, 2005; January 4, July 24, 2006; February 11, September 27, 2007.
Carlo M. DeFerrari to author, December 16, 2002.
Ron Lerch to author, September 18, 2007.
Deborah Melendy Norman to author, September 17, 2004; July 24, 28, August 24, September 7, 8, 15, 20, November 27, 2005; June 5, October 21, 2006; November 1, 2007.
Phil Reader to author, May 17, 2006.
Corinne Stasinos to author, April 30, 2007.
Beatriz C. Wing to author, March 16, 17, 18, 2006.

Diocese of Monterey Archives

Mission San Juan Bautista baptismal and marriage records.
Mission Carmel baptismal, marriage, and death records.

Fresno Public Library

California Death Index, 1905–39.

Huntington Library

Tiburcio Vasquez–Charles B. Darwin correspondence file.

Patsy Ludwig Collection

San Jose Pueblo Index transcript, 1842–43.
Vasquez family genealogical notes.

Marin History Museum

Pedro Sais biographical file.

Monterey County Historical Society

Daniel Martin. Diary.
Mexican Archives of Monterey. Oficios, vols. 9, 13, 14.

Monterey Public Library, California History Room Archives

Assessment List of Taxable Property for the County of Monterey, 1850.
Book of Deeds, vol. A.
City Assessor's Book, 1851–52.
Great Register of Monterey County, 1890
Libro de casamientos, 1847.
Monterey County Jail Register, 1850–72.
Monterey difuntos.
Padrón de familias del cuartel, 1833.
Padrón del vendario del rancho de San Isidro, 1833.
William Pyburn Papers, series 1.
Solares de Monterey, 1834.

Morgan Hill Public Library

Tennant Family/Twenty-One Mile House file.
"The 21 Mile House and Vasquez, the Bandit," undated ms.

National Archives

John P. Harrington Field Notes (1934–35).
Homestead Application No. 6292, George Allen.
Homestead Application No. 9634, Agustín Hernández.
Homestead Application No. 7046, Lorenzo Vasquez.
Register of Enlistments in the United States Army.
U.S. Census Population Schedules, 1850–1920.

Deborah Melendy Norman Collection

Juanita Burton Hinman, "Did Tiburcio Vasquez Really Hide?" and "The Trail Back," unpublished memoirs.
James B. McGrury, "Glimpses into the Days of Tiburcio Vasquez," unpublished memoir.

Palmdale Public Library

Margarita Ruiz Hefner to editor of *Lancaster Ledger Gazette,* May 25, 1915.

Sheila Lee Prader Collection

Death certificate, Obispo Arceo.

Phil Reader Collection

Phil Reader, "After the Soap Lake Stage Robbery," unpublished ms.

Elayne Silva Reyna Collection

Memoir of Donald McAnaney.

San Juan Bautista Public Library

Memoir of Estolano Larios.

San Mateo County Museum

Evelin Bjorgan, "The Berryessa Family," unpublished ms., 1952.

Santa Clara County Recorder's Office

Index Register of Deaths in Santa Clara County, 1873–1905.

Santa Clara University Archives

Mission Santa Clara Baptismal Records.
Mission Santa Clara Cemetery Record Book no. 1.

Dan Schmidt Collection

George de Álvarez, recollections, undated clipping from *King City Rustler-Herald,* 1951.
Donna Hull, "And Then There Were Three Thousand," unpublished memoir.
Alma Jean Russell, "The Tully Family of Bitterwater," unpublished memoir.
William Steglich, "The Salt of the Earth," undated clipping from *King City Rustler-Herald,* 1951.
Amelia Taylor, "Historical Piece on San Benito County," from undated Hollister newspaper.
Edgar Raymond Tully, recollections, undated clipping from *King City Rustler-Herald,* 1951.

William B. Secrest Collection

James M. Chambers, "An Experience with Tiburcio Vasquez, Notorious Outlaw Chief," unpublished memoir.

Corinne Stasinos Collection

James Hefner family genealogical notes.

University of California Santa Cruz Library

"Nigger Dave Boffman," Leon Rowland files.

Ventura County Museum

Lucy Escandon de Barker, "Dr. M.A.R. de Poli and the Escandon Family," unpublished ms., 1918.
Edwin M. Sheridan, Historical Writings.

COURT RECORDS

Agustín Hernández (1841). Criminal case no. 1894, vol. 10, Mexican Archives of Monterey County. Monterey Public Library.

Estate of Antonio M. Vasquez (1890). Probate case no. 492, Monterey County Superior Court Clerk.

People v. Abelardo Salazar (1867). County Court case no. 1300, Santa Clara County Superior Court Clerk.

People v. Alejandro Ramos (1851). District Court Minutes, vol. A, pp. 53, 56. Monterey County Archives.

People v. Alexander Ramos (1851). Monterey Mayor's Court Docket Book, City Records Project. Monterey Public Library.

People v. Jesus Mindosa [sic] *and Tebruzzo Baskes* [sic] (1859). Amador County Court of Sessions, Book A, pp. 405–15. Amador County Superior Court Clerk.

People v. Juan, an Indian, and Jose, an Indian (1857). Case no. 110, Court of Sessions, Los Angeles County. Huntington Library.

People v. Juan Soto and Pancho Galindo (1867). County Court case nos. 1311 and 1312. Santa Clara County Superior Court Clerk.

People v. Pedro Sais (1866). Case no. 430, Sonoma County Justice Court records. California State Archives.

People v. Tiburcio Basquez (1857). Case no. 109, Register of Actions, Court of Sessions, Los Angeles County. Huntington Library.

People v. Tiburcio Basques (1866). Case no. 432, Sonoma County Justice Court. California State Archives.

People v. Tiburcio Vasquez (1867). Case no. 105 (old series), Sonoma County Court. California State Archives.

People v. Tiburcio Vasquez (1875). District Court case files. Santa Clara County Superior Court Clerk.

People v. Tiburcio Vasquez (1875). 49 Cal. 560. California Supreme Court published reports.

NEWSPAPERS

Alameda County Gazette (San Leandro)
Bakersfield Daily Californian
Bakersfield Southern Californian
Castroville Argus
Chicago Inter Ocean
Chicago Tribune
El Clamor Público (Los Angeles)
La Crónica (Los Angeles)
Fresno Bee
Fresno Expositor
Fresno Republican
Gilroy Advocate
Gilroy Dispatch
Gonzales Tribune
Hanford Sentinel
Havilah Miner
Hollister Advance
Hollister Central Californian
Hollister Enterprise
Hollister Free Lance

Hollister Pacific Coast
Independence Inyo Independent
Kern County Weekly Courier (Bakersfield)
Little Rock (Ark.) Republican
Los Angeles Express
Los Angeles Herald
Los Angeles Star
Los Angeles Times
Marin County Journal (San Rafael)
Marin County Tocsin (San Rafael)
Martinez Contra Costa Gazette
Marysville Daily Appeal
Modesto News
Monterey Beacon
Monterey Democrat
Monterey Gazette
Monterey Herald
Monterey Republican
Napa Register
Nevada City Democrat
New York Times
New York Tribune
Oakland Tribune
Panamint News
Petaluma Journal and Argus
Philadelphia Inquirer
Reno Nevada State Journal
Russian River Flag (Healdsburg)
Sacramento Union
Salinas Californian
Salinas Daily Post
Salinas Democrat
Salinas Index
Salinas Index Journal
Salinas Standard
San Bernardino Guardian
San Diego Union
San Diego World
San Francisco Alta California
San Francisco Bulletin
San Francisco California Police Gazette
San Francisco Call
San Francisco Chronicle
San Francisco Examiner
San Francisco Herald
San Francisco Post
San Jose Mercury/ San Jose Weekly Mercury
San Jose Mercury Herald

San Jose Mercury-News
San Jose Morning Guide
San Jose News
San Jose Patriot
San Jose Pioneer
San Jose Semi-Weekly Tribune
San Jose Telegraph
San Jose Times
San Luis Obispo Standard
San Luis Obispo Tribune
Santa Barbara Gazette
Santa Barbara News and Review
Santa Barbara Times
Santa Clara Argus
Santa Cruz (formerly *Monterey*) *Sentinel*
Santa Cruz Surf
Santa Fe Weekly Gazette
Santa Rosa Sonoma Democrat
Soledad Bee
Sonora Union Democrat
Stockton Daily Independent
Stockton San Joaquin Republican
Stockton Times
Tulare Daily Times
Ukiah Mendocino Herald
Ventura Signal
Virginia City (Nev.) *Territorial Enterprise*
Visalia Weekly Delta
Watsonville Pajaronian
Yuma Sentinel

BOOKS AND ARTICLES

Acuña, Rodolfo. *Occupied America: A History of Chicanos.* New York: Harper and Row, 1981.

Akers Chacón, Justin, and Mike Davis. *No One Is Illegal: Fighting Racism and State Violence on the U.S.-Mexico Border.* Chicago: Haymarket Books, 2006.

Allen, Frederick. *A Decent, Orderly Lynching.* Norman: University of Oklahoma Press, 2004.

Angel, Myron. *History of San Luis Obispo County.* Oakland, Calif.: Thompson and West, 1883.

Annual Report of the Board of State Prison Directors for the Year 1858. Appendix to the Journals of the Senate of the Tenth Session of the Legislature of the State of California. Sacramento: State Printer, 1859.

Asbury, Herbert. *The Barbary Coast.* New York: Alfred A. Knopf, 1933.

Bailey, Richard. *Kern County Place Names.* Bakersfield, Calif.: Kern County Historical Society, 1967.

Baker, Joseph. *Past & Present of Alameda County, California.* Chicago: S. J. Clarke Publishing Co., 1914.

Bancroft, Hubert Howe. *California Pastoral.* San Francisco: History Company, 1888.

———. *History of California.* 7 vols. San Francisco: History Company, 1884–90.

————. *Pioneer Register and Index.* Los Angeles: Dawson's Book Shop, 1964.

————. *Popular Tribunals.* 2 vols. San Francisco: History Company, 1887.

Barrows, Henry D., and Luther A. Ingersoll. *Memorial and Biographical History of the Coast Counties of Central California.* Chicago: Lewis Publishing Co., 1893.

Beers, George A. *The California Outlaw: Tiburcio Vasquez.* Comp. by Robert Greenwood. Reprint, Los Gatos, Calif.: Talisman Press, 1960.

————. *Vasquez; or, the Hunted Bandits of the San Joaquin.* New York: R. M. De Witt, 1875.

Blok, Anton. "The Peasant and the Brigand: Social Banditry Reconsidered." *Comparative Studies in Society and History* 14 (1972): 494–503.

Boessenecker, John. *Against the Vigilantes: The Recollections of Dutch Charley Duane.* Norman: University of Oklahoma Press, 1999.

————. *Badge and Buckshot: Lawlessness in Old California.* Norman: University of Oklahoma Press, 1988.

————. "California Bandidos: Social Bandits or Sociopaths?" *Southern California Quarterly* 80, no. 4 (Fall 1998): 419–34.

————. *Gold Dust and Gunsmoke.* New York: John Wiley and Sons, 1999.

————. *Lawman: The Life and Times of Harry N. Morse.* Norman: University of Oklahoma Press, 1998.

Bolton, Herbert. *Anza's California Expeditions.* 5 vols. Berkeley: University of California Press, 1930.

Brewer, William H. *Up and Down California in 1860–1864.* Berkeley: University of California Press, 1966.

Buhle, Paul, and Dan Georgakas. *The Immigrant Left in the United States.* Albany: State University of New York Press, 1996.

Burciaga, José Antonio. "Tiburcio Vasquez, a Chicano Perspective." *The Californians* 3, no. 3 (May–June 1985): 8–9, 12–13.

Burnham, A. M. (as told to Mary Goodrich). "I Knew Vasquez." *Touring Topics* 22, no. 7 (July 1930): 60–61, 71.

Buschlen, John Preston. *Senor Plummer: The Life and Laughter of an Old Californian by Don Juan.* Hollywood, Calif.: Murray and Gee, 1943.

Camarillo, Albert. *Chicanos in a Changing Society: From Mexican Pueblos to American Barrios in Santa Barbara and Southern California, 1848–1930.* Cambridge, Mass.: Harvard University Press, 1979.

Campbell, Leon G. "The First Californios: Presidial Society in Spanish California, 1769–1822." *Journal of the West* 11, no. 4 (October 1972): 582–95.

Carrigan, William D. "The Lynching of Persons of Mexican Origin or Descent in the United States, 1848 to 1928." *Journal of Social History* 37, no. 2 (Winter 2003): 411–38.

Castillo, Pedro, and Albert Camarillo. *Furia y muerte: Los bandidos chicanos.* Los Angeles: University of California, 1973.

Cerruti, Henry. *Ramblings in California.* Berkeley: Friends of the Bancroft Library, 1954.

Chalfant, W. A. *The Story of Inyo.* Los Angeles: W. A. Chalfant, 1933.

Chickering, Allen L. "Bandits, Borax and Bears: A Trip to Searles Lake in 1874." *California Historical Society Quarterly* 17, no. 2 (June 1938): 99–104.

Clark, Donald Thomas. *Monterey County Place Names.* Carmel Valley, Calif.: Kestrel Press, 1991.

Cleland, Robert Glass. *The Cattle on a Thousand Hills.* San Marino, Calif.: Huntington Library, 1951.

Colton, Walter. *Deck and Port.* New York: A. S. Barnes, 1850.

Crongeyer, Sven. *Sixgun Sound: The Early History of the Los Angeles County Sheriff's Department*. Fresno, Calif.: Craven Street Books, 2006.

Dakin, Susana Bryant. *A Scotch Paisano: Hugo Reid's Life in California, 1832–1852*. Berkeley: University of California Press, 1939.

Edwards, E. I. *Freeman's, A Stage Stop on the Mojave*. Glendale, Calif.: La Siesta Press, 1964.

Egan, Ferol. *Frémont: Explorer for a Restless Nation*. Garden City, N.Y.: Doubleday and Co., 1977.

Fitzgerald, O. P. "A California Bandit: My Three Meetings with Vasquez" *Century Magazine* 63, no. 5 (March 1902): 739–43.

Friedman, Lawrence. *Crime and Punishment in American History*. New York: Basic Books, 1993.

Frusetta, Peter C. *Beyond the Pinnacles*. Tres Pinos, Calif.: Peter C. Frusetta, 1990.

Garcés, Francisco. *On the Trail of a Spanish Pioneer: The Diary and Itinerary of Francisco Garcés in His Travels through Sonora, Arizona, and California, 1775–1776*. New York: Francis P. Harper, 1900.

Gay, Antoinette G. *Calle de Alvarado*. Monterey, Calif.: Monterey Trader Press, 1936.

Glenn, Evelyn Nakano. *Unequal Freedom: How Race and Gender Shaped American Citizenship and Labor*. Cambridge, Mass.: Harvard University Press, 2002.

Griswold del Castillo, Richard. *The Los Angeles Barrio, 1850–1890: A Social History*. Berkeley: University of California Press, 1979.

Guinn, J. M. *History and Biographical Record of Monterey and San Benito Counties*. 2 vols. Los Angeles: Historic Record Co., 1910.

———. *History of California and Extended History of Its Southern Coast Counties*. Los Angeles: Historic Record Co., 1907.

Gutiérrez, David Gregory. *Walls and Mirrors: Mexican Americans, Mexican Immigrants, and the Politics of Ethnicity*. Berkeley: University of California Press, 1995.

Gutmann, Matthew C. *The Romance of Democracy: Compliant Defiance in Contemporary Mexico*. Berkeley: University of California Press, 2002.

Harlow, Neal S. *California Conquered: War and Peace on the Pacific, 1846–1850*. Berkeley: University of California Press, 1982.

Harrell, Nita. *The Sánchez Treasure*. San Juan Bautista, Calif.: San Juan Bautista Historical Publisher, 1975.

Hobsbawm, Eric J. *Bandits*. Englewood Cliffs, N.J.: Prentice-Hall, 1969.

———. *Bandits*. Rev. ed. New York: Pantheon Books, 1982.

———. *Bandits*. Rev. ed. New York: New Press, 2000.

———. *Primitive Rebels: Studies in Archaic Forms of Social Movement in the 19th and 20th Centuries*. New York: W. W. Norton and Co., 1965.

Hoover, Mildred Brooke, Hero Eugene Rensch, and Ethel Grace Rensch. *Historic Spots in California*. Stanford: Stanford University Press, 1966.

Howard, Donald. *Adobes and Indian Middens of Monterey County*. Vol. 2. Monterey: Donald Howard, 2000.

Hoyle, Millard F. *Crimes and Career of Tiburcio Vasquez*. Hollister, Calif.: Hollister Free Lance, 1927.

Jackson, Joseph Henry. *Bad Company*. New York: Charles Scribner's Sons, 1949.

Jacobsen, Joel. *Such Men as Billy the Kid*. Lincoln: University of Nebraska Press, 1994.

Jameson, W. C. *Buried Treasures of California*. Little Rock, Ark.: August House Publishers, 1995.

Johnson, Evin R., and Richard P. Cordone. *Pinnacles Guide*. Glendale, Calif.: La Siesta Press, 1992.

Johnson, Susan Lee. *Roaring Camp: The Social World of the California Gold Rush.* New York: W. W. Norton and Co., 2000.

Keffer, Frank M. *History of San Fernando Valley.* Glendale, Calif.: Stillman Printing Co., 1934.

Kimbro, Edna E. *Historic Structure Report for Rancho San Andres Castro Adobe.* Monterey: California State Parks, 2003.

Koch, Margaret. *Santa Cruz County: Parade of the Past.* Fresno, Calif.: Valley Publishers, 1973.

Lamott, Kenneth. *Chronicles of San Quentin.* New York: David McKay Co., 1961.

Langellier, John Phillip, and Daniel Bernard Rosen. *El Presidio de San Francisco: A History under Spain and Mexico, 1776–1846.* Spokane: Arthur H. Clark Co., 1996.

Langum, David J. *Law and Community on the Mexican California Frontier.* Norman: University of Oklahoma Press, 1987.

———. "Sin, Sex, and Separation in Mexican California." *The Californians* 5, no. 3 (May–June 1987): 44–50.

Larkin, Thomas O. *The Larkin Papers: Personal, Business, and Official Correspondence of Thomas Oliver Larkin, Merchant and United States Consul in California.* Edited by George P. Hammond. Vol. 1. Berkeley: University of California Press, 1951.

Latta, Frank F. *Black Gold in the Joaquin.* Caldwell, Idaho: Caxton Printers, 1949.

———. *Joaquín Murrieta and His Horse Gangs.* Santa Cruz, Calif.: Bear State Books, 1980.

———. *The Saga of Rancho El Tejon.* Santa Cruz, Calif.: Bear State Books, 1976.

Martinez, Benjamin M. *The Sheriffs of Monterey County.* Salinas, Calif.: Monterey County Graphics, 1991.

McAfee, Ward M. "San Quentin: The Forgotten Issue of California's Political History in the 1850s." *Southern California Quarterly* 72, no. 23 (Fall 1990): 235–54.

McGarrahan, William. *The History of the McGarrahan Claim.* San Francisco: William McGarrahan, 1880.

McKanna, Clare V., Jr. "Banditry in California, 1850–1880: Myth and Reality." In *Brand Book Number Eight.* San Diego, Calif.: Corral of the Westerners, 1987.

———. "Crime and Punishment: The Hispanic Experience in San Quentin, 1851–1880." *Southern California Quarterly* 72, no. 1 (Spring 1990): 2–4.

———. "Ethnics and San Quentin Prison Registers: A Comment on Methodology." *Journal of Social History* 18, no. 3 (Spring 1985): 477–82.

———. "The Origins of San Quentin." *California History* 66 (March 1987): 49–54.

———. "San Quentin: Hell Hole in Paradise." *Frontier Times,* October 1984.

McWilliams, Carey. *North from Mexico: The Spanish-Speaking People of the United States.* New York: Greenwood Press, 1968.

Meier, Matt S., and Margo Gutiérrez. *Encyclopedia of the Mexican American Civil Rights Movement.* Westport, Conn.: Greenwood Press, 2000.

A Memorial and Biographical History of the Counties of Fresno, Tulare and Kern, California. Chicago: Lewis Publishing Co., 1892.

Millard, Bailey. *History of the San Francisco Bay Region.* 3 vols. Chicago: American Historical Society, 1924.

Miller, Robert Ryal. *Juan Alvarado, Governor of California, 1836–1842.* Norman: University of Oklahoma Press, 1998.

Milliken, Ralph LeRoy. *California Dons.* Fresno, Calif.: Valley Publishers, 1967.

Miranda, Gloria E. "Hispano Mexican Childrearing Practices in Pre-American Santa Barbara." *Southern California Quarterly* 65, no. 4 (Winter 1983): 307–20.

Mirandé, Alfredo, and Evangelina Enríquez. *La Chicana: The Mexican-American Woman.* Chicago: University of Chicago Press, 1979.

Miser, Ross J. *The Pinnacles Story.* Campbell, Calif.: Gordon Multilith, 1961.

Monroy, Douglas. *Thrown among Strangers: The Making of Mexican Culture in Frontier California.* Berkeley: University of California Press, 1990.

Moreno, Deborah. "Here the Society Is United: 'Respectable' Anglos and Intercultural Marriage in Pre–Gold Rush California." *California History* 80 (Spring 2001): 2–17.

Mortimer, Charles. *Life and Career of Charles Mortimer.* Sacramento: William H. Mills and Co., 1873.

Mullen, Kevin J. *Dangerous Strangers: Minority Newcomers and Criminal Violence in the Urban West, 1850–2000.* New York: Palgrave Macmillan, 2005.

Munro-Fraser, J. P. *History of Contra Costa County.* San Francisco: Alley, Bowen & Co., 1881.

———. *History of Marin County.* San Francisco: Alley, Bowen & Co., 1880.

———. *History of Santa Clara County.* San Francisco: Alley, Bowen & Co., 1881.

Murphy, Celeste G. *The People of the Pueblo.* Portland, Ore.: Binfords and Mort, 1937.

Mutnick, Dorothy. *Some Alta California Pioneers and Descendants.* 5 vols. Pleasant Hill, Calif.: Contra Costa County Historical Society, 1989.

Mylar, Isaac. *Early Days at the Mission San Juan Bautista.* Watsonville, Calif.: Evening Pajaronian, 1929.

Nadeau, Remi. *City-Makers.* Garden City, N.Y.: Doubleday, 1948.

Navarro, Armando. *Mexicano Political Experience in Occupied Aztlan.* Walnut Creek, Calif.: Altamira Press, 2005.

Newmark, Harris. *Sixty Years in Southern California.* New York: Knickerbocker Press, 1916.

Nolan, Frederick. *The Lincoln County War: A Documentary History.* Norman: University of Oklahoma Press, 1992.

Northrop, Marie E. *Spanish-Mexican Families of Early California, 1769–1850.* 2 vols. Burbank: Southern California Genealogical Society, 1984.

———. *Spanish-Mexican Families of Early California, 1769–1850.* Vol. 3: *Los Pobladores de La Reina de Los Angeles.* Burbank, Calif.: Southern California Genealogical Society, 2004.

Nunis, Doyce B., Jr.. *The Trials of Isaac Graham.* Los Angeles: Dawson's Book Shop, 1967.

Oberg, Reta R. *Administrative History of Pinnacles National Monument.* Paicines, Calif.: National Park Service, 1979.

Ochoa, Enrique, and Gilda L. Ochoa. *Latino Los Angeles: Transformations, Communities, and Activism.* Tucson: University of Arizona Press, 2005.

Older, Cora Baggerly. "Vasquez the Outlaw." *San Francisco Call,* February 6–May 22, 1920.

Pacific Coast Business Directory. San Francisco: Henry G. Langley, 1871.

Palmer, Lyman L. *History of Mendocino County.* San Francisco: Alley, Bowen & Co., 1880.

Paredes, Américo. *With His Pistol in His Hand: A Border Ballad and Its Hero.* Austin: University of Texas Press, 1958.

Parker, Linda S. "Superior Court Treatment of Ethnics Charged with Violent Crimes in Three California Counties, 1880–1910." *Southern California Quarterly* 74, no. 3 (Fall 1992): 225–43.

Parker, Paul P. "The Roach-Belcher Feud." *California Historical Society Quarterly* 29, no. 1 (March 1950): 19–28.

Patsis, Steve Dean. "Go West Greek George," *Greek Accent* (July–August 1984): 16–19, 45.

Penfield, Thomas. *Guide to Treasure in California.* Conroe, Tex.: True Treasure Publications, 1972.

Phillips, George Harwood. *Indians and Intruders in Central California.* Norman: University of Oklahoma Press, 1993.

Pierce, Marjorie. *East of the Gabilans.* Santa Cruz, Calif.: Western Tanager Press, 1976.

Pitt, Leonard. *Decline of the Californios*. Berkeley: University of California Press, 1966.

Pourade, Richard F. *The Glory Years*. San Diego, Calif.: Union-Tribune Publishing Co., 1964.

Prassel, Frank Richard. *The Great American Outlaw*. Norman: University of Oklahoma Press, 1993.

Reader, Phil. *A Brief History of the Pajaro Property Protective Society*. Santa Cruz, Calif.: Cliffside Publishing, 1995.

———. *Charole: The Life of Branciforte Bandido Faustino Lorenzana*. Santa Cruz, Calif.: Cliffside Publishing, 1991.

———. *Harlots and Whorehouses*. Santa Cruz, Calif.: Cliffside Publishing, 1995.

Report of the Joint Committee on State Prison Affairs. Appendix to Senate Journals of the Ninth Session of the Legislature of the State of California. Sacramento: State Printer, 1858.

Roddy, William Crane. *The Sanchez File*. San Juan Bautista, Calif.: History Co., 1995.

Rolle, Andrew F. *California: A History*. New York: Thomas Y. Crowell Co., 1969.

Sánchez, Rosaura. *Telling Identities: The Californio Testimonios*. Minneapolis: University of Minnesota Press, 1995.

Sawyer, Eugene. "A Californian Duval." *Overland Monthly and Out West Magazine* 68, no. 1 (January 1917): 37–41.

———. *History of Santa Clara County, California*. Los Angeles: Historic Record Co., 1922.

———. *The Life and Career of Tiburcio Vasquez, the California Bandit and Murderer*. San Francisco: Bacon and Co., 1875.

———. *The Life and Career of Tiburcio Vasquez, the California Stage Robber*. Foreword by Joseph A. Sullivan. Reprint, Oakland: Biobooks, 1944. Citations are to this edition.

Schulz, Margaret J. *Los Angeles County, California, Deaths, 1873–1899*. Burbank, Calif.: Southern California Genealogical Society, 1998.

Secrest, William B. *California Badmen*. Sanger, Calif.: Quill Driver Books/Word Dancer Press, 2007.

———. *California Feuds*. Sanger, Calif.: Quill Driver Books/Word Dancer Press, 2005.

———. *Dangerous Trails: Five Desperadoes of the Old West Coast*. Stillwater, Okla.: Barbed Wire Press, 1995.

———. "Kingston Raid!" *Quarterly of the National Association for Outlaw and Lawman History* 5, no. 1 (October 1979): 12–13.

———. *Lawmen and Desperadoes*. Spokane, Wash.: Arthur H. Clark Co., 1994.

———. *The Man from the Rio Grande*. Spokane, Wash.: Arthur H. Clark Co., 2005.

———. "The Return of Chavez." *True West* 25, no. 3 (January–February 1978): 10.

———. "Riders with Vasquez." *Real West* (October 1986): 22–23.

Shay, Anthony. "Fandangos and Bailes: Dancing and Dance Events in Early California." *Southern California Quarterly* 64, no. 2 (Summer 1982): 99–105.

Sheridan, Sol N. *History of Ventura County*. 2 vols. Chicago: S. J. Clarke Publishing Co., 1926.

Shillingberg, William B. *Tombstone, A.T.: A History of Early Mining, Milling, and Mayhem*. Spokane, Wash.: Arthur H. Clark Co., 1999.

Shumate, Albert, ed. *Boyhood Days: Ygnacio Villegas' Reminiscences of California in the 1850s* San Francisco: California Historical Society, 1983.

Slatta, Richard W. "Eric J. Hobsbawm's Social Bandit: A Critique and Revision." *A Contracorriente: A Journal on Social History and Literature in Latin America* 1, no. 2 (Spring 2004): 22–30.

Slotkin, Richard. *Gunfighter Nation*. New York: Atheneum, 1992.

Small, Kathleen E. *History of Tulare County, California*. Vol. 1. Chicago: S. J. Clarke Publishing Co., 1926.

Smith, Wallace. *Garden of the Sun.* Ed. and Rev. William B. Secrest, Jr. Fresno, Calif.: Linden Publishing, 2004.

Spitzzeri, Paul R. "On a Case-by-Case Basis: Ethnicity and Los Angeles Courts, 1850–1875." *California History* 83, no. 2 (Fall 2005): 26–39.

Standart, M. Collette. "The Sonora Migration to California, 1848–1856: A Study in Prejudice." *Southern California Quarterly* 58 (Fall 1976): 340–50.

Starr, Kevin. *California: A History.* New York: Modern Library, 2005.

Steckmesser, Kent Ladd. "Robin Hood and the American Outlaw." *Journal of American Folklore* 79 (April–June 1966): 348–55.

Stephens, L. Dow. *Life Sketches of a Jayhawker of '49.* San Jose, Calif.: Notta Bros., 1916.

Stevenson, Robert Louis. *Across the Plains.* London: Chattus and Windus, 1892.

———. "The Old Pacific Capital." *Fraser's Magazine* 22 (November 1880): 647–57.

Stiles, T. J. *Jesse James, Last Rebel of the Civil War.* New York: Alfred A. Knopf, 2002.

Suchlicki, Jaime. *Mexico: From Montezuma to NAFTA, Chiapas, and Beyond.* New York: Brassey's, 1996.

Tefertiller, Casey. *Wyatt Earp: The Life Behind the Legend.* New York: John Wiley and Sons, 1997.

Thornton, Bruce. *Searching for Joaquín.* San Francisco: Encounter Books, 2003.

Thrall, Will H. "The Haunts and Hideouts of Tiburcio Vasquez." *Southern California Historical Society Quarterly* 30, no. 2 (June 1948): 81–96.

———. "Vasquez, the Bandit." *Westways* (February 1953): 12–13.

Thrapp, Dan L. *Encyclopedia of Frontier Biography.* 3 vols. Glendale, Calif.: Arthur H. Clark Co., 1988.

Truman, Benjamin C. *The Life, Adventures, and Capture of Tiburcio Vasquez, The Great California Bandit and Murderer.* Los Angeles: Los Angeles Star, 1874.

Utley, Robert M. *High Noon in Lincoln.* Albuquerque: University of New Mexico Press, 1987.

Vandor, Paul E. *The History of Fresno County, California.* 2 vols. Los Angeles: Historic Record Co., 1919.

Varley, James F. *The Legend of Joaquín Murrieta.* Twin Falls, Idaho: Big Lost River Press, 1995.

Vigil, James Diego. *From Indians to Chicanos: The Dynamics of Mexican-American Culture.* Prospect Heights, Ill.: Waveland Press, 1998.

Walter, William W. *The Great Understander.* Aurora, Ill.: William W. Walter, 1931.

Walton, John. *Storied Land: Community and Memory in Monterey.* Berkeley: University of California Press, 2001.

Wanamaker, Marc. "Vasquez Rocks: The Southland's Most Famous 'Rock Star.'" *California Territorial Quarterly* 53 (Spring 2003): 30–43.

Williams, Mary Floyd. *Papers of the San Francisco Committee of Vigilance of 1851.* Berkeley: University of California Press, 1919.

Wilson, Neill C. *Silver Stampede.* New York: Macmillan, 1937.

Winchell, Lilbourne A. *History of Fresno County and the San Joaquin Valley.* Fresno, Calif.: Arthur H. Cawston, 1933.

Winther, Oscar O. "The Story of San Jose, 1777–1869." *California Historical Society Quarterly* 14, no. 1 (March 1935): 4–10.

Wood, Raymund F. *Mariana La Loca, Prophetess of the Cantua and Alleged Spouse of Joaquin Murrieta.* Fresno, Calif.: Fresno County Historical Society, 1970.

Index